Pro ASP.NET MVC 4

Adam Freeman

Apress®

Pro ASP.NET MVC 4

ISBN-13 (pbk): 978-1-4302-4236-9

ISBN-13 (electronic): 978-1-4302-4237-6

President and Publisher: Paul Manning
Lead Editor: Ewan Buckingham
Technical Reviewer: Fabio Claudio Ferracchiati
Editorial Board: Steve Anglin, Mark Beckner, Ewan Buckingham, Gary Cornell, Louise Corrigan, Morgan Ertel, Jonathan Gennick, Jonathan Hassell, Robert Hutchinson, Michelle Lowman, James Markham, Matthew Moodie, Jeff Olson, Jeffrey Pepper, Douglas Pundick, Ben Renow-Clarke, Dominic Shakeshaft, Gwenan Spearing, Matt Wade, Tom Welsh
Coordinating Editor: Christine Ricketts
Copy Editors: Laura Lawrie and Kimberly Burton-Weisman
Compositor: Christine Ricketts
Indexer: SPi Global
Artist: SPi Global
Cover Designer: Anna Ishchenko

Distributed to the book trade worldwide by Springer Science+Business Media New York, 233 Spring Street, 6th Floor, New York, NY 10013. Phone 1-800-SPRINGER, fax (201) 348-4505, e-mail orders-ny@springer-sbm.com, or visit www.springeronline.com. Apress Media, LLC is a California LLC and the sole member (owner) is Springer Science + Business Media Finance Inc (SSBM Finance Inc). SSBM Finance Inc is a Delaware corporation.

For information on translations, please e-mail rights@apress.com, or visit www.apress.com.

Apress and friends of ED books may be purchased in bulk for academic, corporate, or promotional use. eBook versions and licenses are also available for most titles. For more information, reference our Special Bulk Sales–eBook Licensing web page at www.apress.com/bulk-sales.

Any source code or other supplementary materials referenced by the author in this text is available to readers at www.apress.com. For detailed information about how to locate your book's source code, go to www.apress.com/source-code/.

Dedicated to my lovely wife, Jacqui Griffyth.

Contents at a Glance

Contents

About the Author

Adam Freeman is an experienced IT professional who has held senior positions in a range of companies, most recently serving as chief technology officer and chief operating officer of a global bank. Now retired, he spends his time writing and running.

About the Technical Reviewer

Fabio Claudio Ferracchiati is a senior consultant and a senior analyst/developer using Microsoft technologies. He works for Brain Force (http://www.brainforce.com) in its Italian branch (http://www.brainforce.it). He is a Microsoft Certified Solution Developer for .NET, a Microsoft Certified Application Developer for .NET, a Microsoft Certified Professional, and a prolific author and technical reviewer. Over the past 10 years, he's written articles for Italian and international magazines and coauthored more than 10 books on a variety of computer topics.

Acknowledgments

I would like to thank everyone at Apress for working so hard to bring this book to print. In particular, I would like to thank Ewan Buckingham for commissioning and editing this title and Christine Ricketts for keeping track of everything. I would also like to thank the technical reviewer, Fabio, whose efforts made this book far better than it otherwise would have been.

—Adam Freeman

P A R T   1

Introducing ASP.NET MVC 4

ASP.NET MVC is a radical shift for web developers using the Microsoft platform. It emphasizes clean architecture, design patterns, and testability, and it doesn't try to conceal how the Web works.

The first part of this book is designed to help you understand broadly the foundational ideas of ASP.NET MVC, including the new features in ASP.NET MVC 4, and to experience in practice what the framework is like to use.

CHAPTER 1

■ ■ ■

What's the Big Idea?

ASP.NET MVC is a Web development framework from Microsoft that combines the effectiveness and tidiness of model-view-controller (MVC) architecture, the most up-to-date ideas and techniques from agile development, and the best parts of the existing ASP.NET platform. It's a complete alternative to traditional ASP.NET Web Forms, delivering considerable advantages for all but the most trivial of Web development projects. In this chapter, you'll learn why Microsoft originally created ASP.NET MVC, how it compares to its predecessors and alternatives, and, finally, what's new in ASP.NET MVC 4.

A Brief History of Web Development

To understand the distinctive aspects and design goals of ASP.NET MVC, it's worth considering the history of Web development so far—brief though it may be. Over the years, Microsoft's Web development platforms have demonstrated increasing power and, unfortunately, increasing complexity. As shown in Table 1-1, each new platform tackled the specific shortcomings of its predecessor.

Table 1-1. Microsoft's Lineage of Web Development Technologies

Period	Technology	Strengths	Weaknesses
Jurassic	Common Gateway Interface (CGI)[*]	Simple Flexible Only option at the time	Runs outside the Web server, so is resource-intensive (spawns a separate operating system process per request) Low-level
Bronze age	Microsoft Internet Database Connector (IDC)	Runs inside Web server	Just a wrapper for SQL queries and templates for formatting result sets
1996	Active Server Pages (ASP)	General purpose	Interpreted at runtime Encourages "spaghetti code"

3

Period	Technology	Strengths	Weaknesses
2002/03	ASP.NET Web Forms 1.0/1.1	Compiled "Stateful" UI Vast infrastructure Encourages object-oriented programming	Heavy on bandwidth Ugly HTML Untestable
2005	ASP.NET Web Forms 2.0		
2007	ASP.NET AJAX		
2008	ASP.NET Web Forms 3.5		
2009	ASP.NET MVC 1.0		
2010	ASP.NET MVC 2.0 ASP.NET Web Forms 4.0		
2011	ASP.NET MVC 3.0		
2012	ASP.NET MVC 4.0 ASP.NET Web Forms 4.5		

CGI is a standard means of connecting a Web server to an arbitrary executable program that returns dynamic content. The specification is maintained by the National Center for Supercomputing Applications (NCSA).

Traditional ASP.NET Web Forms

ASP.NET was a huge shift when it first arrived in 2002. Figure 1-1 illustrates Microsoft's technology stack as it appeared then.

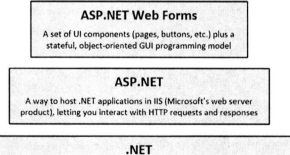

Figure 1-1. The ASP.NET Web Forms technology stack

With Web Forms, Microsoft attempted to hide both HTTP (with its intrinsic statelessness) and HTML (which at the time was unfamiliar to many developers) by modeling the user interface (UI) as a hierarchy of server-side control objects. Each control kept track of its own state across requests (using the View State facility), rendering itself as HTML when needed and automatically connecting client-side events (for example, a button click) with the corresponding server-side event handler code. In effect, Web Forms is a giant abstraction layer designed to deliver a classic event-driven graphical user interface (GUI) over the Web.

The idea was to make Web development feel just the same as Windows Forms development. Developers no longer needed to work with a series of independent HTTP requests and responses; we could now think in terms of a stateful UI. We could forget about the Web and its stateless nature, and instead build UIs using a drag-and-drop designer, and imagine—or at least pretend—that everything was happening on the server.

What Is Wrong with ASP.NET Web Forms?

Traditional ASP.NET Web Forms development was great in principle, but reality proved more complicated. Over time, the use of Web Forms in real-world projects highlighted some shortcomings:

- *View State weight*: The actual mechanism for maintaining state across requests (known as View State) results in large blocks of data being transferred between the client and server. This data can reach hundreds of kilobytes in even modest Web applications, and it goes back and forth with *every* request, leading to slower response times and increasing the bandwidth demands of the server.

- *Page life cycle*: The mechanism for connecting client-side events with server-side event handler code, part of the page life cycle, can be extraordinarily complicated and delicate. Few developers have success manipulating the control hierarchy at runtime without getting View State errors or finding that some event handlers mysteriously fail to execute.

- *False sense of separation of concerns*: ASP.NET's *code-behind* model provides a means to take application code out of its HTML markup and into a separate code-behind class. This has been widely applauded for separating logic and presentation, but, in reality, developers are encouraged to mix presentation code (for example, manipulating the server-side control tree) with their application logic (for example, manipulating database data) in these same monstrous code-behind classes. The end result can be fragile and unintelligible.

- *Limited control over HTML*: Server controls render themselves as HTML, but not necessarily the HTML you want. In early version of ASP.NET 4 the HTML output failed to meet with Web standards or make good use of Cascading Style Sheets (CSS), and server controls generated unpredictable and complex ID attribute values that are hard to access using JavaScript. These problems are much improved in in ASP.NET 4 and ASP.NET 4.5, but it can still be tricky to get the HTML you expect.

- *Leaky abstraction*: Web Forms tries to hide away HTML and HTTP wherever possible. As you try to implement custom behaviors, you frequently fall out of the abstraction, which forces you to reverse-engineer the postback event mechanism or perform obtuse acts to make it generate the desired HTML. Plus, all this abstraction can act as a frustrating barrier for competent Web developers.

- *Low testability*: The designers of ASP.NET could not have anticipated that automated testing would become an essential component of software development. Not surprisingly, the tightly coupled architecture they designed is unsuitable for unit testing. Integration testing can be a challenge, too.

ASP.NET has kept moving. Version 2.0 added a set of standard application components that can reduce the amount of code you need to write yourself. The AJAX release in 2007 was Microsoft's response to the Web 2.0/AJAX frenzy of the day, supporting rich client-side interactivity while keeping developers' lives simple. Things improved a lot with the ASP.NET 4 release, which embraced Web standard in a serious way for the first time. The most recent release, ASP.NET 4.5, actually takes some of the features from ASP.NET MVC and applies them to the Web Forms world, which addresses some of the more troublesome issues—but, even so, many of the intrinsic limitations remain.

Web Development Today

Outside Microsoft, Web development technology has been progressing rapidly and in several different directions since Web Forms was first released. Aside from AJAX, there have been other major developments.

Web Standards and REST

The drive for Web standards compliance has increased in recent years. Web sites are consumed on a greater variety of devices and browsers than ever before, and Web standards (for HTML, CSS, JavaScript, and so forth) remain our one great hope for enjoying a decent browsing experience everywhere—even on the Internet-enabled refrigerator. Modern Web platforms can't afford to ignore the business case and the weight of developer enthusiasm for Web standards compliance.

HTML5 is starting to enter mainstream use and provides the Web developer with rich capabilities that allow the client to perform work that was previously the exclusive responsibility of the server. These new capabilities and the increasing maturity of JavaScript libraries such as jQuery, jQuery UI, and jQuery Mobile means that standards have become ever more important and form the critical foundation for ever richer Web apps.

▓ **Note** We touch on HTML5, jQuery, and its cousins in this book, but we don't go into depth, because these are topics in their own right. If you want more complete coverage, then Apress publishes Adam's books on these subjects: *Pro jQuery*, *Pro JavaScript for Web Apps,* and *The Definitive Guide to HTML5*.

At the same time, Representational State Transfer (REST) has become the dominant architecture for application interoperability over HTTP, completely overshadowing SOAP (the technology behind ASP.NET's original approach to Web services). REST describes an application in terms of resources (URIs) representing real-world entities and standard operations (HTTP methods) representing available operations on those resources. For example, you might PUT a new `http://www.example.com/Products/Lawnmower` or DELETE `http://www.example.com/Customers/Arnold-Smith`.

Today's Web applications don't serve just HTML; often they must also serve JSON or XML data to various client technologies including AJAX, Silverlight, and native smartphone applications. This happens naturally with REST, which eliminates the historical distinction between Web services and Web applications—but requires an approach to HTTP and URL handling that has not easily been supported by ASP.NET Web Forms.

Agile and Test-Driven Development

It is not just Web development that has moved on in the last decade—software development as a whole has shifted toward *agile* methodologies. This can mean a lot of different things, but it is largely about running software projects as adaptable processes of discovery and resisting the encumbrance and restrictions of excessive forward planning. Enthusiasm for agile methodologies tends to go hand-in-hand with a particular set of development practices and tools (usually open source) that promote and assist these practices.

Test-driven development (TDD), and its latest incarnation, *behavior-driven development (BDD)*, are two obvious examples. The idea is to design your software by first describing examples of desired behaviors (known as *tests* or *specifications*), so at any time you can verify the stability and correctness of your application by executing your suite of specifications against the implementation. There's no shortage of .NET tools to support TDD/BDD, but these tend to not work well with Web Forms:

- *Unit testing tools* let you specify the behavior of individual classes or other small code units in isolation. These can be effectively applied only to software that has been designed as a set of independent modules, so that each test can be run in isolation. Unfortunately, few Web Forms applications can be tested this way. Following the framework's guidance to put logic into event handlers or even use server controls that directly query databases, developers typically end up tightly coupling their own application logic to the Web Forms runtime environment. This is death for unit testing.

- *UI automation tools* let you simulate a series of user interactions against a complete running instance of your application. In theory, these can be used with Web Forms, but they can break down whenever you make a slight change to your page layout. Without special attention, Web Forms starts generating totally different HTML structures and element IDs, rendering your existing test suite useless.

The .NET open source and independent software vendor (ISV) community has produced no end of top-quality unit testing frameworks (NUnit and xUnit), mocking frameworks (Moq and Rhino Mocks), inversion-of-control containers (Ninject and AutoFac), continuous integration servers (Cruise Control and TeamCity), object-relational mappers (NHibernate and Subsonic), and the like. Proponents of these tools and techniques have found a common voice, publishing and organizing conferences under the shared brand ALT.NET. Traditional ASP.NET Web Forms is not amenable to these tools and techniques because of its monolithic design, so from this vocal group of experts and industry thought leaders, Web Forms gets little respect.

Ruby on Rails

In 2004, Ruby on Rails was a quiet, open source contribution from an unknown player. Suddenly fame hit, transforming the rules of Web development. It's not that Ruby on Rails contained revolutionary technology but that the concept took existing ingredients and blended them in such a compelling and appealing way as to put existing platforms to shame.

Ruby on Rails (or just Rails, as it is commonly called) embraced an MVC architecture (which we describe shortly). By applying MVC and working in tune with the HTTP protocol instead of against it, by promoting conventions instead of the need for configuration, and by integrating an object-relational mapping (ORM) tool into its core, Rails applications more or less fell into place without much effort. It was as if this was how Web development should have been all along; as if we had suddenly realized we had been fighting our tools all these years and now the war was over.

Rails shows that Web standards compliance and RESTfulness don't need to be hard. It also shows that agile development and TDD work best when the framework is designed to support them. The rest of the Web development world has been catching up ever since.

Sinatra

Thanks to Rails, there were soon a lot of Web developers using Ruby as their main programming language. But in such an intensively innovative community, it was only a matter of time before alternatives to Rails would appear. The best known, Sinatra, emerged in 2007.

Sinatra discards almost all of the standard Rails-style infrastructure (routing, controllers, views, and so on) and merely maps URL patterns to Ruby code blocks. A visitor requests a URL, which causes a Ruby code block to be executed, and data is sent back to the browser—that's it. It's an incredibly simple kind of Web development, but it's found a niche in two main areas. First, for those building RESTful Web services, it just gets the job done fast (we touch on REST in Chapter 25). Second, because Sinatra can be connected to an extensive range of open-source HTML templating and ORM technologies, it's often used as a foundation on which to assemble a custom Web framework to suit the architectural needs of whatever project is at hand.

Sinatra has yet to take any serious market share from full-stack MVC platforms such as Rails (or ASP.NET MVC). We mention it here simply to illustrate the Web development industry's ongoing trend toward simplification, and because Sinatra acts as an opposing force against other frameworks amassing ever more core features.

Node.js

Another significant trend is the movement toward using JavaScript as a primary programming language. AJAX first showed us that JavaScript is important; jQuery showed us that it could be powerful and elegant; and Google's open-source V8 JavaScript engine showed us that it could be incredibly fast. Today, JavaScript is becoming a serious server-side programming language. It serves as the data storage and querying language for several nonrelational databases, including CouchDB and Mongo, and it is used as a general-purpose language in server-side platforms such as Node.js.

Node.js has been around since 2009 and gained wide acceptance very quickly. Architecturally, it's similar to Sinatra, in that it doesn't apply the MVC pattern. It is a more low-level way of connecting HTTP requests to your code. Its key innovations are as follows:

- *Using JavaScript*: Developers need to work only in a single language, from client-side code, through server-side logic, and even into data-querying logic via CouchDB or the like.

- *Being completely asynchronous*: Node.js's core API simply doesn't expose any way of blocking a thread while waiting for input/output (I/O) or any other operation. All I/O is implemented by beginning the operation and then later receiving a callback when the I/O is completed. This means that Node.js makes extremely efficient use of system resources and may handle tens of thousands of concurrent requests per CPU (alternative platforms tend to be limited to about one hundred concurrent requests per CPU).

Like Sinatra, Node.js is a niche technology. Most businesses building real applications in limited time frames typically need the infrastructure in full-stack frameworks such as Ruby on Rails and ASP.NET MVC. Node.js is mentioned here only to put some of ASP.NET MVC's design into context against industry trends. For example, ASP.NET MVC includes *asynchronous controllers* (which we describe in Chapter 17). This is a way to handle HTTP requests with nonblocking I/O and scale up to handle more requests per CPU. And as you will learn, ASP.NET MVC integrates very well with sophisticated JavaScript code running in the browser.

Key Benefits of ASP.NET MVC

ASP.NET has been a great commercial success, but, as discussed, the rest of the Web development world has moved on, and even though Microsoft has kept dusting the cobwebs off Web Forms, its essential design has started to look quite antiquated.

In October 2007, at the very first ALT.NET conference in Austin, Texas, Microsoft vice president Scott Guthrie announced and demonstrated a brand new MVC Web development platform, built on the core ASP.NET platform, clearly designed as a direct response to the evolution of technologies such as Rails and as a reaction to the criticisms of Web Forms. The following sections describe how this new platform overcame the Web Forms limitations and brought ASP.NET back to the cutting edge.

MVC Architecture

It is important to distinguish between the MVC architectural pattern and the ASP.NET MVC Framework. The MVC pattern is not new—it dates back to 1978 and the Smalltalk project at Xerox PARC—but it has gained enormous popularity today as a pattern for Web applications, for the following reasons:

- User interaction with an MVC application follows a natural cycle: the user takes an action, and in response the application changes its data model and delivers an updated view to the user. And then the cycle repeats. This is a very convenient fit for Web applications delivered as a series of HTTP requests and responses.

- Web applications necessitate combining several technologies (databases, HTML, and executable code, for example), usually split into a set of tiers or layers. The patterns that arise from these combinations map naturally onto the concepts in MVC.

The ASP.NET MVC Framework implements the MVC pattern and, in doing so, provides greatly improved separation of concerns. In fact, ASP.NET MVC implements a modern variant of the MVC pattern that is especially suitable for Web applications. You will learn more about the theory and practice of this architecture in Chapter 3.

By embracing and adapting the MVC pattern, the ASP.NET MVC Framework provides strong competition to Ruby on Rails and similar platforms, and brings the MVC pattern into the mainstream of the .NET world. By capitalizing on the experience and best practices discovered by developers using other platforms, ASP.NET MVC has, in many ways, pushed forward beyond what even Rails can offer.

Extensibility

Your desktop PC's internal components are independent pieces that interact only across standard, publicly documented interfaces. You can easily take out your graphics card or hard disk and replace it with another one from a different manufacturer, confident that it will fit in the slot and work. The MVC Framework is also built as a series of independent components—satisfying a .NET interface or built on an abstract base class—so that you can easily replace components, such as the routing system, the view engine, the controller factory, and so on, with a different one of your own implementation.

The ASP.NET MVC designers set out to give you three options for each MVC Framework component:

- Use the *default* implementation of the component as it stands (which should be enough for most applications).

- Derive a *subclass* of the default implementation to tweak its behavior.

- *Replace* the component entirely with a new implementation of the interface or abstract base class.

It is like the provider model from ASP.NET 2.0, but taken much further—right into the heart of the MVC Framework. You'll learn all about the various components, and how and why you might want to tweak or replace each of them, starting in Chapter 12.

Tight Control over HTML and HTTP

ASP.NET MVC recognizes the importance of producing clean, standards-compliant markup. Its built-in HTML helper methods produce standards-compliant output, but there is a more significant philosophical change compared with Web Forms. Instead of spewing out huge swathes of HTML over which you have little control, the MVC Framework encourages you to craft simple, elegant markup styled with CSS.

Of course, if you do want to throw in some ready-made widgets for complex UI elements such as date pickers or cascading menus, ASP.NET MVC's "no special requirements" approach to markup makes it easy to use best-of-breed UI libraries such as jQuery UI or the Yahoo YUI Library. JavaScript developers will be pleased to learn that ASP.NET MVC meshes so well with the popular jQuery library that Microsoft ships jQuery as a built-in part of the default ASP.NET MVC project template, and even lets you directly reference the jQuery .js file on Microsoft's own content delivery network (CDN) servers.

ASP.NET MVC–generated pages don't contain any View State data, so they can be hundreds of kilobytes smaller than typical pages from ASP.NET Web Forms. Despite today's fast broadband connections, this economy of bandwidth still gives an enormously improved end-user experience.

Like Ruby on Rails, ASP.NET MVC works in tune with HTTP. You have total control over the requests passing between the browser and server, so you can fine-tune your user experience as much as you like. AJAX is made easy, and there aren't any automatic postbacks to interfere with client-side state. Any developer who primarily focuses on the Web will almost certainly find this to be hugely freeing and the workday more satisfying.

Testability

The MVC architecture gives you a great start in making your application maintainable and testable because you naturally separate different application concerns into different, independent software pieces. Yet the ASP.NET MVC designers didn't stop there. To support unit testing, they took the framework's component-oriented design and made sure that each separate piece is structured to meet the requirements of unit testing and mocking tools.

They added Visual Studio wizards to create starter unit test projects on your behalf, which are integrated with open-source unit test tools such as NUnit and xUnit as well as Microsoft's own MSTest. Even if you have never written a unit test before, you will be off to a great start.

In this book, you will see examples of how to write clean, simple unit tests for ASP.NET MVC controllers and actions that supply fake or mock implementations of framework components to simulate any scenario, using a variety of testing and mocking strategies.

Testability is not only a matter of unit testing. ASP.NET MVC applications work well with UI automation testing tools, too. You can write test scripts that simulate user interactions without needing to guess which HTML element structures, CSS classes, or IDs the framework will generate, and you do not have to worry about the structure changing unexpectedly.

Powerful Routing System

The style of URLs has evolved as Web application technology has improved. URLs like this one:

```
/App_v2/User/Page.aspx?action=show%20prop&prop_id=82742
```

are increasingly rare, replaced with a simpler, cleaner format like this:

```
/to-rent/chicago/2303-silver-street
```

There are some good reasons for caring about the structure of URLs. First, search engines give considerable weight to keywords found in a URL. A search for "rent in Chicago" is much more likely to turn up the simpler URL. Second, many Web users are now savvy enough to understand a URL, and appreciate the option of navigating by typing it into their browser's address bar. Third, when someone understands the structure of a URL, they are more likely to link to it, share it with a friend, or even read it aloud over the phone. Fourth, it doesn't expose the technical details, folder, and file name structure of your application to the whole public Internet, so you are free to change the underlying implementation without breaking all your incoming links.

Clean URLs were hard to implement in earlier frameworks, but ASP.NET MVC uses the `System.Web.Routing` facility to provide clean URLs by default. This gives you control over your URL schema and its relationship to your application, offering you the freedom to create a pattern of URLs that is meaningful and useful to your users, without the need to conform to a predefined pattern. And, of course, this means you can easily define a modern REST-style URL schema if you wish. You'll find a thorough treatment of routing and URL best practices in Chapters 13 and 14.

Built on the Best Parts of the ASP.NET Platform

Microsoft's existing ASP.NET platform provides a mature, well-proven set of components and facilities for developing effective and efficient Web applications.

First and most obviously, as ASP.NET MVC is based on the .NET platform, you have the flexibility to write code in any .NET language and access the same API features—not just in MVC itself but in the extensive .NET class library and the vast ecosystem of third-party .NET libraries.

Second, ready-made ASP.NET platform features—such as master pages, forms authentication, membership, roles, profiles, and internationalization—can reduce the amount of code you need to develop and maintain any Web application, and these features are just as effective when used in the MVC Framework as they are in a classic Web Forms project. You can reuse some Web Forms built-in server controls, as well as your own custom controls from earlier ASP.NET projects, in an ASP.NET MVC application (as long as they don't depend on Web Forms–specific notions, such as View State).

Modern API

Since its inception in 2002, Microsoft's .NET platform has evolved relentlessly, supporting and even defining the state-of-the-art aspects of modern programming.

ASP.NET MVC 4 is built for .NET 4.5, so its API can take full advantage of recent language and runtime innovations, including the `await` keyword, extension methods, lambda expressions, anonymous and dynamic types, and Language Integrated Query (LINQ). Many of the MVC Framework's API methods and coding patterns follow a cleaner, more expressive composition than was possible with earlier platforms.

ASP.NET MVC Is Open Source

Unlike with previous Microsoft Web development platforms, you are free to download the original source code for ASP.NET MVC, and even modify and compile your own version of it. This is invaluable when your debugging trail leads into a system component, and you want to step into its code (and even read the original programmers' comments). It's also useful if you are building an advanced component and want to see what development possibilities exist, or how the built-in components actually work.

Additionally, this ability is great if you do not like the way something works, if you find a bug, or if you just want to access something that's otherwise inaccessible, because you can simply change it yourself. However, you'll need to keep track of your changes and reapply them if you upgrade to a newer version of the framework. ASP.NET MVC is licensed under the Microsoft Public License (Ms-PL, `http://www.opensource.org/licenses/ms-pl.html`), an Open Source Initiative (OSI)–approved open source license. This means that you can change the source code, deploy it, and even redistribute your

changes publicly as a derivative project. You can download the MVC source code from
`http://aspnetwebstack.codeplex.com`.

Who Should Use ASP.NET MVC?

As with any new technology, the fact of ASP.NET MVC's existence isn't a compelling reason to adopt it. Here, we will give you our view of how the MVC Framework compares with the most obvious alternatives. We have tried to be as unbiased as two people writing a book about the MVC Framework can be, but we know that there is a limit to our objectivity. The following sections are technology-based comparisons. When selecting a Web application framework, you should also consider the skills of your team, the work involved in porting any existing projects, and your relationship with, and confidence in, the technology source.

Comparisons with ASP.NET Web Forms

We have already detailed the weaknesses and limitations in traditional ASP.NET Web Forms, and how ASP.NET MVC overcomes many of those problems. That does not mean that Web Forms is dead, however. Microsoft has repeatedly stated that both technologies are being actively developed and actively supported, and that there are no plans to retire Web Forms. In some ways, your choice between the two is a matter of development philosophy. Consider these points:

- Web Forms takes the view that UIs should be *stateful* and, to that end, adds a sophisticated abstraction layer on top of HTTP and HTML, using View State and postbacks to create the effect of statefulness. This makes it suitable for drag-and-drop Windows Forms–style development, in which you pull UI widgets onto a canvas and fill in code for their event handlers.

- MVC embraces HTTP's true stateless nature, working with it rather than fighting against it. The MVC Framework requires you to understand how Web applications actually work. Given that understanding, it provides a simple, powerful, modern approach to writing Web applications, with tidy code that's easier to extend and maintain over time, and that's free of bizarre complications and painful limitations.

There are certainly cases where Web Forms is at least as good as, and probably better than, MVC. The obvious example is small, intranet-type applications that are largely about binding grids directly to database tables or stepping users through a wizard. Web Forms drag-and-drop development strengths can outweigh its weaknesses when you don't need to worry about bandwidth consumption or search engine optimization.

If, on the other hand, you are writing applications for the Internet or larger intranet applications, you will be attracted by the bandwidth efficiencies, better browser compatibility, and better support for automated testing that MVC offers.

Migrating from Web Forms to MVC

If you have an existing ASP.NET Web Forms project that you are considering migrating to MVC, you will be pleased to know that the two technologies can coexist in the same application. This provides an opportunity to migrate existing applications gradually, especially if the application is partitioned into layers with domain model or business logic constrained separately to the Web Forms pages. In some cases, you might even deliberately design an application to be a hybrid of the two technologies.

Comparisons with Ruby on Rails

Rails has become a benchmark against which other Web platforms are compared. Developers and companies who are in the Microsoft .NET world will find ASP.NET MVC far easier to adopt and learn, whereas developers and companies that work in Python or Ruby on Linux or Mac OS X will find an easier path to Rails. It's unlikely that you would migrate from Rails to ASP.NET MVC or vice versa. There are some real differences in scope between the two technologies.

Rails is a *holistic* development platform, meaning that it handles the complete stack, right from database source control, through ORM, to handling requests with controllers and actions—all topped off with built-in automated testing tools.

The ASP.NET MVC Framework focuses on handling Web requests in an MVC-pattern with controllers and actions. It does not have a built-in ORM tool, a built-in automated testing tool, or a system for managing database migrations. This is because the .NET platform already has an enormous range of choices for these functions, and you can use any of them. For example, if you're looking for an ORM tool, you might use NHibernate, Subsonic, Microsoft's Entity Framework, or one of the many other mature solutions available. Such is the luxury of the .NET platform, although this does mean that these components are not as tightly integrated into ASP.NET MVC as the equivalents are into Rails.

Comparisons with MonoRail

MonoRail is an earlier .NET-based MVC Web application platform, created as part of the open source Castle project and in development since 2003. In many ways, MonoRail acted as the prototype for ASP.NET MVC. MonoRail demonstrated how a Rails-like MVC architecture could be built on top of ASP.NET and established patterns, practices, and terminology that are used throughout Microsoft's implementation.

We don't see MonoRail as a serious competitor. It is probably the most popular .NET Web application platform created outside Redmond, and it did achieve reasonably widespread adoption in its day. However, since the launch of ASP.NET MVC, the MonoRail project is rarely heard of. The momentum of enthusiasm and innovation in the .NET Web development world is now focused on ASP.NET MVC.

What's New in ASP.NET MVC 4?

Version 4 of the MVC Framework provides a number of improvements over version 3. There are some significant new features such as support for *Web API* applications (which we describe in Chapter 25), support for mobile devices (Chapter 24) and some useful optimization techniques for sending content to clients (Chapter 24).

In addition, there are lots of small improvements, such as a simplified syntax for Razor views, a better organized system for providing core configuration information in MVC applications and some new template options for Visual Studio MVC projects.

Summary

In this chapter, we have described how Web development has evolved at tremendous speed from the primordial swamp of the CGI executable to the latest high-performance, standards-compliant, agile platforms. We reviewed the strengths, weaknesses, and limitations of ASP.NET Web Forms, Microsoft's main Web platform since 2002, and the changes in the wider Web development industry that forced Microsoft to respond with something new.

You saw how the ASP.NET MVC platform addresses the weaknesses of ASP.NET Web Forms, and how its modern design delivers advantages to developers who want to write high-quality, maintainable code.

In the next chapter, you'll see the MVC Framework in action, learning the simple mechanisms that yield all these benefits. By Chapter 7, you'll be ready for a realistic e-commerce application built with a clean architecture, proper separation of concerns, automated tests, and beautifully minimal markup.

CHAPTER 2

■ ■ ■

Your First MVC Application

The best way to appreciate a software development framework is to jump right in and use it. In this chapter, you'll create a simple data-entry application using the ASP.NET MVC Framework. We will take things a step at a time so you can see how an ASP.NET MVC application is constructed. To keep things simple, we will skip over some of the technical details for the moment; but don't worry—if you are new to MVC, you will find plenty to keep you interested. Where we use something without explaining it, we provide a reference to the chapter in which you can find all the details.

Preparing the Workstation

The only preparation you need to make to develop MVC 4 application is to install Visual Studio 2012, which contains everything you need to get started, including a built-in application server for running and debugging your MVC applications, an administration-free edition of SQL Server for developing database-driven applications, tools for unit testing and—of course—a code editor compiler and debugger.

There are several different editions of Visual Studio 2012, but we will be using the one that Microsoft makes available free-of-charge, called *Visual Studio Express 2012 for Web*. Microsoft adds some nice features to the paid-for editions of Visual Studio, but you will not need them for this book and all of figures that you see throughout this book have been taken using the Express edition, which you can download from http://www.microsoft.com/visualstudio/eng/products/visual-studio-express-products. There are several different versions of Visual Studio 2012 Express, each of which is used for a different kind of development—make sure that you get the Web version, which supports MVC applications.

Once you have installed Visual Studio, you are ready to go. Microsoft has really improved the scope of the features in the Visual Studio Express and there is nothing else you need to follow along with this book.

■ **Tip**　We have used Windows 8 throughout this book, but you can use Visual Studio 2012 and develop MVC 4 applications quite happily on earlier versions of Windows. See the system requirements for Visual Studio 2012 for details of which versions and patch levels are supported).

Creating a New ASP.NET MVC Project

We are going to start by creating a new MVC project in Visual Studio. Select New ↗Project from the File menu to open the New Project dialog. If you select the Web templates in the Visual C# section, you will see that one of the available project types is ASP.NET MVC 4 Web Application. Select this project type, as shown in Figure 2-1.

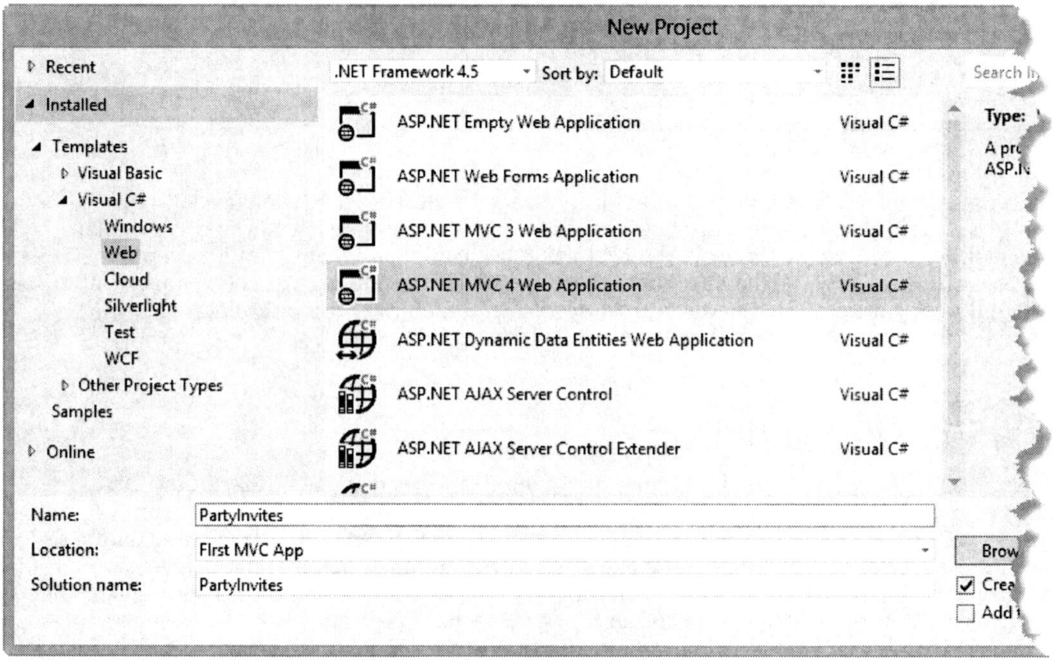

Figure 2-1. The Visual Studio MVC 4 project template

▓ **Caution**　　　　　Visual Studio 2012 includes support for MVC 3 as well as MVC 4, so you'll also see the old templates available alongside the new. When creating a new project, be careful to select the right one.

Set the name of the new project to PartyInvites and click the OK button to continue. You will see another dialog box, shown in Figure 2-2, which asks you to choose between three different types of MVC project templates.

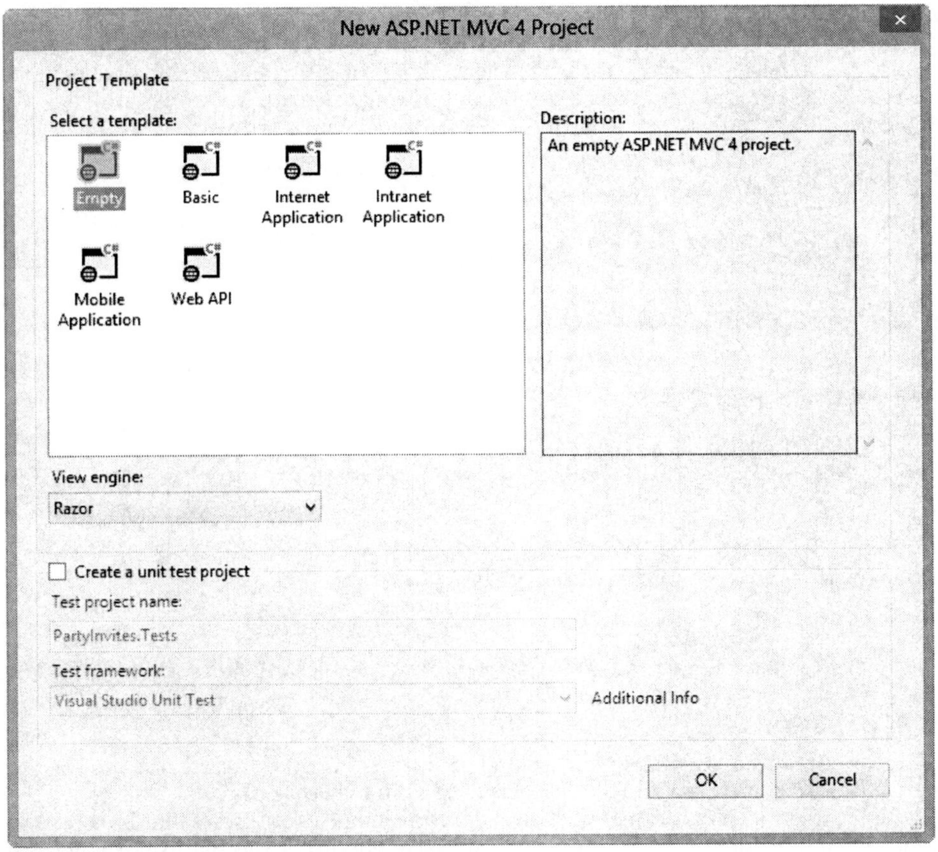

Figure 2-2. Selecting a type of MVC 4 project

The different MVC project templates create projects with varying amounts of basic support for features such as authentication, navigation and visual styles. For this chapter, we are going to keep things simple. Select the Empty option, which creates a project with a basic folder structure, but without any of the files required to create an MVC app. We will add the files we need as we go through the chapter and explain what we are doing each time.

Click the OK button to create the new project.

▦ **Note** In Figure 2-2, you can see a drop-down menu that lets you specify the view engine for the project. With MVC 3, Microsoft introduced a new and improved *view engine* called Razor, which we'll be using Razor throughout this book. We recommend that you do the same. But if you want to use the regular ASP.NET view engine (known as the ASPX engine), this is where you select it. We'll explain all about Razor and what a view engine does in Chapters 5 and 18.

Once Visual Studio creates the project, you will see a number of files and folders displayed in the Solution Explorer window. This is the default structure for an MVC 4 project. You can try to run the application now by selecting Start Debugging from the Debug menu (if it prompts you to enable debugging, just click the OK button). You can see the result in Figure 2-3. Because we started with the empty project template, the application does not contain anything to run, so we see a 404 Not Found Error.

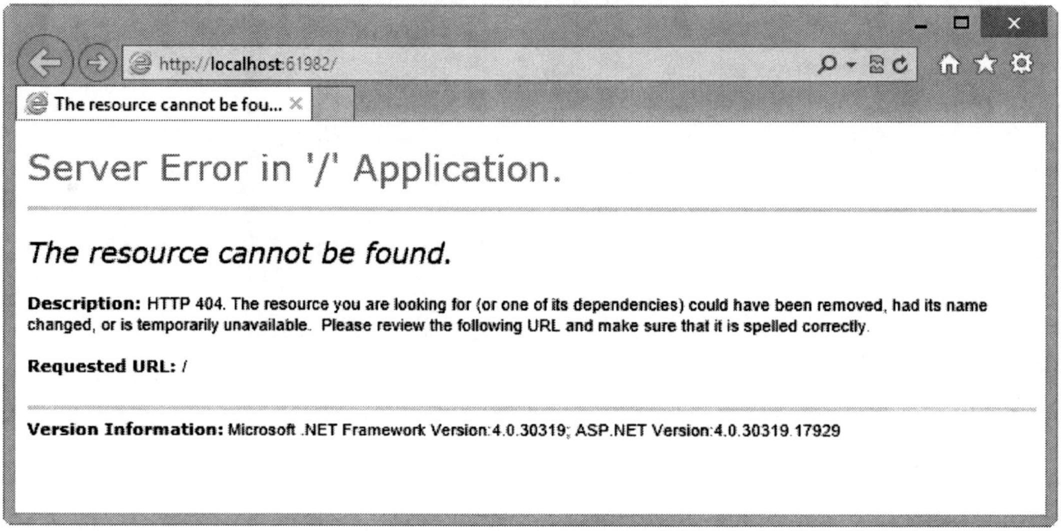

Figure 2-3. Trying to run an empty project

When you are finished, be sure to stop debugging by closing the browser window that shows the error, or by going back to Visual Studio and selecting Stop Debugging from the Debug menu.

Visual Studio opens the browser to display the project and you can change the browser that is used through the toolbar menu shown in Figure 2-4. You can see that we have Microsoft Internet Explorer and Google Chrome installed.

Figure 2-4. Changing the browser that Visual Studio uses to run the project

We will be using Internet Explorer 10 throughout this book. All of the modern Web browsers are pretty good these days, but we will stick with IE because we know that it is so widely installed.

Adding the First Controller

In MVC architecture, incoming requests are handled by *controllers*. In ASP.NET MVC, controllers are just simple C# classes (usually inheriting from System.Web.Mvc.Controller, the framework's built-in controller base class). Each public method in a controller is known as an *action method*, meaning you can invoke it from the Web via some URL to perform an action. The MVC convention is to put controllers in a folder called Controllers, which Visual Studio created for us when it set up the project. You do not need to follow this or most other MVC conventions, but we recommend that you do—not least because it will help you make sense of the examples in this book.

To add a controller to our project, right click the Controllers folder in the Visual Studio Solution Explorer window and choose Add and then Controller from the pop-up menus, as shown in Figure 2-5.

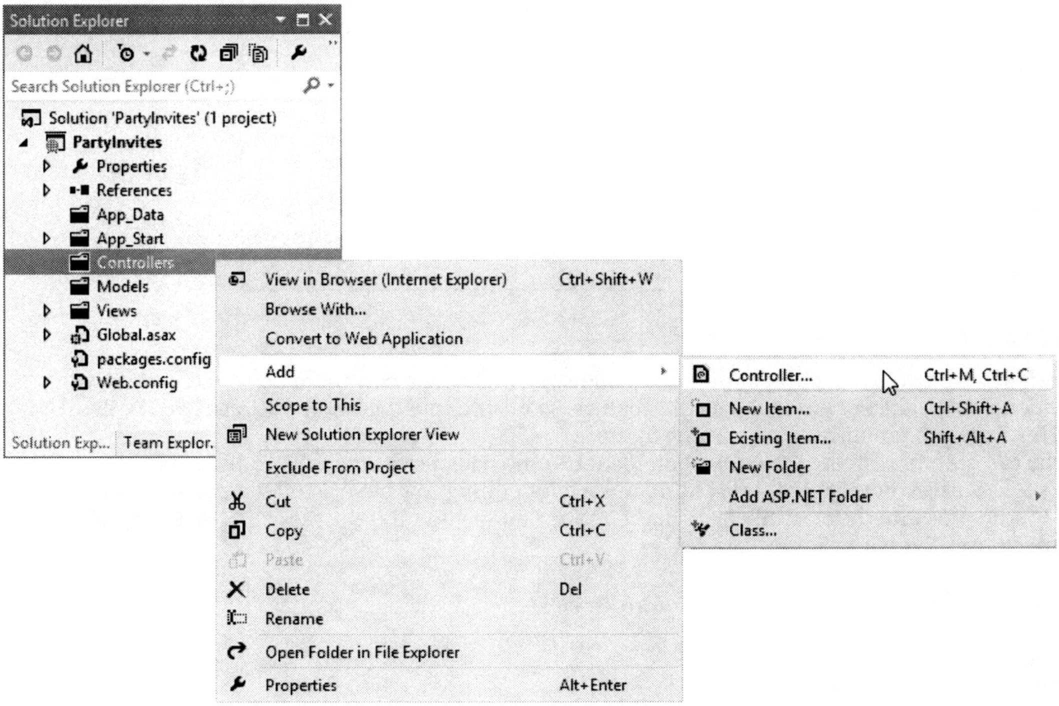

Figure 2-5. Adding a controller to the MVC project

When the Add Controller dialog appears, set the name to HomeController, as shown in Figure 2-6. This is another convention: the names we give to controllers should be descriptive and end with Controller.

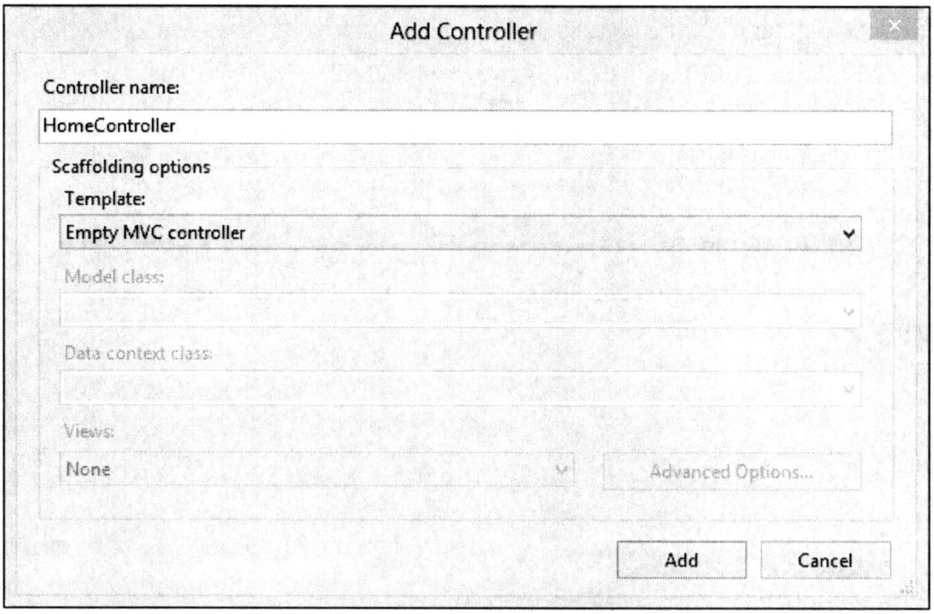

Figure 2-6. Setting the name for the controller

The **Scaffolding options** section of the dialog allows us to create a controller using a template with common functions. We are not going to use this feature, so ensure that the **Empty MVC controller** item is selected in the **Template** menu, as shown in the figure.

Click the **Add** button to create the controller. Visual Studio will create a new C# code file in the **Controllers** folder called **HomeController.cs** and open it for editing. We have listed the default contents that Visual Studio puts into the class file in Listing 2-1. You can see that the class is called **HomeController** and it is derived from **System.Web.Mvc.Controller**.

Listing 2-1. The default contents of the HomeController class

```
using System;
using System.Collections.Generic;
using System.Linq;
using System.Web;
using System.Web.Mvc;

namespace PartyInvites.Controllers {
    public class HomeController : Controller {

        public ActionResult Index() {
            return View();
        }
    }
}
```

A good way of getting started with MVC is to make a couple of simple changes to the controller class. Edit the code in the HomeController.cs file so that it matches Listing 2-2—we have highlighted the changes so they are easier to see.

Listing 2-2. Modifying the HomeController Class

```
using System;
using System.Collections.Generic;
using System.Linq;
using System.Web;
using System.Web.Mvc;

namespace PartyInvites.Controllers {
    public class HomeController : Controller {

        public string Index() {
            return "Hello World";
        }
    }
}
```

We have not created anything exciting, but it makes for a nice demonstration. We have changed the action method called Index so that it returns the string "Hello, world". Run the project again by selecting Start Debugging from the Visual Studio Debug menu. The browser will display the result of the Index action method, as shown in Figure 2-7.

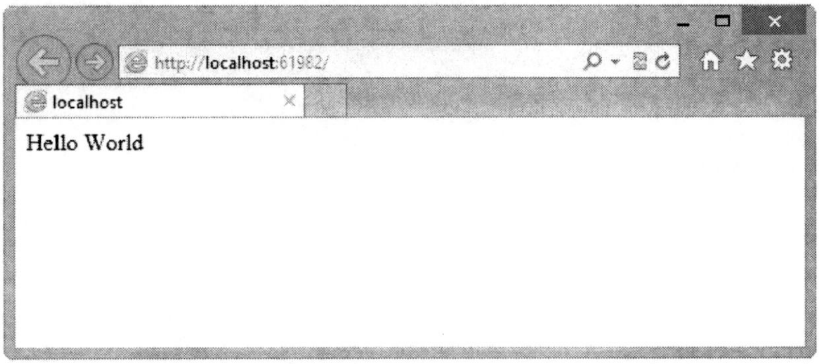

Figure 2-7. The output from our controller action method

Understanding Routes

As well as models, views, and controllers, MVC applications use the ASP.NET *routing system*, which decides how URLs map to particular controllers and actions. When Visual Studio creates the MVC project, it adds some default routes to get us started. You can request any of the following URLs, and they will be directed to the Index action on the HomeController:

- /
- /Home
- /Home/Index

21

So, when a browser requests http://*yoursite*/ or http://*yoursite*/Home, it gets back the output from HomeController's Index method. You can try this yourself by changing the URL in the browser. At the moment, it will be http://localhost:61982/, except that the port part may be different. If you append /Home or /Home/Index to the URL and hit return, you will see the same Hello World result from the MVC application.

This is a good example of benefiting from following MVC conventions. In this case, the convention is that we will have a controller called HomeController and that it will be the starting point for our MVC application. The default routes that Visual Studio creates for a new project assume that we will follow this convention. And since we *did* follow the convention, we got support for the URLs in the preceding list.

If we had *not* followed the convention, we would need to modify the routes to point to whatever controller we had created instead. For this simple example, the default configuration is all we need.

■ **Tip** You can see and edit your routing configuration by opening the Global.asax.cs file. In Chapter 7, you'll set up custom routing entries, and in Chapters 13 and 14 you'll learn much more about what routing can do.

Rendering Web Pages

The output from the previous example wasn't HTML—it was just the string "Hello World". To produce an HTML response to a browser request, we need to create a *view*.

Creating and Rendering a View

The first thing we need to do is modify our Index action method, as shown in Listing 2-3.

Listing 2-3. Modifying the Controller to Render a View

```
using System;
using System.Collections.Generic;
using System.Linq;
using System.Web;
using System.Web.Mvc;

namespace PartyInvites.Controllers {
    public class HomeController : Controller {

        public ViewResult Index() {
            return View();
        }
    }
}
```

The changes in Listing 2-3 are shown in bold. When we return a ViewResult object from an action method, we are instructing MVC to render a view. We create the ViewResult by calling the View method with no parameters. This tells MVC to render the *default* view for the action.

If you run the application at this point, you can see the MVC Framework trying to find a default view to use, as shown in the error message displayed in Figure 2-8.

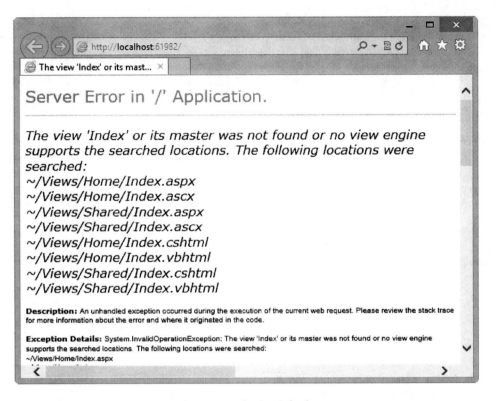

Figure 2-8. The MVC Framework trying to find a default view

This error message is quite helpful. It explains not only that MVC could not find a view for our action method, but it shows where it looked. This is another nice illustration of an MVC convention: views are associated with action methods by a naming convention. Our action method is called Index and our controller is called Home and you can see from Figure 2-8 that MVC is trying to find different files in the Views folder that have that name.

To create a view, stop the debugger and right-click the action method in the HomeController.cs code file (either on the method name or inside the method body) and select Add View from the pop-up menu. This opens the Add View dialog, which is shown in Figure 2-9.

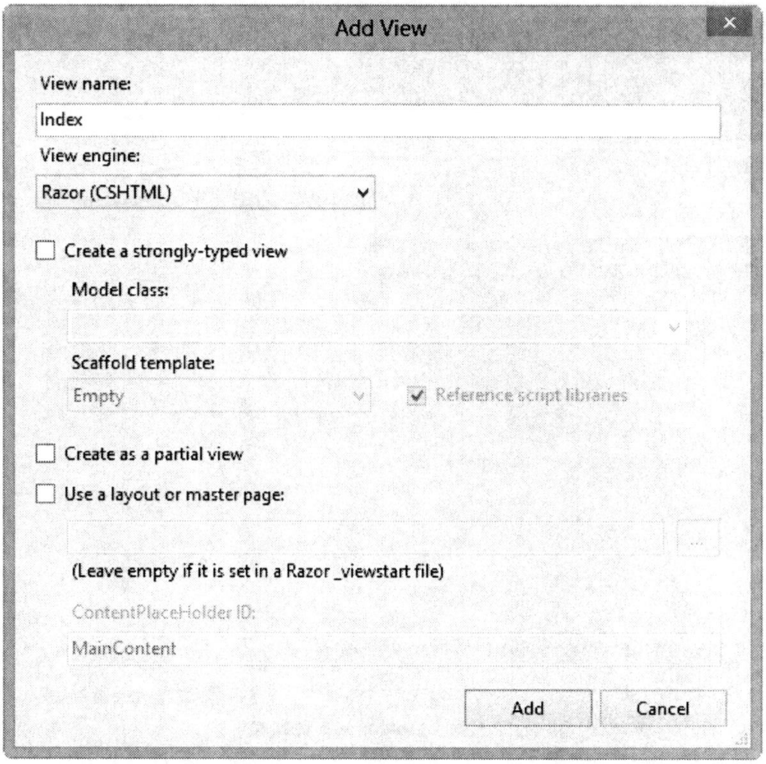

Figure 2-9. The Add View dialog

Uncheck Use a layout or master page. We are not using layouts in this example, but we will see them in use in Chapter 7. Click the Add button and Visual Studio will create a new file called Index.cshtml, in the Views/Home folder. If you look back at the error message in Figure 2-8, you will see that the new file is one of those that the MVC tried to find.

■ **Tip**   The .cshtml file extension denotes a C# view that will be processed by Razor. Previous versions of MVC relied on the ASPX view engine, for which view files have the .aspx extension.

Visual Studio opens the Index.cshtml file for editing. You'll see that this file contains mostly HTML. The exception is the part that looks like this:

```
@{
    Layout = null;
}
```

This is an expression that will be interpreted by the Razor view engine. This is a pretty simple example. It just tells Razor that we chose not to use a master page. We are going to ignore Razor for the moment and come back to it later. Make the addition to the Index.cshtml file that is shown in bold in Listing 2-4.

Listing 2-4. Adding to the View HTML

```
@{
    Layout = null;
}

<!DOCTYPE html>

<html>
<head>
    <meta name="viewport" content="width=device-width" />
    <title>Index</title>
</head>
<body>
    <div>
        Hello World (from the view)
    </div>
</body>
</html>
```

The addition displays another simple message. Select **Start Debugging** from the **Debug** menu to run the application and test our view. You should see something similar to Figure 2-10.

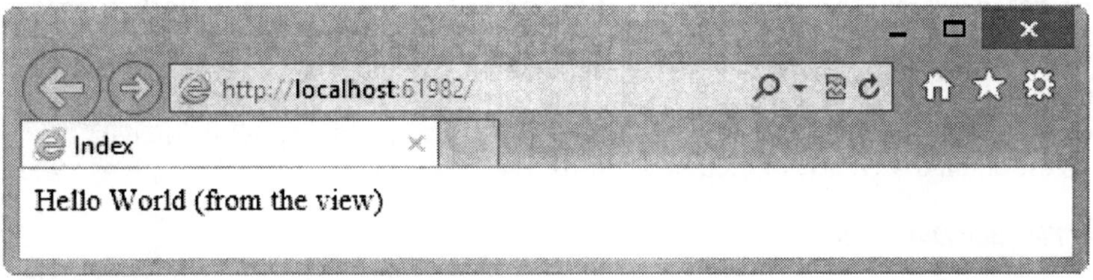

Figure 2-10. Testing the view

When we first edited the `Index` action method, it returned a string value. This meant that MVC did nothing except pass the string value as-is to the browser. Now that the `Index` method returns a `ViewResult`, we instruct MVC to render a view and return HTML. We didn't tell MVC which view should be used, so it used the naming convention to find one automatically. The convention is that the view has the name of the action method and is contained in a folder named after the controller—`~/Views/Home/Index.cshtml`.

We can return other results from action methods besides strings and `ViewResult` objects. For example, if we return a `RedirectResult`, we cause the browser to be redirected to another URL. If we return an `HttpUnauthorizedResult`, we force the user to log in. These objects are collectively known as *action results*, and they are all derived from the `ActionResult` class. The action result system lets us encapsulate and reuse common responses in actions. We'll tell you more about them and show some complex uses as we move through the book.

Adding Dynamic Output

The whole point of a Web application platform is to construct and display *dynamic* output. In MVC, it is the controller's job to construct some data and pass it to the view, which is responsible for rendering it to HTML.

One way to pass data from the controller to the view is by using the `ViewBag` object, which is a member of the `Controller` base class. `ViewBag` is a dynamic object to which you can assign arbitrary properties, making those values available in whatever view is subsequently rendered. Listing 2-5 demonstrates passing some simple dynamic data in this way in the `HomeController.cs` file.

Listing 2-5. Setting Some View Data

```
using System;
using System.Collections.Generic;
using System.Linq;
using System.Web;
using System.Web.Mvc;

namespace PartyInvites.Controllers {
    public class HomeController : Controller {

        public ViewResult Index() {
            int hour = DateTime.Now.Hour;
            ViewBag.Greeting = hour < 12 ? "Good Morning" : "Good Afternoon";
            return View();
        }
    }
}
```

We provide data for the view when we assign a value to the `ViewBag.Greeting` property. The `ViewBag` is an example of a dynamic object and the `Greeting` property didn't exist until the moment we assigned a value—this allows us to pass data from the controller to the view in a free and fluid manner, without having to define classes ahead of time.

We refer to the `ViewBag.Greeting` property again in the view to get the data value, as illustrated in Listing 2-6, which shows the change we made to the `Index.cshtml` file.

Listing 2-6. Retrieving a ViewBag Data Value

```
@{
    Layout = null;
}

<!DOCTYPE html>

<html>
<head>
    <meta name="viewport" content="width=device-width" />
    <title>Index</title>
</head>
<body>
    <div>
        @ViewBag.Greeting World (from the view)
    </div>
</body>
</html>
```

The addition to Listing 2-6 is a Razor expression. When we call the `View` method in the controller's `Index` method, the MVC framework locates the `Index.cshtml` view file and asks the Razor view engine to parse the file's content. Razor looks for expressions like the one we added in the listing and processes them—in this example, processing the expression means inserting the value we assigned to the `ViewBag.Greeting` property in the action method into the view.

There's nothing special about the property name `Greeting`; you could replace this with any property name and it would work the same and you can pass multiple data values from your controller to the view by assigning values to more than one property. We can see our first dynamic MVC output by running the project, as shown in Figure 2-11.

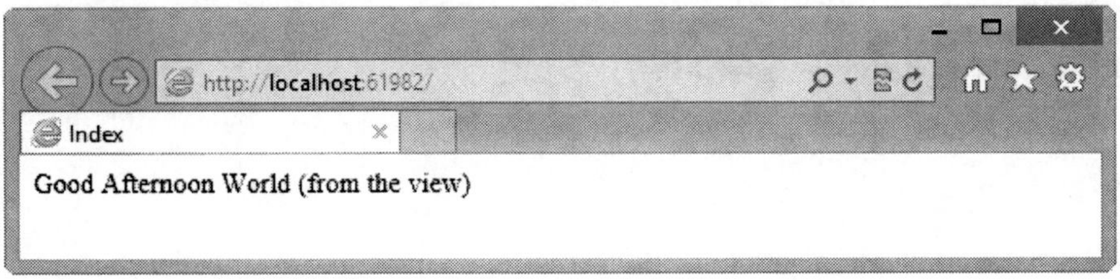

Figure 2-11. A dynamic response from MVC

Creating a Simple Data-Entry Application

In the rest of this chapter, we will explore more of the basic MVC features by building a simple data-entry application. We are going to pick up the pace in this section. Our goal is to demonstrate MVC in action, so we will skip over some of the explanations as to how things work behind the scenes. But don't worry—we'll revisit these topics in depth in later chapters.

Setting the Scene

We are going to imagine that a friend has decided to host a New Year's Eve party and that she has asked us to create a Web site that allows her invitees to electronically RSVP. She has asked for four key features:

- A home page that shows information about the party

- A form that can be used to RSVP

- Validation for the RSVP form, which will display a thank-you page

- RSVPs e-mailed to the party host when complete

In the following sections, we'll build up the MVC project we created at the start of the chapter and add these features. We can knock the first item off the list by applying what we covered earlier—we can add some HTML to our existing view that gives details of the party. Listing 2-7 shows the additions we have made to the `Views/Home/Index.cshtml` file.

Listing 2-7. Displaying Details of the Party

```
@{
    Layout = null;
}

<!DOCTYPE html>

<html>
```

```
<head>
    <meta name="viewport" content="width=device-width" />
    <title>Index</title>
</head>
<body>
    <div>
        @ViewBag.Greeting World (from the view)
        <p>We're going to have an exciting party.<br />
        (To do: sell it better. Add pictures or something.)
        </p>
    </div>
</body>
</html>
```

We are on our way. If you run the application, you'll see the details of the party—well, the placeholder for the details, but you get the idea—as shown in Figure 2-12.

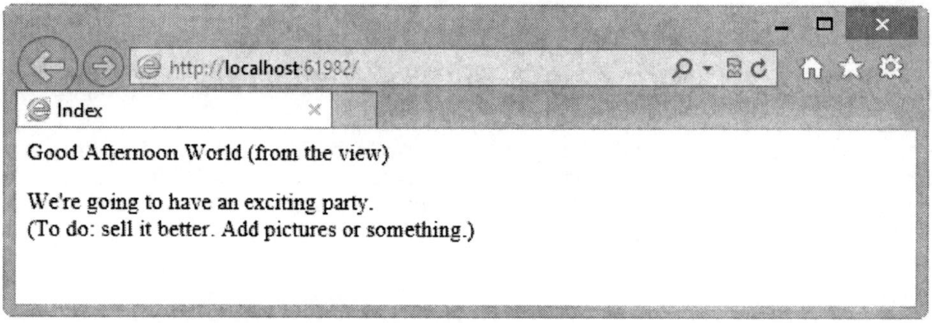

Figure 2-12. Adding to the view HTML

Designing a Data Model

In MVC, the *M* stands for *model*, and it is the most important part of the application. The model is the representation of the real-world objects, processes, and rules that define the subject, known as the *domain*, of our application. The model, often referred to as a *domain model*, contains the C# objects (known as *domain objects*) that make up the universe of our application and the methods that let us manipulate them. The views and controllers expose the domain to our clients in a consistent manner and a well-designed MVC application starts with a well-designed model, which is then the focal point as we add controllers and views.

We don't need a complex model for the PartyInvites application, but we will create one domain class which we will call GuestResponse. This object will be responsible for storing, validating, and confirming an RSVP.

Adding a Model Class

The MVC convention is that the classes that make up a model are placed inside the Models folder. Right click Models in the Solution Explorer window and select Add followed by Class from the pop-up menus. Set the file name to GuestResponse.cs and click the Add button to create the class. Edit the contents of the class to match Listing 2-8.

■ **Tip**   If you don't have a Class menu item, then you probably left the Visual Studio debugger running. Visual Studio restricts the changes you can make to a project while it is running the application.

Listing 2-8. The GuestResponse Domain Class

```
namespace PartyInvites.Models {
    public class GuestResponse {
        public string Name { get; set; }
        public string Email { get; set; }
        public string Phone { get; set; }
        public bool? WillAttend { get; set; }
    }
}
```

■ **Tip**   You may have noticed that the WillAttend property is a *nullable* bool, which means that it can be true, false, or null. We explain the rationale for this in the "Adding Validation" section later in the chapter.

Linking Action Methods

One of our application goals is to include an RSVP form, so we need to add a link to it from our Index.cshtml view, as shown in Listing 2-9.

Listing 2-9. Adding a Link to the RSVP Form

```
@{
    Layout = null;
}

<!DOCTYPE html>

<html>
<head>
    <meta name="viewport" content="width=device-width" />
    <title>Index</title>
</head>
<body>
    <div>
        @ViewBag.Greeting World (from the view)
        <p>We're going to have an exciting party.<br />
        (To do: sell it better. Add pictures or something.)
        </p>
        @Html.ActionLink("RSVP Now", "RsvpForm")
    </div>
</body>
</html>
```

Html.ActionLink is an HTML *helper method*. The MVC Framework comes with a collection of built-in helper methods that are convenient for rendering HTML links, text inputs, checkboxes, selections, and even custom controls. The ActionLink method takes two parameters: the first is the text to display in the link, and the second is the action to perform when the user clicks the link. We explain the rest of the HTML helper methods in Chapters 19-21. You can see the link we have added in Figure 2-13.

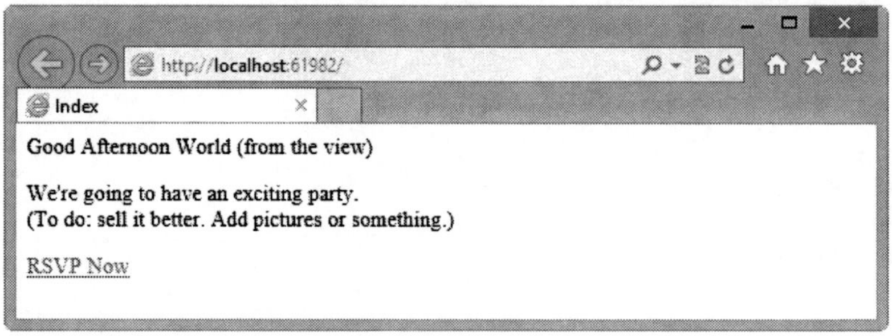

Figure 2-13. Adding a link to the view

If you roll your mouse over the link in the browser, you will see that the link points to http://*yourserver*/Home/RsvpForm. The Html.ActionLink method has inspected our application's URL routing configuration and determined that /Home/RsvpForm is the URL for an action called RsvpForm on a controller called HomeController. Notice that, unlike traditional ASP.NET applications, MVC URLs do not correspond to physical files. Each action method has its own URL, and MVC uses the ASP.NET routing system to translate these URLs into actions.

Creating the Action Method

You will see a 404 Not Found error if you click the link. That's because we have not created the action method that corresponds to the /Home/RsvpForm URL yet. We do this by adding a method called RsvpForm to our HomeController class, as shown in Listing 2-10.

Listing 2-10. Adding a New Action Method to the Controller

```
using System;
using System.Collections.Generic;
using System.Linq;
using System.Web;
using System.Web.Mvc;

namespace PartyInvites.Controllers {
    public class HomeController : Controller {

        public ViewResult Index() {
            int hour = DateTime.Now.Hour;
            ViewBag.Greeting = hour < 12 ? "Good Morning" : "Good Afternoon";
            return View();
        }

        public ViewResult RsvpForm() {
            return View();
        }
    }
}
```

Adding a Strongly Typed View

We are going to add a view for our RsvpForm action method, but we are going to do something slightly different—we are going to create a *strongly typed* view. A strongly typed view is intended to render a specific domain type, and if we specify the type we want to work with (GuestResponse in this example), MVC can create some helpful shortcuts to make it easier.

▓ **Caution** Make sure your MVC project is compiled before proceeding. If you have created the GuestResponse class but not compiled it, MVC won't be able to create a strongly typed view for this type. To compile your application, select Build Solution from the Visual Studio Build menu.

Right-click inside the RsvpForm action method and choose Add View from the pop-up menu to create the view. In the Add View dialog, check the Create a strongly-typed view option and select GuestResponse from the drop-down menu. Uncheck Use a layout or master page and ensure that Razor is selected as the view engine and that the Scaffold template option is set to Empty, as shown in Figure 2-14.

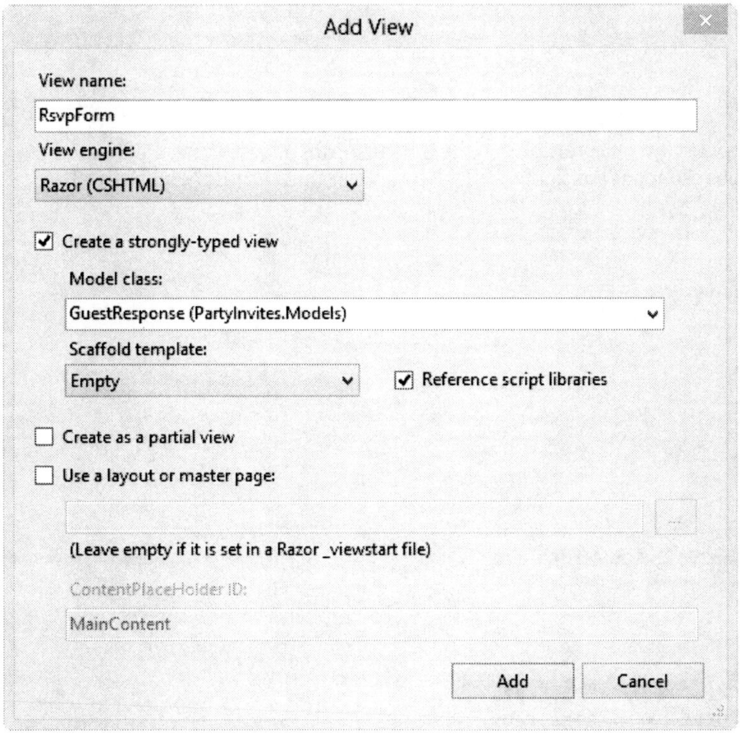

Figure 2-14. Adding a strongly typed view

Click the Add button and Visual Studio will create a new file called RvspForm.cshtml and open it for editing. You can see the initial contents in Listing 2-11. As you will note, this is another skeletal HTML file, but it contains a @model Razor expression. As you will see in a moment, this is the key to a strongly typed view and the convenience it offers.

Listing 2-12. The initial contents of the RsvpForm.cshtml file

```
@model PartyInvites.Models.GuestResponse

@{
    Layout = null;
}

<!DOCTYPE html>

<html>
<head>
    <meta name="viewport" content="width=device-width" />
    <title>RsvpForm</title>
</head>
<body>
    <div>

    </div>
</body>
</html>
```

Building the Form

Now that we have created the strongly typed view, we can build out the contents of `RsvpForm.cshtml` to make it into an HTML form for editing `GuestResponse` objects. Edit the view so that it matches Listing 13.

Listing 2-13. Creating a Form View

```
@model PartyInvites.Models.GuestResponse

@{
    Layout = null;
}

<!DOCTYPE html>

<html>
<head>
    <meta name="viewport" content="width=device-width" />
    <title>RsvpForm</title>
</head>
<body>
    @using (Html.BeginForm()) {
        <p>Your name: @Html.TextBoxFor(x => x.Name) </p>
        <p>Your email: @Html.TextBoxFor(x => x.Email)</p>
        <p>Your phone: @Html.TextBoxFor(x => x.Phone)</p>
        <p>
            Will you attend?
            @Html.DropDownListFor(x => x.WillAttend, new[] {
                new SelectListItem() {Text = "Yes, I'll be there",
                    Value = bool.TrueString},
                new SelectListItem() {Text = "No, I can't come",
```

```
                    Value = bool.FalseString}
                }, "Choose an option")
            </p>
            <input type="submit" value="Submit RSVP" />
        }
    </body>
</html>
```

For each property of the `GuestResponse` model class, we use an HTML helper method to render a suitable HTML `input` control. These methods let you select the property that the `input` element relates to using a lambda expression, like this:

```
@Html.TextBoxFor(x => x.Phone)
```

The HTML `TextBoxFor` helper method generates the HTML for an `input` element, sets the `type` parameter to `text`, and sets the `id` and `name` attributes to `Phone`, the name of the selected domain class property, like this:

```
<input id="Phone" name="Phone" type="text" value="" />
```

This handy feature works because our `RsvpForm` view is strongly typed, and we have told MVC that `GuestResponse` is the type that we want to render with this view, so the HTML helper methods can infer which data type we want to read properties from via the `@model` expression.

Don't worry if you aren't familiar with C# lambda expressions. We provide an overview in Chapter 4—but an alternative to using lambda expressions is to refer to name of the model type property as a string, like this:

```
@Html.TextBox("Email")
```

We find that the lambda expression technique prevents us from mistyping the name of the model type property, because Visual Studio IntelliSense pops up and lets us pick the property automatically, as shown in Figure 2-15.

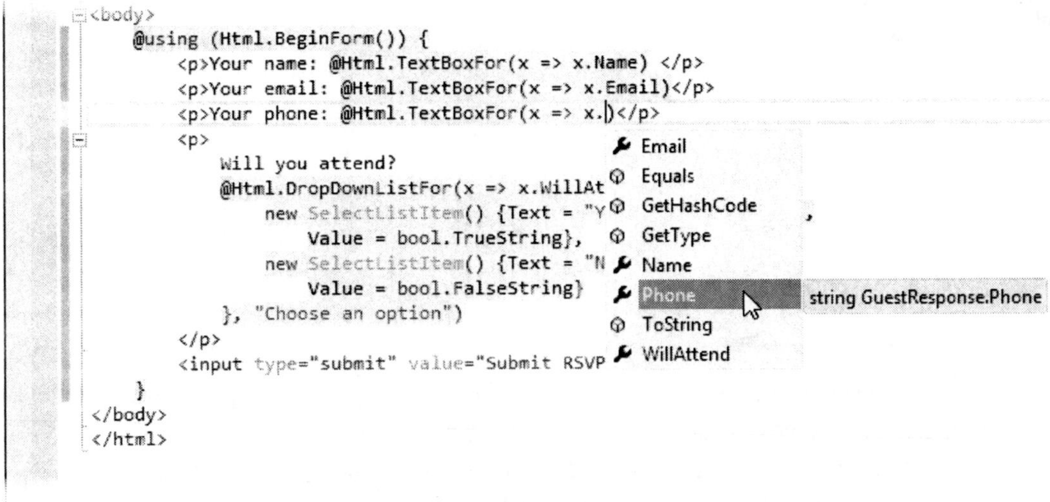

Figure 2-15. Visual Studio IntelliSense for lambda expressions in HTML helper methods

Another convenient helper method is `Html.BeginForm`, which generates an HTML form element configured to postback to the action method. Because we have not passed any parameters to the helper method, it assumes we want to postback to the same URL. A neat trick is to wrap this in a C# `using` statement, like this:

```
@using (Html.BeginForm()) {
    ...form contents go here...
}
```

Normally, when applied like this, the `using` statement ensures that an object is disposed of when it goes out of scope. It is commonly used for database connections, for example, to make sure that they are closed as soon as a query has completed. (This application of the `using` keyword is different from the kind that brings classes in a namespace into scope in a class.)

Instead of disposing of an object, the `HtmlBeginForm` helper closes the HTML `form` element when it goes out of scope. This means that the `Html.BeginForm` helper method creates both parts of a form element, like this:

```
<form action="/Home/RsvpForm" method="post">
    ...form contents go here...
</form>
```

Don't worry if you are not familiar with disposing of C# objects. The point here is to demonstrate how to create a form using the HTML helper method. You can see the form in the `RsvpForm` view when you run the application and click the `RSVP Now` link. Figure 2-16 shows the result.

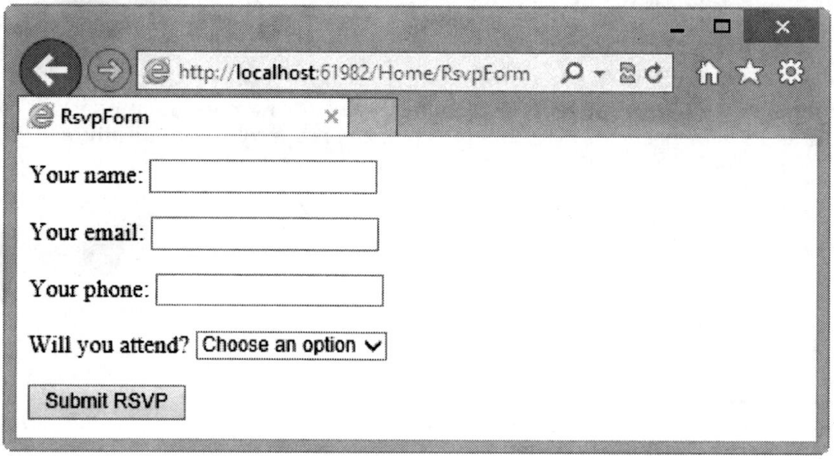

Figure 2-16. The RspvForm view

■ **Note**   This is not a book about CSS or Web design. For the most part, we will be creating examples whose appearance might be described as dated (although we prefer the term *classic*, which feels less disparaging). MVC views generate very clean and pure HTML, and you have total control over the layout of elements and the classes they are assigned to, so you will have no problems using design tools or off-the-shelf templates to make your MVC project pretty.

Handling Forms

We have not told MVC what we want to do when the form is posted to the server. As things stand, clicking the `Submit RSVP` button just clears any values you have entered into the form. That is because the form posts back to the `RsvpForm` action method in the `Home` controller, which just tells MVC to render the view again.

■ **Note** You might be surprised that the input data is lost when the view is rendered again. If so, you have probably been developing applications with ASP.NET Web Forms, which automatically preserves data in this situation. We will show you how to achieve the same effect with MVC shortly.

To receive and process submitted form data, we're going to do a clever thing. We will add a second `RsvpForm` action method in order to create the following:

- *A method that responds to HTTP GET requests*: A `GET` request is what a browser issues normally each time someone clicks a link. This version of the action will be responsible for displaying the initial blank form when someone first visits `/Home/RsvpForm`.

- *A method that responds to HTTP POST requests*: By default, forms rendered using `Html.BeginForm()` are submitted by the browser as a `POST` request. This version of the action will be responsible for receiving submitted data and deciding what to do with it.

Handing `GET` and `POST` requests in separate C# methods helps to keep our code tidy, since the two methods have different responsibilities. Both action methods are invoked by the same URL, but MVC makes sure that the appropriate method is called, based on whether we are dealing with a `GET` or `POST` request. Listing 2-14 shows the changes we need to apply to the `HomeController` class.

Listing 2-14. Adding an Action Method to Support POST Requests

```
using System;
using System.Collections.Generic;
using System.Linq;
using System.Web;
using System.Web.Mvc;
using PartyInvites.Models;

namespace PartyInvites.Controllers {
    public class HomeController : Controller {

        public ViewResult Index() {
            int hour = DateTime.Now.Hour;
            ViewBag.Greeting = hour < 12 ? "Good Morning" : "Good Afternoon";
            return View();
        }

        [HttpGet]
        public ViewResult RsvpForm() {
```

```
            return View();
        }

        [HttpPost]
        public ViewResult RsvpForm(GuestResponse guestResponse) {
            // TODO: Email response to the party organizer
            return View("Thanks", guestResponse);
        }
    }
}
```

We have added the HttpGet attribute to our existing RsvpForm action method. This tells MVC that this method should be used only for GET requests. We then added an overloaded version of RsvpForm, which takes a GuestResponse parameter and applies the HttpPost attribute. The attribute tells MVC that the new method will deal with POST requests. Notice that we also imported the PartyInvites.Models namespace—this is just so we can refer to the GuestResponse model type without needing to qualify the class name. We will explain how our additions to the listing work in the sections that follow.

Using Model Binding

The first overload of the RsvpForm action method renders the same view as before. It generates the form shown in Figure 2-16. The second overload is more interesting because of the parameter, but given that the action method will be invoked in response to an HTTP POST request, and that the GuestResponse type is a C# class, how are the two connected?

The answer is *model binding*, an extremely useful MVC feature whereby incoming data is parsed and the key/value pairs in the HTTP request are used to populate properties of domain model types. This process is the opposite of using the HTML helper methods; that is, when creating the form data to send to the client, we generated HTML input elements where the values for the id and name attributes were derived from the model class property names.

In contrast, with model binding, the names of the input elements are used to set the values of the properties in an instance of the model class, which is then passed to our POST-enabled action method.

Model binding is a powerful and customizable feature that eliminates the grind and toil of dealing with HTTP requests directly and lets us work with C# objects rather than dealing with Request.Form[ ] and Request.QueryString[ ] values. The GuestResponse object that is passed as the parameter to our action method is automatically populated with the data from the form fields. We will dive into the detail of model binding, including how it can be customized, in Chapter 22.

Rendering Other Views

The second overload of the RsvpForm action method also demonstrates how we can tell MVC to render a specific view in response to a request, rather than the default view. Here is the relevant statement:

```
return View("Thanks", guestResponse);
```

This call to the View method tells MVC to find and render a view called Thanks and to pass our GuestResponse object to the view. To create the view we have specified, right-click inside one of the HomeController methods and select Add View from the pop-up menu. Set the name of the view to Thanks, as shown in Figure 2-17.

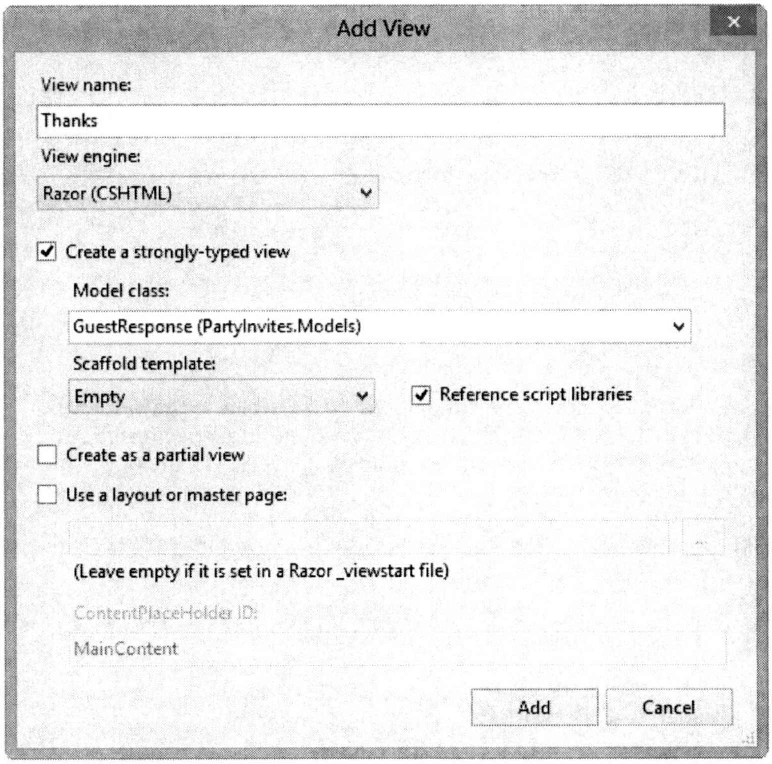

Figure 2-17. Adding the Thanks view

We are going to create another strongly typed view, so check that box in the **Add View** dialog. The data class we select for the view must correspond with the class we pass to the view using the **View** method, so ensure that **GuestResponse** is selected from the drop-down list. Ensure that the **Use a layout or master page** option is not checked, that **View engine** is set to **Razor**, and the **Scaffold template** option is set to **Empty**.

Click **Add** to create the new view. Because the view is associated with the **Home** controller, MVC creates the view as ~/Views/Home/Thanks.cshtml. Edit the new view so that it matches Listing 2-15—we have highlighted the markup you need to add.

Listing 2-15. The Thanks View

```
@model PartyInvites.Models.GuestResponse

@{
    Layout = null;
}

<!DOCTYPE html>

<html>
<head>
    <meta name="viewport" content="width=device-width" />
```

```
        <title>Thanks</title>
    </head>
    <body>
        <div>
            <h1>Thank you, @Model.Name!</h1>
            @if (Model.WillAttend == true) {
                @:It's great that you're coming. The drinks are already in the fridge!
            } else {
                @:Sorry to hear that you can't make it, but thanks for letting us know.
            }
        </div>
    </body>
</html>
```

The Thanks view uses Razor to display content based on the value of the GuestResponse properties that we passed to the View method in the RsvpForm action method. The Razor @model operator specifies the domain model type that the view is strongly typed with. To access the value of a property in the domain object, we use Model.*PropertyName*. For example, to get the value of the Name property, we call Model.Name. Don't worry if the Razor syntax doesn't make sense—we will explain it in detail in Chapter 5.

Now that we have created the Thanks view, we have a basic working example of handling a form with MVC.

Start the application in Visual Studio, click the RSVP Now link, add some data to the form, and click the Submit RSVP button. You will see the result shown in Figure 2-18 (although it might differ if your name is not Joe and you said you could not attend).

Figure 2-18. The rendered Thanks view

Adding Validation

We are now in a position to add validation to our application. If we did not do this, our users could enter nonsense data or even submit an empty form.

In an MVC application, validation is typically applied in the domain model, rather than in the user interface. This means that we define our validation criteria in one place, and it takes effect in any place the model class is used. ASP.NET MVC supports declarative validation rules defined with attributes from the System.ComponentModel.DataAnnotations namespace. Listing 2-16 shows how these attributes can be applied to the GuestResponse model class.

Listing 2-16. Applying Validation to the GuestResponse Model Class

```
using System.ComponentModel.DataAnnotations;

namespace PartyInvites.Models {

    public class GuestResponse {

        [Required(ErrorMessage = "Please enter your name")]
        public string Name { get; set; }

        [Required(ErrorMessage = "Please enter your email address")]
        [RegularExpression(".+\\@.+\\..+",
            ErrorMessage = "Please enter a valid email address")]
        public string Email { get; set; }

        [Required(ErrorMessage = "Please enter your phone number")]
        public string Phone { get; set; }

        [Required(ErrorMessage = "Please specify whether you'll attend")]
        public bool? WillAttend { get; set; }
    }
}
```

The validations rules are shown in bold. MVC automatically detects the attributes and uses them to validate data during the model-binding process. Notice that we have imported the namespace that contains the validations, so we can refer to them without needing to qualify their names.

■ **Tip**   As noted earlier, we used a nullable bool for the WillAttend property. We did this so that we could apply the Required validation attribute. If we used a regular bool, the value we received through model binding could be only true or false, and we wouldn't be able to tell if the user had selected a value. A nullable bool has three possible values: true, false, and null. The null value will be used if the user hasn't selected a value, and this causes the Required attribute to report a validation error.

We can check to see if there has been a validation problem using the ModelState.IsValid property in our controller class. Listing 2-17 shows how to do this in our POST-enabled RsvpForm action method.

Listing 2-17. Checking for Form Validation Errors

```
...
[HttpPost]
public ViewResult RsvpForm(GuestResponse guestResponse) {
    if (ModelState.IsValid) {
        // TODO: Email response to the party organizer
        return View("Thanks", guestResponse);
    } else {
        // there is a validation error
        return View();
    }
}
```

...

If there are no validation errors, we tell MVC to render the Thanks view as we did previously. If there are validation errors, we re-render the RsvpForm view by calling the View method without any parameters.

Just displaying the form when there is an error is not very helpful—we need to provide the user with some indication of what the problem is and why we couldn't accept their form submission. We do this by using the Html.ValidationSummary helper method in the RsvpForm view, as shown in Listing 2-18.

Listing 2-18. Using the Html.ValidationSummary Help Method

```
@model PartyInvites.Models.GuestResponse

@{
    Layout = null;
}

<!DOCTYPE html>

<html>
<head>
    <meta name="viewport" content="width=device-width" />
    <title>RsvpForm</title>
</head>
<body>
    @using (Html.BeginForm()) {
        @Html.ValidationSummary()
        <p>Your name: @Html.TextBoxFor(x => x.Name) </p>
        <p>Your email: @Html.TextBoxFor(x => x.Email)</p>
        <p>Your phone: @Html.TextBoxFor(x => x.Phone)</p>
        <p>
            Will you attend?
            @Html.DropDownListFor(x => x.WillAttend, new[] {
                new SelectListItem() {Text = "Yes, I'll be there",
                    Value = bool.TrueString},
                new SelectListItem() {Text = "No, I can't come",
                    Value = bool.FalseString}
            }, "Choose an option")
        </p>
        <input type="submit" value="Submit RSVP" />
    }
</body>
</html>
```

If there are no errors, the Html.ValidationSummary method creates a hidden list item as a placeholder in the form. MVC makes the placeholder visible and adds the error messages defined by the validation attributes. You can see how this appears in Figure 2-19.

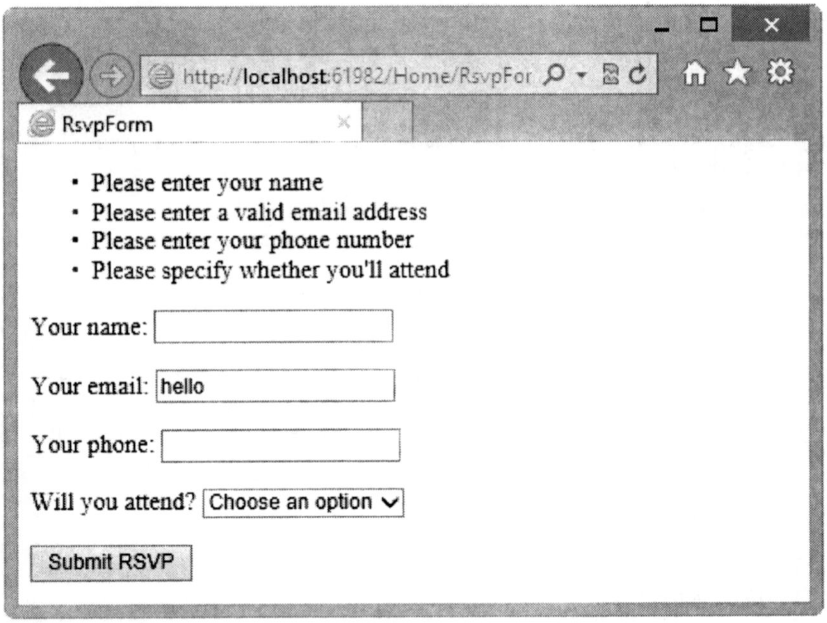

Figure 2-19. The validation summary

The user won't be shown the Thanks view until all of the validation constraints we applied to the GuestResponse class have been satisfied. Notice that the data we entered into the form was preserved and displayed again when the view was rendered with the validation summary. This is another benefit we get from model binding.

▓ **Note** If you have worked with ASP.NET Web Forms, you will know that Web Forms has a concept of "server controls" that retain state by serializing values into a hidden form field called __VIEWSTATE. ASP.NET MVC model binding is not related to the Web Forms concepts of server controls, postbacks, or View State. ASP.NET MVC does not inject a hidden __VIEWSTATE field into your rendered HTML pages.

Highlighting Invalid Fields

The HTML helper methods that create text boxes, drop-downs, and other elements have a very handy feature that can be used in conjunction with model binding. The same mechanism that preserves the data that a user entered in a form can also be used to highlight individual fields that failed the validation checks.

When a model class property has failed validation, the HTML helper methods will generate slightly different HTML. As an example, here is the HTML that a call to Html.TextBoxFor(x => x.Name) generates when there is no validation error:

```
<input data-val="true" data-val-required="Please enter your name" id="Name" name="Name"
    type="text" value="" />
```

And here is the HTML the same call generates when the user doesn't provide a value (which is a validation error because we applied the Required attribute to the Name property in the GuestResponse model class):

```
<input class="input-validation-error" data-val="true" data-val-required="Please enter your
name" id="Name" name="Name" type="text" value="" />
```

We have highlighted the difference in bold. This helper method added a class called input-validation-error. We can take advantage of this feature by creating a style sheet that contains CSS styles for this class and the others that different HTML helper methods apply.

The convention in MVC projects is that static content, such as CSS style sheets, is placed into a folder called Content. We created the Content folder by right clicking on the PartyInvites project in the Solution Explorer and selecting Add ↗ New Folder from the pop-up menu. We created the style sheet by right clicking on the Content folder, selecting Add ↗ New Item and picking the Style Sheet item in the Add New Item dialog. We called our style sheet Site.css, which is the name that Visual Studio uses when you create a project using an MVC template other than Empty. You can see the contents of the Content/Site.css file in Listing 2-19.

Listing 2-19. The contents of the Content/Site.css file

```
.field-validation-error     {color: #f00;}
.field-validation-valid     { display: none;}
.input-validation-error     { border: 1px solid #f00; background-color: #fee; }
.validation-summary-errors { font-weight: bold; color: #f00;}
.validation-summary-valid  { display: none;}
```

To use this style sheet, we add a new reference to the head section of RsvpForm view, as shown in Listing 2-20. You add link elements to views just as you would to a regular static HTML file.

Listing 2-20. Adding the link element to the RsvpForm view

```
@model PartyInvites.Models.GuestResponse

@{
    Layout = null;
}

<!DOCTYPE html>

<html>
<head>
    <meta name="viewport" content="width=device-width" />
    <link rel="stylesheet" type="text/css" href="~/Content/Site.css" />
    <title>RsvpForm</title>
</head>
<body>
    @using (Html.BeginForm()) {
        @Html.ValidationSummary()
        <p>Your name: @Html.TextBoxFor(x => x.Name) </p>
        <p>Your email: @Html.TextBoxFor(x => x.Email)</p>
        <p>Your phone: @Html.TextBoxFor(x => x.Phone)</p>
        <p>
```

```
            Will you attend?
            @Html.DropDownListFor(x => x.WillAttend, new[] {
                new SelectListItem() {Text = "Yes, I'll be there",
                    Value = bool.TrueString},
                new SelectListItem() {Text = "No, I can't come",
                    Value = bool.FalseString}
            }, "Choose an option")
        </p>
        <input type="submit" value="Submit RSVP" />
    }
</body>
</html>
```

■ **Tip** If you have used MVC 3, you might have been expecting us to have added the CSS file to the view by specifying the href attribute as @Href("~/Content/Site.css") or @Url.Content("~/Content/Site.css"). With MVC 4, Razor automatically detects attributes that begin with ~/ and automatically inserts the @Href or @Url call for you.

Now a more visually obvious validation error will be displayed when data is submitted that causes a validation error, as shown in Figure 2-20.

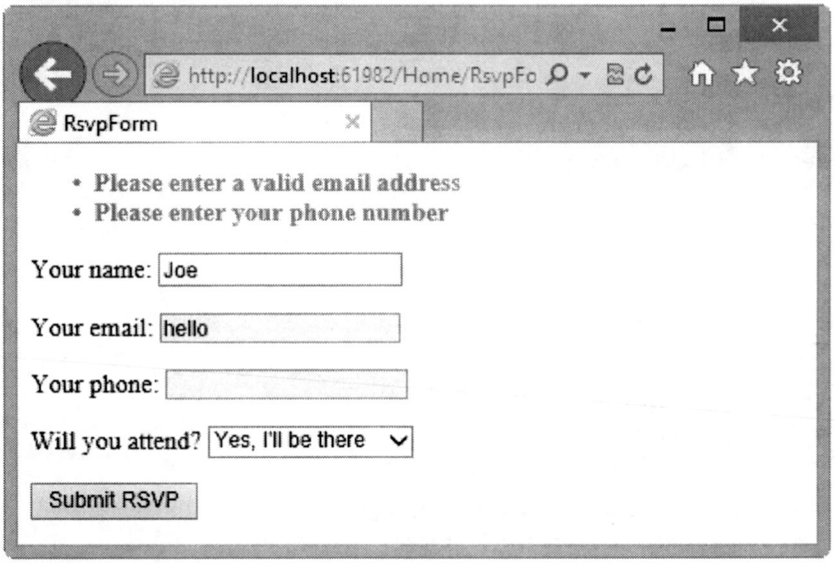

Figure 2-20. Automatically highlighted validation errors

Completing the Example

The last requirement for our sample application is to e-mail completed RSVPs to our friend, the party organizer. We could do this by adding an action method to create and send an e-mail message using the e-mail classes in the .NET Framework. Instead, we are going to use the WebMail helper method. This is not part of the MVC framework, but it does let us complete this example without getting mired in the details of setting up other means of sending e-mail.

■ **Note** We used the WebMail helper because it lets us demonstrate sending an e-mail message with a minimum of effort. Typically, however, we would prefer to put this functionality in an action method. We will explain why when we describe the MVC architecture pattern in Chapter 3.

We want the e-mail message to be sent as we render the Thanks view. Listing 2-21 show the changes that we need to apply.

Listing 2-21. Using the WebMail Helper

```
@model PartyInvites.Models.GuestResponse

@{
    Layout = null;
}

<!DOCTYPE html>

<html>
<head>
    <meta name="viewport" content="width=device-width" />
    <title>Thanks</title>
</head>
<body>
    @{
        try {
            WebMail.SmtpServer = "smtp.example.com";
            WebMail.SmtpPort = 587;
            WebMail.EnableSsl = true;
            WebMail.UserName = "mySmtpUsername";
            WebMail.Password = "mySmtpPassword";
            WebMail.From = "rsvps@example.com";

            WebMail.Send("party-host@example.com", "RSVP Notification",
                Model.Name + " is " + ((Model.WillAttend ?? false) ? "" : "not")
                    + "attending");

        } catch (Exception) {
            @:<b>Sorry - we couldn't send the email to confirm your RSVP.</b>
        }
    }
    <div>
```

```
        <h1>Thank you, @Model.Name!</h1>
        @if (Model.WillAttend == true) {
            @:It's great that you're coming. The drinks are already in the fridge!
        } else {
            @:Sorry to hear that you can't make it, but thanks for letting us know.
        }
    </div>
</body>
</html>
```

We have added a Razor expression that uses the `WebMail` helper to configure the details of our e-mail server, including the server name, whether the server requires SSL connections, and account details. Once we have configured all of the details, we use the `WebMail.Send` method to send the e-mail.

We have enclosed all of the e-mail code in a `try...catch` block so that we can alert the user if the e-mail is not sent. We do this by adding a block of text to the output of the `Thanks` view. A better approach would be to display a separate error view when the e-mail message cannot be sent, but we wanted to keep things simple in our first MVC application.

Summary

In this chapter, we created a new MVC project and used it to construct a simple MVC data-entry application, giving you a first glimpse of the MVC Framework architecture and approach. We skipped over some key features (including Razor syntax, routing, and automated testing), but we will come back to these topics in depth in later chapters.

In the next chapter, we will explore the MVC architecture, design patterns, and techniques that we will use throughout the book.

CHAPTER 3

■ ■ ■

The MVC Pattern

In Chapter 7 we are going to start building a more complex ASP.NET MVC example. Before we start digging into the details of the ASP.NET MVC Framework, we want to make sure you are familiar with the MVC design pattern and the thinking behind it. In this chapter, we describe the following:

- The MVC architecture pattern

- Domain models and repositories

- Creating loosely coupled systems using dependency injection (DI)

- The basics of automated testing

You might already be familiar with some of the ideas and conventions we discuss in this chapter, especially if you have done advanced ASP.NET or C# development. If not, we encourage you to read this chapter carefully—a good understanding of what lies behind MVC can help put the features of the framework into context as we continue through the book.

The History of MVC

The term *model-view-controller* has been in use since the late 1970s and arose from the Smalltalk project at Xerox PARC where it was conceived as a way to organize some early GUI applications. Some of the fine detail of the original MVC pattern was tied to Smalltalk-specific concepts, such as *screens* and *tools*, but the broader concepts are still applicable to applications—and they are especially well suited to Web applications.

Interactions with an MVC application follow a natural cycle of user actions and view updates, where the view is assumed to be stateless. This fits nicely with the HTTP requests and responses that underpin a Web application.

Further, MVC forces a *separation of concerns*—the domain model and controller logic is decoupled from the user interface. In a Web application, this means that the mess of HTML is kept apart from the rest of the application, which makes maintenance and testing simpler and easier. It was Ruby on Rails that led to renewed mainstream interest in MVC and it remains the poster child for the MVC pattern. Many other MVC frameworks have since emerged and demonstrated the benefits of MVC—including, of course, ASP.NET MVC.

Understanding the MVC Pattern

In high-level terms, the MVC pattern means that an MVC application will be split into at least three pieces:

- *Models*, which contain or represent the data that users work with. These can be simple *view models*, which just represent data being transferred between views and controllers; or they can be *domain models*, which contain the data in a business domain as well as the operations, transformations, and rules for manipulating that data.

- *Views*, which are used to render some part of the model as a user interface.

- *Controllers*, which process incoming requests, perform operations on the model, and select views to render to the user.

Models are the definition of the universe your application works in. In a banking application, for example, the model represents everything in the bank that the application supports, such as accounts, the general ledger, and credit limits for customers—as well as the operations that can be used to manipulate the data in the model, such as depositing funds and making withdrawals from the accounts. The model is also responsible for preserving the overall state and consistency of the data—for example, making sure that all transactions are added to the ledger, and that a client doesn't withdraw more money than he is entitled to or more money than the bank has.

Models are also defined by what they are *not* responsible for: models don't deal with rendering UIs or processing requests—those are the responsibilities of *views* and *controllers*. *Views* contain the logic required to display elements of the model to the user—and nothing more. They have no direct awareness of the model and do not directly communicate with the model in any way. *Controllers* are the bridge between views and the model—requests come in from the client and are serviced by the controller, which selects an appropriate view to show the user and, if required, an appropriate operation to perform on the model.

Each piece of the MVC architecture is well-defined and self-contained—this is referred to as the *separation of concerns*. The logic that manipulates the data in the model is contained *only* in the model; the logic that displays data is *only* in the view, and the code that handles user requests and input is contained *only* in the controller. With a clear division between each of the pieces, your application will be easier to maintain and extend over its lifetime, no matter how large it becomes.

Understanding the Domain Model

The most important part of an MVC application is the domain model. We create the model by identifying the real-world entities, operations, and rules that exist in the industry or activity that our application must support, known as the *domain*.

We then create a software representation of the domain—the *domain model*. For our purposes, the domain model is a set of C# types (classes, structs, etc.), collectively known as the *domain types*. The operations from the domain are represented by the methods defined in the domain types, and the domain rules are expressed in the logic inside of these methods—or, as we saw in the previous chapter, by applying C# attributes to the methods. When we create an instance of a domain type to represent a specific piece of data, we create a *domain object*. Domain models are usually persistent and long-lived—there are lots of different ways of achieving this, but relational databases remain the most common choice.

In short, a domain model is the single, authoritative definition of the business data and processes within your application. A *persistent* domain model is also the authoritative definition of the state of your domain representation.

The domain model approach solves many of the problems that arise in the smart UI pattern. Our business logic is contained in one place—if you need to manipulate the data in your model or add a new process or rule, the domain model is the only part of your application that has to be changed.

■ **Tip** A common way of enforcing the separation of the domain model from the rest of an ASP.NET MVC application is to place the model in a separate C# assembly. In this way, you can create references *to* the domain model from other parts of the application but ensure that there are no references in the other direction. This is particularly useful in large-scale projects. We use this approach in the example we start building in Chapter 7.

The ASP.NET Implementation of MVC

In MVC, controllers are C# classes, usually derived from the `System.Web.Mvc.Controller` class. Each `public` method in a class derived from `Controller` is called an *action method*, which is associated with a configurable URL through the ASP.NET routing system. When a request is sent to the URL associated with an action method, the statements in the controller class are executed in order to perform some operation on the domain model and then select a view to display to the client. Figure 3-1 shows the interactions between the controller, model, and view.

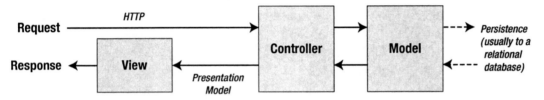

Figure 3-1. The interactions in an MVC application

The ASP.NET MVC Framework provides support for a choice of view engines. Earlier versions of MVC used the standard ASP.NET view engine, which processed `ASPX` pages using a streamlined version of the Web Forms markup syntax. MVC 3 introduced the Razor view engine, which has been refined in MVC 4 and that uses a different syntax entirely (described in Chapter 5). Visual Studio provides IntelliSense support for both view engines, making it a simple matter to inject and respond to view data supplied by the controller.

ASP.NET MVC doesn't apply any constraints on the implementation of your domain model. You can create a model using regular C# objects and implement persistence using any of the databases, object-relational mapping frameworks, or other data tools supported by .NET. Visual Studio creates a `/Models` folder as part of the MVC project template. This is suitable for simple projects, but more complex applications tend to define their domain models in a separate Visual Studio project. We'll discuss implementing a domain model later in this chapter.

Comparing MVC to Other Patterns

MVC is not the only software architecture pattern, of course—there are many others and some of them are, or at least have been, extremely popular. We can learn a lot about MVC by looking at other patterns. In the following sections, we briefly describe different approaches to structuring an application and contrast them with MVC. Some of the patterns are close variations on the MVC theme, whereas others are entirely different.

We are not suggesting that MVC is the perfect pattern for all situations. We are both proponents of picking the best approach to solve the problem at hand. As you will see, there are situations where we feel that some competing patterns are as useful as or better than MVC. We encourage you to make an *informed* and *deliberate* choice when selecting a pattern. The fact that you are reading this book suggests

49

that you already have a certain commitment to the MVC pattern, but we think it is always helpful to maintain the widest possible perspective.

Understanding the Smart UI Pattern

One of the most common design patterns is known as the *smart user interface* (smart UI). Most programmers have created a smart UI application at some point in their careers—we certainly have. If you have used Windows Forms or ASP.NET Web Forms, you have too.

To build a smart UI application, developers construct a user interface—usually by dragging a set of *components* or *controls* onto a design surface or canvas. The controls report interactions with the user by emitting events for button presses, keystrokes, mouse movements, and so on. The developer adds code to respond to these events in a series of *event handlers*—small blocks of code that are called when a specific event on a specific component is emitted. In doing this, we end up with a monolithic application, as shown in Figure 3-2—the code that handles the user interface and the business is all mixed together with no separation of concerns at all. The code that defines the acceptable values for a data input, that queries for data or modifies a user account, ends up in little pieces, coupled together by the order in which events are expected.

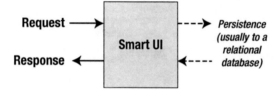

Figure 3-2. The Smart UI pattern

The biggest drawback with this design is that it is difficult to maintain and extend—mixing the domain model and business logic code in with the user interface code leads to duplication, where the same fragment of business logic is copied and pasted to support a newly added component. Finding all of the duplicate parts and applying a fix can be difficult; and in a complex smart UI application, it can be almost impossible to add a new feature without breaking an existing one. Testing a Smart UI application can also be difficult—the only way is to simulate user interactions, which is far from ideal and a difficult basis from which to provide full test coverage.

In the world of MVC, the Smart UI is often referred to as an *anti-pattern*—something that should be avoided at all costs. This antipathy arises—at least in part—because people come to MVC looking for an alternative after spending part of their careers trying to develop and maintain Smart UI applications. That is certainly true for us; we both bear the scars of those long years, but we don't reject the smart UI pattern out of hand. Not everything is rotten in the Smart UI pattern and there are positive aspects to this approach. Smart UI applications are quick and easy to develop—the component and design tool producers have put a lot of effort into making the development experience a pleasant one, and even the most inexperienced programmer can produce something professional-looking and reasonably functional in just a few hours.

The biggest weakness of Smart UI applications—maintainability—doesn't arise in small development efforts. If you are producing a simple tool for a small audience, a Smart UI application can be a perfect solution. The additional complexity of an MVC application simply isn't warranted.

Finally, Smart UIs are ideal for user interface prototyping—those design surface tools are *really* good. If you are sitting with a customer and want to capture the requirements for the look and flow of the interface, a Smart UI tool can be a quick and responsive way to generate and test different ideas.

Understanding the Model-View Architecture

The area in which maintenance problems tend to arise in a Smart UI application is in the business logic, which ends up so diffused across the application that making changes or adding features becomes a fraught process. An improvement in this area is offered by the *model-view* architecture, which pulls out the business logic into a separate domain model. In doing this, the data, processes, and rules are all concentrated in one part of the application, as shown in Figure 3-3.

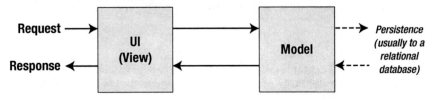

Figure 3-3. The model-view pattern

The model-view architecture is a big improvement over the monolithic Smart UI pattern—it is much easier to maintain, for example. However, two problems arise. The first is that since the UI and the domain model are so closely integrated, it can be difficult to perform unit testing on either. The second problem arises from practice, rather than the definition of the pattern. The model typically contains a mass of data access code—this need not be the case, but it usually is—and this means that the data model does not contain just the business data, operations, and rules.

Understanding Classic Three-Tier Architectures

To address the problems of the model-view architecture, the *three-tier* or *three-layer* pattern separates the persistence code from the domain model and places it in a new component called the *data access layer* (DAL). This is shown in Figure 3-4.

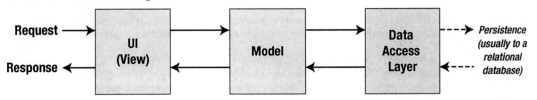

Figure 3-4. The three-tier pattern

This is a big step forward. The three-tier architecture is the most widely used pattern for business applications—it has no constraints on how the UI is implemented and provides good separation of concerns without being too complicated. And, with some care, the DAL can be created so that unit testing is relatively easy. You can see the obvious similarities between a classic three-tier application and the MVC pattern. The difference is that when the UI layer is directly coupled to a click-and-event GUI framework (such as Windows Forms or ASP.NET Web Forms), it becomes almost impossible to perform automated unit tests. And because the UI part of a three-tier application can be very complex, there's a lot of code that can't be rigorously tested.

In the worst scenario, the three-tier pattern's lack of enforced discipline in the UI tier means that many such applications end up as thinly disguised Smart UI applications, with no real separation of concerns. This gives the worst possible outcome—an untestable, unmaintainable application that is excessively complex.

Understanding Variations on MVC

We've already explored the core design principles of MVC applications, especially as they apply to the ASP.NET MVC implementation. Others interpret aspects of the pattern differently and have added to, adjusted, or otherwise adapted MVC to suit the scope and subject of their projects. In the following sections, we will provide a brief overview of the two most prevalent variations on the MVC theme. Understanding these variations is not essential to working with ASP.NET MVC. We have included this information for completeness and because you have heard of these variations elsewhere.

Understanding the Model-View-Presenter Pattern

Model-view-presenter (MVP) is a variation on MVC that is designed to fit more easily with stateful GUI platforms such as Windows Forms or ASP.NET Web Forms—this is a worthwhile attempt to get the best aspects of the Smart UI pattern, without the problems it usually brings.

In this pattern, the presenter has the same responsibilities as an MVC controller—but it also takes a more direct relationship to a stateful view, directly managing the values displayed in the UI components according to the user's inputs and actions. There are two implementations of this pattern:

- The *passive view* implementation, in which the view contains no logic—it is a container for UI controls that are directly manipulated by the presenter.

- The *supervising controller* implementation, in which the view may be responsible for some elements of presentation logic, such as data binding, and has been given a reference to a data source from the domain models.

The difference between these two approaches relates to how intelligent the view is. Either way, the presenter is decoupled from the GUI framework, which makes the presenter logic simpler and suitable for unit testing.

Understanding the Model-View-View Model Pattern

The *model-view-view model* (MVVM) pattern is the most recent variation on MVC. It originated in 2005 with the Microsoft team developing the technology that would become the Windows Presentation Foundation (WPF) and Silverlight.

In the MVVM pattern, models and views have the same roles as they do in MVC. The difference is the MVVM concept of a *view model*, which is an abstract representation of a user interface—typically a C# class that exposes both properties for the data to be displayed in the UI and operations on the data that can be invoked from the UI. Unlike an MVC controller, an MVVM view model has no notion that a view (or any specific UI technology) exists. An MVVM view uses the WPF/Silverlight *binding* feature to bidirectionally associate properties exposed by controls in the view (items in a drop-down menu, or the effect of pressing a button) with the properties exposed by the view model.

MVVM is closely associated with WPF bindings and so it is not a pattern that is readily applied to other platforms.

■ **Tip** MVC also uses the term *view model* but refers to a simple model class that is used only to pass data from a controller to a view. We differentiate between view models and domain models, which are sophisticated representations of data, operations, and rules.

Applying Domain-Driven Development

We have already described how a *domain model* represents the real world in your application, containing representations of your objects, processes, and rules. The domain model is the heart of an MVC application—everything else, including views and controllers, is just a means to interact with the domain model.

ASP.NET MVC does not dictate the technology used for the domain model. You are free to select any technology that will interoperate with the .NET Framework—and there are lots of choices. However, ASP.NET MVC does provide infrastructure and conventions to help connect the classes in the domain model with the controllers and views, and with the MVC Framework itself. There are three key features:

- *Model binding* is a convention-based feature that populates model objects automatically using incoming data, usually from an HTML form post.

- *Model metadata* lets you describe the meaning of your model classes to the framework. For example, you can provide human-readable descriptions of their properties or give hints about how they should be displayed. The MVC Framework can then automatically render a display or an editor UI for your model classes into your views.

- *Validation,* which is performed during model binding and applies rules that can be defined as metadata.

We briefly touched on model binding and validation when we built our first MVC application in Chapter 2—and we will return to these topics and investigate further in Chapters 22 and 23. For the moment, we are going to put the ASP.NET implementation of MVC aside and think about domain modeling as an activity in its own right. We are going to create a simple domain model using .NET and SQL Server, using a few core techniques from the world of *domain-driven development* (DDD).

Modeling an Example Domain

You have probably experienced the process of brainstorming a domain model. It usually involves developers, business experts, and copious quantities of coffee, cookies, and whiteboard pens. After a while, the people in the room converge on a common understanding and a first draft of the domain model emerges. (We are skipping over the many hours of disagreement and arguing that seems inevitable at this stage in the process. Suffice to say that the developers will spend the first hours askance at demands from the business experts for features that are taken directly from science fiction, while the business experts will express surprise and concern that time and cost estimates for the application are similar to what NASA requires to reach Mars. The coffee is essential in resolving such standoffs—eventually everyone's bladder is so full that progress will be made and compromises reached, just to bring the meeting to an end).

You might end up with something similar to Figure 3-5, which is the starting point for this example—a simple domain model for an auction application.

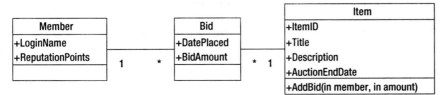

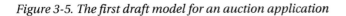

Figure 3-5. The first draft model for an auction application

This model contains a set of Members, which each hold a set of Bids. Each Bid is for an Item, and each Item can hold multiple Bids from different Members.

Ubiquitous Language

A key benefit of implementing your domain model as a distinct component is that you can adopt the language and terminology of your choice. You should try to find terminology for its objects, operations, and relationships that makes sense not just to developers, but to your business experts as well. We recommend that you adopt the domain terminology when it already exists—for example, if what a developer would refer to as *users* and *roles* are known as *agents* and *clearances* in the domain, we recommend you adopt the latter terms in your domain model.

And when modeling concepts that the domain experts do not have terms for, you should come to a common agreement about how you will refer to them, creating a ubiquitous language that runs throughout the domain model.

Developers tend to speak in the language of the code—the names of classes, database tables and so on. Business experts do not understand these terms—and nor should they have to. A business expert with a little technical knowledge is a dangerous thing, because he will be constantly filtering his requirements through his understanding of what the technology is capable of—when this happens, you do not get a true understanding of what the business requires.

This approach also helps to avoid overgeneralization in an application. Programmers have a tendency to want to model every possible business reality, rather than the specific one that the business requires. In the auction model, we thus might end up replacing *members* and *items* with a general notion of *resources* linked by *relationships*. When we create a domain model that is not constrained to match the domain being modeled, we miss the opportunity to gain any real insight in the business processes—and, in the future, we end up representing changes in business processes as awkward corner-cases in our elegant but overly abstract meta-world. Constraints are not limitations—they are insights that direct your development efforts in the right direction.

The link between the ubiquitous language and the domain model should not be a superficial one— DDD experts suggest that any change to the ubiquitous language should result in a change to the model. If you let the model drift out of sync with the business domain, you effectively create an intermediate language that maps from the model to the domain—and that spells disaster in the long term. You will create a special class of people who can speak both languages and they will then start filtering requirements through their incomplete understanding of both languages.

Aggregates and Simplification

Figure 3-5 provides a good starting point for our domain model, but it doesn't offer any useful guidance about implementing the model using C# and SQL Server. If we load a Member into memory, should we also load her Bids and the Items associated with them? And, if so, do we need to load all of the other Bids for those Items, and the Members who made those bids? When we delete an object, should we delete related objects, too—and, if so, which ones? If we choose to implement persistence using a document store instead of a relational database, which collections of objects would represent a single document? We don't know, and our domain model doesn't give us any of the answers to this question.

The DDD way of answering these questions is to arrange domain objects into groups called *aggregates*—Figure 3-6 shows how we might aggregate the objects in our auction domain model.

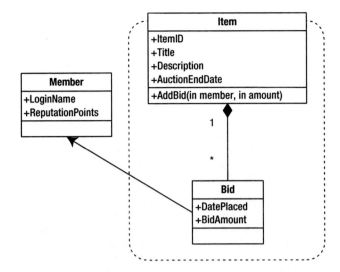

Figure 3-6. The auction domain model with aggregates

An aggregate entity groups together several domain model objects—there is a *root entity* that is used to identify the entire aggregate, and it acts as the "boss" for validation and persistence operations. The aggregate is treated as a single unit with regard to data changes, so we need to create aggregates that represent relationships that make sense in the context of the domain model and create operations that correspond logically to real business processes—that is, we need to create aggregates by grouping objects that are changed as a group.

A key DDD rule is that objects outside of a particular instance of an aggregate can hold persistent references to only the root entity, not to any other object inside of the aggregate (in fact, the identity of a non-root object need be unique only within its aggregate). This rule reinforces the notion of treating the objects inside an aggregate as a single unit.

In our example, Members and Items are both aggregate roots, whereas Bids can be accessed only in the context of the Item that is the root entity of their aggregate. Bids are allowed to hold references to Members (which are root entities), but Members can't directly reference Bids (because they are not).

One of the benefits of aggregates is that it simplifies the set of relationships between objects in the domain model—and often, this can give additional insight into the nature of the domain that is being modeled. In essence, creating aggregates constrains the relationships between domain model objects so that they are more like the relationships that exist in the real-world domain. Listing 3-1 illustrates how our domain model might look like when expressed in C#.

Listing 3-1. The C# Auction Domain Model

```csharp
public class Member {
    public string LoginName { get; set; } // The unique key
    public int ReputationPoints { get; set; }
}

public class Item {
    public int ItemID { get; private set; } // The unique key
    public string Title { get; set; }
    public string Description { get; set; }
    public DateTime AuctionEndDate { get; set; }
```

```
    public IList<Bid> Bids { get; set; }
}

public class Bid {
    public Member Member { get; set; }
    public DateTime DatePlaced { get; set; }
    public decimal BidAmount { get; set; }
}
```

Notice how we are easily able to capture the unidirectional nature of the relationship between `Bids` and `Members`. We have also been able to model some other constraints—for example, `Bids` are immutable (representing the common auction convention that bids can't be changed once they are made). Applying aggregation has allowed us to create a more useful and accurate domain model, which we have been able to represent in C# with ease.

In general, aggregates add structure and accuracy to a domain model. They make it easier to apply validation (the root entity becomes responsible for validating the state of all objects in the aggregate) and are obvious units for persistence. And, because aggregates are essentially the atomic units of our domain model, they are also suitable units for transaction management and cascade deletes from databases.

On the other hand, they impose restrictions that can sometimes appear artificial—because often they *are* artificial. Aggregates arise naturally in document databases, but they are not a native concept in SQL Server, nor in most ORM tools, so to implement them well, your team will need discipline and effective communication.

Defining Repositories

At some point, we will need to add persistence for our domain model—this will usually be done through a relational, object, or document database. Persistence is not part of our domain model—it is an *independent* or *orthogonal concern* in our separation of concerns pattern. This means that we don't want to mix the code that handles persistence with the code that defines the domain model.

The usual way to enforce separation between the domain model and the persistence system is to define *repositories*—these are object representations of the underlying database (or file store or whatever you have chosen). Rather than work directly with the database, the domain model calls the methods defined by the repository, which in turn makes calls to the database to store and retrieve the model data— this allows us to isolate the model from the implementation of the persistence.

The convention is to define separate data models for each aggregate, because aggregates are the natural unit for persistence. In the case of our auction, for example, we might create two repositories— one for `Members` and one for `Items` (note that we don't need a repository for `Bids`, because they will be persisted as part of the `Items` aggregate). Listing 3-2 shows how these repositories might be defined.

Listing 3-2. C# Repository Classes for the Member and Item Domain Classes

```
public class MembersRepository {

    public void AddMember(Member member) {
        /* Implement me */
    }
    public Member FetchByLoginName(string loginName) {
        /* Implement me */ return null;
    }
    public void SubmitChanges() {
        /* Implement me */
```

```
    }
}
public class ItemsRepository {

    public void AddItem(Item item) {
        /* Implement me */
    }

    public Item FetchByID(int itemID) {
        /* Implement me */  return null;
    }

    public IList<Item> ListItems(int pageSize, int pageIndex) {
        /* Implement me */ return null;
    }
    public void SubmitChanges() {
        /* Implement me */
    }
}
```

Notice that the repositories are concerned only with loading and saving data—they contain no domain logic at all. We can complete the repository classes by adding statements to each method that perform the store and retrieve operations for the appropriate persistence mechanism. In Chapter 7, we will start to build a more complex and realistic MVC application and, as part of that process, we'll show you how to use the Entity Framework to implement your repositories.

Building Loosely Coupled Components

As we have said, one of most important features of the MVC pattern is that it enables separation of concerns. We want the components in our application to be as independent as possible and to have as few interdependencies as we can manage.

In our ideal situation, each component knows nothing about any other component and only deals with other areas of the application through abstract interfaces. This is known as *loose coupling*, and it makes testing and modifying our application easier.

A simple example will help put things in context. If we are writing a component called MyEmailSender that will send e-mails, we would implement an interface that defines all of the public functions required to send an e-mail, which we would call IEmailSender.

Any other component of our application that needs to send an e-mail—let's say a password reset helper called PasswordResetHelper, can then send an e-mail by referring only to the methods in the interface. There is no direct dependency between PasswordResetHelper and MyEmailSender, as shown by Figure 3-7.

Figure 3-7. Using interfaces to decouple components

By introducing IEmailSender, we ensure that there is no direct dependency between PasswordResetHelp and MyEmailSender. We could replace MyEmailSender with another e-mail provider or even use a mock implementation for testing purposes. We return to the topic of mock implementations in Chapter 6.

■ **Note** Not every relationship needs to be decoupled using an interface. The decision is really about how complex the application is, what kind of testing is required, and what the long-term maintenance is likely to be. For example, we might choose not to decouple the controllers from the domain model in a small and simple ASP.NET MVC application.

Using Dependency Injection

Interfaces help us decouple components, but we still face a problem—C# doesn't provide a built-in way to easily create objects that implement interfaces, except to create an instance of the concrete component. We end up with the code in Listing 3-3.

Listing 3-3. Instantiating Concrete Classes to Get an Interface Implementation

```
public class PasswordResetHelper {

    public void ResetPassword() {

        IEmailSender mySender = new MyEmailSender();

        //...call interface methods to configure e-mail details...

        mySender.SendEmail();
    }
}
```

We are only part of the way to loosely coupled components—the PasswordResetHelper class is configuring and sending e-mails through the IEmailSender interface, but to create an object that implements that interface, it had to create an instance of MyEmailSender.

We have made things worse—now PasswordResetHelper depends on IEmailSender and MyEmailSender, as shown in Figure 3-8.

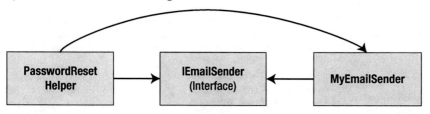

Figure 3-8. Components which are tightly coupled after all

What we need is a way to obtain objects that implement a given interface without having to create the implementing object directly. The solution to this problem is called *dependency injection* (DI), also known as *Inversion of Control* (IoC).

DI is a design pattern that completes the loose coupling we started by adding the `IEmailSender` interface to our simple example. As we describe DI, you might wonder what the fuss is about, but bear with us—this is an important concept that is central to effective MVC development.

There are two parts to the DI pattern. The first is that we remove any dependencies on concrete classes from our component—in this case `PasswordResetHelper`. We do this by passing implementations of the required interfaces to the class constructor, as shown in Listing 3-4.

Listing 3-4. Removing Dependencies from the PasswordResetHelper Class

```
public class PasswordResetHelper {
    private IEmailSender emailSender;

    public PasswordResetHelper(IEmailSender emailSenderParam) {
        emailSender = emailSenderParam;
    }

    public void ResetPassword() {
        // ...call interface methods to configure e-mail details...
        emailSender.SendEmail();
    }
}
```

We have broken the dependency between `PasswordResetHelper` and `MyEmailSender`—the `PasswordResetHelper` constructor demands an object that implements the `IEmailSender` interface, but it does not know, or care, what the object is and is no longer responsible for creating it.

The dependencies are injected into the `PasswordResetHelper` at runtime—that is to say, an instance of some class that implements the `IEmailSender` interface will be created and passed to the `PasswordResetHelper` constructor during instantiation. There is no compile-time dependency between `PasswordResetHelper` and any class that implements the interfaces it depends on.

■ **Note** The `PasswordResetHelper` class demands its dependencies be injected using its constructor—this is known as *constructor injection*. We could also allow the dependencies to be injected through a public property, known as *setter injection*.

Because the dependencies are dealt with at runtime, we can decide which interface implementations are going to be used when we run the application—we can choose between different e-mail providers, or inject a mocked implementation for testing. We have achieved the dependency relationships we were aiming for in Figure 3-8.

An MVC-Specific DI Example

Let's go back to the auction domain model we created earlier and apply DI to it. The goal is to create a controller class, which we'll call `AdminController`, that uses the repository `MembersRepository` for persistence without directly coupling `AdminController` and `MembersRepository` together. We'll start by defining an interface that will decouple our two classes—we will call it `IMembersRepository`—and change the `MembersRepository` class to implement the interface as shown in Listing 3-5.

Listing 3-5. The IMembersRepository Interface

```
public interface IMembersRepository {

    void AddMember(Member member);
    Member FetchByLoginName(string loginName);
    void SubmitChanges();
}

public class MembersRepository : IMembersRepository {
    public void AddMember(Member member) {
        /* Implement me */
    }

    public Member FetchByLoginName(string loginName) {
        /* Implement me */
    }

    public void SubmitChanges() {
        /* Implement me */
    }
}
```

We can now write a controller class that depends on the IMembersRepository interface, as shown in Listing 3-6.

Listing 3-6. The AdminController Class

```
public class AdminController : Controller {
    IMembersRepository membersRepository;

    public AdminController(IMembersRepository repositoryParam) {
        membersRepository = repositoryParam;
    }

    public ActionResult ChangeLoginName(string oldLoginParam, string newLoginParam) {
        Member member = membersRepository.FetchByLoginName(oldLoginParam);
        member.LoginName = newLoginParam;
        membersRepository.SubmitChanges();
        // ... now render some view
        return View();
    }
}
```

The AdminController class demands an implementation of the IMembersRepository interface as a constructor parameter—this will be injected at runtime, allowing AdminController to operate on an instance of a class that implements the interface without being coupled to that implementation.

Using a Dependency Injection Container

We have resolved our dependency issue—we are going to inject our dependencies into the constructors of our classes at runtime. But we still have one more issue to resolve—how do we instantiate the concrete implementation of interfaces without creating dependencies somewhere else in our application?

The answer is a dependency injection container, also known as an IoC container. This is a component that acts as a broker between the dependencies that a class like `PasswordResetHelper` demands and the concrete implementation of those dependencies, such as `MyEmailSender`.

We register the set of interfaces or abstract types that our application uses with the DI container, and tell it which concrete classes should be instantiated to satisfy dependencies. So, we would register the `IEmailSender` interface with the container and specify that an instance of `MyEmailSender` should be created whenever an implementation of `IEmailSender` is required. Whenever we need an `IEmailSender`, such as to create an instance of `PasswordResetHelper`, we go to the DI container and are given an implementation of the class we registered as the default concrete implementation of that interface—in this case, `MyEmailSender`.

We do not need to create the DI container ourselves—there are some great open source and freely licensed implementations available. The one we like is called Ninject and you can get details at `www.ninject.org`. We'll introduce you to using Ninject in Chapter 6.

■ **Tip**   Microsoft created its own DI container, called Unity. We are going to use Ninject, however, because we like it and it demonstrates the ability to mix and match tools when using MVC. If you want more information about Unity, see `unity.codeplex.com`.

The role of a DI container may seem simple and trivial, but that is not the case. A good DI container, such as Ninject, has some very clever features:

- *Dependency chain resolution*: If you request a component that has its own dependencies (e.g., constructor parameters), the container will satisfy those dependencies, too. So, if the constructor for the `MyEmailSender` class requires an implementation of the `INetworkTransport` interface, the DI container will instantiate the default implementation of that interface, pass it to the constructor of `MyEmailSender` and return the result as the default implementation of `IEmailSender`.

- *Object lifecycle management*: If you request a component more than once, should you get the same instance each time or a fresh new instance? A good DI container will let you configure the lifecycle of a component, allowing you to select from predefined options including *singleton* (the same instance each time), *transient* (a new instance each time), *instance-per-thread, instance-per-HTTP-request, instance-from-a-pool*, and many others.

- *Configuration of constructor parameter values*: If the constructor for our implementation of the `INetworkTransport` interface requires a string called `serverName`, for example, you should be able to set a value for it in your DI container configuration. It is a crude but simple configuration system that removes any need for your code to pass around connection strings, server addresses, and so forth.

You might be tempted to write your own DI container. We think that's a great experimental project if you have some time to kill and want to learn a lot about C# and .NET reflection. If you want a DI container to use in a production MVC application, however, we recommend you use one of the established DI containers, such as Ninject.

Getting Started with Automated Testing

The ASP.NET MVC Framework is designed to make it as easy as possible to set up automated tests and use development methodologies such as test-driven development (TDD), which we'll explain later in this chapter. ASP.NET MVC provides an ideal platform for automated testing and Visual Studio has some great testing features—between them they make designing and running tests simple and easy.

In broad terms, Web application developers today focus on two kinds of automated testing. The first is *unit testing*, which is a way to specify and verify the behavior of individual classes (or other small units of code) in isolation from the rest of the application. The second type is *integration testing*, which is a way to specify and verify the behavior of multiple components working together, up to and including the entire Web application.

Both kinds of testing can be extremely valuable in Web applications. Unit tests, which are simple to create and run, are brilliantly precise when you are working on algorithms, business logic, or other backend infrastructure.

The value of integration testing is that it can model how a user will interact with the UI, and can cover the entire technology stack that your application uses, including the Web server and database. Integration testing tends to be better at detecting new bugs that have arisen in old features; this is known as *regression testing*.

Understanding Unit Testing

In the .NET world, you create a separate test project in your Visual Studio solution to hold *test fixtures*. This project will be created when you first add a unit test, or can be set up automatically when you use an MVC project template. A *test fixture* is a C# class that defines a set of test methods—one method for each behavior you want to verify. A test project can contain multiple test fixture classes.

■ **Note** We'll show you how to create a test project and populate it with unit tests in Chapter 6. The goal for this chapter is just to introduce the concept of unit testing and give you an idea of what a test fixture looks like and how it is used.

Listing 3-7 contains an example test fixture that tests the behavior of the `AdminContoller.ChangeLoginName` method, which we defined in Listing 3-6.

Listing 3-7. An Example Test Fixture

```
[TestClass]
public class AdminControllerTest {

    [TestMethod]
    public void CanChangeLoginName() {

        // Arrange (set up a scenario)
        Member bob = new Member() { LoginName = "Bob" };
        FakeMembersRepository repositoryParam = new FakeMembersRepository();
        repositoryParam.Members.Add(bob);
        AdminController target = new AdminController(repositoryParam);
        string oldLoginParam = bob.LoginName;
```

```
        string newLoginParam = "Anastasia";

        // Act (attempt the operation)
        target.ChangeLoginName(oldLoginParam, newLoginParam);

        // Assert (verify the result)
        Assert.AreEqual(newLoginParam, bob.LoginName);
        Assert.IsTrue(repositoryParam.DidSubmitChanges);
    }

    private class FakeMembersRepository : IMembersRepository {
        public List<Member> Members = new List<Member>();
        public bool DidSubmitChanges = false;

        public void AddMember(Member member) {
            throw new NotImplementedException();
        }

        public Member FetchByLoginName(string loginName) {
            return Members.First(m => m.LoginName == loginName);
        }

        public void SubmitChanges() {
            DidSubmitChanges = true;
        }
    }
}
```

The test fixture is the CanChangeLoginName method. Notice that the method is decorated with the TestMethod attribute and that the class it belongs to—called AdminControllerTest—is decorated with the TestClass attribute—this is how Visual Studio finds the test fixture.

The CanChangeLoginName method follows a pattern known as *arrange/act/assert* (A/A/A). *Arrange* refers to setting up the conditions for the test, *act* refers to performing the test, and *assert* refers to verifying that the result was the one that was required. Being consistent about the structure of your unit test methods make them easier to read—something you'll appreciate when your project contains hundreds of unit tests.

The test fixture in Listing 3-7 uses a test-specific fake implementation of the IMembersRepository interface to simulate a specific condition—in this case, when there is a single member, Bob, in the repository. Creating the fake repository and the Member are done in the *arrange* section of the test.

Next, the method being tested—AdminController.ChangeLoginName—is called. This is the *act* section of the test. Finally, we check the results using a pair of Assert calls (this is the *assert* part of the test). We run the test by using the Visual Studio Test menu and get visual feedback about the tests as they are performed, as shown in Figure 3-9.

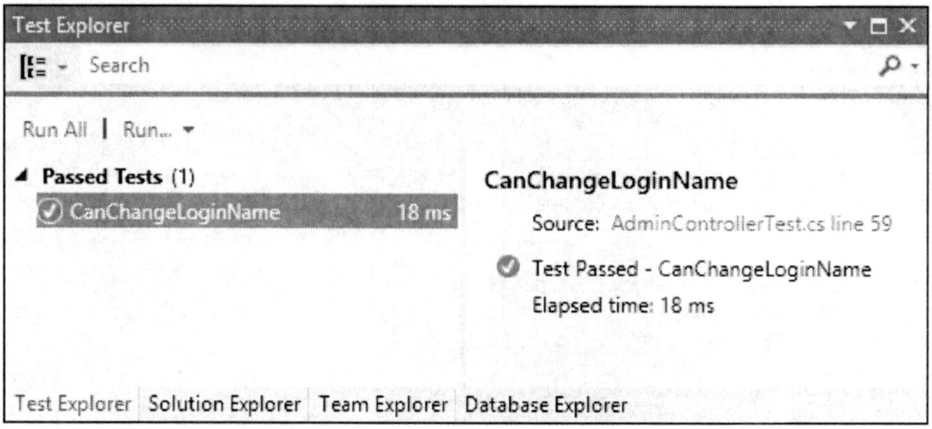

Figure 3-9. Visual feedback on the progress of unit tests

If the test fixture runs without throwing any unhandled exceptions and all of the `Assert` statements pass without problems, the `Test Results` window shows a green light—if not, you get a red light and details of what went wrong.

■ **Note** You can see how our use of DI has helped us with unit testing. We were able to create a fake implementation of the repository and inject it into the controller to create a very specific scenario. We are big fans of DI and this is one of the reasons.

It might seem like we have gone to a lot of effort to test a simple method, but it wouldn't require much more code to test something far more complex. If you find yourself considering skipping small tests like this one, consider that test fixtures like this one help to uncover bugs that can sometimes be hidden in more complex tests.

As we go through the book, you'll see examples of more complex and concise tests—one improvement we can make is to eliminate test-specific fake classes like `FakeMembersRepository` by using a *mocking tool*—we'll show you how to do this in Chapter 6.

Using TDD and the Red-Green-Refactor Workflow

With test-driven development (TDD), you use unit tests to help design your code. This can be an odd concept if you are used to testing after you have finished coding, but there is a lot of sense in this approach. The key concept is a development workflow called red-green-refactor. It works like this:

- Determine that you need to add a new feature or method to your application.

- Write the test that will validate the behavior of the new feature when it is written.

- Run the test and get a red light

- Write the code that implements the new feature.

- Run the test again and correct the code until you get a green light.

- Refactor the code if required—for example, reorganize the statements, rename the variables and so on.

- Run the test to confirm that your changes have not changed the behavior of your additions.

This workflow is repeated for every feature you add. Let's walk through an example so you can see how it works. Let's imagine the behavior we want is the ability to add a bid to an item, but only if the bid is higher than all previous bids for that item. First, we will add a stub method to the Item class, as shown in Listing 3-8.

Listing 3-8. Adding a Stub Method to the Item Class

```
using System;
using System.Collections.Generic;

namespace TheMVCPattern.Models {
    public class Item {
        public int ItemID { get; private set; } // The unique key
        public string Title { get; set; }
        public string Description { get; set; }
        public DateTime AuctionEndDate { get; set; }
        public IList<Bid> Bids { get; private set; }

        public void AddBid(Member memberParam, decimal amountParam) {
            throw new NotImplementedException();
        }
    }
}
```

It is obvious that the AddBid method, shown in bold, doesn't display the required behavior, but do not let that stop you—the key to TDD is to test for the right behavior *before* implementing the feature. We are going to test for three different aspects of the behavior we are seeking to implement:

- When there are no bids, any bid value can be added.

- When there are existing bids, a higher value bid can be added.

- When there are existing bids, a lower value bid cannot be added.

To do this, we create three test methods, which are shown in Listing 3-9.

Listing 3-9. Three Test Fixtures

```
[TestMethod()]
public void CanAddBid() {

    // Arrange - set up the scenario
    Item target = new Item();
    Member memberParam = new Member();
    Decimal amountParam = 150M;

    // Act - perform the test
    target.AddBid(memberParam, amountParam);
```

```
    // Assert - check the behavior
    Assert.AreEqual(1, target.Bids.Count());
    Assert.AreEqual(amountParam, target.Bids[0].BidAmount);
}

[TestMethod()]
[ExpectedException(typeof(InvalidOperationException))]
public void CannotAddLowerBid() {

    // Arrange
    Item target = new Item();
    Member memberParam = new Member();
    Decimal amountParam = 150M;

    // Act
    target.AddBid(memberParam, amountParam);
    target.AddBid(memberParam, amountParam - 10);
}

[TestMethod()]
public void CanAddHigherBid() {

    // Arrange
    Item target = new Item();
    Member firstMember = new Member();
    Member secondMember = new Member();
    Decimal amountParam = 150M;

    // Act
    target.AddBid(firstMember, amountParam);
    target.AddBid(secondMember, amountParam + 10);

    // Assert
    Assert.AreEqual(2, target.Bids.Count());
    Assert.AreEqual(amountParam + 10, target.Bids[1].BidAmount);
}
```

You can see that we have created a unit test for each of the behaviors that we want to see. The test methods follow the arrange/act/assert pattern to create, test, and validate one aspect of the overall behavior. The CannotAddLowerBid method doesn not have an assert part in the method body because a successful test is an exception being thrown, which we assert by applying the ExpectedException attribute on the test method.

■ **Note** Notice how the test that we perform in the CannotAddLowerBid unit test method will shape our implementation of the AddBid method. We validate the result from the test by ensuring that an exception is thrown and that it is an instance of System.InvalidOperationException. Writing a unit test before you write the code can help you think about how different kinds of outcomes should be expressed before you get bogged down in the implementation.

As we'd expect, all of these tests fail when we run them, as shown in Figure 3-10.

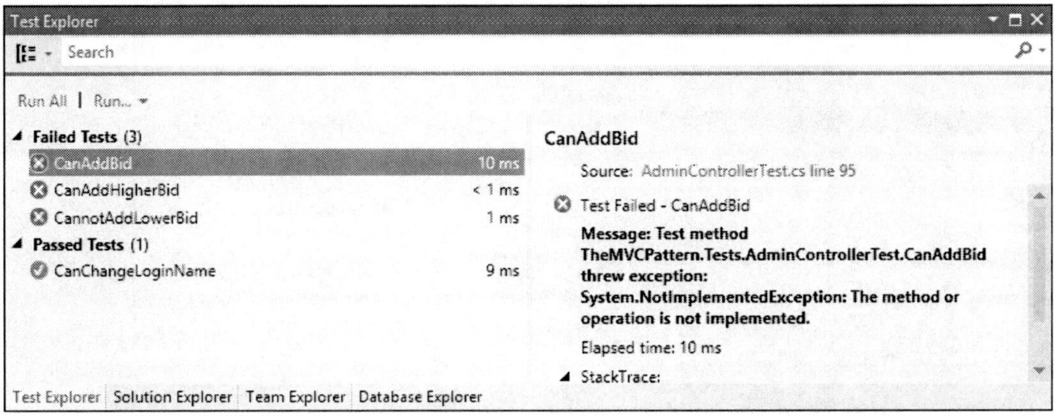

Figure 3-10. Running the unit tests for the first time

We can now implement our first pass at the **AddBid** method, as shown in Listing 3-10.

Listing 3-10. Implementing the AddBid Method

```csharp
using System;
using System.Collections.Generic;

namespace TheMVCPattern.Models {
    public class Item {
        public int ItemID { get; private set; } // The unique key
        public string Title { get; set; }
        public string Description { get; set; }
        public DateTime AuctionEndDate { get; set; }
        public IList<Bid> Bids { get; set; }

        public Item() {
            Bids = new List<Bid>();
        }

        public void AddBid(Member memberParam, decimal amountParam) {
            Bids.Add(new Bid() {
                BidAmount = amountParam,
                DatePlaced = DateTime.Now,
                Member = memberParam
            });
        }
    }
}
```

We have added an initial implementation of the **AddBid** method to the **Item** class. We have also added a simple constructor so we can create instances of **Item** and ensure that the collection of **Bid** objects is properly initialized. Running the unit tests again generates better results, as shown in Figure 3-11.

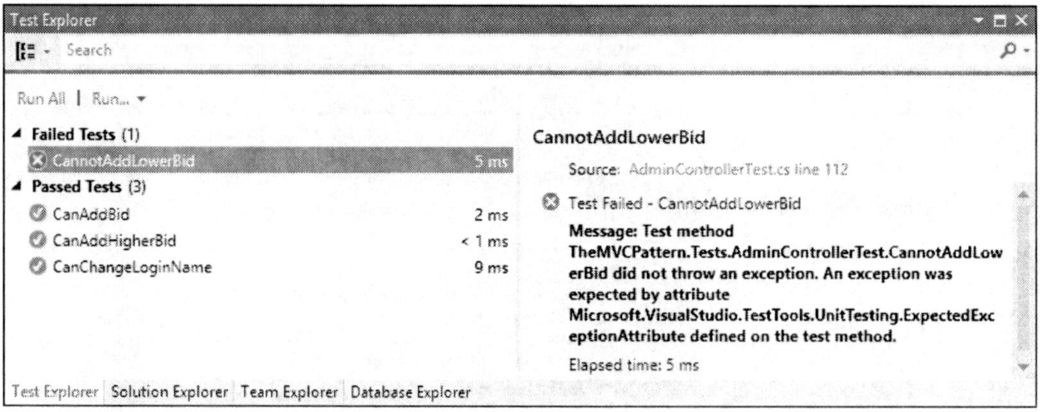

Figure 3-11. Running unit tests against our initial implementation

Two of the three unit tests have passed. The one that has failed is `CannotAddLowerBid`—we did not add any checks to make sure that a bid is higher than previous bids on the item. We have to modify our implementation to put this logic in place, as shown in Listing 3-11.

Listing 3-11. Improving the Implementation of the AddBid Method

```csharp
using System;
using System.Collections.Generic;
using System.Linq;

namespace TheMVCPattern.Models {
    public class Item {
        public int ItemID { get; private set; } // The unique key
        public string Title { get; set; }
        public string Description { get; set; }
        public DateTime AuctionEndDate { get; set; }
        public IList<Bid> Bids { get; set; }

        public Item() {
            Bids = new List<Bid>();
        }

        public void AddBid(Member memberParam, decimal amountParam) {

            if (Bids.Count() == 0 || amountParam > Bids.Max(e => e.BidAmount)) {
                Bids.Add(new Bid() {
                    BidAmount = amountParam,
                    DatePlaced = DateTime.Now,
                    Member = memberParam
                });
            } else {
                throw new InvalidOperationException("Bid amount too low");
            }
        }
    }
}
```

You can see that we have expressed the error condition in such a way as to satisfy the unit test we wrote before we started coding—that is, we throw an `InvalidOperationException` when a bid is received that is too low.

■ **Note**   We have used the Language Integrated Query (LINQ) feature to check that a bid is valid. Do not worry if you are not familiar with LINQ or the lambda expression we used (the `=>` notation)—we will give you an introduction to the C# features that are essential to MVC development in Chapter 6.

Each time we change the implementation of the `AddBid` method, we run our unit tests again—the results are shown in Figure 3-12.

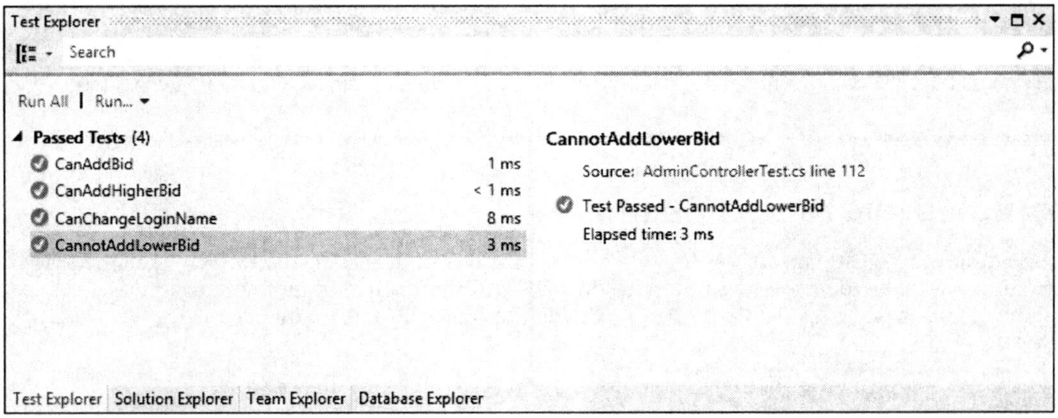

Figure 3-12. Successful unit test results

Success! We have implemented our new feature such that it passes all of the unit tests. The last step is to take a moment and be sure that our tests really do test all aspects of the behavior or feature we are implementing. If so, we are done. If not, then we add more tests and repeat the cycle—and we keep going until we are confident that we have a comprehensive set of tests and an implementation that passes them all.

This cycle is the essence of TDD. There is a lot to recommend it as a development style—not least because it makes a programmer think about how a change or enhancement should behave *before* the coding starts. You always have a clear end-point in view and a way to check that you are there. And if you have unit tests that cover the rest of your application, you can be sure that your additions have not changed the behavior elsewhere.

GETTING THE UNIT TEST RELIGION

If you do not currently unit test your code, you might find the process awkward and disruptive—more typing, more testing, more iterations. If you *do* perform unit tests, you already know what a difference it makes—fewer bugs, better-designed software, and fewer surprises when you make a change.

Going from a nontester to a tester can be tough—it means adopting a new habit and sticking with it long enough to get the benefits. Our first few attempts to embrace testing failed because of unexpected shifts in due dates—it's hard to convince yourself that doing something that feels like extra work is worthwhile when time is tight.

We have both become adherents of unit testing and are convinced that it is a great style of development. ASP.NET MVC is an ideal candidate for adopting unit testing if you have never tried before—or if you have tried and given up. The Microsoft team has made unit testing incredibly easy by separating the key classes from the underlying technology, which means we can create mock implementation of key features and test corner-case situations that would be incredibly difficult to replicate otherwise. We will show you examples of unit testing MVC applications throughout this book. We encourage you to follow along and try unit testing for yourself.

Understanding Integration Testing

For Web applications, the most common approach to integration testing is *UI automation*, which means simulating or automating a Web browser to exercise the application's entire technology stack by reproducing the actions that a user would perform, such as pressing buttons, following links, and submitting forms.

The two best-known open source browser automation options for .NET developers are

- *Selenium RC* (http://seleniumhq.org/), which consists of a Java "server" application that can send automation commands to Internet Explorer, Firefox, Safari, or Opera, plus clients for .NET, Python, Ruby, and multiple others so that you can write test scripts in the language of your choice. Selenium is powerful and mature; its only drawback is that you have to run its Java server.

- *WatiN* (http://watin.org), a .NET library that can send automation commands to Internet Explorer or Firefox. Its API isn't as powerful as Selenium, but it comfortably handles most common scenarios and is easy to set up—you need only reference a single DLL.

Integration testing is an ideal complement to unit testing. Although unit testing is well suited to validating the behavior of individual components at the server, integration testing lets you create tests that are client-focused, recreating the actions of a user. As a result, it can highlight problems that come from the interaction between components—hence the term *integration* testing. And because integration testing for a Web application is done through the browser, you can test that JavaScript behaviors work the way they are supposed to—something that is very difficult with unit testing.

There are some drawbacks, too—integration testing takes more time. It takes longer to create the tests and longer to perform them. And integration tests can be brittle—if you change the id attribute of an element that is checked in a test, for example, the test can (and usually will) fail.

As a consequence of the additional time and effort required, integration testing is often done at key project milestones—perhaps after a weekly source code check-in, or when major functional blocks are completed. Integration testing is every bit as useful as unit testing and it can highlight problems that unit testing cannot. The time required to set up and run integration testing is worthwhile, and we encourage you to add it to your development process.

We are not going to get into integration testing in this book. That is not because we do not think it is useful—it is, which is why we urged you to add it to your process—but because it goes beyond the focus of this book. The ASP.NET MVC Framework has been specifically designed to make unit testing easy and simple, and we need to include unit testing to give you a full flavor of how to build a good MVC application. Integration testing is a separate art and what is true when performing integration testing on any Web application is also true for MVC.

Summary

In this chapter we have introduced you to the MVC architectural pattern and compared it to some other patterns you may have seen or heard of before. We discussed the significance of the domain model and created a simple example. We also introduced dependency injection, which allows us to decouple components to enforce a strict separation between the parts of our application. We demonstrated some simple unit tests and we saw how decoupled components and dependency injection make unit testing simple and easy. Along the way, we demonstrated our enthusiasm for test-driven development and showed how we write the unit tests before we write our application code. Finally, we touched on integration testing and compared it to unit testing.

CHAPTER 4

■ ■ ■

Essential Language Features

C# is a feature-rich language, and not all programmers are familiar with all of the features we will rely on in this book. In this chapter, we are going to look at the C# language features that a good MVC programmer needs to know.

We provide only a short summary of each feature. If you want more in-depth coverage of C# or LINQ, three of Adam's books may be of interest. For a complete guide to C#, try *Introducing Visual C#*; for in-depth coverage of LINQ, check out *Pro LINQ in C#*; and for a detailed examination of the .NET support for asynchronous programming see *Pro .Net Parallel Programming in C#*. All of these books are published by Apress.

Creating the Example Project

To demonstrate the language features in this part of the book, we have created a new Visual Studio `ASP.NET MVC 4 Web Application` project called `LanguageFeatures` and selected the `Empty` template option. The features are not specific to MVC, but Visual Studio Express 2012 for Web doesn't support creating projects that can write to the console, so you will have to create an MVC app if you want to follow along with the examples.

We will need a simple controller to demonstrate these language features, so we have created the `HomeController.cs` file in the `Controllers` folder, using the technique we showed you in Chapter 2. You can see the initial contents of the `Home` controller in Listing 4-1.

Listing 4-1. The Initial Content of the Home Controller

```
using LanguageFeatures.Models;
using System;
using System.Collections.Generic;
using System.Linq;
using System.Web;
using System.Web.Mvc;

namespace LanguageFeatures.Controllers {
    public class HomeController : Controller {

        public string Index() {
            return "Navigate to a URL to show an example";
        }
    }
}
```

We will create action methods for each example, so the result from the `Index` action method is a basic message to keep the project simple. To display the results from our action methods, we added a view called `Result.cshtml` in the `Views/Home` folder. You can see the contents of the view file in Listing 4-2.

Listing 4-2. The Contents of the Result View File

```
@model String

@{
    Layout = null;
}

<!DOCTYPE html>

<html>
<head>
    <meta name="viewport" content="width=device-width" />
    <title>Result</title>
</head>
<body>
    <div>
        @Model
    </div>
</body>
</html>
```

You can see that this is a strongly typed view, where the model type is `String` – these are not complex examples and we can easily represent the results as a simple string.

Using Automatically Implemented Properties

The C# property feature lets you expose a piece of data from a class in a way that decouples the data from how it is set and retrieved. Listing 4-3 contains a simple example in a class called `Product`, which we have added to the `Models` folder of the `LanguageFeatures` project.

Listing 4-3. Defining a Property

```
using System;
using System.Collections.Generic;
using System.Linq;
using System.Web;

namespace LanguageFeatures.Models {
    public class Product {
        private string name;

        public string Name {
            get { return name; }
            set { name = value; }
        }
    }
}
```

The property, called Name, is shown in bold. The statements in the **get** code block (known as the *getter*) are performed when the value of the property is read, and the statements in the **set** code block are performed when a value is assigned to the property (the special variable **value** represents the assigned value). A property is consumed by other classes as though it were a field, as shown in Listing 4-4, which shows the AutoProperty action method we added to the Home controller.

Listing 4-4. Consuming a Property

```
using LanguageFeatures.Models;
using System;
using System.Collections.Generic;
using System.Linq;
using System.Web;
using System.Web.Mvc;

namespace LanguageFeatures.Controllers {
    public class HomeController : Controller {

        public string Index() {
            return "Navigate to a URL to show an example";
        }

        public ViewResult AutoProperty() {
            // create a new Product object
            Product myProduct = new Product();

            // set the property value
            myProduct.Name = "Kayak";

            // get the property
            string productName = myProduct.Name;

            // generate the view
            return View("Result",
                (object)String.Format("Product name: {0}", productName));
        }
    }
}
```

You can see that the property value is read and set just like a regular field. Using properties is preferable to using fields because you can change the statements in the get and set blocks without needing to change all the classes that depend on the property.

■**Tip**   You may notice that we have cast the second argument to the View method to an object in Listing 4. This is because the View method has an overload that accepts two String arguments and which has a different meaning to the overload that accepts a String and an object. To avoid calling the wrong one, we explicitly cast the second argument. We return to the View method and all of its overloads in Chapter 18.

You can see the effect of this example by starting the project and navigating to /Home/AutoProperty (which targets the AutoProperty action method and will the pattern for testing each example in this chapter. Because we are only passing a string from the action method to the view, we are going to show you the results as text, rather than a screen shot. Here is the result of targeting the action method in Listing 4:

Product name: Kayak

All well and good, but it becomes tedious when you have a class that has a lot of properties, all of which mediate access to a field. We end up with something that is needlessly verbose, as shown in Listing 4-5, which shows how these properties appear in the Product.cs file.

Listing 4-5. Verbose Property Definitions

```csharp
using System;
using System.Collections.Generic;
using System.Linq;
using System.Web;

namespace LanguageFeatures.Models {

    public class Product {
        private int productID;
        private string name;
        private string description;
        private decimal price;
        private string category;

        public int ProductID {
            get { return productID; }
            set { productID = value; }
        }

        public string Name {
            get { return name; }
            set { name = value; }
        }

        public string Description {
            get { return description; }
            set { description = value; }
        }

        //...and so on...
    }
}
```

We want the flexibility of properties, but we do not need custom getters and setters at the moment. The solution is an *automatically implemented property*, also known as an *automatic property*. With an automatic property, you can create the pattern of a field-backed property, without defining the field or specifying the code in the getter and setter, as Listing 4-6 shows.

Listing 4-6. Using Automatically Implemented Properties

```csharp
using System;
using System.Collections.Generic;
using System.Linq;
using System.Web;

namespace LanguageFeatures.Models {

    public class Product {
        public int ProductID { get; set; }
        public string Name { get; set; }
        public string Description { get; set; }
        public decimal Price { get; set; }
        public string Category { set; get; }
    }
}
```

There are a couple of points to note when using automatic properties. The first is that we do not define the bodies of the getter and setter. The second is that we do not define the field that the property is backed by. Both of these are done for us by the C# compiler when we build our class. Using an automatic property is no different from using a regular property; the code in the action method in Listing 4-4 will work without any modification.

By using automatic properties, we save ourselves some typing, create code that is easier to read, and still preserve the flexibility that a property provides. If the day comes when we need to change the way a property is implemented, we can then return to the regular property format. Let's imagine we need to change the way the Name property is composed, as shown in Listing 4-7.

Listing 4-7. Reverting from an Automatic to a Regular Property

```csharp
using System;
using System.Collections.Generic;
using System.Linq;
using System.Web;

namespace LanguageFeatures.Models {

    public class Product {
        private string name;

        public int ProductID { get; set; }

        public string Name {
            get {
                return ProductID + name;
            }
            set {
                name = value;
            }
        }

        public string Description { get; set; }
        public decimal Price { get; set; }
        public string Category { set; get; }
    }
}
```

■**Note** Notice that we must implement both the getter and setter to return to a regular property. C# does not support mixing automatic- and regular-style getters and setters in a single property.

Using Object and Collection Initializers

Another tiresome programming task is constructing a new object and then assigning values to the properties, as illustrated by Listing 4-8, which shows the addition of a `CreateProduct` action method to the Home controller.

Listing 4-8. Constructing and Initializing an Object with Properties

```
using LanguageFeatures.Models;
using System;
using System.Collections.Generic;
using System.Linq;
using System.Web;
using System.Web.Mvc;

namespace LanguageFeatures.Controllers {
    public class HomeController : Controller {

        public string Index() {
            return "Navigate to a URL to show an example";
        }

        public ViewResult AutoProperty() {
            // ...statements omitted for brevity...
        }

        public ViewResult CreateProduct() {

            // create a new Product object
            Product myProduct = new Product();

            // set the property values
            myProduct.ProductID = 100;
            myProduct.Name = "Kayak";
            myProduct.Description = "A boat for one person";
            myProduct.Price = 275M;
            myProduct.Category = "Watersports";

            return View("Result",
                (object)String.Format("Category: {0}", myProduct.Category));
        }
    }
}
```

We must go through three stages to create a `Product` object and produce a result: create the object, set the parameter values, and then call the `View` method so we can display the result through the view.

Fortunately, we can use the *object initializer* feature, which allows us to create and populate the `Product` instance in a single step, as shown in Listing 4-9.

Listing 4-9. Using the Object Initializer Feature

```
...
public ViewResult CreateProduct() {

    // create and populate a new Product object
    Product myProduct = new Product {
        ProductID = 100, Name = "Kayak",
        Description = "A boat for one person",
        Price = 275M, Category = "Watersports"
    };

    return View("Result",
        (object)String.Format("Category: {0}", myProduct.Category));
}
...
```

The braces ({}) after the call to the `Product` name form the *initializer*, which we use to supply values to the parameters as part of the construction process. The same feature lets us initialize the contents of collections and arrays as part of the construction process, as demonstrated by Listing 4-10.

Listing 4-10. Initializing Collections and Arrays

```
using LanguageFeatures.Models;
using System;
using System.Collections.Generic;
using System.Linq;
using System.Web;
using System.Web.Mvc;

namespace LanguageFeatures.Controllers {
    public class HomeController : Controller {

        public string Index() {
            return "Navigate to a URL to show an example";
        }

        // ...other action methods omitted for brevity...

        public ViewResult CreateCollection() {
            string[] stringArray = { "apple", "orange", "plum" };

            List<int> intList = new List<int> { 10, 20, 30, 40 };

            Dictionary<string, int> myDict = new Dictionary<string, int> {
                { "apple", 10 }, { "orange", 20 }, { "plum", 30 }
            };

            return View("Result", (object)stringArray[1]);
        }
    }
}
```

The listing demonstrates how to construct and initialize an array and two classes from the generic collection library. This feature is a syntax convenience—it just makes C# more pleasant to use but does not have any other impact or benefit.

Using Extension Methods

Extension methods are a convenient way of adding methods to classes that you do not own and so cannot modify directly. Listing 4-11 shows the `ShoppingCart` class, which we added to the `Models` folder and which represents a collection of `Product` objects.

Listing 4-11. The ShoppingCart Class

```
using System;
using System.Collections.Generic;
using System.Linq;
using System.Web;

namespace LanguageFeatures.Models {

    public class ShoppingCart {
        public List<Product> Products { get; set; }
    }
}
```

This is a very simple class that acts as a wrapper around a `List` of `Product` objects (we only need a basic class for this example). Suppose that we need to be able to determine the total value of the `Product` objects in the `ShoppingCart` class, but we cannot modify the class itself, perhaps because it comes from a third party and we do not have the source code. Fortunately, we can use an extension method to get the functionality we need. Listing 4-12 shows the `MyExtensionMethods` class, which we also added to the `Models` folder.

Listing 4-12. Defining an Extension Method

```
namespace LanguageFeatures.Models {

    public static class MyExtensionMethods {

        public static decimal TotalPrices(this ShoppingCart cartParam) {
            decimal total = 0;
            foreach (Product prod in cartParam.Products) {
                total += prod.Price;
            }
            return total;
        }
    }
}
```

The `this` keyword in front of the first parameter marks `TotalPrices` as an extension method. The first parameter tells .NET which class the extension method can be applied to—`ShoppingCart` in our case. We can refer to the instance of the `ShoppingCart` that the extension method has been applied to by using the `cartParam` parameter. Our method enumerates through the `Products` in the `ShoppingCart` and returns the sum of the `Product.Price` property. Listing 4-13 shows how we apply an extension method in a new action method called `UseExtension` that we added to the `Home` controller.

■**Note** Extension methods do not let you break through the access rules that classes define for their methods, fields, and properties. You can extend the functionality of a class by using an extension method, but using only the class members that you had access to anyway.

Listing 4-13. Applying an Extension Method

```
using LanguageFeatures.Models;
using System;
using System.Collections.Generic;
using System.Linq;
using System.Web;
using System.Web.Mvc;

namespace LanguageFeatures.Controllers {
    public class HomeController : Controller {

        public string Index() {
            return "Navigate to a URL to show an example";
        }

        // ...other action methods omitted for brevity...

        public ViewResult UseExtension() {
            // create and populate ShoppingCart
            ShoppingCart cart = new ShoppingCart {
                Products = new List<Product> {
                    new Product {Name = "Kayak", Price = 275M},
                    new Product {Name = "Lifejacket", Price = 48.95M},
                    new Product {Name = "Soccer ball", Price = 19.50M},
                    new Product {Name = "Corner flag", Price = 34.95M}
                }
            };

            // get the total value of the products in the cart
            decimal cartTotal = cart.TotalPrices();

            return View("Result",
                (object)String.Format("Total: {0:c}", cartTotal));
        }
    }
}
```

The key statement is this one:

```
...
decimal cartTotal = cart.TotalPrices();
...
```

As you can see, we call the TotalPrices method on a ShoppingCart object as though it were part of the ShoppingCart class, even though it is an extension method defined by a different class altogether. .NET will find your extension classes if they are in the scope of the current class, meaning that they are part of the same namespace or in a namespace that is the subject of a **using** statement. Here is the result from the UseExtension action method:

Total: $378.40

Applying Extension Methods to an Interface

We can also create extension methods that apply to an interface, which allows us to call the extension method on all of the classes that implement the interface. Listing 4-14 shows the ShoppingCart class updated to implement the IEnumerable<Product> interface.

Listing 4-14. Implementing an Interface in the ShoppingCart Class

```
using System;
using System.Collections;
using System.Collections.Generic;
using System.Linq;
using System.Web;

namespace LanguageFeatures.Models {

    public class ShoppingCart: IEnumerable<Product> {

        public List<Product> Products { get; set; }

        public IEnumerator<Product> GetEnumerator() {
            return Products.GetEnumerator();
        }

        IEnumerator IEnumerable.GetEnumerator() {
            return GetEnumerator();
        }
    }
}
```

We can now update our extension method so that it deals with IEnumerable<Product>, as shown in Listing 4-15.

Listing 4-15. An Extension Method That Works on an Interface

```
using System.Collections.Generic;

namespace LanguageFeatures.Models {

    public static class MyExtensionMethods {

        public static decimal TotalPrices(this IEnumerable<Product> productEnum) {
            decimal total = 0;
            foreach (Product prod in productEnum) {
                total += prod.Price;
            }
            return total;
        }
    }
}
```

The first parameter type has changed to IEnumerable<Product>, which means that the foreach loop in the method body works directly on Product objects. Otherwise, the extension method is unchanged. The switch to the interface means that we can calculate the total value of the Product objects enumerated by any IEnumerable<Product>, which includes instances of ShoppingCart but also arrays of Products, as shown in Listing 4-16.

Listing 4-16. Applying an Extension Method to Different Implementations of the Same Interface

```
using LanguageFeatures.Models;
using System;
using System.Collections.Generic;
using System.Linq;
using System.Web;
using System.Web.Mvc;

namespace LanguageFeatures.Controllers {
    public class HomeController : Controller {

        public string Index() {
            return "Navigate to a URL to show an example";
        }

        // ...other action methods omitted for brevity...

        public ViewResult UseExtensionEnumerable() {

            IEnumerable<Product> products = new ShoppingCart {
                Products = new List<Product> {
                    new Product {Name = "Kayak", Price = 275M},
                    new Product {Name = "Lifejacket", Price = 48.95M},
                    new Product {Name = "Soccer ball", Price = 19.50M},
                    new Product {Name = "Corner flag", Price = 34.95M}
                }
            };

            // create and populate an array of Product objects
            Product[] productArray = {
                new Product {Name = "Kayak", Price = 275M},
                new Product {Name = "Lifejacket", Price = 48.95M},
                new Product {Name = "Soccer ball", Price = 19.50M},
                new Product {Name = "Corner flag", Price = 34.95M}
            };

            // get the total value of the products in the cart
            decimal cartTotal = products.TotalPrices();
            decimal arrayTotal = products.TotalPrices();

            return View("Result",
                (object)String.Format("Cart Total: {0}, Array Total: {1}",
                    cartTotal, arrayTotal));

        }
    }
}
```

■**Note**   The way that C# arrays implement the `IEnumerable<T>` interface is a little unusual. You will not find it included in the list of implemented interfaces in the MSDN documentation. The support is handled by the compiler so that code for earlier versions C# will still compile. Odd, but true. We could have used another generic collection class in this example, but we wanted to show off our knowledge of the dark corners of the C# specification. Also odd, but true.

If you start the project and target the action method, you will see the following results, which demonstrate that we get the same result from the extension method, irrespective of how the `Product` objects are collected:

```
Cart Total: 378.40, Array Total: 378.40
```

Creating Filtering Extension Methods

The last thing we want to show you about extension methods is that they can be used to filter collections of objects. An extension method that operates on an `IEnumerable<T>` and that also returns an `IEnumerable<T>` can use the `yield` keyword to apply selection criteria to items in the source data to produce a reduced set of results. Listing 4-17 demonstrates such a method, which we have added to the `MyExtensionMethods` class.

Listing 4-17. A Filtering Extension Method

```csharp
using System.Collections.Generic;

namespace LanguageFeatures.Models {

    public static class MyExtensionMethods {

        public static decimal TotalPrices(this IEnumerable<Product> productEnum) {
            decimal total = 0;
            foreach (Product prod in productEnum) {
                total += prod.Price;
            }
            return total;
        }

        public static IEnumerable<Product> FilterByCategory(
                this IEnumerable<Product> productEnum, string categoryParam) {

            foreach (Product prod in productEnum) {
                if (prod.Category == categoryParam) {
                    yield return prod;
                }
            }
        }
    }
}
```

This extension method, called FilterByCategory, takes an additional parameter that allows us to inject a filter condition when we call the method. Those Product objects whose Category property matches the parameter are returned in the result IEnumerable<Product> and those that do not match are discarded. Listing 4-18 shows this method being used.

Listing 4-18. Using the Filtering Extension Method

```
using LanguageFeatures.Models;
using System;
using System.Collections.Generic;
using System.Linq;
using System.Web;
using System.Web.Mvc;

namespace LanguageFeatures.Controllers {
    public class HomeController : Controller {

        public string Index() {
            return "Navigate to a URL to show an example";
        }

        // ... other action methods omitted for brevity...

        public ViewResult UseFilterExtensionMethod() {

            IEnumerable<Product> products = new ShoppingCart {
                Products = new List<Product> {
                    new Product {Name = "Kayak", Category = "Watersports", Price = 275M},
                    new Product {Name = "Lifejacket", Category = "Watersports",
                        Price = 48.95M},
                    new Product {Name = "Soccer ball", Category = "Soccer",
                        Price = 19.50M},
                    new Product {Name = "Corner flag", Category = "Soccer",
                        Price = 34.95M}
                }
            };

            decimal total = 0;
            foreach (Product prod in products.FilterByCategory("Soccer")) {
                total += prod.Price;
            }

            return View("Result", (object)String.Format("Total: {0}", total));
        }
    }
}
```

When we call the FilterByCategory method on the ShoppingCart, only those Products in the Soccer category are returned. If you start the project and target the UseFilterExtensionMethod action method, you will see the following result, which is the sum of the Soccer product prices:

```
Total: 54.45
```

Using Lambda Expressions

We can use a delegate to make our FilterByCategory method more general. That way, the delegate that will be invoked against each Product can filter the objects in any way we choose, as illustrated by Listing 4-19, which shows the Filter extension method we added to the MyExtensionMethods class.

Listing 4-19. Using a Delegate in an Extension Method

```csharp
using System;
using System.Collections.Generic;

namespace LanguageFeatures.Models {

    public static class MyExtensionMethods {

        public static decimal TotalPrices(this IEnumerable<Product> productEnum) {
            decimal total = 0;
            foreach (Product prod in productEnum) {
                total += prod.Price;
            }
            return total;
        }

        public static IEnumerable<Product> FilterByCategory(
                this IEnumerable<Product> productEnum, string categoryParam) {

            foreach (Product prod in productEnum) {
                if (prod.Category == categoryParam) {
                    yield return prod;
                }
            }
        }

        public static IEnumerable<Product> Filter(
            this IEnumerable<Product> productEnum, Func<Product, bool> selectorParam) {

            foreach (Product prod in productEnum) {
                if (selectorParam(prod)) {
                    yield return prod;
                }
            }
        }
    }
}
```

We have used a Func as the filtering parameter, which means that we do not need to define the delegate as a type. The delegate takes a Product parameter and returns a bool, which will be true if that Product should be included in the results. The other end of this arrangement is a little verbose, as illustrated by Listing 4-20, which shows the changes we made to the UseFilterExtensionMethod extension method.

Listing 4-20. Using the Filtering Extension Method with a Func

```
...
public ViewResult UseFilterExtensionMethod() {

    // create and populate ShoppingCart
    IEnumerable<Product> products = new ShoppingCart {
        Products = new List<Product> {
            new Product {Name = "Kayak", Category = "Watersports", Price = 275M},
            new Product {Name = "Lifejacket", Category = "Watersports", Price = 48.95M},
            new Product {Name = "Soccer ball", Category = "Soccer", Price = 19.50M},
            new Product {Name = "Corner flag", Category = "Soccer", Price = 34.95M}
        }
    };

    Func<Product, bool> categoryFilter = delegate(Product prod) {
        return prod.Category == "Soccer";
    };

    decimal total = 0;

    foreach (Product prod in products.Filter(categoryFilter)) {
        total += prod.Price;
    }
    return View("Result", (object)String.Format("Total: {0}", total));
}
...
```

We took a step forward, in the sense that we can now filter the Product objects using any criteria specified in the delegate, but we must define a Func for each kind of filtering that we want, which is not ideal. The less verbose alternative is to use a *lambda expression*, which is a concise format for expressing a method body in a delegate. We can use it to replace our delegate definition, as shown in Listing 4-21.

Listing 4-21. Using a Lambda Expression to Replace a Delegate Definition

```
...
public ViewResult UseFilterExtensionMethod() {

    // create and populate ShoppingCart
    IEnumerable<Product> products = new ShoppingCart {
        Products = new List<Product> {
            new Product {Name = "Kayak", Category = "Watersports", Price = 275M},
            new Product {Name = "Lifejacket", Category = "Watersports", Price = 48.95M},
            new Product {Name = "Soccer ball", Category = "Soccer", Price = 19.50M},
            new Product {Name = "Corner flag", Category = "Soccer", Price = 34.95M}
        }
    };

    Func<Product, bool> categoryFilter = prod => prod.Category == "Soccer";

    decimal total = 0;

    foreach (Product prod in products.Filter(categoryFilter)) {
        total += prod.Price;
    }
    return View("Result", (object)String.Format("Total: {0}", total));
}
...
```

The lambda expression is shown in bold. The parameter is expressed without specifying a type, which will be inferred automatically. The => characters are read aloud as "goes to" and links the parameter to the result of the lambda expression. In our example, a Product parameter called prod goes to a bool result, which will be true if the Category parameter of prod is equal to Soccer. We can make our syntax even tighter by doing away with the Func entirely, as shown in Listing 4-22.

Listing 4-22. A Lambda Expression Without a Func

```
...
public ViewResult UseFilterExtensionMethod() {

    IEnumerable<Product> products = new ShoppingCart {
        Products = new List<Product> {
            new Product {Name = "Kayak", Category = "Watersports", Price = 275M},
            new Product {Name = "Lifejacket", Category = "Watersports", Price = 48.95M},
            new Product {Name = "Soccer ball", Category = "Soccer", Price = 19.50M},
            new Product {Name = "Corner flag", Category = "Soccer", Price = 34.95M}
        }
    };

    decimal total = 0;

    foreach (Product prod in products.Filter(prod => prod.Category == "Soccer")) {
        total += prod.Price;
    }
    return View("Result", (object)String.Format("Total: {0}", total));
}
...
```

In this example, we have supplied the lambda expression as the parameter to the Filter method. This is a nice and natural way of expressing the filter we want to apply. We can combine multiple filters by extending the result part of the lambda expression, as shown in Listing 4-23.

Listing 4-23. Extending the Filtering Expressed by the Lambda Expression

```
...
public ViewResult UseFilterExtensionMethod() {

    IEnumerable<Product> products = new ShoppingCart {
        Products = new List<Product> {
            new Product {Name = "Kayak", Category = "Watersports", Price = 275M},
            new Product {Name = "Lifejacket", Category = "Watersports", Price = 48.95M},
            new Product {Name = "Soccer ball", Category = "Soccer", Price = 19.50M},
            new Product {Name = "Corner flag", Category = "Soccer", Price = 34.95M}
        }
    };

    decimal total = 0;

    foreach (Product prod in products
            .Filter(prod => prod.Category == "Soccer" || prod.Price > 20)) {
        total += prod.Price;
    }
    return View("Result", (object)String.Format("Total: {0}", total));
}
...
```

This revised lambda expression will match Product objects that are in the Soccer category or whose Price property is greater than 20.

OTHER FORMS FOR LAMBDA EXPRESSIONS

We don't need to express the logic of our delegate in the lambda expression. We can as easily call a method, like this:

```
prod => EvaluateProduct(prod)
```

If we need a lambda expression for a delegate that has multiple parameters, we must wrap the parameters in parentheses, like this:

```
(prod, count) => prod.Price > 20 && count > 0
```

And, finally, if we need logic in the lambda expression that requires more than one statement, we can do so by using braces ({}) and finishing with a return statement, like this:

```
(prod, count) => {
    //...multiple code statements
    return result;
}
```

You do not need to use lambda expressions in your code, but they are a neat way of expressing complex functions simply and in a manner that is readable and clear. We like them a lot, and you will see them used liberally throughout this book.

Using Automatic Type Inference

The C# var keyword allows you to define a local variable without explicitly specifying the variable type, as demonstrated by Listing 4-24. This is called *type inference*, or *implicit typing*.

Listing 4-24. Using Type Inference

```
..
var myVariable = new Product { Name = "Kayak", Category = "Watersports", Price = 275M };

string name = myVariable.Name;   // legal
int count = myVariable.Count;    // compiler error
...
```

It is not that myVariable does not have a type. It is just that we are asking the compiler to infer it from the code. You can see from the statements that follow that the compiler will allow only members of the inferred class—Product in this case—to be called.

Using Anonymous Types

By combining object initializers and type inference, we can create simple data-storage objects without needing to define the corresponding class or struct. Listing 4-25 shows an example.

Listing 4-25. Creating an Anonymous Type

```
...
var myAnonType = new {
    Name = "MVC",
    Category = "Pattern"
};

...
```

In this example, myAnonType is an anonymously typed object. This does not mean that it is dynamic in the sense that JavaScript variables are dynamically typed. It just means that the type definition will be created automatically by the compiler. Strong typing is still enforced. You can get and set only the properties that have been defined in the initializer, for example.

The C# compiler generates the class based on the name and type of the parameters in the initializer. Two anonymously typed objects that have the same property names and types will be assigned to the same automatically generated class. This means we can create arrays of anonymously typed objects, as demonstrated by Listing 4-26, which shows the CreateAnonArray action method we added to the Home controller.

Listing 4-26. Creating an Array of Anonymously Typed Objects

```
using LanguageFeatures.Models;
using System;
using System.Collections.Generic;
using System.Linq;
using System.Text;
using System.Web;
using System.Web.Mvc;

namespace LanguageFeatures.Controllers {
    public class HomeController : Controller {

        public string Index() {
            return "Navigate to a URL to show an example";
        }

        // ...other action methods omitted for brevity...
        public ViewResult CreateAnonArray() {

            var oddsAndEnds = new[] {
                new { Name = "MVC", Category = "Pattern"},
                new { Name = "Hat", Category = "Clothing"},
                new { Name = "Apple", Category = "Fruit"}
            };

            StringBuilder result = new StringBuilder();
            foreach (var item in oddsAndEnds) {
```

```
            result.Append(item.Name).Append(" ");
        }

        return View("Result", (object)result.ToString());
    }
  }
}
```

Notice that we use **var** to declare the variable array. We must do this because we do not have a type to specify, as we would in a regularly typed array. Even though we have not defined a class for any of these objects, we can still enumerate the contents of the array and read the value of the **Name** property from each of them. This is important, because without this feature, we would not be able to create arrays of anonymously typed objects at all. Or, rather, we could create the arrays, but we would not be able to do anything useful with them. You will see the following results if you run the example and target the action method:

MVC Hat Apple

Performing Language Integrated Queries

All of the features we have described so far are put to good use in the LINQ feature. We love LINQ. It is a wonderful and strangely compelling addition to .NET. If you have never used LINQ, you have been missing out. LINQ is a SQL-like syntax for querying data in classes. Imagine that we have a collection of **Product** objects, and we want to find the three highest prices and pass them to the **View** method. Without LINQ, we would end up with something similar to Listing 4-27, which shows the **FindProducts** action method we added to the **Home** controller.

Listing 4-27. Querying Without LINQ

```
...
public ViewResult FindProducts() {

    Product[] products = {
        new Product {Name = "Kayak", Category = "Watersports", Price = 275M},
        new Product {Name = "Lifejacket", Category = "Watersports", Price = 48.95M},
        new Product {Name = "Soccer ball", Category = "Soccer", Price = 19.50M},
        new Product {Name = "Corner flag", Category = "Soccer", Price = 34.95M}
    };

    // define the array to hold the results
    Product[] foundProducts = new Product[3];
    // sort the contents of the array
    Array.Sort(products, (item1, item2) => {
        return Comparer<decimal>.Default.Compare(item1.Price, item2.Price);
    });
    // get the first three items in the array as the results
    Array.Copy(products, foundProducts, 3);

    // create the result
    StringBuilder result = new StringBuilder();
    foreach (Product p in foundProducts) {
```

```
        result.AppendFormat("Price: {0} ", p.Price);
    }

    return View("Result", (object)result.ToString());
}
...
```

With LINQ, we can significantly simplify the querying process, as demonstrated in Listing 4-28.

Listing 4-28. Using LINQ to Query Data

```
...
public ViewResult FindProducts() {

    Product[] products = {
        new Product {Name = "Kayak", Category = "Watersports", Price = 275M},
        new Product {Name = "Lifejacket", Category = "Watersports", Price = 48.95M},
        new Product {Name = "Soccer ball", Category = "Soccer", Price = 19.50M},
        new Product {Name = "Corner flag", Category = "Soccer", Price = 34.95M}
    };

    var foundProducts = from match in products
                        orderby match.Price descending
                        select new {
                            match.Name,
                            match.Price
                        };

    // create the result
    int count = 0;
    StringBuilder result = new StringBuilder();
    foreach (var p in foundProducts) {
        result.AppendFormat("Price: {0} ", p.Price);
        if (++count == 3) {
            break;
        }
    }

    return View("Result", (object)result.ToString());
}
...
```

This is a lot neater. You can see the SQL-like query shown in bold. We order the Product objects in descending order and use the select keyword to return an anonymous type that contains just the Name and Price properties. This style of LINQ is known as *query syntax*, and it is the kind that developers find most comfortable when they start using LINQ. The wrinkle in this query is that it returns one anonymously typed object for every Product in the array that we used in the source query, so we need to play around with the results to get the first three and print out the details.

However, if we are willing to forgo the simplicity of the query syntax, we can get a lot more power from LINQ. The alternative is the *dot-notation syntax*, or *dot notation*, which is based on extension methods. Listing 4-29 shows how we can use this alternative syntax to process our Product objects.

Listing 4-29. Using LINQ Dot Notation

```
...
public ViewResult FindProducts() {

    Product[] products = {
        new Product {Name = "Kayak", Category = "Watersports", Price = 275M},
        new Product {Name = "Lifejacket", Category = "Watersports", Price = 48.95M},
        new Product {Name = "Soccer ball", Category = "Soccer", Price = 19.50M},
        new Product {Name = "Corner flag", Category = "Soccer", Price = 34.95M}
    };

    var foundProducts = products.OrderByDescending(e => e.Price)
                            .Take(3)
                            .Select(e => new {
                                e.Name,
                                e.Price
                            });

    StringBuilder result = new StringBuilder();
    foreach (var p in foundProducts) {
        result.AppendFormat("Price: {0} ", p.Price);
    }

    return View("Result", (object)result.ToString());
}
...
```

We will be the first to admit that this LINQ query, shown in bold, is not as nice to look at as the one expressed in query syntax, but not all LINQ features have corresponding C# keywords. For the serious LINQ programmer, we need to switch to using extension methods. Each of the LINQ extension methods the listing is applied to an IEnumerable<T> and returns an IEnumerable<T> too, which allows us to chain the methods together to form complex queries.

■**Note**   All of the LINQ extension methods are in the System.Linq namespace, which you must bring into scope with a using statement before you can make queries. Visual Studio adds the System.Linq namespace to controller classes automatically, but you may need to add it manually elsewhere in your MVC project.

The OrderByDescending method rearranges the items in the data source. In this case, the lambda expression returns the value we want used for comparisons. The Take method returns a specified number of items from the front of the results (this is what we couldn't do using query syntax). The Select method allows us to project our results, specifying the result we want. In this case, we are projecting an anonymous object that contains the Name and Price properties. Notice that we have not even needed to specify the names of the properties in the anonymous type. C# has inferred this from the properties we picked in the Select method.

Table 4-1 describes the most useful LINQ extension methods. We use LINQ liberally throughout the result of this book, and you may find it useful to return to this table when you see an extension method that you have not encountered before. All of the LINQ methods shown in the table operate on IEnumerable<T>.

Table 4-1. Some Useful LINQ Extension Methods

Extension Method	Description	Deferred
All	Returns true if all the items in the source data match the predicate	No
Any	Returns true if at least one of the items in the source data matches the predicate	No
Contains	Returns true if the data source contains a specific item or value	No
Count	Returns the number of items in the data source	No
First	Returns the first item from the data source	No
FirstOrDefault	Returns the first item from the data source or the default value if there are no items	No
Last	Returns the last item in the data source	No
LastOrDefault	Returns the last item in the data source or the default value if there are no items	No
Max Min	Returns the largest or smallest value specified by a lambda expression	No
OrderBy OrderByDescending	Sorts the source data based on the value returned by the lambda expression	Yes
Reverse	Reverses the order of the items in the data source	Yes
Select	Projects a result from a query	Yes
SelectMany	Projects each data item into a sequence of items and then concatenates all of those resulting sequences into a single sequence	Yes
Single	Returns the first item from the data source or throws an exception if there are multiple matches	No
SingleOrDefault	Returns the first item from the data source or the default value if there are no items, or throws an exception if there are multiple matches	No
Skip SkipWhile	Skips over a specified number of elements, or skips while the predicate matches	Yes
Sum	Totals the values selected by the predicate	No

Extension Method	Description	Deferred
Take TakeWhile	Selects a specified number of elements from the start of the data source or selects items while the predicate matches	Yes
ToArray ToDictionary ToList	Converts the data source to an array or other collection type	No
Where	Filters items from the data source that do not match the predicate	Yes

Understanding Deferred LINQ Queries

You will notice that Table 4-1 includes a column called Deferred. There is an interesting variation in the way that the extension methods are executed in a LINQ query. A query that contains only deferred methods is not executed until the items in the result are enumerated, as demonstrated by Listing 4-30, which shows a simple change to the FindProducts action method.

Listing 4-30. Using Deferred LINQ Extension Methods in a Query

```
...
public ViewResult FindProducts() {

    Product[] products = {
        new Product {Name = "Kayak", Category = "Watersports", Price = 275M},
        new Product {Name = "Lifejacket", Category = "Watersports", Price = 48.95M},
        new Product {Name = "Soccer ball", Category = "Soccer", Price = 19.50M},
        new Product {Name = "Corner flag", Category = "Soccer", Price = 34.95M}
    };

    var foundProducts = products.OrderByDescending(e => e.Price)
                    .Take(3)
                    .Select(e => new {
                        e.Name,
                        e.Price
                    });

    products[2] = new Product { Name = "Stadium", Price = 79600M };

    StringBuilder result = new StringBuilder();
    foreach (var p in foundProducts) {
        result.AppendFormat("Price: {0} ", p.Price);
    }

    return View("Result", (object)result.ToString());
}
...
```

Between defining the LINQ query and enumerating the results, we have changed one of the items in the products array. The output from this example is as follows:

```
Price: 79600 Price: 275 Price: 48.95
```

You can see that the query is not evaluated until the results are enumerated, and so the change we made—introducing Stadium into the Product array—is reflected in the output.

■**Tip** One interesting feature that arises from deferred LINQ extension methods is that queries are evaluated from scratch every time the results are enumerated, meaning that you can perform the query repeatedly as the source data for the changes.

By contrast, using any of the nondeferred extension methods causes a LINQ query to be performed immediately. Listing 4-31 shows the SumProducts action method we added to the Home controller.

Listing 4-31. An Immediately Executed LINQ Query

```
...
public ViewResult SumProducts() {

    Product[] products = {
        new Product {Name = "Kayak", Category = "Watersports", Price = 275M},
        new Product {Name = "Lifejacket", Category = "Watersports", Price = 48.95M},
        new Product {Name = "Soccer ball", Category = "Soccer", Price = 19.50M},
        new Product {Name = "Corner flag", Category = "Soccer", Price = 34.95M}
    };

    var results = products.Sum(e => e.Price);

    products[2] = new Product { Name = "Stadium", Price = 79500M };

    return View("Result",
        (object)String.Format("Sum: {0:c}", results));
}
...
```

This example uses the Sum method, which is not deferred, and produces the following result:

```
Sum: $378.40
```

You can see that the Stadium item, with its much higher price, has not been included in the results—this is because the result from the Sum method are evaluated as soon as the method is called, rather than being deferred until the results are used.

LINQ AND THE IQUERYABLE<T> INTERFACE

LINQ comes in different varieties, although using it is always pretty much the same. One variety is LINQ to Objects, which is what we have been using in the examples so far in this chapter. LINQ to Objects lets you query C# objects that are resident in memory. Another variety, LINQ to XML, is a very convenient and powerful way to create, process, and query XML content. Parallel LINQ is a superset of LINQ to Objects that supports executing LINQ queries concurrently over multiple processors or cores.

Of particular interest to us is LINQ to Entities, which allows LINQ queries to be performed on data obtained from the Entity Framework. The Entity Framework is Microsoft's ORM framework, which is part of the broader ADO.NET platform. An ORM allows you to work with relational data using C# objects, and it is the mechanism we will use in this book to access data stored in databases.
You will see how the Entity Framework and LINQ to Entities are used in Chapter 4, but we wanted to mention the IQueryable<T> interface while we are introducing LINQ.

The IQueryable<T> interface is derived from IEnumerable<T> and is used to signify the result of a query executed against a specific data source. In our examples, this will be a SQL Server database. There is no need to use IQueryable<T> directly. One of the nice features of LINQ is that the same query can be performed on multiple types of data source (objects, XML, databases, and so on). When you see us use IQueryable<T> in examples in later chapters, it is because we want to make it clear that we are dealing with data that has come from the database.

Using Async Methods

One of the big additions to C# in .NET 4.5 is improvements in the way that *asynchronous methods* are dealt with. Asynchronous methods perform go off and do work in the background and notify you when they are complete, allowing your code take care of other business while the background work is happening. Asynchronous methods are an important tool in removing bottlenecks from code and allow applications to take advantage of multiple processors and processor cores to perform work in parallel.

C# and .NET has some excellent support for asynchronous methods, but the code tends to be verbose and developers who are not used to parallel programming often get bogged down by the unusual syntax. As a simple example, Listing 4-32 shows an asynchronous method called GetPageLength, which we have defined in a class called MyAsyncMethods and added to the Models folder.

Listing 4-32. A Simple Asynchronous Method

```
using System.Net.Http;
using System.Threading.Tasks;

namespace LanguageFeatures.Models {

    public class MyAsyncMethods {

        public static Task<long?> GetPageLength() {

            HttpClient client = new HttpClient();
```

```
        var httpTask = client.GetAsync("http://apress.com");

        // we could do other things here while we are waiting
        // for the HTTP request to complete

        return httpTask.ContinueWith((Task<HttpResponseMessage> antecedent) => {
            return antecedent.Result.Content.Headers.ContentLength;
        });
    }
  }
}
```

This is a simple method that uses a `System.Net.Http.HttpClient` object to request the contents of the Apress home page and returns its length. We have highlighted the part of the method that tends to cause confusion, which is an example of a *task continuation*.

.NET represents work that will be done asynchronously as a `Task`. Task objects are strongly typed based on the result that the background work produces. So, when we call the `HttpClient.GetAsync` method, what we get back is a `Task<HttpResponseMessage>`. This tells us that the request will be performed in the background and that the result of the request will be an `HttpResponseMessage` object.

▓**Tip**   When we use words like *background*, we are skipping over a lot of detail in order to make the key points that are important to the world of MVC. The .NET support for asynchronous methods and parallel programming in general is excellent and we encourage you to learn more about it if you want to create truly high-performing applications that can take advantage of multicore and multiprocessor hardware. We come back to asynchronous methods for MVC in Chapter 17.

The part that most programmers get bogged down with the *continuation*, which is the mechanism by which you specify what you want to happen when the background task is completed. In the example, we have used the `ContinueWith` method to process the `HttpResponseMessage` object we get from the `HttpClient.GetAsync` method, which we do using a lambda expression that returns the value of a property that returns the length of the content we get from the Apress Web server. Notice that we use the `return` keyword twice:

```
...
return httpTask.ContinueWith((Task<HttpResponseMessage> antecedent) => {
    return antecedent.Result.Content.Headers.ContentLength;
});
...
```

This is the part that makes heads hurt. The first use of the `return` keyword specifies that we are returning a `Task<HttpResponseMessage>` object, which, when the task is complete, will `return` the length of the `ContentLength` header. The `ContentLength` header returns a `long?` result (a nullable long value) and this means that the result of our `GetPageLength` method is `Task<long?>`, like this:

```
...
public static Task<long?> GetPageLength() {
...
```

Do not worry if this does not make sense—you are not alone in your confusion and this is a very simple example. Complex asynchronous operations can chain large numbers of tasks together using the ContinueWith method, which creates code that can be hard to read and harder to maintain.

Applying the async and await Keywords

Microsoft has introduced two new keywords to C# that are specifically intended to simplify using asynchronous methods, like HttpClient.getAsync. The new keywords are async and await and you can see how we have used them to simplify our example method in Listing 4-33.

Listing 4-33. Using the async and await Keywords

```
using System.Net.Http;
using System.Threading.Tasks;

namespace LanguageFeatures.Models {

    public class MyAsyncMethods {

        public async static Task<long?> GetPageLength() {

            HttpClient client = new HttpClient();

            var httpMessage = await client.GetAsync("http://apress.com");

            // we could do other things here while we are waiting
            // for the HTTP request to complete
            return httpMessage.Content.Headers.ContentLength;
        }
    }
}
```

We used the await keyword when calling the asynchronous method. This tells the C# compiler that we want to wait for the result of the Task that the GetAsync method returns and then carry on executing other statements in the same method.

Applying the await keyword means we can treat the result from the GetAsync method as though it were a regular method and just assign the HttpResponseMessage object that it returns to a variable. And, even better, we can then use the return keyword in the normal way to produce a result from other method—in this case, the value of the ContentLength property. This is a much more natural looking method and it means we do not have to worry about the ContinueWith method and multiple uses of the return keyword.

When you use the await keyword, you must also add the async keyword to the method signature, as we have done in the example. And the method result type does not change—our example GetPageLength method still returns a Task<long?>. This is because the await and async are implemented using some clever compiler tricks, meaning that they allow us to use more natural syntax, but they do not change what is happening in the methods to which they are applied. Someone who is calling our GetPageLength method still has to deal with a Task<long?> result because there is still a background operation that produces a nullable long—although, of course, that programmer can also choose to use the await and async keywords as well.

■**Note**   You will have noticed that we did not provide an MVC example for you to test out the `async` and `await` keywords. This is because using asynchronous methods in MVC controllers requires a special technique, and we have a lot of information to present to you before we introduce it in Chapter 17.

Summary

In this chapter, we started by giving an overview of the key C# language features that an effective MVC programmer needs to know about. These features are combined in LINQ, which we will use to query data throughout this book. As we said, we are big fans of LINQ, and it plays an important role in MVC applications. We also showed you the new `async` and `await` keywords, which make it easier to work with asynchronous methods—this is a topic that we will return to in Chapter 17 when we show you an advanced technique for integrating asynchronous programming into your MVC controllers.

In the next chapter, we turn our attention to the Razor View Engine, which is the mechanism by which we insert dynamic data into views.

CHAPTER 5

Working with Razor

Razor is the name of the view engine that Microsoft introduced in MVC 3 and that has been revised in MVC 4 (although the changes are relatively minor). A view engine processes ASP.NET content and looks for instructions, typically to insert dynamic content into the output sent to a browser. Microsoft maintains two view engines—the ASPX engine works on the <% and %> tags that have been the mainstay of ASP.NET development for many years and the Razor engine that works on regions of content denoted with the @ character.

By and large, if you are familiar with the <% %> syntax, you will not have too many problems with Razor, although there are a few new rules. In this section, we will give you a quick tour of the Razor syntax so you can recognize the new elements when you see them. We are not going to supply an exhaustive Razor reference in this chapter; think of this more as a crash course in the syntax. We explore Razor in depth as we continue through the book.

■ **Tip**   Razor is closely associated with MVC development, but with the introduction of ASP.NET 4.5, the Razor view engine is support for ASP.NET Web Pages development as well.

Creating the Example Project

To demonstrate the features and syntax of Razor, we have created a new Visual Studio project using the ASP.NET MVC 4 Web Application template and selected the Empty option.

Defining the Model

We are going to use a very simple domain model and reproduce the same Product domain class we used in the first part of the chapter. Add a class file to your Models folder called Product.cs and ensure that the contents match those shown in Listing 5-1.

Listing 5-1. Creating a Simple Domain Model Class

```
namespace Razor.Models {

    public class Product {

        public int ProductID { get; set; }
        public string Name { get; set; }
        public string Description { get; set; }
        public decimal Price { get; set; }
        public string Category { set; get; }
    }
}
```

Defining the Controller

To add a controller to the project, right click the **Controllers** folder in your project and select **Add** and then **Controller** from the pop-up menus. Set the name to **HomeController** and select **Empty MVC Controller** for the **Template** option, as shown in Figure 5-1.

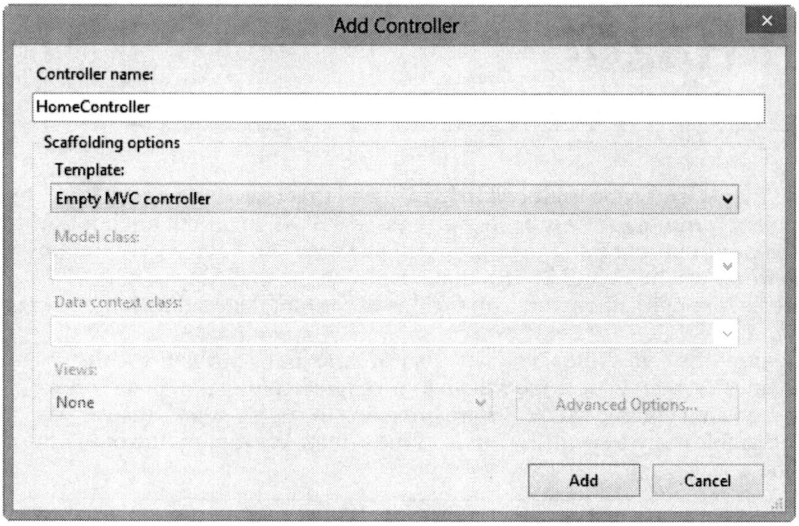

Figure 5-1. Creating the ProductController

Click the **Add** button to create the **Controller** class, and then edit the contents of the file so that they match Listing 5-2.

Listing 5-2. A Simple Controller

```
using Razor.Models;
using System;
using System.Collections.Generic;
using System.Web.Mvc;

namespace Razor.Controllers {
    public class HomeController : Controller {
        Product myProduct = new Product {
            ProductID = 1,
            Name = "Kayak",
            Description = "A boat for one person",
            Category = "Watersports",
            Price = 275M
        };

        public ActionResult Index() {
            return View(myProduct);
        }
    }
}
```

We have defined an action method called `Index`, in which we create and populate the properties of a `Product` object. We pass the `Product` to the `View` method so that it is used as the model when the view is rendered. We do not specify the name of a view file when we call the `View` method, so the default view for the action method will be used (we will create the view file next).

Creating the View

To create the view, right-click the `Index` method of the `HomeController` class and select **Add View**. Check the option to create a strongly typed view and select the `Product` class from the drop-down list, as shown in Figure 5-2.

■ **Note** If you do not see the `Product` class in the drop-down list, compile your project and try creating the view again. Visual Studio will not recognize model classes until they are compiled.

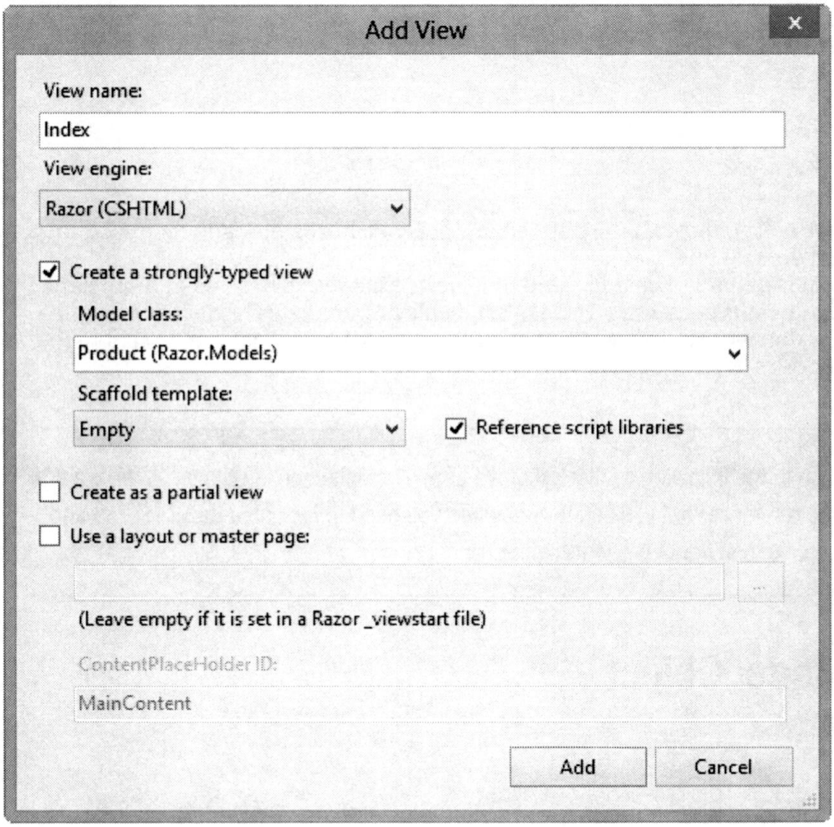

Figure 5-2. Adding the Index view

Ensure that the option to use a layout or master page is unchecked, as shown in the figure. Click **Add** to create the view, which will appear in the **Views/Product** folder as **Index.cshtml**. The view file will be opened for editing and you will see that this is the same basic view file that we created in the previous chapter, as shown in Listing 5-3.

Listing 5-3. A Simple Razor View

```
@model Razor.Models.Product

@{
    Layout = null;
}

<!DOCTYPE html>

<html>
<head>
    <meta name="viewport" content="width=device-width" />
    <title>Index</title>
</head>
<body>
    <div>

    </div>
</body>
</html>
```

In the sections that follow, we will go through the different aspects of a Razor view and demonstrate some the different things you can do with one.

When learning about Razor, it is helpful to bear in mind that views exist to express one or more parts of the model to the user—and that means generating HTML that displays data that is retrieved from one or more objects. If you remember that we are always trying to build an HTML page that can be sent to the client, then everything that Razor does begins to make sense.

■ **Note** We repeat some information in the following sections that we already touched on in Chapter 2. We want to provide you with a single place in the reference that you can turn to when you need to look up a Razor feature and we thought that a small amount of duplication made this worthwhile.

Working with the Model Object

Let's start with the first line in the view:

```
...
@model Razor.Models.Product
...
```

Razor statements start with the @ character. In this case, we the @model statement declares the type of the model object that we will pass to the view from the action method. This allows us to refer to the methods, fields, and properties of the view model object through @Model, as shown in Listing 5-4, which shows a simple addition to the Index view.

Listing 5-4. Referring to a View Model Object Property in a Razor View

```
@model Razor.Models.Product

@{
    Layout = null;
}

<!DOCTYPE html>

<html>
<head>
    <meta name="viewport" content="width=device-width" />
    <title>Index</title>
</head>
<body>
    <div>
        @Model.Name
    </div>
</body>
</html>
```

■ **Note** Notice that we declared the view model object type using @model (lower case m) and access the Name property using @Model (upper case M). This is slightly confusing when you start working with Razor, but it becomes second nature pretty quickly.

If you start the project, you'll see the output shown in Figure 5-3. You do not have to target a specific URL because the default convention in an MVC project is that a request for the root URL (/) is directed to the Index action method in the Home controller—although we will show you how to change that in Chapter 13.

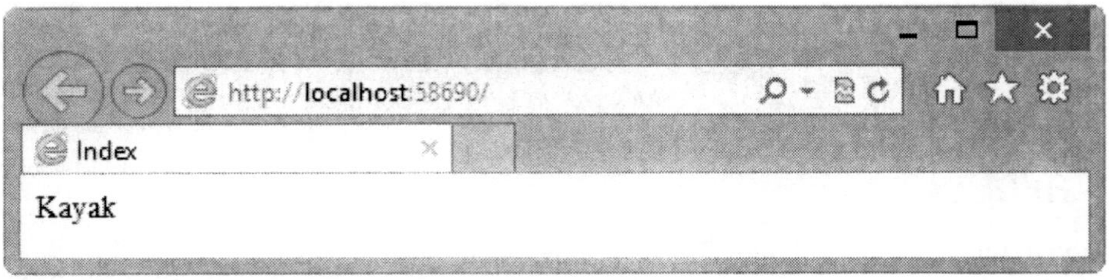

Figure 5-3. The Effect of Reading a Property Value in the View

By using the @model expression, we tell MVC what kind of object we will be working with and Visual Studio takes advantage of this in a couple of ways. First, as you are writing your view, Visual Studio will pop up suggestions of member names when you type @model followed by a period, as shown in Figure 5-4.

105

This is very similar to the way that autocomplete for lambda expressions passed to HTML helper methods works, which we described in Chapter 4.

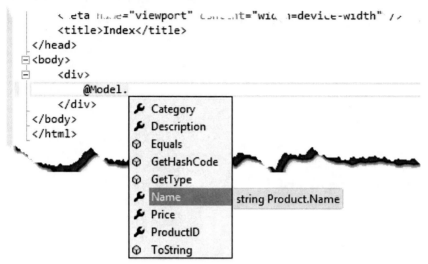

Figure 5-4. Visual Studio Offering Suggestions for Member Names Based on the @Model Expression

Equally useful is that Visual Studio will flag errors when there are problems with the view model object members you are referring to. You can see an example of this in Figure 5-5, where we have tried to reference the `@Model.NotARealProperty` method. Visual Studio has realized that the `Product` class we specified at the model type does not have such a property and has highlighted an error in the editor.

Figure 5-5. Visual Studio Reporting a Problem with an @Model Expression

Working with Layouts

The other Razor expression in the `Index.cshtml` view file is this one:

```
...
@{
    Layout = null;
}
...
```

This is an example of a Razor *code block*, which allows us to include C# statements in a view. The code block is opened with @{ and closed with } and the statements it contains are evaluated when the view is rendered.

This particular code block sets the value of the Layout property to null. As we will explain in detail in Chapter 18, Razor views are compiled into C# classes in an MVC application and the base class that is used defines the Layout property. We'll show you how this all works in Chapter 18, but the effect of setting the Layout property to null is to tell the MVC framework that our view is self-contained and will render all of the content that we need to return to the client.

Self-contained views are fine for simple example apps, but a real project can have dozens of views and layouts are effectively templates that contain markup that you use to create consistency across your Web—this could be to ensure that the right JavaScript libraries are included in the result or that a common look and feel is used throughout your app.

Creating the Layout

To create a layout, right click on the Views folder in the Solution Explorer, click Add New Item from the Add menu and select the MVC 4 Layout Page (Razor) template, as shown in Figure 5-6.

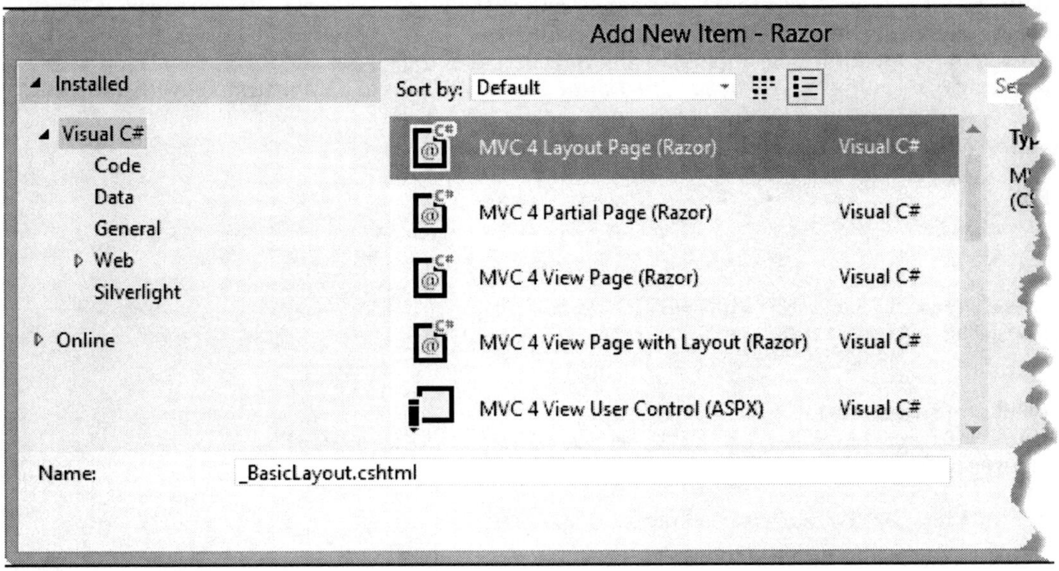

Figure 5-6. Creating a New Layout

Set the name of the file to _BasicLayout.cshtml and click the Add button to create the file. Listing 5-5 shows the contents of the file as it is created by Visual Studio.

■ **Note** Files in the Views folder whose names begin with an underscore (_) are not returned to the user, which allows us to use the file name to differentiate between views that we want to render and the files that support them. Layouts, which are support files, are prefixed with an underscore.

Listing 5-5. The Initial Contents of a Layout

```
<!DOCTYPE html>

<html>
<head>
    <meta name="viewport" content="width=device-width" />
    <title>@ViewBag.Title</title>
</head>
<body>
    <div>
        @RenderBody()
    </div>
</body>
</html>
```

Layouts are a specialized form of view and you can see that we have highlighted the @ expressions in the listing. The call to the @RenderBody method inserts the contents of the view specified by the action method into the layout markup. The other Razor expression in the layout looks for a property called Title in the ViewBag in order to set the contents of the title element.

Any elements in the layout will be applied to any view that uses the layout and this is why layouts are essentially templates. In Listing 5-6, we have added some simple markup to demonstrate how this works.

Listing 5-6. Adding Elements to a Layout

```
<!DOCTYPE html>

<html>
<head>
    <meta name="viewport" content="width=device-width" />
    <title>@ViewBag.Title</title>
</head>
<body>
    <h1>Product Information</h1>
    <div style="padding: 20px; border: solid medium black; font-size: 20pt">
        @RenderBody()
    </div>
    <h2>Visit <a href="http://apress.com">Apress</a></h2>
</body>
</html>
```

We have added a couple of header elements and applied some CSS styles to the div element which contains the @RenderBody expression, just to make it clear what content comes from the layout and what comes from the view.

Applying a Layout

To apply the layout to our view, we just need to set the value of the Layout property. We can also remove the elements that provide the structure of a complete HTML page, because these will come from the layout. You can how we have applied the layout in Listing 5-7, which shows a drastically simplified Index.cshtml file.

> ▪ **Tip** We have also set a value for the ViewBag.Title property, which will be used as the contents of the title element in the HTML document sent back to the user—this is optional, but good practice. If there is no value for the property, the MVC framework will return an empty title element.

Listing 5-7. Using the Layout Property to Specify a View File

```
@model Razor.Models.Product

@{
    ViewBag.Title = "Product Name";
    Layout = "~/Views/_BasicLayout.cshtml";
}

Product Name: @Model.Name
```

The transformation is pretty dramatic, even for such a simple view. What we are left with is focused on presenting data from the view model object to the user, and the HTML document structure is gone.

Using layouts has a number of benefits. It allows us to simplify our views (as the listing demonstrates), it allows us to create common HTML that we can apply to multiple views, and it makes maintenance easier because we can change the common HTML in one place and know that it will be applied wherever the layout is used. To see the effect of the layout, run the example app. The results are shown in Figure 5-7.

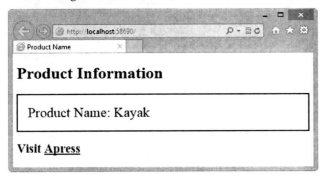

Figure 5-7. The Effect of Applying a Simple Layout to a View

Using a View Start File

We still have a tiny wrinkle to sort out, which is that we have to specify the layout file we want in every view. That means that if we need to rename the layout file, we are going to have to find every view that refers to it and make a change, which will be an error-prone process and counter to the general theme of easy maintenance that runs through the MVC framework.

We can resolve this by using a view start file. When it renders a view, the MVC framework will look for a file called _ViewStart.cshtml. The contents of this file will be treated as though they were contained in the view file itself and we can use this feature to automatically set a value for the Layout property.

To create a view start file, add a new layout file to the Views folder using the process that we showed you earlier. Set the name of the file to _ViewStart.cshtml and set the contents so that they match those shown in Listing 5-8.

Listing 5-8. Creating a View Start File

```
@{
    Layout = "~/Views/_BasicLayout.cshtml";
}
```

Our view start file contains a value for the Layout property, which means that we can remove the corresponding statement from the Index.cshtml file, as shown in Listing 5-9.

Listing 5-9. Updating the View to Reflect the Use of a View Start File

```
@model Razor.Models.Product

@{
    ViewBag.Title = "Product Name";
}

Product Name: @Model.Name
```

We do not have to specify that we want to use the view start file in any way. The MVC framework will locate the file and use its contents automatically. The values defined in the view file take precedence, which makes it easy to override the view start file.

■ **Caution**   It is important to understand the difference between omitting the Layout property from the view file and setting it to null. If your view is self-contained and you do not want to use a layout, then set the Layout property to null. If you omit the Layout property, then the MVC framework will assume that you *do* want a layout and that it should use the value it finds in the view start file.

Demonstrating Shared Layouts

As a quick and simple demonstration of how layouts are shared, we have added a new action method to the Home controller called NameAndPrice. You can see the definition of this method in Listing 5-10, which shows the changes we made to the /Controllers/HomeController.cs file.

Listing 5-10. Adding a New Action Method to the Home Controller

```
using Razor.Models;
using System;
using System.Web.Mvc;

namespace Razor.Controllers {
    public class HomeController : Controller {
        Product myProduct = new Product {
            ProductID = 1,
            Name = "Kayak",
            Description = "A boat for one person",
            Category = "Watersports",
            Price = 275M
```

```
    };

    public ActionResult Index() {
        return View(myProduct);
    }

    public ActionResult NameAndPrice() {
        return View(myProduct);
    }
  }
}
```

The action method just passes the myProduct object to the view method, just like the Index action method does—this is not something that you would do in a real project, but we are demonstrating Razor functionality and so a very simple example suits our needs.

Right-click on the NameAndPrice method in the editor and select Add View from the pop-up menu to display the Add View dialog. Check the Create a strongly-typed view option and pick the Product class from the drop-down list. Check the Use a layout or master page option as shown in Figure 5-8.

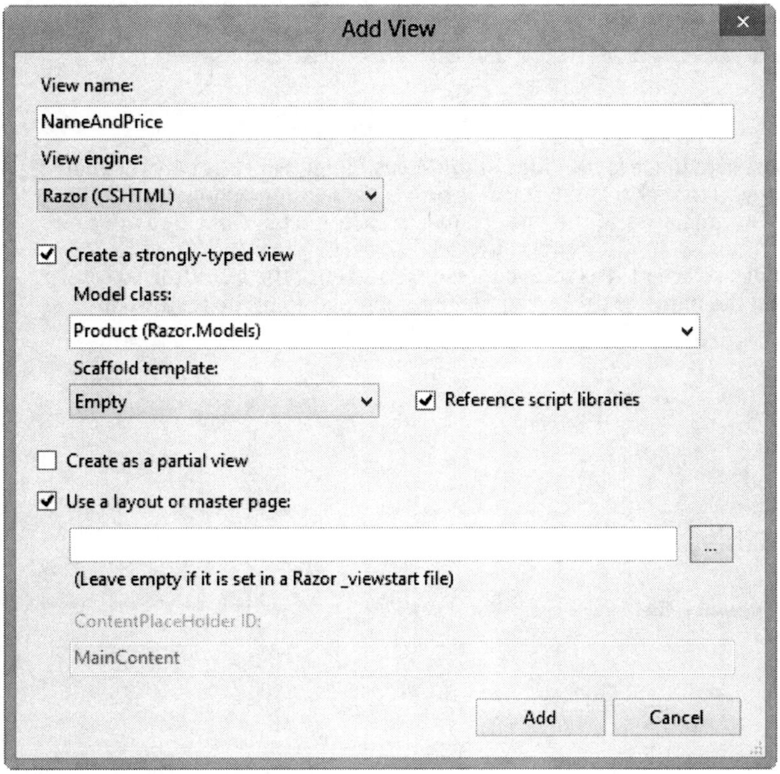

Figure 5-8. Creating a View that Uses a Layout

Notice the text beneath the Use a layout option. It says that if you should leave the textbox empty if you have specified the view you want to use in a view start file. If you were to click the Add button at this point, the view would be created without a C# statement that sets the value of the Layout property.

We are going to explicitly specify the view, so click on the button with an ellipsis label (...) that is to the right of the text box. Visual Studio will present you with a dialog that allows you to select a layout file, as shown in Figure 5-9.

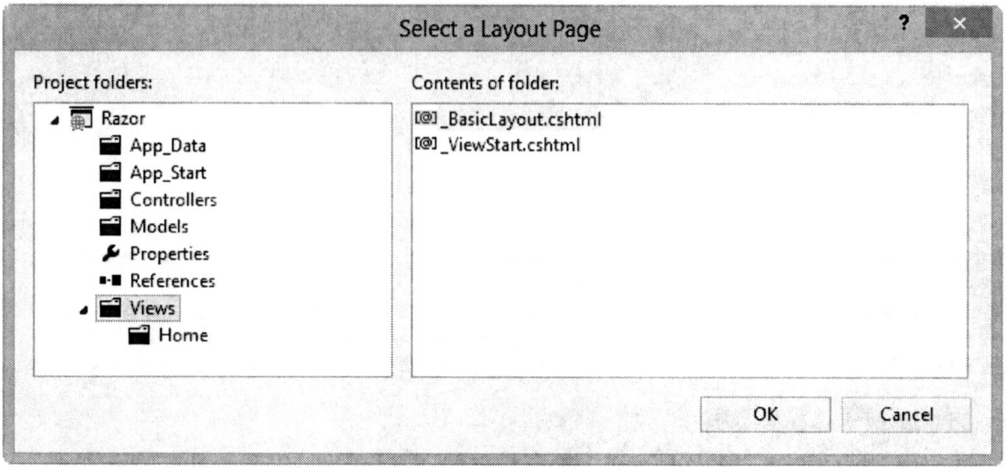

Figure 5-9. Selecting the Layout File

The convention for an MVC project is to place layout files in the Views folder, which is why the dialog presents the contents of that folder for you to pick from. But this is only a convention, which is why the left-hand panel of the dialog lets you navigate around the project, just in case you have decided not to follow the convention.

We have only defined one layout file, so select **_BasicLayout.cshtml** and click the OK button to return to the **Add View** dialog. You will see that the name of the layout file has been placed in the textbox, as shown in Figure 5-10.

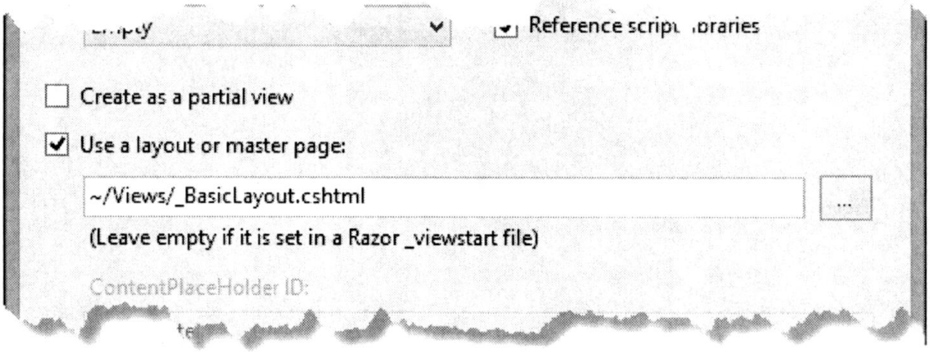

Figure 5-10. Specifying a Layout File When Creating a View

Click the **Add** button to create the **/Views/Home/NameAndPrice.cshtml** file. You can see the contents of this file in Listing 5-11.

Listing 5-11. The Contents of the NameAndPrice View

```
@model Razor.Models.Product

@{
    ViewBag.Title = "NameAndPrice";
    Layout = "~/Views/_BasicLayout.cshtml";
}

<h2>NameAndPrice</h2>
```

Visual Studio uses slightly different default content for view files when you specify a layout, but you can see that the result contains the same Razor expressions we used when we applied the layout to a view ourselves. To complete this example, Listing 5-12 shows a simple addition to the `NameAndPrice.cshtml` file that displays data values from the view model object.

Listing 5-12. Adding to the NameAndPrice Layout

```
@model Razor.Models.Product

@{
    ViewBag.Title = "NameAndPrice";
    Layout = "~/Views/_BasicLayout.cshtml";
}

<h2>NameAndPrice</h2>
The product name is @Model.Name and it costs $@Model.Price
```

If you start the app and navigate to `/Home/NameAndPrice`, you will see the results shown by Figure 5-11. As you might have expected, the common elements and styles defined in the layout have been applied to the view, demonstrating how a layout can be used as a template to create a common look and feel (albeit a simple and unattractive one in this example).

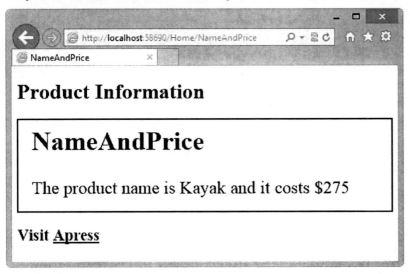

Figure 5-11. The Content in the Layout File Applied to the NameAndPrice View

▓ **Note** We would have got the same result if we had left the textbox in the Add View dialog empty and relied on the view start file. We specified the file explicitly only because we wanted to show you the Visual Studio feature which helps you make a selection.

Using Razor Expressions

Now that we have shown you the basics of views and layouts, we are going to turn to the different kinds of expressions that Razor supports and how you can use them to create view content.

In a good MVC Framework application, there is a clear separation between the roles that the action method and view perform. For this chapter, the rules are simple and we have summarized them in Table 5-1.

Table 5-1. The roles plated by the Action Method and the View

Component	Does Do	Doesn't Do
Action Method	Passes a view model object to the view	Pass formatted data to the view
View	Uses the view model object to present content to the user	Change any aspect of the view model object

We are going to come back to this theme again and again throughout this book. To get the best from the MVC Framework, you need to respect and enforce the separation between the different parts of the app. As you will see, you can do quite a lot with Razor, including using C# statements—but you must not use Razor to perform business logic or manipulate your domain model objects in any way.

Equally, you should not format the data that your action method passed to the view. Instead, let the view figure out data it needs to display. You can see a very simple example of this in the previous section of this chapter. We defined an action method called NameAndPrice, which displays the value of the Name and Price properties of a Product object. Even though we knew which properties we needed to display, we passed the complete Product object to the view model, like this:

```
...
public ActionResult NameAndPrice() {
    return View(myProduct);
}
...
```

We then used the Razor @Model expression in the view to get the value of the properties we were interested in, like this:

```
...
The product name is @Model.Name and it costs $@Model.Price
...
```

We could have created the string we want to display in the action method and passed it as the view model object to the view. It would have worked, but taking this approach undermines the benefit of the MVC pattern and reduces our ability to respond to changes in the future. As we said, we will return to this theme again, but you should remember that the MVC Framework does not enforce proper use of the MVC pattern and that you must remain aware of the effect of the design and coding decisions you make.

Inserting Data Values

The simplest thing you can do with a Razor expression is to insert a data value into the markup. You can do this using the @Model expression to refer to properties and methods defined by the view model object or use the @ViewBag expression to refer to properties you have defined dynamically using the view bag feature (which we introduced in Chapter 2).

You have already seen example of both these expressions, but for completeness, we have added a new action method to the Home controller called DemoExpressions that passes data to the view using a model object and the view bag. You can see the definition of the new action method in Listing 5-13.

Listing 5-13. The DemoExpression Action Method

```
using Razor.Models;
using System;
using System.Web.Mvc;

namespace Razor.Controllers {
    public class HomeController : Controller {
        Product myProduct = new Product {
            ProductID = 1,
            Name = "Kayak",
            Description = "A boat for one person",
            Category = "Watersports",
            Price = 275M
        };

        public ActionResult Index() {
            return View(myProduct);
        }

        public ActionResult NameAndPrice() {
            return View(myProduct);
        }

        public ActionResult DemoExpression() {

            ViewBag.ProductCount = 1;
            ViewBag.ExpressShip = true;
            ViewBag.ApplyDiscount = false;
            ViewBag.Supplier = null;

            return View(myProduct);
        }
    }
}
```

We have created a strongly-typed view called DemoExpression.cshtml to shows these basic expression types, and you can see the contents of the view file in Listing 5-14.

Listing 5-14. The Contents of the DemoExpression View File

```
@model Razor.Models.Product

@{
    ViewBag.Title = "DemoExpression";
}

<table>
    <thead>
        <tr><th>Property</th><th>Value</th></tr>
    </thead>
    <tbody>
        <tr><td>Name</td><td>@Model.Name</td></tr>
        <tr><td>Price</td><td>@Model.Price</td></tr>
        <tr><td>Stock Level</td><td>@ViewBag.ProductCount</td></tr>
    </tbody>
</table>
```

For this example, we have created a simple HTML table and used the properties from the model object and the view bag to populate some of the cell values. You can see the result of starting the app and navigating to the /Home/DemoExpression URL in Figure 5-12. This is just a reconfirmation of the basic Razor expressions that we have been using in the examples so far.

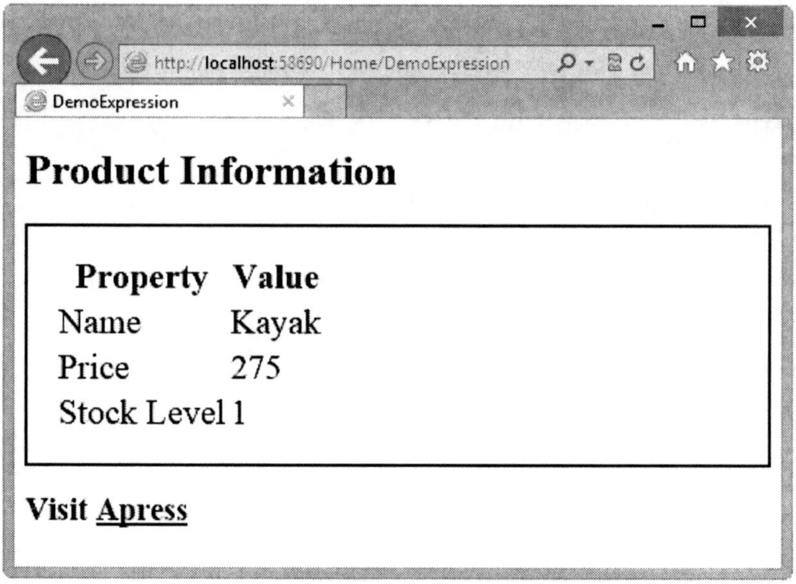

Figure 5-12. Using Basic Razor Expressions to Insert Data Values into the HTML Markup

The result is not pretty because we have not applied any CSS styles to the HTML elements that the view and the layout generate, but the example serves to reinforce the way in which the basic Razor expressions can be used to display the data passed from the action method to the view.

Setting Attribute Values

All of our examples so far have set the content of elements, but you can also use Razor expressions to set the value of element attributes. Listing 5-15 shows how we have changed the DemoExpression view to use view bag properties to attribute values. The way that Razor handles attributes in MVC 4 is pretty clever and this is one of the areas that have been improved since MVC 3.

Listing 5-15. Using a Razor Expression to Set an Attribute Value

```
@model Razor.Models.Product

@{
    ViewBag.Title = "DemoExpression";
    Layout = "~/Views/_BasicLayout.cshtml";
}

<table>
    <thead>
        <tr><th>Property</th><th>Value</th></tr>
    </thead>
    <tbody>
        <tr><td>Name</td><td>@Model.Name</td></tr>
        <tr><td>Price</td><td>@Model.Price</td></tr>
        <tr><td>Stock Level</td><td>@ViewBag.ProductCount</td></tr>
    </tbody>
</table>

<div data-discount="@ViewBag.ApplyDiscount" data-express="@ViewBag.ExpressShip"
    data-supplier="@ViewBag.Supplier">
    The containing element has data attributes
</div>


Discount:<input type="checkbox" checked="@ViewBag.ApplyDiscount" />
Express:<input type="checkbox" checked="@ViewBag.ExpressShip" />
Supplier:<input type="checkbox" checked="@ViewBag.Supplier" />
```

We have started by using basic Razor expressions to set the value for some data attributes on a div element. Data attributes, which are attributes whose names are prefixed by name-, have been an informal way of creating custom attributes for many years and have been made part of the formal standard as part of HTML5. We have used the values of the ApplyDiscount, ExpressShip and Supplier view bag properties to set the value of these attributes.

Start the example app, target the action method, and look at the HTML source that has been used to render the page. You will see that Razor has set the value of the attributes like this:

```
...
<div data-discount="False" data-express="True" data-supplier="">
    The containing element has data attributes
</div>
...
```

The False and True values correspond to the Boolean view bag values, but Razor has done something sensible for the property whose value is null, which is to render an empty string.

But things get much more interesting when we look at the second of our additions to the view, which are a series of checkboxes whose checked attribute is set to the same view bag properties that we used for the data attributes. The HTML that Razor has rendered is as follows:

```
...
Discount: <input type="checkbox" />
Express:  <input type="checkbox" checked="checked" />
Supplier: <input type="checkbox" />
...
```

In MVC 4, Razor has gained awareness of the way that attributes such as checked are used, where the presence of the attribute rather than its value, changes the configuration of the element. If Razor had inserted False or null or the empty string as the value of the checked attribute, then the checkbox that the browser displays would be checked. Instead, Razor has deletes the attribute from the element entirely when the value is false or null, creating an effect that is consistent with the view data, as shown in Figure 5-13.

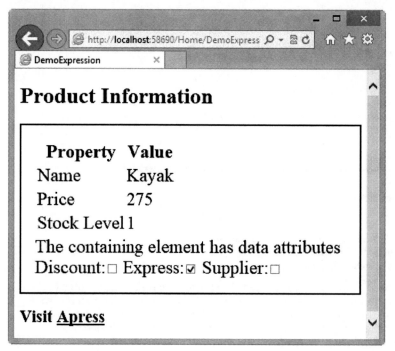

Figure 5-13. The Effect of Deleting Attributes Whose Presence Configures Their Element

Using Conditional Statements

Razor is able to process conditional statements, which means that we can tailor the output from our views based on the values in our view data. We are starting to get to the heart of Razor, which allows you to create complex and fluid layouts that are still reasonably simple to read and maintain. In Listing 5-16, we have updated our DemoExpression.cshtml view file to include a conditional statement.

Listing 5-16. Using a Conditional Razor Statement

```
@model Razor.Models.Product

@{
    ViewBag.Title = "DemoExpression";
    Layout = "~/Views/_BasicLayout.cshtml";
}

<table>
    <thead>
        <tr><th>Property</th><th>Value</th></tr>
    </thead>
    <tbody>
        <tr><td>Name</td><td>@Model.Name</td></tr>
        <tr><td>Price</td><td>@Model.Price</td></tr>
        <tr>
            <td>Stock Level</td>
            <td>
            @switch ((int)ViewBag.ProductCount) {
                case 0:
                    @: Out of Stock
                    break;
                case 1:
                    <b>Low Stock (@ViewBag.ProductCount)</b>
                    break;
                default:
                    @ViewBag.ProductCount
                    break;
            }
            </td>
        </tr>
    </tbody>
</table>
```

To start a conditional statement, you place an @ character in front of the C# conditional keyword, which is switch in this example. You terminate the code block with a close brace character (}) just as you would with a regular C# code block.

■ **Tip**   Notice that we have had to cast the value of the ViewBag.ProductCount property to an int in order to use it with a switch statement. This is required because the switch statement only works with a specific set of types and it cannot evaluate a dynamic property without it being cast like this.

Inside of the Razor code block, you can include HTML elements and data values into the view output just by defining the HTML and Razor expressions, like this:

```
...
<b>Low Stock (@ViewBag.ProductCount)</b>
...
@ViewBag.ProductCount
...
```

We do not have to put the elements or expressions in quotes or denote them in any special way—the Razor engine will interpret these as output to be processed in the normal way. However, if you want to insert literal text into the view when it is not contained in an HTML element, then you need to give Razor a helping hand and prefix the line like this:

```
...
@: Out of Stock
...
```

The @: characters prevent Razor from interpreting this as a C# statement, which is the default behavior when it encounters text. You can see the result of our conditional statement in Figure 5-14.

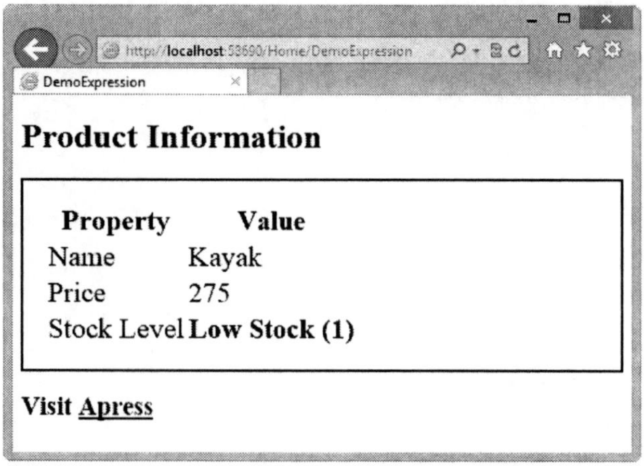

Figure 5-14. Using a Switch Statement in a Razor View

Conditional statements are important in Razor views because they allow you to adapt your content to the data values that the view receives from the action method. As an additional demonstration, Listing 5-17 shows the addition of an **if** statement to the **DemoExpression.cshtml** view—as you might imagine, this is a very commonly used conditional statement.

Listing 5-17. Using an if Statement in a Razor View

```
@model Razor.Models.Product

@{
    ViewBag.Title = "DemoExpression";
    Layout = "~/Views/_BasicLayout.cshtml";
}

<table>
    <thead>
        <tr><th>Property</th><th>Value</th></tr>
    </thead>
    <tbody>
        <tr><td>Name</td><td>@Model.Name</td></tr>
        <tr><td>Price</td><td>@Model.Price</td></tr>
        <tr>
            <td>Stock Level</td>
```

```
        <td>
            @if (ViewBag.ProductCount == 0) {
                @:Out of Stock
            } else if (ViewBag.ProductCount == 1) {
                <b>Low Stock (@ViewBag.ProductCount)</b>
            } else {
                @ViewBag.ProductCount
            }
        </td>
    </tr>
    </tbody>
</table>
```

This conditional statement produces the same results as the `switch` statement, but we just wanted to demonstrate how you can mesh C# conditional statements with Razor views. We explain how this all works in Chapter 18, when we explore views in depth.

Enumerating Arrays and Collections

When writing an MVC application, you will often want to enumerate the contents of an array or some other kind of collection of objects and generate content that details each one. To demonstrate how this is done, we have defined a new action method in the `Home` controller called `DemoArray` which you can see in Listing 5-18.

Listing 5-18. The DemoArray Action Method

```
using Razor.Models;
using System;
using System.Collections.Generic;
using System.Web.Mvc;

namespace Razor.Controllers {
    public class HomeController : Controller {
        Product myProduct = new Product {
            ProductID = 1,
            Name = "Kayak",
            Description = "A boat for one person",
            Category = "Watersports",
            Price = 275M
        };

        // ...other action methods omitted for brevity...

        public ActionResult DemoArray() {

            Product[] array = {
                new Product {Name = "Kayak", Price = 275M},
                new Product {Name = "Lifejacket", Price = 48.95M},
                new Product {Name = "Soccer ball", Price = 19.50M},
                new Product {Name = "Corner flag", Price = 34.95M}
            };
            return View(array);
        }
    }
}
```

This action method creates `Product[]` object that contains some simple data values and passes them to the `View` method so that the data is rendered using the default view.

Visual Studio will not offer you options for arrays and collections when you create a view, so you have to manually enter details of the type you require in the **Add View** dialog. You can see how we have done this in Figure 5-15, which show how we created the `DemoArray.cshtml` view and specified that the view model type is `Razor.Models.Product[]`.

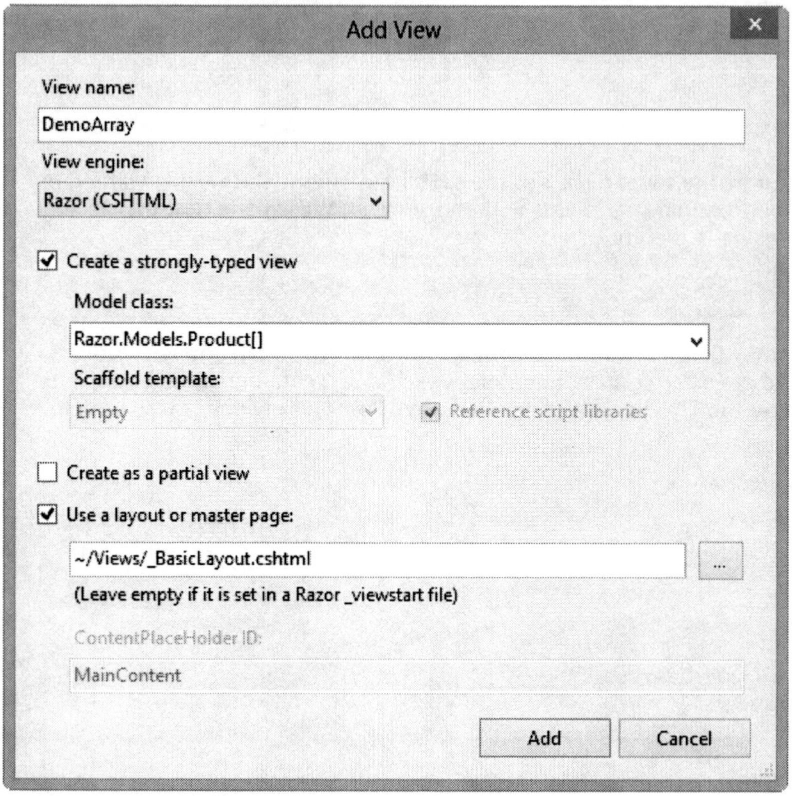

Figure 5-15. Manually Setting the View Model Type for a Strongly Typed View

You can see the contents of the `DemoArray.cshtml` view file in Listing 5-19, including the additions we made to render details of the array items to the user.

Listing 5-19. The Contents of the DemoArray.html File

```
@model Razor.Models.Product[]

@{
    ViewBag.Title = "DemoArray";
    Layout = "~/Views/_BasicLayout.cshtml";
}

@if (Model.Length > 0) {
    <table>
```

```
        <thead><tr><th>Product</th><th>Price</th></tr></thead>
        <tbody>
            @foreach (Razor.Models.Product p in Model) {
                <tr>
                    <td>@p.Name</td>
                    <td>$@p.Price</td>
                </tr>
            }
        </tbody>
    </table>
} else {
    <h2>No product data</h2>
}
```

We have used an @if statement to vary the content based on the length of the array that we are working with and a @foreach expression to enumerate the contents of the array and generate a row in an HTML table for each of them. You can see how these expressions match their C# counterparts and how we have created a local variable called p in the foreach loop and then referred to its properties using the Razor expressions @p.Name and @p.Price.

The result is that we generate an h2 element if the array is empty and produce one row per array item in an HTML table otherwise. Because our data is static in this example, you will always see the same result, which we have shown in Figure 5-16.

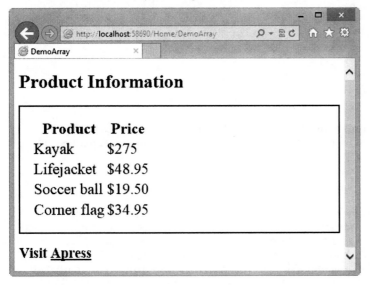

Figure 5-16. Generating Elements Using a Foreach Statement

Dealing with Namespaces

You will notice that we had to refer to the Product class by its fully qualified name in the foreach loop in the last example, like this:

```
...
@foreach (Razor.Models.Product p in Model) {
...
```

This can become annoying in a complex view, where you will have many references to view model and other classes. We can tidy up our views by applying the @using expression to being a namespace into context for a view, just like we would for a regular C# class. Listing 5-20 shows how we have applied the @using expression to the DemoArray.cshtml view we created previously.

Listing 5-20. Applying the @using Expression

```
@using Razor.Models
@model Product[]

@{
    ViewBag.Title = "DemoArray";
    Layout = "~/Views/_BasicLayout.cshtml";
}

@if (Model.Length > 0) {
    <table>
        <thead><tr><th>Product</th><th>Price</th></tr></thead>
        <tbody>
            @foreach (Product p in Model) {
                <tr>
                    <td>@p.Name</td>
                    <td>$@p.Price</td>
                </tr>
            }
        </tbody>
    </table>
} else {
    <h2>No product data</h2>
}
```

A view can contain multiple @using expressions. We have used the @using expression to import the Razor.Models namespace, which means that we can remove the namespace from the @model expression and from within the foreach loop.

Summary

In this chapter, we have given you an overview of the Razor view engine and how it can be used to generate HTML. We showed you how to refer to data passed from the controller via the view model object and the view bag, and we showed you how Razor expressions can be used to tailor your response to the user based on the data you are working with. You will see many different examples of how Razor can be used in the rest of the book and we describe how the MVC view mechanism works in detail in Chapter 18. In the next chapter, we describe the essential development and testing tools that underpin the MVC Framework and that help you to get the best from your projects.

CHAPTER 6

■ ■ ■

Essential Tools for MVC

In this chapter, we are going to look at three tools that should be part of every MVC programmer's arsenal: a dependency injection (DI) container, a unit test framework, and a mocking tool.

We have picked three specific implementations of these tools for this book, but there are many alternatives for each type of tool. If you cannot get along with the ones we use, do not worry. There are so many out there, that you are certain to find something that suits the way your mind and workflow operate.

As we noted in Chapter 3, Ninject is our preferred DI container. It is simple, elegant, and easy to use. There are more-sophisticated alternatives, but we like the way that Ninject works with the minimum of configuration. We consider patterns to be starting points, not law, and we have found it easy to tailor our DI with Ninject to suit different projects and workflows. If you do not like Ninject, we recommend trying Unity, which is one of the Microsoft alternatives.

For unit testing, we are going to be using the support that is built in to Visual Studio. We used to use NUnit, which is a most popular .NET unit-testing framework, but Microsoft has made a big push to improve the unit-testing support in Visual Studio (and now includes it in the free Visual Studio editions). The result is a unit test framework that is tightly integrated into the rest of the IDE and which has actually become pretty good.

The third tool we selected is Moq, which is a mocking tool kit. We use Moq to create implementations of interfaces to use in our unit tests. Programmers either love or hate Moq; there is nothing in the middle. Either you will find the syntax elegant and expressive, or you will be cursing every time you try to use it. If you just cannot get along with it, we suggest looking at Rhino Mocks, which is a nice alternative.

We will introduce each of these tools and demonstrate their core features. We do not provide exhaustive coverage of these tools—each could easily fill a book in its own right—but we have given you enough to get started and, critically, to follow the examples in the rest of the book.

■**Note** This chapter assumes that you want all of the benefits that come from the MVC Framework, including an architecture that supports lots of testing and an emphasis on creating applications that are easily modified and maintained. We love this stuff and would not build apps without it, but we know that some readers will just want to understand the features that the MVC Framework offers and not get into the development philosophy and methodology. We are not going to try to convert you—it is a personal decision and you know what you need to best deliver your projects. We suggest that you at least have a quick skim through this chapter to see what is available, but if you are not the unit-testing type then you can skip to the next chapter and see how to build a realistic example MVC app.

Creating the Example Project

We are going to start by creating a simple example project that we will use throughout this chapter. We created a new Visual Studio project using the `ASP.NET MVC 4 Web Application` template and selected the `Empty` option to create an MVC project with no initial content. This is the same kind of project that we started with in all the chapters so far, and we called the project for this example `EssentialTools`.

Creating the Model Classes

Next, add a class file to the `Models` project folder called `Product.cs` and set the content to match Listing 6-1. This is the same model class used in previous chapters, and the only change is that the namespace matches that of the `EssentialTools` project.

Listing 6-1. The Product Model Class

```
namespace EssentialTools.Models {
    public class Product {

        public int ProductID { get; set; }
        public string Name { get; set; }
        public string Description { get; set; }
        public decimal Price { get; set; }
        public string Category { set; get; }
    }
}
```

We also want to add a class that will calculate the total price of a collection of `Product` objects. Add a new class file to the `Models` folder called `LinqValueCalculator.cs` and set the contents to match Listing 6-2.

Listing 6-2. The LinqValueCalculator Class

```
using System.Collections.Generic;
using System.Linq;

namespace EssentialTools.Models {

    public class LinqValueCalculator {

        public decimal ValueProducts(IEnumerable<Product> products) {
            return products.Sum(p => p.Price);
        }
    }
}
```

The `LinqValueCalculator` class defines a single method called `ValueProducts`, which uses the LINQ `Sum` method to add together the value of the `Price` property of each `Product` object in an enumerable passed to the method (a nice LINQ feature that we use often).

Our final model class is called `ShoppingCart` and it represents a collection of `Product` objects and uses a `LinqValueCalculator` to determine the total value. Create a new class file called `ShoppingCart.cs` and ensure that the contents match those shown in Listing 6-3.

Listing 6-3. The ShoppingCart Class

```
using System.Collections.Generic;

namespace EssentialTools.Models {
    public class ShoppingCart {
        private LinqValueCalculator calc;

        public ShoppingCart(LinqValueCalculator calcParam) {
            calc = calcParam;
        }

        public IEnumerable<Product> Products { get; set; }

        public decimal CalculateProductTotal() {
            return calc.ValueProducts(Products);
        }
    }
}
```

Adding the Controller

Add a new controller to the Controllers folder called HomeController and set the content to match Listing 6-4. The Index action method creates an array of Product objects and uses a LinqValueCalculator class to produce the total value, which is passed to the View method. We do not specify a view when we call the View method, so the default will be used.

Listing 6-4. The Home controller#

```
using EssentialTools.Models;
using System.Web.Mvc;
using System.Linq;

namespace EssentialTools.Controllers {
    public class HomeController : Controller {
        private Product[] products = {
            new Product {Name = "Kayak", Category = "Watersports", Price = 275M},
            new Product {Name = "Lifejacket", Category = "Watersports", Price = 48.95M},
            new Product {Name = "Soccer ball", Category = "Soccer", Price = 19.50M},
            new Product {Name = "Corner flag", Category = "Soccer", Price = 34.95M}
        };

        public ActionResult Index() {

            LinqValueCalculator calc = new LinqValueCalculator();

            ShoppingCart cart = new ShoppingCart(calc) { Products = products };

            decimal totalValue = cart.CalculateProductTotal();

            return View(totalValue);
        }
    }
}
```

Adding the View

The last addition to the project is the view. Right-click the Index action method in the Home controller, and then select Add View. Create a view called Index, which is strongly-typed with a decimal view model object. Once you have created the file, modify the contents so that they match Listing 6-5.

Listing 6-5. The Index.cshtml File

```
@model decimal

@{
    Layout = null;
}

<!DOCTYPE html>

<html>
<head>
    <meta name="viewport" content="width=device-width" />
    <title>Value</title>
</head>
<body>
    <div>
        Total value is $@Model
    </div>
</body>
</html>
```

This is a very simple which uses the @Model expression to display the value of the decimal passed from the action method. If you start the project, you will see the total value, as calculated by the LinqValueCalculator class, illustrated by Figure 6-1.

Figure 6-1. Testing the example app

This is a very simple project, but it sets the scene for the different tools and techniques that we describe in this chapter.

Using Ninject

We introduced the idea of DI in Chapter 3. To recap, the idea is to decouple the components in our MVC applications, and we do this with a combination of interfaces and DI. In the sections that follow, we will explain the problem we deliberately created in the example app and show how to use Ninject, our favorite DI package, can be used to solve it.

Understanding the Problem

In the example app, we have created an example of one kind of problem that DI can solve. Our simple example project relies on tightly-coupled classes: the ShoppingCart class is tightly coupled to the LinqValueCalculator class and the HomeController class is tightly coupled to both ShoppingCart and LinqValueCalculator. This means that if we want to replace the LinqValueCalculator class, we have to locate the change the references in the classes that are tightly-coupled to it. This is not a problem with such a simple project, but it becomes a tedious and error-prone process in a real project, especially if we want to between different calculator implementations, rather than just replace one class with another.

Applying an Interface

We can solve part of the problem by using a C# interface to abstract the definition of the calculator functionality from its implementation. To demonstrate this, we have added the IValueCalculator.cs file to the Models folder and created the interface shown in Listing 6-6.

Listing 6-6. The IValueCalculator Interface

```
using System.Collections.Generic;

namespace EssentialTools.Models {
    public interface IValueCalculator {

        decimal ValueProducts(IEnumerable<Product> products);
    }
}
```

We can then implement this interface in the LinqValueCalculator class, as shown in Listing 6-7.

Listing 6-7. Applying the Interface to the LinqValueCalculator Class

```
using System.Collections.Generic;
using System.Linq;

namespace EssentialTools.Models {

    public class LinqValueCalculator: IValueCalculator {

        public decimal ValueProducts(IEnumerable<Product> products) {
            return products.Sum(p => p.Price);
        }
    }
}
```

The interface allows us to break the tight-coupling between the ShoppingCart and LinqValueCalculator class, as shown in Listing 6-8.

Listing 6-8. Applying the Interface to the ShoppingCart Class

```
using System.Collections.Generic;

namespace EssentialTools.Models {
```

```
public class ShoppingCart {
    private IValueCalculator calc;

    public ShoppingCart(IValueCalculator calcParam) {
        calc = calcParam;
    }

    public IEnumerable<Product> Products { get; set; }

    public decimal CalculateProductTotal() {
        return calc.ValueProducts(Products);
    }
}
}
```

We have made some progress, but C# requires us to specify the implementation class for an interface during instantiation, which is fair enough because it needs to know *which* implementation class we want to use. This means that we still have a problem in the Home controller when we create the LinqValueCalculator object:

```
...
public ActionResult Index() {

    IValueCalculator calc = new LinqValueCalculator();

    ShoppingCart cart = new ShoppingCart(calc) { Products = products };

    decimal totalValue = cart.CalculateProductTotal();

    return View(totalValue);
}
...
```

Our goal with Ninject is to reach the point where we specify that we want to instantiate an implementation of the IValueCalculator interface, but the details of which implementation is required are not part of the code in the Home controller.

Adding Ninject to the Visual Studio Project

The easiest way to add Ninject to an MVC project is to use the integrated Visual Studio support for *NuGet*, which makes it easy to install a wide range of packages and keep them up to date. Select Tools ↗ Library Package Manager ↗ Manage NuGet Packages for Solution to open the NuGet packages dialog. Click Online in the left panel and enter Ninject in the search box in the top-right corner of the dialog. You will see a range of Ninject packages similar to the ones shown in Figure 6-2. (You may see a different set of search results, reflecting updates that have been released since we wrote this chapter).

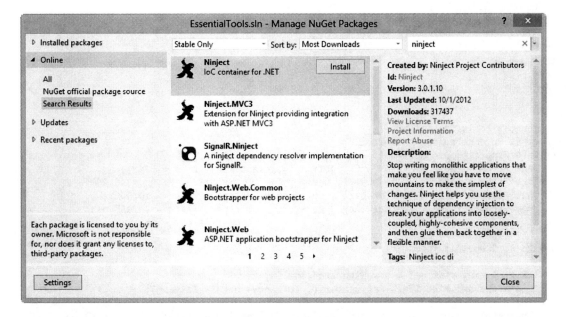

Figure 6-2. Selecting Ninject from the NuGet packages

Click the `Install` button for the Ninject library and Visual Studio will take you through a process of downloading the library and installing it in your project—you will see a Ninject item appearing in the `References` section of the project.

NuGet is an excellent way of getting and maintaining packages used in Visual Studio projects and we recommend that you use it. For this book, however, we need to take a different approach because using NuGet adds a lot of dependency and version tracking information to a project so that it can keep packages in sync and up-to-date. This extra data doubles the size of our simple example projects. It would make the source code download available from `Apress.com` too big for many readers to download.

Instead, we have downloaded the latest version of the library from the Ninject Web site (`www.ninject.org`) and installed it manually by selecting `Add Reference` from the Visual Studio `Project` menu, clicking the `Browse` button, and navigating to the file location where we extracted the contents of the Ninject zip file. We selected the `Ninject.dll` file and added it to the project manually. This has the same effect initial effect as using NuGet, but of course, we do not get the benefit of simple updates and package dependency management.

■**Note**   To be clear, the only reason that we added the Ninject library manually is to keep the size of the source code download that accompanies this book manageable. We use NuGet in our own projects, where an extra few megabytes of data does not make any difference. We recommend that you use NuGet, too.

Getting Started with Ninject

There are three stages to getting the basic Ninject functionality working, and you can see all of them in Listing 6-9, which highlights the changes we have made to the `Home` controller.

Listing 6-9. Adding the Basic Ninject Functionality to the Index Action Method

```
using EssentialTools.Models;
using System.Web.Mvc;
using System.Linq;
using Ninject;

namespace EssentialTools.Controllers {
    public class HomeController : Controller {
        private Product[] products = {
            new Product {Name = "Kayak", Category = "Watersports", Price = 275M},
            new Product {Name = "Lifejacket", Category = "Watersports", Price = 48.95M},
            new Product {Name = "Soccer ball", Category = "Soccer", Price = 19.50M},
            new Product {Name = "Corner flag", Category = "Soccer", Price = 34.95M}
        };

        public ActionResult Index() {

            IKernel ninjectKernel = new StandardKernel();
            ninjectKernel.Bind<IValueCalculator>().To<LinqValueCalculator>();

            IValueCalculator calc = ninjectKernel.Get<IValueCalculator>();

            ShoppingCart cart = new ShoppingCart(calc) { Products = products };

            decimal totalValue = cart.CalculateProductTotal();

            return View(totalValue);
        }
    }
}
```

The first stage is to prepare Ninject for use. We need to create an instance of a Ninject *kernel*, which is the object we will use to communicate with Ninject and request implementations of interfaces. Here is the statement that creates the kernel from the listing:

```
...
IKernel ninjectKernel = new StandardKernel();
...
```

We need to create an implementation of the `Ninject.IKernel` interface, which we do by creating a new instance of the `StandardKernel` class. This allows us to perform the second stage, which is to set up the relationship between the interfaces in our application and the implementation classes we want to work with. Here is the statement from the listing that does that:

```
...
ninjectKernel.Bind<IValueCalculator>().To<LinqValueCalculator>();
...
```

Ninject uses C# type parameters to create a relationship: we set the interface we want to work with as the type parameter for the `Bind` method and call the `To` method on the result it returns. We set the implementation class we want instantiated as the type parameter for the `To` method. This statement tells Ninject that when it is asked for an implementation of the `IValueCalculator` interface, it should service the request by creating a new instance of the `LinqValueCalculator` class.

The last step is to actually use Ninject, which we do through the **Get** method, as follows:

```
...
IValueCalculator calc = ninjectKernel.Get<IValueCalculator>();
...
```

The type parameter used for the **Get** method tells Ninject which interface we are interested in and the result from this method is an instance of the implementation type we specified with the **To** method a moment ago.

Setting up MVC Dependency Injection

The result of the three steps we showed you in the previous listing is that the knowledge about which implementation class should be used to fulfill requests for the **IValueCalculator** interface has been set up in Ninject. But, of course, we have not improved our application any, because that knowledge is still defined in the **Home** controller—meaning that the **Home** controller is still tightly-coupled with the **LinqValueCalculator** class.

In the following sections, we will show you how to embed Ninject at the heart of the example MVC application, which will allow us to simplify the controller, expands the Ninject influence has so that it works across the app and sets us up for some nice examples of some additional Ninject features.

Creating the Dependency Resolver

The first change we are going to make is to create a *custom dependency resolver*. The MVC Framework uses a dependency resolver to create instances of the classes it needs to service requests. By creating a custom resolver, we ensure that Ninject is used whenever an object is going to be created.

Add a new folder to the example project called **Infrastructure** and add a new class file called **NinjectDependencyResolver.cs**. Ensure that the contents of this file match those shown in Listing 6-10.

Listing 6-10. The Contents of the NinjectDependencyResolver.cs File

```csharp
using System;
using System.Collections.Generic;
using System.Web.Mvc;
using Ninject;
using Ninject.Parameters;
using Ninject.Syntax;
using System.Configuration;
using EssentialTools.Models;

namespace EssentialTools.Infrastructure {
    public class NinjectDependencyResolver : IDependencyResolver {
        private IKernel kernel;

        public NinjectDependencyResolver() {
            kernel = new StandardKernel();
            AddBindings();
        }

        public object GetService(Type serviceType) {
            return kernel.TryGet(serviceType);
        }
```

```
        public IEnumerable<object> GetServices(Type serviceType) {
            return kernel.GetAll(serviceType);
        }

        private void AddBindings() {
            kernel.Bind<IValueCalculator>().To<LinqValueCalculator>();
        }
    }
}
```

The MVC Framework will call the GetService or GetServices methods when it needs an instance of a class to service an incoming request. The job of a dependency resolver is to create that instance—a task that we fulfill by calling the Ninject TryGet and GetAll methods. The TryGet method works like the Get method we used previously, but it returns null when there is no suitable binding, rather than throwing an exception. The GetAll method supports multiple bindings for a single type, which is used when there are several different service providers available.

Our dependency resolver class is also where we have set up our Ninject bindings. In the AddBindings method, we use the Bind and To methods to set up the relationship between the IValueCalculator interface and the LinqValueCalculator class.

Register the Dependency Resolver

We have to tell the MVC Framework that we want to use our own dependency resolver, which we do by modifying the Global.asax.cs file. You can see the addition we have made to the MVCApplication class that this file contains in Listing 6-11.

Listing 6-11. Registering the Dependency Resolver

```
using EssentialTools.Infrastructure;
using System.Web.Http;
using System.Web.Mvc;
using System.Web.Routing;

namespace EssentialTools {
    public class MvcApplication : System.Web.HttpApplication {
        protected void Application_Start() {
            AreaRegistration.RegisterAllAreas();

            DependencyResolver.SetResolver(new NinjectDependencyResolver());

            WebApiConfig.Register(GlobalConfiguration.Configuration);
            FilterConfig.RegisterGlobalFilters(GlobalFilters.Filters);
            RouteConfig.RegisterRoutes(RouteTable.Routes);

        }
    }
}
```

With this addition, Ninject will be offered the opportunity to create any object instance that the MVC Framework requires, putting DI right in the core of our example MVC application.

Refactoring the Home Controller

The final step is to refactor the Home controller so that it takes advantage of the facilities we set up in the previous sections. You can see the changes we made in Listing 6-12.

Listing 6-12. Refactoring the Home Controller

```
using EssentialTools.Models;
using System.Web.Mvc;
using System.Linq;

namespace EssentialTools.Controllers {
    public class HomeController : Controller {
        private Product[] products = {
            new Product {Name = "Kayak", Category = "Watersports", Price = 275M},
            new Product {Name = "Lifejacket", Category = "Watersports", Price = 48.95M},
            new Product {Name = "Soccer ball", Category = "Soccer", Price = 19.50M},
            new Product {Name = "Corner flag", Category = "Soccer", Price = 34.95M}
        };
        private IValueCalculator calc;

        public HomeController(IValueCalculator calcParam) {
            calc = calcParam;
        }

        public ActionResult Index() {
            ShoppingCart cart = new ShoppingCart(calc) { Products = products };

            decimal totalValue = cart.CalculateProductTotal();

            return View(totalValue);
        }
    }
}
```

The main change we have made here is to add a class constructor that accepts an implementation of the IValueCalculator interface. We have not specified *which* implementation we want to work with, and we have added an instance variable called calc that we can use to refer to the IValueCalculator we receive in the constructor throughout the controller class.

The other change we have made is to remove any mention of the Ninject code or the LinqValueCalculator class—we have broken the tight-coupling between the HomeController and LinqValueCalculator class at last. If you run the example, you will see the result shown in Figure 6-3. We got this same result when we were instantiating the LinqValueCalculator class directly in the controller, of course.

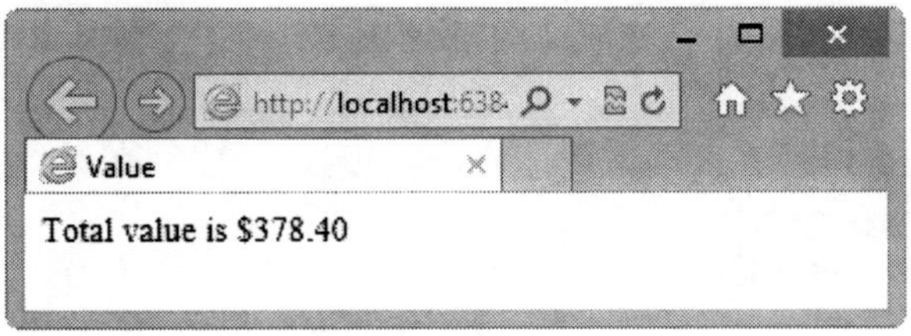

Figure 6-3. The effect of running the example app

What we have created is an example of *constructor injection*, which is one form of dependency injection. Here is what happened when you ran the example app and Internet Explorer made the request for the root URL of the app:

1. The MVC Framework received the request and figured out that the request is intended for the Home controller (we will explain how the MVC framework figures this stuff out in Chapter 15).

2. The MVC Framework asked our custom dependency resolver class to create a new instance of the HomeController class, specifying the class using the Type parameter of the GetService method.

3. Our dependency resolver asked Ninject to create a new HomeController class by passing on the Type object to the TryGet method.

4. Ninject inspected the HomeController constructor and found that it requires an IValueCalculator implementation, which it knows that it has a binding for.

5. Ninject creates an instance of the LinqValueCalculator class and uses it to create a new instance of the HomeController class.

6. Ninject passes the newly-created HomeController instance to the custom dependency resolver, which returns it to the MVC Framework. The MVC Framework uses the controller instance to service the request.

We have labored this slightly because DI can be a bit mind-bending when you see it used for the first time. One benefit of the approach we have taken here is that any controller can declare that it requires an IValueCalculator in its constructor and Ninject will be used, through our custom dependency resolver, creates an instance of the implementation we specified in the AddBindings method.

The best part is that we only have to modify our dependency resolver class when we want to replace the LinqValueCalculator with another implementation, because this is the only place where we have to specify the implementation that is used to satisfy requests for the IValueCalculator interface.

Creating Chains of Dependency

When you ask Ninject to create a type, it examines the couplings between that type and other types. If there are additional dependencies, Ninject automatically resolves them and creates instances of all of the classes that are required. To demonstrate this feature, we have added a file called Discount.cs to the Models folder in the project and defined a new interface and a class that implements it, as shown in Listing 6-13.

Listing 6-13. Defining a New Interface and Implementation

```
namespace EssentialTools.Models {

    public interface IDiscountHelper {
        decimal ApplyDiscount(decimal totalParam);
    }

    public class DefaultDiscountHelper : IDiscountHelper {

        public decimal ApplyDiscount(decimal totalParam) {
            return (totalParam - (10m / 100m * totalParam));
        }
    }
}
```

The IDiscountHelper defines the ApplyDiscount method, which will apply a discount to a decimal value. The DefaultDiscounterHelper class implements the interface and applies a fixed 10 percent discount. We have modified the LinqValueCalculator class so that it has uses the IDiscountHelper interface when it performs calculations, as shown in Listing 6-14.

Listing 6-14. Adding a Dependency in the LinqValueCalculator Class

```
using System.Collections.Generic;
using System.Linq;

namespace EssentialTools.Models {

    public class LinqValueCalculator: IValueCalculator {
        private IDiscountHelper discounter;

        public LinqValueCalculator(IDiscountHelper discountParam) {
            discounter = discountParam;
        }

        public decimal ValueProducts(IEnumerable<Product> products) {
            return discounter.ApplyDiscount(products.Sum(p => p.Price));
        }
    }
}
```

The newly added constructor for the class takes an implementation of the IDiscountHelper interface, which is then used in the ValueProducts method to apply a discount to the cumulative value of the Product objects being processed.

We bind the IDiscountHelper interface to the implementation class with the Ninject kernel in the NinjectDependencyResolver class, just as we did for IValueCalculator, as shown in Listing 6-15.

Listing 6-15. Binding Another Interface to Its Implementation

```
using System;
using System.Collections.Generic;
using System.Web.Mvc;
using Ninject;
using Ninject.Parameters;
using Ninject.Syntax;
using System.Configuration;
using EssentialTools.Models;

namespace EssentialTools.Infrastructure {
    public class NinjectDependencyResolver : IDependencyResolver {
        private IKernel kernel;

        public NinjectDependencyResolver() {
            kernel = new StandardKernel();
            AddBindings();
        }

        public object GetService(Type serviceType) {
            return kernel.TryGet(serviceType);
```

```
        }

        public IEnumerable<object> GetServices(Type serviceType) {
            return kernel.GetAll(serviceType);
        }

        private void AddBindings() {
            kernel.Bind<IValueCalculator>().To<LinqValueCalculator>();
            kernel.Bind<IDiscountHelper>().To<DefaultDiscountHelper>();
        }
    }
}
```

We have created a dependency chain, which Ninject resolves effortlessly using the binding that we defined in the custom dependency resolver. In order to satisfy a request for the HomeController class, Ninject realizes that it needs to create an implementation for the IValueCalculator class, and it does this by looking at its bindings and seeing that our policy for this interface is to use the LinqValueCalculator class. But in order to create a LinqValueCalculator object, Ninject realizes that it needs to use an IDiscountHelper implementation and so it looks at the bindings and creates a DefaultDiscountHelper object. It creates the DefaultDiscountHelper and passes it to the constructor of the LinqValueCalculator object, which it passes in turn to the constructor of the HomeController class, which is then used to service the request from the user. Ninject checks every class it instantiates for dependencies in this way, no matter how long or complex the chain of dependencies is.

Specifying Property and Constructor Parameter Values

We can configure the classes that Ninject creates by providing details of values we want applied to properties when we bind the interface to its implementation. To demonstrate this feature, we have revised the DefaultDiscountHelper class so that it defines a DiscountSize property, which is used to calculate the discount amount, as shown in Listing 6-16.

Listing 6-16. Adding a Property to an Implementation Class

```
namespace EssentialTools.Models {

    public interface IDiscountHelper {
        decimal ApplyDiscount(decimal totalParam);
    }

    public class DefaultDiscountHelper : IDiscountHelper {

        public decimal DiscountSize { get; set; }

        public decimal ApplyDiscount(decimal totalParam) {
            return (totalParam - (DiscountSize / 100m * totalParam));
        }
    }
}
```

When we bind the concrete class to the type with Ninject, we can use the WithPropertyValue method to set the value for the DiscountSize property in the DefaultDiscountHelper class. You can see the change we have made to the AddBindings method in the NinjectDependencyResolver class, as shown in Listing 6-17.

Listing 6-17. Using the Ninject WithPropertyValue Method

```
...
private void AddBindings() {
    kernel.Bind<IValueCalculator>().To<LinqValueCalculator>();
    kernel.Bind<IDiscountHelper>()
        .To<DefaultDiscountHelper>().WithPropertyValue("DiscountSize", 50M);
}
...
```

Notice that we must supply the name of the property to set as a string value. We do not need to change any other binding, nor change the way we use the Get method to obtain an instance of the ShoppingCart class.

The property value is set following construction of the DefaultDiscountHelper class, and has the effect of halving the total value of the items. The result from this change is shown in Figure 6-4.

Figure 6-4. The effect of applying a discount through a property when resolving the dependency chain

If you have more than one property value you need to set, you can chain calls to the WithPropertyValue method to cover them all. We can do the same thing with constructor parameters. Listing 6-18 shows the DefaultDiscounterHelper class reworked so that the size of the discount is passed as a constructor parameter.

Listing 6-18. Using a Constructor Property in an Implementation Class

```
namespace EssentialTools.Models {

    public interface IDiscountHelper {
        decimal ApplyDiscount(decimal totalParam);
    }

    public class DefaultDiscountHelper : IDiscountHelper {
        public decimal discountSize;

        public DefaultDiscountHelper(decimal discountParam) {
            discountSize = discountParam;
        }

        public decimal ApplyDiscount(decimal totalParam) {
            return (totalParam - (discountSize / 100m * totalParam));
        }
    }
}
```

To bind this class using Ninject, we specify the value of the constructor parameter using the WithConstructorArgument method in the AddBindings method, as shown in Listing 6-19.

Listing 6-19. Binding to a Class That Requires a Constructor Parameter

```
...
private void AddBindings() {
    kernel.Bind<IValueCalculator>().To<LinqValueCalculator>();
    kernel.Bind<IDiscountHelper>()
            .To<DefaultDiscountHelper>().WithConstructorArgument("discountParam", 50M);
}
...
```

This technique allows you to inject a value into the constructor. Once again, we can chain these method calls together to supply multiple values and mix and match with dependencies. Ninject will figure out what we need and create it accordingly.

■**Tip**   Notice that we did not just change the `WithPropertyValue` call to `WithConstructorArgument`. We also changed the name of the member being targeted so that it matches the C# convention for parameters names.

Using Conditional Binding

Ninject supports a number of conditional binding methods that allow us to specify which classes should be used to respond to requests for particular requests. To demonstrate this feature, we have added a new file to the `Models` folder of the example project called `FlexibleDiscountHelper.cs`, the contents of which you can see in Listing 6-20.

Listing 6-20. The Contents of the FlexibleDiscountHelper.cs File

```
namespace EssentialTools.Models {
    public class FlexibleDiscountHelper : IDiscountHelper {

        public decimal ApplyDiscount(decimal totalParam) {
            decimal discount = totalParam > 100 ? 70 : 25;
            return (totalParam - (discount / 100m * totalParam));
        }
    }
}
```

The `FlexibleDiscountHelper` class applies different discounts based on the magnitude of the total that is being discounted. We can then modify the `AddBindings` method of the `NinjectDependencyResolver` to tell Ninject when we want to use the `FlexibleDiscountHelper` and when we want to use the `DefaultDiscountHelper`, as shown in Listing 6-21.

Listing 6-21. Updating the AddBindings Method to Use Conditional Binding

```
...
private void AddBindings() {
    kernel.Bind<IValueCalculator>().To<LinqValueCalculator>();
    kernel.Bind<IDiscountHelper>()
            .To<DefaultDiscountHelper>().WithConstructorArgument("discountParam", 50M);
```

```
kernel.Bind<IDiscountHelper>().To<FlexibleDiscountHelper>()
    .WhenInjectedInto<LinqValueCalculator>();
```

}
...

The new binding specifies that when the FlexibleDiscountHelper class should be used as the implementation of the IDiscountHelper interface when Ninject is going to inject the implementation into the LinqValueCalculator object.

We have left the original binding for IDiscountHelper in place. Ninject tries to find the best match and it helps to have a default binding for the same class or interface, so that Ninject has a fallback if the criteria for a conditional binding cannot be satisfied. Ninject supports a number of different conditional binding methods, the most useful of which we have listed in Table 6-1.

Table 6-1. Ninject Conditional Binding Methods

Method	Effect
When(predicate)	Binding is used when the predicate—a lambda expression—evaluates to true.
WhenClassHas<T>()	Binding is used when the class being injected is annotated with the attribute whose type is specified by T.
WhenInjectedInto<T>()	Binding is used when the class being injected into is of type T.

Unit Testing with Visual Studio

There are a lot of .NET unit-testing packages, many of which are open source and freely available. In this book, we are going to use the built-in unit test support that comes with Visual Studio, but there are other .NET unit-test packages are available. The most popular is probably NUnit, but all of the test packages do much the same thing. The reason we have selected the Visual Studio support is that we like the integration with the rest of the IDE, although with Visual Studio 2012, Microsoft has made it possible to integrate third-party testing libraries into the IDE to create a similar experience to the one you get with the built-in test tools.

To demonstrate the Visual Studio unit-test support, we are going to add a new implementation of the IDiscountHelper interface to the example project. Create a new file in the Models folder called MinimumDiscountHelper.cs. Ensure that the contents match those shown in Listing 6-22.

Listing 6-22. The Contents of the MinumumDiscountHelper.cs File

```
using System;

namespace EssentialTools.Models {
    public class MinimumDiscountHelper : IDiscountHelper {

        public decimal ApplyDiscount(decimal totalParam) {
            throw new NotImplementedException();
        }
    }
}
```

Our objective in this example is to make the `MinimumDiscountHelper` demonstrate the following behaviors:

- If the total is greater than $100, the discount will be 10 percent.

- If the total is between $10 and $100 inclusive, the discount will be $5.

- No discount will be applied on totals less than $10.

- An `ArgumentOutOfRangeException` will be thrown for negative totals.

Our `MinimumDiscountHelper` class does not implement any of these behaviors yet—we are going to follow the Test Driven Development (TDD) approach of writing the unit tests and only then implementing the code.

Creating the Unit Test Project

The first step we need to take is to create the unit test project, which we do by right-clicking the top-level item in the Solution Explorer (which is labeled `Solution 'EssentialTools'` for our example app) and selecting `Add ➐ New Project` from the pop-up menu.

■**Tip**   You can choose to create a test project when you create a new MVC project: there is a `Create a unit test project` option on the dialog where you choose the initial content for the MVC project.

This will open the `Add New Project` dialog. Select `Test` from the `Visual C#` templates section in the left-panel and ensure that `Unit Test Project` is selected in the middle panel, as shown in Figure 6-5.

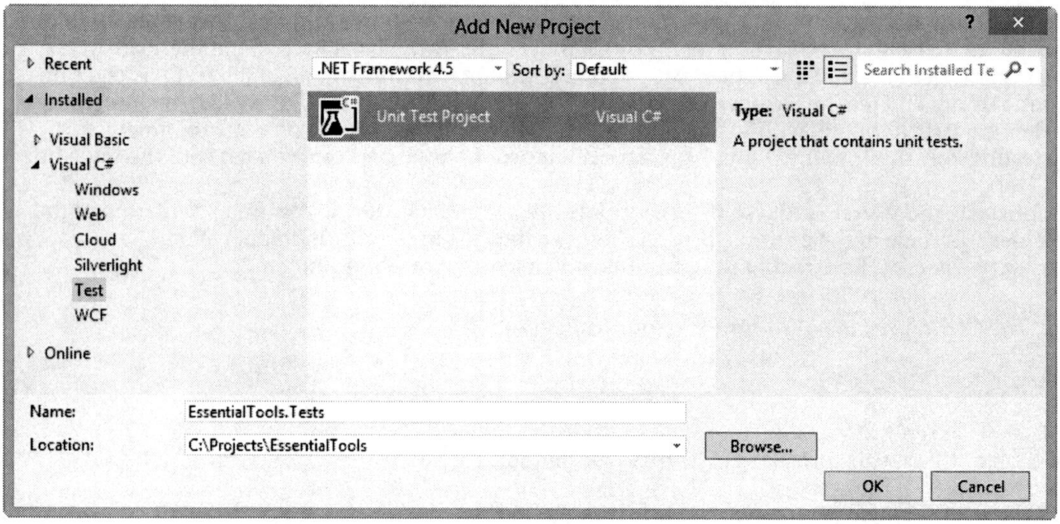

Figure 6-5. Creating the unit test project

Set the project name to EssentialTools.Tests and click the OK button to create the new project, which will be added to the current Visual Studio solution alongside the MVC application project.

We need to add a reference to the test project so that we can use it to perform tests on the classes in the MVC project. Right-click the References item for the EssentialTools.Tests project in the Solution Explorer, and then select Add Reference from the pop-up menu. Click Solution in the left-hand panel and check the box next to the EssentialTools item, as shown in Figure 6-6.

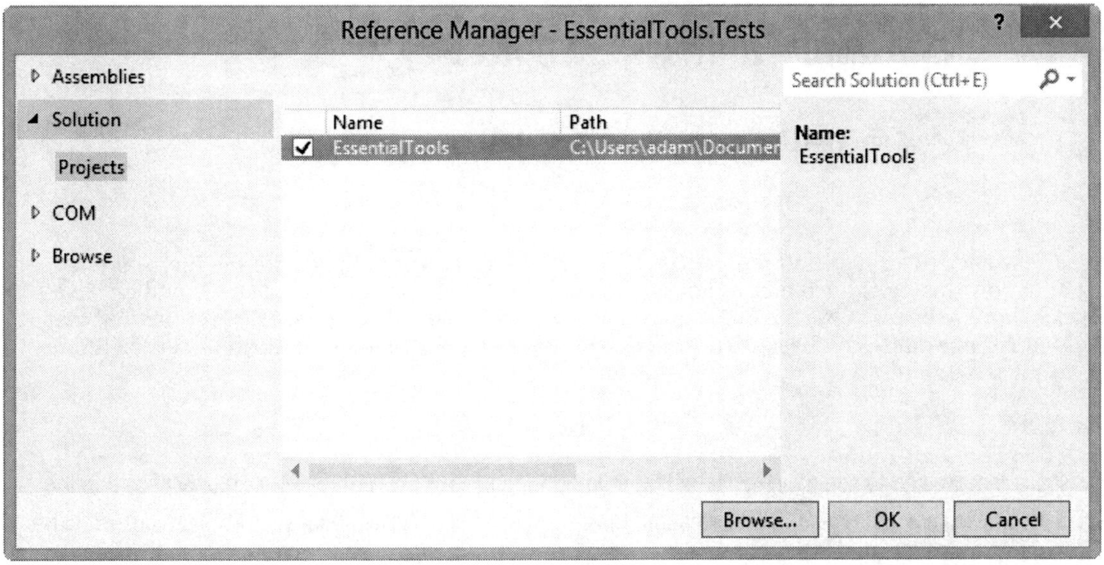

Figure 6-6. Adding a reference to the MVC project

Creating the Unit Tests

We will add our unit tests to the UnitTest1.cs file in the EssentialTools.Tests project. The paid-for Visual Studio editions have some nice features for automatically generating test methods for a class that are not available in the Express edition, but we can still create useful and meaningful tests (and our experience of the automatically generated tests has been one of variable success). To get started, we have made the changes shown in Listing 6-23.

Listing 6-23. Adding the Test Methods to the UnitTest1.cs File

```
using System;
using Microsoft.VisualStudio.TestTools.UnitTesting;
using EssentialTools.Models;

namespace EssentialTools.Tests {

    [TestClass]
    public class UnitTest1 {

        private IDiscountHelper getTestObject() {
            return new MinimumDiscountHelper();
        }
```

143

```
        [TestMethod]
        public void Discount_Above_100() {
            // arrange
            IDiscountHelper target = getTestObject();
            decimal total = 200;

            // act
            var discountedTotal = target.ApplyDiscount(total);

            // assert
            Assert.AreEqual(total * 0.9M, discountedTotal);
        }
    }
}
```

We have just added a single unit test. A class that contains tests is annotated with the TestClass attribute and individual tests are methods annotated with the TestMethod attribute. Not all methods in a unit test class have to be unit tests. To demonstrate this, we have defined the getTestObject method that we will use to arrange our tests—because this method does not have a TestMethod attribute, Visual Studio will not treat it as a unit test.

■**Tip**　　Notice that we had to add a using statement to import the EssentialTools.Models namespace into the test class. Test classes are just regular C# classes and have no special knowledge about your MVC project—it is the TestClass and TestMethod attributes which add the testing magic to the project.

You can see that we have followed the arrange/act/assert (A/A/A) pattern in the unit test method. There are countless conventions about how to name unit tests, but our guidance is simply that you use names that make it clear what the test is checking. Our unit test method is called Discount_Above_100, which is clear and meaningful to us. But all that really matters is that you (and your team) understand whatever naming pattern you settle on, so you adopt a different naming scheme if you do not like ours.

In our test method, we get set up by calling the getTestObject method, which creates an instance of the object we are going to test—the MinimumDiscountHelper class in this case. We also define the total value that we are going to test against. This is the *arrange* section of our unit test.

For the *act* section of the test, we call the MinimumDiscountHelper.ApplyDiscount method and assign the result to the discountedTotal variable. Finally, for the assert section of the test, we use the Assert.AreEqual method to check that the value we got back from the ApplyDiscount method is 90% of the total that we started with.

The Assert class has a range of static methods that you can use in your tests. The class can be found in the Microsoft.VisualStudio.TestTools.UnitTesting namespace along with some additional classes that can be useful for setting up and performing tests. You can learn more about classes in the namespace at http://msdn.microsoft.com/en-us/library/ms182530.aspx.

The Assert class is the one that we use the most and we have summarized the most important methods in Table 6-2 (although there are lot more and worth exploring).

Table 6-2. Static Assert Methods

Method	Description
`AreEqual<T>(T, T)` `AreEqual<T>(T, T, string)`	Asserts that two objects of type T have the same value.
`AreNotEqual<T>(T, T)` `AreNotEqual<T>(T, T, string)`	Asserts that two objects of type T do not have the same value.
`AreSame<T>(T, T)` `AreSame<T>(T, T, string)`	Asserts that two variables refer to the same object.
`AreNotSame<T>(T, T)` `AreNotSame<T>(T, T, string)`	Asserts that two variables refer to different objects.
`Fail()` `Fail(string)`	Fails an assertion—no conditions are checked.
`Inconclusive()` `Inconclusive(string)`	Indicates that the result of the unit test cannot be definitively established.
`IsTrue(bool)` `IsTrue(bool, string)`	Asserts that a `bool` value is true—most often used to evaluate an expression that returns a `bool` result.
`IsFalse(bool)` `IsFalse(bool, string)`	Asserts that a `bool` value is false.
`IsNull(object)` `IsNull(object, string)`	Asserts that a variable is not assigned an object reference.
`IsNotNull(object)` `IsNotNull(object, string)`	Asserts that a variable is assigned an object reference.
`IsInstanceOfType(object, Type)` `IsInstanceOfType(object, Type, string)`	Asserts that an object is of the specified type or is derived from the specified type.
`IsNotInstanceOfType(object, Type)` `IsNotInstanceOfType(object, Type, string)`	Asserts that an object is not of the specified type.

Each of the static methods in the **Assert** class allows you to check some aspect of your unit test. An exception is thrown if an assertion fails, and this means that the entire unit test fails. Each unit test is treated separately, so other tests will continue to be performed.

Each of these methods is overloaded with a version that takes a **string** parameter. The string is included as the message element of the exception if the assertion fails. The **AreEqual** and **AreNotEqual** methods have a number of overloads that cater to comparing specific types. For example, there is a version that allows strings to be compared without taking case into account.

■**Tip**   One noteworthy member of the `Microsoft.VisualStudio.TestTools.UnitTesting` namespace is the `ExpectedException` attribute. This is an assertion that succeeds only if the unit test throws an exception of the type specified by the `ExceptionType` parameter. This is a neat way of ensuring that exceptions are thrown without needing to mess around with `try...catch` blocks in your unit test.

Now that we have shown you how one unit test is put together, we have added tests to the test project to validate the other behaviors we described for our `MinimumDiscountHelper`. You can see the additions in Listing 6-24, but these unit tests are so short and simple (which is generally a characteristic of unit tests) that we are not going to explain them in detail.

Listing 6-24. Defining the Remaining Tests

```
using System;
using Microsoft.VisualStudio.TestTools.UnitTesting;
using EssentialTools.Models;

namespace EssentialTools.Tests {

    [TestClass]
    public class UnitTest1 {

        private IDiscountHelper getTestObject() {
            return new MinimumDiscountHelper();
        }

        [TestMethod]
        public void Discount_Above_100() {
            // arrange
            IDiscountHelper target = getTestObject();
            decimal total = 200;

            // act
            var discountedTotal = target.ApplyDiscount(total);

            // assert
            Assert.AreEqual(total * 0.9M, discountedTotal);
        }

        [TestMethod]
        public void Discount_Between_10_And_100() {
            //arrange
            IDiscountHelper target = getTestObject();

            // act
            decimal TenDollarDiscount = target.ApplyDiscount(10);
            decimal HundredDollarDiscount = target.ApplyDiscount(100);
            decimal FiftyDollarDiscount = target.ApplyDiscount(50);

            // assert
            Assert.AreEqual(5, TenDollarDiscount, "$10 discount is wrong");
            Assert.AreEqual(95, HundredDollarDiscount, "$100 discount is wrong");
```

```
        Assert.AreEqual(45, FiftyDollarDiscount, "$50 discount is wrong");
    }

    [TestMethod]
    public void Discount_Less_Than_10() {
        //arrange
        IDiscountHelper target = getTestObject();

        // act
        decimal discount5 = target.ApplyDiscount(5);
        decimal discount0 = target.ApplyDiscount(0);

        // assert
        Assert.AreEqual(5, discount5);
        Assert.AreEqual(0, discount0);

    }

    [TestMethod]
    [ExpectedException(typeof(ArgumentOutOfRangeException))]
    public void Discount_Negative_Total() {
        //arrange
        IDiscountHelper target = getTestObject();

        // act
        target.ApplyDiscount(-1);
    }
  }
}
```

Running the Unit Tests (and Failing)

Visual Studio 2012 has introduced a more useful Test Explorer window for managing and running tests. Select Windows ↗ Test Explorer from the Visual Studio Test menu to see the new window and click the Run All button near the top-left corner. You will see results similar to the ones shown in Figure 6-7.

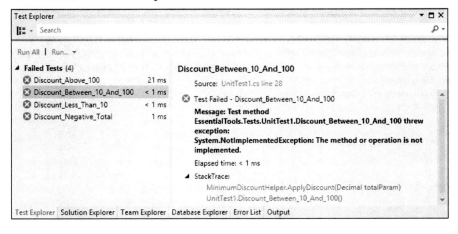

Figure 6-7. Running the tests in the project

You can see the list of tests we defined in the left-hand panel of the Test Explorer window. All of the tests have failed, of course, because we have yet to implement the method we are testing. You can click any of the tests in the window and details of why it has failed will be displayed in the right-panel of the window. The Test Explorer window provides a range of different ways to select and filter unit tests and to choose which tests are run. For our simple example project, however, we will just run all of the tests by clicking the Run All button.

Implementing the Feature

We have reached the point where we can implement the feature, safe in the knowledge that we will be able to check that the code works as expected when we are finished. For all of our preparation, the implementation of the MinimumDiscountHelper class is pretty simple and is shown in Listing 6-25.

Listing 6-25. The Implementation of the MinimumDiscountHelper Class

```
using System;

namespace EssentialTools.Models {
    public class MinimumDiscountHelper : IDiscountHelper {

        public decimal ApplyDiscount(decimal totalParam) {
            if (totalParam < 0) {
                throw new ArgumentOutOfRangeException();
            } else if (totalParam > 100) {
                return totalParam * 0.9M;
            } else if (totalParam > 10 && totalParam <= 100) {
                return totalParam -5;
            } else {
                return totalParam;
            }
        }
    }
}
```

Testing and Fixing the Code

We have left an error in this code deliberately to demonstrate how iterative unit testing with Visual Studio works and you can see the effect of the error if you click the Run All button in the Test Explorer window. You can see the test results in Figure 6-8.

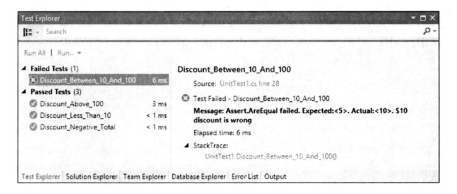

Figure 6-8. The effect of implementing the feature with a bug

Visual Studio always tries to promote the most useful information to the top of the Test Explorer window. In this situation, this means that failed tests are displayed before passed tests.

You can see that we passed three of our unit tests, but we have a problem that has been detected by the Discount_Between_10_And_100 test method. When we click the failed test, we can see that our test expected to get a result of 5, but actually got a value of 10.

At this point, we return to our code and see that we have not implemented our expected behaviors properly—specifically the discounts for totals that are 10 or 100 are not handled properly. The problem is in this statement from the MinumumDiscountHelper class:

```
...
} else if (totalParam > 10 && totalParam < 100) {
...
```

The simple specification that we are working to sets out the behavior for values which are between $10 and $100 *inclusive*, but our implementation excludes those values and only checks for values which are greater than $10, excluding totals which are exactly $10. The solution is simple and is shown in Listing 6-26—only a single character need to be added to change the effect of the **if** statement.

Listing 6-26. Fixing the Feature Code

```csharp
using System;

namespace EssentialTools.Models {
    public class MinimumDiscountHelper : IDiscountHelper {

        public decimal ApplyDiscount(decimal totalParam) {
            if (totalParam < 0) {
                throw new ArgumentOutOfRangeException();
            } else if (totalParam > 100) {
                return totalParam * 0.9M;
            } else if (totalParam >= 10 && totalParam <= 100) {
                return totalParam -5;
            } else {
                return totalParam;
            }
        }
    }
}
```

When we click the Run All button in the Test Explorer window, the results show that we have fixed the problem and that our code has passed all of the tests (see Figure 6-9).

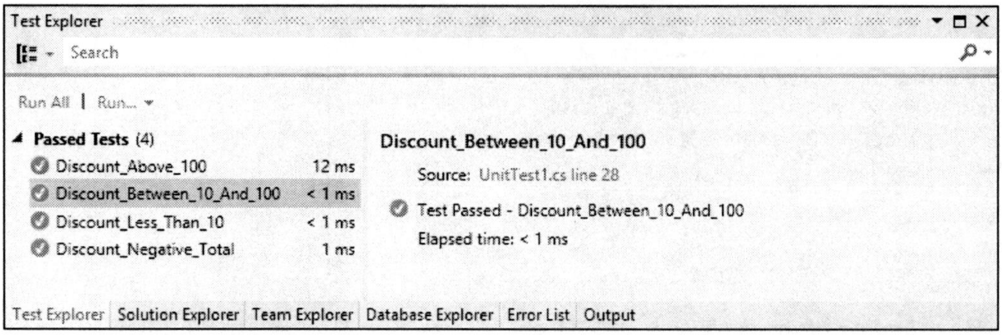

Figure 6-9. Passing all of the unit tests

We have given you a very quick introduction to unit testing, and we will demonstrate unit tests in later chapters as well. The unit test support in Visual Studio is pretty good and we recommend you explore the unit testing documentation on MSDN, which you can find at http://msdn.microsoft.com/en-us/library/dd264975.aspx.

Using Moq

One of the reasons that we were able to keep our tests so simple in the previous section was because we were testing a single class that depended on no other class to function. Such objects exist in real projects, of course, but you will also need to test objects that cannot function in isolation. In these situations, you need to be able to focus on the class or method you are interested in, so that you are not implicitly testing the classes that are depended on as well.

One useful approach is to use *mock objects*, which simulator the functionality of real objects from your project, but in a very specific and controlled way. Mock objects let you narrow the focus of your tests so that you only examine the functionality you are interested in.

The paid-for versions of Visual Studio 2012 include support for creating mock objects through a feature called *fakes*, but we prefer to use a library called Moq, which is simple, easy-to-use and can be used with all Visual Studio editions, including the free ones.

Understanding the Problem

Before we get into the using Moq, we want to demonstrate the problem that we are trying to fix. In this section, we are going to unit test the LinqValueCalculator class, which we defined in the Models folder of the example project. As a reminder, Listing 6-27 shows the definition of the LinqValueCalculator class.

Listing 6-27. The LinqValueCalculator Class

```
using System.Collections.Generic;
using System.Linq;

namespace EssentialTools.Models {
```

```csharp
public class LinqValueCalculator : IValueCalculator {
    private IDiscountHelper discounter;

    public LinqValueCalculator(IDiscountHelper discounterParam) {
        discounter = discounterParam;
    }

    public decimal ValueProducts(IEnumerable<Product> products) {
        return  discounter.ApplyDiscount(products.Sum(p => p.Price));
    }
}
}
```

To test this class, we added a new unit test class to the test project. You do this by right-clicking the test project in the Solution Explorer, selecting Add ↗ Unit Test from the pop-up menu. If your Add menu does not have a Unit Test item, select New Item instead and use the Basic Unit Test template. You can see the changes we made to the new file, which Visual Studio names UnitTest2.cs by default, in Listing 6-28.

Listing 6-28. Adding a Unit Test for the ShoppingCart Class

```csharp
using System;
using Microsoft.VisualStudio.TestTools.UnitTesting;
using EssentialTools.Models;
using System.Linq;

namespace EssentialTools.Tests {
    [TestClass]
    public class UnitTest2 {

        private Product[] products = {
            new Product {Name = "Kayak", Category = "Watersports", Price = 275M},
            new Product {Name = "Lifejacket", Category = "Watersports", Price = 48.95M},
            new Product {Name = "Soccer ball", Category = "Soccer", Price = 19.50M},
            new Product {Name = "Corner flag", Category = "Soccer", Price = 34.95M}
        };

        [TestMethod]
        public void Sum_Products_Correctly() {

            // arrange
            var discounter = new MinimumDiscountHelper();
            var target = new LinqValueCalculator(discounter);
            var goalTotal = products.Sum(e => e.Price);

            // act
            var result = target.ValueProducts(products);

            // assert
            Assert.AreEqual(goalTotal, result);
        }
    }
}
```

The problem we face is that the `LinqValueCalculator` class depends on an implementation of the `IDiscountHelper` interface to operate. In the example, we have used the `MinimumDiscountHelper` class, which presents two different issues.

First, we have made our unit test complex and brittle. In order to create a unit test that works, we need to take into account the discount logic in the `IDiscountHelper` implementation to figure out the expected value from the `ValueProducts` method. The brittleness comes from the fact that our tests will fail if the discount logic in the implementation changes.

Second, and most troubling, we have extended the scope of our unit test so that it implicitly includes the `MinimumDiscountHelper` class. When our unit test fails, we will not know if the problem is in the `LinqValueCalculator` or `MinimumDiscountHelper` class.

Unit tests work best when they are simple and focused, and our current setup does not allow for either of these characteristics. In the sections that follow, we will show you how to add and apply Moq in your MVC project so that you can avoid these problems.

Adding Moq to the Visual Studio Project

Just like with Ninject earlier in the chapter, the easiest way to add Moq to an MVC project is to use the integrated Visual Studio support for *NuGet*, which makes it easy to install a wide range of packages and keep them up to date. Select `Tools ↗ Library Package Manager ↗ Manage NuGet Packages for Solution` to open the NuGet packages dialog.

Click `Online` in the left panel and enter `Moq` in the search box in the top-right corner of the dialog. You will see a range of Moq packages similar to the ones shown in Figure 6-10.

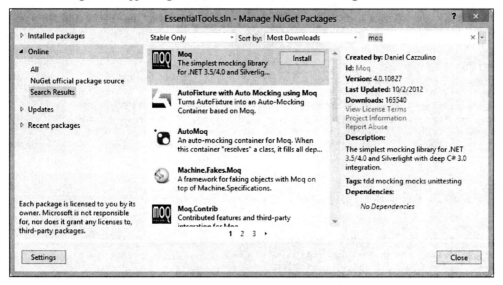

Figure 6-10. Selecting Ninject from the NuGet packages

Click the `Install` button for the Moq library and Visual Studio will take you through a process of downloading the library and installing it in your project—you will see a Moq item appearing in the `References` section of the project.

◼**Caution**   We will be using Moq in the unit test project and not the MVC project—make sure you add the library to the right project.

Once again, we recommend that you use NuGet to get Moq, but we have downloaded the library directly from the project Web site (http://code.google.com/p/moq) and installed it manually, so as to keep the size of the source code download that accompanies this book to a manageable size. We installed it manually by selecting Add Reference from the Visual Studio Project menu, clicking the Browse button, and navigating to the file location where we extracted the contents of the Moq zip file and selected the Moq.dll file.

◼**Note**   We want to repeat the message we gave you when we installed Ninject manually, too: the only reason that we added the Moq library manually is to keep the size of the source code download that accompanies this book manageable. We use NuGet in our own projects, where an extra few megabytes of data does not make any difference and we recommend that you use NuGet, too.

Adding a Mock Object to a Unit Test

Adding a mock object to a unit test means telling Moq what kind of object you want to work with, configuring its behavior and then applying the object to the target being tested. You can see how we have added a mock object to our unit test for the LinqValueCalculator in Listing 6-29.

Listing 6-29. Using a Mock Object in a Unit Test

```
using EssentialTools.Models;
using Microsoft.VisualStudio.TestTools.UnitTesting;
using Moq;
using System.Linq;

namespace EssentialTools.Tests {
    [TestClass]
    public class UnitTest2 {

        private Product[] products = {
            new Product {Name = "Kayak", Category = "Watersports", Price = 275M},
            new Product {Name = "Lifejacket", Category = "Watersports", Price = 48.95M},
            new Product {Name = "Soccer ball", Category = "Soccer", Price = 19.50M},
            new Product {Name = "Corner flag", Category = "Soccer", Price = 34.95M}
        };

        [TestMethod]
        public void Sum_Products_Correctly() {
            // arrange
            Mock<IDiscountHelper> mock = new Mock<IDiscountHelper>();
            mock.Setup(m => m.ApplyDiscount(It.IsAny<decimal>()))
```

```
            .Returns<decimal>(total => total);
        var target = new LinqValueCalculator(mock.Object);

        // act
        var result = target.ValueProducts(products);

        // assert
        Assert.AreEqual(products.Sum(e => e.Price), result);
    }
  }
}
```

The syntax for using Moq is a little odd when you first see it, so we will walk through each stage of the process.

■**Tip**   Bear in mind that there are a number of different mocking libraries available, so the chances are good that you can find an alternative to suit you if you do not like the way that Moq works—although Moq is actually an easy library to use. You can expect some of the other popular libraries to have manuals hundreds of pages long.

Creating a Mock Object

The first step is to tell Moq what kind of mock object you want to work with. Moq relies heavily on generic type parameters, and you can see this in the way that we tell Moq we want to create a mock IDiscountHelper implementation:

```
...
Mock<IDiscountHelper> mock = new Mock<IDiscountHelper>();
...
```

We create a strongly-typed Mock<IDiscountHelper> object, which tells the Moq library the type it will be handling—of course, this is the IDiscountHelper interface for our unit test, but it can be any type that you want to isolate to improve the focus of your unit tests.

Selecting a Method

In addition to creating the strongly-typed Mock object, we also need to specify the way that it behaves— this is at the heart of the mocking process and it allows you to ensure that you establish a baseline behavior in the mock object which you can use to test the functionality of your target object in the unit test. This is the statement from the unit test that sets up the behavior we want:

```
...
mock.Setup(m => m.ApplyDiscount(It.IsAny<decimal>())).Returns<decimal>(total => total);
...
```

We use the Setup method to add a method to our mock object. Moq works using LINQ and lambda expressions. When we call the Setup method, Moq passes us the interface that we have asked it to implement. This is cleverly wrapped up in some LINQ magic that we are not going to get into, but it allows us to select the method we want to configure through a lambda expression. For our unit test, we want to define the behavior of the `ApplyDiscount` method, which is the only method in the `IDiscountHelper` interface and the method we need to test the `LinqValueCalculator` class.

We also have to tell Moq what parameter values we are interested in, which we do using the `It` class, which we have highlighted as follows:

```
...
mock.Setup(m => m.ApplyDiscount(It.IsAny<decimal>())).Returns<decimal>(total => total);
...
```

The `It` class defines a number of methods that are used with generic type parameters. In this case, we have called the `IsAny` method using `decimal` as the generic type. This tells Moq that the behavior we are defining should be applied whenever the `ApplyDiscount` method is called with any decimal value. Table 6-3 shows the methods that the `It` class provides, all of which are static.

Table 6-3. The Methods of the It Class

Method	Description
Is<T>(predicate)	Specifies values of type T that cause the predicate to return `true` (see Listing 6-30 for an example).
IsAny<T>()	Specifies any value of the type T.
IsInRange<T>(min, max, kind)	Matches if the parameter is between the defined values and of type T. The final parameter is a value from the `Range` enumeration and can be either `Inclusive` or `Exclusive`.
IsRegex(expr)	Matches a string parameter if it matches the specified regular expression.

We will show you a more complex example later in this chapter that uses some other `It` methods, but for the moment we will stick with the `IsAny<decimal>` method which allows us to respond to any decimal value.

Defining the Result

The `Returns` method allows us to specify the result that will be returned when our mocked method is called. We specify the type of the result using a type parameter and specify the result itself using a lambda expression. You can see how we have done this for the example:

```
...
mock.Setup(m => m.ApplyDiscount(It.IsAny<decimal>())).Returns<decimal>(total => total);
...
```

By calling `Returns` method with a `decimal` type parameter (i.e. `Returns<decimal>`), we tell Moq that we are going to return a `decimal` value. For the lambda expression, Moq passes us a value of the type we receive in the `ApplyDiscount` method—we create a *pass-through* method in the example, in which we return the value that is passed to the mock `ApplyDiscount` method without performing any operations on it. This is the simplest kind of mock method, but we will show you more-sophisticated examples shortly.

Using the Mock Object

The last step is to use the mock object in the unit test, which we do by reading the value of the `Object` property of the `Mock<IDiscountHelper>` object:

```
...
var target = new LinqValueCalculator(mock.Object);
...
```

To summarize, in our example, the `Object` property returns an implementation of the `IDiscountHelper` interface where the `ApplyDiscount` method returns the value of the `decimal` parameter it is passed.

This makes it very easy to perform our unit test because we can sum the prices of our test `Product` objects ourselves and check that we get the same value back from the `LinqValueCalculator` object:

```
...
Assert.AreEqual(products.Sum(e => e.Price), result);
...
```

The benefit of using Moq in this way is that our unit test only checks the behavior of the `LinqValueCalculator` object and does not depend on any of the real implementations of the `IDiscountHelper` interface in the `Models` folder. This means that when our tests fail, we know that the problem is either in the `LinqValueCalculator` implementation or in the way we set up mock object—and solving a problem from either of these sources is simpler and easier than dealing with a chain of real objects and the interactions between them.

Creating a More Complex Mock Object

We showed you a very simple mock object in the last section, but part of the beauty of Moq is the ability to quickly build up complex behaviors to test different situations. In Listing 6-30, we have added a new unit test to the `UnitTest2.cs` file that mocks a more complex implementation of the `IDiscountHelper` interface—in fact, we have used Moq to model the behavior of the `MinimumDiscountHelper` class.

Listing 6-30. Mocking the Behavior of the MinimumDiscountHelper Class

```
using EssentialTools.Models;
using Microsoft.VisualStudio.TestTools.UnitTesting;
using Moq;
using System.Linq;

namespace EssentialTools.Tests {
    [TestClass]
    public class UnitTest2 {

        private Product[] products = {
            new Product {Name = "Kayak", Category = "Watersports", Price = 275M},
            new Product {Name = "Lifejacket", Category = "Watersports", Price = 48.95M},
            new Product {Name = "Soccer ball", Category = "Soccer", Price = 19.50M},
            new Product {Name = "Corner flag", Category = "Soccer", Price = 34.95M}
        };

        [TestMethod]
        public void Sum_Products_Correctly() {
            // arrange
```

```
        Mock<IDiscountHelper> mock = new Mock<IDiscountHelper>();
        mock.Setup(m => m.ApplyDiscount(It.IsAny<decimal>()))
            .Returns<decimal>(total => total);
        var target = new LinqValueCalculator(mock.Object);

        // act
        var result = target.ValueProducts(products);

        // assert
        Assert.AreEqual(products.Sum(e => e.Price), result);
    }

    private Product[] createProduct(decimal value) {
        return new[] { new Product { Price = value } };
    }

    [TestMethod]
    [ExpectedException(typeof(System.ArgumentOutOfRangeException))]
    public void Pass_Through_Variable_Discounts() {
        // arrange
        Mock<IDiscountHelper> mock = new Mock<IDiscountHelper>();
        mock.Setup(m => m.ApplyDiscount(It.IsAny<decimal>()))
            .Returns<decimal>(total => total);
        mock.Setup(m => m.ApplyDiscount(It.Is<decimal>(v => v == 0)))
            .Throws<System.ArgumentOutOfRangeException>();
        mock.Setup(m => m.ApplyDiscount(It.Is<decimal>(v => v > 100)))
            .Returns<decimal>(total => (total * 0.9M));
        mock.Setup(m => m.ApplyDiscount(It.IsInRange<decimal>(10, 100,
            Range.Inclusive))).Returns<decimal>(total => total - 5);
        var target = new LinqValueCalculator(mock.Object);

        // act
        decimal FiveDollarDiscount = target.ValueProducts(createProduct(5));
        decimal TenDollarDiscount = target.ValueProducts(createProduct(10));
        decimal FiftyDollarDiscount = target.ValueProducts(createProduct(50));
        decimal HundredDollarDiscount = target.ValueProducts(createProduct(100));
        decimal FiveHundredDollarDiscount = target.ValueProducts(createProduct(500));

        // assert
        Assert.AreEqual(5, FiveDollarDiscount, "$5 Fail");
        Assert.AreEqual(5, TenDollarDiscount, "$10 Fail");
        Assert.AreEqual(45, FiftyDollarDiscount, "$50 Fail");
        Assert.AreEqual(95, HundredDollarDiscount, "$100 Fail");
        Assert.AreEqual(450, FiveHundredDollarDiscount, "$500 Fail");
        target.ValueProducts(createProduct(0));
    }
  }
}
```

In unit test terms, replicating the expected behavior of one of the other model classes like would be an odd thing to do, but it is a perfect demonstration of some of the different ways that we can use Moq.

You can see that we have defined four different behaviors for the `ApplyDiscount` method based on the value of the parameter that we receive. The simplest is the catch-all, which returns a value for any `decimal` value, like this:

```
...
mock.Setup(m => m.ApplyDiscount(It.IsAny<decimal>())).Returns<decimal>(total => total);
...
```

This is the same behavior used in the previous example, and we have included it here because it the order in which you call the `Setup` method affects the behavior of the mock object. Moq evaluates the behaviors it has been given in reverse order, so that the most recent calls to the `Setup` method are considered first. This means that you have to take care to create your mock behaviors in order from the most generate to the most specific. The `It.IsAny<decimal>` condition is the most general condition we define in this example and so we apply it first—if we reversed the order of our `Setup` calls, this behavior would capture all of the calls we make to the `ApplyDiscount` method and generate the wrong mock results.

Mocking For Specific Values (and Throwing an Exception)

For our second call to the `Setup` method, we have used the `It.Is` method:

```
...
mock.Setup(m => m.ApplyDiscount(It.Is<decimal>(v => v == 0)))
    .Throws<System.ArgumentOutOfRangeException>();
...
```

The predicate we have passed to the `Is` method returns true if the value passed to the `ApplyDiscount` method is 0. Rather than return a result, we have used the `Throws` method, which causes Moq to throw a new instance of the exception we specify with the type parameter.

We also use the `Is` method to capture values that are greater than 100, like this:

```
...
mock.Setup(m => m.ApplyDiscount(It.Is<decimal>(v => v > 100)))
    .Returns<decimal>(total => (total * 0.9M));
...
```

The `It.Is` method is the most flexible way of setting up specific behaviors for different parameter values because you can use any predicate that returns `true` or `false`. This is the method we use most often when creating complex mock objects.

Mocking For a Range of Values

Our final use of the `It` object is with the `IsInRange` method, which allows us to capture a range of parameter values:

```
...
mock.Setup(m => m.ApplyDiscount(It.IsInRange<decimal>(10, 100, Range.Inclusive)))
    .Returns<decimal>(total => total - 5);
...
```

We have included this for completeness, but in our own projects, we tend to use the Is method and a predicate that does the same thing, like this:

```
...
mock.Setup(m => m.ApplyDiscount(It.Is<decimal>(v => v >= 10 && v <= 100)))
    .Returns<decimal>(total => total - 5);
...
```

The effect is the same, but we find the predicate approach more flexible. Moq has a range of extremely useful features and you can see how many of them are applied by reading the quick start provided at http://code.google.com/p/moq/wiki/QuickStart.

Summary

In this chapter, we looked at the three tools we find essential for effective MVC development—Ninject, the built-in Visual Studio support for unit testing, and Moq. There are many alternatives, both open source and commercial, for all three tools and you will not lack alternatives if you do not get along with the tools we like and use.

You may find that you do not like TDD or unit testing in general, or that you are happy performing DI and mocking manually. That, of course, is entirely your choice. However, we think there are some substantial benefits in using all three tools in the development cycle. If you are hesitant to adopt them because you have never tried them, we encourage you to suspend disbelief and give them a go—at least for the duration of this book.

CHAPTER 7

■ ■ ■

SportsStore—A Real Application

In the previous chapters, we built a quick and simple MVC application. We have looked at the MVC pattern. We have refreshed our memories about the essential C# features and described the kinds of tools that good MVC developers require. Now it is time to put everything together and build a simple but realistic e-commerce application.

Our application, SportsStore, will follow the classic approach taken by online stores everywhere. We will create an online product catalog that customers can browse by category and page, a shopping cart where users can add and remove products, and a checkout where customers can enter their shipping details. We will also create an administration area that includes create, read, update, and delete (CRUD) facilities for managing the catalog—and we will protect it so that only logged-in administrators can make changes.

The application we are going to build is not just a shallow demonstration. Instead, we are going to create a solid and realistic application that adheres to best practices. You might find the going a little slow as we build up the levels of infrastructure we need. Certainly, you *would* get the initial functionality built more quickly with Web Forms, just by dragging and dropping controls bound directly to a database. But the initial investment in an MVC application pays dividends, giving us maintainable, extensible, well-structured code with excellent support for unit testing. We will be able to speed up things once we have the basic infrastructure in place.

UNIT TESTING

We have made quite a big deal about the ease of unit testing in MVC, and about our belief that unit testing is an important part of the development process. You will see this belief demonstrated throughout this part of the book because we have included details of unit tests and techniques as they relate to key MVC features.

But we know this is not a universal belief. If you do not want to unit test, that is fine with us. So, to that end, when we have something to say that is purely about unit testing or TDD, we will put it in a sidebar like this one. If you are not interested in unit testing, you can skip right over these sections, and the SportsStore application will work just fine. You do not need to do any kind of unit testing to get the technology benefits of ASP.NET MVC—although, of course, it is essential if you want the development and testing benefits.

Some of the MVC features we are going to use have their own chapters later in the book. Rather than duplicate everything here, we will tell you just enough to make sense for the example application and point you to the other chapter for in-depth information.

We will call out each step that is needed to build the application, so that you can see how the MVC features fit together. You should pay particular attention when we create views. You will get some odd results if you do not use the same options that we use. To help you with this, we have included figures that show the Add View dialog each time we add a view to the project.

Getting Started

You will need to install the software described in Chapter 2 if you are planning to code the SportsStore application on your own computer as we go. You can also download SportsStore as part of the code archive that accompanies this book (available from apress.com). We have included snapshots of the application project after we added major features, so you can see how the application evolves as it is being built.

You do not need to follow along, of course. We have tried to make the screenshots and code listings as easy to follow as possible, just in case you are reading this book on a train, in a coffee shop, or the like.

Creating the Visual Studio Solution and Projects

We are going to create a Visual Studio solution that contains three projects. One project will contain our domain model, one will be our MVC application, and the third will contain our unit tests. To get started, we created a new Visual Studio solution called SportsStore using the Blank Solution template, which you can find in the Other Project Types section of the New Project dialog, as shown in Figure 7-1. Click the OK button to create the solution.

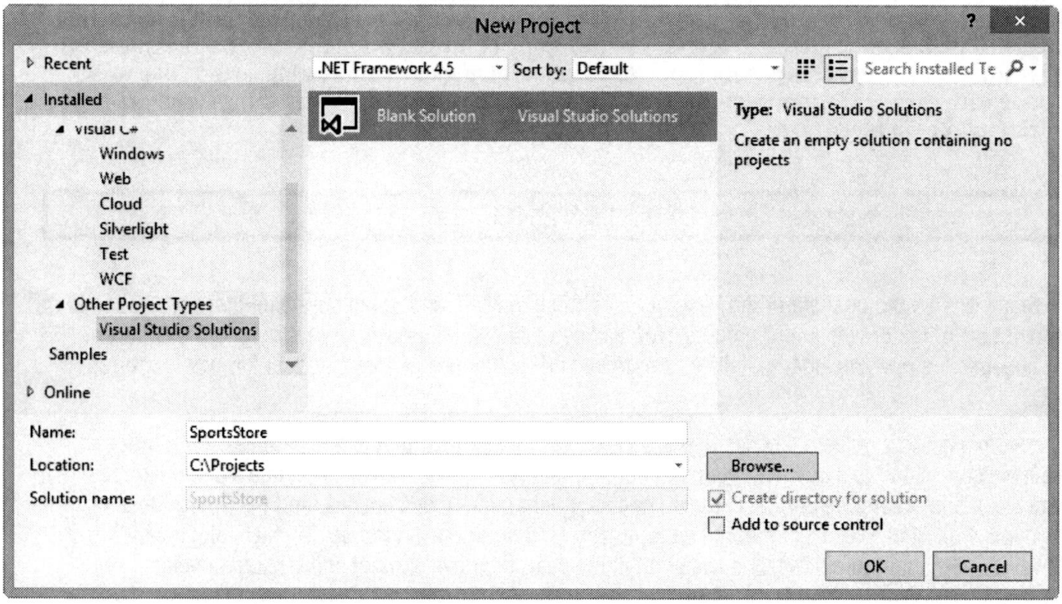

Figure 7-1. Creating a new Visual Studio solution

A Visual Studio solution is a container for one or more projects. We require three projects for our example app, which we have described in Table 7-1. You add a project by right-clicking the Solution entry in the Solution Explorer and selecting Add ↗ New Project from the pop-up menus.

Table 7-1. The Three SportsStore Projects

Project Name	Visual Studio Project Template	Purpose
SportsStore.Domain	Class Library	Holds the domain entities and logic; set up for persistence via a repository created with the Entity Framework.
SportsStore.WebUI	ASP.NET MVC 4 Web Application (choose Basic when prompted to choose a project template)	Holds the controllers and views; acting as the UI for the SportsStore application.
SportsStore.UnitTests	Unit Test Project	Holds the unit tests for the other two projects.

We are using the Basic version of the ASP.NET MVC 4 Web Application template because it contains some use additions, including a set of commonly-used JavaScript libraries in the Scripts folder (including jQuery, jQuery UI, Knockout, and Modernizr), a basic layout in the Views folder, and some CSS styles in the Content folder (including the form validation styles we added manually to a project in Chapter 2).

■**Note**   We describe the JavaScript library files that are included in the Basic MVC project template in Chapter 24. Steve is the creator of the Knockout library. Adam has written about Knockout in his book *Pro JavaScript for Web Apps* (Apress, 2012), along with Modernizr and some other important JavaScript libraries and HTML5 APIs. Adam has also written about jQuery, jQuery UI, and jQuery Mobile in his book *Pro jQuery* (Apress, 2012). As you may gather, this is an area that we both take a great deal of interest in and feel that you cannot create great server-side apps unless you give the client-side some serious attention, too.

You can delete the Class1.cs file in the SportsStore.Domain project—we will not be using it. When you are finished, your Solution Explorer window should look like the one shown in Figure 7-2.

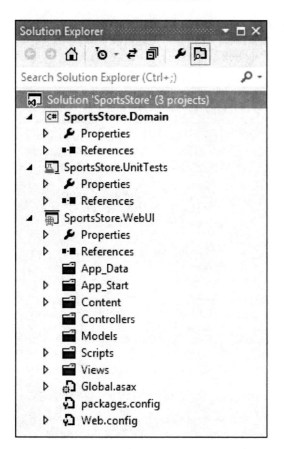

Figure 7-2. The projects shown in the Solution Explorer window

To make debugging easier, right-click the `SportsStore.WebUI` project and select `Set as Startup Project` from the pop-up menu (you will see the name turn bold). This means that when you select `Start Debugging` or `Start without Debugging` from the `Debug` menu, it is this project that will be started.

Adding References

We need to add references to the tool libraries we are going to use for two of the projects we created. The easiest way to add the libraries is to right-click each project, and then select `Manage NuGet Packages` to bring up the NuGet dialog and locate and install the required libraries.

We also need to set up dependencies between projects. Right-click each project in the `Solution Explorer` window, select `Add Reference`, and add the reference to the tool library or one of the other projects from the `Solution` section as required.

You can see details of the projects, the NuGet packages, and the dependencies on other projects in Table 7-2.

■ **Caution**   Take the time to set these relationships up properly. If you do not have the right libraries and project references, you will get into trouble when trying to build the project.

Table 7-2. Required Project Dependencies

Project Name	Tool Dependencies	Project Dependencies	Microsoft References
SportsStore.Domain	None	None	System.Web.Mvc System.ComponentModel .DataAnnotations
SportsStore.WebUI	Ninject Moq	SportsStore.Domain	None
SportsStore.UnitTests	Ninject Moq	SportsStore.Domain SportsStore.WebUI	System.Web.Mvc System.Web Microsoft.CSharp

To add the reference for the System.Web.Mvc assembly to the SportsStore.UnitTests project, right-click the project item in the Solution Explorer, select Add Reference and navigate to the Assemblies ↗ Extensions section. You will find multiple references for assemblies called System.Web.Mvc—make sure you add the one whose version is 4.0.0. Selecting earlier versions will cause problems when testing features that have changed with the latest release. The other Microsoft references are added in the same way, but can be found in the Assemblies ↗ Framework section.

Setting Up the DI Container

In Chapter 6, we showed you how to use Ninject to create a custom dependency resolver that the MVC Framework will use to instantiate objects across the application. For this example, we are going to do something different, which is to create a *custom controller factory*. This is an example of one of the many extension points in the MVC Framework where you can add custom code, which you can use to change the behavior of the MVC Framework or, as we are doing here, limiting DI to one part of the application. The usual pattern is to use a dependency resolver to handle DI and a custom controller factory to change the way that controller classes are located (a topic we return to in Chapter 15), but we are only going to use a controller factory in this example app because we want to show you as many different facets of the MVC Framework as possible.

Create a new folder within the SportsStore.WebUI project called Infrastructure, then create a class called NinjectControllerFactory and edit the class file so that it matches Listing 7-1.

Listing 7-1. The NinjectControllerFactory Class

```
using System;
using System.Web.Mvc;
using System.Web.Routing;
using Ninject;

namespace SportsStore.WebUI.Infrastructure {

    public class NinjectControllerFactory : DefaultControllerFactory {
```

```
        private IKernel ninjectKernel;

        public NinjectControllerFactory() {
            ninjectKernel = new StandardKernel();
            AddBindings();
        }

        protected override IController GetControllerInstance(RequestContext
            requestContext, Type controllerType) {

            return controllerType == null
                ? null
                : (IController)ninjectKernel.Get(controllerType);
        }

        private void AddBindings() {
            // put bindings here
        }
    }
}
```

We have not added any Ninject bindings yet, but we can use the `AddBindings` method when we are ready to do so. We need to tell MVC that we want to use the `NinjectController` class to create controller objects, which we do by making the additions shown in bold in Listing 7-2 to the `Application_Start` method of `Global.asax.cs` in the `SportsStore.WebUI` project.

Listing 7-2. Registering the NinjectControllerFactory with the MVC Framework

```
using SportsStore.WebUI.Infrastructure;
using System.Web.Http;
using System.Web.Mvc;
using System.Web.Optimization;
using System.Web.Routing;

namespace SportsStore.WebUI {

    public class MvcApplication : System.Web.HttpApplication {
        protected void Application_Start() {
            AreaRegistration.RegisterAllAreas();

            WebApiConfig.Register(GlobalConfiguration.Configuration);
            FilterConfig.RegisterGlobalFilters(GlobalFilters.Filters);
            RouteConfig.RegisterRoutes(RouteTable.Routes);
            BundleConfig.RegisterBundles(BundleTable.Bundles);

            ControllerBuilder.Current.SetControllerFactory(new
                NinjectControllerFactory());
        }
    }
}
```

Starting the Application

If you select Start Debugging from the Debug menu, you will see an error page. This is because you have requested a URL that is associated with a controller that Ninject does not have a binding for, as shown in Figure 7-3.

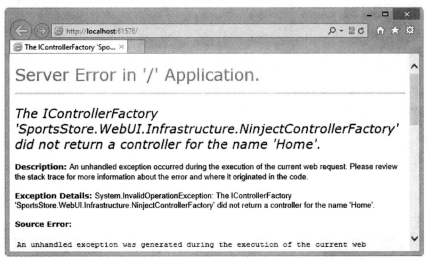

Figure 7-3. The error page

If you have made it this far, your Visual Studio 2012 and ASP.NET MVC development setup is working as expected. You can stop debugging by closing the browser window if your default browser is Internet Explorer. Alternatively, you can switch back to Visual Studio and select Stop Debugging from the Debug menu.

EASIER DEBUGGING

When you run the project from the Debug menu, Visual Studio will create a new browser window to display the application. As a speedier alternative, you can keep your application open in a stand-alone browser window. To do this, assuming you have launched the debugger at least once already, right-click the IIS Express icon in the system tray and select the URL for your app from the pop-up menus, as shown in the following screenshot.

This way, each time you make a change to the application, you will not need to launch a new debugging session to see the effect. You simply compile the solution in Visual Studio by pressing F6 or choosing `Build` ↗ `Build Solution`, and then switch to your browser window and reload the Web page.

Starting the Domain Model

We are going to start with the domain model. Pretty much everything in an MVC application revolves around the domain model, so it is the perfect place to start.

Since this is an e-commerce application, the most obvious domain entity we will need is a product. Create a new folder called `Entities` inside the `SportsStore.Domain` project and then a new C# class called `Product` within it. You can see the structure we are looking for in Figure 7-4.

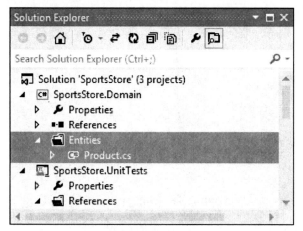

Figure 7-4. Creating the Product class

You are already familiar with the contents of the `Product` class, as we are going to use the same class you saw in the previous chapters. Edit your `Product` class file so that it matches Listing 7-3.

Listing 7-3. The Product Class File

```csharp
namespace SportsStore.Domain.Entities {

    public class Product {
        public int ProductID { get; set; }
        public string Name { get; set; }
        public string Description { get; set; }
        public decimal Price { get; set; }
        public string Category { get; set; }
    }
}
```

We have followed the convention of defining our domain model in a separate Visual Studio project, which means that the class must be marked as `public`. You do not need to follow this convention, but we find that it helps us keep the model separate from the controllers.

Creating an Abstract Repository

We know that we need some way of getting `Product` entities from a database. As we explained in Chapter 3, we want to keep the persistence logic separate from the domain model entities—and we do this by using the *repository pattern*. We do not need to worry about how we are going to implement the persistence for the moment, but we will start the process of defining an interface for it.

Create a new top-level folder inside the `SportsStore.Domain` project called `Abstract` and a new interface called `IProductsRepository`, the contents of which are shown in Listing 7-4. You can add a new interface by right-clicking the `Abstract` folder, selecting `Add ↗ New Item`, and selecting the `Interface` template.

Listing 7-4. The IProductRepository Interface File

```
using System.Linq;
using SportsStore.Domain.Entities;

namespace SportsStore.Domain.Abstract {
    public interface IProductRepository {

        IQueryable<Product> Products { get; }
    }
}
```

This interface uses the `IQueryable<T>` interface to allow a sequence of `Product` objects to be obtained, without saying anything about how or where the data is stored or how it will be retrieved. A class that uses the `IProductRepository` interface can obtain `Product` objects without needing to know anything about where they are coming from or how they will be delivered. This is the essence of the repository pattern. We will revisit this interface throughout the development process to add features.

Making a Mock Repository

Now that we have defined an abstract interface, we could implement the persistence mechanism and hook it up to a database. We are going to do that later in this chapter. In order to be able to start writing other parts of the application, we are going to create a mock implementation of the `IProductRepository` interface. We are going to do this in the `AddBindings` method of our `NinjectControllerFactory` class in the `SportsStore.WebUI` project, as shown in Listing 7-5.

Listing 7-5. Adding the Mock IProductRepository Implementation

```
using System;
using System.Web.Mvc;
using System.Web.Routing;
using Ninject;
using SportsStore.Domain.Entities;
using SportsStore.Domain.Abstract;
using System.Collections.Generic;
using System.Linq;
using Moq;

namespace SportsStore.WebUI.Infrastructure {

    public class NinjectControllerFactory : DefaultControllerFactory {
        private IKernel ninjectKernel;

        public NinjectControllerFactory() {
```

```
        ninjectKernel = new StandardKernel();
        AddBindings();
    }

    protected override IController GetControllerInstance(RequestContext
        requestContext, Type controllerType) {

        return controllerType == null
            ? null
            : (IController)ninjectKernel.Get(controllerType);
    }

    private void AddBindings() {

        Mock<IProductRepository> mock = new Mock<IProductRepository>();
        mock.Setup(m => m.Products).Returns(new List<Product> {
            new Product { Name = "Football", Price = 25 },
            new Product { Name = "Surf board", Price = 179 },
            new Product { Name = "Running shoes", Price = 95 }
        }.AsQueryable());

        ninjectKernel.Bind<IProductRepository>().ToConstant(mock.Object);
    }
}
}
```

We had to add a number of namespaces to the file for this addition, but the process we used to create the mock repository implementation uses the same Moq techniques we introduced in Chapter 4. The AsQueryable method is a LINQ extension method that transforms an IEnumerable<T> into an IQueryable<T>, which we need to match our interface signature.

We want Ninject to return the same mock object whenever it gets a request for an implementation of the IProductRepository interface, which is why we have used the ToConstant method, like this:

```
...
ninjectKernel.Bind<IProductRepository>().ToConstant(mock.Object);
...
```

Rather than create a new instance of the implementation object each time, Ninject will always satisfy requests for the IProductRepository interface with the mock object.

Displaying a List of Products

We could spend the rest of this chapter building out the domain model and the repository, and not touch the UI project at all. We think you would find that boring, though, so we are going to switch tracks and start using the MVC Framework in earnest. We will add features to the model and the repository as we need them.

In this section, we are going to create a controller and an action method that can display details of the products in the repository. For the moment, this will be for only the data in the mock repository, but we will sort that out later. We will also set up an initial *routing configuration* so that MVC knows how to map requests for the application to the controller we are going to create.

Adding a Controller

Right-click the Controllers folder in the SportsStore.WebUI project and select Add ↗ Controller from the pop-up menus. Change the name of the controller to ProductController and ensure that the Template option is set to Empty controller. When Visual Studio opens the file for you to edit, you can remove the default action method that has been added automatically, so that your file looks like the one in Listing 7-6.

Listing 7-6. The Initial Definition of the Product Controller

```
using System;
using System.Collections.Generic;
using System.Linq;
using System.Web;
using System.Web.Mvc;
using SportsStore.Domain.Abstract;
using SportsStore.Domain.Entities;

namespace SportsStore.WebUI.Controllers {
    public class ProductController : Controller {
        private IProductRepository repository;

        public ProductController(IProductRepository productRepository) {
            this.repository = productRepository;
        }
    }
}
```

In addition to removing the Index action method, we have added a constructor that takes an IProductRepository parameter. This will allow Ninject to inject the dependency for the product repository when it instantiates the controller class. We have also imported the SportsStore.Domain namespaces so that we can refer to the repository and model classes without having to quality their names.

Next, we have added an action method, called List, which will render a view showing the complete list of products, as shown in Listing 7-7.

Listing 7-7. Adding an Action Method

```
using System;
using System.Collections.Generic;
using System.Linq;
using System.Web;
using System.Web.Mvc;
using SportsStore.Domain.Abstract;
using SportsStore.Domain.Entities;

namespace SportsStore.WebUI.Controllers {
    public class ProductController : Controller {
        private IProductRepository repository;

        public ProductController(IProductRepository productRepository) {
            this.repository = productRepository;
        }

        public ViewResult List() {
            return View(repository.Products);
        }
    }
}
```

Calling the `View` method like this (without specifying a view name) tells the framework to render the default view for the action method. By passing a `List` of `Product` objects to the `View` method, we are providing the framework with the data with which to populate the `Model` object in a strongly typed view.

Adding the View

Now we need to add the default view for the `List` action method. Right-click the `List` method in the code editor and select `Add View` from the pop-up menu. Name the view `List` and check the option that creates a strongly typed view, as shown in Figure 7-5.

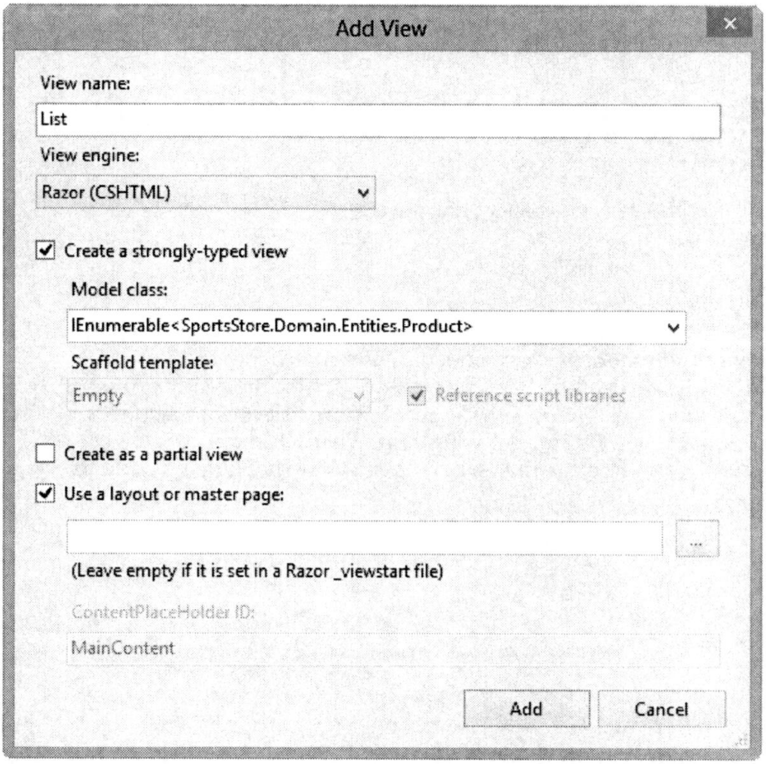

Figure 7-5. Adding the List view

For the model class, enter `IEnumerable<SportsStore.Domain.Entities.Product>`. You will need to type this in; it will not be available from the drop-down list, which does not include enumerations of domain objects.

We will use the default Razor layout which is included in the `Basic` MVC project template later on to add a consistent appearance to our views, so check the option to use a layout but leave the text box empty, as we have done in the figure. Click the `Add` button to create the view.

Rendering the View Data

Knowing that the model in the view is an `IEnumerable<Product>` means we can create a list by using a `foreach` loop in Razor, as shown in Listing 7-8.

Listing 7-8. The List.cshtml View

```
@model IEnumerable<SportsStore.Domain.Entities.Product>

@{
    ViewBag.Title = "Products";
}

@foreach (var p in Model) {
    <div class="item">
        <h3>@p.Name</h3>
        @p.Description
        <h4>@p.Price.ToString("c")</h4>
    </div>
}
```

We have also changed the title of the page. Notice that we do not need to use the Razor text or @: elements to display the view data. This is because each of the content lines in the code body either is a Razor directive or starts with an HTML element.

■ **Tip** Notice that we converted the Price property to a string using the ToString("c") method, which renders numerical values as currency according to the culture settings that are in effect on your server. For example, if the server is set up as en-US, then (1002.3).ToString("c") will return $1,002.30, but if the server is set to en-GB, then the same method will return £1,002.30. You can change the culture setting for your server by adding a section to the <system.web> node in the Web.config file like this: <globalization culture="en-GB" uiCulture="en-GB" />.

Setting the Default Route

All we need to do now is tell the MVC Framework that requests that arrive for the root of our site (http://mysite/) should be mapped to the List action method in the ProductController class. We do this by editing the statement in the RegisterRoutes method in the App_Start/RouteConfig.cs file, as shown in Listing 7-9.

Listing 7-9. Adding the Default Route

```
using System;
using System.Collections.Generic;
using System.Linq;
using System.Web;
using System.Web.Mvc;
using System.Web.Routing;

namespace SportsStore.WebUI {
    public class RouteConfig {
        public static void RegisterRoutes(RouteCollection routes) {
            routes.IgnoreRoute("{resource}.axd/{*pathInfo}");
```

```
        routes.MapRoute(
            name: "Default",
            url: "{controller}/{action}/{id}",
            defaults: new { controller = "Product", action = "List",
                id = UrlParameter.Optional }
        );
    }
  }
}
```

You can see the changes in bold—change Home to Product and Index to List, as shown in the listing. We will cover the ASP.NET routing feature in detail in Chapter 13. For now, it is enough to know that this change directs requests for the default URL to the action method we defined.

■ **Tip** Notice that we have set the value of the controller in Listing 7-9 to be Product and not ProductController, which is the name of the class. This is part of the ASP.NET MVC naming scheme, in which controller classes *always* end in Controller and you omit this part of the name when referring to the class.

Running the Application

We have all the basics in place. We have a controller with an action method that is called when the default URL is requested. That action method relies on a mock implementation of our repository interface, which generates some simple test data. The test data is passed to the view that we associated with the action method, and the view creates a simple list of the details for each product. If you run the application, you can see the result, which we have shown in Figure 7-6.

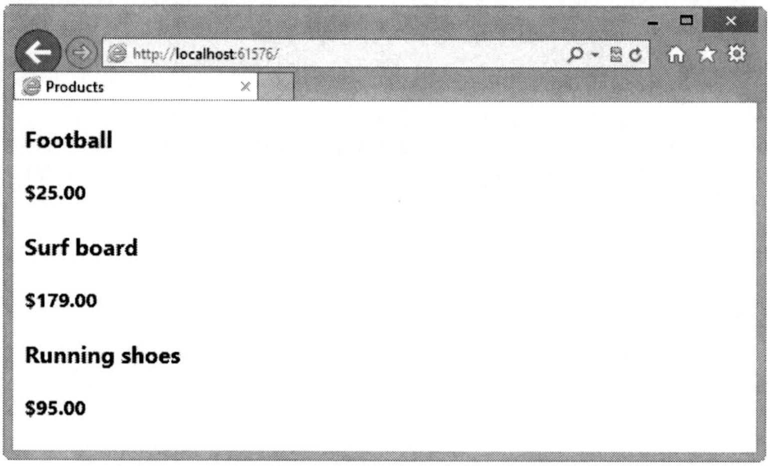

Figure 7-6. Viewing the basic application functionality

This is the typical pattern of development for the ASP.NET MVC Framework. We invest a relatively long period of time getting everything set up, and then the basic functionality of the application starts to come together very quickly.

Preparing a Database

We can already display simple views that contain details of our products, but we are still displaying the test data that our mock IProductRepository returns. Before we can implement a real repository, we need to set up a database and populate it with some data.

We are going to use SQL Server as the database, and we will access the database using the Entity Framework (EF), which is the .NET ORM framework. An ORM framework lets us work with the tables, columns, and rows of a relational database using regular C# objects. We mentioned in Chapter 6 that LINQ can work with different sources of data, and one of these is the Entity Framework. You will see how this simplifies things in a little while.

This is another area where you can choose from a wide range of tools and technologies. Not only are there different relational databases available, but you can also work with object repositories, document stores, and some very esoteric alternatives. There are many ORM frameworks as well, each of which takes a slightly different approach—variations that may give you a better fit for your projects.

We are using the Entity Framework for a couple of reasons. The first is that it is simple and easy to get it up and working. The second is that the integration with LINQ is first rate, and we like using LINQ. The third reason is that it is actually pretty good. The earlier releases were a bit hit-and-miss, but the current versions are elegant and feature-rich.

Creating the Database

One of the nice additions to Visual Studio 2012 and SQL Server 2012 is the *LocalDB* feature, which is an administration-free implementation of the core SQL Server features specifically designed for developers. Using this feature, we can skip the process of setting up a database while we build our project and then deploy to a full SQL Server instance when we deploy. Most MVC apps are deployed to hosted environments that are run by professional administrators and so the LocalDB feature means that database configuration can be left in the hands of DBAs and developers can get on with coding. The LocalDB feature is installed automatically with Visual Studio Express 2012 for Web, but you can download it directly from www.microsoft.com/sqlserver if you prefer.

The first step is to create the database connection in Visual Studio. Open the Database Explorer window from the View menu and click the Connect to Database button (which looks like a power cable with a green plus sign on it).

You will see the Add Connection dialog. Set the server name to (localdb)\v11.0—this is a special name that indicates that you want to use the LocalDB feature. Ensure that the Use Windows Authentication option is checked and set the database name to SportsStore, as shown in Figure 7-7.

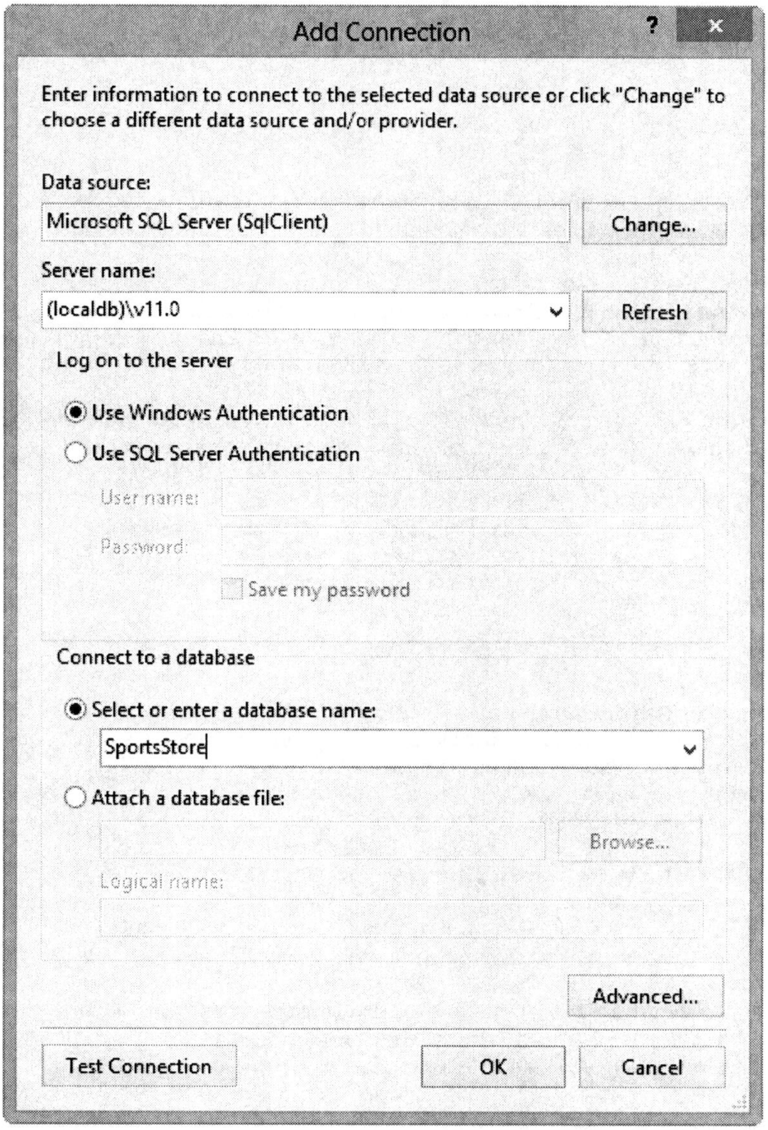

Figure 7-7. Setting up the SportsStore database

Click the OK button and you will be prompted to create the new database. Click the Yes button and a new entry will appear in the **Database Explorer** window. You can expand this item to see the different facets of the newly-created database, as shown in Figure 7-8.

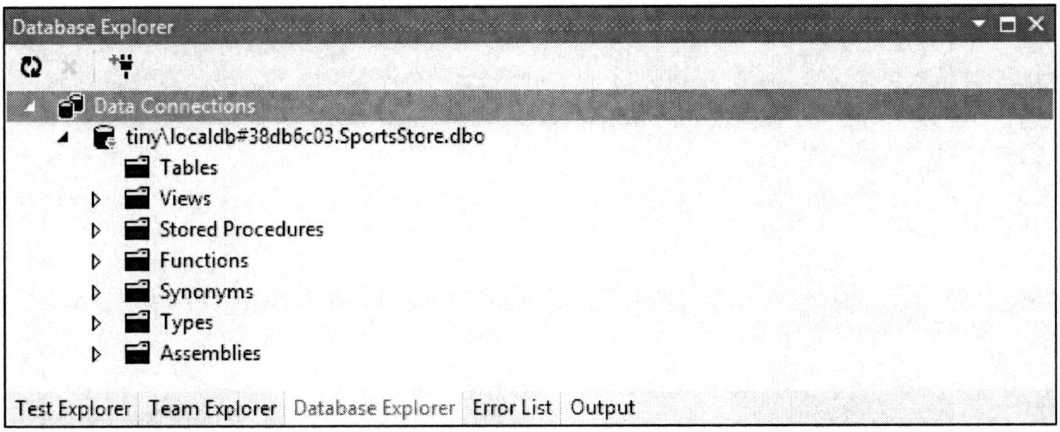

Figure 7-8. The LocalDB database as shown in the Database Explorer window

You should see something very similar, but the name of the database connection will be different, not least because it will include the local PC name (ours is called **tiny**).

Defining the Database Schema

We need only one table in our database, which we will use to store our **Product** data. Using the **Database Explorer** window, expand the database you just created so you can see the **Tables** item and right-click it. Select **Add New Table** from the menu, as shown in Figure 7-9.

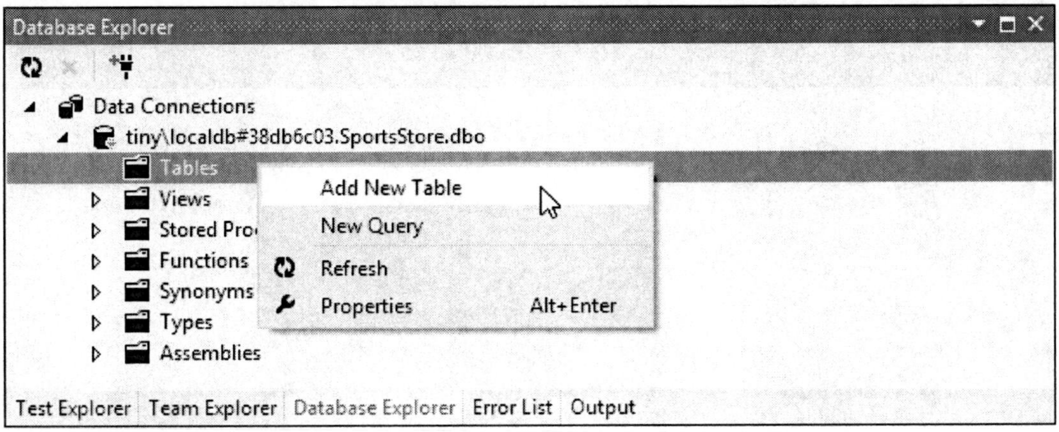

Figure 7-9. Adding a new table

A designer for creating a new table will be displayed. You can create new database tables using the visual part of the designer, but we will use the T-SQL window because it is a more concise and accurate way of describing the table specification we require. Enter the SQL statement shown in Listing 7-10 and click the **Update** button in the top-left corner of the table design window.

Listing 7-10. The SQL Statement to Create the Table in the SportsStore Database

```
CREATE TABLE Products
(
    [ProductID] INT NOT NULL PRIMARY KEY IDENTITY,
    [Name] NVARCHAR(100) NOT NULL,
    [Description] NVARCHAR(500) NOT NULL,
    [Category] NVARCHAR(50) NOT NULL,
    [Price] DECIMAL(16, 2) NOT NULL
)
```

This statement creates a table called Products, which has columns for the different properties we defined in our Product model class earlier in the chapter.

■ **Tip** Setting the IDENTITY property for the ProductID column means that SQL Server will generate a unique primary key value when we add data to this table. When using a database in a Web application, it can be very difficult to generate unique primary keys because requests from users arrive concurrently. Enabling this feature means we can store new table rows and rely on SQL Server to sort out unique values for us.

When you click the Update button, you will be shown a summary of the effect of the statement, as shown in Figure 7-10.

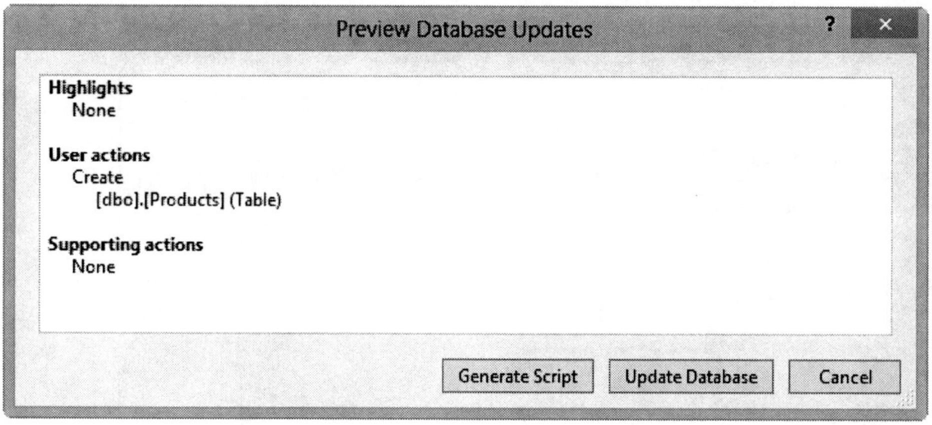

Figure 7-10. The summary of the effect of the SQL statement

Click the Update Database button to execute the SQL and create the Products table in the database. You will be able to see the effect the update has if you click the Refresh button in the Database Explorer window. The Tables section shows the new Product table and details of each of the rows.

■ **Tip** After you have updated the database, you can close the dbo.Products window. Visual Studio will offer you the chance to save the SQL script used to create the database. You do not need to save the script for this chapter, but it can be useful in real projects if you need to configure multiple databases.

Adding Data to the Database

We are going to manually add some data to the database so that we have something to work with until we add the catalog administration features in Chapter 10.

In the Database Explorer window, expand the Tables item of the SportsStore database, right-click the Products table, and select Show Table Data. Enter the data shown in Figure 7-11. You can move from row to row by using the Tab key. At the end of each row, pressing tab will move to the next row and update the data in the database.

■ **Note** You must leave the ProductID column empty. It is an identity column so SQL Server will generate a unique value when you tab to the next row.

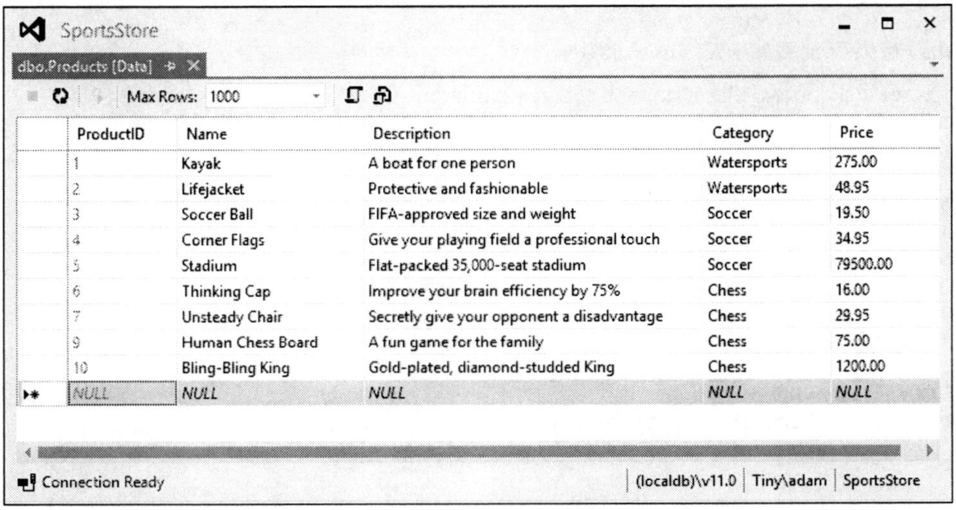

Figure 7-11. Adding data to the Products table

Creating the Entity Framework Context

The latest versions of the Entity Framework include a nice feature called *code-first*. The idea is that we can define the classes in our model and then generate a database from those classes.

This is great for green-field development projects, but these are few and far between. Instead, we are going to show you a variation on code-first, where we associate our model classes with an existing database. The first step is to add Entity Framework version 5.0 to our SportsStore.Domain project. Right-click the References item in the Solution Explorer, and then select Manage NuGet Packages from the pop-up menu. Enter entity in the search box and select find the EntityFramework package, as shown in Figure 7-12, and then click the Install button. Visual Studio will download and install the latest version of Entity Framework package.

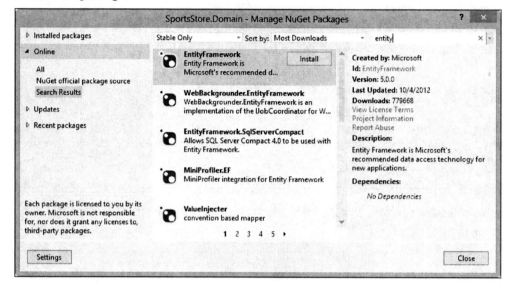

Figure 7-12. Adding the EntityFramework library package

The next step is to create a context class that will associate our simple model with the database. Create a new folder called Concrete and add a new class called EFDbContext within it. Edit the contents of the class file so they match Listing 7-11.

Listing 7-11. The EFDbContext Class

```
using SportsStore.Domain.Entities;
using System.Data.Entity;

namespace SportsStore.Domain.Concrete {

    public class EFDbContext : DbContext {
        public DbSet<Product> Products { get; set; }
    }
}
```

To take advantage of the code-first feature, we need to create a class that is derived from System.Data.Entity.DbContext. This class then automatically defines a property for each table in the database that we want to work with.

The name of the property specifies the table, and the type parameter of the DbSet result specifies the model that the Entity Framework should use to represent rows in that table. In our case, the property name is Products and the type parameter is Product. We want the Product model type to be used to represent rows in the Products table.

We need to tell the Entity Framework how to connect to the database, and we do that by adding a database connection string to the Web.config file in the SportsStore.WebUI project with the same name as the context class, as shown in Listing 7-12.

■ **Tip**   Notice that we have switched project here. We define the model and the repository logic in the SportsStore.Domain project, but the database connection information is put in the Web.config file in the SportsStore.WebUI project.

Listing 7-12. Adding a Database Connection

```
...
<connectionStrings>
    <add name="EFDbContext" connectionString="Data Source=(localdb)\v11.0;Initial
        Catalog=SportsStore;Integrated Security=True"
        providerName="System.Data.SqlClient"/>
  </connectionStrings>
...
```

■ **Caution**   We have had to split the connection string across multiple lines to fit it on the page, but it is important to put everything on a single line in the Web.config file.

There will be another add element in the connectionsStrings section of the Web.config file. Visual Studio creates this element by default and you can either ignore it or, as we have, delete it from the Web.config file.

Creating the Product Repository

We now have everything we need to implement the IProductRepository class for real. Add a class to the Concrete folder of the SportsStore.Domain project called EFProductRepository. Edit your class file so it matches Listing 7-13.

Listing 7-13. EFProductRepostory.cs

```
using SportsStore.Domain.Abstract;
using SportsStore.Domain.Entities;
using System.Linq;

namespace SportsStore.Domain.Concrete {

    public class EFProductRepository : IProductRepository {
        private EFDbContext context = new EFDbContext();

        public IQueryable<Product> Products {
            get { return context.Products; }
        }
    }
}
```

This is our repository class. It implements the IProductRepository interface and uses an instance of EFDbContext to retrieve data from the database using the Entity Framework. You will see how we work with the Entity Framework (and how simple it is) as we add features to the repository.

The last stage is to replace the Ninject binding for our mock repository with a binding for our real one. Edit the NinjectControllerFactory class in the SportsStore.WebUI project so that the AddBindings method looks like Listing 7-14.

Listing 7-14. Adding the Real Repository Binding

```
using System;
using System.Web.Mvc;
using System.Web.Routing;
using Ninject;
using SportsStore.Domain.Entities;
using SportsStore.Domain.Abstract;
using System.Collections.Generic;
using System.Linq;
using Moq;
using SportsStore.Domain.Concrete;

namespace SportsStore.WebUI.Infrastructure {

    public class NinjectControllerFactory : DefaultControllerFactory {
        private IKernel ninjectKernel;

        public NinjectControllerFactory() {
            ninjectKernel = new StandardKernel();
            AddBindings();
        }

        protected override IController GetControllerInstance(RequestContext
            requestContext, Type controllerType) {

            return controllerType == null
                ? null
                : (IController)ninjectKernel.Get(controllerType);
        }

        private void AddBindings() {
            ninjectKernel.Bind<IProductRepository>().To<EFProductRepository>();
        }
    }
}
```

The new binding is shown in bold. It tells Ninject that we want to create instances of the EFProductRepository class to service requests for the IProductRepository interface. All that remains now is to run the application again. The results are shown in Figure 7-13, and you can see that our list now contains the product data we put into the database.

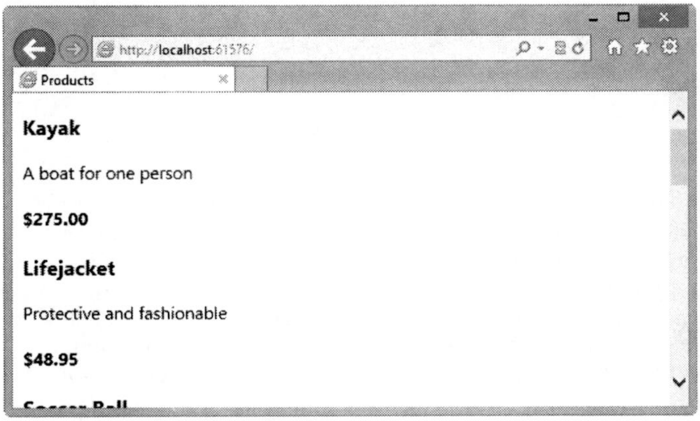

Figure 7-13. The result of implementing the real repository

This approach to getting the Entity Framework to present a SQL Server database as a series of model objects is simple and easy and it allows us to keep our focus on the MVC Framework. But, of course, we are skipping over a lot of the detail in how the Entity Framework operates and the huge number of different configuration options that are available. We like the Entity Framework a lot and we recommend that you spend some time getting to know it in detail. A good place to start is the Microsoft site for the Entity Framework: http://msdn.microsoft.com/data/ef.

Adding Pagination

You can see from Figure 7-13 that all of the products in the database are displayed on a single page. In this section, we will add support for pagination so that we display a number of products on a page, and the user can move from page to page to view the overall catalog. To do this, we are going to add a parameter to the List method in the Product controller, as shown in Listing 7-15.

Listing 7-15. Adding Pagination Support to the Product Controller List Method

```
using System;
using System.Collections.Generic;
using System.Linq;
using System.Web;
using System.Web.Mvc;
using SportsStore.Domain.Abstract;
using SportsStore.Domain.Entities;

namespace SportsStore.WebUI.Controllers {
    public class ProductController : Controller {
        private IProductRepository repository;
        public int PageSize = 4;

        public ProductController(IProductRepository productRepository) {
            this.repository = productRepository;
        }

        public ViewResult List(int page = 1) {
            return View(repository.Products
```

```
        .OrderBy(p => p.ProductID)
        .Skip((page - 1) * PageSize)
        .Take(PageSize));
    }
  }
}
```

The additions to the controller class are shown in bold. The PageSize field specifies that we want four products per page. We will come back and replace this with a better mechanism later on. We have added an *optional parameter* to the List method. This means that if we call the method without a parameter (List()), our call is treated as though we had supplied the value we specified in the parameter definition (List(1)). The effect of this is that we get the first page when we do not specify a page value. LINQ makes pagination very simple. In the List method, we get the Product objects from the repository, order them by the primary key, skip over the products that occur before the start of our page, and then take the number of products specified by the PageSize field.

UNIT TEST: PAGINATION

We can unit test the pagination feature by creating a mock repository, injecting it into the constructor of the ProductController class, and then calling the List method to request a specific page. We can then compare the Product objects we get with what we would expect from the test data in the mock implementation. See Chapter 6 for details of how to set up unit tests. Here is the unit test we created for this purpose:

```
using Microsoft.VisualStudio.TestTools.UnitTesting;
using Moq;
using SportsStore.Domain.Abstract;
using SportsStore.Domain.Entities;
using SportsStore.WebUI.Controllers;
using System.Collections.Generic;
using System.Linq;

namespace SportsStore.UnitTests {
    [TestClass]
    public class UnitTest1 {

        [TestMethod]
        public void Can_Paginate() {

            // Arrange
            Mock<IProductRepository> mock = new Mock<IProductRepository>();
            mock.Setup(m => m.Products).Returns(new Product[] {
                new Product {ProductID = 1, Name = "P1"},
                new Product {ProductID = 2, Name = "P2"},
                new Product {ProductID = 3, Name = "P3"},
                new Product {ProductID = 4, Name = "P4"},
                new Product {ProductID = 5, Name = "P5"}
            }.AsQueryable());

            ProductController controller = new ProductController(mock.Object);
```

```
            controller.PageSize = 3;

            // Act
            IEnumerable<Product> result =
                (IEnumerable<Product>)controller.List(2).Model;

            // Assert
            Product[] prodArray = result.ToArray();
            Assert.IsTrue(prodArray.Length == 2);
            Assert.AreEqual(prodArray[0].Name, "P4");
            Assert.AreEqual(prodArray[1].Name, "P5");
        }
    }
}
```

Notice how easy it is to get the data that is returned from a controller method. We call the `Model` property on the result to get the `IEnumerable<Product>` sequence that we generated in the `List` method. We can then check that the data is what we want. In this case, we converted the sequence to an array, and checked the length and the values of the individual objects.

Displaying Page Links

If you run the application, you will see that there are only four items shown on the page. If you want to view another page, you can append query string parameters to the end of the URL, like this:

`http://localhost:23081/?page=2`

You will need to change the port part of the URL to match whatever port your ASP.NET development server is running on. Using these query strings, we can navigate our way through the catalog of products.

Of course, only we know this. There is no way for customers to figure out that these query string parameters can be used, and even if there were, we can be pretty sure that customers are not going to want to navigate this way. We need to render some page links at the bottom of the each list of products so that customers can navigate between pages. To do this, we are going to implement a reusable HTML helper method, similar to the `Html.TextBoxFor` and `Html.BeginForm` methods we used in Chapter 2. Our helper will generate the HTML markup for the navigation links we need.

Adding the View Model

To support the HTML helper, we are going to pass information to the view about the number of pages available, the current page, and the total number of products in the repository. The easiest way to do this is to create a view model, which we mentioned briefly in Chapter 3. Add the class shown in Listing 7-16, called `PagingInfo`, to the `Models` folder in the `SportsStore.WebUI` project.

Listing 7-16. The PagingInfo View Model Class

```
using System;

namespace SportsStore.WebUI.Models {

    public class PagingInfo {
        public int TotalItems { get; set; }
```

```
        public int ItemsPerPage { get; set; }
        public int CurrentPage { get; set; }

        public int TotalPages {
            get { return (int)Math.Ceiling((decimal)TotalItems / ItemsPerPage); }
        }
    }
}
```

A view model is not part of our domain model. It is just a convenient class for passing data between the controller and the view. To emphasize this, we have put this class in the SportsStore.WebUI project to keep it separate from the domain model classes.

Adding the HTML Helper Method

Now that we have the view model, we can implement the HTML helper method, which we are going to call PageLinks. Create a new folder in the SportsStore.WebUI project called HtmlHelpers and add a new static class called PagingHelpers. The contents of the class file are shown in Listing 7-17.

Listing 7-17. The PagingHelpers Class

```
using System;
using System.Text;
using System.Web.Mvc;
using SportsStore.WebUI.Models;

namespace SportsStore.WebUI.HtmlHelpers {

    public static class PagingHelpers {

        public static MvcHtmlString PageLinks(this HtmlHelper html,
                                              PagingInfo pagingInfo,
                                              Func<int, string> pageUrl) {

            StringBuilder result = new StringBuilder();
            for (int i = 1; i <= pagingInfo.TotalPages; i++) {
                TagBuilder tag = new TagBuilder("a"); // Construct an <a> tag
                tag.MergeAttribute("href", pageUrl(i));
                tag.InnerHtml = i.ToString();
                if (i == pagingInfo.CurrentPage)
                    tag.AddCssClass("selected");
                result.Append(tag.ToString());
            }

            return MvcHtmlString.Create(result.ToString());
        }
    }
}
```

The PageLinks extension method generates the HTML for a set of page links using the information provided in a PagingInfo object. The Func parameter provides the ability to pass in a delegate that will be used to generate the links to view other pages.

UNIT TEST: CREATING PAGE LINKS

To test the PageLinks helper method, we call the method with test data and compare the results to our expected HTML. The unit test method is as follows:

```
using Microsoft.VisualStudio.TestTools.UnitTesting;
using Moq;
using SportsStore.Domain.Abstract;
using SportsStore.Domain.Entities;
using SportsStore.WebUI.Controllers;
using SportsStore.WebUI.Models;
using System;
using System.Collections.Generic;
using System.Linq;
using System.Web.Mvc;
using SportsStore.WebUI.HtmlHelpers;

namespace SportsStore.UnitTests {
    [TestClass]
    public class UnitTest1 {

        [TestMethod]
        public void Can_Paginate() {
            // ...statements removed for brevity...
        }

        [TestMethod]
        public void Can_Generate_Page_Links() {

            // Arrange - define an HTML helper - we need to do this
            // in order to apply the extension method
            HtmlHelper myHelper = null;

            // Arrange - create PagingInfo data
            PagingInfo pagingInfo = new PagingInfo {
                CurrentPage = 2,
                TotalItems = 28,
                ItemsPerPage = 10
            };

            // Arrange - set up the delegate using a lambda expression
            Func<int, string> pageUrlDelegate = i => "Page" + i;

            // Act
            MvcHtmlString result = myHelper.PageLinks(pagingInfo, pageUrlDelegate);

            // Assert
            Assert.AreEqual(result.ToString(), @"<a href=""Page1"">1</a>"
                + @"<a class=""selected"" href=""Page2"">2</a>"
                + @"<a href=""Page3"">3</a>");
        }
    }
}
```

This test verifies the helper method output by using a literal string value that contains double quotes. C# is perfectly capable of working with such strings, as long as we remember to prefix the string with @ and use two sets of double quotes ("") in place of one set of double quotes. We must also remember not to break the literal string into separate lines, unless the string we are comparing to is similarly broken. For example, the literal we use in the test method has wrapped onto two lines because the width of a printed page is narrow. We have not added a newline character; if we did, the test would fail.

An extension method is available for use only when the namespace that contains it is in scope. In a code file, this is done with a `using` statement; but for a Razor view, we must add a configuration entry to the `Web.config` file, or add a `@using` statement to the view itself. There are, confusingly, two `Web.config` files in a Razor MVC project: the main one, which resides in the root directory of the application project, and the view-specific one, which is in the `Views` folder. The change we need to make is to the `Views/Web.config` file and is shown in Listing 7-18.

Listing 7-18. Adding the HTML Helper Method Namespace to the Views/Web.config File

```
...
<system.web.webPages.razor>
    <host factoryType="System.Web.Mvc.MvcWebRazorHostFactory, System.Web.Mvc,
        Version=4.0.0.0, Culture=neutral, PublicKeyToken=31BF3856AD364E35" />
    <pages pageBaseType="System.Web.Mvc.WebViewPage">
    <namespaces>
      <add namespace="System.Web.Mvc" />
      <add namespace="System.Web.Mvc.Ajax" />
      <add namespace="System.Web.Mvc.Html" />
      <add namespace="System.Web.Optimization"/>
      <add namespace="System.Web.Routing" />
      <add namespace="SportsStore.WebUI.HtmlHelpers"/>
    </namespaces>
  </pages>
</system.web.webPages.razor>
...
```

Every namespace that we need to refer to in a Razor view needs to be declared either in this way or in the view itself with a `@using` statement.

Adding the View Model Data

We are not quite ready to use our HTML helper method. We have yet to provide an instance of the `PagingInfo` view model class to the view. We could do this using the view bag feature, but we would rather wrap all of the data we are going to send from the controller to the view in a single view model class. To do this, add a new class called `ProductsListViewModel` to the `Models` folder of the `SportsStore.WebUI` project. The contents of this class are shown in Listing 7-19.

Listing 7-19. The ProductsListViewModel class

```
using System.Collections.Generic;
using SportsStore.Domain.Entities;

namespace SportsStore.WebUI.Models {
    public class ProductsListViewModel {
```

```
        public IEnumerable<Product> Products { get; set; }
        public PagingInfo PagingInfo { get; set; }
    }
}
```

We can now update the List method in the `ProductController` class to use the `ProductsListViewModel` class to provide the view with details of the products to display on the page and details of the pagination, as shown in Listing 7-20.

Listing 7-20. Updating the List Method

```
using System;
using System.Collections.Generic;
using System.Linq;
using System.Web;
using System.Web.Mvc;
using SportsStore.Domain.Abstract;
using SportsStore.Domain.Entities;
using SportsStore.WebUI.Models;

namespace SportsStore.WebUI.Controllers {
    public class ProductController : Controller {
        private IProductRepository repository;
        public int PageSize = 4;

        public ProductController(IProductRepository productRepository) {
            this.repository = productRepository;
        }

        public ViewResult List(int page = 1) {

            ProductsListViewModel model = new ProductsListViewModel {
                Products = repository.Products
                .OrderBy(p => p.ProductID)
                .Skip((page - 1) * PageSize)
                .Take(PageSize),
                PagingInfo = new PagingInfo {
                    CurrentPage = page,
                    ItemsPerPage = PageSize,
                    TotalItems = repository.Products.Count()
                }
            };

            return View(model);
        }
    }
}
```

These changes pass a `ProductsListViewModel` object as the model data to the view.

```
                    UNIT TEST: PAGE MODEL VIEW DATA
```

We need to ensure that the correct pagination data is being sent by the controller to the view. Here is the unit test we have added to our test project to address this:

```
[TestMethod]
public void Can_Send_Pagination_View_Model() {

    // Arrange
    Mock<IProductRepository> mock = new Mock<IProductRepository>();
    mock.Setup(m => m.Products).Returns(new Product[] {
        new Product {ProductID = 1, Name = "P1"},
        new Product {ProductID = 2, Name = "P2"},
        new Product {ProductID = 3, Name = "P3"},
        new Product {ProductID = 4, Name = "P4"},
        new Product {ProductID = 5, Name = "P5"}
    }.AsQueryable());

    // Arrange
    ProductController controller = new ProductController(mock.Object);
    controller.PageSize = 3;

    // Act
    ProductsListViewModel result = (ProductsListViewModel)controller.List(2).Model;

    // Assert
    PagingInfo pageInfo = result.PagingInfo;
    Assert.AreEqual(pageInfo.CurrentPage, 2);
    Assert.AreEqual(pageInfo.ItemsPerPage, 3);
    Assert.AreEqual(pageInfo.TotalItems, 5);
    Assert.AreEqual(pageInfo.TotalPages, 2);
}
```

We also need to modify our earlier pagination unit test, contained in the Can_Paginate method. It relies on the List action method returning a ViewResult whose Model property is a sequence of Product objects, but we have wrapped that data inside another view model type. Here is the revised test:

```
[TestMethod]
public void Can_Paginate() {

    // Arrange
    // - create the mock repository
    Mock<IProductRepository> mock = new Mock<IProductRepository>();
    mock.Setup(m => m.Products).Returns(new Product[] {
        new Product {ProductID = 1, Name = "P1"},
        new Product {ProductID = 2, Name = "P2"},
        new Product {ProductID = 3, Name = "P3"},
        new Product {ProductID = 4, Name = "P4"},
        new Product {ProductID = 5, Name = "P5"}
    }.AsQueryable());
```

```
    // create a controller and make the page size 3 items
    ProductController controller = new ProductController(mock.Object);
    controller.PageSize = 3;

    // Action
    ProductsListViewModel result = (ProductsListViewModel)controller.List(2).Model;

    // Assert
    Product[] prodArray = result.Products.ToArray();
    Assert.IsTrue(prodArray.Length == 2);
    Assert.AreEqual(prodArray[0].Name, "P4");
    Assert.AreEqual(prodArray[1].Name, "P5");
}
```

We would usually create a common setup method, given the degree of duplication between these two test methods. However, since we are delivering the unit tests in individual sidebars like this one, we are going to keep everything separate, so you can see each test on its own.

At the moment, the view is expecting a sequence of Product objects, so we need to update List.cshtml, as shown in Listing 7-21, to deal with the new view model type.

Listing 7-21. Updating the List.cshtml View

```
@model SportsStore.WebUI.Models.ProductsListViewModel

@{
    ViewBag.Title = "Products";
}

@foreach (var p in Model.Products) {
    <div class="item">
        <h3>@p.Name</h3>
        @p.Description
        <h4>@p.Price.ToString("c")</h4>
    </div>
}
```

We have changed the @model directive to tell Razor that we are now working with a different data type. We also needed to update the foreach loop so that the data source is the Products property of the model data.

Displaying the Page Links

We have everything in place to add the page links to the List view. We created the view model that contains the paging information, updated the controller so that this information is passed to the view, and changed the @model directive to match the new model view type. All that remains is to call our HTML helper method from the view, which you can see in Listing 7-22.

Listing 7-22. Calling the HTML Helper Method

```
@model SportsStore.WebUI.Models.ProductsListViewModel

@{
    ViewBag.Title = "Products";
}

@foreach (var p in Model.Products) {
    <div class="item">
        <h3>@p.Name</h3>
        @p.Description
        <h4>@p.Price.ToString("c")</h4>
    </div>
}
```

<div class="pager">

   @Html.PageLinks(Model.PagingInfo, x => Url.Action("List", new {page = x}))

</div>

If you run the application, you will see that we have added page links, as illustrated in Figure 7-14. The style is still pretty basic, and we will fix that later in the chapter. What is important at the moment is that the links take us from page to page in the catalog and let us explore the products for sale.

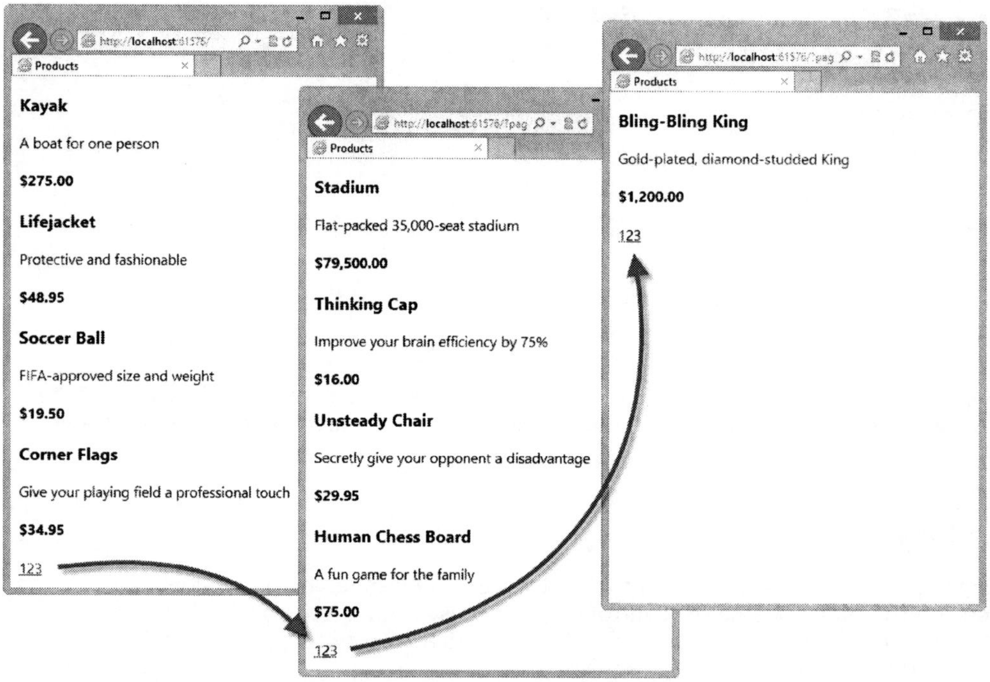

Figure 7-14. Displaying page navigation links

WHY NOT JUST USE A GRIDVIEW?

If you have worked with ASP.NET before, you might think that was a lot of work for a pretty unimpressive result. It has taken us pages and pages just to get a page list. If we were using Web Forms, we could have done the same thing using the ASP.NET Web Forms `GridView` control, right out of the box, by hooking it up directly to our `Products` database table.

What we have accomplished so far does not look like much, but it is very different from dragging a `GridView` onto a design surface. First, we are building an application with a sound and maintainable architecture that involves proper separation of concerns. Unlike the simplest use of `GridView`, we have not directly coupled the UI and the database—an approach that gives quick results but that causes pain and misery over time. Second, we have been creating unit tests as we go, and these allow us to validate the behavior of our application in a natural way that is nearly impossible with a Web Forms `GridView` control.

Finally, bear in mind that a lot of this chapter has been given over to creating the underlying infrastructure on which the application is built. We need to define and implement the repository only once, for example, and now that we have, we will be able to build and test new features quickly and easily, as the following chapters will demonstrate.

Improving the URLs

We have the page links working, but they still use the query string to pass page information to the server, like this:

`http://localhost/?page=2`

We can do better, specifically by creating a scheme that follows the pattern of *composable URLs*. A composable URL is one that makes sense to the user, like this one:

`http://localhost/Page2`

Fortunately, MVC makes it very easy to change the URL scheme because it uses the ASP.NET *routing* feature. All we need to do is add a new route to the `RegisterRoutes` method in the `RouteConfig.cs` file, which you will find in the `App_Start` folder. You can see the change we made to this file in Listing 7-23.

Listing 7-23. Adding a New Route

```
using System;
using System.Collections.Generic;
using System.Linq;
using System.Web;
using System.Web.Mvc;
using System.Web.Routing;

namespace SportsStore.WebUI {
    public class RouteConfig {
        public static void RegisterRoutes(RouteCollection routes) {
            routes.IgnoreRoute("{resource}.axd/{*pathInfo}");
```

```
routes.MapRoute(
    name: null,
    url: "Page{page}",
    defaults: new { Controller = "Product", action = "List" }
);

routes.MapRoute(
    name: "Default",
    url: "{controller}/{action}/{id}",
    defaults: new { controller = "Product", action = "List",
        id = UrlParameter.Optional }
);
        }
    }
}
```

It is important that you add this route before the Default one that is already in the file. As you will see in Chapter 13, routes are processed in the order they are listed, and we need our new route to take precedence over the existing one.

This is the only alteration we need to make to change the URL scheme for our product pagination. The MVC Framework is tightly integrated with the routing function, and so a change like this is automatically reflected in the result produced by the Url.Action method (which is what we use in the List.cshtml view to generate our page links). Do not worry if routing does not make sense to you at the moment—we will explain it in detail in Chapter 13. If you run the application and navigate to a page, you will see the new URL scheme in action, as illustrated in Figure 7-15.

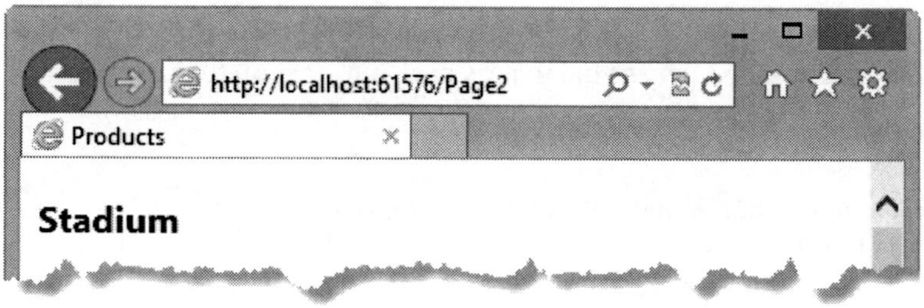

Figure 7-15. The new URL scheme displayed in the browser

Styling the Content

We have built a great deal of infrastructure, and our application is really starting to come together, but we have not paid any attention to its appearance. Even though this book is not about Web design or CSS, the SportsStore application design is so miserably plain that it undermines its technical strengths. In this section, we will put some of that right.

■ **Note** In this part of the chapter, we will ask you to add CSS styles without explaining their meaning. Adam provides detailed coverage of CSS in his book *The Definitive Guide to HTML5* (Apress, 2011).

We are going to implement a classic two-column layout with a header, as shown in Figure 7-16.

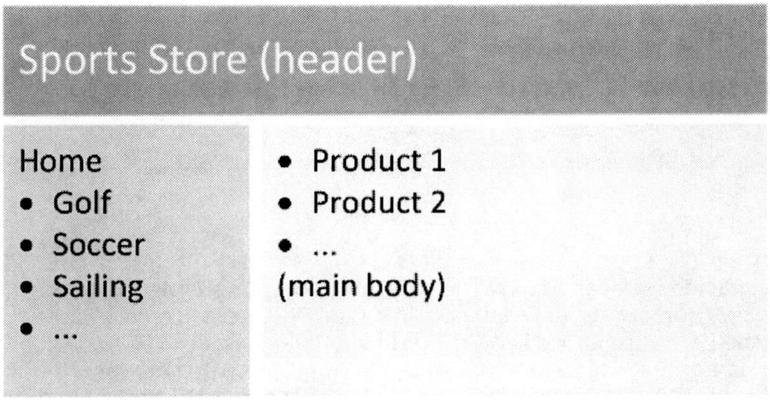

Figure 7-16. The design goal for the SportsStore application

Defining Common Content in the Layout

In Chapter 5, we explained how Razor layouts work and are applied. When we created the `List.cshtml` view for the `Product` controller, we asked you to check the option to use a layout, but leave the box that specifies a layout blank. This has the effect of using the default layout, `_Layout.cshtml`, which can be found in the `Views/Shared` folder of the `SportsStore.WebUI` project. Open this file and change the content so that it matches Listing 7-24.

Listing 7-24. Modifying the Default Razor Layout

```
<!DOCTYPE html>
<html>
<head>
    <meta charset="utf-8" />
    <meta name="viewport" content="width=device-width" />
    <title>@ViewBag.Title</title>
    <link href="~/Content/Site.css" type="text/css" rel="stylesheet" />
</head>
<body>
    <div id="header">
        <div class="title">SPORTS STORE</div>
    </div>
    <div id="categories">
        We will put something useful here later
    </div>
    <div id="content">
        @RenderBody()
    </div>
</body>
</html>
```

■ **Note** You will notice that we had you remove @Styles and @Scripts Razor tags from the view. These are new additions to Razor in MVC 4 and we introduce them properly in Chapter 24 when we talk about the ways in which you can optimize the content that your MVC application delivers to clients. For the moment, we want to keep the focus on the core MVC features.

Adding CSS Styles

The HTML markup in Listing 7-24 is characteristic of an ASP.NET MVC application. It is simple and purely semantic. It describes the content, but says nothing about how it should be laid out on the screen. We will use CSS to tell the browser how the elements we just added should be laid out.

Visual Studio creates a CSS file for us automatically when we create a MVC project using the Basic option. This file, called Site.css, can be found in the Content folder of the SportsStore.WebUI project and one of the changes we had you make to the _Layout.cshtml file was to add a link element to reference this file:

```
...
<link href="~/Content/Site.css" type="text/css" rel="stylesheet" />
...
```

Open the Site.css file and add the styles shown in Listing 7-25 to the bottom of the file (do not remove the existing content in Site.css). You do not need to type these in by hand. You can download the CSS additions and the rest of the project as part of the code samples that accompany this book.

Listing 7-25. Defining CSS

```
...
BODY { font-family: Cambria, Georgia, "Times New Roman"; margin: 0; }
DIV#header DIV.title, DIV.item H3, DIV.item H4, DIV.pager A {
    font: bold 1em "Arial Narrow", "Franklin Gothic Medium", Arial;
}
DIV#header { background-color: #444; border-bottom: 2px solid #111; color: White; }
DIV#header DIV.title { font-size: 2em; padding: .6em; }
DIV#content { border-left: 2px solid gray; margin-left: 9em; padding: 1em; }
DIV#categories { float: left; width: 8em; padding: .3em; }

DIV.item { border-top: 1px dotted gray; padding-top: .7em; margin-bottom: .7em; }
DIV.item:first-child { border-top:none; padding-top: 0; }
DIV.item H3 { font-size: 1.3em; margin: 0 0 .25em 0; }
DIV.item H4 { font-size: 1.1em; margin:.4em 0 0 0; }

DIV.pager { text-align:right; border-top: 2px solid silver;
    padding: .5em 0 0 0; margin-top: 1em; }
DIV.pager A { font-size: 1.1em; color: #666; text-decoration: none;
    padding: 0 .4em 0 .4em; }
DIV.pager A:hover { background-color: Silver; }
DIV.pager A.selected { background-color: #353535; color: White; }
...
```

If you run the application, you will see that we have improved the appearance—at least a little, anyway. The changes are shown in Figure 7-17.

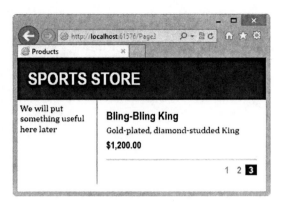

Figure 7-17. The design-enhanced SportsStore application

Creating a Partial View

As a finishing trick for this chapter, we are going to refactor the application to simplify the `List.cshtml` view. We are going to create a *partial view*, which is a fragment of content that is embedded in another view. Partial views are contained within their own files and are reusable across multiple views, which can help reduce duplication—especially if you need to render the same kind of data in several places in your application.

To add the partial view, right-click the `/Views/Shared` folder in the `SportsStore.WebUI` project and select Add ↗ View from the pop-up menu. Set the name of the view to `ProductSummary`. We want to display details of a product, so select the `Product` class from the `Model class` drop-down menu or type the qualified class name. Check the `Create as a partial view` option, as shown in Figure 7-18.

Figure 7-18. Creating a partial view

Click the Add button, and Visual Studio will create a partial view file at
Views/Shared/ProductSummary.cshtml. A partial view is very similar to a regular view, except that when it is
rendered, it produces a fragment of HTML, rather than a full HTML document. If you open the
ProductSummary view, you will see that it contains only the model view directive, which is set to our
Product domain model class. Apply the changes shown in Listing 7-26.

Listing 7-26. Adding Markup to the ProductSummary Partial View

```
@model SportsStore.Domain.Entities.Product

<div class="item">
    <h3>@Model.Name</h3>
    @Model.Description
    <h4>@Model.Price.ToString("c")</h4>
</div>
```

Now we need to update Views/Products/List.cshtml so that it uses the partial view. You can see the
change in Listing 7-27.

Listing 7-27. Using a Partial View from List.cshtml

```
@model SportsStore.WebUI.Models.ProductsListViewModel

@{
    ViewBag.Title = "Products";
}

@foreach (var p in Model.Products) {
    Html.RenderPartial("ProductSummary", p);
}

<div class="pager">
    @Html.PageLinks(Model.PagingInfo, x => Url.Action("List", new {page = x}))
</div>
```

We have taken the markup that was previously in the foreach loop in the List.cshtml view and
moved it to the new partial view. We call the partial view using the Html.RenderPartial helper method.
The parameters are the name of the view and the view model object.

■ **Tip** The RenderPartial method does not return HTML markup like most other helper methods. Instead, it
writes content directly to the response stream, which is why we must call it like a complete line of C#, using a
semicolon. This is slightly more efficient than buffering the rendered HTML from the partial view, since it will be
written to the response stream anyway. If you prefer a more consistent syntax, you can use the Html.Partial
method, which does the same as the RenderPartial method, but returns an HTML fragment and can be used as
@Html.Partial("ProductSummary", p).

Switching to a partial view like this is good practice, but it does not change the appearance of the
application. If you run it, you will see that the display remains as before, as shown in Figure 7-19.

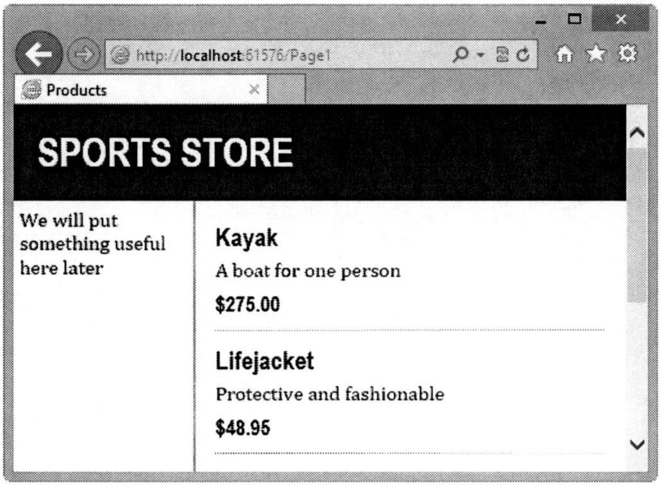

Figure 7-19. Applying a partial view

Summary

In this chapter, we have built most of the core infrastructure for the SportsStore application. It does not have many features that you could demonstrate to a client at this point, but behind the scenes, we have the beginnings of a domain model with a product repository that is backed by SQL Server and the Entity Framework. We have a single controller, `ProductController`, that can produce paginated lists of products, and we have set up DI and a clean and friendly URL scheme.

If this chapter felt like a lot of setup for little benefit, then the next chapter will balance the equation. Now that we have the fundamental elements out of the way, we can forge ahead and add all of the customer-facing features: navigation by category, a shopping cart, and a checkout process.

CHAPTER 8

■ ■ ■

SportsStore: Navigation

In the previous chapter, we set up the core infrastructure of the SportsStore application. Now we will use the infrastructure to add key features to the application, and you will start to see how the investment in the basic plumbing pays off. We will be able to add important customer-facing features simply and easily. Along the way, you will see some additional features that the MVC Framework provides.

Adding Navigation Controls

The SportsStore application will be a lot more usable if we let customers navigate products by category. We will do this in three parts:

- Enhance the `List` action model in the `ProductController` class so that it is able to filter the `Product` objects in the repository.

- Revisit and enhance our URL scheme and revise our rerouting strategy.

- Create the category list that will go into the sidebar of the site, highlighting the current category and linking to others.

Filtering the Product List

We are going to start by enhancing our view model class, `ProductsListViewModel`, which we added to the `SportsStore.WebUI` project in the last chapter. We need to communicate the current category to the view in order to render our sidebar, and this is as good a place to start as any. Listing 8-1 shows the changes we made.

Listing 8-1. Enhancing the ProductsListViewModel Class

```
using System.Collections.Generic;
using SportsStore.Domain.Entities;

namespace SportsStore.WebUI.Models {
    public class ProductsListViewModel {

        public IEnumerable<Product> Products { get; set; }
        public PagingInfo PagingInfo { get; set; }
        public string CurrentCategory { get; set; }
    }
}
```

We added a new property called CurrentCategory. The next step is to update the ProductController class so that the List action method will filter Product objects by category and use the new property we added to the view model to indicate which category has been selected. The changes are shown in Listing 8-2.

Listing 8-2. Adding Category Support to the List Action Method

```
using System;
using System.Collections.Generic;
using System.Linq;
using System.Web;
using System.Web.Mvc;
using SportsStore.Domain.Abstract;
using SportsStore.Domain.Entities;
using SportsStore.WebUI.Models;

namespace SportsStore.WebUI.Controllers {
    public class ProductController : Controller {
        private IProductRepository repository;
        public int PageSize = 4;

        public ProductController(IProductRepository productRepository) {
            this.repository = productRepository;
        }

        public ViewResult List(string category, int page = 1) {

            ProductsListViewModel viewModel = new ProductsListViewModel {
                Products = repository.Products
                    .Where(p => category == null || p.Category == category)
                    .OrderBy(p => p.ProductID)
                    .Skip((page - 1) * PageSize)
                    .Take(PageSize),
                PagingInfo = new PagingInfo {
                    CurrentPage = page,
                    ItemsPerPage = PageSize,
                    TotalItems = repository.Products.Count()
                },
                CurrentCategory = category
            };
            return View(viewModel);
        }
    }
}
```

We have made three changes to the action method. First, we added a new parameter called category. This category parameter is used by the second change, which is an enhancement to the LINQ query—if category is not null, only those Product objects with a matching Category property are selected. The last change is to set the value of the CurrentCategory property we added to the ProductsListViewModel class. However, these changes mean that the value of PagingInfo.TotalItems is incorrectly calculated—we will fix this in a while.

UNIT TEST: UPDATING EXISTING UNIT TESTS

We have changed the signature of the List action method, which will prevent some of our existing unit test methods from compiling. To address this, pass null as the first parameter to the List method in those unit tests that work with the controller. For example, in the Can_Paginate test, the action section of the unit test becomes as follows:

```
...
[TestMethod]
public void Can_Paginate() {

    // Arrange
    Mock<IProductRepository> mock = new Mock<IProductRepository>();
    mock.Setup(m => m.Products).Returns(new Product[] {
        new Product {ProductID = 1, Name = "P1"},
        new Product {ProductID = 2, Name = "P2"},
        new Product {ProductID = 3, Name = "P3"},
        new Product {ProductID = 4, Name = "P4"},
        new Product {ProductID = 5, Name = "P5"}
    }.AsQueryable());

    // create a controller and make the page size 3 items
    ProductController controller = new ProductController(mock.Object);
    controller.PageSize = 3;

    // Act
    ProductsListViewModel result
        = (ProductsListViewModel)controller.List(null, 2).Model;

    // Assert
    Product[] prodArray = result.Products.ToArray();
    Assert.IsTrue(prodArray.Length == 2);
    Assert.AreEqual(prodArray[0].Name, "P4");
    Assert.AreEqual(prodArray[1].Name, "P5");
}
...
```

By using null, we receive all of the Product objects that the controller gets from the repository, which is the same situation we had before we added the new parameter.

Even with these small changes, we can start to see the effect of the filtering. For instance, suppose that you start the application and select a category using the query string, like the following:

```
http://localhost:61576/?category=Soccer
```

You will see only the products in the Soccer category, as shown in Figure 8-1.

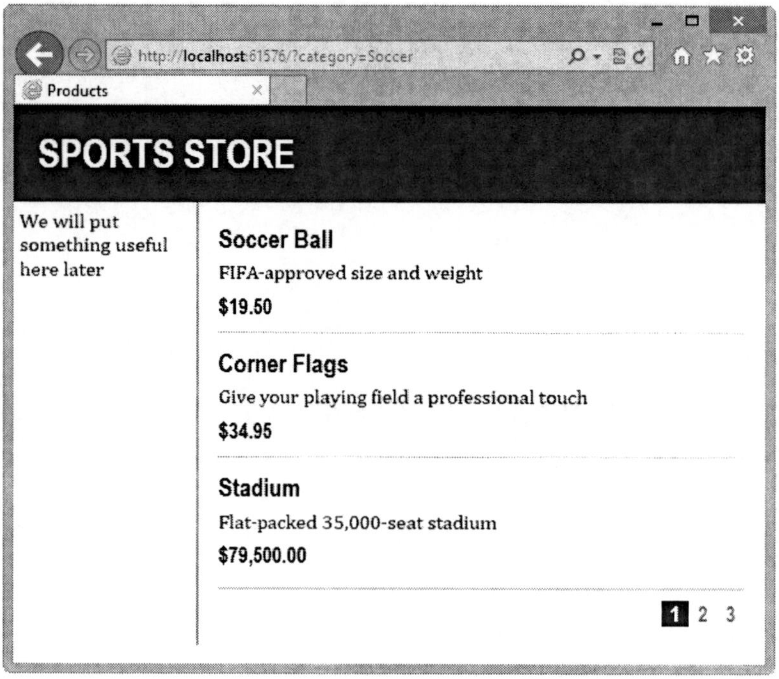

Figure 8-1. Using the query string to filter by category

UNIT TEST: CATEGORY FILTERING

We need a unit test to properly test the category filtering function, to ensure that we can filter correctly and receive only products in a specified category. Here is the test:

```
...
[TestMethod]
public void Can_Filter_Products() {

    // Arrange
    // - create the mock repository
    Mock<IProductRepository> mock = new Mock<IProductRepository>();
    mock.Setup(m => m.Products).Returns(new Product[] {
        new Product {ProductID = 1, Name = "P1", Category = "Cat1"},
        new Product {ProductID = 2, Name = "P2", Category = "Cat2"},
        new Product {ProductID = 3, Name = "P3", Category = "Cat1"},
        new Product {ProductID = 4, Name = "P4", Category = "Cat2"},
        new Product {ProductID = 5, Name = "P5", Category = "Cat3"}
    }.AsQueryable());

    // Arrange - create a controller and make the page size 3 items
    ProductController controller = new ProductController(mock.Object);
```

```
        controller.PageSize = 3;

        // Action
        Product[] result = ((ProductsListViewModel)controller.List("Cat2", 1).Model)
            .Products.ToArray();

        // Assert
        Assert.AreEqual(result.Length, 2);
        Assert.IsTrue(result[0].Name == "P2" && result[0].Category == "Cat2");
        Assert.IsTrue(result[1].Name == "P4" && result[1].Category == "Cat2");
    }
...
```

This test creates a mock repository containing `Product` objects that belong to a range of categories. One specific category is requested using the `Action` method, and the results are checked to ensure that the results are the right objects in the right order.

Refining the URL Scheme

No one wants to see or use ugly URLs such as /?category=Soccer. To address this, we are going to revisit our routing scheme to create an approach to URLs that suits us (and our customers) better. To implement our new scheme, change the `RegisterRoutes` method in the `App_Start/RouteConfig.cs` file to match Listing 8-3, replacing the contents of the method that we used in the last chapter.

Listing 8-3. The New URL Scheme

```
using System;
using System.Collections.Generic;
using System.Linq;
using System.Web;
using System.Web.Mvc;
using System.Web.Routing;

namespace SportsStore.WebUI {
    public class RouteConfig {
        public static void RegisterRoutes(RouteCollection routes) {

            routes.IgnoreRoute("{resource}.axd/{*pathInfo}");

            routes.MapRoute(null,
                "",
                new {
                    controller = "Product", action = "List",
                    category = (string)null, page = 1
                }
            );

            routes.MapRoute(null,
                "Page{page}",
                new { controller = "Product", action = "List", category = (string)null },
                new { page = @"\d+" }
```

```
        );

        routes.MapRoute(null,
            "{category}",
            new { controller = "Product", action = "List", page = 1 }
        );

        routes.MapRoute(null,
            "{category}/Page{page}",
            new { controller = "Product", action = "List" },
            new { page = @"\d+" }
        );

        routes.MapRoute(null, "{controller}/{action}");
    }
  }
}
```

■ **Caution**   It is important to add the new routes in Listing 8-3 in the order they are shown. Routes are applied in the order in which they are defined, and you will get some odd effects if you change the order.

Table 8-1 describes the URL scheme that these routes represent. We will explain the routing system in detail in Chapter 13.

Table 8-1. Route Summary

URL	Leads To
/	Lists the first page of products from all categories.
/Page2	Lists the specified page (in this case, page 2), showing items from all categories.
/Soccer	Shows the first page of items from a specific category (in this case, the Soccer category).
/Soccer/Page2	Shows the specified page (in this case, page 2) of items from the specified category (in this case, Soccer).
/Anything/Else	Calls the Else action method on the Anything controller.

The ASP.NET routing system is used by MVC to handle *incoming* requests from clients, but it also requests *outgoing* URLs that conform to our URL scheme and that we can embed in Web pages. This way, we make sure that all of the URLs in the application are consistent.

■ **Note** We show you how to unit test routing configurations in Chapter 13.

The `Url.Action` method is the most convenient way of generating outgoing links. In the previous chapter, we used this helper method in the `List.cshtml` view in order to display the page links. Now that we have added support for category filtering, we need to go back and pass this information to the helper method, as shown in Listing 8-4.

Listing 8-4. Adding Category Information to the Pagination Links

```
@model SportsStore.WebUI.Models.ProductsListViewModel

@{
    ViewBag.Title = "Products";
}

@foreach (var p in Model.Products) {
    Html.RenderPartial("ProductSummary", p);
}

<div class="pager">
        @Html.PageLinks(Model.PagingInfo, x => Url.Action("List",
            new {page = x, category = Model.CurrentCategory}))
</div>
```

Prior to this change, the links we were generating for the pagination links were like this:

```
http://<myserver>:<port>/Page2
```

If the user clicked a page link like this, the category filter he applied would be lost, and he would be presented with a page containing products from all categories. By adding the current category, which we have taken from the view model, we generate URLs like this instead:

```
http://<myserver>:<port>/Chess/Page2
```

When the user clicks this kind of link, the current category will be passed to the `List` action method, and the filtering will be preserved. After you have made this change, you can visit a URL such as `/Chess` or `/Soccer`, and you will see that the page link at the bottom of the page correctly includes the category.

Building a Category Navigation Menu

We need to provide the customers with a way to select a category. This means that we need to present them with a list of the categories available and indicate which, if any, they've selected. As we build out the application, we will use this list of categories in multiple controllers, so we need something that is self-contained and reusable.

The ASP.NET MVC Framework has the concept of *child actions*, which are perfect for creating items such as a reusable navigation control. A child action relies on the HTML helper method called `RenderAction`, which lets you include the output from an arbitrary action method in the current view. In this case, we can create a new controller (we will call ours `NavController`) with an action method (`Menu`, in this case) that renders a navigation menu and inject the output from that method into the layout.

This approach gives us a real controller that can contain whatever application logic we need and that can be unit tested like any other controller. It's a really nice way of creating smaller segments of an application while preserving the overall MVC Framework approach.

Creating the Navigation Controller

Right-click the Controllers folder in the SportsStore.WebUI project and select Add Controller from the pop-up menu. Set the name of the new controller to NavController, select the Empty MVC controller option from the Template menu, and click Add to create the class.

Remove the Index method that Visual Studio creates by default and add the Menu action method shown in Listing 8-5.

Listing 8-5. The Menu Action Method

```
using System;
using System.Collections.Generic;
using System.Linq;
using System.Web;
using System.Web.Mvc;

namespace SportsStore.WebUI.Controllers {
    public class NavController : Controller {

        public string Menu() {
            return "Hello from NavController";
        }
    }
}
```

This method returns a static message string but it is enough to get us started while we integrate the child action into the rest of the application. We want the category list to appear on all pages, so we are going to render the child action in the layout, rather than in a specific view. Edit the Views/Shared/_Layout.cshtml file so that it calls the RenderAction helper method, as shown in Listing 8-6.

Listing 8-6. Adding the RenderAction Call to the Razor Layout

```
<!DOCTYPE html>
<html>
<head>
    <meta charset="utf-8" />
    <meta name="viewport" content="width=device-width" />
    <title>@ViewBag.Title</title>
    <link href="~/Content/Site.css" type="text/css" rel="stylesheet" />
</head>
<body>
    <div id="header">
        <div class="title">SPORTS STORE</div>
    </div>
    <div id="categories">
        @{ Html.RenderAction("Menu", "Nav"); }
    </div>
    <div id="content">
        @RenderBody()
    </div>
</body>
</html>
```

We have removed the placeholder text that we added in Chapter 7 and replaced it with a call to the RenderAction method. The parameters to this method are the action method we want to call (Menu) and the controller we want to use (Nav).

■ **Note** The RenderAction method writes its content directly to the response stream, just like the RenderPartial method introduced in Chapter 5. This means that the method returns void, and therefore cannot be used with a regular Razor @ tag. Instead, we must enclose the call to the method inside a Razor code block (and remember to terminate the statement with a semicolon). You can use the Action method as an alternative if you do not like this code-block syntax.

If you run the application, you will see that the output of the Menu action method is included in every page, as shown in Figure 8-2.

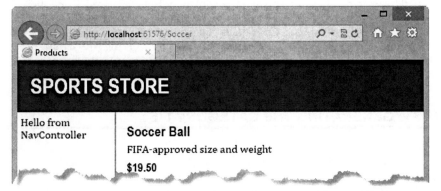

Figure 8-2. Displaying the output from the Menu action method

Generating Category Lists

We can now return to the controller and generate a real set of categories. We do not want to generate the category URLs in the controller. We are going to use a helper method in the view to do that. All we need to do in the Menu action method is create the list of categories, which we have done in Listing 8-7.

Listing 8-7. Implementing the Menu Method

```
using SportsStore.Domain.Abstract;
using System;
using System.Collections.Generic;
using System.Linq;
using System.Web;
using System.Web.Mvc;

namespace SportsStore.WebUI.Controllers {
    public class NavController : Controller {
```

```
        private IProductRepository repository;

        public NavController(IProductRepository repo) {
            repository = repo;
        }

        public PartialViewResult Menu() {
            IEnumerable<string> categories = repository.Products
                                    .Select(x => x.Category)
                                    .Distinct()
                                    .OrderBy(x => x);

            return PartialView(categories);
        }
    }
}
```

Our first change is to add constructor that accepts an IProductRepository implementation as its argument – the implementation will be provided by Ninject when the controller is instantiated, using the bindings that we set up in the previous chapter.

Our second change is to the Menu action method, which now uses a LINQ query to obtain a list of categories from the repository and pass them to the view. Notice that, since we are working with a partial view in this controller, we call the PartialView method in the action method and that the result is a PartialViewResult object.

UNIT TEST: GENERATING THE CATEGORY LIST

The unit test for our ability to produce a category list is relatively simple. Our goal is to create a list that is sorted in alphabetical order and contains no duplicates. The simplest way to do this is to supply some test data that *does* have duplicate categories and that is *not* in order, pass this to the NavController, and assert that the data has been properly cleaned up. Here is the unit test we used:

```
...
[TestMethod]
public void Can_Create_Categories() {

    // Arrange
    // - create the mock repository
    Mock<IProductRepository> mock = new Mock<IProductRepository>();
    mock.Setup(m => m.Products).Returns(new Product[] {
        new Product {ProductID = 1, Name = "P1", Category = "Apples"},
        new Product {ProductID = 2, Name = "P2", Category = "Apples"},
        new Product {ProductID = 3, Name = "P3", Category = "Plums"},
        new Product {ProductID = 4, Name = "P4", Category = "Oranges"},
    }.AsQueryable());

    // Arrange - create the controller
    NavController target = new NavController(mock.Object);

    // Act = get the set of categories
```

```
        string[] results = ((IEnumerable<string>)target.Menu().Model).ToArray();

        // Assert
        Assert.AreEqual(results.Length, 3);
        Assert.AreEqual(results[0], "Apples");
        Assert.AreEqual(results[1], "Oranges");
        Assert.AreEqual(results[2], "Plums");
    }
    ...
```

We created a mock repository implementation that contains repeating categories and categories that are not in order. We assert that the duplicates are removed and that alphabetical ordering is imposed.

Creating the Partial View

Since the navigation list is just part of the overall page, it makes sense to create a partial view for the Menu action method. Right-click the Menu method in the NavController class and select Add View from the pop-up menu.

Leave the view name as Menu, check the option to create a strongly typed view, and enter IEnumerable<string> as the model class type, as shown in Figure 8-3.

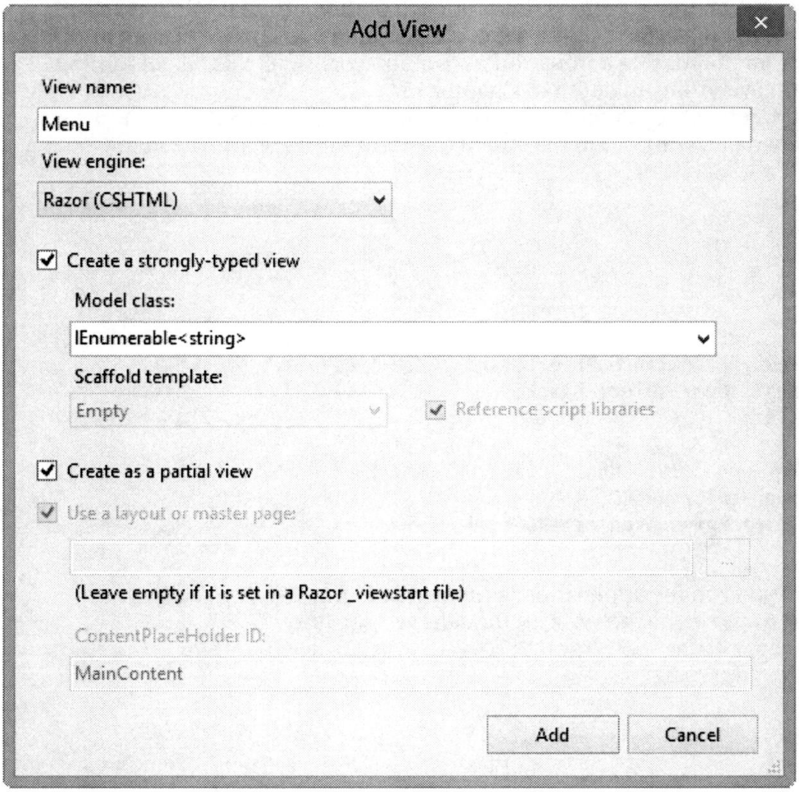

Figure 8-3. Creating the Menu partial view

Check the `Create as a partial view` option and click the `Add` button to create the view. Edit the view contents so that they match those shown in Listing 8-8.

Listing 8-8. The Menu Partial View

```
@model IEnumerable<string>

@Html.ActionLink("Home", "List", "Product")

@foreach (var link in Model) {
    @Html.RouteLink(link, new {
        controller = "Product",
        action = "List",
        category = link,
        page = 1
    })
}
```

We have added a link called Home that will appear at the top of the category list and will take the user back to the first page of the list of all products with no category filter. We did this using the `ActionLink` helper method, which generates an HTML anchor element using the routing information we configured earlier.

We then enumerated the category names and created links for each of them using the `RouteLink` method. This is similar to `ActionLink`, but it lets us supply a set of name/value pairs that are taken into account when generating the URL from the routing configuration. Do not worry if all this talk of routing does not make sense yet—we explain everything in depth in Chapter 13.

The links we generate will look pretty ugly by default, so we have defined some CSS that will improve their appearance. Add the styles shown in Listing 8-9 to the end of the `/Content/Site.css` file in the `SportsStore.WebUI` project.

Listing 8-9. CSS for the Category Links

```
...
DIV#categories A
{
    font: bold 1.1em "Arial Narrow","Franklin Gothic Medium",Arial; display: block;
    text-decoration: none; padding: .6em; color: Black;
    border-bottom: 1px solid silver;
}
DIV#categories A.selected { background-color: #666; color: White; }
DIV#categories A:hover { background-color: #CCC; }
DIV#categories A.selected:hover { background-color: #666; }
...
```

You can see the category links if you run the application, as shown in Figure 8-4. If you click a category, the list of items is updated to show only items from the selected category.

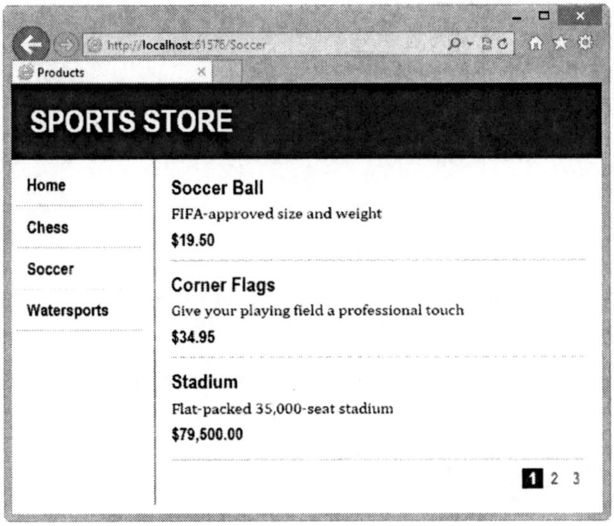

Figure 8-4. The category links

Highlighting the Current Category

At present, we do not indicate to users which category they are viewing. It might be something that the customer could infer from the items in the list, but we prefer to provide some solid visual feedback.

We could do this by creating a view model that contains the list of categories and the selected category, and in fact, this is exactly what we would usually do. But for variety we are we are going to use the view bag feature we introduced in Chapter 2. This feature allows us to pass data from the controller to the view without using a view model. Listing 8-10 shows the changes to the Menu action method in the Nav controller.

Listing 8-10. Using the View Bag Feature

```
using SportsStore.Domain.Abstract;
using System;
using System.Collections.Generic;
using System.Linq;
using System.Web;
using System.Web.Mvc;

namespace SportsStore.WebUI.Controllers {
    public class NavController : Controller {
        private IProductRepository repository;

        public NavController(IProductRepository repo) {
            repository = repo;
        }

        public PartialViewResult Menu(string category = null) {

            ViewBag.SelectedCategory = category;
```

```
            IEnumerable<string> categories = repository.Products
                            .Select(x => x.Category)
                            .Distinct()
                            .OrderBy(x => x);

        return PartialView(categories);
    }
  }
}
```

We have added a parameter to the Menu action method called **category**. The value for this parameter will be provided automatically by the routing configuration. Inside the method body, we have dynamically created a SelectedCategory property in the ViewBag object and set its value to be the category parameter value. As we explained in Chapter 2, the ViewBag is a dynamic object and we create new properties simply by setting values for them.

UNIT TEST: REPORTING THE SELECTED CATEGORY

We can test that the Menu action method correctly adds details of the selected category by reading the value of the ViewBag property in a unit test, which is available through the ViewResult class. Here is the test:

```
...
[TestMethod]
public void Indicates_Selected_Category() {

    // Arrange
    // - create the mock repository
    Mock<IProductRepository> mock = new Mock<IProductRepository>();
    mock.Setup(m => m.Products).Returns(new Product[] {
        new Product {ProductID = 1, Name = "P1", Category = "Apples"},
        new Product {ProductID = 4, Name = "P2", Category = "Oranges"},
    }.AsQueryable());

    // Arrange - create the controller
    NavController target = new NavController(mock.Object);

    // Arrange - define the category to selected
    string categoryToSelect = "Apples";

    // Action
    string result = target.Menu(categoryToSelect).ViewBag.SelectedCategory;

    // Assert
    Assert.AreEqual(categoryToSelect, result);
}
...
```

Notice that we do not need to cast the property value from the ViewBag. This is one the advantages of using the ViewBag object in preference to ViewData.

Now that we are providing information about which category is selected, we can update the view to take advantage of this, and add a CSS class to the HTML anchor element that represents the selected category. Listing 8-11 shows the changes to the Menu.cshtml partial view.

Listing 8-11. Highlighting the Selected Category

```
@model IEnumerable<string>

@Html.ActionLink("Home", "List", "Product")

@foreach (var link in Model) {
    @Html.RouteLink(link, new {
        controller = "Product",
        action = "List",
        category = link,
        page = 1
    },
    new {
        @class = link == ViewBag.SelectedCategory ? "selected" : null
    })
}
```

We have taken advantage of an overloaded version of the RouteLink method, which lets us provide an object whose properties will be added to the HTML anchor element as attributes. In this case, the link that represents the currently selected category is assigned the selected CSS class.

░ **Note** Notice that we used @class in the anonymous object we passed as the new parameter to the RouteLink helper method. This is not a Razor tag. We are using a standard C# language feature to avoid a conflict between the HTML keyword class (used to assign a CSS style to an element) and the C# use of the same word (used to denote a .NET class). The @ character allows us to use reserved C# keywords without confusing the compiler. If we just called the parameter class (without the @), the compiler would assume we are defining a new C# type. When we use the @ character, the compiler knows we want to create a parameter in the anonymous type *called* class, and we get the result we need.

Running the application shows the effect of the category highlighting, which you can also see in Figure 8-5.

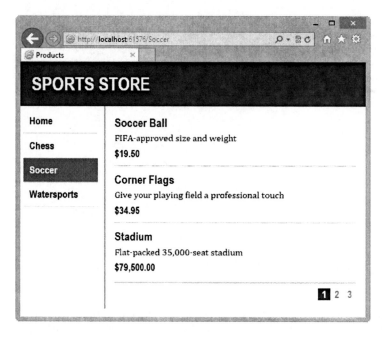

Figure 8-5. Highlighting the selected category

Correcting the Page Count

We need to correct the page links so that they work correctly when a category is selected. Currently, the number of page links is determined by the total number of products in the repository and not the number of products in the selected category. This means that the customer can click the link for page 2 of the Chess category and end up with an empty page because there are not enough chess products to fill the second page. You can see how this looks in Figure 8-6.

Figure 8-6. Displaying the wrong page links when a category is selected

We can fix this by updating the `List` action method in `ProductController` so that the pagination information takes the categories into account. You can see the required changes in Listing 8-12.

Listing 8-12. Creating Category-Aware Pagination Data

```
...
public ViewResult List(string category, int page = 1) {

    ProductsListViewModel viewModel = new ProductsListViewModel {
        Products = repository.Products
            .Where(p => category == null || p.Category == category)
            .OrderBy(p => p.ProductID)
            .Skip((page - 1) * PageSize)
            .Take(PageSize),
        PagingInfo = new PagingInfo {
            CurrentPage = page,
            ItemsPerPage = PageSize,
            TotalItems = category == null ?
                repository.Products.Count() :
                repository.Products.Where(e => e.Category == category).Count()
        },
        CurrentCategory = category
    };
    return View(viewModel);
}
...
```

If a category is selected, we return the number of items in that category; if not, we return the total number of products.

UNIT TEST: CATEGORY-SPECIFIC PRODUCT COUNTS

Testing that we are able to generate the current product count for different categories is very simple—we create a mock repository that contains known data in a range of categories and then call the `List` action method requesting each category in turn. Here is the unit test:

```
...
[TestMethod]
public void Generate_Category_Specific_Product_Count() {
    // Arrange
    // - create the mock repository
    Mock<IProductRepository> mock = new Mock<IProductRepository>();
    mock.Setup(m => m.Products).Returns(new Product[] {
        new Product {ProductID = 1, Name = "P1", Category = "Cat1"},
        new Product {ProductID = 2, Name = "P2", Category = "Cat2"},
        new Product {ProductID = 3, Name = "P3", Category = "Cat1"},
        new Product {ProductID = 4, Name = "P4", Category = "Cat2"},
        new Product {ProductID = 5, Name = "P5", Category = "Cat3"}
    }.AsQueryable());

    // Arrange - create a controller and make the page size 3 items
```

```
        ProductController target = new ProductController(mock.Object);
        target.PageSize = 3;

        // Action - test the product counts for different categories
        int res1 = ((ProductsListViewModel)target
            .List("Cat1").Model).PagingInfo.TotalItems;
        int res2 = ((ProductsListViewModel)target
            .List("Cat2").Model).PagingInfo.TotalItems;
        int res3 = ((ProductsListViewModel)target
            .List("Cat3").Model).PagingInfo.TotalItems;
        int resAll = ((ProductsListViewModel)target
            .List(null).Model).PagingInfo.TotalItems;

        // Assert
        Assert.AreEqual(res1, 2);
        Assert.AreEqual(res2, 2);
        Assert.AreEqual(res3, 1);
        Assert.AreEqual(resAll, 5);
    }
    ...
```

Notice that we also call the List method specifying no category to make sure we get the right total count as well.

Now when we view a category, the links at the bottom of the page correctly reflect the number of products in the category, as shown in Figure 8-7.

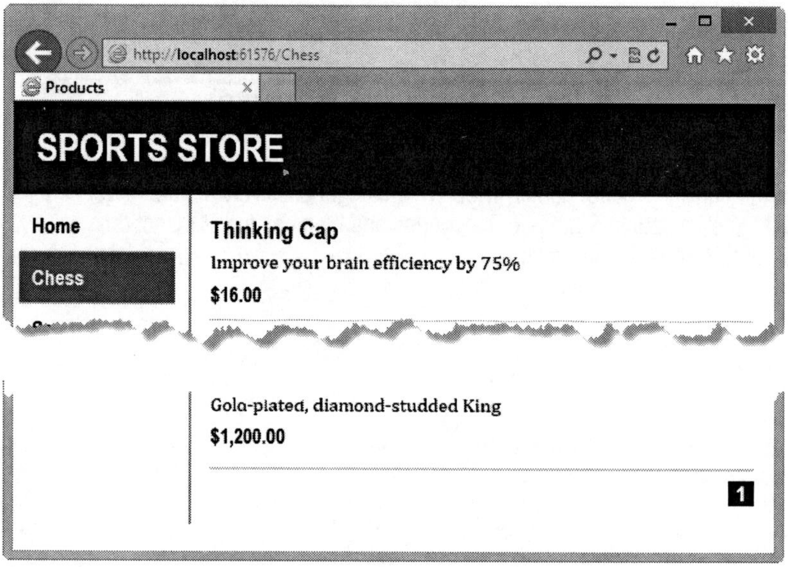

Figure 8-7. Displaying category-specific page counts

Building the Shopping Cart

Our application is progressing nicely, but we cannot sell any products until we implement a shopping cart. In this section, we will create the shopping cart experience shown in Figure 8-8. This will be familiar to anyone who has ever made a purchase online.

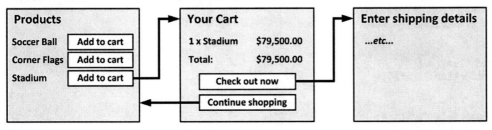

Figure 8-8. The basic shopping cart flow

An `Add to cart` button will be displayed alongside each of the products in our catalog. Clicking this button will show a summary of the products the customer has selected so far, including the total cost. At this point, the user can click the `Continue shopping` button to return to the product catalog, or click the `Checkout now` button to complete the order and finish the shopping session.

Defining the Cart Entity

A shopping cart is part of our application's business domain, so it makes sense to represent a cart by creating an entity in our domain model. Add a class file called `Cart` to the `Entities` folder in the `SportsStore.Domain` project and define the classes shown in Listing 8-13.

Listing 8-13. The Cart and CartLine classes

```
using System;
using System.Collections.Generic;
using System.Linq;
using System.Text;
using System.Threading.Tasks;

namespace SportsStore.Domain.Entities {

    public class Cart {
        private List<CartLine> lineCollection = new List<CartLine>();

        public void AddItem(Product product, int quantity) {
            CartLine line = lineCollection
                .Where(p => p.Product.ProductID == product.ProductID)
                .FirstOrDefault();

            if (line == null) {
                lineCollection.Add(new CartLine { Product = product,
                    Quantity = quantity });
            } else {
                line.Quantity += quantity;
            }
```

```
        }

        public void RemoveLine(Product product) {
            lineCollection.RemoveAll(l => l.Product.ProductID == product.ProductID);
        }

        public decimal ComputeTotalValue() {
            return lineCollection.Sum(e => e.Product.Price * e.Quantity);

        }
        public void Clear() {
            lineCollection.Clear();
        }

        public IEnumerable<CartLine> Lines {
            get { return lineCollection; }
        }
    }

    public class CartLine {
        public Product Product { get; set; }
        public int Quantity { get; set; }
    }
}
```

The Cart class uses CartLine, defined in the same file, to represent a product selected by the customer and the quantity the user wants to buy. We have defined methods to add an item to the cart, remove a previously added item from the cart, calculate the total cost of the items in the cart, and reset the cart by removing all of the selections. We have also provided a property that gives access to the contents of the cart using an IEnumerble<CartLine>. This is all straightforward stuff, easily implemented in C# with the help of a little LINQ.

UNIT TEST: TESTING THE CART

The Cart class is relatively simple, but it has a range of important behaviors that we must ensure work properly. A poorly functioning cart would undermine the entire SportsStore application. We have broken down the features and tested them individually. We created a new unit test file in the SportsStore.UnitTests project called CartTests.cs to contain these tests.

The first behavior relates to when we add an item to the cart. If this is the first time that a given Product has been added to the cart, we want a new CartLine to be added. Here is the test, including the unit test class definition:

```
using System;
using Microsoft.VisualStudio.TestTools.UnitTesting;
using SportsStore.Domain.Entities;
using System.Linq;

namespace SportsStore.UnitTests {
```

```
[TestClass]
public class CartTests {

    [TestMethod]
    public void Can_Add_New_Lines() {

        // Arrange - create some test products
        Product p1 = new Product { ProductID = 1, Name = "P1" };
        Product p2 = new Product { ProductID = 2, Name = "P2" };

        // Arrange - create a new cart
        Cart target = new Cart();

        // Act
        target.AddItem(p1, 1);
        target.AddItem(p2, 1);
        CartLine[] results = target.Lines.ToArray();

        // Assert
        Assert.AreEqual(results.Length, 2);
        Assert.AreEqual(results[0].Product, p1);
        Assert.AreEqual(results[1].Product, p2);
    }

}
}
```

However, if the customer has already added a Product to the cart, we want to increment the quantity of the corresponding CartLine and not create a new one. Here is the test:

```
..
[TestMethod]
public void Can_Add_Quantity_For_Existing_Lines() {

    // Arrange - create some test products
    Product p1 = new Product { ProductID = 1, Name = "P1" };
    Product p2 = new Product { ProductID = 2, Name = "P2" };

    // Arrange - create a new cart
    Cart target = new Cart();

    // Act
    target.AddItem(p1, 1);
    target.AddItem(p2, 1);
    target.AddItem(p1, 10);
    CartLine[] results = target.Lines.OrderBy(c => c.Product.ProductID).ToArray();

    // Assert
    Assert.AreEqual(results.Length, 2);
    Assert.AreEqual(results[0].Quantity, 11);
    Assert.AreEqual(results[1].Quantity, 1);
}
```

...

We also need to check that users can change their mind and remove products from the cart. This feature is implemented by the RemoveLine method. Here is the test:

```
...
[TestMethod]
public void Can_Remove_Line() {

    // Arrange - create some test products
    Product p1 = new Product { ProductID = 1, Name = "P1" };
    Product p2 = new Product { ProductID = 2, Name = "P2" };
    Product p3 = new Product { ProductID = 3, Name = "P3" };

    // Arrange - create a new cart
    Cart target = new Cart();
    // Arrange - add some products to the cart
    target.AddItem(p1, 1);
    target.AddItem(p2, 3);
    target.AddItem(p3, 5);
    target.AddItem(p2, 1);

    // Act
    target.RemoveLine(p2);

    // Assert
    Assert.AreEqual(target.Lines.Where(c => c.Product == p2).Count(), 0);
    Assert.AreEqual(target.Lines.Count(), 2);
}
...
```

The next behavior we want to test is our ability to calculate the total cost of the items in the cart. Here's the test for this behavior:

```
...
[TestMethod]
public void Calculate_Cart_Total() {

    // Arrange - create some test products
    Product p1 = new Product { ProductID = 1, Name = "P1", Price = 100M};
    Product p2 = new Product { ProductID = 2, Name = "P2" , Price = 50M};

    // Arrange - create a new cart
    Cart target = new Cart();

    // Act
    target.AddItem(p1, 1);
    target.AddItem(p2, 1);
    target.AddItem(p1, 3);
    decimal result = target.ComputeTotalValue();
```

```
    // Assert
    Assert.AreEqual(result, 450M);
}
...
```

The final test is very simple. We want to ensure that the contents of the cart are properly removed when we reset it. Here is the test:

```
...
[TestMethod]
public void Can_Clear_Contents() {

    // Arrange - create some test products
    Product p1 = new Product { ProductID = 1, Name = "P1", Price = 100M };
    Product p2 = new Product { ProductID = 2, Name = "P2", Price = 50M };

    // Arrange - create a new cart
    Cart target = new Cart();

    // Arrange - add some items
    target.AddItem(p1, 1);
    target.AddItem(p2, 1);

    // Act - reset the cart
    target.Clear();

    // Assert
    Assert.AreEqual(target.Lines.Count(), 0);
}
...
```

Sometimes, as in this case, the code required to test the functionality of a type is much longer and much more complex than the type itself. Do not let that put you off writing the unit tests. Defects in simple classes, especially ones that play such an important role as Cart does in our application, can have huge impacts.

Adding the Add to Cart Buttons

We need to edit the Views/Shared/ProductSummary.cshtml partial view to add the buttons to the product listings. The changes are shown in Listing 8-14.

Listing 8-14. Adding the Buttons to the Product Summary Partial View

```
@model SportsStore.Domain.Entities.Product

<div class="item">
    <h3>@Model.Name</h3>
    @Model.Description

    @using(Html.BeginForm("AddToCart", "Cart")) {
        @Html.HiddenFor(x => x.ProductID)
```

```
        @Html.Hidden("returnUrl", Request.Url.PathAndQuery)
        <input type="submit" value="+ Add to cart" />
    }

    <h4>@Model.Price.ToString("c")</h4>
</div>
```

We have added a Razor block that creates a small HTML form for each product in the listing. When this form is submitted, it will invoke the **AddToCart** action method in the **Cart** controller (we will implement this method in just a moment).

■ **Note** By default, the BeginForm helper method creates a form that uses the HTTP POST method. You can change this so that forms use the GET method, but you should think carefully about doing so. The HTTP specification requires that GET requests must be *idempotent*, meaning that they must not cause changes, and adding a product to a cart is definitely a change. We will have more to say on this topic in Chapter 14, including an explanation of what can happen if you ignore the need for idempotent GET requests.

We want to keep the styling of these buttons consistent with the rest of the application, so add the CSS shown in Listing 8-15 to the end of the **Content/Site.css** file.

Listing 8-15. Styling the Buttons

```
...
FORM { margin: 0; padding: 0; }
DIV.item FORM { float:right; }
DIV.item INPUT {
    color:White; background-color: #333; border: 1px solid black; cursor:pointer;
}
...
```

CREATING MULTIPLE HTML FORMS IN A PAGE

Using the Html.BeginForm helper in each product listing means that every Add to cart button is rendered in its own separate HTML form element. This may be surprising if you have been developing with ASP.NET Web Forms, which imposes a limit of one form per page. ASP.NET MVC does not limit the number of forms per page, and you can have as many as you need.

There is no technical requirement for us to create a form for each button. However, since each form will postback to the same controller method, but with a different set of parameter values, it is a nice and simple way to deal with the button presses.

Implementing the Cart Controller

We need to create a controller to handle the Add to cart button presses. Create a new controller called CartController and edit the content so that it matches Listing 8-16.

Listing 8-16. Creating the Cart Controller

```
using SportsStore.Domain.Abstract;
using SportsStore.Domain.Entities;
using System;
using System.Collections.Generic;
using System.Linq;
using System.Web;
using System.Web.Mvc;

namespace SportsStore.WebUI.Controllers {

    public class CartController : Controller {
        private IProductRepository repository;

        public CartController(IProductRepository repo) {
            repository = repo;
        }

        public RedirectToRouteResult AddToCart(int productId, string returnUrl) {
            Product product = repository.Products
                .FirstOrDefault(p => p.ProductID == productId);

            if (product != null) {
                GetCart().AddItem(product, 1);
            }
            return RedirectToAction("Index", new { returnUrl });
        }

        public RedirectToRouteResult RemoveFromCart(int productId, string returnUrl) {
            Product product = repository.Products
                .FirstOrDefault(p => p.ProductID == productId);

            if (product != null) {
                GetCart().RemoveLine(product);
            }
            return RedirectToAction("Index", new { returnUrl });
        }

        private Cart GetCart() {

            Cart cart = (Cart)Session["Cart"];
            if (cart == null) {
                cart = new Cart();
                Session["Cart"] = cart;
            }
            return cart;
        }
    }
}
```

There are a few points to note about this controller. The first is that we use the ASP.NET session state feature to store and retrieve `Cart` objects. This is the purpose of the `GetCart` method. ASP.NET has a nice session feature that uses cookies or URL rewriting to associate requests from a user together, to form a single browsing session. A related feature is session state, which allows us to associate data with a session. This is an ideal fit for our `Cart` class. We want each user to have their own cart, and we want the cart to be persistent between requests. Data associated with a session is deleted when a session expires (typically because a user has not made a request for a while), which means that we do not need to manage the storage or life cycle of the `Cart` objects. To add an object to the session state, we set the value for a key on the `Session` object, like this:

```
...
Session["Cart"] = cart;
...
```

To retrieve an object again, we simply read the same key, like this:

```
...
Cart cart = (Cart)Session["Cart"];
...
```

■ **Tip**   Session state objects are stored in the memory of the ASP.NET server by default, but you can configure a range of different storage approaches, including using a SQL database.

For the `AddToCart` and `RemoveFromCart` methods, we have used parameter names that match the `input` elements in the HTML forms we created in the `ProductSummary.cshtml` view. This allows the MVC Framework to associate incoming form `POST` variables with those parameters, meaning we do not need to process the form ourselves.

Displaying the Contents of the Cart

The final point to note about the `Cart` controller is that both the `AddToCart` and `RemoveFromCart` methods call the `RedirectToAction` method. This has the effect of sending an HTTP redirect instruction to the client browser, asking the browser to request a new URL. In this case, we have asked the browser to request a URL that will call the `Index` action method of the `Cart` controller.

We are going to implement the `Index` method and use it to display the contents of the `Cart`. If you refer back to Figure 8-8, you will see that this is our workflow when the user clicks the `Add to cart` button.

We need to pass two pieces of information to the view that will display the contents of the cart: the `Cart` object and the URL to display if the user clicks the `Continue shopping` button. We will create a simple view model class for this purpose. Create a new class called `CartIndexViewModel` in the `Models` folder of the `SportsStore.WebUI` project. The contents of this class are shown in Listing 8-17.

Listing 8-17. The CartIndexViewModel Class

```
using SportsStore.Domain.Entities;

namespace SportsStore.WebUI.Models {
    public class CartIndexViewModel {
        public Cart Cart { get; set; }
        public string ReturnUrl { get; set; }
    }
}
```

Now that we have the view model, we can implement the **Index** action method in the **Cart** controller class, as shown in Listing 8-18.

Listing 8-18. The Index Action Method

```
using SportsStore.Domain.Abstract;
using SportsStore.Domain.Entities;
using SportsStore.WebUI.Models;
using System;
using System.Collections.Generic;
using System.Linq;
using System.Web;
using System.Web.Mvc;

namespace SportsStore.WebUI.Controllers {

    public class CartController : Controller {
        private IProductRepository repository;

        public CartController(IProductRepository repo) {
            repository = repo;
        }

        public ViewResult Index(string returnUrl) {
            return View(new CartIndexViewModel {
                Cart = GetCart(),
                ReturnUrl = returnUrl
            });
        }

        // ...other action methods omitted for brevity...
    }

}
```

The last step is to display the contents of the cart is to create the new view. Right-click the **Index** method and select **Add View** from the pop-up menu. Set the name of the view to **Index**, check the option to create a strongly typed view, and select **CartIndexViewModel** as the model class, as shown in Figure 8-9.

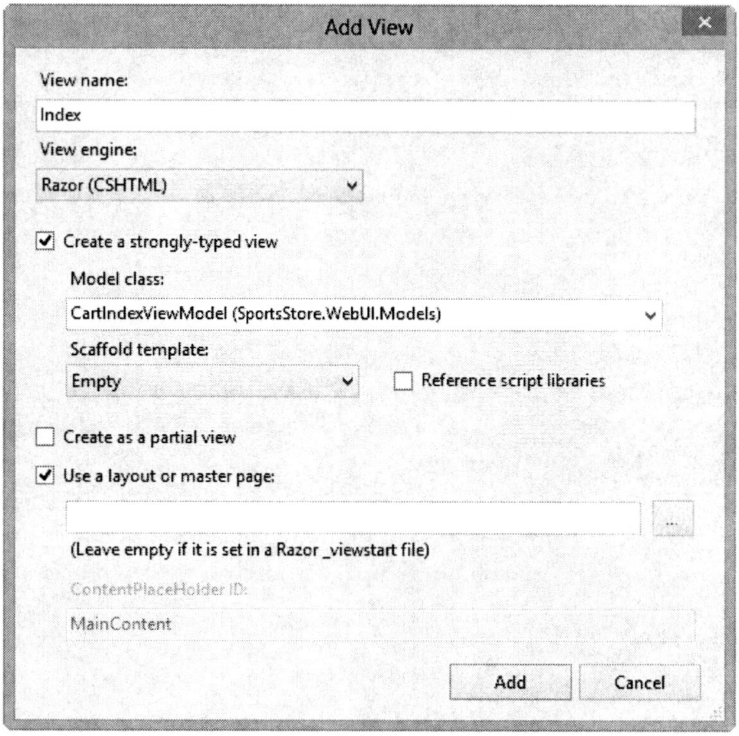

Figure 8-9. Adding the Index view

We want the contents of the cart to be displayed consistently with the rest of the application pages, so ensure that the option to use a layout is checked, and leave the text box empty so that we use the default _Layout.cshtml file. Click **Add** to create the view and edit the contents so that they match Listing 8-19.

Listing 8-19. The Index View

```
@model SportsStore.WebUI.Models.CartIndexViewModel

@{
    ViewBag.Title = "Sports Store: Your Cart";
}

<h2>Your cart</h2>
<table width="90%" align="center">
    <thead><tr>
        <th align="center">Quantity</th>
        <th align="left">Item</th>
        <th align="right">Price</th>
        <th align="right">Subtotal</th>
    </tr></thead>
    <tbody>
        @foreach(var line in Model.Cart.Lines) {
            <tr>
```

```
                <td align="center">@line.Quantity</td>
                <td align="left">@line.Product.Name</td>
                <td align="right">@line.Product.Price.ToString("c")</td>
                <td align="right">@((line.Quantity
                    * line.Product.Price).ToString("c"))</td>
            </tr>
        }
    </tbody>
    <tfoot><tr>
        <td colspan="3" align="right">Total:</td>
        <td align="right">
            @Model.Cart.ComputeTotalValue().ToString("c")
        </td>
    </tr></tfoot>
</table>
<p align="center" class="actionButtons">
    <a href="@Model.ReturnUrl">Continue shopping</a>
</p>
```

The view looks more complicated than it is. It just enumerates the lines in the cart and adds rows for each of them to an HTML table, along with the total cost per line and the total cost for the cart. The final step is to add some more CSS. Add the styles shown in Listing 8-20 to the Site.css file.

Listing 8-20. CSS for Displaying the Contents of the Cart

```
...
H2 { margin-top: 0.3em }
TFOOT TD { border-top: 1px dotted gray; font-weight: bold; }
.actionButtons A, INPUT.actionButtons {
    font: .8em Arial; color: White; margin: .5em;
    text-decoration: none; padding: .15em 1.5em .2em 1.5em;
    background-color: #353535; border: 1px solid black;
}
...
```

We now have the basic functions of the shopping cart in place. First, products are listed along with a button to add them to the cart, as shown in Figure 8-10.

Figure 8-10. The Add to cart button

And second, when we click the `Add to cart button`, the appropriate product is added to our cart and a summary of the cart is displayed, as shown in Figure 8-11. We can click the `Continue shopping` button and return to the product page we came from—all very nice and slick.

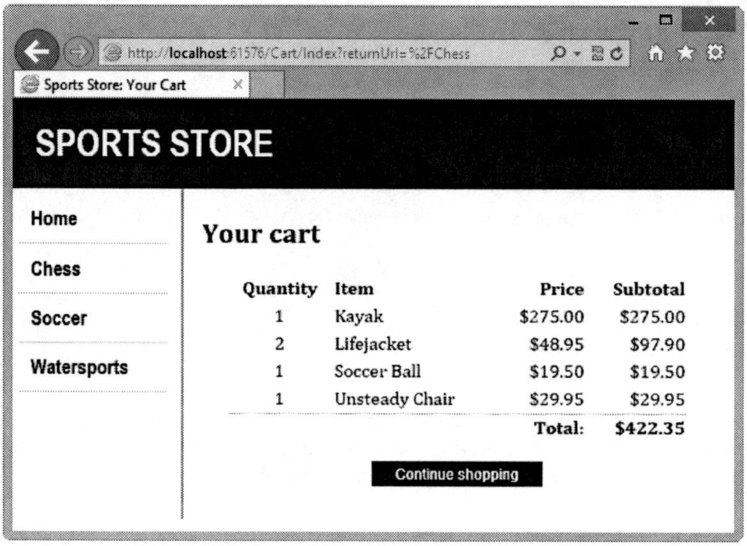

Figure 8-11. Displaying the contents of the shopping cart

Summary

In this chapter, we have started to flesh out the customer-facing parts of the SportsStore app. We provided the means by which the user can navigate by category and put the basic building blocks in place for adding items to a shopping cart. We have more work to do, which we will continue in the next chapter.

CHAPTER 9

■ ■ ■

SportsStore: Completing the Cart

In this chapter, we continue to build out our SportsStore example app. In the previous chapter, we added the basic support for a shopping cart and now we are going to improve on and complete that functionality.

Using Model Binding

The MVC Framework uses a system called *model binding* to create C# objects from HTTP requests in order to pass them as parameter values to action methods. This is how MVC processes forms, for example. The framework looks at the parameters of the action method that has been targeted, and uses a *model binder* to get the values of the form input elements and convert them to the type of the parameter with the same name.

Model binders can create C# types from any information that is available in the request. This is one of the central features of the MVC Framework. We are going to create a custom model binder to improve our `CartController` class.

We like using the session state feature in the `Cart` controller to store and manage our `Cart` objects, but we *do not* like the way we have to go about it. It does not fit the rest of our application model, which is based around action method parameters. We cannot properly unit test the `CartController` class unless we mock the `Session` parameter of the base class, and that means mocking the `Controller` class and a whole bunch of other stuff we would rather not deal with.

To solve this problem, we are going to create a custom model binder that obtains the `Cart` object contained in the session data. The MVC Framework will then be able to create `Cart` objects and pass them as parameters to the action methods in our `CartController` class. The model binding feature is very powerful and flexible. We go into a lot more depth about this feature in Chapter 22, but this is a nice example to get us started.

Creating a Custom Model Binder

We create a custom model binder by implementing the `IModelBinder` interface. Create a new folder in the `SportsStore.WebUI` project called `Binders` and create a `CartModelBinder` class inside that folder. Listing 9-1 shows the definition of the `CartModelBinder` class.

Listing 9-1. The CartModelBinder Class

```
using System;
using System.Web.Mvc;
using SportsStore.Domain.Entities;

namespace SportsStore.WebUI.Binders {

    public class CartModelBinder : IModelBinder {
```

```
        private const string sessionKey = "Cart";

        public object BindModel(ControllerContext controllerContext,
            ModelBindingContext bindingContext) {

            // get the Cart from the session
            Cart cart = (Cart)controllerContext.HttpContext.Session[sessionKey];
            // create the Cart if there wasn't one in the session data
            if (cart == null) {
                cart = new Cart();
                controllerContext.HttpContext.Session[sessionKey] = cart;
            }
            // return the cart
            return cart;
        }
    }
}
```

The `IModelBinder` interface defines one method: `BindModel`. The two parameters are provided to make creating the domain model object possible. The `ControllerContext` provides access to all the information that the controller class has, which includes details of the request from the client. The `ModelBindingContext` gives you information about the model object you are being asked to build and some tools for making the binding process easier. We will come back to this class in Chapter 22.

For our purposes, the `ControllerContext` class is the one we are interested in. It has the `HttpContext` property, which in turn has a `Session` property that lets us get and set session data. We obtain the `Cart` by reading a key value from the session data, and create a `Cart` if there is not one there already.

We need to tell the MVC Framework that it can use our `CartModelBinder` class to create instances of `Cart`. We do this in the `Application_Start` method of `Global.asax`, as shown in Listing 9-2.

Listing 9-2. Registering the CartModelBinder Class

```
using SportsStore.Domain.Entities;
using SportsStore.WebUI.Binders;
using SportsStore.WebUI.Infrastructure;
using System.Web.Http;
using System.Web.Mvc;
using System.Web.Optimization;
using System.Web.Routing;

namespace SportsStore.WebUI {

    public class MvcApplication : System.Web.HttpApplication {
        protected void Application_Start() {
            AreaRegistration.RegisterAllAreas();

            WebApiConfig.Register(GlobalConfiguration.Configuration);
            FilterConfig.RegisterGlobalFilters(GlobalFilters.Filters);
            RouteConfig.RegisterRoutes(RouteTable.Routes);
            BundleConfig.RegisterBundles(BundleTable.Bundles);

            ControllerBuilder.Current
                .SetControllerFactory(new NinjectControllerFactory());
            ModelBinders.Binders.Add(typeof(Cart), new CartModelBinder());
        }
    }
}
```

We can now update the CartController class to remove the GetCart method and rely on our model binder, which the MVC Framework will apply automatically. Listing 9-3 shows the changes.

Listing 9-3. Relying on the Model Binder in CartController

```
using SportsStore.Domain.Abstract;
using SportsStore.Domain.Entities;
using SportsStore.WebUI.Models;
using System;
using System.Collections.Generic;
using System.Linq;
using System.Web;
using System.Web.Mvc;

namespace SportsStore.WebUI.Controllers {

    public class CartController : Controller {
        private IProductRepository repository;

        public CartController(IProductRepository repo) {
            repository = repo;
        }

        public ViewResult Index(Cart cart, string returnUrl) {
            return View(new CartIndexViewModel {
                Cart = cart,
                ReturnUrl = returnUrl
            });
        }

        public RedirectToRouteResult AddToCart(Cart cart, int productId,
                string returnUrl) {
            Product product = repository.Products
                .FirstOrDefault(p => p.ProductID == productId);

            if (product != null) {
                cart.AddItem(product, 1);
            }
            return RedirectToAction("Index", new { returnUrl });
        }

        public RedirectToRouteResult RemoveFromCart(Cart cart, int productId,
                string returnUrl) {
            Product product = repository.Products
                .FirstOrDefault(p => p.ProductID == productId);

            if (product != null) {
                cart.RemoveLine(product);
            }
            return RedirectToAction("Index", new { returnUrl });
        }
    }
}
```

233

We have removed the GetCart method and added a Cart parameter to each of the action methods. When the MVC Framework receives a request that requires, say, the AddToCart method to be invoked, it begins by looking at the parameters for the action method. It looks at the list of binders available and tries to find one that can create instances of each parameter type. Our custom binder is asked to create a Cart object, and it does so by working with the session state feature. Between our binder and the default binder, the MVC Framework is able to create the set of parameters required to call the action method, allowing us to refactor the controller so that it has no knowledge of how Cart objects are created when requests are received.

There are a few benefits to using a custom model binder like this. The first is that we have separated the logic used to create a Cart from that of the controller, which allows us to change the way we store Cart objects without needing to change the controller. The second benefit is that any controller class that works with Cart objects can simply declare them as action method parameters and take advantage of the custom model binder. The third benefit, and the one we think is most important, is that we can now unit test the Cart controller without needing to mock a lot of ASP.NET plumbing.

UNIT TEST: THE CART CONTROLLER

We can unit test the CartController class by creating Cart objects and passing them to the action

- The AddToCart method should add the selected product to the customer's cart.

- After adding a product to the cart, we should be redirected to the Index view.

- The URL that the user can follow to return to the catalog should be correctly passed to the Index action method.

methods. We want to test three different aspects of this controller:
Here are the unit tests we added to the CartTests.cs file in the SportsStore.UnitTests project:

```
using System;
using Microsoft.VisualStudio.TestTools.UnitTesting;
using SportsStore.Domain.Entities;
using System.Linq;
using Moq;
using SportsStore.Domain.Abstract;
using SportsStore.WebUI.Controllers;
using System.Web.Mvc;
using SportsStore.WebUI.Models;

namespace SportsStore.UnitTests {
    [TestClass]
    public class CartTests {

        //...existing test methods omitted for brevity...

        [TestMethod]
        public void Can_Add_To_Cart() {

            // Arrange - create the mock repository
            Mock<IProductRepository> mock = new Mock<IProductRepository>();
            mock.Setup(m => m.Products).Returns(new Product[] {
                new Product {ProductID = 1, Name = "P1", Category = "Apples"},
            }.AsQueryable());
```

```
        // Arrange - create a Cart
        Cart cart = new Cart();

        // Arrange - create the controller
        CartController target = new CartController(mock.Object);

        // Act - add a product to the cart
        target.AddToCart(cart, 1, null);

        // Assert
        Assert.AreEqual(cart.Lines.Count(), 1);
        Assert.AreEqual(cart.Lines.ToArray()[0].Product.ProductID, 1);
    }

    [TestMethod]
    public void Adding_Product_To_Cart_Goes_To_Cart_Screen() {
        // Arrange - create the mock repository
        Mock<IProductRepository> mock = new Mock<IProductRepository>();
        mock.Setup(m => m.Products).Returns(new Product[] {
            new Product {ProductID = 1, Name = "P1", Category = "Apples"},
        }.AsQueryable());

        // Arrange - create a Cart
        Cart cart = new Cart();

        // Arrange - create the controller
        CartController target = new CartController(mock.Object);

        // Act - add a product to the cart
        RedirectToRouteResult result = target.AddToCart(cart, 2, "myUrl");

        // Assert
        Assert.AreEqual(result.RouteValues["action"], "Index");
        Assert.AreEqual(result.RouteValues["returnUrl"], "myUrl");
    }

    [TestMethod]
    public void Can_View_Cart_Contents() {
        // Arrange - create a Cart
        Cart cart = new Cart();

        // Arrange - create the controller
        CartController target = new CartController(null);

        // Act - call the Index action method
        CartIndexViewModel result
            = (CartIndexViewModel)target.Index(cart, "myUrl").ViewData.Model;

        // Assert
        Assert.AreSame(result.Cart, cart);
        Assert.AreEqual(result.ReturnUrl, "myUrl");
    }
    }
}
```

Completing the Cart

Now that we have introduced our custom model binder, it is time to complete the cart functionality by adding two new features. The first feature will allow the customer to remove an item from the cart. The second feature will display a summary of the cart at the top of the page.

Removing Items from the Cart

We have already defined and tested the RemoveFromCart action method in the controller, so letting the customer remove items is just a matter of exposing this method in a view, which we are going to do by adding a Remove button in each row of the cart summary. The changes to Views/Cart/Index.cshtml are shown in Listing 9-4.

Listing 9-4. Introducing a Remove Button

```
...
<tbody>
    @foreach(var line in Model.Cart.Lines) {
        <tr>
            <td align="center">@line.Quantity</td>
            <td align="left">@line.Product.Name</td>
            <td align="right">@line.Product.Price.ToString("c")</td>
            <td align="right">@((line.Quantity
                * line.Product.Price).ToString("c"))</td>
            <td>
                @using (Html.BeginForm("RemoveFromCart", "Cart")) {
                    @Html.Hidden("ProductId", line.Product.ProductID)
                    @Html.HiddenFor(x => x.ReturnUrl)
                    <input class="actionButtons" type="submit"
                        value="Remove" />
                }
            </td>
        </tr>
    }
</tbody>
...
```

■ **Note** We can use the strongly typed Html.HiddenFor helper method to create a hidden field for the ReturnUrl model property, but we need to use the string-based Html.Hidden helper to do the same for the Product ID field. If we had written Html.HiddenFor(x => line.Product.ProductID), the helper would render a hidden field with the name line.Product.ProductID. The name of the field would not match the names of the parameters for the CartController.RemoveFromCart action method, which would prevent the default model binders from working, so the MVC Framework would not be able to call the method.

You can see the Remove buttons at work by running the application, adding some items to the shopping cart, and then clicking one of them. The result is illustrated in Figure 9-1.

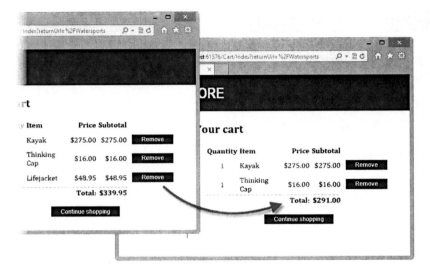

Figure 9-1. Removing an item from the shopping cart

Adding the Cart Summary

We have a functioning cart, but we have an issue with the way we have integrated the cart into the interface. Customers can tell what is in their cart only by viewing the cart summary screen. And they can view the cart summary screen only by adding a new a new item to the cart.

To solve this problem, we are going to add a widget that summarizes the contents of the cart and that can be clicked to display the cart contents. We will do this in much the same way that we added the navigation widget—as an action whose output we will inject into the Razor layout.

To start, we need to add the simple method shown in Listing 9-5 to the CartController class.

Listing 9-5. Adding the Summary Method to the Cart Controller

```
...
public PartialViewResult Summary(Cart cart) {
    return PartialView(cart);
}
...
```

You can see that this is a very simple method. It just needs to render a view, supplying the current Cart (which will be obtained using our custom model binder) as view data. We need to create a partial view that will be rendered in response to the Summary method being called. Right-click the Summary method and select Add View from the pop-up menu. Set the name of the view to Summary, check the option for a strongly typed view, and set the model class to be Cart, as shown in Figure 9-2. We want a partial view because we are going to inject it into our overall page, so check the Create as a partial view option.

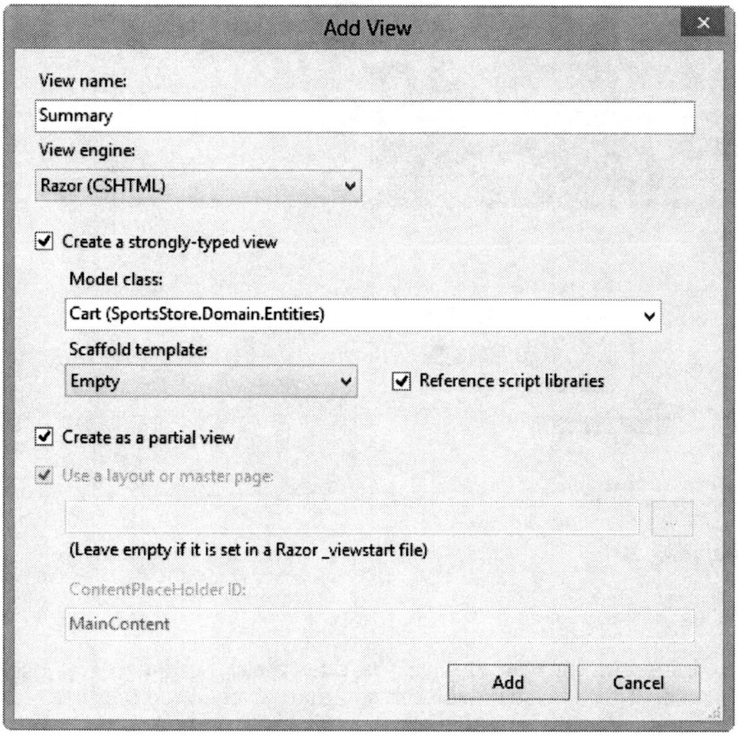

Figure 9-2. Adding the Summary view

Edit the new partial view so that it matches Listing 9-6.

Listing 9-6. The Summary Partial View

```
@model SportsStore.Domain.Entities.Cart

<div id="cart">
    <span class="caption">
        <b>Your cart:</b>
        @Model.Lines.Sum(x => x.Quantity) item(s),
        @Model.ComputeTotalValue().ToString("c")
    </span>

    @Html.ActionLink("Checkout", "Index", "Cart",
        new { returnUrl = Request.Url.PathAndQuery }, null)
</div>
```

This is a simple view that displays the number of items in the cart, the total cost of those items, and a link that shows the contents of the cart to the user. Now that we have defined the view that is returned by the Summary action method, we can include the rendered result in the _Layout.cshtml file, as shown in Listing 9-7.

Listing 9-7. Adding the Cart Summary Partial View to the Layout

```
<!DOCTYPE html>
<html>
<head>
    <meta charset="utf-8" />
    <meta name="viewport" content="width=device-width" />
    <title>@ViewBag.Title</title>
    <link href="~/Content/Site.css" type="text/css" rel="stylesheet" />
</head>
<body>
    <div id="header">
        @{Html.RenderAction("Summary", "Cart");}
        <div class="title">SPORTS STORE</div>
    </div>
    <div id="categories">
        @{ Html.RenderAction("Menu", "Nav"); }
    </div>
    <div id="content">
        @RenderBody()
    </div>
</body>
</html>
```

The last step is to add some additional CSS rules to format the elements in the partial view. Add the styles in Listing 9-8 to the `Site.css` file in the `SportsStore.WebUI` project.

Listing 9-8. Adding Styles to Site.css

```
...
DIV#cart { float:right; margin: .8em; color: Silver;
   background-color: #555; padding: .5em .5em .5em 1em; }
DIV#cart A { text-decoration: none; padding: .4em 1em .4em 1em; line-height:2.1em;
   margin-left: .5em; background-color: #333; color:White; border: 1px solid black;}
...
```

You can see the cart summary by running the application. The item count and total increase as you add items to the cart, as shown by Figure 9-3.

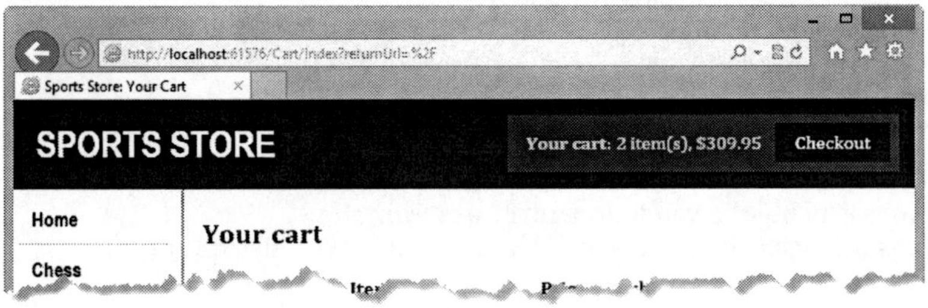

Figure 9-3. The cart summary widget

With this addition, we now let customers know what is in their cart and provide an obvious way to check out from the store. You can see, once again, how easy it is to use `RenderAction` to incorporate the rendered output from an action method in a Web page. This is a nice technique for breaking down the functionality of an application into distinct, reusable blocks.

Submitting Orders

We have now reached the final customer feature in SportsStore: the ability to check out and complete an order. In the following sections, we will extend our domain model to provide support for capturing the shipping details from a user and add a feature to process those details.

Extending the Domain Model

Add a class called ShippingDetails to the Entities folder of the SportsStore.Domain project. This is the class we will use to represent the shipping details for a customer. The contents are shown in Listing 9-9.

Listing 9-9. The ShippingDetails Class

```
using System.ComponentModel.DataAnnotations;

namespace SportsStore.Domain.Entities {

    public class ShippingDetails {
        [Required(ErrorMessage = "Please enter a name")]
        public string Name { get; set; }

        [Required(ErrorMessage = "Please enter the first address line")]
        public string Line1 { get; set; }
        public string Line2 { get; set; }
        public string Line3 { get; set; }

        [Required(ErrorMessage = "Please enter a city name")]
        public string City { get; set; }

        [Required(ErrorMessage = "Please enter a state name")]
        public string State { get; set; }

        public string Zip { get; set; }

        [Required(ErrorMessage = "Please enter a country name")]
        public string Country { get; set; }

        public bool GiftWrap { get; set; }
    }
}
```

You can see from Listing 9-9 that we are using the validation attributes from the System.ComponentModel.DataAnnotations namespace, just as we did in Chapter 2. We will explore validation further in Chapter 23.

■ **Note** The ShippingDetails class does not have any functionality, so there is nothing that we can sensibly unit test.

Adding the Checkout Process

Our goal is to reach the point where users are able to enter their shipping details and submit their order. To start this off, we need to add a Checkout now button to the cart summary view. Listing 9-10 shows the change we need to apply to the `Views/Cart/Index.cshtml` file.

Listing 9-10. Adding the Checkout Now Button

```
...
</table>
<p align="center" class="actionButtons">
    <a href="@Model.ReturnUrl">Continue shopping</a>
    @Html.ActionLink("Checkout now", "Checkout")
</p>
...
```

This single change generates a link that, when clicked, calls the Checkout action method of the Cart controller. You can see how this button appears in Figure 9-4.

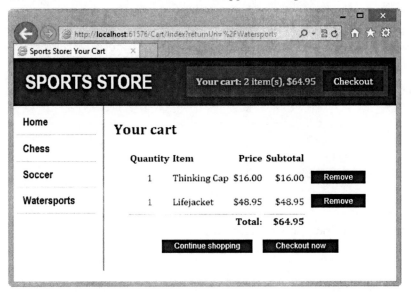

Figure 9-4. The Checkout Now button

As you might expect, we now need to define the Checkout method in the CartController class, as shown in Listing 9-11.

Listing 9-11. The Checkout Action Method

```
...
public ViewResult Checkout() {
    return View(new ShippingDetails());
}
...
```

The `Checkout` method returns the default view and passes a new `ShippingDetails` object as the view model. To create the corresponding view, right-click the `Checkout` method, select **Add View**, and fill in the dialog box as shown in Figure 9-5. We are going to use the `ShippingDetails` domain class as the basis for the strongly typed view. Check the option to use a layout, because we are rendering a full page and want it to be consistent with the rest of the application.

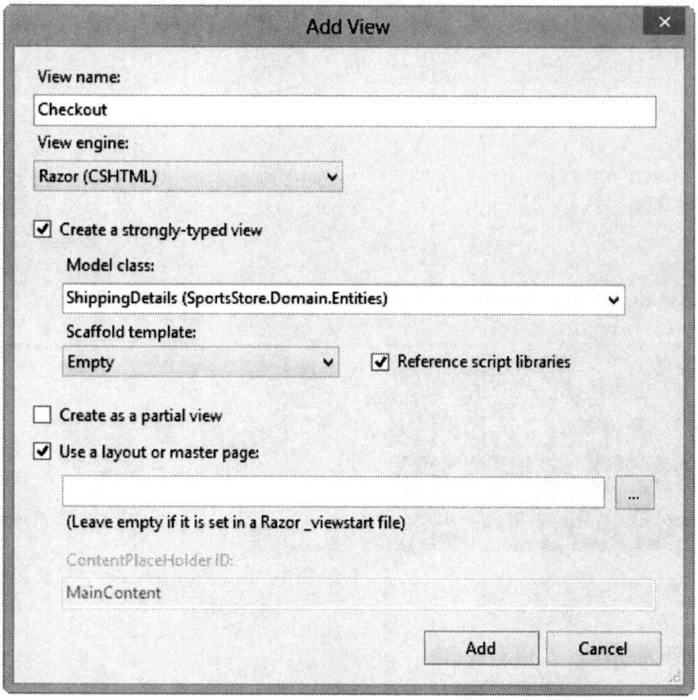

Figure 9-5. Adding the Checkout view

Set the contents of the view to match the markup shown in Listing 9-12.

Listing 9-12. The Checkout.cshtml View

```
@model SportsStore.Domain.Entities.ShippingDetails

@{
    ViewBag.Title = "SportStore: Checkout";
}

<h2>Check out now</h2>
Please enter your details, and we'll ship your goods right away!
@using (Html.BeginForm()) {
    <h3>Ship to</h3>
    <div>Name: @Html.EditorFor(x => x.Name)</div>

    <h3>Address</h3>
    <div>Line 1: @Html.EditorFor(x => x.Line1)</div>
    <div>Line 2: @Html.EditorFor(x => x.Line2)</div>
```

```
<div>Line 3: @Html.EditorFor(x => x.Line3)</div>
<div>City: @Html.EditorFor(x => x.City)</div>
<div>State: @Html.EditorFor(x => x.State)</div>
<div>Zip: @Html.EditorFor(x => x.Zip)</div>
<div>Country: @Html.EditorFor(x => x.Country)</div>

<h3>Options</h3>
<label>
    @Html.EditorFor(x => x.GiftWrap)
    Gift wrap these items
</label>

<p align="center">
    <input class="actionButtons" type="submit" value="Complete order" />
</p>
}
```

You can see how this view is rendered by running the application, adding an item to the shopping cart, and clicking the Checkout now button. As you can see in Figure 9-6, the view is rendered as a form for collecting the customer's shipping details.

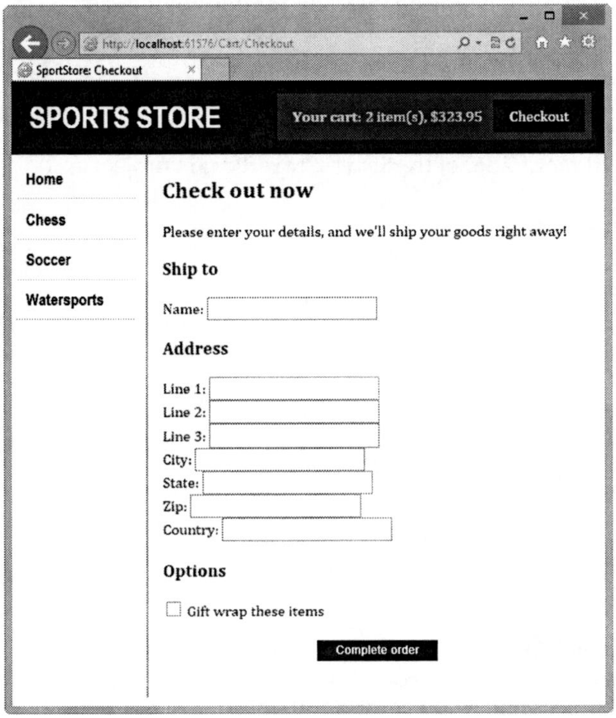

Figure 9-6. The shipping details form

We have rendered the input elements for each of the form fields using the Html.EditorFor helper method. This is an example of a *templated helper method*. We let the MVC Framework work out what kind

243

of input element a view model property requires, instead of specifying it explicitly (by using Html.TextBoxFor, for example).

We will explain templated helper methods in detail in Chapter 20, but you can see from the figure that the MVC Framework is smart enough to render a checkbox for bool properties (such as the gift wrap option) and text boxes for the string properties.

■ **Tip** We could go further and replace most of the markup in the view with a single call to the Html.EditorForModel helper method, which would generate the labels and inputs for all the properties in the ShippingDetails view model class. However, we wanted to separate the elements so that the name, address, and options appear in different regions of the form, so it is simple to refer to each property directly.

Implementing the Order Processor

We need a component in our application to which we can hand details of an order for processing. In keeping with the principles of the MVC model, we are going to define an interface for this functionality, write an implementation of the interface, and then associate the two using our DI container, Ninject.

Defining the Interface

Add a new interface called IOrderProcessor to the Abstract folder of the SportsStore.Domain project and edit the contents so that they match Listing 9-13.

Listing 9-13. The IOrderProcessor Interface

```
using SportsStore.Domain.Entities;

namespace SportsStore.Domain.Abstract {

    public interface IOrderProcessor {

        void ProcessOrder(Cart cart, ShippingDetails shippingDetails);
    }
}
```

Implementing the Interface

Our implementation of IOrderProcessor is going to deal with orders by e-mailing them to the site administrator. We are simplifying the sales process, of course. Most e-commerce sites would not simply e-mail an order, and we have not provided support for processing credit cards or other forms of payment. But we want to keep things focused on MVC, and so e-mail it is.

Create a new class called EmailOrderProcessor in the Concrete folder of the SportsStore.Domain project and edit the contents so that they match Listing 9-14. This class uses the built-in SMTP support included in the .NET Framework library to send an e-mail.

Listing 9-14. The EmailOrderProcessor Class

```
using System.Net.Mail;
using System.Text;
using SportsStore.Domain.Abstract;
using SportsStore.Domain.Entities;
using System.Net;

namespace SportsStore.Domain.Concrete {

    public class EmailSettings {
        public string MailToAddress = "orders@example.com";
        public string MailFromAddress = "sportsstore@example.com";
        public bool UseSsl = true;
        public string Username = "MySmtpUsername";
        public string Password = "MySmtpPassword";
        public string ServerName = "smtp.example.com";
        public int ServerPort = 587;
        public bool WriteAsFile = false;
        public string FileLocation = @"c:\sports_store_emails";
    }

    public class EmailOrderProcessor :IOrderProcessor {
        private EmailSettings emailSettings;

        public EmailOrderProcessor(EmailSettings settings) {
            emailSettings = settings;
        }

        public void ProcessOrder(Cart cart, ShippingDetails shippingInfo) {

            using (var smtpClient = new SmtpClient()) {

                smtpClient.EnableSsl = emailSettings.UseSsl;
                smtpClient.Host = emailSettings.ServerName;
                smtpClient.Port = emailSettings.ServerPort;
                smtpClient.UseDefaultCredentials = false;
                smtpClient.Credentials
                    = new NetworkCredential(emailSettings.Username,
                        emailSettings.Password);

                if (emailSettings.WriteAsFile) {
                    smtpClient.DeliveryMethod
                        = SmtpDeliveryMethod.SpecifiedPickupDirectory;
                    smtpClient.PickupDirectoryLocation = emailSettings.FileLocation;
                    smtpClient.EnableSsl = false;
                }

                StringBuilder body = new StringBuilder()
                    .AppendLine("A new order has been submitted")
                    .AppendLine("---")
                    .AppendLine("Items:");

                foreach (var line in cart.Lines) {
```

```
                    var subtotal = line.Product.Price * line.Quantity;
                    body.AppendFormat("{0} x {1} (subtotal: {2:c}", line.Quantity,
                                        line.Product.Name,
                                        subtotal);
                }

            body.AppendFormat("Total order value: {0:c}", cart.ComputeTotalValue())
                .AppendLine("---")
                .AppendLine("Ship to:")
                .AppendLine(shippingInfo.Name)
                .AppendLine(shippingInfo.Line1)
                .AppendLine(shippingInfo.Line2 ?? "")
                .AppendLine(shippingInfo.Line3 ?? "")
                .AppendLine(shippingInfo.City)
                .AppendLine(shippingInfo.State ?? "")
                .AppendLine(shippingInfo.Country)
                .AppendLine(shippingInfo.Zip)
                .AppendLine("---")
                .AppendFormat("Gift wrap: {0}",
                    shippingInfo.GiftWrap ? "Yes" : "No");

            MailMessage mailMessage = new MailMessage(
                            emailSettings.MailFromAddress,    // From
                            emailSettings.MailToAddress,      // To
                            "New order submitted!",           // Subject
                            body.ToString());                 // Body

            if (emailSettings.WriteAsFile) {
                mailMessage.BodyEncoding = Encoding.ASCII;
            }

            smtpClient.Send(mailMessage);
        }
    }
  }
}
```

To make things simpler, we have defined the EmailSettings class in Listing 9-14 as well. An instance of this class is demanded by the EmailOrderProcessor constructor and contains all the settings that are required to configure the .NET e-mail classes.

■ **Tip**   Do not worry if you do not have an SMTP server available. If you set the EmailSettings.WriteAsFile property to true, the e-mail messages will be written as files to the directory specified by the FileLocation property. This directory must exist and be writable. The files will be written with the .eml extension, but they can be read with any text editor.

Registering the Implementation

Now that we have an implementation of the IOrderProcessor interface and the means to configure it, we can use Ninject to create instances of it. Edit the NinjectControllerFactory class in the SportsStore.WebUI project and make the changes shown in Listing 9-15 to the AddBindings method.

Listing 9-15. Adding Ninject Bindings for IOrderProcessor

```
using System;
using System.Web.Mvc;
using System.Web.Routing;
using Ninject;
using SportsStore.Domain.Entities;
using SportsStore.Domain.Abstract;
using System.Collections.Generic;
using System.Linq;
using Moq;
using SportsStore.Domain.Concrete;
using System.Configuration;

namespace SportsStore.WebUI.Infrastructure {

    public class NinjectControllerFactory : DefaultControllerFactory {
        private IKernel ninjectKernel;

        public NinjectControllerFactory() {
            ninjectKernel = new StandardKernel();
            AddBindings();
        }

        protected override IController GetControllerInstance(RequestContext
            requestContext, Type controllerType) {

            return controllerType == null
                ? null
                : (IController)ninjectKernel.Get(controllerType);
        }

        private void AddBindings() {
            ninjectKernel.Bind<IProductRepository>().To<EFProductRepository>();

            EmailSettings emailSettings = new EmailSettings {
                WriteAsFile = bool.Parse(ConfigurationManager
                    .AppSettings["Email.WriteAsFile"] ?? "false")
            };

            ninjectKernel.Bind<IOrderProcessor>()
                .To<EmailOrderProcessor>()
                .WithConstructorArgument("settings", emailSettings);
        }
    }
}
```

We created an EmailSettings object, which we use with the Ninject WithConstructorArgument method so that we can inject it into the EmailOrderProcessor constructor when new instances are created to service requests for the IOrderProcessor interface. In Listing 9-15, we specified a value for only one of the EmailSettings properties: WriteAsFile. We read the value of this property using the ConfigurationManager.AppSettings property, which allows us to access application settings we have placed in the Web.config file (the one in the root project folder), which are shown in Listing 9-16.

Listing 9-16. Application Settings in the Web.config File

```
...
<appSettings>
  <add key="webpages:Version" value="2.0.0.0" />
  <add key="webpages:Enabled" value="false" />
  <add key="PreserveLoginUrl" value="true" />
  <add key="ClientValidationEnabled" value="true" />
  <add key="UnobtrusiveJavaScriptEnabled" value="true" />
  <add key="Email.WriteAsFile" value="true"/>
</appSettings>
...
```

Completing the Cart Controller

To complete the CartController class, we need to modify the constructor so that it demands an implementation of the IOrderProcessor interface and add a new action method that will handle the HTTP form POST when the user clicks the Complete order button. Listing 9-17 shows both changes.

Listing 9-17. Completing the CartController Class

```
using SportsStore.Domain.Abstract;
using SportsStore.Domain.Entities;
using SportsStore.WebUI.Models;
using System;
using System.Collections.Generic;
using System.Linq;
using System.Web;
using System.Web.Mvc;

namespace SportsStore.WebUI.Controllers {

    public class CartController : Controller {
        private IProductRepository repository;
        private IOrderProcessor orderProcessor;

        public CartController(IProductRepository repo, IOrderProcessor proc) {
            repository = repo;
            orderProcessor = proc;
        }

        public ViewResult Index(Cart cart, string returnUrl) {
            return View(new CartIndexViewModel {
                Cart = cart,
                ReturnUrl = returnUrl
            });
```

```
        }

        public ViewResult Summary(Cart cart) {
            return View(cart);
        }

        [HttpPost]
        public ViewResult Checkout(Cart cart, ShippingDetails shippingDetails) {
            if (cart.Lines.Count() == 0) {
                ModelState.AddModelError("", "Sorry, your cart is empty!");
            }

            if (ModelState.IsValid) {
                orderProcessor.ProcessOrder(cart, shippingDetails);
                cart.Clear();
                return View("Completed");
            } else {
                return View(shippingDetails);
            }
        }

        public ViewResult Checkout() {
            return View(new ShippingDetails());
        }

        // ...other action methods omitted for brevity...
    }
}
```

You can see that the Checkout action method we have added is decorated with the HttpPost attribute, which means that it will be invoked for a POST request—in this case, when the user submits the form. Once again, we are relying on the model binder system, both for the ShippingDetails parameter (which is created automatically using the HTTP form data) and the Cart parameter (which is created using our custom binder).

▓ **Note** The change in constructor forces us to update the unit tests we created for the CartController class. Passing null for the new constructor parameter will let the unit tests compile.

The MVC Framework checks the validation constraints that we applied to ShippingDetails using the data annotation attributes in Listing 9-17, and any violations are passed to our action method through the ModelState property. We can see if there are any problems by checking the ModelState.IsValid property. Notice that we call the ModelState.AddModelError method to register an error message if there are no items in the cart. We will explain how to display such errors shortly, and we will have much more to say about model binding and validation in Chapters 22 and 23.

UNIT TEST: ORDER PROCESSING

To complete the unit testing for the CartController class, we need to test the behavior of the new overloaded version of the Checkout method. Although the method looks short and simple, the use of MVC Framework model binding means that there is a lot going on behind the scenes that needs to be tested.

We should process an order only if there are items in the cart *and* the customer has provided us with valid shipping details. Under all other circumstances, the customer should be shown an error. Here is the first test method:

```
...
[TestMethod]
public void Cannot_Checkout_Empty_Cart() {

    // Arrange - create a mock order processor
    Mock<IOrderProcessor> mock = new Mock<IOrderProcessor>();
    // Arrange - create an empty cart
    Cart cart = new Cart();
    // Arrange - create shipping details
    ShippingDetails shippingDetails = new ShippingDetails();
    // Arrange - create an instance of the controller
    CartController target = new CartController(null, mock.Object);

    // Act
    ViewResult result = target.Checkout(cart, shippingDetails);

    // Assert - check that the order hasn't been passed on to the processor
    mock.Verify(m => m.ProcessOrder(It.IsAny<Cart>(), It.IsAny<ShippingDetails>()),
        Times.Never());
    // Assert - check that the method is returning the default view
    Assert.AreEqual("", result.ViewName);
    // Assert - check that we are passing an invalid model to the view
    Assert.AreEqual(false, result.ViewData.ModelState.IsValid);
}
...
```

This test ensures that we cannot check out with an empty cart. We check this by ensuring that the ProcessOrder of the mock IOrderProcessor implementation is never called, that the view that the method returns is the default view (which will redisplay the data entered by customers and give them a chance to correct it), and that the model state being passed to the view has been marked as invalid. This may seem like a belt-and-braces set of assertions, but we need all three to be sure that we have the right behavior. The next test method works in much the same way, but injects an error into the view model to simulate a problem reported by the model binder (which would happen in production when the customer enters invalid shipping data):

```
...
[TestMethod]
public void Cannot_Checkout_Invalid_ShippingDetails() {

    // Arrange - create a mock order processor
```

```
        Mock<IOrderProcessor> mock = new Mock<IOrderProcessor>();
        // Arrange - create a cart with an item
        Cart cart = new Cart();
        cart.AddItem(new Product(), 1);

        // Arrange - create an instance of the controller
        CartController target = new CartController(null, mock.Object);
        // Arrange - add an error to the model
        target.ModelState.AddModelError("error", "error");

        // Act - try to checkout
        ViewResult result = target.Checkout(cart, new ShippingDetails());

        // Assert - check that the order hasn't been passed on to the processor
        mock.Verify(m => m.ProcessOrder(It.IsAny<Cart>(), It.IsAny<ShippingDetails>()),
            Times.Never());
        // Assert - check that the method is returning the default view
        Assert.AreEqual("", result.ViewName);
        // Assert - check that we are passing an invalid model to the view
        Assert.AreEqual(false, result.ViewData.ModelState.IsValid);
}
...
```

Having established that an empty cart or invalid details will prevent an order from being processed, we need to ensure that we do process orders when appropriate. Here is the test:

```
...
[TestMethod]
public void Can_Checkout_And_Submit_Order() {
    // Arrange - create a mock order processor
    Mock<IOrderProcessor> mock = new Mock<IOrderProcessor>();
    // Arrange - create a cart with an item
    Cart cart = new Cart();
    cart.AddItem(new Product(), 1);
    // Arrange - create an instance of the controller
    CartController target = new CartController(null, mock.Object);

    // Act - try to checkout
    ViewResult result = target.Checkout(cart, new ShippingDetails());

    // Assert - check that the order has been passed on to the processor
    mock.Verify(m => m.ProcessOrder(It.IsAny<Cart>(), It.IsAny<ShippingDetails>()),
        Times.Once());
    // Assert - check that the method is returning the Completed view
    Assert.AreEqual("Completed", result.ViewName);
    // Assert - check that we are passing a valid model to the view
    Assert.AreEqual(true, result.ViewData.ModelState.IsValid);
}
...
```

Notice that we did not need to test that we can identify valid shipping details. This is handled for us automatically by the model binder using the attributes we applied to the properties of the ShippingDetails class.

Displaying Validation Errors

If users enter invalid shipping information, the individual form fields that contain the problems will be highlighted, but no message will be displayed. Worse, if users try to check out an empty cart, we do not let them complete the order, but they will not see any error message at all. To address this, we need to add a validation summary to the view, much as we did back in Chapter 2. Listing 9-18 shows the addition to Checkout.cshtml view.

Listing 9-18. Adding a Validation Summary

```
...
<h2>Check out now</h2>
Please enter your details, and we'll ship your goods right away!
@using (Html.BeginForm()) {

    @Html.ValidationSummary()

    <h3>Ship to</h3>
    <div>Name: @Html.EditorFor(x => x.Name)</div>
...
```

Now when customers provide invalid shipping data or try to check out an empty cart, they are shown useful error messages, as shown in Figure 9-7.

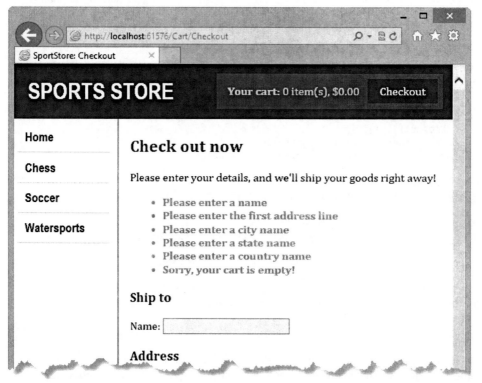

Figure 9-7. Displaying validation messages

Displaying a Summary Page

To complete the checkout process, we will show customers a page that confirms the order has been processed and thanks them for their business. Right-click any of the action methods in the **CartController** class and select **Add View** from the pop-up menu. Set the name of the view to **Completed**, as shown in Figure 9-8.

Figure 9-8. Creating the Completed view

We do not want this view to be strongly typed because we are not going to pass any view models between the controller and the view. We do want to use a layout, so that the summary page will be consistent with the rest of the application. Click the **Add** button to create the view and edit the content so that it matches Listing 9-19.

Listing 9-19. The Completed.cshtml View

```
@{
    ViewBag.Title = "SportsStore: Order Submitted";
}

<h2>Thanks!</h2>
Thanks for placing your order. We'll ship your goods as soon as possible.
```

Now customers can go through the entire process, from selecting products to checking out. If they provide valid shipping details (and have items in their cart), they will see the summary page when they click the `Complete order` button, as shown in Figure 9-9.

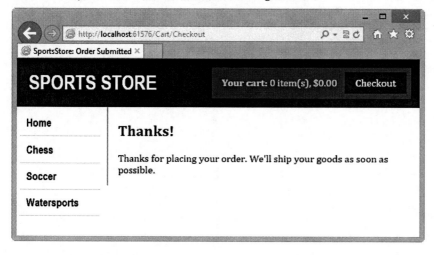

Figure 9-9. The thank-you page

Summary

We have completed all the major parts of the customer-facing portion of SportsStore. It might not be enough to worry Amazon, but we have a product catalog that can be browsed by category and page, a neat shopping cart, and a simple checkout process.

The well-separated architecture means we can easily change the behavior of any piece of the application without worrying about causing problems or inconsistencies elsewhere. For example, we could process orders by storing them in a database, and it would not have any impact on the shopping cart, the product catalog, or any other area of the application.

In the next chapter, we will complete the SportsStore application by adding the administration features, which will let us manage the product catalog and upload, store, and display images for each product.

■ ■ ■

CHAPTER 10

SportsStore: Administration

In this chapter, we continue to build the SportsStore application in order to give the site administrator a way of managing the product catalog. We will add support for creating, editing, and removing items from the product repository, as well as for uploading and displaying images alongside products in the catalog.

Adding Catalog Management

The convention for managing collections of items is to present the user with two types of pages: a *list* page and an *edit* page, as shown in Figure 10-1.

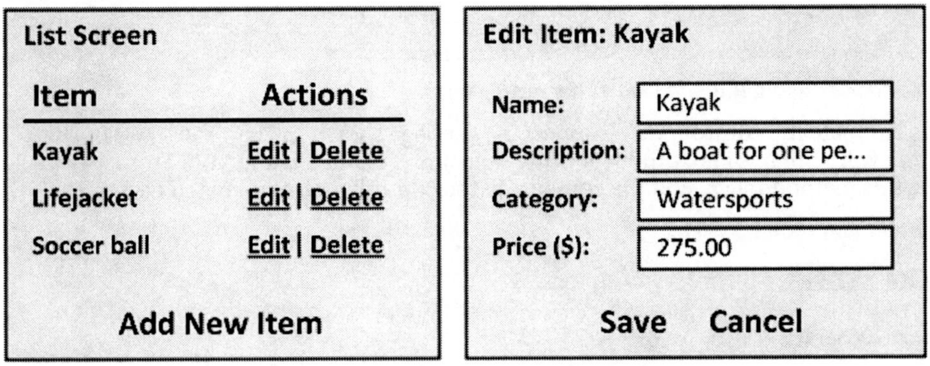

List Screen

Item	Actions
Kayak	Edit | Delete
Lifejacket	Edit | Delete
Soccer ball	Edit | Delete

Add New Item

Edit Item: Kayak

Name:	Kayak
Description:	A boat for one pe...
Category:	Watersports
Price ($):	275.00

Save   Cancel

Figure 10-1. Sketch of a CRUD UI for the product catalog

Together, these pages allow a user to create, read, update, and delete items in the collection. Collectively, these actions are known as *CRUD*. Developers need to implement CRUD so often that Visual Studio tries to help by offering to generate MVC controllers that have action methods for CRUD operations and view templates that support them.

Creating a CRUD Controller

We will create a new controller to handle our administration functions. Right-click the `Controllers` folder of the `SportsStore.WebUI` project and select `Add ➤ Controller` from the pop-up menu. Set the name of the controller to `AdminController` and ensure that `Empty MVC Controller` is selected from the `Template` drop-down list, as shown in Figure 10-2.

■ **Tip** Visual Studio has some templates for controller classes that include CRUD methods. As we mentioned, we do not like these templates and prefer to build our controller classes from the ground up.

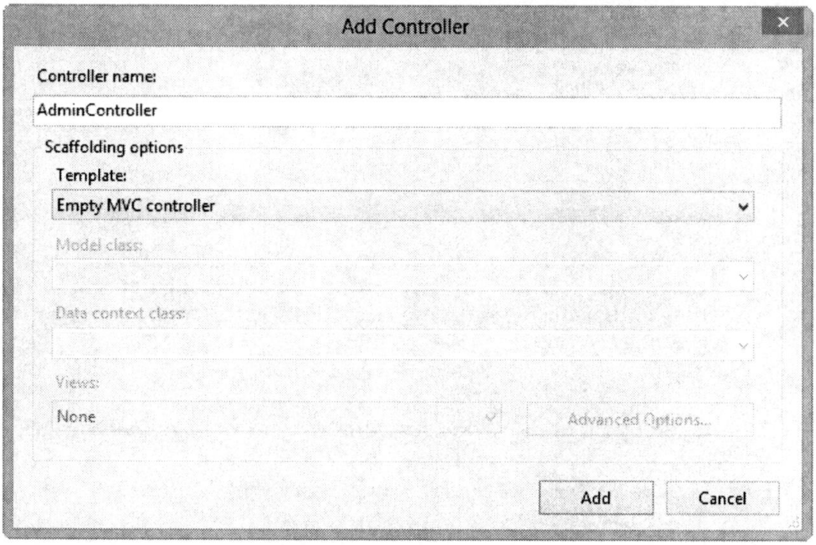

Figure 10-2. Creating a controller using the Add Controller dialog box

Click the **Add** button to create the controller. To support the list page shown in Figure 10-1, we need to add an action method that will display all the products in the repository. Following the MVC Framework conventions, we will call this method **Index**. Edit the contents of the controller class to match Listing 10-1.

Listing 10-1. The Index Action Method

```
using SportsStore.Domain.Abstract;
using System;
using System.Collections.Generic;
using System.Linq;
using System.Web;
using System.Web.Mvc;

namespace SportsStore.WebUI.Controllers {

    public class AdminController : Controller {
        private IProductRepository repository;

        public AdminController(IProductRepository repo) {
            repository = repo;
        }

        public ViewResult Index() {
            return View(repository.Products);
        }
    }
}
```

UNIT TEST: THE INDEX ACTION

The behavior that we care about for the Index method is that it correctly returns the Product objects that are in the repository. We can test this by creating a mock repository implementation and comparing the test data with the data returned by the action method. Here is the unit test, which we placed into a new unit test file called AdminTests.cs:

```
using Microsoft.VisualStudio.TestTools.UnitTesting;
using Moq;
using SportsStore.Domain.Abstract;
using SportsStore.Domain.Entities;
using SportsStore.WebUI.Controllers;
using System;
using System.Collections.Generic;
using System.Linq;
using System.Web.Mvc;

namespace SportsStore.UnitTests {
    [TestClass]
    public class AdminTests {

        [TestMethod]
        public void Index_Contains_All_Products() {
            // Arrange - create the mock repository
            Mock<IProductRepository> mock = new Mock<IProductRepository>();
            mock.Setup(m => m.Products).Returns(new Product[] {
                new Product {ProductID = 1, Name = "P1"},
                new Product {ProductID = 2, Name = "P2"},
                new Product {ProductID = 3, Name = "P3"},
            }.AsQueryable());

            // Arrange - create a controller
            AdminController target = new AdminController(mock.Object);


            // Action
            Product[] result = ((IEnumerable<Product>)target.Index().
                ViewData.Model).ToArray();

            // Assert
            Assert.AreEqual(result.Length, 3);
            Assert.AreEqual("P1", result[0].Name);
            Assert.AreEqual("P2", result[1].Name);
            Assert.AreEqual("P3", result[2].Name);
        }
    }
}
```

Creating a New Layout

We are going to create a new layout to use with the SportsStore administration views. It will be a simple layout that provides a single point where we can apply changes to all the administration views.

To create the layout, right-click the `Views/Shared` folder in the `SportsStore.WebUI` project and select **Add ➤ New Item**. Select the `MVC 4 Layout Page (Razor)` template and set the name to `_AdminLayout.cshtml`, as shown in Figure 10-3. Click the **Add** button to create the new file.

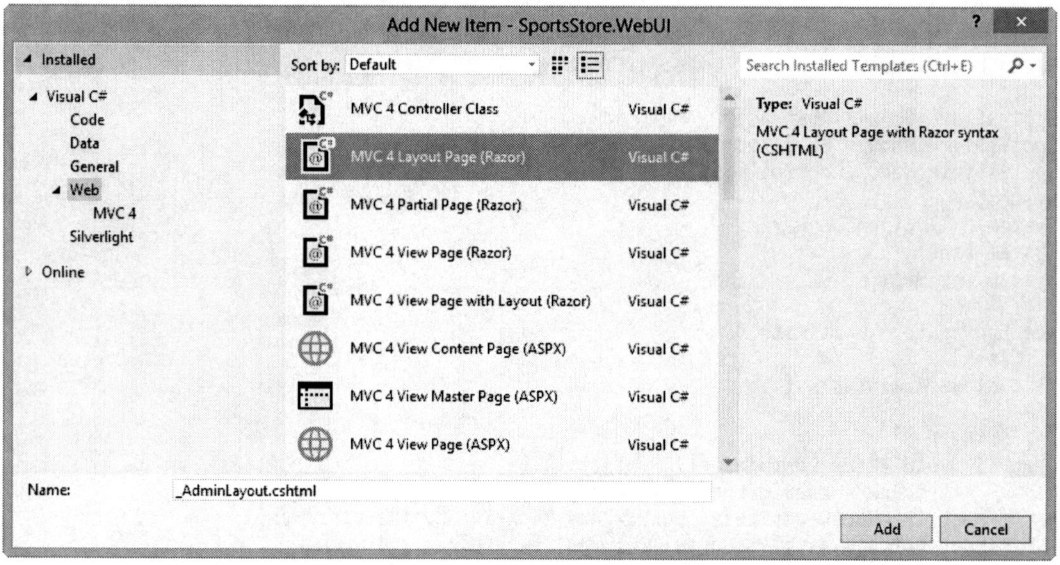

Figure 10-3. Creating a new Razor layout

As we explained previously, the convention is to start the layout name with an underscore (_). Razor is also used by another Microsoft technology called WebMatrix, which uses the underscore to prevent layout pages from being served to browsers. MVC does not need this protection, but the convention for naming layouts is carried over to MVC applications anyway.

We want to create a reference to a CSS file in the layout, as shown in Listing 10-2.

Listing 10-2. The _AdminLayout.cshtml File

```
<!DOCTYPE html>

<html>
<head>
    <meta name="viewport" content="width=device-width" />
    <link href="~/Content/Admin.css" rel="stylesheet" type="text/css" />
    <title></title>
</head>
<body>
    <div>
        @RenderBody()
    </div>
</body>
</html>
```

The addition (shown in bold) is a reference to a CSS file called `Admin.css` in the `Content` folder. To create the `Admin.css` file, right-click the `Content` folder, select `Add` ➤ `New` Item, select the `Style Sheet` template, and set the name to `Admin.css`, as shown in Figure 10-4.

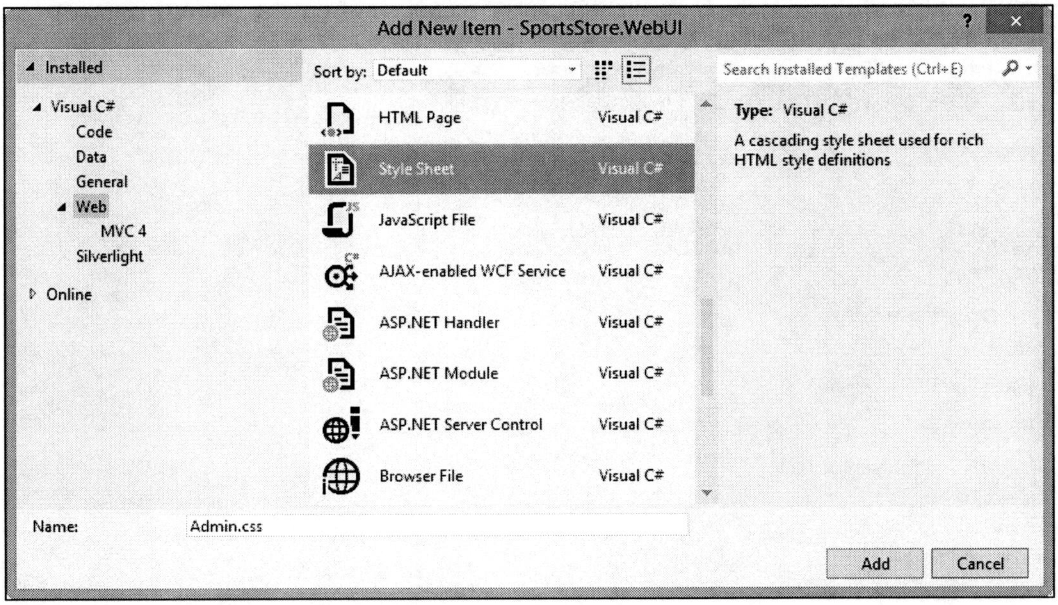

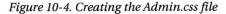

Figure 10-4. Creating the Admin.css file

Replace the contents of the `Admin.css` file with the styles shown in Listing 10-3.

Listing 10-3. The CSS Styles for the Admin Views

```
...
BODY, TD { font-family: Segoe UI, Verdana }
H1 { padding: .5em; padding-top: 0; font-weight: bold;
     font-size: 1.5em; border-bottom: 2px solid gray; }
DIV#content { padding: .9em; }
TABLE.Grid TD, TABLE.Grid TH { border-bottom: 1px dotted gray; text-align:left; }
TABLE.Grid { border-collapse: collapse; width:100%; }
TABLE.Grid TH.NumericCol, Table.Grid TD.NumericCol {
    text-align: right; padding-right: 1em; }
FORM {margin-bottom: 0px;    }
DIV.Message { background: gray; color:White; padding: .2em; margin-top:.25em; }

.field-validation-error { color: red; display: block; }
.field-validation-valid { display: none; }
.input-validation-error { border: 1px solid red; background-color: #ffeeee; }
.validation-summary-errors { font-weight: bold; color: red; }
.validation-summary-valid { display: none; }
...
```

Implementing the List View

Now that we have created the new layout, we can add a view to the project for the Index action method of the Admin controller. Right-click inside the Index method and select Add View from the pop-up menu. Set the name of the view to Index, as shown in Figure 10-5.

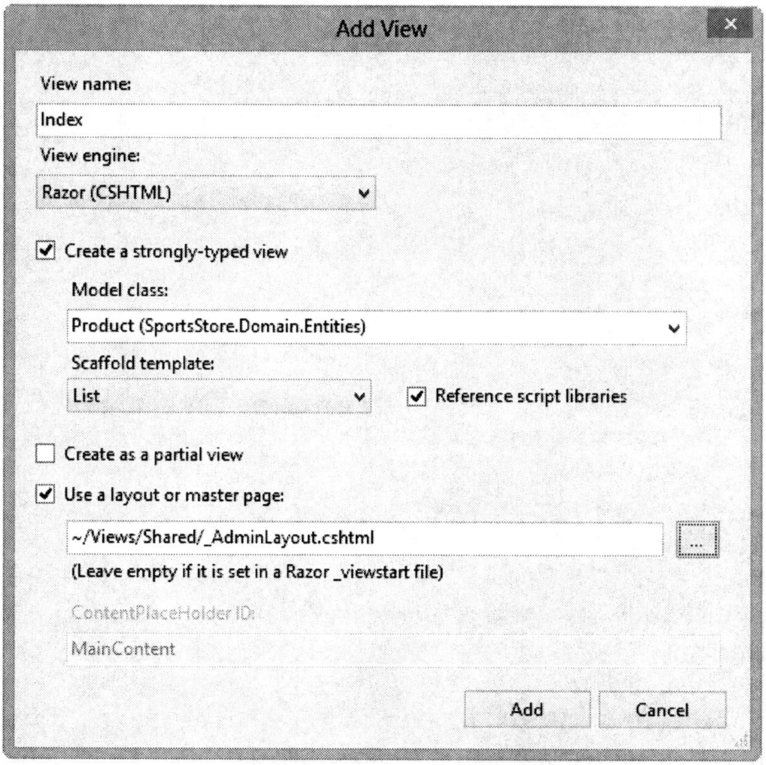

Figure 10-5. Creating the Index view

We are going to use a *scaffold view*, which is where Visual Studio looks at the class we select for a strongly-typed view and creates a view containing markup tailored for that model type. To do this, select Product from the list of model classes and List for the scaffold template, as shown in Figure 10-5.

▨ **Note** When using the List scaffold, Visual Studio assumes you are working with an IEnumerable sequence of the model view type, so you can just select the singular form of the class from the list.

We want to apply our newly created layout, so check the option to use a layout for the view and select the _AdminLayout.cshtml file from the Views/Shared folder. Click the Add button to create the view. The scaffold view that Visual Studio creates is shown in Listing 10-4 (which we have tidied up slightly to make it more compact and readable on the page).

Listing 10-4. The Scaffold for List Views

```
@model IEnumerable<SportsStore.Domain.Entities.Product>

@{
    ViewBag.Title = "Index";
    Layout = "~/Views/Shared/_AdminLayout.cshtml";
}
<h2>Index</h2>
<p>
    @Html.ActionLink("Create New", "Create")
</p>
<table>
    <tr>
        <th>@Html.DisplayNameFor(model => model.Name)</th>
        <th>@Html.DisplayNameFor(model => model.Description)</th>
        <th>@Html.DisplayNameFor(model => model.Price)</th>
        <th>@Html.DisplayNameFor(model => model.Category)</th>
        <th></th>
    </tr>

@foreach (var item in Model) {
    <tr>
        <td>@Html.DisplayFor(modelItem => item.Name)</td>
        <td>@Html.DisplayFor(modelItem => item.Description)</td>
        <td>@Html.DisplayFor(modelItem => item.Price)</td>
        <td>@Html.DisplayFor(modelItem => item.Category)</td>
        <td>
            @Html.ActionLink("Edit", "Edit", new { id=item.ProductID }) |
            @Html.ActionLink("Details", "Details", new { id=item.ProductID }) |
            @Html.ActionLink("Delete", "Delete", new { id=item.ProductID })
        </td>
    </tr>
}

</table>
```

Visual Studio looks at the type of view model object and generates elements in a table that correspond to the properties it defines. You can see how this view is rendered by starting the application and navigating to the /Admin/Index URL. Figure 10-6 shows the results.

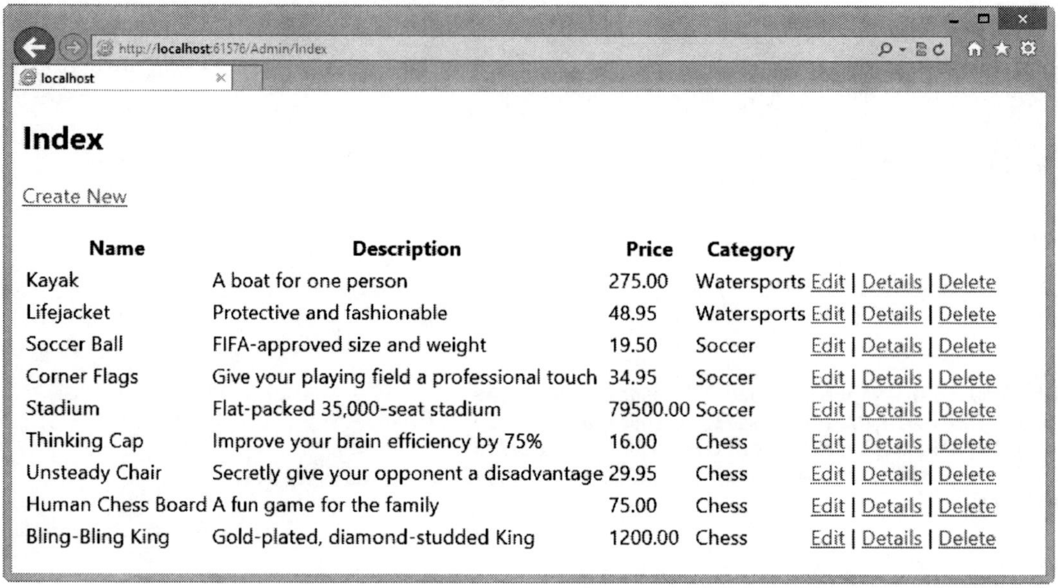

Figure 10-6. Rendering the scaffold List view

The scaffold view does a pretty good job of setting things up for us. We have columns for each of the properties in the Product class and links for other CRUD operations that refer to action methods in the same controller. That said, the markup is a little verbose. Also, we want something that ties in with the CSS we created earlier. Edit your Index.cshtml file to match Listing 10-5.

Listing 10-5. Modifying the Index.cshtml View

```
@model IEnumerable<SportsStore.Domain.Entities.Product>

@{
    ViewBag.Title = "Admin: All Products";
    Layout = "~/Views/Shared/_AdminLayout.cshtml";
}

<h1>All Products</h1>
<table class="Grid">
    <tr>
        <th>ID</th>
        <th>Name</th>
        <th class="NumericCol">Price</th>
        <th>Actions</th>
    </tr>
    @foreach (var item in Model) {
        <tr>
            <td>@item.ProductID</td>
            <td>@Html.ActionLink(item.Name, "Edit", new { item.ProductID })</td>
            <td class="NumericCol">@item.Price.ToString("c")</td>
            <td>
                @using (Html.BeginForm("Delete", "Admin")) {
                    @Html.Hidden("ProductID", item.ProductID)
```

```
                    <input type="submit" value="Delete"/>
                }
            </td>
        </tr>
    }
</table>
<p>@Html.ActionLink("Add a new product", "Create")</p>
```

This view presents the information in a more compact form, omitting some of the properties from the **Product** class and using a different approach to lay out the links to specific products. You can see how this view renders in Figure 10-7.

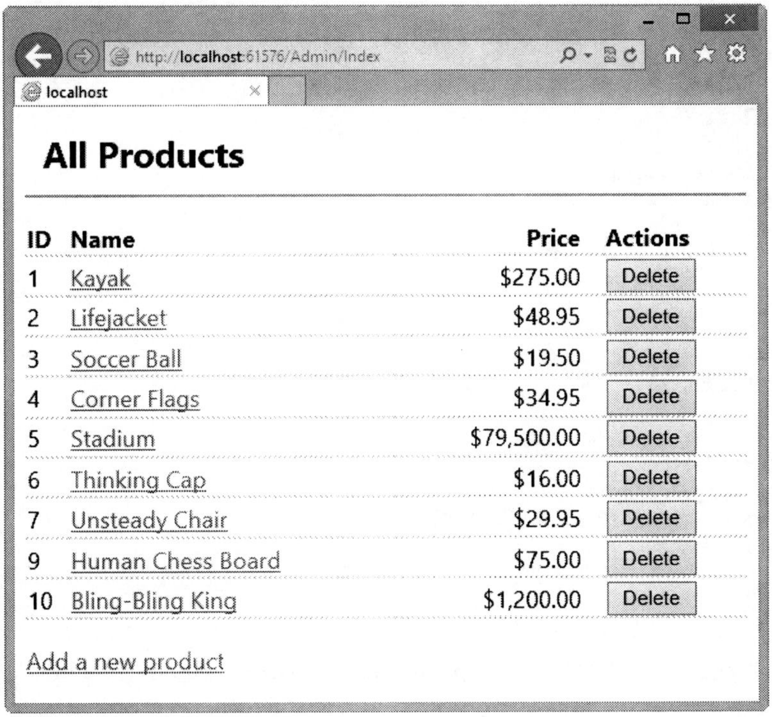

Figure 10-7. Rendering the modified Index view

Now we have a nice list page. The administrator can see the products in the catalog, and there are links or buttons to add, delete, and inspect items. In the following sections, we will add the functionality to support each of these actions.

Editing Products

To provide create and update features, we will add a product-editing page similar to the one shown in Figure 10-1. There are two parts to this job:

- Display a page that will allow the administrator to change values for the properties of a product.

- Add an action method that can process those changes when they are submitted.

Creating the Edit Action Method

Listing 10-6 shows the Edit method we have added to the AdminController class. This is the action method we specified in the calls to the Html.ActionLink helper method in the Index view.

Listing 10-6. The Edit Method

```
using SportsStore.Domain.Abstract;
using SportsStore.Domain.Entities;
using System;
using System.Collections.Generic;
using System.Linq;
using System.Web;
using System.Web.Mvc;

namespace SportsStore.WebUI.Controllers {

    public class AdminController : Controller {
        private IProductRepository repository;

        public AdminController(IProductRepository repo) {
            repository = repo;
        }

        public ViewResult Index() {
            return View(repository.Products);
        }

        public ViewResult Edit(int productId) {
            Product product = repository.Products
                .FirstOrDefault(p => p.ProductID == productId);
            return View(product);
        }
    }
}
```

This simple method finds the product with the ID that corresponds to the productId parameter and passes it as a view model object.

UNIT TEST: THE EDIT ACTION METHOD

We want to test for two behaviors in the Edit action method. The first is that we get the product we ask for when we provide a valid ID value. Obviously, we want to make sure that we are editing the product we expected. The second behavior is that we do not get any product at all when we request an ID value that is not in the repository. Here are the test methods we added to the AdminTests.cs unit test file:

```
...
[TestMethod]
public void Can_Edit_Product() {

    // Arrange - create the mock repository
```

```
    Mock<IProductRepository> mock = new Mock<IProductRepository>();
    mock.Setup(m => m.Products).Returns(new Product[] {
        new Product {ProductID = 1, Name = "P1"},
        new Product {ProductID = 2, Name = "P2"},
        new Product {ProductID = 3, Name = "P3"},
    }.AsQueryable());

    // Arrange - create the controller
    AdminController target = new AdminController(mock.Object);

    // Act
    Product p1 = target.Edit(1).ViewData.Model as Product;
    Product p2 = target.Edit(2).ViewData.Model as Product;
    Product p3 = target.Edit(3).ViewData.Model as Product;

    // Assert
    Assert.AreEqual(1, p1.ProductID);
    Assert.AreEqual(2, p2.ProductID);
    Assert.AreEqual(3, p3.ProductID);
}

[TestMethod]
public void Cannot_Edit_Nonexistent_Product() {

    // Arrange - create the mock repository
    Mock<IProductRepository> mock = new Mock<IProductRepository>();
    mock.Setup(m => m.Products).Returns(new Product[] {
        new Product {ProductID = 1, Name = "P1"},
        new Product {ProductID = 2, Name = "P2"},
        new Product {ProductID = 3, Name = "P3"},
    }.AsQueryable());

    // Arrange - create the controller
    AdminController target = new AdminController(mock.Object);

    // Act
    Product result = (Product)target.Edit(4).ViewData.Model;

    // Assert
    Assert.IsNull(result);
}
...
```

Creating the Edit View

Now that we have an action method, we can create a view for it to render. Right-click in the Edit action method, and then select Add View. Leave the view name as Edit, check the option for a strongly typed view, and ensure that the Product class is selected as the model class, as shown in Figure 10-8.

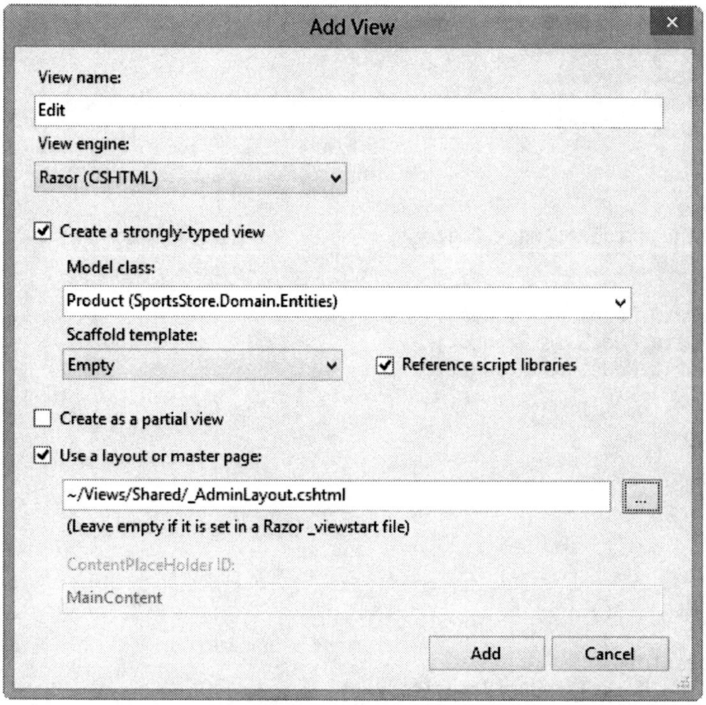

Figure 10-8. Creating the Edit view

There is a scaffold view for the Edit CRUD operation, which you can select if you are interested in seeing what Visual Studio creates. We will use our own markup again, so we have selected `Empty` from the list of scaffold options. Do not forget to check the option to apply a layout to the view and select `_AdminLayout.cshtml` as the view to use. Click the `Add` button to create the view, which will be placed in the `Views/Admin` folder. Edit the view so that the content matches Listing 10-7.

Listing 10-7. The Edit View

```
@model SportsStore.Domain.Entities.Product

@{
    ViewBag.Title = "Admin: Edit " + @Model.Name;
    Layout = "~/Views/Shared/_AdminLayout.cshtml";
}

<h1>Edit @Model.Name</h1>

@using (Html.BeginForm()) {
    @Html.EditorForModel()
    <input type="submit" value="Save" />
    @Html.ActionLink("Cancel and return to List", "Index")
}
```

Instead of writing out markup for each of the labels and inputs by hand, we have called the `Html.EditorForModel` helper method. This method asks the MVC Framework to create the editing interface for us, which it does by inspecting the model type—in this case, the `Product` class.

To see the page that is generated from the Edit view, run the application and navigate to /Admin/Index. Click one of the product names, and you will see the page shown in Figure 10-9.

Figure 10-9. The page generated using the EditorForModel helper method

Let's be honest—the EditorForModel method is convenient, but it does not produce the most attractive results. In addition, we do not want the administrator to be able to see or edit the ProductID attribute, and the text box for the Description property is far too small.

We can give the MVC Framework directions about how to create editors for properties by using *model metadata*. This allows us to apply attributes to the properties of the new model class to influence the output of the Html.EditorForModel method. Listing 10-8 shows how to use metadata on the Product class in the SportsStore.Domain project.

Listing 10-8. Using Model Metadata

```
using System.ComponentModel.DataAnnotations;
using System.Web.Mvc;

namespace SportsStore.Domain.Entities {

    public class Product {

        [HiddenInput(DisplayValue = false)]
        public int ProductID { get; set; }
        public string Name { get; set; }

        [DataType(DataType.MultilineText)]
        public string Description { get; set; }
        public decimal Price { get; set; }
        public string Category { get; set; }
    }
}
```

The HiddenInput attribute tells the MVC Framework to render the property as a hidden form element, and the DataType attribute allows us to specify how a value is presented and edited. In this case, we have selected the MultilineText option. The HiddenInput attribute is part of the System.Web.Mvc namespace and the DataType attribute is part of the System.ComponentModel.DataAnnotations namespace, which is why we had you add references to the assemblies for these namespace to the SportsStore.Domain project in Chapter 7.

Figure 10-10 shows the Edit page once the metadata has been applied. You can no longer see or edit the ProductId property, and you have a multiline text box for entering the description. However, the UI still looks pretty poor.

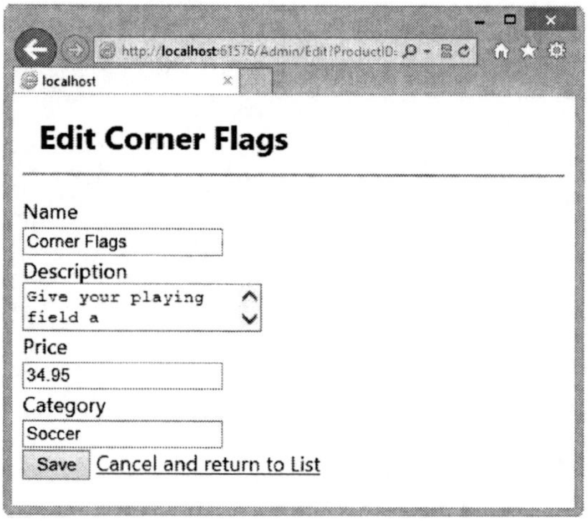

Figure 10-10. The effect of applying metadata

We can make some simple improvements using CSS. When the MVC Framework creates the input fields for each property, it assigns different CSS classes to them. When you look at the source for the page shown in Figure 10-10, you can see that the **textarea** element that has been created for the product description has been assigned the "**text-box-multi-line**" CSS class:

```
...
<textarea class="text-box multi-line" id="Description" name="Description">
    Give your playing field a professional touch
</textarea>
...
```

Other HTML elements are assigned similar classes and we can improve the appearance of the Edit view, by adding the styles shown in Listing 10-9 to the Admin.css file in the Content folder of the SportsStore.WebUI project. These styles target the different classes that are added to the HTML elements by the EditorForModel helper method.

Listing 10-9. CSS Styles for the Editor Elements

```
...
.editor-field { margin-bottom: .8em; }
.editor-label { font-weight: bold; }
.editor-label:after { content: ":" }
.text-box { width: 25em; }
.multi-line { height: 5em; font-family: Segoe UI, Verdana; }
...
```

Figure 10-11 shows the effect these styles have on the Edit view. The rendered view is still pretty basic, but it is functional and it will do for our administration needs.

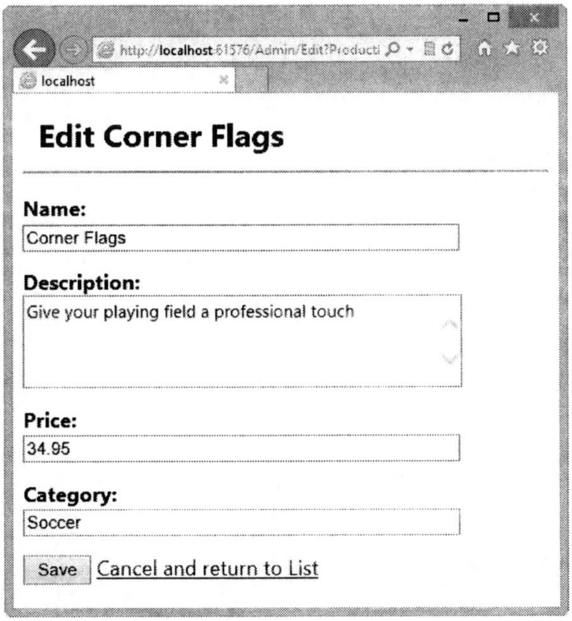

Figure 10-11. Applying CSS to the editor elements

As you saw in this example, the page a templated helper method like EditorForModel creates will not always meet your requirements. We will discuss using and customizing template helper methods in detail in Chapter 20.

Updating the Product Repository

Before we can process edits, we need to enhance the product repository so that we can save changes. First, we will add a new method to the IProductRepository interface, as shown in Listing 10-10. (As a reminder, you will find this interface in the Abstract folder of the SportsStore.Domain project).

Listing 10-10. Adding a Method to the Repository Interface

```
using System.Linq;
using SportsStore.Domain.Entities;

namespace SportsStore.Domain.Abstract {
    public interface IProductRepository {

        IQueryable<Product> Products { get; }

        void SaveProduct(Product product);
    }
}
```

We can then add this method to our Entity Framework implementation of the repository, the Concrete/EFProductRepository class, as shown in Listing 10-11.

Listing 10-11. Implementing the SaveProduct Method

```
using SportsStore.Domain.Abstract;
using SportsStore.Domain.Entities;
using System.Linq;

namespace SportsStore.Domain.Concrete {

    public class EFProductRepository : IProductRepository {
        private EFDbContext context = new EFDbContext();

        public IQueryable<Product> Products {
            get { return context.Products; }
        }

        public void SaveProduct(Product product) {

            if (product.ProductID == 0) {
                context.Products.Add(product);
            } else {
                Product dbEntry = context.Products.Find(product.ProductID);
                if (dbEntry != null) {
                    dbEntry.Name = product.Name;
                    dbEntry.Description = product.Description;
                    dbEntry.Price = product.Price;
                    dbEntry.Category = product.Category;
                }
            }
            context.SaveChanges();
        }
    }
}
```

The implementation of the SaveChanges method adds a product to the repository if the ProductID is 0; otherwise, it applies any changes to the existing entry in the database.

We do not want to go into details of the Entity Framework because, as we explained earlier, it is a topic in itself—but there is a something in the SaveProduct method that has a bearing on the design of the MVC application.

We know we need to perform an update when we receive a Product parameter that has a ProductID that is not zero. We do this by getting a Product object from the repository with the same ProductID and updating each of the properties so they match the parameter object.

We do this because the Entity Framework keeps track of the objects that it creates from the database. The object passed to the SaveChanges method is created by the MVC Framework using the default model binder, which means that the Entity Framework does not know anything about the parameter object and will not apply an update to the database. There are lots of ways of resolving this issue and we have taken the simplest one, which is to locate the corresponding object that the Entity Framework *does* know about and update it explicitly.

An alternative approach would be to create a custom model binder that only obtains objects from the repository. This may seem like a more elegant approach, but it would require us to add a find capability to our repository interface so we could locate Product objects by ProductID values.

The drawback with this approach is that we would have started to add functionality to the abstract definition of the repository in order to work around limitations of a concrete implementation. If we switch repository implementations in the future, we run the risk of having to implement a find capability that may not be readily supported by the new storage technology. It can be tempting to use the flexibility of the MVC Framework to avoid workarounds like the one in the SaveProduct method, but doing so can compromise the design of your application.

Handling Edit POST Requests

At this point, we are ready to implement an overload of the Edit action method in the Admin controller that will handle POST requests when the administrator clicks the Save button. The new method is shown in Listing 10-12.

Listing 10-12. Adding the POST-Handling Edit Action Method

```
using SportsStore.Domain.Abstract;
using SportsStore.Domain.Entities;
using System;
using System.Collections.Generic;
using System.Linq;
using System.Web;
using System.Web.Mvc;

namespace SportsStore.WebUI.Controllers {

    public class AdminController : Controller {
        private IProductRepository repository;

        public AdminController(IProductRepository repo) {
            repository = repo;
        }

        public ViewResult Index() {
            return View(repository.Products);
        }

        public ViewResult Edit(int productId) {
            Product product = repository.Products
                .FirstOrDefault(p => p.ProductID == productId);
            return View(product);
        }

        [HttpPost]
        public ActionResult Edit(Product product) {
            if (ModelState.IsValid) {
                repository.SaveProduct(product);
                TempData["message"] = string.Format("{0} has been saved", product.Name);
                return RedirectToAction("Index");
            } else {
                // there is something wrong with the data values
                return View(product);
            }
        }
    }
}
```

We check that the model binder has been able to validate the data submitted to the user by reading the value of the ModelState.IsValid property. If everything is OK, we save the changes to the repository, and then invoke the Index action method to return the user to the list of products. If there is a problem with the data, we render the Edit view again so that the user can make corrections.

After we have saved the changes in the repository, we store a message using the *Temp Data* feature. This is a key/value dictionary similar to the session data and view bag features we have used previously. The key difference from session data is that temp data is deleted at the end of the HTTP request.

Notice that we return the ActionResult type from the Edit method. We've been using the ViewResult type until now. ViewResult is derived from ActionResult, and it is used when you want the framework to render a view. However, other types of ActionResults are available, and one of them is returned by the RedirectToAction method. We use that in the Edit action method to invoke the Index action method.

We cannot use ViewBag in this situation because the user is being redirected. ViewBag passes data between the controller and view, and it cannot hold data for longer than the current HTTP request. We could have used the session data feature, but then the message would be persistent until we explicitly removed it, which we would rather not have to do. So, the Temp Data feature is the perfect fit. The data is restricted to a single user's session (so that users do not see each other's TempData) and will persist until we have read it. We will read the data in the view rendered by the action method to which we have redirected the user.

UNIT TEST: EDIT SUBMISSIONS

For the POST-processing Edit action method, we need to make sure that valid updates to the Product object that the model binder has created are passed to the product repository to be saved. We also want to check that invalid updates—where a model error exists—are not passed to the repository. Here are the test methods:

```
...
[TestMethod]
public void Can_Save_Valid_Changes() {

    // Arrange - create mock repository
    Mock<IProductRepository> mock = new Mock<IProductRepository>();
    // Arrange - create the controller
    AdminController target = new AdminController(mock.Object);
    // Arrange - create a product
    Product product = new Product {Name = "Test"};

    // Act - try to save the product
    ActionResult result = target.Edit(product);

    // Assert - check that the repository was called
    mock.Verify(m => m.SaveProduct(product));
    // Assert - check the method result type
    Assert.IsNotInstanceOfType(result, typeof(ViewResult));
}

[TestMethod]
public void Cannot_Save_Invalid_Changes() {

    // Arrange - create mock repository
```

```
    Mock<IProductRepository> mock = new Mock<IProductRepository>();
    // Arrange - create the controller
    AdminController target = new AdminController(mock.Object);
    // Arrange - create a product
    Product product = new Product { Name = "Test" };
    // Arrange - add an error to the model state
    target.ModelState.AddModelError("error", "error");

    // Act - try to save the product
    ActionResult result = target.Edit(product);

    // Assert - check that the repository was not called
    mock.Verify(m => m.SaveProduct(It.IsAny<Product>()), Times.Never());
    // Assert - check the method result type
    Assert.IsInstanceOfType(result, typeof(ViewResult));
}
...
```

Displaying a Confirmation Message

We are going to deal with the message we stored using TempData in the _AdminLayout.cshtml layout file. By handling the message in the template, we can create messages in any view that uses the template without needing to create additional Razor blocks. Listing 10-13 shows the change to the file.

Listing 10-13. Handling the ViewBag Message in the Layout

```html
<!DOCTYPE html>

<html>
<head>
    <meta name="viewport" content="width=device-width" />
    <link href="~/Content/Admin.css" rel="stylesheet" type="text/css" />
    <title></title>
</head>
<body>
    <div>
        @if (TempData["message"] != null) {
            <div class="Message">@TempData["message"]</div>
        }
        @RenderBody()
    </div>
</body>
</html>
```

■ **Tip**   The benefit of dealing with the message in the template like this is that users will see it displayed on whatever page is rendered after they have saved a change. At the moment, we return them to the list of products, but we could change the workflow to render some other view, and the users will still see the message (as long as the next view also uses the same layout).

We how have all the elements we need to test editing products. Run the application, navigate to the `Admin/Index` URL, and make some edits. Click the **Save** button. You will be returned to the list view, and the `TempData` message will be displayed, as shown in Figure 10-12.

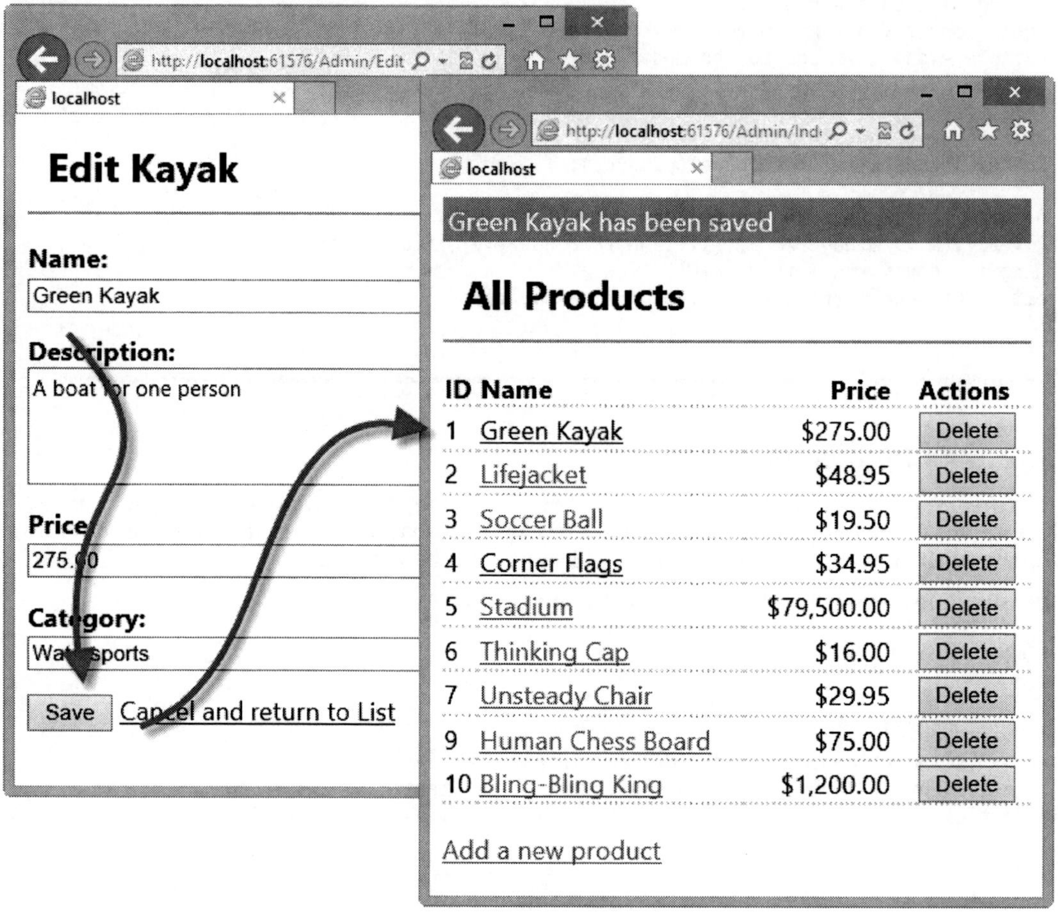

Figure 10-12. Editing a product and seeing the TempData message

The message will disappear if you reload the product list screen, because `TempData` is deleted when it is read. That is very convenient, since we do not want old messages hanging around.

Adding Model Validation

As is always the case, we need to add validation rules to our model entity. At the moment, the administrator could enter negative prices or blank descriptions, and SportsStore would happily store that data in the database. Listing 10-14 shows how we have applied data annotations attributes to the `Product` class, just as we did for the `ShippingDetails` class in the previous chapter.

Listing 10-14. Applying Validation Attributes to the Product Class

```
using System.ComponentModel.DataAnnotations;
using System.Web.Mvc;

namespace SportsStore.Domain.Entities {

    public class Product {

        [HiddenInput(DisplayValue = false)]
        public int ProductID { get; set; }

        [Required(ErrorMessage = "Please enter a product name")]
        public string Name { get; set; }

        [DataType(DataType.MultilineText)]
        [Required(ErrorMessage = "Please enter a description")]
        public string Description { get; set; }

        [Required]
        [Range(0.01, double.MaxValue, ErrorMessage = "Please enter a positive price")]
        public decimal Price { get; set; }

        [Required(ErrorMessage = "Please specify a category")]
        public string Category { get; set; }
    }
}
```

■ **Note** We have reached the point with the Product class where there are more attributes than properties. Don't worry if you feel that the attributes make the class unreadable. You can move the attributes into a different class and tell MVC where to find them. We will show you how to do this in Chapter 23.

When we used the Html.EditorForModel helper method to create the form elements to edit a Product, the MVC Framework added the markup and applied the CSS classes needed to display validation errors inline. Figure 10-13 shows how this appears when you edit a product and enter data that breaks the validation rules we applied to the Product class.

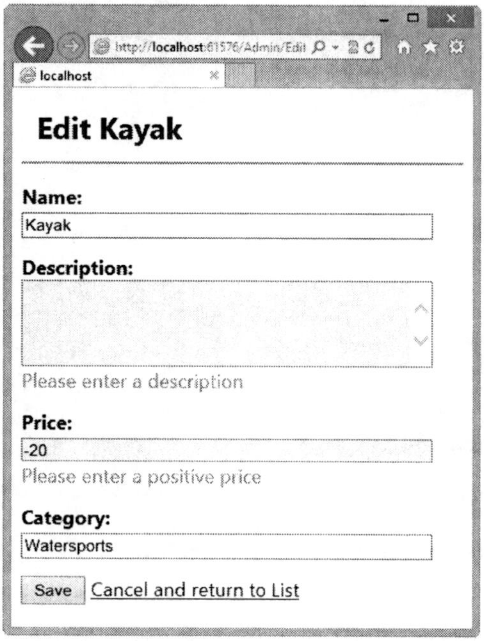

Figure 10-13. Data validation when editing products

Enabling Client-Side Validation

At present, our data validation is applied only when the administrator submits edits to the server. Most Web users expect immediate feedback if there are problems with the data they have entered. This is why Web developers often want to perform *client-side validation*, where the data is checked in the browser using JavaScript. The MVC Framework can perform client-side validation based on the data annotations we applied to the domain model class.

This feature is enabled by default, but it has not been working because we have not added links to the required JavaScript libraries. The simplest place to add these links is in the _AdminLayout.cshtml file, so that client validation can work on any page that uses this layout. Listing 10-15 shows the changes to the layout. The MVC client-side validation feature is based on the jQuery JavaScript library, which can be deduced from the name of the script files.

Listing 10-15. Importing JavaScript Files for Client-Side Validation

```
<!DOCTYPE html>

<html>
<head>
    <meta name="viewport" content="width=device-width" />
    <link href="~/Content/Admin.css" rel="stylesheet" type="text/css" />
    <script src="~/Scripts/jquery-1.7.1.js"></script>
    <script src="~/Scripts/jquery.validate.min.js"></script>
    <script src="~/Scripts/jquery.validate.unobtrusive.min.js"></script>
    <title></title>
</head>
<body>
```

```
    <div>
        @if (TempData["message"] != null) {
            <div class="Message">@TempData["message"]</div>
        }
        @RenderBody()
    </div>
</body>
</html>
```

With these additions, client-side validation will work for our administration views. The appearance of error messages to the user is the same because the CSS classes that are used by the server validation are also used by the client-side validation—but the response is immediate and does not require a request to be sent to the server. In most situations, client-side validation is a useful feature, but if, for some reason, you do not want to validate at the client, you need to use the following statements:

```
...
HtmlHelper.ClientValidationEnabled = false;
HtmlHelper.UnobtrusiveJavaScriptEnabled = false;
...
```

If you put these statements in a view or in a controller, then client-side validation is disabled only for the current action. You can disable client-side validation for the entire application by using those statements in the Application_Start method of Global.asax or by adding values to the Web.config file, like this:

```
...
<configuration>
    <appSettings>
        <add key="ClientValidationEnabled" value="false"/>
        <add key="UnobtrusiveJavaScriptEnabled" value="false"/>
    </appSettings>
</configuration>
...
```

Creating New Products

Next, we will implement the Create action method, which is the one specified by the Add a new product link in the product list page. This will allow the administrator to add new items to the product catalog. Adding the ability to create new products will require only one small addition and one small change to our application. This is a great example of the power and flexibility of a well-thought-out MVC application. First, add the Create method, shown in Listing 10-16, to the AdminController class.

Listing 10-16. Adding the Create Action Method to the Admin Controller

```
...
public ViewResult Create() {
    return View("Edit", new Product());
}
...
```

The Create method does not render its default view. Instead, it specifies that the Edit view should be used. It is perfectly acceptable for one action method to use a view that is usually associated with another view. In this case, we inject a new Product object as the view model so that the Edit view is populated with empty fields.

This leads us to the modification. We would usually expect a form to postback to the action that rendered it, and this is what the Html.BeginForm assumes by default when it generates an HTML form.

However, this does not work for our `Create` method, because we want the form to be posted back to the `Edit` action so that we can save the newly created product data. To fix this, we can use an overloaded version of the `Html.BeginForm` helper method to specify that the target of the form generated in the `Edit` view is the `Edit` action method of the `Admin` controller, as shown in Listing 10-17, which illustrated the change we have made to the `Views/Admin/Edit.cshtml` view file.

Listing 10-17. Explicitly Specifying an Action Method and Controller for a Form

```
@model SportsStore.Domain.Entities.Product

@{
    ViewBag.Title = "Admin: Edit " + @Model.Name;
    Layout = "~/Views/Shared/_AdminLayout.cshtml";
}

<h1>Edit @Model.Name</h1>

@using (Html.BeginForm("Edit", "Admin")) {
    @Html.EditorForModel()
    <input type="submit" value="Save" />
    @Html.ActionLink("Cancel and return to List", "Index")
}
```

Now the form will always be posted to the `Edit` action, regardless of which action rendered it. We can create products by clicking the `Add a new product` link and filling in the details, as shown in Figure 10-14.

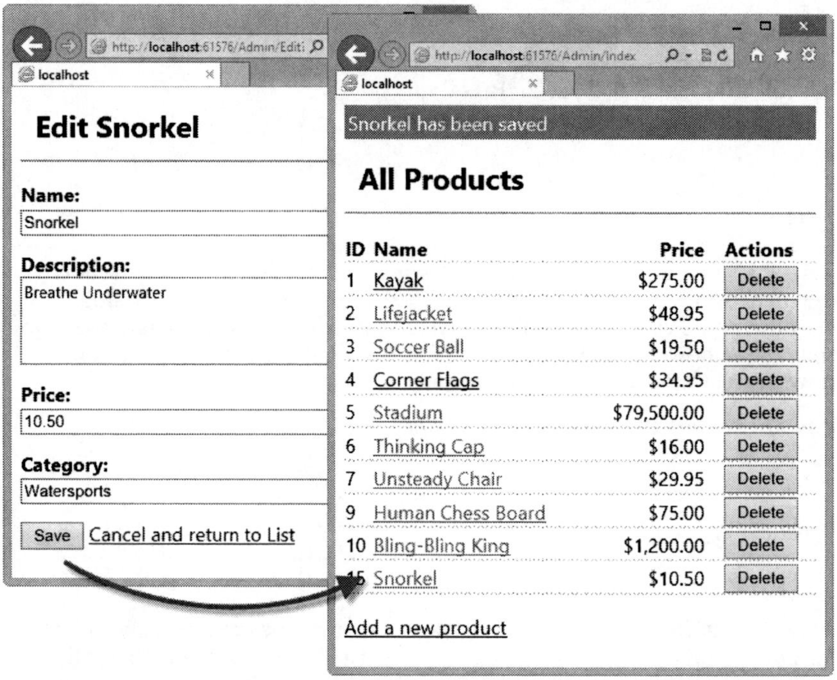

Figure 10-14. Adding a new product to the catalog

Deleting Products

Adding support for deleting items is fairly simple. First, we add a new method to the IProductRepository interface, as shown in Listing 10-18.

Listing 10-18. Adding a Method to Delete Products

```
using System.Linq;
using SportsStore.Domain.Entities;

namespace SportsStore.Domain.Abstract {
    public interface IProductRepository {

        IQueryable<Product> Products { get; }

        void SaveProduct(Product product);

        Product DeleteProduct(int productID);
    }
}
```

Next, we implement this method in our Entity Framework repository class, EFProductRepository, as shown in Listing 10-19.

Listing 10-19. Implementing Deletion Support in the Entity Framework Repository Class

```
using SportsStore.Domain.Abstract;
using SportsStore.Domain.Entities;
using System.Linq;

namespace SportsStore.Domain.Concrete {

    public class EFProductRepository : IProductRepository {
        private EFDbContext context = new EFDbContext();

        public IQueryable<Product> Products {
            get { return context.Products; }
        }

        public void SaveProduct(Product product) {

            if (product.ProductID == 0) {
                context.Products.Add(product);
            } else {
                Product dbEntry = context.Products.Find(product.ProductID);
                if (dbEntry != null) {
                    dbEntry.Name = product.Name;
                    dbEntry.Description = product.Description;
                    dbEntry.Price = product.Price;
                    dbEntry.Category = product.Category;
                }
            }
            context.SaveChanges();
        }
```

```
    public Product DeleteProduct(int productID) {
        Product dbEntry = context.Products.Find(productID);
        if (dbEntry != null) {
            context.Products.Remove(dbEntry);
            context.SaveChanges();
        }
        return dbEntry;
    }
  }
}
```

The final step is to implement a Delete action method in the Admin controller. This action method should support only POST requests, because deleting objects is not an idempotent operation. As we will explain in Chapter 14, browsers and caches are free to make GET requests without the user's explicit consent, so we must be careful to avoid making changes as a consequence of GET requests. Listing 10-20 shows the new action method.

Listing 10-20. The Delete Action Method

```
...
[HttpPost]
public ActionResult Delete(int productId) {
    Product deletedProduct = repository.DeleteProduct(productId);
    if (deletedProduct != null) {
        TempData["message"] = string.Format("{0} was deleted",
            deletedProduct.Name);
    }
    return RedirectToAction("Index");
}
...
```

UNIT TEST: DELETING PRODUCTS

We want to test the basic behavior of the Delete action method, which is that when a valid ProductID is passed as a parameter, the action method calls the DeleteProduct method of the repository and passes the correct ProductID value to be deleted. Here is the test:

```
...
[TestMethod]
public void Can_Delete_Valid_Products() {

    // Arrange - create a Product
    Product prod = new Product { ProductID = 2, Name = "Test" };

    // Arrange - create the mock repository
    Mock<IProductRepository> mock = new Mock<IProductRepository>();
    mock.Setup(m => m.Products).Returns(new Product[] {
        new Product {ProductID = 1, Name = "P1"},
        prod,
        new Product {ProductID = 3, Name = "P3"},
    }.AsQueryable());
```

```
    // Arrange - create the controller
    AdminController target = new AdminController(mock.Object);

    // Act - delete the product
    target.Delete(prod.ProductID);

    // Assert - ensure that the repository delete method was
    // called with the correct Product
    mock.Verify(m => m.DeleteProduct(prod.ProductID));
}
...
```

You can see the new function at work simply by clicking one of the **Delete** buttons in the product list page, as shown in Figure 10-15. As shown in the figure, we have taken advantage of the **TempData** variable to display a message when a product is deleted from the catalog.

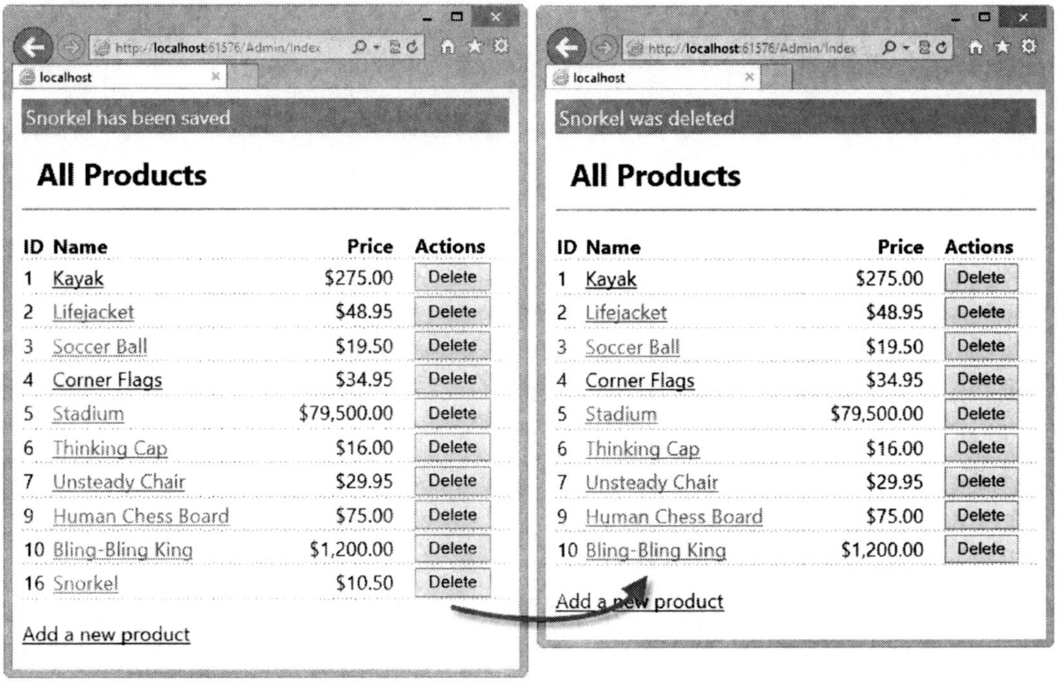

Figure 10-15. Deleting a product from the catalog

Summary

In this chapter, we introduced the administration capability and showed you how to implement CRUD operations that allow the administrator to create, read, update, and delete products from the repository. In the next chapter, we will show you how to secure the administration functions so that they are not available to all users, and we will add the finishing touches to complete the SportsStore functionality.

CHAPTER 11

■ ■ ■

SportsStore: Security & Finishing Touches

In the previous chapter, we added support for administering the SportsStore application, and it will not have escaped your attention that anyone would be able to modify the product catalog if we deployed the application right now. All someone would need to know is that the administration features are available using the `Admin/Index` URL. In this chapter, we are going to show you how to prevent random people from using the administration functions by password-protecting access to the entire `Admin` controller.

Once we have the security in place, we will complete the SportsStore app by adding support for product images. This may seem like a simple feature, but it requires some interesting MVC techniques.

Securing the Administration Controller

Because ASP.NET MVC is built on the core ASP.NET platform, we have access to the ASP.NET Forms Authentication facility, which is a general-purpose system for keeping track of who is logged in. But for our example application, we will simply show you how to set up the most basic of configurations.

If you open the `Web.config` file (the one in the root directory of the project), you will be able to find a section entitled `authentication`, like this one:

```
...
<authentication mode="Forms">
    <forms loginUrl="~/Account/Login" timeout="2880"/>
</authentication>
...
```

As you can see, forms authentication is enabled automatically in an MVC application created with the `Basic` template. The `loginUrl` attribute tells ASP.NET which URL users should be directed to when they need to authenticate themselves—in this case, the `~/Account/Login` page. The `timeout` attribute specifies how long a user remains authenticated for after logging in. By default, this is 48 hours (2,880 minutes).

■ **Note** The main alternative to forms authentication is *Windows authentication,* where the operating system credentials are used to identify users. This is a great facility if you are deploying intranet applications and all of your users are in the same Windows domain, but it is not suitable for Internet applications.

If you create an MVC application project using the `Internet Application` or `Mobile Application` options, Visual Studio will automatically create an `AccountController` class, which will handle authentication requests using the ASP.NET *membership* feature.

We selected the `Basic` option when we created the `SportStore.WebUI` project, which means that forms authentication is enabled in the `Web.config` file, but we are responsible for creating the controller that will process authentication. This means that we can implement any authentication model we choose, which is useful because the ASP.NET membership feature is overkill for our example project where a much simpler authentication will suffice for an introduction in the MVC security features.

To start, we will create a username and password that will grant access to the SportsStore administration features. Listing 11-1 shows the changes to apply to the authentication section of the `Web.config` file.

Listing 11-1. Defining a Username and Password

```
...
<authentication mode="Forms">
  <forms loginUrl="~/Account/Login" timeout="2880">
    <credentials passwordFormat="Clear">
      <user name="admin" password="secret" />
    </credentials>
  </forms>
</authentication>
...
```

We have kept things very simple and hard-code a username (`admin`) and password (`secret`) in the `Web.config` file. Our focus in this chapter is applying basic security to an MVC application, so hard-coded credentials suit us just fine.

■ **Caution** Obviously, we don't recommend deploying a real application with such a basic level of security. We just want to demonstrate the core MVC Framework security features and static and hard-coded passwords are not adequate for real projects.

Applying Authorization with Filters

The MVC Framework has a powerful feature called *filters*. These are .NET attributes that you can apply to an action method or a controller class. They introduce additional logic when a request is processed. Different kinds of filters are available, and you can create your own custom filters, too, as we will explain in Chapter 16. The filter that interests us at the moment is the default authorization filter, `Authorize`. We will apply it to the `AdminController` class, as shown in Listing 11-2.

Listing 11-2. Adding the Authorize Attribute to the Controller Class

```
using SportsStore.Domain.Abstract;
using SportsStore.Domain.Entities;
using System;
using System.Collections.Generic;
using System.Linq;
using System.Web;
using System.Web.Mvc;

namespace SportsStore.WebUI.Controllers {
```

```
[Authorize]
public class AdminController : Controller {
    private IProductRepository repository;

    public AdminController(IProductRepository repo) {
        repository = repo;
    }

    // ...action methods omitted for brevity...
    }
}
```

When applied without any parameters, the Authorize attribute grants access to the controller action methods if the user is authenticated. This means that if you are authenticated, you are automatically authorized to use the administration features. This is fine for SportsStore, where there is only one set of restricted action methods and only one user.

■ **Note** You can apply filters to an individual action method or to a controller. When you apply a filter to a controller, it works as though you had applied it to every action method in the controller class. In Listing 11-2, we applied the Authorize filter to the class, so all of the action methods in the Admin controller are available only to authenticated users.

You can see the effect that the Authorize filter has by running the application and navigating to the /Admin/Index URL. You will see an error similar to the one shown in Figure 11-1.

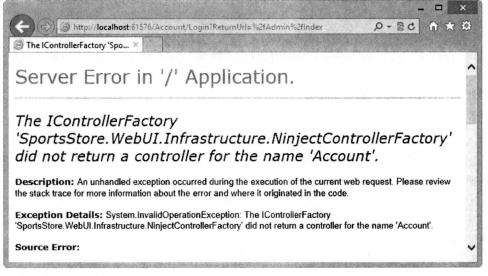

Figure 11-1. The effect of the Authorize filter

When you try to access the Index action method of the Admin controller, the MVC Framework detects the Authorize filter. Because you have not been authenticated, you are redirected to the URL specified in the `Web.config` forms authentication section: `/Account/Login`. We have not created the `Account` controller yet—which is what causes the error shown in the figure—but the fact that the MVC Framework has tried to instantiate an `AccountController` class shows us that the Authorize attribute is working.

Creating the Authentication Provider

Using the forms authentication feature requires us to call two static methods of the `System.Web.Security.FormsAuthentication` class:

- The `Authenticate` method lets us validate credentials supplied by the user.

- The `SetAuthCookie` method adds a cookie to the response to the browser, so that users do not need to authenticate every time they make a request.

The problem with calling static methods from within action methods is that it makes unit testing the controller difficult. Mocking frameworks such as Moq can mock only instance members. This problem arises because the `FormsAuthentication` class predates the unit-testing-friendly design of MVC.

The best way to address this is to decouple the controller from the class with the static methods using an interface, which offers the additional benefit that this fits in with the broader MVC design pattern and makes it easier to switch to a different authentication system later.

We start by defining the authentication provider interface. Create a new folder called `Abstract` in the `Infrastructure` folder of the `SportsStore.WebUI` project and add a new interface called `IAuthProvider`. The contents of this interface are shown in Listing 11-3.

Listing 11-3. The IAuthProvider Interface

```
namespace SportsStore.WebUI.Infrastructure.Abstract {
    public interface IAuthProvider {

        bool Authenticate(string username, string password);
    }
}
```

We can now create an implementation of this interface that acts as a wrapper around the static methods of the `FormsAuthentication` class. Create another new folder in `Infrastructure`—this time called `Concrete`—and create a new class called `FormsAuthProvider`. The contents of this class are shown in Listing 11-4.

Listing 11-4. The FormsAuthProvider Class

```
using System.Web.Security;
using SportsStore.WebUI.Infrastructure.Abstract;

namespace SportsStore.WebUI.Infrastructure.Concrete {

    public class FormsAuthProvider : IAuthProvider {

        public bool Authenticate(string username, string password) {

            bool result = FormsAuthentication.Authenticate(username, password);
            if (result) {
                FormsAuthentication.SetAuthCookie(username, false);
            }
            return result;
        }
    }
}
```

The implementation of the `Authenticate` method calls the static `FormsAuthentication` methods that we wanted to keep out of the controller. The final step is to register the `FormsAuthProvider` in the `AddBindings` method of the `NinjectControllerFactory` class, as shown in Listing 11-5 (the changes are shown in bold).

Listing 11-5. Adding the Authentication Provider Ninject Binding

```
using System;
using System.Web.Mvc;
using System.Web.Routing;
using Ninject;
using SportsStore.Domain.Entities;
using SportsStore.Domain.Abstract;
using System.Collections.Generic;
using System.Linq;
using Moq;
using SportsStore.Domain.Concrete;
using System.Configuration;
using SportsStore.WebUI.Infrastructure.Abstract;
using SportsStore.WebUI.Infrastructure.Concrete;

namespace SportsStore.WebUI.Infrastructure {

    public class NinjectControllerFactory : DefaultControllerFactory {
        private IKernel ninjectKernel;

        public NinjectControllerFactory() {
            ninjectKernel = new StandardKernel();
            AddBindings();
        }

        protected override IController GetControllerInstance(RequestContext
            requestContext, Type controllerType) {

            return controllerType == null
                ? null
                : (IController)ninjectKernel.Get(controllerType);
        }

        private void AddBindings() {
            ninjectKernel.Bind<IProductRepository>().To<EFProductRepository>();

            EmailSettings emailSettings = new EmailSettings {
                WriteAsFile = bool.Parse(ConfigurationManager
                    .AppSettings["Email.WriteAsFile"] ?? "false")
            };

            ninjectKernel.Bind<IOrderProcessor>()
                .To<EmailOrderProcessor>()
                .WithConstructorArgument("settings",emailSettings);

            ninjectKernel.Bind<IAuthProvider>().To<FormsAuthProvider>();
        }
    }
}
```

Creating the Account Controller

The next task is to create the `Account` controller and the `Login` action method referred to in the `Web.config` file. In fact, we will create two versions of the `Login` method. The first will render a view that contains a login prompt, and the other will handle the `POST` request when users submit their credentials.

To get started, we will create a view model class that we will pass between the controller and the view. Add a new class to the `Models` folder of the `SportsStore.WebUI` project called `LoginViewModel` and edit the content so that it matches Listing 11-6.

Listing 11-6. The LoginViewModel Class

```
using System.ComponentModel.DataAnnotations;

namespace SportsStore.WebUI.Models {

    public class LoginViewModel {
        [Required]
        public string UserName { get; set; }

        [Required]
        [DataType(DataType.Password)]
        public string Password { get; set; }
    }
}
```

This class contains properties for the username and password, and uses data annotation attributes to specify that values for both are required. In addition, we use the `DataType` attribute to tell the MVC Framework how we want the editor for the `Password` property displayed.

Given that there are only two properties, you might be tempted to do without a view model and rely on the `ViewBag` to pass data to the view. However, it is good practice to define view models so that the data passed from the controller to the view and from the model binder to the action method is typed consistently. This allows us to use template view helpers more easily.

Next, create a new controller called `AccountController`, as shown in Listing 11-7.

Listing 11-7. The AccountController Class

```
using System.Web.Mvc;
using SportsStore.WebUI.Infrastructure.Abstract;
using SportsStore.WebUI.Models;

namespace SportsStore.WebUI.Controllers {

    public class AccountController : Controller {
        IAuthProvider authProvider;

        public AccountController(IAuthProvider auth) {
            authProvider = auth;
        }

        public ViewResult Login() {
            return View();
        }

        [HttpPost]
```

```
public ActionResult Login(LoginViewModel model, string returnUrl) {

    if (ModelState.IsValid) {
        if (authProvider.Authenticate(model.UserName, model.Password)) {
            return Redirect(returnUrl ?? Url.Action("Index", "Admin"));
        } else {
            ModelState.AddModelError("", "Incorrect username or password");
            return View();
        }
    } else {
        return View();
    }
}
```

Creating the View

Right click in one of the action methods in the Account controller class and select Add View from the pop-up menu. Create a strongly typed view called Login that uses LoginViewModel as the view model type, as shown in Figure 11-2. Check the option to use a layout and select the _AdminLayout.cshtml file.

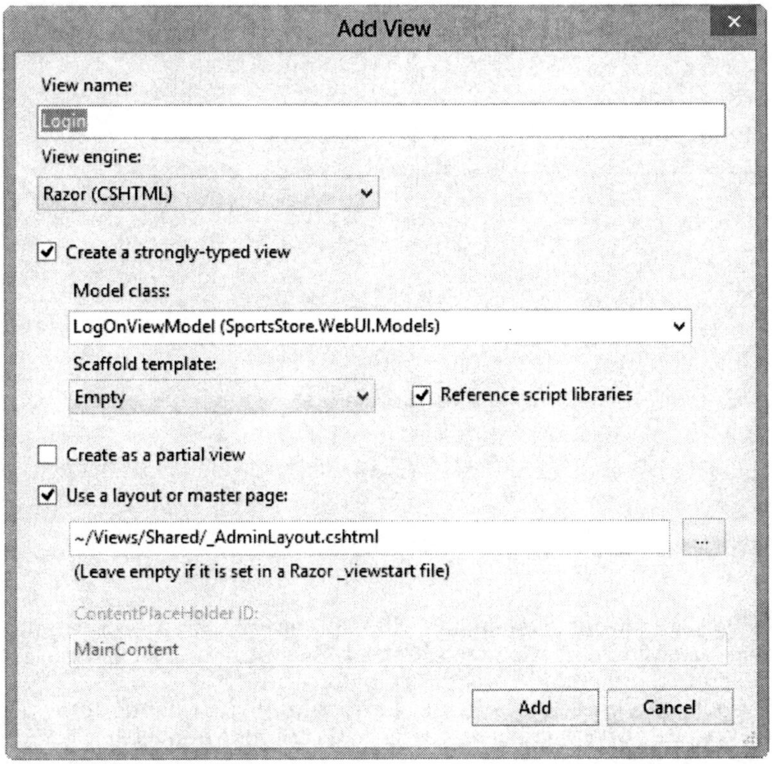

Figure 11-2. Adding the Login view

Click the Add button to create the view and edit the markup so that it matches Listing 11-8.

Listing 11-8. The Login View

```
@model SportsStore.WebUI.Models.LoginViewModel

@{
    ViewBag.Title = "Admin: Log In";
    Layout = "~/Views/Shared/_AdminLayout.cshtml";
}

<h1>Log In</h1>

<p>Please log in to access the administrative area:</p>
@using(Html.BeginForm()) {
    @Html.ValidationSummary(true)
    @Html.EditorForModel()
    <p><input type="submit" value="Log in" /></p>
}
```

You can see how the view appears by starting the app and navigating to the /Admin/Index URL, as shown in Figure 11-3.

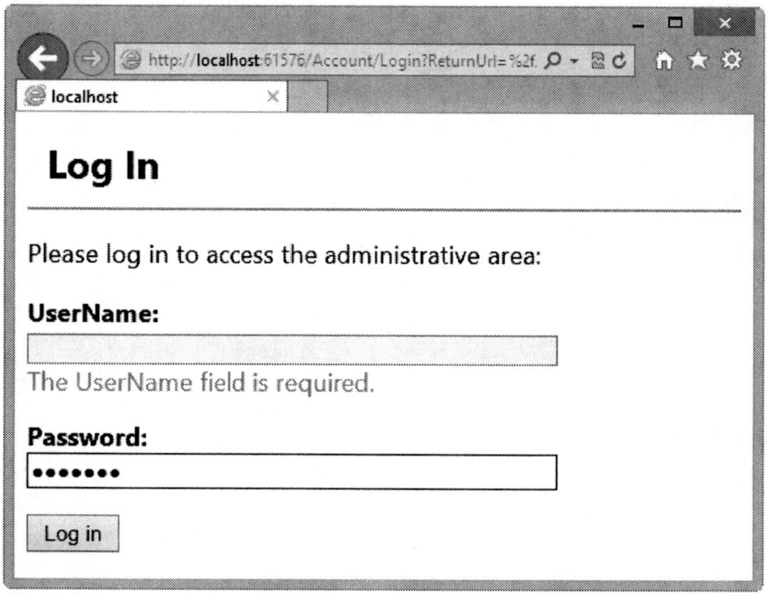

Figure 11-3. The Login view

The DataType attribute has led the MVC Framework to render the editor for the Password property as an HTML password-input element, which means that the characters in the password are not visible. The Required attribute that we applied to the properties of the view model are enforced using client-side validation (we included the required JavaScript libraries in the _AdminLayout.cshtml file in Chapter 10). Users can submit the form only after they have provided both a username and password, and the authentication is performed at the server when we call the FormsAuthentication.Authenticate method.

■ **Caution** In general, using client-side data validation is a good idea. It offloads some of the work from your server and gives users immediate feedback about the data they are providing. However, you should not be tempted to perform authentication at the client, as this would typically involve sending valid credentials to the client so they can be used to check the username and password that the user has entered, or at least trusting the client's report of whether they have successfully authenticated. Authentication must always be done at the server.

When we receive bad credentials, we add an error to the ModelState and re-render the view. This causes our message to be displayed in the validation summary area, which we have created by calling the Html.ValidationSummary helper method in the view.

■ **Note** Notice that we call the Html.ValidationSummary helper method with a bool parameter value of true in Listing 11-8. Doing so excludes any property validation messages from being displayed. If we had not done this, any property validation errors would be duplicated in the summary area and next to the corresponding input element.

UNIT TEST: AUTHENTICATION

Testing the Account controller requires us to check two behaviors: a user should be authenticated when valid credentials are supplied, and a user should *not* be authenticated when invalid credentials are supplied. We can perform these tests by creating mock implementations of the IAuthProvider interface and checking the type and nature of the result of the controller Login method. We created the following tests in a new unit test file called AdminSecurityTests.cs:

```
using Microsoft.VisualStudio.TestTools.UnitTesting;
using Moq;
using SportsStore.WebUI.Controllers;
using SportsStore.WebUI.Infrastructure.Abstract;
using SportsStore.WebUI.Models;
using System.Web.Mvc;

namespace SportsStore.UnitTests {
    [TestClass]
    public class AdminSecurityTests {

        [TestMethod]
        public void Can_Login_With_Valid_Credentials() {

            // Arrange - create a mock authentication provider
            Mock<IAuthProvider> mock = new Mock<IAuthProvider>();
            mock.Setup(m => m.Authenticate("admin", "secret")).Returns(true);

            // Arrange - create the view model
```

```
            LoginViewModel model = new LoginViewModel {
                UserName = "admin",
                Password = "secret"
            };

            // Arrange - create the controller
            AccountController target = new AccountController(mock.Object);

            // Act - authenticate using valid credentials
            ActionResult result = target.Login(model, "/MyURL");

            // Assert
            Assert.IsInstanceOfType(result, typeof(RedirectResult));
            Assert.AreEqual("/MyURL", ((RedirectResult)result).Url);
        }

        [TestMethod]
        public void Cannot_Login_With_Invalid_Credentials() {

            // Arrange - create a mock authentication provider
            Mock<IAuthProvider> mock = new Mock<IAuthProvider>();
            mock.Setup(m => m.Authenticate("badUser", "badPass")).Returns(false);

            // Arrange - create the view model
            LoginViewModel model = new LoginViewModel {
                UserName = "badUser",
                Password = "badPass"
            };

            // Arrange - create the controller
            AccountController target = new AccountController(mock.Object);

            // Act - authenticate using valid credentials
            ActionResult result = target.Login(model, "/MyURL");

            // Assert
            Assert.IsInstanceOfType(result, typeof(ViewResult));
            Assert.IsFalse(((ViewResult)result).ViewData.ModelState.IsValid);
        }
    }
}
```

This takes care of protecting the SportsStore administration functions. Users will be allowed to access these features only after they have supplied valid credentials and received a cookie, which will be attached to subsequent requests.

Image Uploads

We are going to complete the SportsStore user experience with something a little more sophisticated, We will add the ability for the administrator to upload product images and store them in the database so that they are displayed in the product catalog.

Extending the Database

Open the Visual Studio Database Explorer window and navigate to the Products table in the database we created in Chapter 7. The name of the data connection may have changed to be EFDbContext, which is the name we assigned to the connection in the Web.config file in Chapter 7. Visual Studio is a little bit inconsistent about when it renames the connection, so you might also see the original name that was shown when the connection was created.

Right-click the table and select Open Table Definition from the pop-up menu. Add definitions for the two new columns that are shown in Figure 11-4. Make sure that you set the details of the columns correctly and do not forget to check the Allow Nulls option for both new columns.

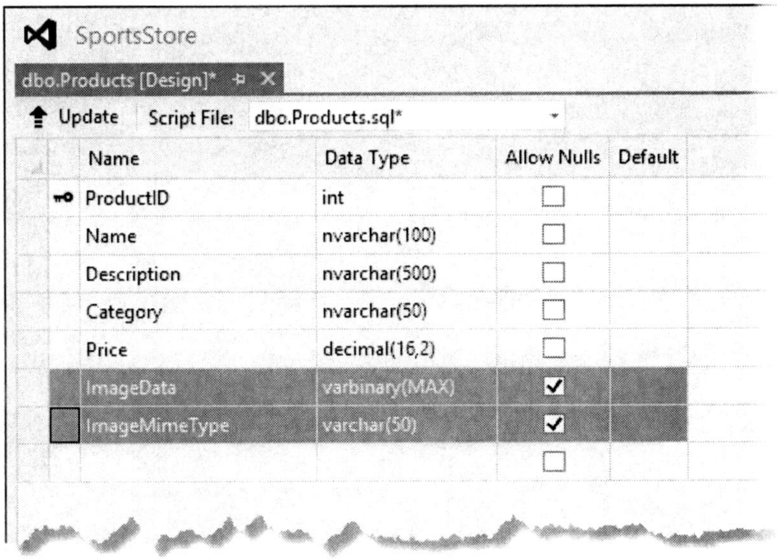

Figure 11-4. Adding new columns to the Products table

Click the Update button so that Visual Studio figures out what SQL statements need to be sent to the database to update the database, which will be displayed in the Preview Database Updates dialog, as shown in Figure 11-5.

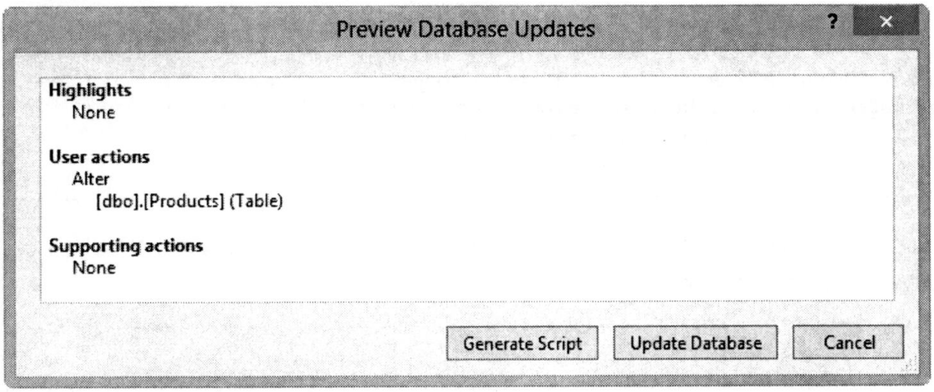

Figure 11-5. The preview of database updates

Click the Update Database button to create the new columns in the database.

Enhancing the Domain Model

We need to add two new fields to the Products class in the SportsStore.Domain project that correspond to the columns we added to the database. The additions are shown in bold in Listing 11-9.

Listing 11-9. Adding Properties to the Product Class

```
using System.ComponentModel.DataAnnotations;
using System.Web.Mvc;

namespace SportsStore.Domain.Entities {

    public class Product {

        [HiddenInput(DisplayValue=false)]
        public int ProductID { get; set; }

        [Required(ErrorMessage = "Please enter a product name")]
        public string Name { get; set; }

        [Required(ErrorMessage = "Please enter a description")]
        [DataType(DataType.MultilineText)]
        public string Description { get; set; }

        [Required]
        [Range(0.01, double.MaxValue, ErrorMessage = "Please enter a positive price")]
        public decimal Price { get; set; }

        [Required(ErrorMessage = "Please specify a category")]
        public string Category { get; set; }

        public byte[] ImageData { get; set; }

        [HiddenInput(DisplayValue = false)]
        public string ImageMimeType { get; set; }
    }
}
```

We do not want either of these new properties to be visible when the MVC Framework renders an editor for us. To that end, we use the HiddenInput attribute on the ImageMimeType property. We do not need to do anything with the ImageData property, because the framework doesn't render an editor for byte arrays. It does this only for "simple" types, such as int, string, DateTime, and so on.

■ **Caution**   Make sure that the names of the properties that you add to the Product class exactly match the names you gave to the new columns in the database.

Creating the Upload User Interface Elements

Our next step is to add support for handling file uploads. This involves creating a UI that the administrator can use to upload an image. Modify the `Views/Admin/Edit.cshtml` view so that it matches Listing 11-10 (the additions are in bold).

Listing 11-10. Adding Support for Images

```
@model SportsStore.Domain.Entities.Product

@{
    ViewBag.Title = "Admin: Edit " + @Model.Name;
    Layout = "~/Views/Shared/_AdminLayout.cshtml";
}

<h1>Edit @Model.Name</h1>

@using (Html.BeginForm("Edit", "Admin",
    FormMethod.Post, new { enctype = "multipart/form-data" })) {

    @Html.EditorForModel()

    <div class="editor-label">Image</div>
    <div class="editor-field">
        @if (Model.ImageData == null) {
            @:None
        } else {
            <img width="150" height="150"
                src="@Url.Action("GetImage", "Product", new { Model.ProductID })" />
        }
        <div>Upload new image: <input type="file" name="Image" /></div>
    </div>

    <input type="submit" value="Save" />
    @Html.ActionLink("Cancel and return to List", "Index")
}
```

You may already be aware that Web browsers will upload files properly only when the HTML `form` element defines an `enctype` value of `multipart/form-data`. In other words, for a successful upload, the `form` element must look like this:

```
<form action="/Admin/Edit" enctype="multipart/form-data" method="post">
...
</form>
```

Without the `enctype` attribute, the browser will transmit only the name of the file and not its content, which is no use to us at all. To ensure that the `enctype` attribute appears, we must use an overload of the `Html.BeginForm` helper method that lets us specify HTML attributes, like this:

```
...
@using (Html.BeginForm("Edit", "Admin", FormMethod.Post,
    new { enctype = "multipart/form-data" })) {
...
```

Notice that if the `Product` being displayed has a non-null `ImageData` property value, we add an `img` element and set its source to be the result of calling the `GetImage` action method of the `Product` controller. We will implement this shortly.

Saving Images to the Database

We need to enhance the `POST` version of the `Edit` action method in the `AdminController` class so that we take the image data that has been uploaded to us and save it in the database. Listing 11-11 shows the changes that are required.

Listing 11-11. Handling Image Data in the AdminController Class

```
...
[HttpPost]
public ActionResult Edit(Product product, HttpPostedFileBase image) {
    if (ModelState.IsValid) {
        if (image != null) {
            product.ImageMimeType = image.ContentType;
            product.ImageData = new byte[image.ContentLength];
            image.InputStream.Read(product.ImageData, 0, image.ContentLength);
        }
        repository.SaveProduct(product);
        TempData["message"] = string.Format("{0} has been saved", product.Name);
        return RedirectToAction("Index");
    } else {
        // there is something wrong with the data values
        return View(product);
    }
}
...
```

We have added a new parameter to the `Edit` method, which the MVC Framework uses to pass the uploaded file data to us. We check to see if the parameter value is `null`; if it is not, we copy the data and the MIME type from the parameter to the `Product` object so that it is saved to the database.

▓ **Note** You'll need to update your unit tests to reflect the new parameter in Listing 11-11. Providing a `null` parameter value will satisfy the compiler.

We must also update the `EFProductRepository` class in the `SportsStore.Domain` project to ensure that the values assigned to the `ImageData` and `ImageMimeType` properties are stored in the database. Listing 11-12 shows the required changes so the `SaveProduct` method.

Listing 11-12. Ensuring that the image values are stored in the database

```
...
public void SaveProduct(Product product) {

    if (product.ProductID == 0) {
        context.Products.Add(product);
    } else {
        Product dbEntry = context.Products.Find(product.ProductID);
```

```
        if (dbEntry != null) {
            dbEntry.Name = product.Name;
            dbEntry.Description = product.Description;
            dbEntry.Price = product.Price;
            dbEntry.Category = product.Category;
            dbEntry.ImageData = product.ImageData;
            dbEntry.ImageMimeType = product.ImageMimeType;
        }
    }
    context.SaveChanges();
}
...
```

Implementing the GetImage Action Method

In Listing 11-10, we added an `img` element whose content was obtained through a `GetImage` action method. We are going to implement this so that we can display images contained in the database. Listing 11-13 shows the method we added to the `ProductController` class.

Listing 11-13. The GetImage Action Method

```
...
public FileContentResult GetImage(int productId) {
    Product prod = repository.Products.FirstOrDefault(p => p.ProductID == productId);
    if (prod != null) {
        return File(prod.ImageData, prod.ImageMimeType);
    } else {
        return null;
    }
}
...
```

This method tries to find a product that matches the ID specified by the parameter. The `FileContentResult` class is returned from an action method when we want to return a file to the client browser, and instances are created using the `File` method of the base controller class. We'll discuss the different types of results you can return from action methods in Chapter 15.

UNIT TEST: RETRIEVING IMAGES

We want to make sure that the `GetImage` method returns the correct MIME type from the repository and make sure that no data is returned when we request a product ID that doesn't exist. Here are the test methods we created, which we added to a new unit test file called `ImageTests.cs`:

```
using Microsoft.VisualStudio.TestTools.UnitTesting;
using Moq;
using SportsStore.Domain.Abstract;
using SportsStore.Domain.Entities;
using SportsStore.WebUI.Controllers;
using System.Linq;
using System.Web.Mvc;

namespace SportsStore.UnitTests {
    [TestClass]
```

```csharp
public class ImageTests {

    [TestMethod]
    public void Can_Retrieve_Image_Data() {

        // Arrange - create a Product with image data
        Product prod = new Product {
            ProductID = 2,
            Name = "Test",
            ImageData = new byte[] { },
            ImageMimeType = "image/png"
        };

        // Arrange - create the mock repository
        Mock<IProductRepository> mock = new Mock<IProductRepository>();
        mock.Setup(m => m.Products).Returns(new Product[] {
            new Product {ProductID = 1, Name = "P1"},
            prod,
            new Product {ProductID = 3, Name = "P3"}
        }.AsQueryable());

        // Arrange - create the controller
        ProductController target = new ProductController(mock.Object);

        // Act - call the GetImage action method
        ActionResult result = target.GetImage(2);

        // Assert
        Assert.IsNotNull(result);
        Assert.IsInstanceOfType(result, typeof(FileResult));
        Assert.AreEqual(prod.ImageMimeType, ((FileResult)result).ContentType);
    }

    [TestMethod]
    public void Cannot_Retrieve_Image_Data_For_Invalid_ID() {

        // Arrange - create the mock repository
        Mock<IProductRepository> mock = new Mock<IProductRepository>();
        mock.Setup(m => m.Products).Returns(new Product[] {
            new Product {ProductID = 1, Name = "P1"},
            new Product {ProductID = 2, Name = "P2"}
        }.AsQueryable());

        // Arrange - create the controller
        ProductController target = new ProductController(mock.Object);

        // Act - call the GetImage action method
        ActionResult result = target.GetImage(100);

        // Assert
        Assert.IsNull(result);
    }
}
}
```

When dealing with a valid product ID, we check that we get a `FileResult` result from the action method and that the content type matches the type in our mock data. The `FileResult` class does not let us access the binary contents of the file, so we must be satisfied with a less-than-perfect test. When we request an invalid product ID, we simply check to ensure that the result is `null`.

The administrator can now upload images for products. You can try this yourself by starting the application, navigating to the **/Admin/Index** URL and editing one of the products. Figure 11-6 shows an example.

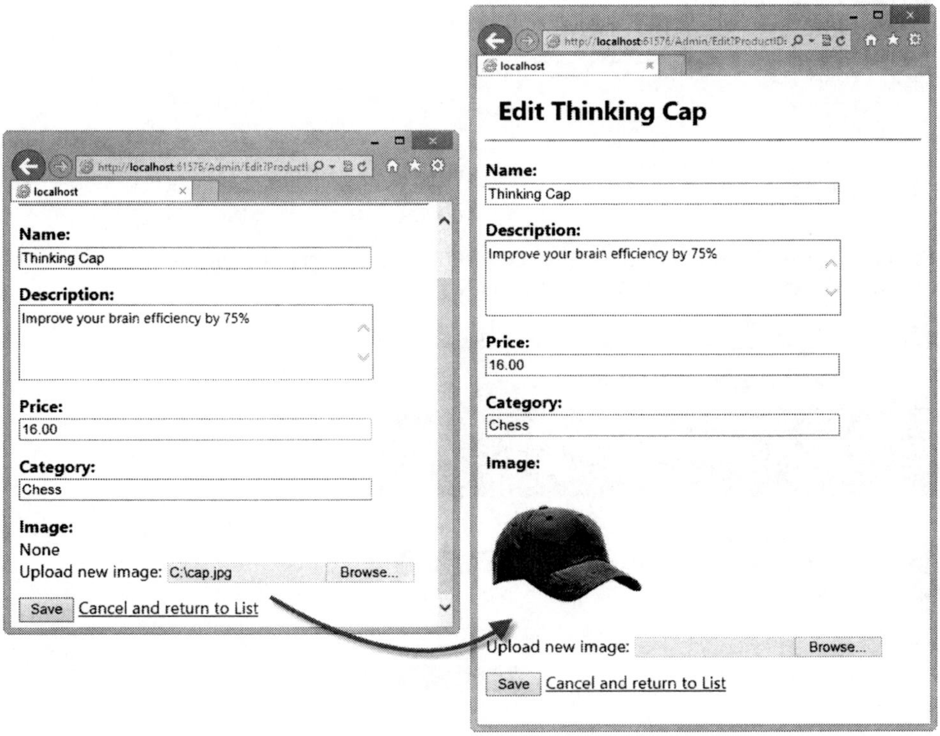

Figure 11-6. Adding an image to a product listing

Displaying Product Images

All that remains is to display the images alongside the product description in the product catalog. Edit the **Views/Shared/ProductSummary.cshtml** view to reflect the changes shown in bold in Listing 11-14.

Listing 11-14. Displaying Images in the Product Catalog

```
@model SportsStore.Domain.Entities.Product

<div class="item">

    @if (Model.ImageData != null) {
        <div style="float:left;margin-right:20px">
            <img width="75" height="75" src="@Url.Action("GetImage", "Product",
                new { Model.ProductID })" />
```

```
        </div>
}

<h3>@Model.Name</h3>
@Model.Description

<div class="item">

@using(Html.BeginForm("AddToCart", "Cart")) {
    @Html.HiddenFor(x => x.ProductID)
    @Html.Hidden("returnUrl", Request.Url.PathAndQuery)
    <input type="submit" value="+ Add to cart" />
}

</div>

    <h4>@Model.Price.ToString("c")</h4>
</div>
```

With these changes in place, the customers will see images displayed as part of the product description when they browse the catalog, as shown in Figure 11-7.

Figure 11-7. Displaying product images

Summary

In this and previous chapters, we have demonstrated how the ASP.NET MVC Framework can be used to create a realistic e-commerce application. This extended example has introduced many of the framework's key features: controllers, action methods, routing, views, model binding, metadata, validation, layouts, authentication, and more. You have also seen how some of the key technologies related to MVC can be used. These included the Entity Framework, Ninject, Moq, and the Visual Studio support for unit testing.

We have ended up with an application that has a clean, component-oriented architecture that separates out the various concerns, leaving us with a code base that will be easy to extend and maintain. The second part of this book digs deep into each MVC Framework component to give you a complete guide to its capabilities.

P A R T   2

ASP.NET MVC 4 in Detail

So far, you've learned about why the ASP.NET MVC Framework exists and have gained an understanding of its architecture and underlying design goals. You've taken it for a good, long test-drive by building a realistic e-commerce application. Now it's time to open the hood and expose the full details of the framework's machinery.

In Part 2 of this book, we'll look at the details. We'll start with an exploration of the structure of an ASP.NET MVC application and the way that requests are processed. We then focus on individual features, such as routing (Chapters 13 and 14), controllers and actions (Chapters 15-17), the MVC view and helper system (Chapters 18-21), and the way that MVC works with domain models (Chapters 22 and 23).

In the final chapters of this book, we show you the MVC Framework features that make client-side development easier (Chapters 24 and 25) and show you how to prepare and deploy an MVC Framework application (Chapter 26).

CHAPTER 12

■ ■ ■

Overview of MVC Projects

We are going to provide some additional context before we start diving into the details of specific MVC Framework features. This chapter gives an overview of the structure and nature of an ASP.NET MVC application, including the default project structure and naming conventions that you must follow.

Working with Visual Studio MVC Projects

When you create a new MVC project, Visual Studio gives you a choice between different starting points: Empty, Basic, Internet Application, Intranet Application, Mobile Application and Web API, as shown in Figure 12-1.

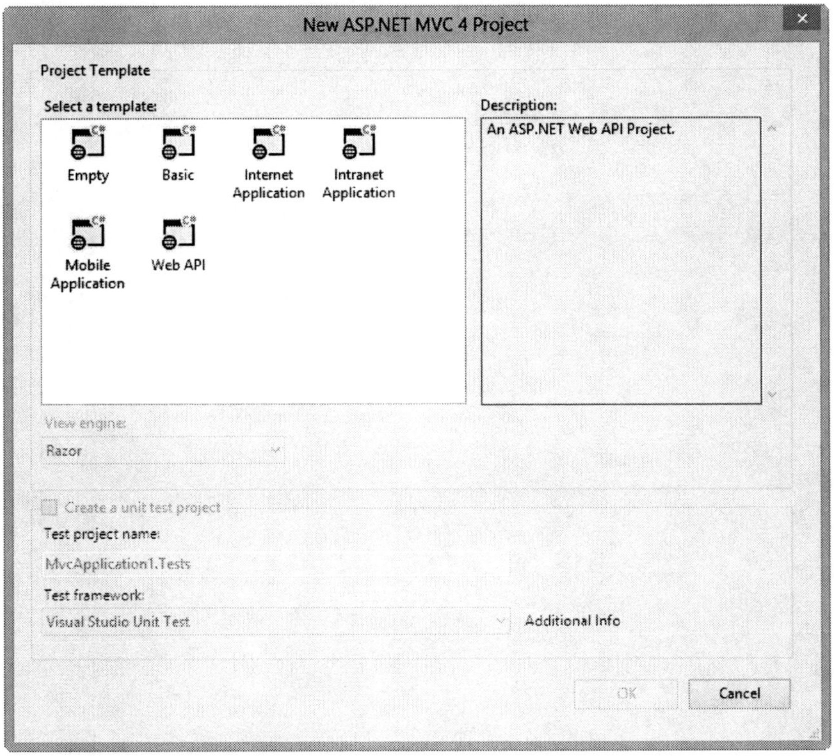

Figure 12-1. Choosing the initial configuration of an MVC project

We have already shown you the first two templates in previous chapters. The Empty project template is the one we used in Chapter 2 for the RSVP application and it contains only the bare minimum of files required by the MVC Framework.

We used the Basic project template in Chapter 7 when we created the SportsStore application and it supplements the structure created for Empty projects with some layouts, JavaScript library files and some CSS styles used for HTML form elements and validation. It is the Basic template that we use in our own projects because the script files and other additions are useful, but we are still free to implement the important parts of the project ourselves, just as we did for the SportsStore application.

The Internet Application and Intranet Application templates fill out the project to give a more complete starting point, using different authentication mechanisms that are suited to internet and intranet applications. The Mobile Application template is a variation on the Internet Application template which is optimized for mobile devices (we will explain the new MVC 4 features for targeting mobile devices in Chapter 24). The final template, Web API, creates a project which gets you started with the new MVC 4 Web API feature, which we explain in Chapter 25.

You can see the difference between three of the most diverse templates in Figure 12-2, where we have shown the contents of the Solution Explorer for the Basic, Internet Application and Intranet Application templates.

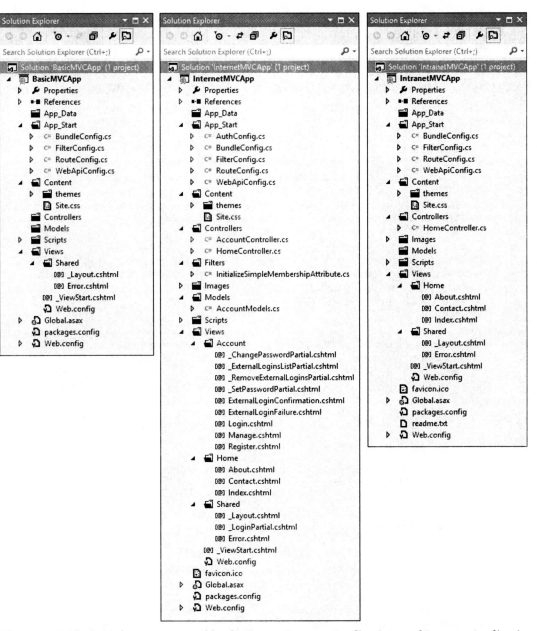

Figure 12-2. The initial content created by the Empty, Internet Application, and Intranet Application templates

You can see that the Internet Application project is the most complex and this is because it implements a complete user management and authentication system, which requires a lot of different views. The Intranet Application project is able to rely on Windows authentication to handle tasks like user management and password changes, while the Basic template makes no default provision for authentication at all.

We mainly use the `Empty` and `Basic` templates and recommend that you do the same. The default functionality in the other project templates is a little too general to be useful and require a lot of work to be useful. We get better results by building our projects from scratch.

Whichever template you choose, you will notice that the resulting projects have very similar structures. Some of the items in an MVC project have special roles, which are hard-coded into ASP.NET or the MVC Framework. Others are subject to naming conventions. We have described each of these files and folders in Table 12-1.

Table 12-1. Summary of MVC Project Items

Folder or File	Description	Notes
/App_Data	This folder is where you put private data, such as XML files or databases if you are using SQL Server Express, SQLite, or other file-based repositories.	IIS will not serve the contents of this folder.
/App_Start	This folder contains some core configuration settings for your project, including the definition of routes and filters and content bundles.	We describe routes in Chapter 13, filters in Chapter 16 and content bundles in Chapter 24.
/bin	The compiled assembly for your MVC application is placed here, along with any referenced assemblies that are not in the GAC.	IIS will not serve the contents of this directory. You won't see the bin directory in the Solution Explorer window unless you click the Show All Files button. Since these are binary files generated on compilation, you should not normally store them in source control.
/Content	This is where you put static content such as CSS files and images.	This is a convention but not required. You can put your static content anywhere that suits you.
/Controllers	This is where you put your controller classes.	This is a convention. You can put your controller classes anywhere you like, because they are all compiled into the same assembly.
/Models	This is where you put your view model and domain model classes, although all but the simplest applications benefit from defining the domain model in a dedicated project, as we demonstrated for SportsStore.	This is a convention. You can define your model classes anywhere in the project or in a separate project.

Folder or File	Description	Notes
/Scripts	This directory is intended to hold the JavaScript libraries for your application. Visual Studio adds the libraries for jQuery and several other popular JavaScript libraries.	This is a convention. You can put script files in any location, as they are really just another type of static content. See Chapter 24 for more information about managing script files
/Views	This directory holds views and partial views, usually grouped together in folders named after the controller with which they are associated.	The /Views/Web.config file prevents IIS from serving the content of these directories. Views must be rendered through an action method.
/Views/Shared	This directory holds layouts and views which are not specific to a single controller.	
/Views/Web.config	This is *not* the configuration file for your application. It contains the configuration required to make views work with ASP.NET and prevents views from being served by IIS and the namespaces imported into views by default.	
/Global.asax	This is the global ASP.NET application class. Its code-behind class (Global.asax.cs) is the place to register routing configuration, as well as set up any code to run on application initialization or shutdown, or when unhandled exceptions occur.	The Global.asax file has the same role in an MVC application as it does in a Web Forms application.
/Web.config	This is the configuration file for your application. We'll explain more about its role later in the chapter.	The Web.config file has the same role in an MVC application as it does in a Web Forms application.

WebTable 12-2 describes the folders and files that have special meanings if they exist in an MVC project.

Table 12-2. Summary of Optional MVC Project Items

Folder or File	Description
/Areas	Areas are a way of partitioning a large application into smaller pieces. We'll explain how areas work in Chapter 13.
/App_GlobalResources /App_LocalResources	These contain resource files used for localizing Web Forms pages.

Folder or File	Description
/App_Browsers	This folder contains .browser XML files that describe how to identify specific Web browsers, and what such browsers are capable of (whether they support JavaScript, for example).
/App_Themes	This folder contains Web Forms themes (including .skin files), which influence how Web Forms controls are rendered.

■ **Note** Except for /Areas, the items in Table 12-2 are part of the core ASP.NET platform and are not particularly relevant for MVC applications. Adam goes into detail about the underlying ASP.NET features in his books *Applied ASP.NET 4.5 in Context* and *Pro ASP.NET 4.5*, both published by Apress.

Understanding MVC Conventions

There are two kinds of conventions in an MVC project. The first kind is really just suggestions as to how you might like to structure your project. For example, it is conventional to put your JavaScript files in the Scripts folder. This is where other MVC developers would expect to find them, and where Visual Studio puts the initial JavaScript files for a new MVC project. But you are free to rename the Scripts folder, or remove it entirely and put your scripts anywhere you like. That would not prevent the MVC Framework from running your application.

The other kind of convention arises from the principle of *convention over configuration*, which was one of the main selling points that made Ruby on Rails so popular. Convention over configuration means that you don't need to explicitly configure associations between controllers and their views, for example. You just follow a certain naming convention for your files, and everything just works. There is less flexibility in changing your project structure when dealing with this kind of convention. The following sections explain the conventions that are used in place of configuration.

■ **Tip** All of the conventions can be changed if you are using a custom view engine, which we cover in Chapter 18, but this is not a step to be taken lightly and for the most part these are the conventions you will be dealing with in MVC projects.

Following Conventions for Controller Classes

Controller classes must have names that end with Controller, such as ProductController, AdminController, and HomeController.

When referencing a controller from elsewhere in the project, such as when using an HTML helper method, you specify the first part of the name (such as Product), and the MVC Framework automatically appends Controller to the name and starts looking for the controller class.

■ **Tip** You can change this behavior by creating your own implementation of the IControllerFactory interface, which we describe in Chapter 17.

Following Conventions for Views

Views and partial views go into the folder /Views/*Controllername*. For example, a view associated with the ProductController class would go in the /Views/Product folder.

■ **Tip** Notice that we omit the Controller part of the class from the Views folder; we use the folder /Views/Product, *not* /Views/ProductController. This may seem counterintuitive at first, but it quickly becomes second nature.

The MVC Framework expects that the default view for an action method should be named after that method. For example, the default view associated with an action method called List should be called List.cshtml. Thus, for the List action method in the ProductController class, the default view is expected to be /Views/Product/List.cshtml.

The default view is used when you return the result of calling the View method in an action method, like this:

```
return View();
```

You can specify a different view by name, like this:

```
return View("MyOtherView");
```

Notice that we do not include the file name extension or the path to the view. When looking for a view, the MVC Framework looks in the folder named after the controller and then in the /Views/Shared folder. This means that we can put views that will be used by more than one controller in the /Views/Shared folder and the framework will find them.

Following Conventions for Layouts

The naming convention for layouts is to prefix the file with an underscore (_) character, and layout files are placed in the /Views/Shared folder. Visual Studio creates a layout called _Layout.cshtml when all but the Empty project template is used. This layout is applied to all views by default through the /Views/_ViewStart.cshtml file.

If you do not want the default layout applied to views, you can change the settings in _ViewStart.cshtml (or delete the file entirely) to specify another layout in the view, like this:

```
@{
    Layout = "~/Views/Shared/MyLayout.cshtml";
}
```

Or you can disable any layout for a given view, like this:

```
@{
    Layout = null;
}
```

Debugging MVC Applications

You can debug an ASP.NET MVC application in exactly the same way as you debug an ASP.NET Web Forms application. The Visual Studio debugger is a powerful and flexible tool, with many features and uses. We can only scratch the surface in this book, but in the sections that follow we show you how to set up the debugger and perform different debugging activities on your MVC project.

Creating the Project

To demonstrate using the debugger, we have created a new MVC project using the Basic template. We have called our project DebuggingDemo and checked the option to create a unit test project, as shown in Figure 12-3.

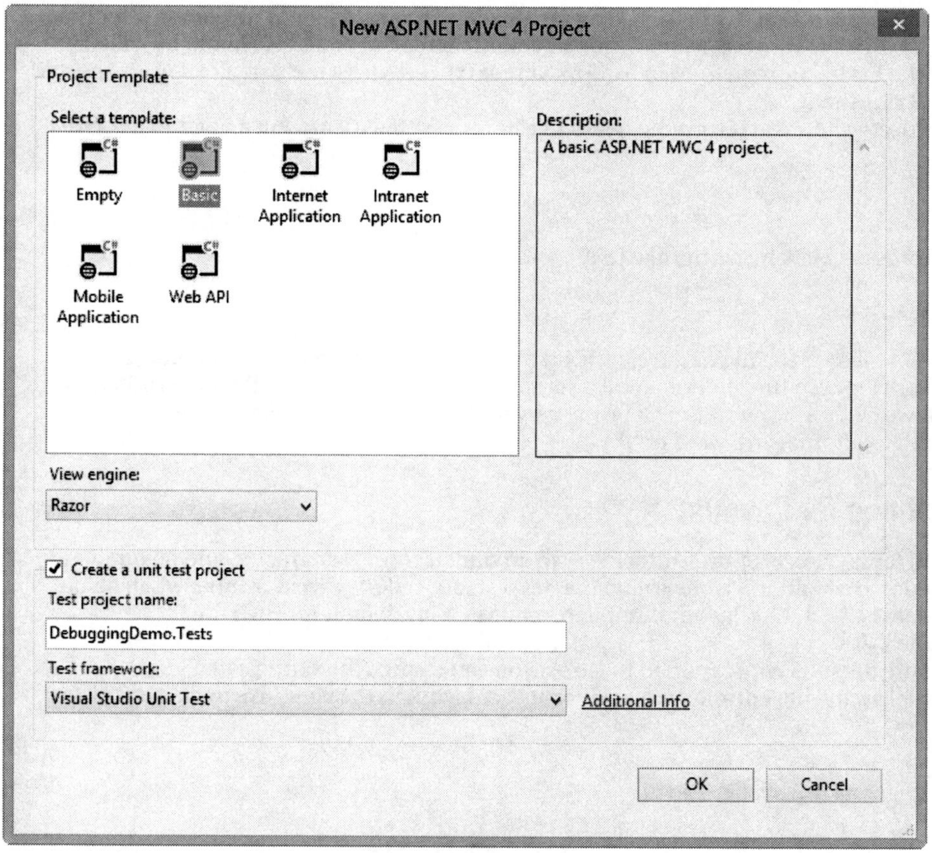

Figure 12-3. Creating the DebuggingDemo project

Create a new controller called Home and set the contents to match Listing 12-1. The statements in the action methods do not do anything interesting, but we will use them to demonstrate different debugging features.

Listing 12-1. The initial contents of the Home controller

```
using System.Web.Mvc;

namespace DebuggingDemo.Controllers {

    public class HomeController : Controller {

        public ActionResult Index() {

            int firstVal = 10;
            int secondVal = 5;
            int result = firstVal / secondVal;

            ViewBag.Message = "Welcome to ASP.NET MVC!";

            return View(result);
        }
    }
}
```

Right-click on the Index action method and select Add View from the popup menu and create a new view. Set the Model class to int and uncheck the option to use a layout, as shown in Figure 12-4.

Figure 12-4. Creating the view

Click the **Add** button and edit the contents of the view to match Listing 12-2. This is a very simple view, which just displays the view model value and the view bag property that we defined in the **Index** action method.

Listing 12-2. The initial contents of the Index.cshtml view

```
@model int

@{
    Layout = null;
}

<!DOCTYPE html>

<html>
<head>
    <meta name="viewport" content="width=device-width" />
    <link href="~/Content/Site.css" rel="stylesheet" type="text/css" />
    <title>Index</title>
</head>
<body>
    <h2 class="message">@ViewData["Message"]</h2>
    <p>
        The calculation result value is: @Model
    </p>
</body>
</html>
```

The last preparatory step we need to make is to add a style to the `/Content/Site.css` file, as shown in Listing 12-3.

Listing 12-3. Adding a style to the /Content/Site.css file

```
...
.message {
    font-size: 20pt;
    text-decoration: underline;
}
...
```

Launching the Visual Studio Debugger

Debugging in an MVC Framework application is controlled in a different way to other kinds of Visual Studio application. Visual Studio configures debugging by default, but it is useful to understand how to change the configuration.

The important setting is in the `Web.config` file in the root project folder and can be found in the `system.web` element, as shown in Listing 12-4.

Listing 12-4. The debug attribute in the Web.config file

```
...
<system.web>
  <httpRuntime targetFramework="4.5" />
  <compilation debug="true" targetFramework="4.5" />
```

```
<pages>
  <namespaces>
    <add namespace="System.Web.Helpers" />
    <add namespace="System.Web.Mvc" />
    <add namespace="System.Web.Mvc.Ajax" />
    <add namespace="System.Web.Mvc.Html" />
    <add namespace="System.Web.Routing" />
    <add namespace="System.Web.WebPages" />
  </namespaces>
</pages>
</system.web>
...
```

A lot of compilation in an MVC Framework project is done when the application is running in IIS, and so you need to ensure that the debug attribute on the compilation attribute is set to true during the development process. This ensure that the debugger is able to operate on the classes files produced through on-demand compilation

---

■ **Caution** Do not deploy your application to a production server without disabling the debug settings. We explain why this is in Chapter 26.

In addition to the Web.config file, we need to ensure that Visual Studio includes debugging information in the class files that it creates—this isn't critical, but it can cause problems if the different debug settings are not in sync. Ensure that the Debug configuration is selected in the Visual Studio toolbar, as shown in Figure 12-5.

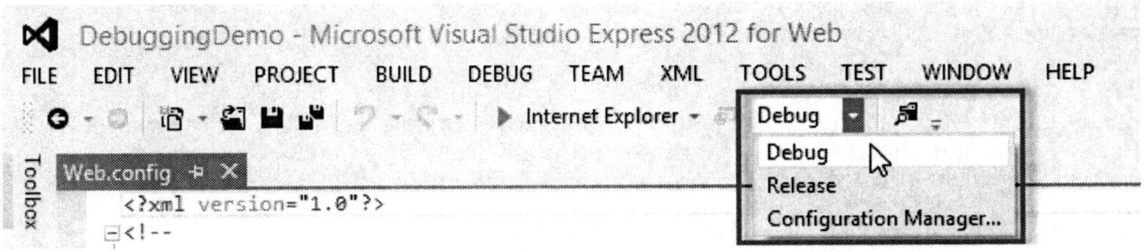

Figure 12-5. Selecting the Debug configuration

To debug an MVC Framework application, select Start Debugging from the Visual Studio Debug menu or click on the green arrow in the Visual Studio toolbar (which you can see in Figure 12-4, next to the name of the browser that will be used to display the app—Internet Explorer in this case).

If you the debug attribute in the Web.config file is set to false when you start the debugger, then Visual Studio will display the dialog shown in Figure 12-6. Select the option which allows Visual Studio to edit the Web.config file and click the OK button and the debugger will start.

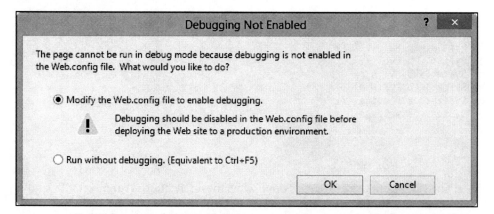

Figure 12-6. The dialog that Visual Studio displays when the Web.config file disables debugging

At this point, your application will be started and displayed in a new browser window, as shown in Figure 12-7.

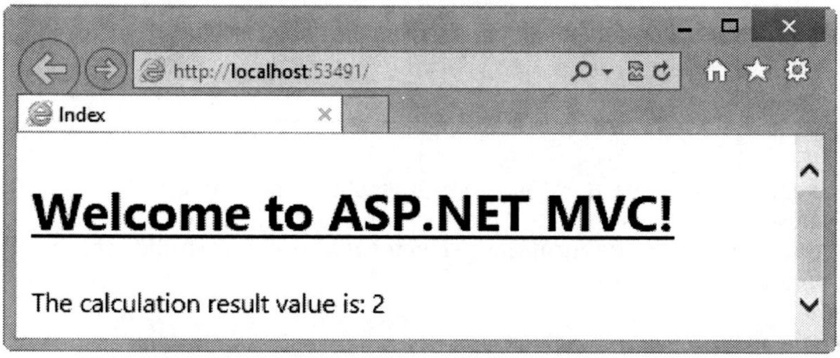

Figure 12-7. Running the debugger

The debugger will be attached to your application, but you will not notice any difference until the debugger breaks (we explain what this means in the next section). To stop the debugger, select `Stop Debugging` from the Visual Studio `Debug` menu or close the browser window.

Causing the Visual Studio Debugger to Break

An application that is running with the debugger attached will behave normally until a *break* occurs, at which point the execution of the application is halted and control is turned over to the debugger. At this point, you can inspect and control the state of the application. Breaks occur for two main reasons: when a breakpoint is reached and when an unhandled exception arises. You will see examples of both in the following sections.

■ **Tip**   You can manually break the debugger at any time by selecting `Break All` from the Visual Studio `Debug` menu while the debugger is running.

Using Breakpoints

A *breakpoint* is an instruction that tells the debugger to halt execution of the application and hand control to the programmer. At this point, you can inspect the state of the application and see what is happening and, optionally, resume execution again.

To create a breakpoint, right-click a code statement and select **Breakpoint ➤ Insert Breakpoint** from the pop-up menu. As a demonstration, apply a breakpoint to the first statement in the **Index** action method of the **Home** controller and you will see a red dot appear in the margin of the text editor, as shown in Figure 12-8.

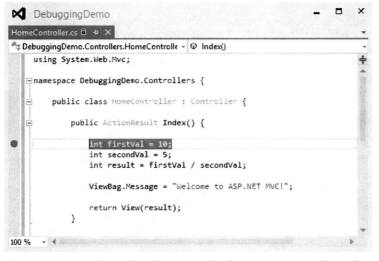

Figure 12-8. Applying a breakpoint to the first statement to the Index action method

To see the effect of the breakpoint, start the debugger by selecting **Start Debugging** from the Visual Studio **Debug** menu. The application will run until the statement to which the breakpoint has been applied is reached, at which the debugger will break, halting execution of the application and transferring control back to us.

Visual Studio highlights the point at which the execution has been stopped with yellow highlights, as shown in Figure 12-9.

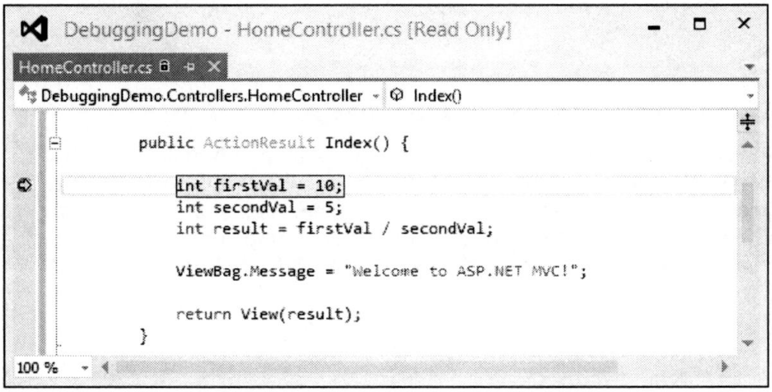

```
public ActionResult Index() {
    int firstVal = 10;
    int secondVal = 5;
    int result = firstVal / secondVal;

    ViewBag.Message = "Welcome to ASP.NET MVC!";

    return View(result);
}
```

Figure 12-9. Hitting a breakpoint

315

> ■ **Note** A breakpoint is triggered only when the statement it is associated with is executed. Our example breakpoint was reached as soon as we started the application because it is inside the action method that is called when a request for the default URL is received. If you place a breakpoint inside another action method, you must use the browser to request a URL associated with that method. This can mean working with the application in the way a user would or navigating directly to the URL in the browser window.

Once you have control of the application's execution, you can move to the next statement, follow execution into other methods and generally explore the state of your application—you can do this using the toolbar buttons or using the items in the Visual Studio Debug menu.

In addition to giving you control of the execution of the app, Visual Studio provides you with a lot of useful information about the state of your app—in fact, there is so much information that we do not have room in this book to show you anything but the basics.

Viewing Data Values in the Code Editor

The most common use for breakpoints is to try and track down bugs in your code. Before you can fix a bug, you have to figure out what is going on and one of the most useful features that Visual Studio provides is the ability to view and monitor the values of variables right in the code editor.

As an example, start the app using the debugger and wait until the breakpoint we added in the previous section is reached. When the debugger breaks, move the mouse pointer over the statement that defines the **result** variable. You will see a small pop-up which shows you the current value, as illustrated by Figure 12-10. It can be hard to make out the pop-up, so we have shown a magnified version in the figure.

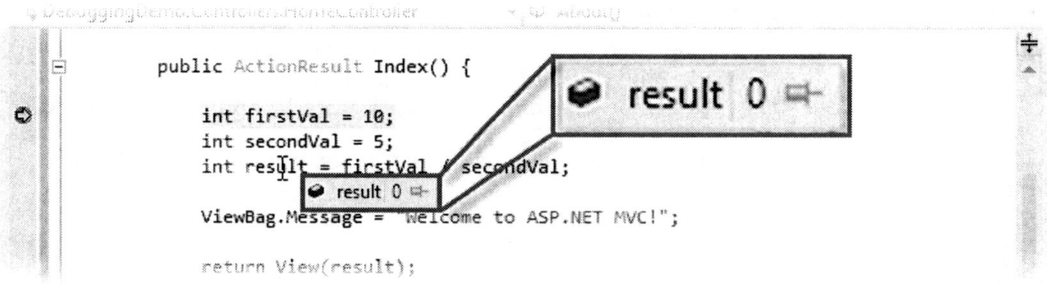

Figure 12-10. Displaying the value of a variable in the Visual Studio code editor

The execution of the statements in the Index action method has not reached the point where a value has been assigned to the **result** variable, so Visual Studio shows us the default value, which is 0 for the **int** type. Select the **Step Over** menu (or press F10) item in the Visual Studio **Debug** menu to advance the point of execution until the statement which defines the **ViewBar.Message** property and hold your mouse over the **result** variable again. We executed the statement that assigns a value to the **result** variable, and you can see the effect in Figure 12-11.

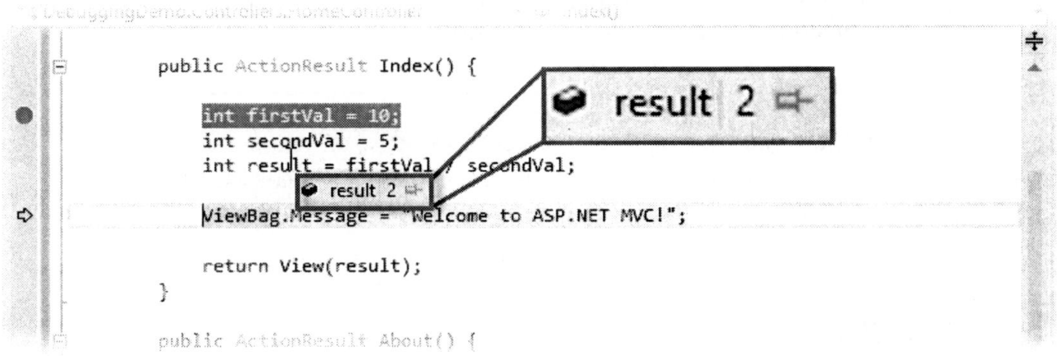

Figure 12-11. The effect of assigning a value of a variable

We use this feature a lot when we start the process of tracking down a bug, because it gives you an immediate insight into what is going on inside your app and is especially useful for spotting null values, which indicate that a variable has not been assigned a value (a cause of many bugs, in our experience).

You will notice that there is a pushpin icon to the right of the value in the po-pup. If you click on this, the pop-up becomes permanent and will indicate when the value of the variable changes—this allows you to monitor one or more variables and see when they change and what their new values are.

Viewing Application State in the Debugger Windows

Visual Studio provides a number of different windows that you can use to get information about your app while the execution has been halted following a breakpoint. A complete list of the windows available is shown on the Debug ➤ Windows menu, but two of the most useful are the Locals and Call Stack windows. The Locals window automatically displays the value of all of the variables in the current scope, as Figure 12-12 illustrates. This gives you an all-in-one view of the variables, which are likely to be of interest.

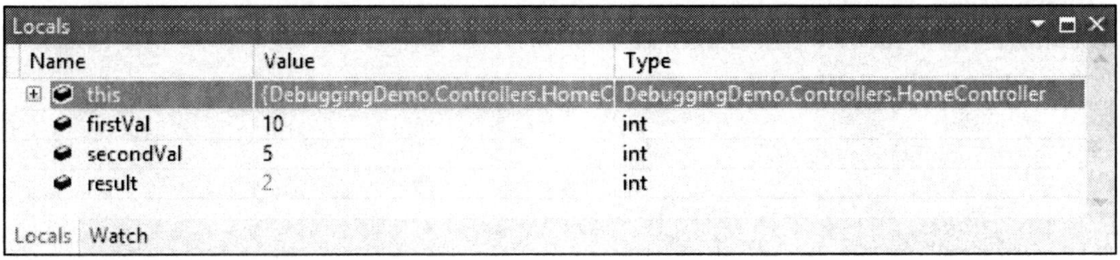

Figure 12-12. The Locals window

Variables whose values were changed by the previously executed statement are shown in red—in the figure, the result variable is red because we have just executed the statement that assigns a value.

The set of variables shown in the Locals window changes as you navigate through the application, but if you want to keep an eye on a variable globally, then right-click on one of the items shown in the Locals window and select the Add Watch option. The items in the Watch window don't change as you execute statement in the app, providing you with a fixed point of reference.

The Call Stack window shows you the sequence of calls that have led to the current statement being executed. This can be very helpful if you are trying to figure out odd behavior because you can unwind the call stack and explore the circumstances that led to the breakpoint being triggered. (We have not shown you the Call Stack window in a figure because our simple example app doesn't have enough call depth to provide a useful insight—but we recommend you explore this and the other Visual Studio windows to get more of an idea of what information the debugger is able to provide.)

■ **Tip**   You can add breakpoints to views. This can be very helpful for inspecting the values of view model properties, for example. You add a breakpoint to a view just as we did in the code file: right-click the Razor statement that you are interested in and select `Breakpoint` ➤ `Insert Breakpoint`.

Breaking on Exceptions

Unhandled exceptions are a fact of development. One of the reasons that we do a lot of unit and integration testing in our projects is to minimize the likelihood that such an exception will occur in production. The Visual Studio debugger will break automatically when it sees an unhandled exception.

■ **Note**   Only *unhandled* exceptions cause the debugger to break. An exception becomes *handled* if you catch and handle it in a `try...catch` block. Handled exceptions are a useful programming tool. They are used to represent the scenario where a method was unable to complete its task and needs to notify its caller. Unhandled exceptions are bad, because they represent an unexpected condition that we didn't try to compensate for (and because they drop the user into an error page).

To demonstrate breaking on an exception, we have made a small change to the `Index` action method, as shown in Listing 12-5.

Listing 12-5. Adding a Statement That Will Cause an Exception

```
using System.Web.Mvc;

namespace DebuggingDemo.Controllers {

    public class HomeController : Controller {

        public ActionResult Index() {

            int firstVal = 10;
            int secondVal = 0;
            int result = firstVal / secondVal;

            ViewBag.Message = "Welcome to ASP.NET MVC!";

            return View(result);
        }
    }
}
```

We changed the value of the `secondVal` variable to be 0, which will cause an exception in the statement that divides `firstVal` by `secondVal`.

■ **Note** We also removed the breakpoint from the Index action method by right clicking on the breakpoint icon in the margin and selecting `Delete Breakpoint` from the pop-up menu.

When you start the debugger, the application will run until the exception is thrown—at which point the exception helper pop-up will appear, as shown in Figure 12-13.

```
public class HomeController : Controller {

    public ActionResult Index() {

        int firstVal = 10;
        int secondVal = 0;
        int result = firstVal / secondVal;

        ViewBag.Message = "Welcome to ASP.NET MVC!";

        return View(result);
    }
}
```

```
! DivideByZeroException was unhandled by user code          ×

Attempted to divide by zero.

Troubleshooting tips:
Make sure the value of the denominator is not zero before performing a division operation.
Get general help for this exception.

Search for more Help Online...

Exception settings:
☑ Break when this exception type is user-unhandled

Actions:
View Detail...
Enable editing
Copy exception detail to the clipboard
Open exception settings
```

Figure 12-13. The exception helper

The exception helper gives you details of the exception. When the debugger breaks on an exception, you can inspect the application state and control execution, just as when a breakpoint is hit.

Using Edit and Continue

An interesting Visual Studio debugging features is called *Edit and Continue*. When the debugger breaks, you can edit you code and then continue debugging. Visual Studio recompiles your application and re-creates the state of your application at the moment of the debugger break.

Enabling Edit and Continue

We need to enable Edit and Continue in two places:

- In the `Edit and Continue` section of the `Debugging` options (select `Options` from the Visual Studio `Tools` menu), make sure that `Enable Edit and Continue` is checked, as shown in Figure 12-14.

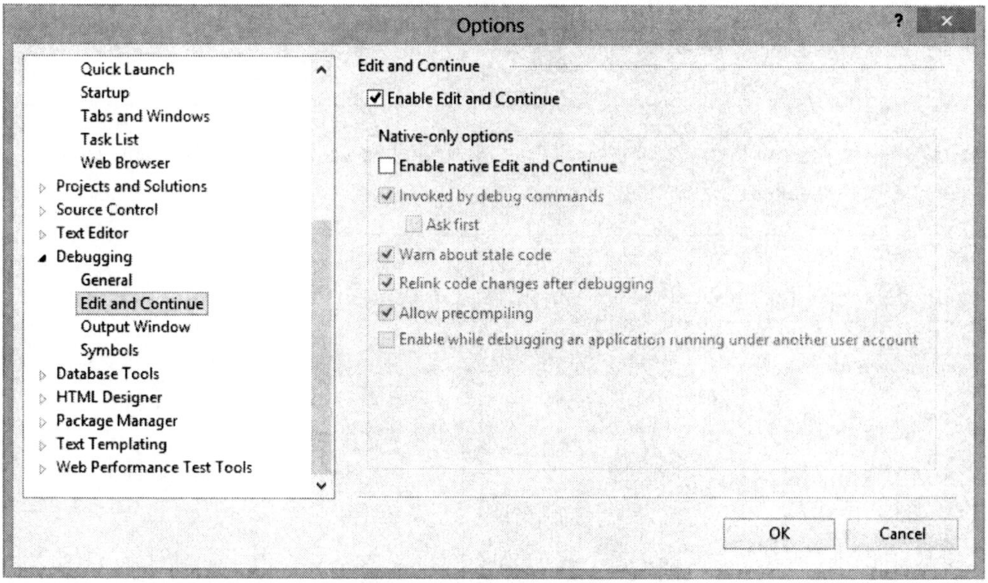

Figure 12-14. Enabling Edit and Continue in the Options dialog box

- In the project properties (select `DebuggingDemo Properties` from the Visual Studio `Project` menu), click the `Web` section and ensure that `Enable Edit and Continue` is checked, as shown in Figure 12-15.

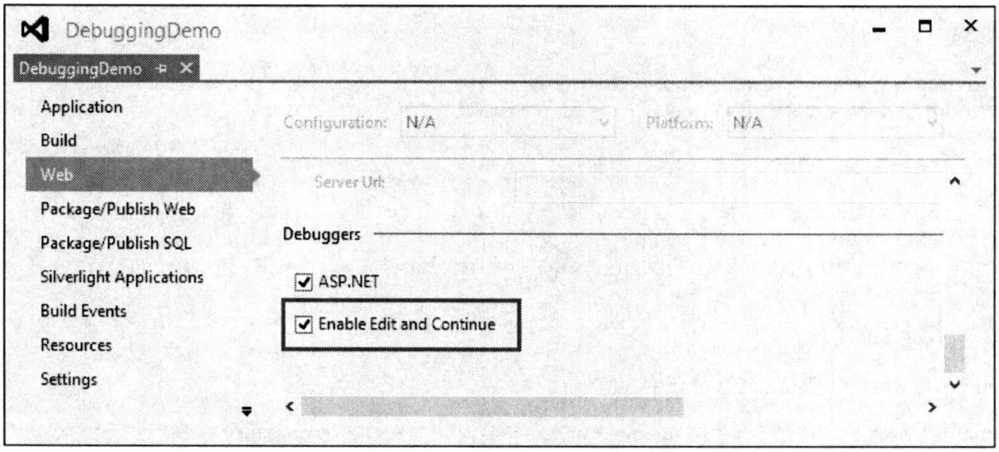

Figure 12-15. Enabling Edit and Continue in the project properties

Modifying the Project

The Edit and Continue feature is somewhat picky. There are some conditions under which it cannot work. One such condition is present in the `Index` action method of the `HomeController` class: the use of dynamic objects. To work around this, we have commented out the line that uses the view bag in the `HomeController.cs` class, as shown in Listing 12-6.

Listing 12-6. Removing the ViewBag Call from the Index Method

```
using System.Web.Mvc;

namespace DebuggingDemo.Controllers {

    public class HomeController : Controller {

        public ActionResult Index() {

            int firstVal = 10;
            int secondVal = 0;
            int result = firstVal / secondVal;

            // This statement has been commented out
            //ViewBag.Message = "Welcome to ASP.NET MVC!";

            return View(result);
        }
    }
}
```

We need to make a corresponding change in the `Index.cshtml` view, as shown in Listing 12-7.

Listing 12-7. Removing the ViewBag Call from the View

```
@model int

@{
    Layout = null;
}

<!DOCTYPE html>

<html>
<head>
    <meta name="viewport" content="width=device-width" />
    <link href="~/Content/Site.css" rel="stylesheet" type="text/css" />
    <title>Index</title>
</head>
<body>
    <!-- This element has been commented out -->
    <!--<h2 class="message">@ViewData["Message"]</h2>-->
    <p>
        The calculation result value is: @Model
    </p>
</body>
</html>
```

Editing and Continuing

We are ready for a demonstration of the Edit and Continue feature. Begin by selecting `Start Debugging` from the Visual Studio `Debug` menu. The application will be started with the debugger attached and run until it reaches the line where we perform a simple calculation in the `Index` method. The value of the second parameter is zero, which causes an exception to be thrown. At this point, the debugger halts execution, and the exception helper pops up (just like the one shown in Figure 12-13).

Click the Enable editing link in the exception helper window. In the code editor, move your mouse over the secondVal variable and click on the value in the popup that appears. Enter 5 as the new value, as shown in Figure 12-16.

```
public ActionResult Index() {

    int firstVal = 10;
    int secondVal = 0;
    int result = firstVal / secondVal;
                                        secondVal 5
    // This statement has been commented out
    //ViewBag.Message = "Welcome to ASP.NET MVC!";

    return View(result);
```

Figure 12-16. Changing the value of a variable

Now select Continue from the Visual Studio Debug menu to resume execution of the application. The new value you assigned to the variable is used to generate the value for the result variable, producing the output shown in Figure 12-17.

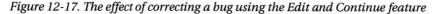

Figure 12-17. The effect of correcting a bug using the Edit and Continue feature

Take a moment to reflect on what happened here. We started the application with a bug in it—an attempt to divide a value by zero. The debugger detected the exception and stopped executing the program. We edited the code to fix the bug, replacing the reference to the variable with the literal value 5. We then told the debugger to continue the execution.

At this point, Visual Studio recompiled our application so that our change was included in the build process, restarted execution, re-created the state that led to the exception, and then carried on as normal. The browser received the rendered result, which reflected our correction.

Without Edit and Continue, we would have needed to stop the application, make our changes, compile the application, and restart the debugger. We would then use the browser to repeat the steps that we took up to the moment of the debugger break. It is avoiding this last step that can be the most important. Complex bugs may require many steps through the application to re-create, and the ability to test potential fixes without needing to repeat those steps over and over can save the programmer's time and sanity.

Summary

In this chapter, we have shown you the structure of a Visual Studio MVC project and how the various parts fit together. We also touched on one of the most important characteristics of the MVC Framework: convention. These are topics that we will return to again and again in the chapters that follow, as we dig deeper into how the MVC Framework operates.

CHAPTER 13

■ ■ ■

URL Routing

Before the introduction of the MVC Framework, ASP.NET assumed that there was a direct relationship between requested URLs and the files on the server hard disk. The job of the server was to receive the request from the browser and deliver the output from the corresponding file, as follows:

Request URL	Corresponding File
http://mysite.com/default.aspx	e:\webroot\default.aspx
http://mysite.com/admin/login.aspx	e:\webroot\admin\login.aspx
http://mysite.com/articles/AnnualReview	File not found! Send error 404.

This approach works just fine for Web Forms, where each ASPX page is both a file and a self-contained response to a request. It doesn't make sense for an MVC application, where requests are processed by action methods in controller classes, and there is no one-to-one correlation to the files on the disk.

To handle MVC URLs, the ASP.NET platform uses the *routing system*. In this chapter, we will show you how to set up and use the routing system to create powerful and flexible URL handling for your projects. As you will see, the routing system lets you create any pattern of URLs you desire, and express them in a clear and concise manner. The routing system has two functions:

- Examine an *incoming URL* and Figure 13-out for which controller and action the request is intended. As you might expect, this is what we want the routing system to do when we receive a client request.

- Generate *outgoing URLs*. These are the URLs that appear in the HTML rendered from our views so that a specific action will be invoked when the user clicks the link (at which point, it has become an incoming URL again).

In this chapter, we will focus on defining routes and using them to process incoming URLs so that the user can reach your controllers and actions. Then, in the next chapter, we will show you how to use those same routes to generate the outgoing URLs you will need to include in your views, as well as show you how to customize the routing system and use a related feature called *areas*.

Creating the Example Project

To demonstrate the routing system, we need a project to which we can add routes. We have created a new MVC application using the Basic template, and we called the project UrlsAndRoutes.

▒ **Tip**   We have included a number of different unit tests in this chapter and if you want to recreate them you will need to check the `Create a unit test project` option when you select the `Basic` template option and use NuGet to add Moq to the unit test project.

To demonstrate the route feature, we are going to add some simple controllers to the example application. In this chapter, we only care about the way in which URLs interpreted in order to call action methods, so the view models we use are string values in the view bag which report the controller and action method name. First, create a Home controller and set its contents to match those in Listing 13-1.

Listing 13-1. The Contents of the Home Controller

```
using System;
using System.Collections.Generic;
using System.Linq;
using System.Web;
using System.Web.Mvc;

namespace UrlsAndRoutes.Controllers {
    public class HomeController : Controller {

        public ActionResult Index() {
            ViewBag.Controller = "Home";
            ViewBag.Action = "Index";
            return View("ActionName");
        }

    }
}
```

Create a Customer controller and set its contents to match Listing 13-2.

Listing 13-2. The Contents of the Customer Controller

```
using System;
using System.Collections.Generic;
using System.Linq;
using System.Web;
using System.Web.Mvc;

namespace UrlsAndRoutes.Controllers {
    public class CustomerController : Controller {

        public ActionResult Index() {
            ViewBag.Controller = "Customer";
            ViewBag.Action = "Index";
            return View("ActionName");
        }

        public ActionResult List() {
            ViewBag.Controller = "Customer";
            ViewBag.Action = "List";
            return View("ActionName");
        }
    }
}
```

Create a second controller called Admin and edits its contents to match the code shown in Listing 13-3.

Listing 13-3. The Contents of the Admin Controller

```
using System;
using System.Collections.Generic;
using System.Linq;
using System.Web;
using System.Web.Mvc;

namespace UrlsAndRoutes.Controllers {
    public class AdminController : Controller {

        public ActionResult Index() {
            ViewBag.Controller = "Admin";
            ViewBag.Action = "Index";
            return View("ActionName");
        }
    }
}
```

We specified the ActionName view in all of the action methods in these controllers, which allows us to define one view and use it throughout the example application. Add a new view called ActionName.cshtml in the /Views/Shared folder and set its contents to match those shown in Listing 13-4.

Listing 13-4. The Contents of the ActionName.cshtml View

```
@{
    Layout = null;
}

<!DOCTYPE html>

<html>
<head>
    <meta name="viewport" content="width=device-width" />
    <title>ActionName</title>
</head>
<body>
    <div>The controller is: @ViewBag.Controller</div>
    <div>The action is: @ViewBag.Action</div>
</body>
</html>
```

If you start the example app, you will see an error like the one shown in Figure 13-1.

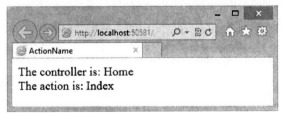

Figure 13-1. Running the example app

Introducing URL Patterns

The routing system works its magic using a set of *routes*. These routes collectively compose the URL *schema* or *scheme* for an application, which is the set of URLs that your application will recognize and respond to.

We do not need to manually type out all of the individual URLs we are willing to support. Instead, each route contains a *URL pattern*, which is compared to an incoming URL. If the pattern matches the URL, then it is used by the routing system to process that URL. Let's start with an URL for our example application:

```
http://mysite.com/Admin/Index
```

URLs can be broken down into *segments*. These are the parts of the URL, excluding the hostname and query string, that are separated by the / character. In the example URL, there are two segments, as shown in Figure 13-2.

Figure 13-2. *The segments in an example URL*

The first segment contains the word `Admin`, and the second segment contains the word `Index`. To the human eye, it is obvious that the first segment relates to the controller and the second segment relates to the action. But, of course, we need to express this relationship in a way that the routing system can understand. Here is a URL pattern that does this:

```
{controller}/{action}
```

When processing an incoming request, the job of the routing system is to match the URL that has been requested to a pattern and extract values from the URL for the *segment variables* defined in the pattern. The segment variables are expressed using braces (the { and } characters). The example pattern has two segment variables with the names `controller` and `action`, and so the value of the `controller` segment variable will be `Admin` and the value of the `action` segment variable will be `Index`.

We say match to *a* pattern, because an MVC application will usually have several routes and the routing system will compare the incoming URL to the URL pattern of each route until it finds a match.

■ **Note** The routing system does not have any special knowledge of controllers and actions. It just extracts values for the segment variables and passes them along the request pipeline. It is later in the request processing pipeline, when the request reaches the MVC Framework proper, that meaning is assigned to the `controller` and `action` variables. This is why the routing system can be used with Web Forms and the Web API (we introduce the Web API Chapter 25).

By default, a URL pattern will match any URL that has the correct number of segments. For example, the pattern {controller}/{action} will match any URL that has two segments, as illustrated by Table 13-1.

Table 13-1. Matching URLs

Request URL	Segment Variables
`http://mysite.com/Admin/Index`	`controller = Admin` `action = Index`
`http://mysite.com/Index/Admin`	`controller = Index` `action = Admin`
`http://mysite.com/Apples/Oranges`	`controller = Apples` `action = Oranges`
`http://mysite.com/Admin`	No match—too few segments
`http://mysite.com/Admin/Index/Soccer`	No match—too many segments

Table 13-1 highlights two key behaviors of URL patterns:

- URL patterns are *conservative*, and will match only URLs that have the same number of segments as the pattern. You can see this in the fourth and fifth examples in the table.

- URL patterns are *liberal*. If a URL *does* have the correct number of segments, the pattern will extract the value for the segment variable, whatever it might be.

These are the default behaviors, which are the keys to understanding how URL patterns function. We show you how to change the defaults later in this chapter.

As we already mentioned, the routing system does not know anything about an MVC application, and so URL patterns will match even when there is no controller or action that corresponds to the values extracted from a URL. You can see this demonstrated in the second example in Table 13-1. We have transposed the `Admin` and `Index` segments in the URL, and so the values extracted from the URL have also been transposed, even though there is no `Index` controller in the example project.

Creating and Registering a Simple Route

Once you have a URL pattern in mind, you can use it to define a route. Routes are defined in the `RouteConfig.cs` file, which is in the `App_Start` project folder. You can see the initial content that Visual Studio defines for this file in Listing 13-5.

Listing 13-5. The Default Contents of the RouteConfig.cs File

```
using System;
using System.Collections.Generic;
using System.Linq;
using System.Web;
using System.Web.Mvc;
using System.Web.Routing;

namespace UrlsAndRoutes {
    public class RouteConfig {
        public static void RegisterRoutes(RouteCollection routes) {
```

```
        routes.IgnoreRoute("{resource}.axd/{*pathInfo}");

        routes.MapRoute(
            name: "Default",
            url: "{controller}/{action}/{id}",
            defaults: new { controller = "Home", action = "Index",
                id = UrlParameter.Optional }
        );
    }
}
}
```

The static `RegisterRoutes` method that is defined in the `RouteConfig.cs` file is called from the `Global.asax.cs` file, which sets up some of the core MVC features when the application is started. You can see the default contents of the `Global.asax.cs` file in Listing 13-6, and we have highlighted the call to the `RouteConfig.RegisterRoutes` method, which is made from the `Application_Start` method.

Listing 13-6. The Default Contents of the Global.asax.cs

```
using System;
using System.Collections.Generic;
using System.Linq;
using System.Web;
using System.Web.Http;
using System.Web.Mvc;
using System.Web.Optimization;
using System.Web.Routing;

namespace UrlsAndRoutes {
    public class MvcApplication : System.Web.HttpApplication {
        protected void Application_Start() {
            AreaRegistration.RegisterAllAreas();

            WebApiConfig.Register(GlobalConfiguration.Configuration);
            FilterConfig.RegisterGlobalFilters(GlobalFilters.Filters);
            RouteConfig.RegisterRoutes(RouteTable.Routes);
            BundleConfig.RegisterBundles(BundleTable.Bundles);
        }
    }
}
```

The `Application_Start` method is called by the underlying ASP.NET platform when the MVC application is first started, which leads to the `RouteConfig.RegisterRoutes` method being called. The parameter to this method is the value of the static `RouteTable.Routes` property, which is an instance of the `RouteCollection` class (the features of which we describe shortly).

■ **Tip**   The other calls made in the `Application_Start` method are covered in other chapters. We describe the `AreaRegistration.RegisterAllAreas` method in Chapter 14, the `WebApiConfig.Register` method in Chapter 25, the `FilterConfig.RegisterGlobalFilters` method in Chapter 16 and the `BundleConfig.RegisterBundles` method in Chapter 24.

Listing 13-7 shows how to create a route using the example URL pattern from the previous section in the `RegisterRoutes` method of the `RouteConfig.cs` file (we have removed all of the other statements in the method so we can focus on the example).

Listing 13-7. Registering a Route

```
using System;
using System.Collections.Generic;
using System.Linq;
using System.Web;
using System.Web.Mvc;
using System.Web.Routing;

namespace UrlsAndRoutes {
    public class RouteConfig {
        public static void RegisterRoutes(RouteCollection routes) {

            Route myRoute = new Route("{controller}/{action}", new MvcRouteHandler());
            routes.Add("MyRoute", myRoute);
        }
    }
}
```

We create a new `Route` using our URL pattern as a constructor parameter, which we express as a string. We also pass an instance of `MvcRouteHandler` to the constructor. Different ASP.NET technologies provide different classes to tailor the routing behavior, and this is the class we use for ASP.NET MVC applications. Once we have created the route, we add it to the `RouteCollection` object using the `Add` method, passing in the name we want the route to be known by and the route we have created.

■ **Tip** Naming your routes is optional—and there is a philosophical argument that doing so sacrifices some of the clean separation of concerns that otherwise comes from routing. We are pretty relaxed about naming, but we explain why this can be a problem in the "Generating a URL from a Specific Route" section later in this chapter.

A more convenient way of registering routes is to use the `MapRoute` method defined by the `RouteCollection` class. Listing 13-8 shows how we can use this method to register our route, which has the same effect as the previous example, but is a cleaner syntax.

Listing 13-8. Registering a Route Using the MapRoute Method

```
using System;
using System.Collections.Generic;
using System.Linq;
using System.Web;
using System.Web.Mvc;
using System.Web.Routing;

namespace UrlsAndRoutes {
    public class RouteConfig {
        public static void RegisterRoutes(RouteCollection routes) {

            routes.MapRoute("MyRoute", "{controller}/{action}");
        }
    }
}
```

This approach is slightly more compact, mainly because we do not need to create an instance of the MvcRouteHandler class. The MapRoute method is solely for use with MVC applications. ASP.NET Web Forms applications can use the MapPageRoute method, also defined in the RouteCollection class.

Using the Simple Route

You can see the effect of the changes we made to the routing by running the example application. When the browser tries to navigate to the root URL for the application, you will see an error—but if you navigate to a route that matches our {controller}/{action} pattern, you will see a result like the one shown in Figure 13-3, which illustrates the effect of navigating to /Admin/Index.

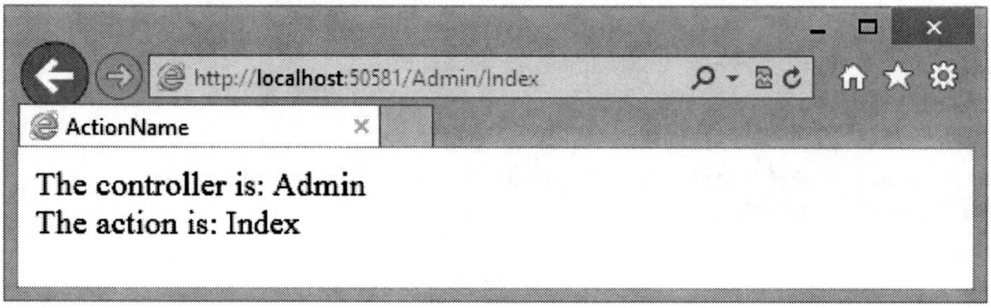

Figure 13-3. Navigating using a simple route

Our simple route does not tell the MVC Framework how to respond to requests for the root URL and only supports a single, very specific, URL pattern. We have, temporarily taken a step back from the functionality that Visual Studio adds to the RouteConfig.cs file when it creates the MVC project. We will show you how to build more complex patterns and routes throughout the rest of this chapter.

UNIT TEST: TESTING INCOMING URLS

We recommend that you unit test your routes to make sure they process incoming URLs as expected, even if you choose not to unit test the rest of your application. URL schemas can get pretty complex in large applications, and it is easy to create something that has unexpected results.

In previous chapters, we have avoided creating common helper methods to be shared among tests in order to keep each unit test description self-contained. For this chapter, we are taking a different approach. Testing the routing schema for an application is most readily done when you can batch several tests in a single method, and this becomes much easier with some helper methods.

To test routes, we need to mock three classes from the MVC Framework: HttpRequestBase, HttpContextBase, and HttpResponseBase (this last class is required for testing outgoing URLs, which we cover in the next chapter). Together, these classes re-create enough of the MVC infrastructure to support the routing system. We added a new Unit Tests file called RouteTests.cs to the unit test project and our first addition is the helper method that creates the mock HttpContextBase objects, as follows:

```
using System;
using Microsoft.VisualStudio.TestTools.UnitTesting;
using System.Web;
using System.Web.Routing;
```

```
using Moq;
using System.Reflection;

namespace UrlsAndRoutes.Tests {
    [TestClass]
    public class RouteTests {

        private HttpContextBase CreateHttpContext(string targetUrl = null,
                                                  string httpMethod = "GET") {
            // create the mock request
            Mock<HttpRequestBase> mockRequest = new Mock<HttpRequestBase>();
            mockRequest.Setup(m => m.AppRelativeCurrentExecutionFilePath)
                .Returns(targetUrl);
            mockRequest.Setup(m => m.HttpMethod).Returns(httpMethod);

            // create the mock response
            Mock<HttpResponseBase> mockResponse = new Mock<HttpResponseBase>();
            mockResponse.Setup(m => m.ApplyAppPathModifier(
                It.IsAny<string>())).Returns<string>(s => s);

            // create the mock context, using the request and response
            Mock<HttpContextBase> mockContext = new Mock<HttpContextBase>();
            mockContext.Setup(m => m.Request).Returns(mockRequest.Object);
            mockContext.Setup(m => m.Response).Returns(mockResponse.Object);

            // return the mocked context
            return mockContext.Object;
        }
    }
}
```

The setup here is simpler than it looks. We expose the URL we want to test through the
AppRelativeCurrentExecutionFilePath property of the HttpRequestBase class, and expose the
HttpRequestBase through the Request property of the mock HttpContextBase class.
Our next helper method lets us test a route:

```
...
private void TestRouteMatch(string url, string controller, string action,
    object routeProperties = null, string httpMethod = "GET") {

    // Arrange
    RouteCollection routes = new RouteCollection();
    RouteConfig.RegisterRoutes(routes);
    // Act - process the route
    RouteData result
        = routes.GetRouteData(CreateHttpContext(url, httpMethod));
    // Assert
    Assert.IsNotNull(result);
    Assert.IsTrue(TestIncomingRouteResult(result, controller,
        action, routeProperties));
}
...
```

The parameters of this method let us specify the URL to test, the expected values for the `controller` and `action` segment variables, and an `object` that contains the expected values for any additional variables we have defined. We will show you how to create such variables later in the chapter. We also defined a parameter for the HTTP method, which we will explain in the "Constraining Routes" section.

The `TestRouteMatch` method relies on another method, `TestIncomingRouteResult`, to compare the result obtained from the routing system with the segment variable values we expect. This method uses .NET reflection so that we can use an anonymous type to express any additional segment variables. Do not worry if this method doesn't make sense, as this is just to make testing more convenient; it is not a requirement for understanding MVC. Here is the `TestIncomingRouteResult` method:

```
...
private bool TestIncomingRouteResult(RouteData routeResult,
    string controller, string action, object propertySet = null) {

    Func<object, object, bool> valCompare = (v1, v2) => {
        return StringComparer.InvariantCultureIgnoreCase
            .Compare(v1, v2) == 0;
    };

    bool result = valCompare(routeResult.Values["controller"], controller)
        && valCompare(routeResult.Values["action"], action);

    if (propertySet != null) {
        PropertyInfo[] propInfo = propertySet.GetType().GetProperties();
        foreach (PropertyInfo pi in propInfo) {
            if (!(routeResult.Values.ContainsKey(pi.Name)
                    && valCompare(routeResult.Values[pi.Name],
                    pi.GetValue(propertySet, null)))) {

                result = false;
                break;
            }
        }
    }
    return result;
}
...
```

We also need a method to check that a URL does not work. As you will see, this can be an important part of defining a URL schema.

```
...
private void TestRouteFail(string url) {
    // Arrange
    RouteCollection routes = new RouteCollection();
    RouteConfig.RegisterRoutes(routes);
    // Act - process the route
    RouteData result = routes.GetRouteData(CreateHttpContext(url));
    // Assert
    Assert.IsTrue(result == null || result.Route == null);
}
...
```

`TestRouteMatch` and `TestRouteFail` contain calls to the `Assert` method, which throws an exception if the assertion fails. Because C# exceptions are propagated up the call stack, we can create simple test methods that can test a set of URLs and get the test behavior we require. Here is a test method that tests the route we defined in Listing 13-8:

```
...
[TestMethod]
public void TestIncomingRoutes() {

    // check for the URL that we hope to receive
    TestRouteMatch("~/Admin/Index", "Admin", "Index");
    // check that the values are being obtained from the segments
    TestRouteMatch("~/One/Two", "One", "Two");

    // ensure that too many or too few segments fails to match
    TestRouteFail("~/Admin/Index/Segment");
    TestRouteFail("~/Admin");
}
...
```

This test uses the `TestRouteMatch` method to check the URL we are expecting and also checks a URL in the same format to make sure that the `controller` and `action` values are being obtained properly using the URL segments. We also use the `TestRouteFail` method to make sure that our application won't accept URLs that have a different number of segments. When testing, we must prefix the URL with the tilde (~) character, because this is how the ASP.NET Framework presents the URL to the routing system.

Notice that we didn't need to define the routes in the test methods. This is because we are loading them directly using the `RegisterRoutes` method in the `RouteConfig` class.

Defining Default Values

The reason that we got an error when we requested the default URL for the application is that it didn't match the route we had defined. The default URL is expressed as ~/ to the routing system and there are no segments in this string that can be matched to the `controller` and `action` variables defined by our simple route pattern.

We explained earlier that URL patterns are conservative, in that they will match only URLs with the specified number of segments. We also said that this was the default behavior. One way to change this behavior is to use *default values*. A default value is applied when the URL doesn't contain a segment that can be matched to the value. Listing 13-9 provides an example of a route that contains a default value.

■ **Note** From here on in, when we show you a new routing configuration, we have applied the changes to the `RegisterRoutes` method of the `RouteConfig` class.

Listing 13-9. Providing a Default Value in a Route

```
using System;
using System.Collections.Generic;
using System.Linq;
using System.Web;
using System.Web.Mvc;
using System.Web.Routing;

namespace UrlsAndRoutes {
    public class RouteConfig {
        public static void RegisterRoutes(RouteCollection routes) {

            routes.MapRoute("MyRoute", "{controller}/{action}",
                new { action = "Index" });
        }
    }
}
```

Default values are supplied as properties in an anonymous type. In Listing 13-9, we have provided a default value of Index for the action variable. This route will match all two-segment URLs, as it did previously. For example, if the URL http://mydomain.com/Home/Index is requested, the route will extract Home as the value for the controller and Index as the value for the action.

But now that we have provided a default value for the action segment, the route will also match single-segment URLs as well. When processing a single-segment URL, the routing system will extract the controller value from the sole URL segment, and use the default value for the action variable. In this way, we can request the URL http://mydomain.com/Home and invoke the Index action method on the Home controller.

We can go further and define URLs that do not contain any segment variables at all, relying on just the default values to identify the action and controller. We can map the default URL using default values for both, as shown in Listing 13-10.

Listing 13-10. Providing Action and Controller Default Values in a Route

```
using System;
using System.Collections.Generic;
using System.Linq;
using System.Web;
using System.Web.Mvc;
using System.Web.Routing;

namespace UrlsAndRoutes {
    public class RouteConfig {
        public static void RegisterRoutes(RouteCollection routes) {

            routes.MapRoute("MyRoute", "{controller}/{action}",
                new { controller = "Home", action = "Index" });
        }
    }
}
```

By providing default values for both the controller and action variables, we have created a route that will match URLs that have zero, one, or two segments, as shown in Table 13-2.

Table 13-2. Matching URLs

Number of Segments	Example	Maps To
0	mydomain.com	controller = Home action = Index
1	mydomain.com/Customer	controller = Customer action = Index
2	mydomain.com/Customer/List	controller = Customer action = List
3	mydomain.com/Customer/List/All	No match—too many segments

The fewer segments we receive in the incoming URL, the more we rely on the default values, up until the point we receive a URL with no segments and only default values are used. You can see the effect of the default values by starting the example app again—this time, when the browser requests the root URL for the application, the default values for the `controller` and `action` segment variables will be used, which will lead the MVC Framework to invoke the Index action method on the Home controller, as shown in Figure 13-4.

Figure 13-4. Using default values to broaden the scope of a route

UNIT TESTING: DEFAULT VALUES

We do not need to take any special actions if we use our helper methods to test routes that define default values. Here are the revisions we made to the `TestIncomingRoutes` test method in the `RouteTests.cs` file for the route we defined in Listing 13-10:

```
...
[TestMethod]
public void TestIncomingRoutes() {
    TestRouteMatch("~/", "Home", "Index");
    TestRouteMatch("~/Customer", "Customer", "Index");
    TestRouteMatch("~/Customer/List", "Customer", "List");
    TestRouteFail("~/Customer/List/All");
}
...
```

The only point of note is that we must specify the default URL as ~/, as this is how ASP.NET presents the URL to the routing system. If we specify the empty string ("") that we used to define the route or /, the routing system will throw an exception, and the test will fail.

Using Static URL Segments

Not all of the segments in a URL pattern need to be variables. You can also create patterns that have static segments. Suppose that we want to match a URL like this to support URLs that are prefixed with `Public`:

`http://mydomain.com/Public/Home/Index`

We can do so by using a pattern like the one shown in Listing 13-11.

Listing 13-11. A URL Pattern with Static Segments

```
using System;
using System.Collections.Generic;
using System.Linq;
using System.Web;
using System.Web.Mvc;
using System.Web.Routing;

namespace UrlsAndRoutes {
    public class RouteConfig {
        public static void RegisterRoutes(RouteCollection routes) {

            routes.MapRoute("MyRoute", "{controller}/{action}",
                new { controller = "Home", action = "Index" });

            routes.MapRoute("", "Public/{controller}/{action}",
                new { controller = "Home", action = "Index" });
        }
    }
}
```

This new pattern will match only URLs that contain three segments, the first of which *must* be `Customers`. The other two segments can contain any value, and will be used for the `controller` and `action` variables. If the last two segments are omitted, then the default values will be used.

We can also create URL patterns that have segments containing both static and variable elements, such as the one shown in Listing 13-12.

Listing 13-12. A URL Pattern with a Mixed Segment

```
using System;
using System.Collections.Generic;
using System.Linq;
using System.Web;
using System.Web.Mvc;
using System.Web.Routing;

namespace UrlsAndRoutes {
    public class RouteConfig {
        public static void RegisterRoutes(RouteCollection routes) {
```

```
        routes.MapRoute("", "X{controller}/{action}");

        routes.MapRoute("MyRoute", "{controller}/{action}",
            new { controller = "Home", action = "Index" });

        routes.MapRoute("", "Public/{controller}/{action}",
            new { controller = "Home", action = "Index" });
        }
    }
}
```

The pattern in this route matches any two-segment URL where the first segment starts with the letter X. The value for `controller` is taken from the first segment, excluding the X. The `action` value is taken from the second segment. You can see the effect of this route if you start the application and navigate to /XHome/Index, the result of which is illustrated by Figure 13-5.

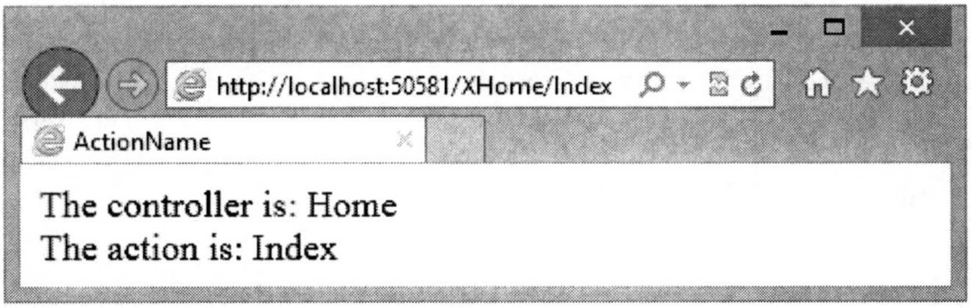

Figure 13-5. Mixing static and variable elements in a single segment

ROUTE ORDERING

In Listing 13-12, we defined a new route and placed it before all of the others in the `RegisterRoutes` method. We did this because routes are applied in the order in which they appear in the `RouteCollection` object. The `MapRoute` method adds a route to the end of the collection, which means that routes are generally applied in the order in which we add them. We say "generally" because there are methods that let us insert routes in specific locations. We tend not to use these methods, because having routes applied in the order in which they are defined makes understanding the routing for an application simpler.

The route system tries to match an incoming URL against the URL pattern of the route that was defined first, and proceeds to the next route only if there is no match. The routes are tried in sequence until a match is found or the set of routes has been exhausted. The result of this is that we must define out most specific routes first. The route we added in Listing 13-12 is more specific than the route that follows. Suppose that we reversed the order of the routes, like this:

```
...
routes.MapRoute("MyRoute", "{controller}/{action}",
new { controller = "Home", action = "Index" });

routes.MapRoute("", "X{controller}/{action}");
...
```

337

Then the first route, which matches *any* URL with zero, one, or two segments, will be the one that is used. The more specific route, which is now second in the list, will never be reached. The new route excludes the leading X of a URL, but this won't be done by the older route, Therefore, a URL such as this:

```
http://mydomain.com/XHome/Index
```

will be targeted to a controller called XHome, which does not exist, and so will lead to a 404–Not Found error being sent to the user.

If you have not read the section on unit testing incoming URLs, we suggest you do so now. If you unit test only one part of your MVC application, it should be your URL schema.

We can combine static URL segments and default values to create an alias for a specific URL. This can be useful if you have published your URL schema publicly and it has formed a contract with your user. If you refactor an application in this situation, you need to preserve the previous URL format so that any URL favorites or macro scripts the user has created continue to work. Let us imagine that we used to have a controller called Shop, which has now been replaced by the Home controller. Listing 13-13 shows how we can create a route to preserve the old URL schema.

Listing 13-13. Mixing Static URL Segments and Default Values

```
using System;
using System.Collections.Generic;
using System.Linq;
using System.Web;
using System.Web.Mvc;
using System.Web.Routing;

namespace UrlsAndRoutes {
    public class RouteConfig {
        public static void RegisterRoutes(RouteCollection routes) {

            routes.MapRoute("ShopSchema", "Shop/{action}",
                new { controller = "Home" });

            routes.MapRoute("", "X{controller}/{action}");

            routes.MapRoute("MyRoute", "{controller}/{action}",
                new { controller = "Home", action = "Index" });

            routes.MapRoute("", "Public/{controller}/{action}",
                new { controller = "Home", action = "Index" });
        }
    }
}
```

The route we have added matches any two-segment URL where the first segment is Shop. The action value is taken from the second URL segment. The URL pattern doesn't contain a variable segment for controller, so the default value we have supplied is used. This means that a request for an action on the Shop controller is translated to a request for the Home controller. You can see the effect of this route by starting the app and navigating to the /Shop/Index URL—as Figure 13-6 shows, the route we added causes the MVC Framework to target the Index action method in the Home controller.

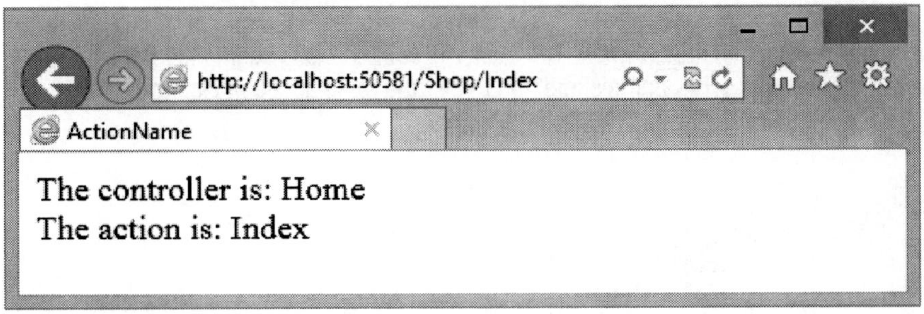

Figure 13-6. Creating an alias to perverse URL schemas

And we can go one step further and create aliases for action methods that have been refactored away as well and are no longer present in the controller. To do this, we simply create a static URL and provide the controller and action values as defaults, as shown in Listing 13-14.

Listing 13-14. Aliasing a Controller and an Action

```
using System;
using System.Collections.Generic;
using System.Linq;
using System.Web;
using System.Web.Mvc;
using System.Web.Routing;

namespace UrlsAndRoutes {
    public class RouteConfig {
        public static void RegisterRoutes(RouteCollection routes) {

            routes.MapRoute("ShopSchema2", "Shop/OldAction",
                new { controller = "Home", action = "Index" });

            routes.MapRoute("ShopSchema", "Shop/{action}",
                new { controller = "Home" });

            routes.MapRoute("", "X{controller}/{action}");

            routes.MapRoute("MyRoute", "{controller}/{action}",
                new { controller = "Home", action = "Index" });

            routes.MapRoute("", "Public/{controller}/{action}",
                new { controller = "Home", action = "Index" });
        }
    }
}
```

Notice that, once again, we have placed our new route so that it is defined first. This is because it is more specific than the routes that follow. If a request for Shop/OldAction were processed by the next defined route, for example, we would get a different result from the one we want. The request would be dealt with using a 404–Not Found error, rather than being translated in order to preserve a contract with our clients.

UNIT TEST: TESTING STATIC SEGMENTS

Once again, we can use our helper methods to routes whose URL patterns contain static segments. Here is the addition we made to the `TestIncomingRoutes` unit test method to test the route added in Listing 13-14:

```
...
[TestMethod]
public void TestIncomingRoutes() {
    TestRouteMatch("~/", "Home", "Index");
    TestRouteMatch("~/Customer", "Customer", "Index");
    TestRouteMatch("~/Shop/Index", "Home", "Index");
    TestRouteMatch("~/Customer/List", "Customer", "List");
    TestRouteFail("~/Customer/List/All");
}
...
```

Defining Custom Segment Variables

The `controller` and `action` segment variables have special meaning to the MVC Framework and, obviously, they correspond to the controller and action method that will be used to service the request. We are not limited to these built-in segment variables—we can also define our own variables, as shown in Listing 13-15. (We have removed the existing routes from the previous section so we can start over.)

Listing 13-15. Defining Additional Variables in a URL Pattern

```
using System;
using System.Collections.Generic;
using System.Linq;
using System.Web;
using System.Web.Mvc;
using System.Web.Routing;

namespace UrlsAndRoutes {
    public class RouteConfig {
        public static void RegisterRoutes(RouteCollection routes) {

            routes.MapRoute("MyRoute", "{controller}/{action}/{id}",
                new { controller = "Home", action = "Index",
                    id = "DefaultId" });
        }
    }
}
```

The route's URL pattern defines the standard `controller` and `action` variables, as well as a custom variable called `id`. This route will match any zero-to-three-segment URL. The contents of the third segment will be assigned to the `id` variable, and if there is no third segment, the default value will be used.

■ **Caution**   Some names are reserved and not available for custom segment variable names. These are
controller, action, and area. The meaning of the first two is obvious, and we will explain the role of areas in the
next chapter.

We can access any of the segment variables in an action method by using the `RouteData.Values`
property. To demonstrate this, we have added an action method to the `HomeController` class called
`CustomVariable`, as shown in Listing 13-16.

Listing 13-16. Accessing a Custom Segment Variable in an Action Method

```
using System;
using System.Collections.Generic;
using System.Linq;
using System.Web;
using System.Web.Mvc;

namespace UrlsAndRoutes.Controllers {
    public class HomeController : Controller {

        public ActionResult Index() {
            ViewBag.Controller = "Home";
            ViewBag.Action = "Index";
            return View("ActionName");
        }

        public ActionResult CustomVariable() {
            ViewBag.Controller = "Home";
            ViewBag.Action = "CustomVariable";
            ViewBag.CustomVariable = RouteData.Values["id"];
            return View();
        }
    }
}
```

This method obtains the value of the custom variable in the route URL pattern and passes it to the
view using the `ViewBag`. Right click on the new action method in the code editor and select `Add View`. Set
the view name to `CustomVariable` and click the `Add` button. Visual Studio will create a new
`CustomVariable.cshtml` file in the `/Views/Home` folder. Edit the view so that it matches the content shown
in Listing 13-17.

Listing 13-17. Displaying the Value of a Custom Segment Variable

```
@{
    Layout = null;
}

<!DOCTYPE html>

<html>
<head>
    <meta name="viewport" content="width=device-width" />
    <title>Custom Variable</title>
</head>
<body>
```

```
    <div>The controller is: @ViewBag.Controller</div>
    <div>The action is: @ViewBag.Action</div>
    <div>The custom variable is: @ViewBag.CustomVariable</div>
</body>
</html>
```

To see the effect of the custom segment variable, start the application and navigate to the URL /Home/CustomVariable/Hello. The CustomVariable action method in the Home controller is called, and the value of the custom segment variable is retrieved from the ViewBag and passed to the view. You can see the results in Figure 13-7.

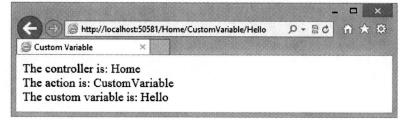

Figure 13-7. Displaying the value of a custom segment variable

We have provided a default value for the id segment variable, which means that you will see the results shown in Figure 13-8 if you navigate to /Home/CustomVariable.

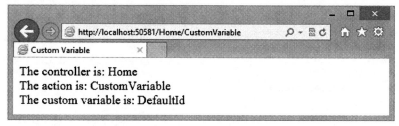

Figure 13-8. The default value for a custom segment variable

UNIT TEST: TESTING CUSTOM SEGMENT VARIABLES

We included support for testing custom segment variables in our test helper methods. The TestRouteMatch method has an optional parameter that accepts an anonymous type containing the names of the properties we want to test for and the values we expect. Here are the changes we made to the TestIncomingRoutes test method to test the route defined in Listing 13-15:

```
...
[TestMethod]
public void TestIncomingRoutes() {
    TestRouteMatch("~/", "Home", "Index", new { id = "DefaultId" });
    TestRouteMatch("~/Customer", "Customer", "index", new { id = "DefaultId" });
    TestRouteMatch("~/Customer/List", "Customer", "List",
        new { id = "DefaultId" });
    TestRouteMatch("~/Customer/List/All", "Customer", "List", new { id = "All" });
    TestRouteFail("~/Customer/List/All/Delete");
}
...
```

Using Custom Variables as Action Method Parameters

Using the RouteData.Values property is only one way to access custom route variables. The other way is much more elegant. If we define parameters to our action method with names that match the URL pattern variables, the MVC Framework will pass the values obtained from the URL as parameters to the action method. For example, the custom variable we defined in the route in Listing 13-15 is called id. We can modify the CustomVariable action method so that it has a matching parameter, as shown in Listing 13-18.

Listing 13-18. Mapping a Custom URL Segment Variable to an Action Method Parameter

```
using System;
using System.Collections.Generic;
using System.Linq;
using System.Web;
using System.Web.Mvc;

namespace UrlsAndRoutes.Controllers {
    public class HomeController : Controller {

        public ActionResult Index() {
            ViewBag.Controller = "Home";
            ViewBag.Action = "Index";
            return View("ActionName");
        }

        public ActionResult CustomVariable(string id) {
            ViewBag.Controller = "Home";
            ViewBag.Action = "CustomVariable";
            ViewBag.CustomVariable = id;
            return View();
        }
    }
}
```

When the routing system matches a URL against the route we defined in Listing 13-15, the value of the third segment in the URL is assigned to the custom variable id. The MVC Framework compares the list of segment variables with the list of action method parameters, and if the names match, passes the values from the URL to the method.

We have defined the id parameter as a string, but the MVC Framework will try to convert the URL value to whatever parameter type we define. If we declared the id parameter as an int or a DateTime, then we would receive the value from the URL parsed to an instance of that type. This is an elegant and useful feature that removes the need for us to handle the conversion ourselves.

■ **Note** The MVC Framework uses the model binding system to convert the values contained in the URL to .NET types and can handle much more complex situations than shown in this example. We cover model binding in Chapter 22.

343

Defining Optional URL Segments

An *optional* URL segment is one that the user does not need to specify, but for which no default value is specified. Listing 13-19 shows an example, and we specify that a segment variable is optional by setting the default value to `UrlParameter.Optional`.

Listing 13-19. Specifying an Optional URL Segment

```
using System;
using System.Collections.Generic;
using System.Linq;
using System.Web;
using System.Web.Mvc;
using System.Web.Routing;

namespace UrlsAndRoutes {
    public class RouteConfig {
        public static void RegisterRoutes(RouteCollection routes) {

            routes.MapRoute("MyRoute", "{controller}/{action}/{id}",
                new { controller = "Home", action = "Index",
                    id = UrlParameter.Optional });
        }
    }
}
```

This route will match URLs whether or not the `id` segment has been supplied. Table 13-3 shows how this works for different URLs.

Table 13-3. Matching URLs with an Optional Segment Variable

Segments	Example URL	Maps To
0	mydomain.com	controller = Home action = Index
1	mydomain.com/Customer	controller = Customer action = Index
2	mydomain.com/Customer/List	controller = Customer action = List
3	mydomain.com/Customer/List/All	controller = Customer action = List id = All
4	mydomain.com/Customer/List/All/Delete	No match—too many segments

As you can see from the table, the `id` variable is added to the set of variables only when there is a corresponding segment in the incoming URL. This feature is useful if you need to know whether the user supplied a value for a segment variable. When no value has been supplied for an optional segment variable, the value of the corresponding parameter will be null. We have updated our controller to respond when no value is provided for the id segment variable in Listing 13-20.

Listing 13-20. Checking to see if a value has been supplied for an optional segment variable

```
using System;
using System.Collections.Generic;
using System.Linq;
using System.Web;
using System.Web.Mvc;

namespace UrlsAndRoutes.Controllers {
    public class HomeController : Controller {

        public ActionResult Index() {
            ViewBag.Controller = "Home";
            ViewBag.Action = "Index";
            return View("ActionName");
        }

        public ActionResult CustomVariable(string id) {
            ViewBag.Controller = "Home";
            ViewBag.Action = "CustomVariable";
            ViewBag.CustomVariable = id == null ? "<no value>" : id;
            return View();
        }
    }
}
```

You can see the result of starting the application and navigating to the /Home/CustomVariable controller URL (which doesn't define a value for the id segment variable) in Figure 13-9.

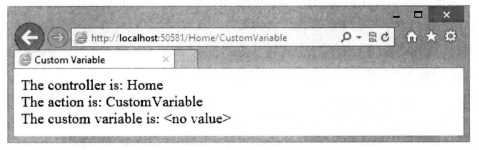

Figure 13-9. Detecting when a URL doesn't contain a value for an optional segment variable

Using Optional URL Segments to Enforce Separation of Concerns

Some developers who are very focused on the separation of concerns in the MVC pattern do not like putting the default values for segment variables into the routes for an application. If this is an issue, you can use the C# optional parameters along with an optional segment variable in the route to define the default values for action method parameters. As an example, Listing 13-21 shows how we have modified the CustomVariable action method to define a default value for the id parameter that will be used if the URL doesn't contain a value.

Listing 13-21. Defining a Default Value for an Action Method Parameter

```
...
public ActionResult CustomVariable(string id = "DefaultId") {
    ViewBag.Controller = "Home";
    ViewBag.Action = "CustomVariable";
    ViewBag.CustomVariable = id;
    return View();
}
...
```

There will always be a value for the id parameter (either one from the URL or the default), so we have removed the code which deals with the null value. This action method combined with the route we defined in Listing 13-19 is functionality equivalent to this route, which we defined in Listing 13-15:

```
...
routes.MapRoute("MyRoute", "{controller}/{action}/{id}",
    new { controller = "Home", action = "Index", id = "DefaultId" });
...
```

The difference is that the default value for the id segment variable is defined in the controller code and not in the routing definition.

UNIT TESTING: OPTIONAL URL SEGMENTS

The only issue to be aware of when testing optional URL segments is that the segment variable will not be added to the RouteData.Values collection unless a value was found in the URL. This means that you should not include the variable in the anonymous type unless you are testing a URL that contains the optional segment. Here are our changes to the TestIncomingRoutes unit test method for the route defined in Listing 13-19.

```
...
[TestMethod]
public void TestIncomingRoutes() {

    TestRouteMatch("~/", "Home", "Index");
    TestRouteMatch("~/Customer", "Customer", "index");
    TestRouteMatch("~/Customer/List", "Customer", "List");
    TestRouteMatch("~/Customer/List/All", "Customer", "List", new { id = "All" });
    TestRouteFail("~/Customer/List/All/Delete");
}
...
```

Defining Variable-Length Routes

Another way of changing the default conservatism of URL patterns is to accept a variable number of URL segments. This allows you to route URLs of arbitrary lengths in a single route. You define support for variable segments by designating one of the segment variables as a *catchall,* done by prefixing it with an asterisk (*), as shown in Listing 13-22.

Listing 13-22. Designating a Catchall Variable

```
using System;
using System.Collections.Generic;
using System.Linq;
using System.Web;
using System.Web.Mvc;
using System.Web.Routing;

namespace UrlsAndRoutes {
    public class RouteConfig {
        public static void RegisterRoutes(RouteCollection routes) {

            routes.MapRoute("MyRoute", "{controller}/{action}/{id}/{*catchall}",
                new { controller = "Home", action = "Index",
                    id = UrlParameter.Optional });
        }
    }
}
```

We have extended the route from the previous example to add a catchall segment variable, which is we imaginatively called catchall. This route will now match *any* URL, irrespective of the number of segments it contains or the value of any of those segments. The first three segments are used to set values for the controller, action, and id variables, respectively. If the URL contains additional segments, they are all assigned to the catchall variable, as shown in Table 13-4.

Table 13-4. Matching URLs with a Catchall Segment Variable

Segments	Example URL	Maps To
0	/	controller = Home action = Index
1	/Customer	controller = Customer action = Index
2	/Customer/List	controller = Customer action = List
3	/Customer/List/All	controller = Customer action = List id = All
4	/Customer/List/All/Delete	controller = Customer action = List id = All catchall = Delete
5	/Customer/List/All/Delete/Perm	controller = Customer action = List id = All catchall = Delete/Perm

There is no upper limit to the number of segments that the URL pattern in this route will match. Notice that the segments captured by the catchall are presented in the form *segment/segment/segment*. We are responsible for processing the string to break out the individual segments.

UNIT TEST: TESTING CATCHALL SEGMENT VARIABLES

We can treat a catchall variable just like a custom variable. The only difference is that we must expect multiple segments to be concatenated in a single value, such as *segment/segment/segment*. Notice that we will not receive the leading or trailing / character. Here are the changes to the `TestIncomingRoutes` method that demonstrate testing for a catchall segment, using the route defined in Listing 13-22 and the URLs shown in Table 13-4:

```
...
[TestMethod]
public void TestIncomingRoutes() {

    TestRouteMatch("~/", "Home", "Index");
    TestRouteMatch("~/Customer", "Customer", "Index");
    TestRouteMatch("~/Customer/List", "Customer", "List");
    TestRouteMatch("~/Customer/List/All", "Customer", "List", new { id = "All" });
    TestRouteMatch("~/Customer/List/All/Delete", "Customer", "List",
        new { id = "All", catchall = "Delete" });
    TestRouteMatch("~/Customer/List/All/Delete/Perm", "Customer", "List",
        new { id = "All", catchall = "Delete/Perm" });
}
...
```

Prioritizing Controllers by Namespaces

When an incoming URL matches a route, the MVC Framework takes the value of the `controller` variable and looks for the appropriate name. For example, when the value of the `controller` variable is Home, then the MVC Framework looks for a controller called `HomeController`. This is an *unqualified* class name, which means that the MVC Framework doesn't know what to do if there are two or more classes called `HomeController` in different namespaces.

To demonstrate the problem, create a new folder in the root of example project called `AdditionalControllers` and add a new Home controller, setting the contents to match those in Listing 13-23.

Listing 13-23. Adding a Second Home Controller to the Example Project

```
using System;
using System.Collections.Generic;
using System.Linq;
using System.Web;
using System.Web.Mvc;

namespace UrlsAndRoutes.AdditionalControllers {
    public class HomeController : Controller {
```

```
        public ActionResult Index() {
            ViewBag.Controller = "Additional Controllers - Home";
            ViewBag.Action = "Index";
            return View("ActionName");
        }
    }
}
```

When you start the app, you will see the error shown in Figure 13-10.

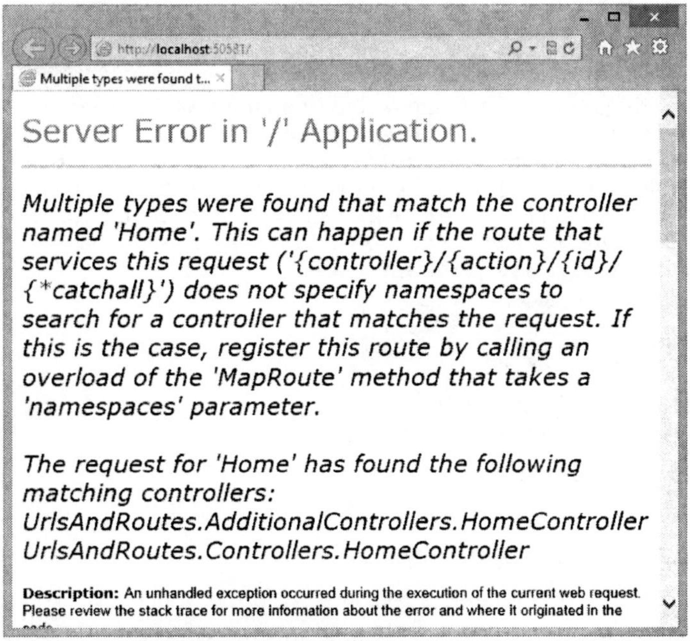

Figure 13-10. The error displayed when there are two controllers with the same name

The MVC Framework searched for a class called HomeController and found two: one in our original project and one in our AdditionalControllers project. If you read the text of the error shown in Figure 13-10, you can see that the MVC Framework helpfully tells us which classes it has found.

This problem arises more often than you might expect, especially if you are working on a large MVC project that uses libraries of controllers from other development teams or third-party suppliers. It is natural to name a controller relating to user accounts AccountController, for example, and it is only a matter of time before you encounter a naming clash.

To address this problem, we can tell the MVC Framework to give preference to certain namespaces when attempting to resolve the name of a controller class, as demonstrated in Listing 13-24.

Listing 13-24. Specifying Namespace Resolution Order

```
using System;
using System.Collections.Generic;
using System.Linq;
using System.Web;
using System.Web.Mvc;
using System.Web.Routing;
```

```
namespace UrlsAndRoutes {
    public class RouteConfig {
        public static void RegisterRoutes(RouteCollection routes) {

            routes.MapRoute("MyRoute", "{controller}/{action}/{id}/{*catchall}",
                new { controller = "Home", action = "Index",
                    id = UrlParameter.Optional
                },
                new[] { "URLsAndRoutes.AdditionalControllers" });
        }
    }
}
```

We express the namespaces as an array of strings and in the listing we have told the MVC Framework to look in the URLsAndRoutes.AdditionalControllers namespace before looking anywhere else.

If a suitable controller cannot be found in that namespace, then the MVC Framework will default to its regular behavior and look in all of the available namespaces. If you start the app once you have made this addition to the route, you will see the result shown in Figure 13-11, which shows that the request for the root URL, which is translated in to a request for the Index action method in the Home controller, has been sent to the controller we defined in the AdditionalControllers namespace.

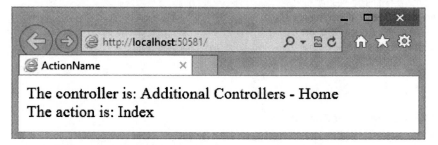

Figure 13-11. Giving priority to controllers in a specified namespaces

The namespaces added to a route are given equal priority. The MVC Framework does not check the first namespace before moving on to the second and so forth. For example, suppose that we added both of our project namespaces to the route, like this:

```
...
routes.MapRoute("MyRoute", "{controller}/{action}/{id}/{*catchall}",
    new { controller = "Home", action = "Index",
        id = UrlParameter.Optional
    },
    new[] { "URLsAndRoutes.AdditionalControllers", "UrlsAndRoutes.Controllers" });
...
```

We would see the same error as shown in Figure 13-10, because the MVC Framework is trying to resolve the controller class name in *all* of the namespaces we added to the route. If we want to give preference to a single controller in one namespace, but have all other controllers resolved in another namespace, we need to create multiple routes, as shown in Listing 13-25.

Listing 13-25. Using Multiple Routes to Control Namespace Resolution

```
using System;
using System.Collections.Generic;
using System.Linq;
```

```
using System.Web;
using System.Web.Mvc;
using System.Web.Routing;

namespace UrlsAndRoutes {
    public class RouteConfig {
        public static void RegisterRoutes(RouteCollection routes) {

            routes.MapRoute("AddContollerRoute", "Home/{action}/{id}/{*catchall}",
                new { controller = "Home", action = "Index",
                    id = UrlParameter.Optional },
                new[] { "URLsAndRoutes.AdditionalControllers" });

            routes.MapRoute("MyRoute", "{controller}/{action}/{id}/{*catchall}",
                new { controller = "Home", action = "Index",
                    id = UrlParameter.Optional },
                new[] { "URLsAndRoutes.Controllers" });
        }
    }
}
```

Our first route applies when the user explicitly requests a URL whose first segment is Home and will target the Home controller in the AdditionalControllers folder. All other requests, including those where no first segment is specified, will be handled by controllers in the Controllers folder.

We can tell the MVC Framework to look *only* in the namespaces that we specify. If a matching controller cannot be found, then the framework will not search elsewhere. Listing 13-26 shows how this feature is used.

Listing 13-26. Disabling Fallback Namespaces

```
using System;
using System.Collections.Generic;
using System.Linq;
using System.Web;
using System.Web.Mvc;
using System.Web.Routing;

namespace UrlsAndRoutes {
    public class RouteConfig {
        public static void RegisterRoutes(RouteCollection routes) {

            Route myRoute = routes.MapRoute("AddContollerRoute",
                    "Home/{action}/{id}/{*catchall}",
                new { controller = "Home", action = "Index",
                    id = UrlParameter.Optional },
                new[] { "URLsAndRoutes.AdditionalControllers" });

            myRoute.DataTokens["UseNamespaceFallback"] = false;
        }
    }
}
```

The MapRoute method returns a Route object. We have been ignoring this in previous examples, because we didn't need to make any adjustments to the routes that were created. To disable searching for controllers in other namespaces, we take the `Route` object and set the `UseNamespaceFallback` key in the `DataTokens` collection property to `false`.

This setting will be passed along to the component responsible for finding controllers, which is known as the *controller factory* and which we discuss in detail in Chapter 17. The effect of this addition is that requests that cannot be satisfied by the `Home` controller in the `AdditionalControllers` folder will fail.

Constraining Routes

At the start of the chapter, we described how URL patterns are conservative in how they match segments and liberal in how they match the content of segments. The previous few sections have explained different techniques for controlling the degree of conservatism—making a route match more or fewer segments using default values, optional variables, and so on.

It is now time to look at how we can control the liberalism in matching the content of URL segments—how to restrict the set of URLs that a route will match against. Once we have control over both of these aspects of the behavior of a route, we can create URL schemas that are expressed with laserlike precision.

Constraining a Route Using a Regular Expression

The first technique we will look at is constraining a route using regular expressions. Listing 13-27 contains an example.

Listing 13-27. Using a Regular Expression to Constrain a Route

```
...
public static void RegisterRoutes(RouteCollection routes) {
    routes.MapRoute("MyRoute", "{controller}/{action}/{id}/{*catchall}",
        new { controller = "Home", action = "Index", id = UrlParameter.Optional },
        new { controller = "^H.*"},
        new[] { "URLsAndRoutes.Controllers"});
}
...
```

We define constraints by passing them as a parameter to the `MapRoute` method. Like default values, constraints are expressed as an anonymous type, where the properties of the type correspond to the names of the segment variables we want to constrain.

In this example, we have used a constraint with a regular expression that matches URLs only where the value of the `controller` variable begins with the letter `H`.

■ **Note** Default values are used before constraints are checked. So, for example, if we request the URL /, the default value for `controller`, which is `Home`, is applied. The constraints are then checked, and since the `controller` value beings with `H`, the default URL will match the route.

Constraining a Route to a Set of Specific Values

We can use regular expressions to constrain a route so that only specific values for a URL segment will cause a match. We do this using the bar (|) character, as shown in Listing 13-28.

Listing 13-28. Constraining a Route to a Specific Set of Segment Variable Values

```
...
public static void RegisterRoutes(RouteCollection routes) {

    routes.MapRoute("MyRoute", "{controller}/{action}/{id}/{*catchall}",
        new { controller = "Home", action = "Index", id = UrlParameter.Optional },
        new { controller = "^H.*", action = "^Index$|^About$"},
        new[] { "URLsAndRoutes.Controllers"});
}
...
```

This constraint will allow the route to match only URLs where the value of the action segment is Index or About. Constraints are applied together, so the restrictions imposed on the value of the action variable are combined with those imposed on the controller variable. This means that the route in Listing 13-28 will match URLs only when the controller variable begins with the letter H and the action variable is Index or About. So, now you can see what we mean about creating very precise routes.

Constraining a Route Using HTTP Methods

We can constrain routes so that they match a URL only when it is requested using a specific HTTP method, as demonstrated in Listing 13-29.

Listing 13-29. Constraining a Route Based on an HTTP Method

```
...
public static void RegisterRoutes(RouteCollection routes) {

    routes.MapRoute("MyRoute", "{controller}/{action}/{id}/{*catchall}",
        new { controller = "Home", action = "Index", id = UrlParameter.Optional },
        new { controller = "^H.*", action = "Index|About",
            httpMethod = new HttpMethodConstraint("GET") },
        new[] { "URLsAndRoutes.Controllers" });
}
...
```

The format for specifying an HTTP method constraint is slightly odd. It does not matter what name we give the property, as long as we assign it an instance of the HttpMethodConstraint class. In the listing, we called our constraint property httpMethod to help distinguish it from the value-based constraints we defined previously.

■ **Note** The ability to constrain routes by HTTP method is unrelated to the ability to restrict action methods using attributes such as HttpGet and HttpPost. The route constraints are processed much earlier in the request pipeline, and they determine the name of the controller and action required to process a request. The action method attributes are used to determine which specific action method will be used to service a request by the controller. We provide details of how to handle different kinds of HTTP methods (including the more unusual ones such as PUT and DELETE) in Chapter 14.

We pass the names of the HTTP methods we want to support as string parameters to the constructor of the HttpMethodConstraint class. In the listing, we limited the route to GET requests, but we could have easily added support for other methods, like this:

```
...
httpMethod = new HttpMethodConstraint("GET", "POST") },
...
```

```
┌─────────────────────────────────────────────────────────────────────┐
│                   UNIT TESTING: ROUTE CONSTRAINTS                     │
└─────────────────────────────────────────────────────────────────────┘
```

When testing constrained routes, it is important to test for both the URLs that will match and the URLs you are trying to exclude, which you can do by using the helper methods introduced at the start of the chapter. Here are the changes to the TestIncomingRoutes test method that we used to test the route defined in Listing 13-29:

```
...
[TestMethod]
public void TestIncomingRoutes() {

    TestRouteMatch("~/", "Home", "Index");
    TestRouteMatch("~/Home", "Home", "Index");
    TestRouteMatch("~/Home/Index", "Home", "Index");


    TestRouteMatch("~/Home/About", "Home", "About");
    TestRouteMatch("~/Home/About/MyId", "Home", "About", new { id = "MyId" });
    TestRouteMatch("~/Home/About/MyId/More/Segments", "Home", "About",
        new {
            id = "MyId",
            catchall = "More/Segments"
        });

    TestRouteFail("~/Home/OtherAction");
    TestRouteFail("~/Account/Index");
    TestRouteFail("~/Account/About");
}
...
```

Defining a Custom Constraint

If the standard constraints are not sufficient for your needs, you can define your own custom constraints by implementing the IRouteConstraint interface. To demonstrate this feature, we added an Infrastructure folder to the example project and created a new class file called UserAgentConstraint.cs, the contents of which are shown in Listing 13-30.

Listing 13-30. Creating a Custom Route Constraint

```
using System.Web;
using System.Web.Routing;

namespace UrlsAndRoutes.Infrastructure {
    public class UserAgentConstraint : IRouteConstraint {
```

```
        private string requiredUserAgent;

        public UserAgentConstraint(string agentParam) {
            requiredUserAgent = agentParam;
        }

        public bool Match(HttpContextBase httpContext, Route route, string parameterName,
                          RouteValueDictionary values, RouteDirection routeDirection) {

            return httpContext.Request.UserAgent != null &&
                httpContext.Request.UserAgent.Contains(requiredUserAgent);
        }
    }
}
```

The IRouteConstraint interface defines the Match method, which an implementation can use to indicate to the routing system if its constraint has been satisfied. The parameters for the Match method provide access to the request from the client, the route that is being evaluated, the parameter name of the constraint, the segment variables extracted from the URL, and details of whether the request is to check an incoming or outgoing URL. For our example, we check the value of the UserAgent property of the client request to see if it contains a value that was passed to our constructor. Listing 13-31 shows our custom constraint used in a route.

Listing 13-31. Applying a Custom Constraint in a Route

```
using System;
using System.Collections.Generic;
using System.Linq;
using System.Web;
using System.Web.Mvc;
using System.Web.Routing;
using UrlsAndRoutes.Infrastructure;

namespace UrlsAndRoutes {
    public class RouteConfig {

        public static void RegisterRoutes(RouteCollection routes) {

            routes.MapRoute("ChromeRoute", "{*catchall}",
                new { controller = "Home", action = "Index" },
                new {
                    customConstraint = new UserAgentConstraint("Chrome")
                },
                new[] { "UrlsAndRoutes.AdditionalControllers" });


            routes.MapRoute("MyRoute", "{controller}/{action}/{id}/{*catchall}",
                new { controller = "Home", action = "Index",
                    id = UrlParameter.Optional },
                new[] { "URLsAndRoutes.Controllers" });
        }
    }
}
```

In the listing, we have constrained the first route so that it will match only requests made from browsers whose user-agent string contains `Chrome`. If the route matches, then the request will be sent to the `Index` action method in the `Home` controller defined in the `AdditionalControllers` folder, irrespective of the structure and content of the URL that has been requested. Our URL pattern consists of just a catchall segment variable, which means that the values for the `controller` and `action` segment variables will always be taken from the defaults and not the URL itself.

The second route will match all other requests and target controllers in the `Controllers` folder. The effect of these routes is that one kind of browser always ends up at the same place in the application—you can see this in Figure 13-12, which shows the effect of navigating to the app using Google Chrome.

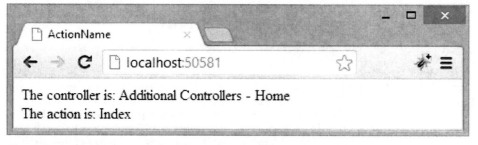

Figure 13-12. Navigating to the app using the Google Chrome browser

Figure 13-13 shows the result of navigating to the example application using Internet Explorer.

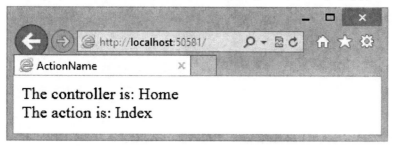

Figure 13-13. Navigating to the app using Internet Explorer

■ **Note** To be clear, because this is the kind of thing we get angry letters about, we are not suggesting that you restrict your application so that it supports only one kind of browser. We used user-agent strings solely to demonstrate custom route constraints and believe in equal opportunities for all browsers. We really hate Web sites that try to force their preference for browsers on users.

Routing Requests for Disk Files

Not all of the requests for an MVC application are for controllers and actions. We still need a way to serve content such as images, static HTML files, JavaScript libraries, and so on. As a demonstration, we have created a file called `StaticContent.html` in the `Content` folder of our example MVC application using the `HTML Page` item template. Listing 13-32 shows this file's contents.

Listing 13-32. The StaticContent.html File

```
<!DOCTYPE html>
<html xmlns="http://www.w3.org/1999/xhtml">
    <head><title>Static HTML Content</title></head>
    <body>
        This is the static html file (~/Content/StaticContent.html)
    </body>
</html>
```

The routing system provides integrated support for serving such content. If you start the application and request the URL /Content/StaticContent.html, you will see the contents of this simple HTML file displayed in the browser, as shown in Figure 13-14.

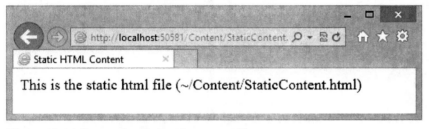

Figure 13-14. Requesting the static content file

By default, the routing system checks to see if a URL matches a disk file *before* evaluating the application's routes, which is why we didn't have to add a route to get the result shown in Figure 13-14.

If there is a match between the requested URL and a disk on the file then the disk file is served and the routes defined by the application are never used. We can reverse this behavior so that our routes are evaluated before disk files are checked by setting the `RouteExistingFiles` property of the `RouteCollection` to `true`, as shown in Listing 13-33.

Listing 13-33. Enabling Route Evaluation Before File Checking

```
public static void RegisterRoutes(RouteCollection routes) {

    routes.RouteExistingFiles = true;

    routes.MapRoute("ChromeRoute", "{*catchall}",
        new { controller = "Home", action = "Index" },
        new {
            customConstraint = new UserAgentConstraint("Chrome")
        },
        new[] { "UrlsAndRoutes.AdditionalControllers" });


    routes.MapRoute("MyRoute", "{controller}/{action}/{id}/{*catchall}",
        new { controller = "Home", action = "Index",
            id = UrlParameter.Optional },
        new[] { "URLsAndRoutes.Controllers" });
}
```

The convention is to place this statement close to the top of the `RegisterRoutes` method, although it will take effect even if you set it after you have defined your routes.

357

Configuring the Application Server

Visual Studio 2012 uses IIS Express as the application server for MVC application projects. Not only do we have to set the `RouteExistingFiles` property to `true` in the `RegisterRoutes` method, we also have to tell IIS Express not to intercept requests for disk files before they are passed to the MVC routing system.

First of all, start IIS Express—the easiest way to do this is to start the MVC application from Visual Studio, which will cause the IIS Express icon to appear on the task bar. Right click on the icon and select `Show All Applications` from the popup menu. Click on `UrlsAndRoutes` in the `Site Name` column to display the IIS configuration information, as shown in Figure 13-15.

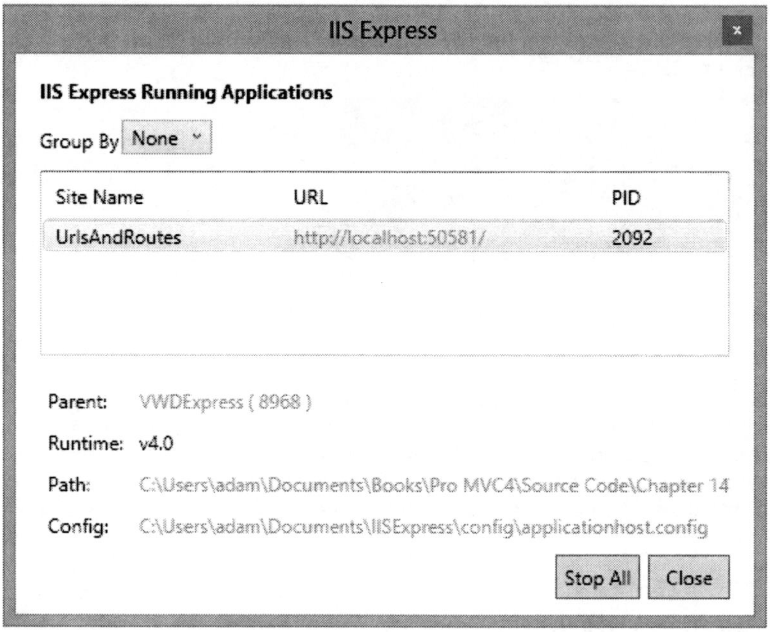

Figure 13-15. The IIS Express configuration information

Click on the `Config` link at the bottom of the window to open the IIS Express configuration file in Visual Studio. Now type `Control+F` and search for `UrlRoutingModule-4.0`. There will be an entry found in the `modules` section of the configuration file and we need to set the `preCondition` attribute to the empty string, like this:

```
<add name="UrlRoutingModule-4.0" type="System.Web.Routing.UrlRoutingModule"
    preCondition="" />
```

Now restart the application in Visual Studio to let the modified settings take effect and navigate to the `/Content/StaticContent.html` URL. Rather than see the contents of the file, you will see the error message shown in Figure 13-16—this error occurs because the request for the HTML file has been passed to the MVC routing system but the route that matches the URL directs the request to the `Content` controller, which does not exist.

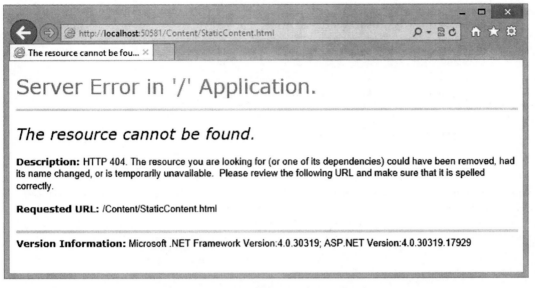

Figure 13-16. Requesting a static content URL which is handled by the routing system

---

■ **Tip**   An alternative approach is to use the Visual Studio development server, which you can activate in the Web section of the project configuration, available when you select `UrlsAndRoutes Properties` item from the Visual Studio `Project` menu. The development server is pretty simple and isn't a cut down version of IIS like IIS Express, and so it doesn't intercept requests in the same way.

Defining Routes for Disk Files

Once the property have been set to `true`, we can define routes that match URLs that correspond to disk files, such as the one shown in Listing 13-34.

Listing 13-34. A Route Whose URL Pattern Corresponds to a Disk File

```
...
public static void RegisterRoutes(RouteCollection routes) {

    routes.RouteExistingFiles = true;

    routes.MapRoute("DiskFile", "Content/StaticContent.html",
        new {
            controller = "Customer",
            action = "List",
        });

    routes.MapRoute("ChromeRoute", "{*catchall}",
        new { controller = "Home", action = "Index" },
```

```
        new {
            customConstraint = new UserAgentConstraint("Chrome")
        },
        new[] { "UrlsAndRoutes.AdditionalControllers" });


    routes.MapRoute("MyRoute", "{controller}/{action}/{id}/{*catchall}",
        new { controller = "Home", action = "Index",
            id = UrlParameter.Optional },
        new[] { "URLsAndRoutes.Controllers" });
}
...
```

This route maps requests for the URL Content/StaticContent.html to the List action of the Customer controller. You can see the URL mapping at work in Figure 13-17, which we created by starting the app and navigating to the /Content/StaticContent.html URL again.

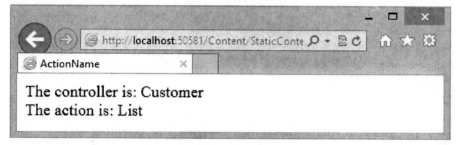

Figure 13-17. Intercepting a request for a disk file using a route

Routing requests intended for disk files requires careful thought, not least because URL patterns will match these kinds of URL as eagerly as any other. For example, as you saw in the previous section, a request for /Content/StaticContent.html will be matched by a URL pattern such as {controller}/{action}. Unless you are careful, you can end up with some exceptionally strange results and reduced performance. So, enabling this option is very much a last resort.

Bypassing the Routing System

Setting the RouteExistingFiles property, which we demonstrated in the previous section, makes the routing system more inclusive. Requests that would normally bypass the routing system are now evaluated against the routes we have defined.

The counterpart to this feature is the ability to make the routing system *less* inclusive and prevent URLs from being evaluated against our routes. We do this by using the IgnoreRoute method of the RouteCollection class, as shown in Listing 13-35.

Listing 13-35. Using the IgnoreRoute Method

```
...
public static void RegisterRoutes(RouteCollection routes) {

    routes.RouteExistingFiles = true;

    routes.IgnoreRoute("Content/{filename}.html");
```

```
routes.MapRoute("DiskFile", "Content/StaticContent.html",
    new {
        controller = "Customer",
        action = "List",
    });

routes.MapRoute("ChromeRoute", "{*catchall}",
    new { controller = "Home", action = "Index" },
    new {
        customConstraint = new UserAgentConstraint("Chrome")
    },
    new[] { "UrlsAndRoutes.AdditionalControllers" });


routes.MapRoute("MyRoute", "{controller}/{action}/{id}/{*catchall}",
    new { controller = "Home", action = "Index",
        id = UrlParameter.Optional },
    new[] { "URLsAndRoutes.Controllers" });
}
...
```

We can use segment variables like {filename} to match a range of URLs. In this case, the URL pattern will match any two-segment URL where the first segment is Content and the second content has the .html extension.

The IgnoreRoute method creates an entry in the RouteCollection where the route handler is an instance of the StopRoutingHandler class, rather than MvcRouteHandler. The routing system is hard-coded to recognize this handler. If the URL pattern passed to the IgnoreRoute method matches, then no subsequent routes will be evaluated, just as when a regular route is matched. It follows, therefore, that where we place the call to the IgnoreRoute method is significant. If you start the app and navigate to the /Content/StaticContent.html URL again, you will see the contents of the HTML file because the StopRoutingHandler object is processed before any other route which might have matched the URL.

Summary

In this chapter, we have taken an in-depth look at the routing system. You have seen how incoming URLs are matched and handled, how to customize routes by changing the way that they match URL segments and by using default values and optional segments. We also showed you to constrain routes to narrow the range of requests that they will match and how to route requests for static content.

In the next chapter, we show you how to generate outgoing URLs from routes in your views and how to use the MVC Framework areas feature, which relies on the routing system and which can be used to manage large and complex MVC Framework applications.

CHAPTER 14

∎∎∎

Advanced Routing Features

In the previous chapter, we showed you how to use the routing system to handle incoming URLs—but this is only part of the story. We also need to be able use our URL schema to generate *outgoing URLs* we can embed in our views, so that users can click links and submit forms back to our application in a way that will target the correct controller and action. In this chapter, we will show you different techniques for generating outgoing URLs, show you how to customize the routing system by replacing the standard MVC routing implementation classes and use the MVC Framework *areas* feature, which allows you to break a large and complex MVC application into manageable chucks. We finish this chapter with some best-practice advice about URL schemas in MVC Framework applications.

Preparing the Example Project

We are going to continue to use the `UrlsAndRoutes` project from the previous chapter, but we need to make a couple of changes before we start.

First, delete the `AdditionalControllers` folder and `HomeController.cs` file that it contains. We created this folder and file to demonstrate how to prioritize namespaces, and we won't need them again. To perform the deletion, right-click on the `AdditionalControllers` folder and select `Delete` from the pop-up menu.

The other change we need to make it to simplify the routes in the application. Edit your `App_Start/RouteConfig.cs` file so that it matches the content shown in Listing 14-1.

Listing 14-1. Simplifying the Example Routes in the RouteConfig.cs File

```
using System;
using System.Collections.Generic;
using System.Linq;
using System.Web;
using System.Web.Mvc;
using System.Web.Routing;
using UrlsAndRoutes.Infrastructure;

namespace UrlsAndRoutes {
    public class RouteConfig {

        public static void RegisterRoutes(RouteCollection routes) {

            routes.MapRoute("MyRoute", "{controller}/{action}/{id}",
                new { controller = "Home", action = "Index",
                    id = UrlParameter.Optional });
        }
    }
}
```

Generating Outgoing URLs in Views

In almost every MVC Framework application, you will want to allow the user to navigate from one view to another, which will usually rely on including a link in the first view that targets the action method that generates the second view.

It is tempting to just add a static a element whose href attribute targets the action method, like this:

```
<a href="/Home/CustomVariable">This is an outgoing URL</a>
```

This HTML element creates a link that will be processed as a request to the CustomVariable action method on the Home controller, with the optional segment variable Hello. Manually defined URLs like this one are quick and simple to create. They are also extremely dangerous and you will break all of the URLs you have hard-coded when you change the URL schema for your application. You then must trawl through all of the views in your application and update all of the references to your controllers and action methods—a process that is tedious, error-prone, and difficult to test.

A much better alternative is to use the routing system to generate outgoing URLs, which ensures that the URLs scheme is used to produce the URLs dynamically and in a way that is guaranteed to reflect the URL schema of the application.

Using the Routing System to Generate an Outgoing URL

The simplest way to generate an outgoing URL in a view is to call the Html.ActionLink helper method within as illustrated by Listing 14-2, which shows the addition we have made to the /Views/Shared/ActionName.cshtml view.

Listing 14-2. Using the Html.ActionLink Helper Method to Generate an Outgoing URL

```
@{
    Layout = null;
}

<!DOCTYPE html>

<html>
<head>
    <meta name="viewport" content="width=device-width" />
    <title>ActionName</title>
</head>
<body>
    <div>The controller is: @ViewBag.Controller</div>
    <div>The action is: @ViewBag.Action</div>
    <div>
        @Html.ActionLink("This is an outgoing URL", "CustomVariable")
    </div>
</body>
</html>
```

The parameters to the ActionLink method are the text for the link and the name of the action method that the link should target. You can see the result of this addition by starting the app and allowing the browser to navigate to the root URL, as illustrated by Figure 14-1.

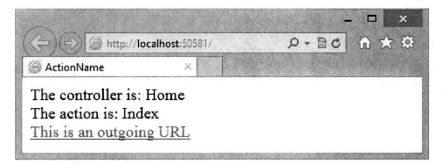

Figure 14-1. Adding an outgoing URL to a view

The HTML that the `ActionLink` method generates is based on the current routing configuration. For example, using the schema defined in Listing 14-1 (and assuming that the view is being rendered by a request to the `Home` controller), we get this HTML:

```
<a href="/Home/CustomVariable">This is an outgoing URL</a>
```

Now, this may seem like we taken the long path to recreate the manually defined URL we showed you earlier, but the benefit of this approach is that it automatically responds to changes in the routing configuration. As a demonstration, we have changed the route defined in added a new route to the `RouteConfig.cs` file, as shown in Listing 14-3.

Listing 14-3. Adding a Route to the Example Application

```
...
public static void RegisterRoutes(RouteCollection routes) {

    routes.MapRoute("NewRoute", "App/Do{action}",
        new { controller = "Home" });

    routes.MapRoute("MyRoute", "{controller}/{action}/{id}",
        new { controller = "Home", action = "Index",
            id = UrlParameter.Optional });
}
...
```

The new route changes the URL schema for requests that target the `Home` controller. If you start the app, you will see that this change is reflected in the HTML that is generated by the `ActionLink` HTML helper method, as follows:

```
<a href="/App/DoCustomVariable">This is an outgoing URL</a>
```

You can see how generating links in this way addresses the issue of maintenance. We were able to change our routing schema and have the outgoing links in our views reflect the change automatically. And, of course an outgoing URL becomes a regular request when you click on the link, and so the routing system is used again to target the action method correctly—as shown in Figure 14-2.

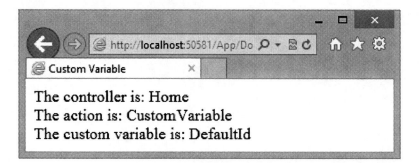

Figure 14-2. The effect of clicking on a link is to make an outgoing URL into an incoming request

UNDERSTANDING OUTBOUND URL ROUTE MATCHING

You have seen how changing the routes that define your URL schema changes the way that outgoing URLs are generated. Applications will usually define several routes, and it is important to understand just how routes are selected for URL generation. The routing system processes the routes in the order that they were added to the `RouteCollection` object passed to the `RegisterRoutes` method. Each route is inspected to see if it is a match, which requires three conditions to be met:

- A value must be available for every segment variable defined in the URL pattern. To find values for each segment variable, the routing system looks first at the values we have provided (using the properties of anonymous type), then the variable values for the current request, and finally at the default values defined in the route. (We return to the second source of these values later in this chapter.)

- None of the values we provided for the segment variables may disagree with the default-only variables defined in the route. These are variables for which default values have been provided, but which do not occur in the URL pattern. For example, in this route definition, `myVar` is a default-only variable:

```
routes.MapRoute("MyRoute", "{controller}/{action}",
    new { myVar = "true" });
```

For this route to be a match, we must take care to not supply a value for `myVar` or to make sure that the value we do supply matches the default value.

- The values for all of the segment variables must satisfy the route constraints. See the "Constraining Routes" section earlier in the chapter for examples of different kinds of constraints.

To be very clear: the routing system doesn't try to find the route that provides the *best* matching route. It finds only the *first* match, at which point it uses the route to generate the URL; any subsequent routes are ignored. For this reason, you should define your most specific routes first. It is important to test your outbound URL generation. If you try to generate a URL for which no matching route can be found, you will create a link that contains an empty `href` attribute, like this:

```
<a href="">About this application</a>
```

The link will render in the view properly, but won't function as intended when the user clicks it. If you are generating just the URL (which we show you how to do later in the chapter), then the result will be `null`, which renders as the empty string in views. You can exert some control over route matching by using named routes. See the "Generating a URL from a Specific Route" section later in this chapter for details.

The first `Route` object meeting these criteria will produce a non-null URL, and that will terminate the URL-generating process. The chosen parameter values will be substituted in for each segment parameter, with any trailing sequence of default values omitted. If you have supplied any explicit parameters that do not correspond to segment parameters or default parameters, then the method will append them as a set of query string name/value pairs.

UNIT TEST: TESTING OUTGOING URLS

The simplest way to test outgoing URL generation is to use the static `UrlHelper.GenerateUrl` method, which has parameters for all of the different ways that you can direct the route generation—for example, by specifying the route name, controller, action, segment values, and so on. Here is a test method that verifies URL generation against the route defined in Listing 14-3, which we added to the `RouteTests.cs` file in the test project (because it uses the test utility methods we defined in the previous chapter):

```
...
[TestMethod]
public void TestIncomingRoutes() {
    // ...code deleted to prevent test failure...
}

[TestMethod]
public void TestOutgoingRoutes() {

    // Arrange
    RouteCollection routes = new RouteCollection();
    RouteConfig.RegisterRoutes(routes);
    RequestContext context = new RequestContext(CreateHttpContext(),
        new RouteData());

    // Act - generate the URL
    string result = UrlHelper.GenerateUrl(null, "Index", "Home", null,
        routes, context, true);

    // Assert
    Assert.AreEqual("/App/DoIndex", result);
}
...
```

We generate a URL rather than a link so that we do not need to worry about testing the surrounding HTML. The `UrlHelper.GenerateUrl` method requires a `RequestContext` object, which we create using the mocked `HttpContextBase` object from the `CreateHttpContext` test helper method. See the unit test for testing incoming URLs presented earlier in this chapter for the full source code for `CreateHttpContext`.

We removed the code from the `TestIncomingRoutes` method because our test code does not reflect the changes we have made to the routes in this chapter and we do not want to keep updating the test because we are focused on outgoing routes.

Targeting Other Controllers

The default version of the `ActionLink` method assumes that you want to target an action method in the same controller that has caused the view to be rendered. To create an outgoing URL that targets a different controller, you can use a different overload that allows you to specify the controller name, as illustrated by Listing 14-4, which shows the change we have made to the `ActionName.cshtml` view.

■ **Caution**   The routing system has no more knowledge of our application when generating outgoing URLs than when processing incoming requests. This means that the values you supply for action methods and controllers are not validated, and you must take care not to specify nonexistent targets.

Listing 14-4. Targeting a Different Controller Using the ActionLink Helper Method

```
@{
    Layout = null;
}

<!DOCTYPE html>

<html>
<head>
    <meta name="viewport" content="width=device-width" />
    <title>ActionName</title>
</head>
<body>
    <div>The controller is: @ViewBag.Controller</div>
    <div>The action is: @ViewBag.Action</div>
    <div>
        @Html.ActionLink("This is an outgoing URL", "CustomVariable")
    </div>
    <div>
        @Html.ActionLink("This targets another controller", "Index", "Admin")
    </div>
</body>
</html>
```

When you render the view, you will see the following HTML generated:

```
<a href="/Admin">This targets another controller</a>
```

Our request for a URL that targets the Index action method on the Admin controller has been expressed as /Admin by the ActionLink method. The routing system is pretty clever and it knows that the route defined in the application will use the Index action method by default, allowing it to omit unneeded segments.

Passing Extra Values

You can pass values for segment variables using an anonymous type, with properties representing the segments. Listing 14-5 provides an example, which we added to the ActionName.cshtml view file.

Listing 14-5. Supplying Values for Segment Variables

```
...
<body>
    <div>The controller is: @ViewBag.Controller</div>
    <div>The action is: @ViewBag.Action</div>
    <div>
        @Html.ActionLink("This is an outgoing URL",
            "CustomVariable", new { id = "Hello" })
    </div>
</body>
...
```

In this example, we have supplied a value for a segment variable called id. If our application uses the route shown in Listing 14-3, then we get the following HTML when we render the view:

```
<a href="/App/DoCustomVariable?id=Hello">This is an outgoing URL</a>
```

Notice that the value we supplied has been added as part of the query string to fit into the URL pattern described by the route we added in Listing 14-3. This is because there is no segment variable that corresponds to id in that route. In Listing 14-6, we have edited the routes in the RouteConfig.cs file so that only a route that does have an id segment is used.

Listing 14-6. Disabling a route in the configuration

```
...
public static void RegisterRoutes(RouteCollection routes) {

    // These statements have been commented out
    //routes.MapRoute("NewRoute", "App/Do{action}",
    //    new { controller = "Home" });

    routes.MapRoute("MyRoute", "{controller}/{action}/{id}",
        new { controller = "Home", action = "Index",
            id = UrlParameter.Optional });
}
...
```

If we start the application again, the URL in the ActionName.cshtml view produces the following HTML element:

```
<a href="/Home/CustomVariable/Hello">This is an outgoing URL</a>
```

This time, the value we assigned to the id property is included as a URL segment, in keeping with the active route in the application configuration. Did we mention that the routing system is pretty clever?

UNDERSTANDING SEGMENT VARIABLE REUSE

When we described the way that routes are matched for outbound URLs, we explained that when trying to find values for each of the segment variables in a route's URL pattern, the routing system will look at the values from the current request. This is a behavior that confuses many programmers and can lead to a lengthy debugging session.

Imagine our application has a single route, as follows:

```
routes.MapRoute("MyRoute", "{controller}/{action}/{color}/{page}");
```

Now imagine that a user is currently at the URL /Catalog/List/Purple/123, and we render a link as follows:

```
@Html.ActionLink("Click me", "List", "Catalog", new {page=789}, null)
```

You might expect that the routing system would be unable to match the route, because we have not supplied a value for the color segment variable, and there is no default value defined. You would, however, be wrong. The routing system *will* match against the route we have defined. It will generate the following HTML:

```
<a href="/Catalog/List/Purple/789">Click me</a>
```

The routing system is keen to make a match against a route, to the extent that it will reuse segment variable values from the incoming URL. In this case, we end up with the value Purple for the color variable, because of the URL from which our imaginary user started.

This is *not* a behavior of last resort. The routing system will apply this technique as part of its regular assessment of routes, even if there is a subsequent route that would match without requiring values from the current request to be reused. The routing system will reuse values only for segment variables that occur earlier in the URL pattern than any parameters that are supplied to the Html.ActionLink method. Suppose we tried to create a link like this:

```
@Html.ActionLink("Click me", "List", "Catalog", new {color="Aqua"}, null)
```

We have supplied a value for color, but not for page. But color appears before page in the URL pattern, and so the routing system *won't* reuse the values from the incoming URL, and the route will not match.

The best way to deal with this behavior is to prevent it from happening. We strongly recommend that you do not rely on this behavior, and that you supply values for all of the segment variables in a URL pattern. Relying on this behavior will not only make your code harder to read, but you end up making assumptions about the order in which your users make requests, which is something that will ultimately bite you as your application enters maintenance.

Specifying HTML Attributes

We have focused on the URL that the `ActionLink` helper method generates, but remember that the method generates a complete HTML anchor (a) element. We can set attributes for this element by providing an anonymous type whose properties correspond to the attributes we require. Listing 14-7 shows how we modified the `ActionName.cshtml` view to set an `id` attribute and assign a class to the HTML a element.

Listing 14-7. Generating an Anchor Element with Attributes

```
...
<body>
    <div>The controller is: @ViewBag.Controller</div>
    <div>The action is: @ViewBag.Action</div>
    <div>
        @Html.ActionLink("This is an outgoing URL",
            "Index", "Home", null, new {id = "myAnchorID",
                @class = "myCSSClass"})
    </div>
</body>
...
```

We have created a new anonymous type that has `id` and `class` properties, and passed it as a parameter to the `ActionLink` method. We passed `null` for the additional segment variable values, indicating that we do not have any values to supply.

▨ **Tip**   Notice that we prepended the `class` property with a @ character. This is a C# language feature that lets us use reserved keywords as the names for class members.

When this call to `ActionLink` is rendered, we get the following HTML:

```
<a class="myCSSClass" href="/" id="myAnchorID">This is an outgoing URL</a>
```

Generating Fully Qualified URLs in Links

All of the links that we have generated so far have contained relative URLs, but we can also use the `ActionLink` helper method to generate fully qualified URLs, as shown in Listing 14-8.

Listing 14-8. Generating a Fully Qualified URL

```
...
<body>
    <div>The controller is: @ViewBag.Controller</div>
    <div>The action is: @ViewBag.Action</div>
    <div>
        @Html.ActionLink("This is an outgoing URL", "Index", "Home",
            "https", "myserver.mydomain.com", " myFragmentName",
            new { id = "MyId"},
            new { id = "myAnchorID", @class = "myCSSClass"})
    </div>
</body>
...
```

This is the `ActionLink` overload with the most parameters, and it allows us to provide values for the protocol (`https`, in our example), the name of the target server (`myserver.mydomain.com`), and the URL fragment (`myFragmentName`), as well as all of the other options you saw previously. When rendered in a view, the call in the Listing 14-generates the following HTML:

```
<a class="myCSSClass"
    href="https://myserver.mydomain.com/Home/Index/MyId#myFragmentName"
    id="myAnchorID">This is an outgoing URL</a>
```

We recommend using relative URLs wherever possible. Fully qualified URLs create dependencies on the way that your application infrastructure is presented to your users. We have seen many large applications that relied on absolute URLs broken by uncoordinated changes to the network infrastructure or domain name policy, which are often outside the control of the programmers.

Generating URLs (and Not Links)

The `Html.ActionLink` helper method generates complete HTML `<a>` elements, which is exactly what we want most of the time. However, there are times when we just need a URL, which may be because we want to display the URL, build the HTML for a link manually, display the value of the URL, or include the URL as a data element in the HTML page being rendered.

In such circumstances, we can use the `Url.Action` method to generate just the URL and not the surrounding HTML. Listing 14-9 shows the changes we have made to the `ActionName.cshtml` file to create a URL with the `Url.Action` helper.

Listing 14-9. Generating a URL Without the Surrounding HTML

```
@{
    Layout = null;
}

<!DOCTYPE html>

<html>
<head>
    <meta name="viewport" content="width=device-width" />
    <title>ActionName</title>
</head>
<body>
    <div>The controller is: @ViewBag.Controller</div>
    <div>The action is: @ViewBag.Action</div>
    <div>This is a URL:
        @Url.Action("Index", "Home", new { id = "MyId" })
    </div>
</body>
</html>
```

The `Url.Action` method works in the same way as the `Html.ActionLink` method, except that it generates only the URL. The overloaded versions of the method and the parameters they accept are the same for both methods, and you can do all of the things with `Url.Action` that we demonstrated with `Html.ActionLink` in the previous sections. You can see how the URL in Listing 14-9 is rendered in the view in Figure 14-3.

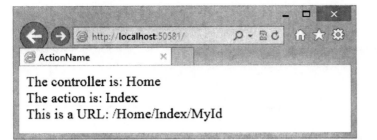

Figure 14-3. Rendering a URL (as opposed to a link) in a view

Generating Outgoing URLs in Action Methods

Mostly, we want to generate outgoing URLs in views, but there are times when we want to do something similar inside an action method. If we just need to generate a URL, we can use the same helper method that we used in the view, as illustrated by Listing 14-10, which shows a new action method we added to the Home controller.

Listing 14-10. Generating an Outgoing URL in an Action Method

```
...
public ViewResult MyActionMethod() {

    string myActionUrl = Url.Action("Index", new { id = "MyID" });
    string myRouteUrl = Url.RouteUrl(new { controller = "Home", action = "Index" });

    //... do something with URLs...
    return View();
}
...
```

For the routing in our example app, the myActionUrl variable would be set to /Home/Index/MyID and the myRouteUrl variable would be set to /, which is consistent with the results that calling these helpers in a view would produce.

A more common requirement is to redirect the client browser to another URL. We can do this by returning the result of calling the RedirectToAction method, as shown in Listing 14-11.

Listing 14-11. Redirecting to Another Action

```
...
public RedirectToRouteResult MyActionMethod() {
    return RedirectToAction("Index");
}
...
```

The result of the RedirectToAction method is a RedirectToRouteResult, which instructs the MVC Framework to issue a redirect instruction to a URL that will invoke the specified action. There are the usual overloaded versions of the RedirectToAction method that specify the controller and values for the segment variables in the generated URL.

If you want to send a redirect using a URL generated from just object properties, you can use the RedirectToRoute method, as shown in Listing 14-12.

Listing 14-12. Redirecting to a URL Generated from Properties in an Anonymous Type

```
...
public RedirectToRouteResult MyActionMethod() {
    return RedirectToRoute(new {
        controller = "Home",
        action = "Index",
        id = "MyID" });
}
```

This method also returns a `RedirectToRouteResult` object and has exactly the same effect as calling the `RedirectToAction` method.

Generating a URL from a Specific Route

In our previous examples, we have left the routing system to select the route which will be used to generate a URL or a link. In this section, we will show you how to control of this process and select specific routes. In Listing 14-13, we have changes the routing information in the `RouteConfig.cs` file to better demonstrate this feature.

Listing 14-13. Changing the Routing Configuration for the Example App

```
...
public static void RegisterRoutes(RouteCollection routes) {
    routes.MapRoute("MyRoute", "{controller}/{action}");
    routes.MapRoute("MyOtherRoute", "App/{action}", new { controller = "Home" });
}
...
```

We have specified names for both of these routes—`MyRoute` and `MyOtherRoute`. There are two reasons for naming your routes:

- As a reminder of the purpose of the route

- So that you can select a specific route to be used to generate an outgoing URL

We have arranged the routes so that the least specific appears first in the list. This means that if we were to generate a link using the `ActionLink` method like this:

```
@Html.ActionLink("Click me", "Index", "Customer")
```

the outgoing link would always be generated using `MyRoute`, as follows:

```
<a href="/Customer/Index">Click me</a>
```

You can override the default route matching behavior by using the `Html.RouteLink` method, which lets you specify which route you want to use, as follows:

```
@Html.RouteLink("Click me", "MyOtherRoute","Index", "Customer")
```

The result is that the link generated by the helper looks like this:

```
<a Length="8" href="/App/Index?Length=5">Click me</a>
```

In this case, the controller we specified, `Customer`, is overridden by the route and the link targets the `Home` controller instead.

```
┌─────────────────────────────────────────────────────────┐
│          DO NOT: THE CASE AGAINST NAMED ROUTES          │
└─────────────────────────────────────────────────────────┘
```

The problem with relying on route names to generate outgoing URLs is that doing so breaks through the separation of concerns that is so central to the MVC design pattern. When generating a link or a URL in a view or action method, we want to focus on the action and controller that the user will be directed to, not the format of the URL that will be used. By bringing knowledge of the different routes into the views or controllers, we are creating dependencies that we would prefer to avoid.

We tend to avoid naming our routes (by specifying null for the route name parameter). We prefer to use code comments to remind ourselves of what each route is intended to do.

Customizing the Routing System

You have seen how flexible and configurable the routing system is, but if it does not meet your requirements, you can customize the behavior. In this section, we will show you the two ways to do this.

Creating a Custom RouteBase Implementation

If you do not like the way that standard Route objects match URLs, or want to implement something unusual, you can derive an alternative class from RouteBase. This gives you control over how URLs are matched, how parameters are extracted, and how outgoing URLs are generated.

To derive a class from RouteBase, you need to implement two methods:

- GetRouteData(HttpContextBase httpContext): This is the mechanism by which *inbound URL matching* works. The framework calls this method on each RouteTable.Routes entry in turn, until one of them returns a non-null value.

- GetVirtualPath(RequestContext requestContext, RouteValueDictionary values): This is the mechanism by which *outbound URL generation* works. The framework calls this method on each RouteTable.Routes entry in turn, until one of them returns a non-null value.

To demonstrate this kind of customization, we are going to create a RouteBase class that will handle legacy URL requests. Imagine that we have migrated an existing application to the MVC Framework, but some users have bookmarked our pre-MVC URLs or hard-coded them into scripts. We still want to support those old URLs. We could handle this using the regular routing system, but this problem provides a nice example for this section.

To begin, we need to create a controller that we will receive our legacy requests. We have called our controller LegacyController, and its contents are shown in Listing 14-14.

Listing 14-14. The LegacyController Class

```csharp
using System.Web.Mvc;

namespace UrlsAndRoutes.Controllers {

    public class LegacyController : Controller {

        public ActionResult GetLegacyURL(string legacyURL) {
            return View((object)legacyURL);
        }
    }
}
```

In this simple controller, the `GetLegacyURL` action method takes the parameter and passes it as a view model to the view. If we were really implementing this controller, we would use this method to retrieve the files that were requested, but as it is, we are simply going to display the URL in a view.

■ **Tip**   Notice that we have cast the parameter to the `View` method in Listing 14-14. One of the overloaded versions of the `View` method takes a string specifying the name of the view to render, and without the cast, this would be the overload that the C# compiler thinks we want. To avoid this, we cast to object so that we call the overload that passes a view model and uses the default view. We could also have solved this by using the overload that takes both the view name and the view model, but we prefer not to make explicit associations between action methods and views if we can help it.

The view that we have associated with this action is called `GetLegacyURL.cshtml` and is shown in Listing 14-15.

Listing 14-15. The GetLegacyURL View

```
@model string

@{
    ViewBag.Title = "GetLegacyURL";
    Layout = null;
}

<h2>GetLegacyURL</h2>


The URL requested was: @Model
```

Once again, this is very simple. We want to demonstrate the custom route behavior, so we are not going to spend any time creating complicated actions and views. We have now reached the point where we can create our derivation of `RouteBase`.

Routing Incoming URLs

We have created a class called `LegacyRoute`, which we put in the `Infrastructure` folder (which is where we like to put support classes that do not really belong anywhere else). The class is shown in Listing 14-16.

Listing 14-16. The LegacyRoute Class

```
using System;
using System.Linq;
using System.Web;
using System.Web.Mvc;
using System.Web.Routing;

namespace UrlsAndRoutes.Infrastructure {

    public class LegacyRoute : RouteBase {
        private string[] urls;
```

```
public LegacyRoute(params string[] targetUrls) {
    urls = targetUrls;
}

public override RouteData GetRouteData(HttpContextBase httpContext) {
    RouteData result = null;

    string requestedURL =
        httpContext.Request.AppRelativeCurrentExecutionFilePath;
    if (urls.Contains(requestedURL, StringComparer.OrdinalIgnoreCase)) {
        result = new RouteData(this, new MvcRouteHandler());
        result.Values.Add("controller", "Legacy");
        result.Values.Add("action", "GetLegacyURL");
        result.Values.Add("legacyURL", requestedURL);
    }
    return result;
}

public override VirtualPathData GetVirtualPath(RequestContext requestContext,
    RouteValueDictionary values) {

    return null;
    }
  }
}
```

This constructor of this class takes a string array that represents the individual URLs that this routing class will support. We will specify these when we register the route later. Of note in this Listing 14-is the GetRouteData method, which is what the routing system calls to see if we can handle an incoming URL.

If we cannot handle the request, then we can just return null, and the routing system will move on to the next route in the list and repeat the process. If we *can* handle the request, we need to return an instance of the RouteData class containing the values for the controller and action variables, and anything else we want to pass along to the action method.

When we create the RouteData object, we need to pass in the handler that we want to deal with the values we generate. We are going to use the standard MvcRouteHandler class, which is what assigns meaning to the controller and action values:

```
result = new RouteData(this, new MvcRouteHandler());
```

For the vast majority of MVC applications, this is the class that you will require, as it connects the routing system to the controller/action model of an MVC application. But you can implement a replacement for MvcRouteHandler, as we will show you in the Creating a Custom Route Handler section later in the chapter.

In this routing implementation, we are willing to route any request for the URLs that were passed to our constructor. When we get such a URL, we add hard-coded values for the controller and action method to the RouteValues object. We also pass along the requested URL as the legacyURL property. Notice that the name of this property matches the name of the parameter of our action method, ensuring that the value we generate here will be passed to the action method via the parameter.

The last step is to register a new route that uses our RouteBase derivation. You can see how to do this in Listing 14-17, which shows the addition to the RouteConfig.cs file.

Listing 14-17. Registering the Custom RouteBase Implementation

```
...
public static void RegisterRoutes(RouteCollection routes) {

    routes.Add(new LegacyRoute(
            "~/articles/Windows_3.1_Overview.html",
            "~/old/.NET_1.0_Class_Library"));

    routes.MapRoute("MyRoute", "{controller}/{action}");
    routes.MapRoute("MyOtherRoute", "App/{action}", new { controller = "Home" });
}
...
```

We create a new instance of our LegacyRoute class and pass in the URLs we want it to route. We then add the object to the RouteCollection using the Add method. Now when we start the application and request one of the legacy URLs we defined, the request is routed by our custom class and directed toward our controller, as shown in Figure 14-4.

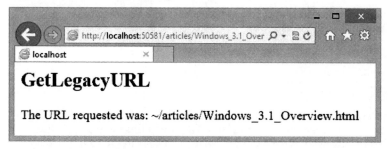

Figure 14-4. Routing requests using a custom RouteBase implementation

Generating Outgoing URLs

To support outgoing URL generation, we need to implement the GetVirtualPath method in our LegacyRoute class. Once again, if we are unable to deal with the request, we let the routing system know by returning null. Otherwise, we return an instance of the VirtualPathData class. Listing 14-18 shows our implementation of this method.

Listing 14-18. Implementing the GetVirtualPath Method

```
...
public override VirtualPathData GetVirtualPath(RequestContext requestContext,
    RouteValueDictionary values) {

    VirtualPathData result = null;

    if (values.ContainsKey("legacyURL") &&
        urls.Contains((string)values["legacyURL"], StringComparer.OrdinalIgnoreCase)) {
        result = new VirtualPathData(this,
            new UrlHelper(requestContext)
                .Content((string)values["legacyURL"]).Substring(1));
    }
    return result;
}
...
```

We have been passing segment variables and other details around using anonymous types, but behind the scenes, the routing system has been converting these into `RouteValueDictionary` objects. Listing 14-19 shows an addition to the `ActionName.cshtml` that generates an outgoing URL using our custom route.

Listing 14-19. Generating an outgoing URL via a custom route

```
@{
    Layout = null;
}

<!DOCTYPE html>

<html>
<head>
    <meta name="viewport" content="width=device-width" />
    <title>ActionName</title>
</head>
<body>
    <div>The controller is: @ViewBag.Controller</div>
    <div>The action is: @ViewBag.Action</div>
    <div>This is a URL:
        @Html.ActionLink("Click me", "GetLegacyURL",
            new { legacyURL = "~/articles/Windows_3.1_Overview.html" })
    </div>
</body>
</html>
```

When this view is rendered the `ActionLink` helper generates the following HTML, just as you would expect:

```
<a href="/articles/Windows_3.1_Overview.html">Click me</a>
```

The anonymous type created with the `legacyURL` property is converted into a `RouteValueDictionary` class that contains a key of the same name. In this example, we decide we can deal with a request for an outbound URL if there is a key named `legacyURL` and if its value is one of the URLs passed to the constructor. We could be more specific and check for `controller` and `action` values, but for a simple example, this is sufficient.

If we get a match, we create a new instance of `VirtualPathData`, passing in a reference to the current object and the outbound URL. We have used the `Content` method of the `UrlHelper` class to convert the application-relative URL to one that can be passed to browsers. The routing system prepends an additional / to the URL, so we must take care to remove the leading character from our generated URL.

Creating a Custom Route Handler

We have relied on the `MvcRouteHandler` in our routes because it connects the routing system to the MVC Framework. And, because our focus is MVC, this is what we want pretty much all of the time. Even so, the routing system lets us define our own route handler by implementing the `IRouteHandler` interface. Listing 14-20 shows the content of the `CustomRouteHandler` class that we added to the `Infrastructure` folder in the example project.

Listing 14-20. Implementing the IRouteHandler Interface

```
using System.Web;
using System.Web.Routing;

namespace UrlsAndRoutes.Infrastructure {

    public class CustomRouteHandler : IRouteHandler {
        public IHttpHandler GetHttpHandler(RequestContext requestContext) {
            return new CustomHttpHandler();
        }
    }

    public class CustomHttpHandler : IHttpHandler {
        public bool IsReusable {
            get { return false; }
        }

        public void ProcessRequest(HttpContext context) {
            context.Response.Write("Hello");
        }
    }
}
```

The purpose of the IRouteHandler interface is to provide a means to generate implementations of the IHttpHandler interface, which is responsible for processing requests. In the MVC implementation of these interfaces, controllers are found, action methods are invoked, views are rendered, and the results are written to the response. Our implementation is a little simpler. It just writes the word Hello to the client (not an HTML document containing that word, but just the text). We can register our custom handler in the RouteConfig.cs file when we define a route, as shown in Listing 14-21.

Listing 14-21. Using a Custom Routing Handler in a Route

```
...
public static void RegisterRoutes(RouteCollection routes) {

    routes.Add(new Route("SayHello", new CustomRouteHandler()));

    routes.Add(new LegacyRoute(
            "~/articles/Windows_3.1_Overview.html",
            "~/old/.NET_1.0_Class_Library"));

    routes.MapRoute("MyRoute", "{controller}/{action}");
    routes.MapRoute("MyOtherRoute", "App/{action}", new { controller = "Home" });
}
...
```

When we request the URL /SayHello, our handler is used to process the request. Figure 14-5 shows the result.

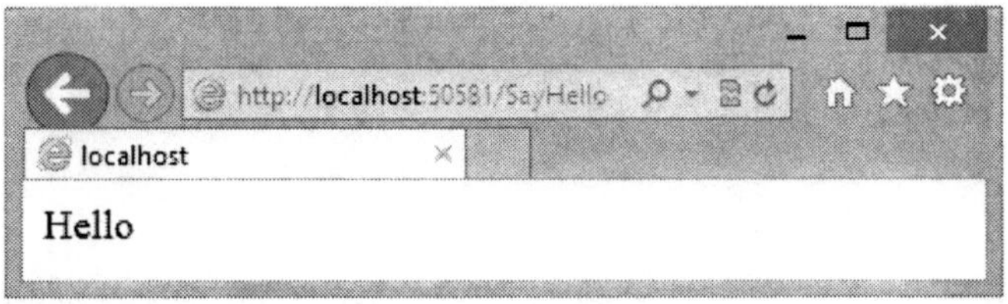

Figure 14-5. Using a custom request handler

Implementing custom route handling means taking on responsibility for functions that are usually handled for you, such as controller and action resolution. But it does give you incredible freedom. You can co-opt some parts of the MVC Framework and ignore others, or even implement an entirely new architectural pattern.

Working with Areas

The MVC Framework supports organizing a Web application into *areas*, where each area represents a functional segment of the application, such as administration, billing, customer support, and so on. This is useful in a large project, where having a single set of folders for all of the controllers, views, and models can become difficult to manage.

Each MVC area is has its own folder structure, allowing you to keep everything separate. This makes it more obvious which project elements relate to each functional area of the application. This helps multiple developers to work on the project without colliding with one another. Areas are supported largely through the routing system, which is why we have chosen to cover this feature alongside our coverage of URLs and routes. In this section, we will show you how to set up and use areas in your MVC projects.

Creating an Area

To add an area to the example MVC application, right-click the project item in the `Solution Explorer` window and select Add ➤ Area. Visual Studio will prompt you for the name of the area, as shown in Figure 14-6. In this case, we have created an area called `Admin`. This is a pretty common area to create, because many Web applications need to separate the customer-facing and administration functions. Click the `Add` button to create the area.

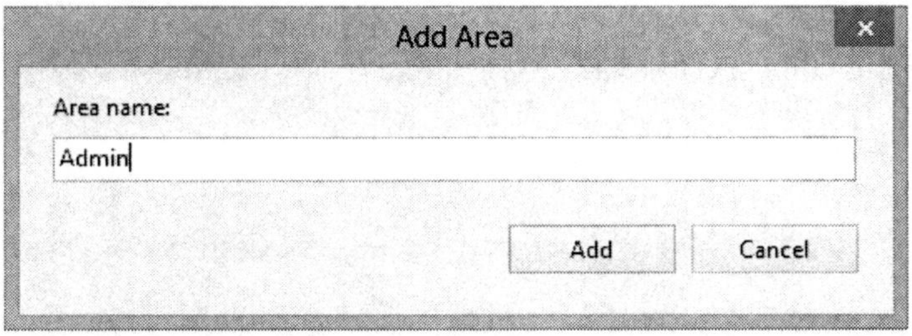

Figure 14-6. Adding an area to an MVC application

After you click Add, you will see some changes applied to the project. First of all, the project contains a new top-level folder called `Areas`. This contains a folder called `Admin`, which represents the area that we just created. If we were to create additional areas, other folders would be created here.

Inside the `Areas/Admin` folder, you will see that we have a mini-MVC project. There are folders called `Controllers`, `Models`, and `Views`. The first two are empty, but the `Views` folder contains a `Shared` folder (and a `Web.config` file that configures the view engine, but we are not interested in the view engine until Chapter 18).

381

The other change is that there is a file called AdminAreaRegistration.cs, which defines the AdminAreaRegistration class, as shown in Listing 14-22.

Listing 14-22. The AdminAreaRegistration Class

```
using System.Web.Mvc;

namespace UrlsAndRoutes.Areas.Admin {
    public class AdminAreaRegistration : AreaRegistration {
        public override string AreaName {
            get {
                return "Admin";
            }
        }

        public override void RegisterArea(AreaRegistrationContext context) {
            context.MapRoute(
                "Admin_default",
                "Admin/{controller}/{action}/{id}",
                new { action = "Index", id = UrlParameter.Optional }
            );
        }
    }
}
```

The interesting part of this class is the RegisterArea method. As you can see from the listing, this method registers a route with the URL pattern Admin/{controller}/{action}/{id}. We can define additional routes in this method, which will be unique to this area.

▪ **Caution**   If you assign names to your routes, you must ensure that they are unique across the entire application and not just the area for which they are intended.

We do not need to take any action to make sure that this registration method is called. It is handled for us automatically by the Application_Start method of Global.asax, which you can see in Listing 14-23.

Listing 14-23. Area Registration Called from Global.asax

```
...
protected void Application_Start() {
    AreaRegistration.RegisterAllAreas();

    WebApiConfig.Register(GlobalConfiguration.Configuration);
    FilterConfig.RegisterGlobalFilters(GlobalFilters.Filters);
    RouteConfig.RegisterRoutes(RouteTable.Routes);
    BundleConfig.RegisterBundles(BundleTable.Bundles);
}
...
```

The call to the static AreaRegistration.RegisterAllAreas method causes the MVC Framework to go through all of the classes in our application, find those that are derived from the AreaRegistration class and call the RegisterArea method on each of them.

■ **Caution** Do not change the order of the statements related to routing in the `Application_Start` method. If you call `RegisterRoutes` before `AreaRegistration.RegisterAllAreas` is called, then your routes will be defined before the area routes. Given that routes are evaluated in order, this will mean that requests for area controllers are likely to be matched against the wrong routes.

The `AreaRegistrationContext` class that is passed to each area's `RegisterArea` method exposes a set of `MapRoute` methods that the area can use to register routes in the same way as your main application does in the `RegisterRoutes` method of `Global.asax`.

■ **Note** The `MapRoute` methods in the `AreaRegistrationContext` class automatically limit the routes you register to the namespace that contains the controllers for the area. This means that when you create a controller in an area, you must leave it in its default namespace; otherwise, the routing system will not be able to find it.

Populating an Area

You can create controllers, views, and models in an area just as you have seen in previous examples. To create a controller, right-click the `Controllers` folder within the `Admin` area and select Add ➤ Controller from the pop-up menu. The `Add Controller` dialog box will be displayed, allowing you to enter the name for your new controller class, as shown in Figure 14-7.

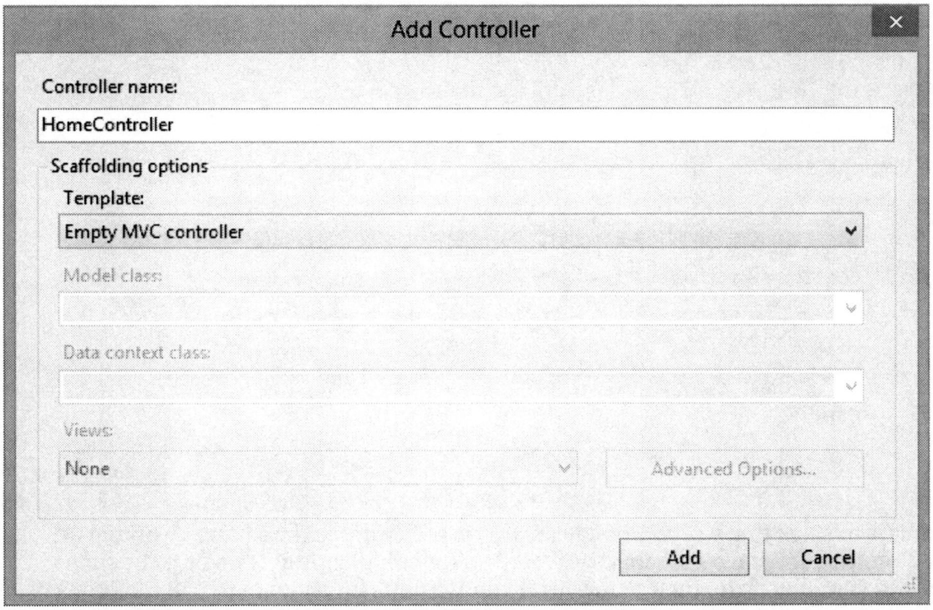

Figure 14-7. Adding a controller to an area

Clicking **Add** creates an empty controller, as shown in Listing 14-24. In this example, we have called our class **HomeController** to demonstrate the separation between areas in an application.

Listing 14-24. A Controller Created Inside an MVC Area

```
using System;
using System.Collections.Generic;
using System.Linq;
using System.Web;
using System.Web.Mvc;

namespace UrlsAndRoutes.Areas.Admin.Controllers {
    public class HomeController : Controller {

        public ActionResult Index() {
            return View();
        }

    }
}
```

To complete this simple example, we can create a view by right-clicking inside the **Index** action method and selecting **Add View** from the pop-up menu. We accepted the default name for our view (**Index**). When you create the view, you will see that it appears in the **Areas/Admin/Views/Home** folder. The view we created is shown in Listing 14-25.

Listing 14-25. A Simple View for an Area Controller

```
@{
    ViewBag.Title = "Index";
    Layout = null;
}

<!DOCTYPE html>

<html>
<head>
    <meta name="viewport" content="width=device-width" />
    <title>Index</title>
</head>
<body>
    <div>
        <h2>Admin Area Index</h2>
    </div>
</body>
</html>
```

The point of all of this is to show that working inside an area is pretty much the same as working in the main part of an MVC project. You have seen that the workflow for creating project items is the same. We created a controller and view that share their names with counterparts in the main part of the project. If you start the application and navigate to **/Admin/Home/Index**, you will see the view that we created, as shown in Figure 14-8.

Figure 14-8. Rendering an area view

Resolving the Ambiguous Controller Issue

Okay, so we lied slightly—areas are not quite as self-contained as they might be. If you navigate to the /Home/Index URL, you will see the error shown in Figure 14-9.

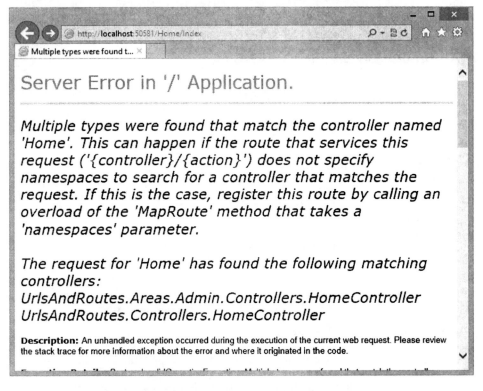

Figure 14-9. The ambiguous controller error

When an area is registered, any routes that we define are limited to the namespace associated with the area. This is how we were able to request /Admin/Home/Index and get the HomeController class in the WorkingWithAreas.Areas.Admin.Controllers namespace.

However, routes defined in the RegisterRoutes method of RouteConfig.cs are not similarly restricted. In Listing 14-26, as a reminder, we have listed the current routing configuration of our example app.

Listing 14-26. The Routing Configuration for the Example MVC App

```
...
public static void RegisterRoutes(RouteCollection routes) {

    routes.Add(new Route("SayHello", new CustomRouteHandler()));

    routes.Add(new LegacyRoute(
            "~/articles/Windows_3.1_Overview.html",
            "~/old/.NET_1.0_Class_Library"));

    routes.MapRoute("MyRoute", "{controller}/{action}");
    routes.MapRoute("MyOtherRoute", "App/{action}", new { controller = "Home" });
}
...
```

The route named MyRoute translates the incoming URL from the browser to the Index action on the Home controller. At that point, we get an error, because there are no namespace restrictions in place for this route and the MVC Framework can see two HomeController classes. To resolve this, we need to prioritize the main controller namespace in all of the routes which might lead to a conflict, as shown in Listing 14-27.

Listing 14-27. Resolving the Area Namespace Conflict

```
...
public static void RegisterRoutes(RouteCollection routes) {

    routes.Add(new Route("SayHello", new CustomRouteHandler()));

    routes.Add(new LegacyRoute(
            "~/articles/Windows_3.1_Overview.html",
            "~/old/.NET_1.0_Class_Library"));

    routes.MapRoute("MyRoute", "{controller}/{action}", null,
        new[] {"UrlsAndRoutes.Controllers"});
    routes.MapRoute("MyOtherRoute", "App/{action}",
        new { controller = "Home" }, new[] { "UrlsAndRoutes.Controllers" });
}
...
```

This change ensures that the controllers in the main project are given priority in resolving requests. Of course, if you want to give preference to the controllers in an area, you can do that instead.

Generating Links to Actions in Areas

You do not need to take any special steps to create links that refer to actions in the same MVC area that the user is already on. The MVC Framework detects that the current request relates to a particular area, and then outbound URL generation will find a match only among routes defined for that area. For example, this addition to the view in our Admin area:

```
@Html.ActionLink("Click me", "About")
```

generates the following HTML:

```
<a href="/Admin/Home/About">Click me</a>
```

To create a link to an action in a different area, or no area at all, you must create a variable called **area** and use it to specify the name of the area you want, like this:

```
@Html.ActionLink("Click me to go to another area", "Index", new { area = "Support" })
```

It is for this reason that **area** is reserved from use as a segment variable name. The HTML generated by this call is as follows (assuming that you created an area called **Support** that has the standard route defined):

```
<a href="/Support/Home">Click me to go to another area</a>
```

If you want to link to an action on one of the top-level controllers (a controller in the /Controllers folder), then you should specify the area as an empty string, like this:

```
@Html.ActionLink("Click me to go to another area", "Index", new { area = "" })
```

URL Schema Best Practices

After all of this, you may be left wondering where to start in designing your own URL schema. You could just accept the default schema that Visual Studio generates for you, but there are some benefits in giving your schema some thought.

In recent years, the design of an applications URLs have been taken increasingly seriously, and a few important design principles have emerged. If you follow these design patterns, you will improve the usability, compatibility, and search-engine rankings of your applications.

Make Your URLs Clean and Human-Friendly

Users notice the URLs in your applications. If you do not agree, then just think back to the last time you tried to send someone an Amazon URL. Here is the URL for this book:

```
http://www.amazon.com/Pro-ASP-NET-MVC-Professional-
Apress/dp/1430242361/ref=la_B001IU0SNK_1_5?ie=UTF8&qid=1349978167&sr=1-5
```

It is bad enough sending someone such a URL by e-mail, but try reading this over the phone. When we needed to do this recently, we ended up looking up the ISBN number and asking the caller to look it up for himself. It would be nice if we could access the book with a URL like this:

```
http://www.amazon.com/books/pro-aspnet-mvc4-framework
```

That is the kind of URL that we *could* read out over the phone and that doesn't look like we dropped something on the keyboard while composing an e-mail message.

▪ **Note** To be very clear, we have only the highest respect for Amazon, who sells more of our books than everyone else combined. We know for a fact that each and every member of the Amazon team is a strikingly intelligent and beautiful person. Not one of them would be so petty as to stop selling our books over something so minor as criticism of their URL format. We love Amazon. We adore Amazon. We just wish they would fix their URLs.

Here are some simple guidelines to make friendly URLs:

- Design URLs to describe their content, not the implementation details of your application. Use **/Articles/AnnualReport** rather than **/Website_v2/CachedContentServer/FromCache/AnnualReport**.

- Prefer content titles over ID numbers. Use **/Articles/AnnualReport** rather than **/Articles/2392**. If you must use an ID number (to distinguish items with identical titles, or to avoid the extra database query needed to find an item by its title), then use both (**/Articles/2392/AnnualReport**). It takes longer to type, but it makes more sense to a human and improves search-engine rankings. Your application can just ignore the title and display the item matching that ID.

- Do not use file name extensions for HTML pages (for example, **.aspx** or **.mvc**), but do use them for specialized file types (such as **.jpg**, **.pdf**, and **.zip**). Web browsers do not care about file name extensions if you set the MIME type appropriately, but humans still expect PDF files to end with **.pdf**.

- Create a sense of hierarchy (for example, **/Products/Menswear/Shirts/Red**), so your visitor can guess the parent category's URL.

- Be case-insensitive (someone might want to type in the URL from a printed page). The ASP.NET routing system is case-insensitive by default.

- Avoid symbols, codes, and character sequences. If you want a word separator, use a dash (as in **/my-great-article**). Underscores are unfriendly, and URL-encoded spaces are bizarre (**/my+great+article**) or disgusting (**/my%20great%20article**).

- Do not change URLs. Broken links equal lost business. When you do change URLs, continue to support the old URL schema for as long as possible via permanent (301) redirections.

- Be consistent. Adopt one URL format across your entire application.

URLs should be short, easy to type, hackable (human-editable), and persistent, and they should visualize site structure. Jakob Nielsen, usability guru, expands on this topic at **http://www.useit.com/alertbox/990321.html**. Tim Berners-Lee, inventor of the Web, offers similar advice (see **http://www.w3.org/Provider/Style/URI**).

GET and POST: Pick the Right One

The rule of thumb is that GET requests should be used for all read-only information retrieval, while POST requests should be used for any operation that changes the application state. In standards-compliance terms, GET requests are for *safe* interactions (having no side effects besides information retrieval), and POST requests are for *unsafe* interactions (making a decision or changing something). These conventions are set by the World Wide Web Consortium (W3C), at **http://www.w3.org/Protocols/rfc2616/rfc2616-sec9.html**.

GET requests are *addressable*—all the information is contained in the URL, so it's possible to bookmark and link to these addresses.

Do not use GET requests for operations that change state. Many Web developers learned this the hard way in 2005, when Google Web Accelerator was released to the public. This application pre-fetched all the content linked from each page, which is legal within the HTTP because GET requests should be safe. Unfortunately, many Web developers had ignored the HTTP conventions and placed simple links to "delete item" or "add to shopping cart" in their applications. Chaos ensued.

One company believed their content management system was the target of repeated hostile attacks, because all their content kept getting deleted. They later discovered that a search-engine crawler had hit upon the URL of an administrative page and was crawling all the delete links. Authentication might protect you from this, but it wouldn't protect you from Web accelerators.

Summary

In this chapter, we have shown you the advanced features of the MVC Framework routing system, showing you how to generate outgoing links and URLs, and how to customize the routing system. Along the way, we introduced the concept of areas and set out our views on how to create a useful and meaningful URL schema.

In the next chapter, we turn to controllers and actions, which are the very heart of the MVC model. We will explain how these work in detail and show you how to use them to get the best results in your application.

■ ■ ■

CHAPTER 15

Controllers and Actions

Every request that comes to your application is handled by a controller. The controller is free to handle the request any way it sees fit, as long as it doesn't stray into the areas of responsibility that belong to the model and view. This means that we do not put business or data storage logic into a controller, nor do we generate user interfaces.

In the ASP.NET MVC Framework, controllers are .NET classes that contain the logic required to handle a request. In Chapter 3, we explained that the role of the controller is to encapsulate your application logic. This means that controllers are responsible for processing incoming requests, performing operations on the domain model, and selecting views to render to the user.

In this chapter, we will show you how controllers are implemented and the different ways that you can use controllers to receive and generate output. The MVC Framework doesn't limit you to generating HTML through views, and we will discuss the other options that are available. We will also show how action methods make unit testing easy and demonstrate how to test each kind of result that an action method can produce.

Introducing the Controller

You've seen the use of controllers in almost all of the chapters so far. Now it is time to take a step back and look behind the scenes. To begin, we need to create a project for our examples.

Preparing the Example Project

To prepare for this chapter, we created a new MVC project called `ControllersAndActions` using the `Empty` template. We chose the `Empty` template because we are going to create all of the controllers and views we need as we go through the chapter.

■ **Tip**   Do not forget to check the option to create a unit test project if you want to follow the example tests we provide in this chapter.

Creating a Controller with IController

In the MVC Framework, controller classes must implement the `IController` interface from the `System.Web.Mvc` namespace, as shown in Listing 15-1.

Listing 15-1. The System.Web.Mvc.IController Interface

```
public interface IController {
    void Execute(RequestContext requestContext);
}
```

This is a very simple interface. The sole method, Execute, is invoked when a request is targeted at the controller class. The MVC Framework knows which controller class has been targeted in a request by reading the value of the controller property generated by the routing data.

You can choose to create controller classes by implementing IController, but it is a pretty low-level interface, and you must do a lot of work to get anything useful done. Listing 15-2 shows a simple controller called BasicController that provides a demonstration.

Listing 15-2. The BasicController Class

```
using System.Web.Mvc;
using System.Web.Routing;

namespace ControllersAndActions.Controllers {

    public class BasicController : IController {

        public void Execute(RequestContext requestContext) {

            string controller = (string)requestContext.RouteData.Values["controller"];
            string action = (string)requestContext.RouteData.Values["action"];

            requestContext.HttpContext.Response.Write(
                string.Format("Controller: {0}, Action: {1}", controller, action));
        }
    }
}
```

To create this class, we right-clicked the Controllers folder in the example project and selected Add ➤ New Class. We then gave the name for our controller, BasicController, and entered the code you see in Listing 15-2.

In our Execute method, we read the value of the controller and action variables from the RouteData object associated with the request and write them to the result. If you run the application and navigate to /Basic/Index, you can see the output generated by our controller, as shown in Figure 15-1.

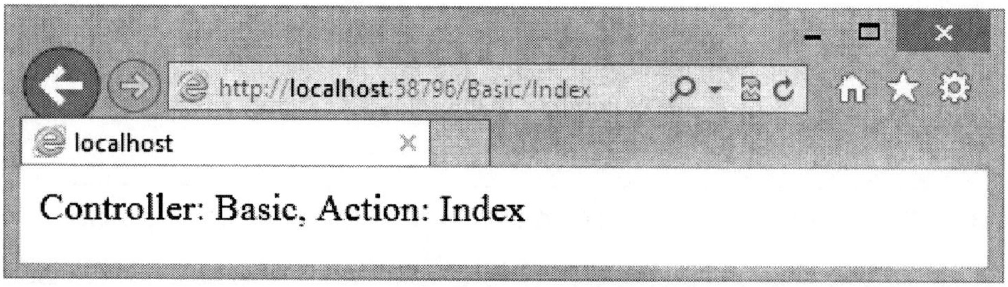

Figure 15-1. A result generated from the BasicController class

Implementing the IController interface allows you to create a class that the MVC Framework recognizes as a controller and sends requests to, but it would be pretty hard to write a complex application. The MVC Framework does not specify how a controller deals with requests, which means that you can create any approach you want.

▨ **Tip**   Notice that the MVC Framework does not impose a view engine on our basic controller. How responses are produced is at the discretion of the controller and the MVC Framework doesn't make any assumptions about the technique that will be used.

Creating a Controller by Deriving from the Controller Class

The MVC Framework is endlessly customizable and extensible. You can implement the IController interface to create any kind of request handling and result generation you require. Do not like action methods? Do not care for rendered views? Then you can just take matters in your own hands and write a better, faster, and more elegant way of handling requests. Or you can build on the features that the MVC Framework team has provided, which is achieved by deriving your controllers from the System.Web.Mvc.Controller class.

System.Web.Mvc.Controller is the class that provides the request handling support that most MVC developers will be familiar with. It's what we have been using in all of our examples in previous chapters.

The Controller class provides three key features:

- *Action methods*: A controller's behavior is partitioned into multiple methods (instead of having just one single Execute() method). Each action method is exposed on a different URL and is invoked with parameters extracted from the incoming request.

- *Action results*: You can return an object describing the result of an action (for example, rendering a view, or redirecting to a different URL or action method), which is then carried out on your behalf. The separation between *specifying results* and *executing them* simplifies unit testing.

- *Filters*: You can encapsulate reusable behaviors (for example, authentication, as you saw in Chapter 11) as filters, and then tag each behavior onto one or more controllers or action methods by putting an [Attribute] in your source code.

Unless you have a *very* specific requirement in mind, the best way to create controllers is to derive from the Controller class, and, as you might hope, this is what Visual Studio does when it creates a new class in response to the Add ➤ Controller menu item. Listing 15-3 shows a simple controller created this way. We have called our class DerivedController.

Listing 15-3. A Simple Controller Derived from the System.Web.Mvc.Controller Class

```
using System.Web.Mvc;

namespace ControllersAndActions.Controllers {

    public class DerivedController : Controller {

        public ActionResult Index() {
            ViewBag.Message = "Hello from the DerivedController Index method";
            return View("MyView");
        }
    }
}
```

The `Controller` base class implements the `Execute` method and takes responsibility for invoking the action method whose name matches the `action` value in the route data.

The `Controller` class is also our link to the Razor view system. In the listing, we return the result of the `View` method, passing in the name of the view we want rendered to the client as a parameter. Listing 15-4 shows this view, called `MyView.cshtml` and located in the `Views/Derived` folder in the project.

Listing 15-4. The MyView.cshtml File

```
@{
    ViewBag.Title = "MyView";
}


<h2>MyView</h2>

Message: @ViewBag.Message
```

If you start the application and navigate to `/Derived/Index`, the action method we have defined will be executed, and the view we named will be rendered, as shown in Figure 15-2.

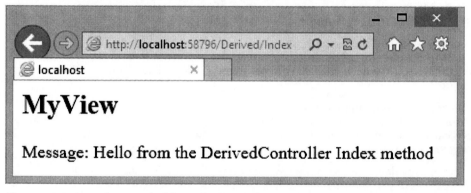

Figure 15-2. A result generated from the DerviedController class

Our job, as a derivation of the `Controller` class, is to implement action methods, obtain whatever input we need to process a request, and generate a suiTable 15-response. The myriad of ways that we can do this are covered in the rest of this chapter.

Receiving Input

Controllers frequently need to access incoming data, such as query string values, form values, and parameters parsed from the incoming URL by the routing system. There are three main ways to access that data:

- Extract it from a set of *context objects*.

- Have the data passed as *parameters* to your action method.

- Explicitly invoke the framework's *model binding* feature.

Here, we will look at the approaches for getting input for your action methods, focusing on using context objects and action method parameters. In Chapter 22, we will cover model binding in depth.

Getting Data from Context Objects

The most direct way to get hold of data is to fetch it yourself. When you create a controller by deriving from the Controller base class, you get access to a set of convenience properties to access information about the request. These properties include Request, Response, RouteData, HttpContext, and Server. Each provides information about a different aspect of the request. We refer to these as *convenience properties*, because they each retrieve different types of data from the request's ControllerContext instance (which can be accessed through the Controller.ControllerContext property). We have described some of the most commonly used context objects in Table 15-1.

Table 15-1. Commonly Used Context Objects

Property	Type	Description
Request.QueryString	NameValueCollection	GET variables sent with this request
Request.Form	NameValueCollection	POST variables sent with this request
Request.Cookies	HttpCookieCollection	Cookies sent by the browser with this request
Request.HttpMethod	string	The HTTP method (verb, such as GET or POST) used for this request
Request.Headers	NameValueCollection	The full set of HTTP headers sent with this request
Request.Url	Uri	The URL requested
Request.UserHostAddress	string	The IP address of the user making this request
RouteData.Route	RouteBase	The chosen RouteTable.Routes entry for this request
RouteData.Values	RouteValueDictionary	Active route parameters (either extracted from the URL or default values)
HttpContext.Application	HttpApplicationStateBase	Application state store
HttpContext.Cache	Cache	Application cache store
HttpContext.Items	IDictionary	State store for the current request
HttpContext.Session	HttpSessionStateBase	State store for the visitor's session
User	IPrincipal	Authentication information about the logged-in user
TempData	TempDataDictionary	Temporary data items stored for the current user

An action method can use any of these context objects to get information about the request, as Listing 15-5 demonstrates in the form of a hypothetical action method.

Listing 15-5. An Action Method Using Context Objects to Get Information About a Request

```
...
public ActionResult RenameProduct() {
    // Access various properties from context objects
    string userName = User.Identity.Name;
    string serverName = Server.MachineName;
    string clientIP = Request.UserHostAddress;
    DateTime dateStamp = HttpContext.Timestamp;
    AuditRequest(userName, serverName, clientIP, dateStamp, "Renaming product");

    // Retrieve posted data from Request.Form
    string oldProductName = Request.Form["OldName"];
    string newProductName = Request.Form["NewName"];
    bool result = AttemptProductRename(oldProductName, newProductName);

    ViewData["RenameResult"] = result;
    return View("ProductRenamed");
}
...
```

You can explore the vast range of available request context information using IntelliSense (in an action method, type this. and browse the pop-up), and the Microsoft Developer Network (look up System.Web.Mvc.Controller and its base classes, or System.Web.Mvc.ControllerContext).

Using Action Method Parameters

As you've seen in previous chapters, action methods can take parameters. This is a neater way to receive incoming data than extracting it manually from context objects, and it makes your action methods easier to read. For example, suppose we have an action method that uses context objects like this:

```
...
public ActionResult ShowWeatherForecast() {
    string city = (string)RouteData.Values["city"];
    DateTime forDate = DateTime.Parse(Request.Form["forDate"]);
    // ... implement weather forecast here ...
    return View();
}
...
```

We can rewrite it to use parameters, like this:

```
...
public ActionResult ShowWeatherForecast(string city, DateTime forDate) {
    // ... implement weather forecast here ...
    return View();
}
...
```

Not only is this easier to read, but it also helps with unit testing—we can test the action method without needing to mock the convenience properties of the controller class.

For completeness, it's worth noting that action methods aren't allowed to have **out** or **ref** parameters. It wouldn't make any sense if they did and ASP.NET MVC will simply throw an exception if it sees such a parameter.

The MVC Framework will provide values for our parameters by checking context objects on our behalf, including `Request.QueryString`, `Request.Form`, and `RouteData.Values`. The names of our parameters are treated case-insensitively, so that an action method parameter called `city` can be populated by a value from `Request.Form["City"]`.

Understanding How Parameters Objects Are Instantiated

The base `Controller` class obtains values for your action method parameters using MVC Framework components called *value providers* and *model binders*.

Value providers represent the set of data items available to your controller. There are built-in value providers that fetch items from `Request.Form`, `Request.QueryString`, `Request.Files`, and `RouteData.Values`. The values are then passed to model binders that try to map them to the types that your action methods require as parameters.

The default model binders can create and populate objects of any .NET type, including collections and project-specific custom types. You saw an example of this in Chapter 10 when form posts from administrators were presented to our action method as a single `Product` object, even though the individual values were dispersed among the elements of the HTML form. We cover value providers and model binders in depth in Chapter 22.

Understanding Optional and Compulsory Parameters

If the MVC Framework cannot find a value for a reference type parameter (such as a `string` or `object`), the action method will still be called, but using a `null` value for that parameter. If a value cannot be found for a value type parameter (such as `int` or `double`), then an exception will be thrown, and the action method will *not* be called. Here is another way to think about it:

- Value-type parameters are compulsory. To make them optional, either specify a default value (see the next section) or change the parameter type to a nullable type (such as `int?` or `DateTime?`), so the MVC Framework can pass `null` if no value is available.

- Reference-type parameters are optional. To make them compulsory (to ensure that a non-`null` value is passed), add some code to the top of the action method to reject `null` values. For example, if the value equals `null`, throw an `ArgumentNullException`.

Specifying Default Parameter Values

If you want to process requests that do not contain values for action method parameters, but you would rather not check for `null` values in your code or have exceptions thrown, you can use the C# optional parameter feature instead. Listing 15-6 provides a demonstration.

Listing 15-6. Using the C# Optional Parameter Feature in an Action Method

```
...
public ActionResult Search(string query= "all", int page = 1) {
    // ...process request...
    return View();
}
...
```

We mark parameters as optional by assigning values when we define them. In the listing, we have provided default values for the **query** and **page** parameters. The MVC Framework will try to obtain values from the request for these parameters, but if there are no values available, the defaults we have specified will be used instead.

For the string parameter, query, this means that we do not need to check for null values. If the request we are processing didn't specify a query, then our action method will be called with the string all. For the int parameter, we do not need to worry about requests resulting in errors when there is no page value. Our method will be called with the default value of 1.

Optional parameters can be used for *literal types*, which are types that you can define without using the new keyword, including string, int, and double.

■ **Caution**   If a request *does* contain a value for a parameter but it cannot be converted to the correct type (for example, if the user gives a nonnumeric string for an int parameter), then the framework will pass the default value for that parameter type (for example, 0 for an int parameter), and will register the attempted value as a validation error in a special context object called ModelState. Unless you check for validation errors in ModelState, you can get into odd situations where the user has entered bad data into a form, but the request is processed as though the user had not entered any data or had entered the default value. See Chapter 23 for details of validation and ModelState, which can be used to avoid such problems.

Producing Output

After a controller has finished processing a request, it usually needs to generate a response. When we created our bare-metal controller by implementing the IController interface directly, we needed to take responsibility for every aspect of processing a request, including generating the response to the client. If we want to send an HTML response, for example, then we must create and assemble the HTML data and send it to the client using the Response.Write method. Similarly, if we want to redirect the user's browser to another URL, we need to call the Response.Redirect method and pass the URL we are interested in directly. Both of these approaches are shown in Listing 15-7, which shows enhancements to the BasicController class.

Listing 15-7. Generating Results in an IController Implementation

```
using System.Web.Mvc;
using System.Web.Routing;

namespace ControllersAndActions.Controllers {

    public class BasicController : IController {

        public void Execute(RequestContext requestContext) {

            string controller = (string)requestContext.RouteData.Values["controller"];
            string action = (string)requestContext.RouteData.Values["action"];

            if (action.ToLower() == "redirect") {
                requestContext.HttpContext.Response.Redirect("/Derived/Index");
            } else {
                requestContext.HttpContext.Response.Write(
                    string.Format("Controller: {0}, Action: {1}",
                    controller, action));
            }
        }
    }
}
```

You can use the same approach when you have derived your controller from the `Controller` class. The `HttpResponseBase` class that is returned when you read the `requestContext.HttpContext.Response` property in your `Execute` method is available through the `Controller.Response` property, as shown in Listing 15-8, which shows enhancements to the `DerivedController` class.

Listing 15-8. Using the Response Property to Generate Output

```
using System.Web.Mvc;

namespace ControllersAndActions.Controllers {

    public class DerivedController : Controller {

        public ActionResult Index() {
            ViewBag.Message = "Hello from the DerivedController Index method";
            return View("MyView");
        }

        public void ProduceOutput() {
            if (Server.MachineName == "TINY") {
                Response.Redirect("/Basic/Index");
            } else {
                Response.Write("Controller: Derived, Action: ProduceOutput");
            }
        }
    }
}
```

The `ProduceOutput` method uses the value of the `Server.MachineName` property to decide what response to send to the client. (TINY is the name of one of our development machines).

This approach works, but it has a few problems:

- The controller classes must contain details of HTML or URL structure, which makes the classes harder to read and maintain.

- It is hard to unit test a controller that generates its response directly to the output. You need to create mock implementations of the `Response` object, and then be able to process the output you receive from the controller in order to determine what the output represents. This can mean parsing HTML for keywords, for example, which is a drawn-out and painful process.

- Handling the fine detail of every response this way is tedious and error-prone. Some programmers will like the absolute control that building a raw controller gives, but normal people get frustrated pretty quickly.

Fortunately, the MVC Framework has a nice feature that addresses all of these issues, called *action results*. The following sections introduce the action result concept and show you the different ways that it can be used to generate responses from controllers.

Understanding Action Results

The MVC Framework uses action results to separate *stating our intentions* from *executing our intentions*. It works very simply.

Instead of working directly with the Response object, we return an object derived from the ActionResult class that describes what we want the response from our controller to be, such as rendering a view or redirecting to another URL or action method.

■ **Note** The system of action results is an example of the *command pattern*. This pattern describes scenarios where you store and pass around objects that describe operations to be performed. See http://en.wikipedia.org/wiki/Command_pattern for more details.

When the MVC Framework receives an ActionResult object from an action method, it calls the ExecuteResult method defined by that object. The action result implementation then deals with the Response object for you, generating the output that corresponds to your intention. A simple example is the CustomRedirectResult class shown in Listing 15-9, which we defined in a new Infrastructure folder we created in the example project.

Listing 15-9. The CustomRedirectResult class

```
using System;
using System.Collections.Generic;
using System.Linq;
using System.Web;
using System.Web.Mvc;

namespace ControllersAndActions.Infrastructure {
    public class CustomRedirectResult : ActionResult {

        public string Url { get; set; }

        public override void ExecuteResult(ControllerContext context) {
            string fullUrl = UrlHelper.GenerateContentUrl(Url, context.HttpContext);
            context.HttpContext.Response.Redirect(fullUrl);
        }
    }
}
```

We based this class on way that the System.Web.Mvc.RedirectResult class works—one of the benefits of the MVC Framework being open source is that you can see how things work behind the scenes. Our CustomRedirectResult class is a lot simpler than the MVC equivalent, but is enough for our purposes in this chapter.

When we create an instance of the RedirectResult class, we pass in the URL we want to redirect the user to. The ExecuteResult method, which will be executed by the MVC Framework when our action method has finished, gets the Response object for the query through the ControllerContext object that the framework provides, and calls either the RedirectPermanent or Redirect method, which is exactly what we were doing manually in Listing 15-8.

You can see how we have used the CustomRedirectResult class in Listing 15-10, which shows how we have changed the Derived controller.

Listing 15-10. Using the CustomRedirectResult class in the Derived Controllers

```
using ControllersAndActions.Infrastructure;
using System.Web.Mvc;

namespace ControllersAndActions.Controllers {

    public class DerivedController : Controller {

        public ActionResult Index() {
            ViewBag.Message = "Hello from the DerivedController Index method";
            return View("MyView");
        }

        public ActionResult ProduceOutput() {
            if (Server.MachineName == "TINY") {
                return new CustomRedirectResult { Url = "/Basic/Index" };
            } else {
                Response.Write("Controller: Derived, Action: ProduceOutput");
                return null;
            }
        }
    }
}
```

Notice that we have had to change the result of the action method to return an `ActionResult`. We return `null` if we do not want the MVC Framework to do anything when our action method has been executed, which is what we have done when we do not return a `CustomRedirectResult` instance.

UNIT TESTING CONTROLLERS AND ACTIONS

Many parts of the MVC Framework are designed to facilitate unit testing, and this is especially true for actions and controllers. There are a few reasons for this support:

> You can test actions and controllers outside a Web server. The context objects are accessed through their base classes (such as `HttpRequestBase`), which are easy to mock.

> You do not need to parse any HTML to test the result of an action method. You can inspect the `ActionResult` object that is returned to ensure that you received the expected result.

> You do not need to simulate client requests. The MVC Framework model binding system allows you to write action methods that receive input as method parameters. To test an action method, you simply call the action method directly and provide the parameter values that interest you.

We will show you how to create unit tests for the different kinds of action results as we go through this chapter.

Do not forget that unit testing isn't the complete story. Complex behaviors in an application arise when action methods are called in sequence. Unit testing is best combined with other testing approaches.

Now that you have seen how our custom action result works, we can switch to the one provided by the MVC Framework, which has more features and has been thoroughly tested by Microsoft. Listing 15-11 shows how we have made the change.

Listing 15-11. Using the built-in RedirectResult object

```
...
public ActionResult ProduceOutput() {
    return new RedirectResult("/Basic/Index");
}
...
```

We have removed the conditional statement from the action method, which means that if you start the application and navigate to the /Derived/ProduceOutput method, your browser will be redirected to the /Basic/Index URL.

To make action method code simpler, the Controller class includes convenience methods for generating different kinds of ActionResult objects. So, as an example, we can achieve the effect in Listing 15-11 by returning the result of the Redirect method, as shown in Listing 15-12.

Listing 15-12. Using a Controller Convenience Method for Creating an Action Result

```
...
public ActionResult ProduceOutput() {
    return Redirect("/Basic/Index");
}
...
```

There is nothing in the action result system that is especially complex, but it helps you to end up with simpler, cleaner and more consistent code, which is easier to read and easier to unit test.

In the case of a redirection, for example, you can simply check that the action method returns an instance of RedirectResult and that the Url property contains the target you expect.

The MVC Framework contains a number of built-in action result types, which are shown in Table 15-2. All of these types are derived from ActionResult, and many of them have convenient helper methods in the Controller class. In the following sections, we will show you how to use these result types.

Table 15-2. Built-in ActionResult Types

Type	Description	Helper Methods
ViewResult	Renders the specified or default view template	View
PartialViewResult	Renders the specified or default partial view template	PartialView
RedirectToRouteResult	Issues an HTTP 301 or 302 redirection to an action method or specific route entry, generating a URL according to your routing configuration	RedirectToAction RedirectToActionPermanent RedirectToRoute RedirectToRoutePermanent

Type	Description	Helper Methods
RedirectResult	Issues an HTTP 301 or 302 redirection to a specific URL	Redirect RedirectPermanent
HttpUnauthorizedResult	Sets the response HTTP status code to 401 (meaning "not authorized"), which causes the active authentication mechanism (forms authentication or Windows authentication) to ask the visitor to log in	None
HttpNotFoundResult	Returns a HTTP 404—Not found error	HttpNotFound
HttpStatusCodeResult	Returns a specified HTTP code	None
EmptyResult	Does nothing	None

Returning HTML by Rendering a View

The most common kind of response from an action method is to generate HTML and send it to the browser. When using the action result system, you do this by creating an instance of the ViewResult class that specifies the view you want rendered in order to generate the HTML, as demonstrated in Listing 15-13.

Listing 15-13. Specifying a View to Be Rendered Using ViewResult

```
using System.Web.Mvc;

namespace ControllersAndActions.Controllers {

    public class ExampleController : Controller {

        public ViewResult Index() {
            return View("Homepage");
        }
    }
}
```

In this listing, we use the View helper method to create an instance of the ViewResult class, which is then returned as the result of the action method.

░ **Note** Notice that that the return type for the action method in the listing is ViewResult. The method would compile and work just as well if we had specified the more general ActionResult type. In fact, some MVC programmers will define the result of every action method as ActionResult, even when they know it will always return a more specific type. We have been particularly diligent in this practice in the examples that follow to make it clear how you can use each result type, but we tend to be more relaxed in real projects.

You specify the view you want rendered using the parameter to the `View` method. In this example, we have specified the `Homepage` view.

■ **Note** We could have created the `ViewResult` object explicitly, (with `return new ViewResult { ViewName = "Homepage" };`). This is a perfectly acceptable approach, but we prefer to use the convenient helper methods defined by the `Controller` class.

When the MVC Framework calls the `ExecuteResult` method of the `ViewResult` object, a search will begin for the view that you have specified. If you are using areas in your project, then the framework will look in the following locations:

- `/Areas/<AreaName>/Views/<ControllerName>/<ViewName>.aspx`

- `/Areas/<AreaName>/Views/<ControllerName>/<ViewName>.ascx`

- `/Areas/<AreaName>/Views/Shared/<ViewName>.aspx`

- `/Areas/<AreaName>/Views/Shared/<ViewName>.ascx`

- `/Areas/<AreaName>/Views/<ControllerName>/<ViewName>.cshtml`

- `/Areas/<AreaName>/Views/<ControllerName>/<ViewName>.vbhtml`

- `/Areas/<AreaName>/Views/Shared/<ViewName>.cshtml`

- `/Areas/<AreaName>/Views/Shared/<ViewName>.vbhtml`

You can see from the list that the framework looks for views that have been created for the legacy ASPX view engine (the `.aspx` and `.ascx` file extensions), even though we specified Razor when we created the project. The framework also looks for C# and Visual Basic .NET Razor templates (the `.cshtml` files are the C# ones and `.vbhtml` are Visual Basic; the Razor syntax is the same in these files, but the code fragments are, as the names suggest, in different languages). The MVC Framework checks to see if each of these files exists in turn. As soon as it locates a match, it uses that view to render the result of the action method.

If you are not using areas, or you are using areas but none of the files in the preceding list have been found, then the framework continues its search, using the following locations:

- `/Views/<ControllerName>/<ViewName>.aspx`

- `/Views/<ControllerName>/<ViewName>.ascx`

- `/Views/Shared/<ViewName>.aspx`

- `/Views/Shared/<ViewName>.ascx`

- `/Views/<ControllerName>/<ViewName>.cshtml`

- `/Views/<ControllerName>/<ViewName>.vbhtml`

- `/Views/Shared/<ViewName>.cshtml`

- `/Views/Shared/<ViewName>.vbhtml`

Once again, as soon as the MVC Framework tests a location and finds a file, then the search stops, and the view that has been found is used to render the response to the client.

We are not using areas in our example application, so the first place that the framework will look will be /Views/Example/Index.aspx. Notice that the Controller part of the class name is omitted, so that creating a ViewResult in ExampleController leads to a search for a directory called Example.

UNIT TEST: RENDERING A VIEW

To test the view that an action method renders, you can inspect the ViewResult object that it returns. This is not quite the same thing—after all, you are not following the process through to check the final HTML that is generated—but it is close enough, as long as you have reasonable confidence that the MVC Framework view system works properly. We added a new Unit Test project to our Visual Studio solution and added a Unit Test file called ActionTests.cs to contain our test methods.

The first situation to test is when an action method selects a specific view, like this:

```
public ViewResult Index() {
    return View("Homepage");
}
```

You can determine which view has been selected by reading the ViewName property of the ViewResult object, as shown in this test method.

```
using System;
using Microsoft.VisualStudio.TestTools.UnitTesting;
using ControllersAndActions.Controllers;
using System.Web.Mvc;

namespace ControllersAndActions.Tests {
    [TestClass]
    public class ActionTests {

        [TestMethod]
        public void ViewSelectionTest() {

            // Arrange - create the controller
            ExampleController target = new ExampleController();

            // Act - call the action method
            ViewResult result = target.Index();

            // Assert - check the result
            Assert.AreEqual("Homepage", result.ViewName);
        }
    }
}
```

A slight variation arises when you are testing an action method that selects the default view, like this one:

```
public ViewResult Index() {
    return View();
}Fa
```

In such situations, you need to accept the empty string ("") for the view name, like this:

```
...
Assert.AreEqual("", result.ViewName);
...
```

The sequence of directories that the MVC Framework searches for a view is another example of convention over configuration. You do not need to register your view files with the framework. You just put them in one of a set of known locations, and the framework will find them. We can take the convention a step further by omitting the name of the view we want rendered when we call the View method, as shown in Listing 15-14.

Listing 15-14. Creating a ViewResult Without Specifying a View

```
using System.Web.Mvc;
using System;

namespace ControllersAndActions.Controllers {

    public class ExampleController : Controller {

        public ViewResult Index() {
            return View();
        }
    }
}
```

When we do this, the MVC Framework assumes that we want to render a view that has the same name as the action method. This means that the call to the View method in Listing 15-14 starts a search for a view called Index.

■ **Note** The effect is that a view that has the same name as the action method is sought, but the name of the view is actually determined from the RouteData.Values["action"] value, which we explained as part of the routing system in Chapters 13 and 14.

There are a number of overridden versions of the View method. They correspond to setting different properties on the ViewResult object that is created. For example, you can override the layout used by a view by explicitly naming an alternative, like this:

```
...
public ViewResult Index() {
    return View("Index", "_AlternateLayoutPage");
}
...
```

SPECIFYING A VIEW BY ITS PATH

The naming convention approach is convenient and simple, but it does limit the views you can render. If you want to render a specific view, you can do so by providing an explicit path and bypass the search phase. Here is an example:

```
using System.Web.Mvc;

namespace ControllersAndActions.Controllers {

    public class ExampleController : Controller {

        public ViewResult Index() {
            return View("~/Views/Other/Index.cshtml");
        }
    }
}
```

When you specify a view like this, the path must begin with / or ~/ and include the file name extension (such as .cshtml for Razor views containing C# code).

If you find yourself using this feature, we suggest that you take a moment and ask yourself what you are trying to achieve. If you are attempting to render a view that belongs to another controller, then you might be better off redirecting the user to an action method in that controller (see the "Redirecting to an Action Method" section later in this chapter for an example). If you are trying to work around the naming scheme because it doesn't suit the way you have organized your project, then see Chapter 18, which explains how to implement a custom search sequence.

Passing Data from an Action Method to a View

We often need to pass data from an action method to a view. The MVC Framework provides a number of different ways of doing this, which we describe in the following sections. In these sections, we touch on the topic of views, which we cover in depth in Chapter 18. In this chapter, we will discuss only enough view functionality to demonstrate the controller features of interest.

Providing a View Model Object

You can send an object to the view by passing it as a parameter to the **View** method, as shown in Listing 15-15.

Listing 15-15. Specifying a View Model Object

```
...
public ViewResult Index() {
    DateTime date = DateTime.Now;
    return View(date);
}
...
```

We have passed a `DateTime` object as the view model. We can access the object in the view using the Razor `Model` keyword, as shown in Listing 15-16.

Listing 15-16. Accessing a View Model in a Razor View

```
@{
    ViewBag.Title = "Index";
}

<h2>Index</h2>

The day is: @(((DateTime)Model).DayOfWeek)
```

The view shown in Listing 15-16 is known as an *untyped* or *weakly typed* view. The view does not know anything about the view model object, and treats it as an instance of `object`. To get the value of the `DayOfWeek` property, we need to cast the object to an instance of `DateTime`. This works, but produces messy views. We can tidy this up by creating strongly typed views, in which we tell the view what the type of the view model object will be, as demonstrated in Listing 15-17.

Listing 15-17. A Strongly Typed View

```
@model DateTime
@{
    ViewBag.Title = "Index";
}

<h2>Index</h2>

The day is: @Model.DayOfWeek
```

We specify the view model type using the Razor `model` keyword. Notice that we use a lowercase `m` when we specify the model type and an uppercase `M` when we read the value. Not only does this help tidy up our view, but Visual Studio supports IntelliSense for strongly typed views, as shown in Figure 15-3.

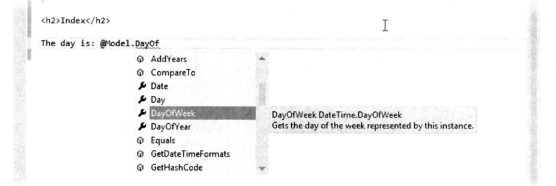

Figure 15-3. IntelliSense support for strongly typed views

UNIT TEST: VIEW MODEL OBJECTS

You can access the view model object passed from the action method to the view through the
ViewResult.ViewData.Model property. Here is a simple action method:

```
public ViewResult Index() {
    return View((object)"Hello, World");
}
```

This action method passes a string as the view model object. We have cast this to object so that the
compiler doesn't think that we want the overload of View that specifies a view name. We can access the
view model object through the ViewData.Model property, as shown in this test method:

```
...

[TestMethod]
public void ViewSelectionTest() {

    // Arrange - create the controller
    ExampleController target = new ExampleController();

    // Act - call the action method
    ViewResult result = target.Index();

    // Assert - check the result
    Assert.AreEqual("Hello, World", result.ViewData.Model);
}

...
```

Passing Data with the View Bag

We introduced the View Bag feature in Chapter 2. This feature allows you to define arbitrary properties on
a dynamic object and access them in a view. The dynamic object is accessed through the
Controller.ViewBag property, as demonstrated in Listing 15-18.

Listing 15-18. Using the View Bag Feature

```
using System;
using System.Web.Mvc;

namespace ControllersAndActions.Controllers {

    public class ExampleController : Controller {

        public ViewResult Index() {

            ViewBag.Message = "Hello";
            ViewBag.Date = DateTime.Now;

            return View();
        }
    }
}
```

In the listing, we have defined properties called Message and Date simply by assigning values to them. Before this point, no such properties existed, and we made no preparations to create them. To read the data back in the view, we simply get the same properties that we set in the action method, as Listing 15-19 shows.

Listing 15-19. Reading Data from the ViewBag

```
@{
    ViewBag.Title = "Index";
}

<h2>Index</h2>

The day is: @ViewBag.Date.DayOfWeek
<p />
The message is: @ViewBag.Message
```

The ViewBag has an advantage over using a view model object in that it is easy to send multiple objects to the view. If we were restricted to using view models, then we would need to create a new type that had string and DateTime members in order to get the same effects as Listings 15-18 and 15-19.

When working with dynamic objects, you can enter any sequence of method and property calls in the view, like this:

```
The day is: @ViewBag.Date.DayOfWeek.Blah.Blah.Blah
```

Visual Studio cannot provide IntelliSense support for any dynamic objects, including the ViewBag, and errors such as this won't be revealed until the view is rendered.

■ **Tip** We like the flexibility of the ViewBag, but we tend to stick to strongly typed views. There is nothing to stop us from using both view models and the View Bag feature in the same view. Both will work alongside each other without interference.

UNIT TEST: VIEWBAG

You can read values from the ViewBag through the ViewResult.ViewBag property. The following test method is for the action method in Listing 15-18:

```
...
[TestMethod]
public void ViewSelectionTest() {

    // Arrange - create the controller
    ExampleController target = new ExampleController();

    // Act - call the action method
    ActionResult result = target.Index();

    // Assert - check the result
    Assert.AreEqual("Hello", result.ViewBag.Message);
}
...
```

Performing Redirections

A common result from an action method is not to produce any output directly, but to redirect the user's browser to another URL. Most of the time, this URL is another action method in the application that generates the output you want the users to see.

THE POST/REDIRECT/GET PATTERN

The most frequent use of a redirect is in action methods that process HTTP POST requests. As we mentioned in the previous chapter, POST requests are used when you want to change the state of an application. If you just return HTML following the processing of a request, you run the risk that the user will click the browser's reload button and resubmit the form a second time, causing unexpected and undesirable results.

To avoid this problem, you can follow the pattern called Post/Redirect/Get. In this pattern, you receive a POST request, process it, and then redirect the browser so that a GET request is made by the browser for another URL. GET requests should not modify the state of your application, so any inadvertent resubmissions of this request won't cause any problems.

When you perform a redirect, you send one of two HTTP codes to the browser:

- Send the HTTP code 302, which is a *temporary* redirection. This is the most frequently used type of redirection and when using the Post/Redirect/Get pattern, this is the code that you want to send.

- Send the HTTP code 301, which indicates a permanent redirection. This should be used with caution, because it instructs the recipient of the HTTP code not to request the original URL ever again and to use the new URL that is included alongside the redirection code. If you are in doubt, use temporary redirections; that is, send code 302.

Redirecting to a Literal URL

The most basic way to redirect a browser is to call the `Redirect` method, which returns an instance of the `RedirectResult` class, as shown in Listing 15-20.

Listing 15-20. Redirecting to a Literal URL

```
using System;
using System.Web.Mvc;

namespace ControllersAndActions.Controllers {

    public class ExampleController : Controller {

        public ViewResult Index() {

            ViewBag.Message = "Hello";
            ViewBag.Date = DateTime.Now;

            return View();
        }

        public RedirectResult Redirect() {
            return Redirect("/Example/Index");
        }
    }
}
```

The URL you want to redirect to is expressed as a string and passed as a parameter to the Redirect method. The Redirect method sends a temporary redirection. You can send a permanent redirection using the RedirectPermanent method, as shown in Listing 15-21.

Listing 15-21. Permanently Redirecting to a Literal URL

```
...
public RedirectResult Redirect() {
    return RedirectPermanent("/Example/Index");
}
...
```

▪ **Tip**   If you prefer, you can use the overloaded version of the Redirect method, which takes a bool parameter that specifies whether or not a redirection is permanent.

UNIT TEST: LITERAL REDIRECTIONS

Literal redirections are easy to test. You can read the URL and whether the redirection is permanent or temporary using the Url and Permanent properties of the RedirectResult class. The following is a test method for the redirection shown in Listing 15-21:

```
...
[TestMethod]
public void RedirectTest() {
    // Arrange - create the controller
    ExampleController target = new ExampleController();

    // Act - call the action method
    RedirectResult result = target.Redirect();

    // Assert - check the result
    Assert.IsFalse(result.Permanent);
    Assert.AreEqual("/Example/Index", result.Url);
}
...
```

Redirecting to a Routing System URL

If you are redirecting the user to a different part of your application, you need to make sure that the URL you send is valid within your URL schema, as described in the previous chapter. The problem with using literal URLs for redirection is that any change in your routing schema means that you need to go through your code and update the URLs.

As an alternative, you can use the routing system to generate valid URLs with the RedirectToRoute method, which creates an instance of the RedirectToRouteResult, as shown in Listing 15-22.

Listing 15-22. Redirecting to a Routing System URL

```
using System;
using System.Web.Mvc;

namespace ControllersAndActions.Controllers {

    public class ExampleController : Controller {

        public ViewResult Index() {

            ViewBag.Message = "Hello";
            ViewBag.Date = DateTime.Now;

            return View();
        }

        public RedirectToRouteResult Redirect() {
            return RedirectToRoute(new {
                controller = "Example",
                action = "Index",
                ID = "MyID"
            });
        }
    }
}
```

The RedirectToRoute method issues a temporary redirection. Use the RedirectToRoutePermanent method for permanent redirections. Both methods take an anonymous type whose properties are then passed to the routing system to generate a URL. For more details of this process, see the Chapter 14.

UNIT TESTING: ROUTED REDIRECTIONS

Here is a unit test we added to the ActionTests.cs file that tests the action method in Listing 15-22:

```
...
[TestMethod]
public void RedirectValueTest() {

    // Arrange - create the controller
    ExampleController target = new ExampleController();

    // Act - call the action method
    RedirectToRouteResult result = target.RedirectToRoute();

    // Assert - check the result
    Assert.IsFalse(result.Permanent);

    Assert.AreEqual("Example", result.RouteValues["controller"]);
    Assert.AreEqual("Index", result.RouteValues["action"]);
    Assert.AreEqual("MyID", result.RouteValues["ID"]);
}
...
```

Redirecting to an Action Method

You can redirect to an action method more elegantly by using the `RedirectToAction` method. This is just a wrapper around the `RedirectToRoute` method that lets you specify values for the action method and the controller without needing to create an anonymous type, as shown in Listing 15-23.

Listing 15-23. Redirecting Using the RedirectToAction Method

```
...
public RedirectToRouteResult RedirectToRoute() {
    return RedirectToAction("Index");
}
...
```

If you just specify an action method, then it is assumed that you are referring to an action method in the current controller. If you want to redirect to another controller, you need to provide the name as a parameter, like this:

```
...
public RedirectToRouteResult Redirect() {
    return RedirectToAction("Index", "Basic");
}
...
```

There are other overloaded versions that you can use to provide additional values for the URL generation. These are expressed using an anonymous type, which does tend to undermine the purpose of the convenience method, but can still make your code easier to read.

■ **Note** The values that you provide for the action method and controller are not verified before they are passed to the routing system. You are responsible for making sure that the targets you specify actually exist.

The `RedirectToAction` method performs a temporary redirection. Use the `RedirectToActionPermanent` for permanent redirections.

PRESERVING DATA ACROSS A REDIRECTION

A redirection causes the browser to submit an entirely new HTTP request, which means that you do not have access to the details of the original request. If you want to pass data from one request to the next, you can use the Temp Data feature.

TempData is similar to `Session` data, except that `TempData` values are marked for deletion when they are read, and they are removed when the request has been processed. This is an ideal arrangement for short-lived data that you want to persist across a redirection. Here is a simple example in an action method that uses the `RedirectToAction` method:

```
...
public RedirectToRouteResult RedirectToRoute() {
    TempData["Message"] = "Hello";
    TempData["Date"] = DateTime.Now;
    return RedirectToAction("Index");
}
...
```

When this method processes a request, it sets values in the TempData collection, and then redirects the user's browser to the Index action method in the same controller. You can read the TempData values back in the target action method, and then pass them to the view, like this:

```
...
public ViewResult Index() {
    ViewBag.Message = TempData["Message"];
    ViewBag.Date = TempData["Date"];
    return View();
}
...
```

A more direct approach would be to read these values in the view, like this:

```
@{
    ViewBag.Title = "Index";
}

<h2>Index</h2>

The day is: @(((DateTime)TempData["Date"]).DayOfWeek)
<p />
The message is: @TempData["Message"]
```

Reading the values in the view means that you do not need to use the View Bag feature in the action method. However, you must cast the TempData results to an appropriate type.
You can get a value from TempData without marking it for removal by using the Peek method, like this:

```
DateTime time = (DateTime)TempData.Peek("Date");
```

You can preserve a value that would otherwise be deleted by using the Keep method, like this:

```
TempData.Keep("Date");
```

The Keep method doesn't protect a value forever. If the value is read again, it will be marked for removal once more. If you want to store items so that they won't be removed when the request is processed then use session data instead.

Returning Errors and HTTP Codes

The last of the built-in ActionResult classes that we will look at can be used to send specific error messages and HTTP result codes to the client. Most applications do not require these features because the MVC Framework will automatically generate these kinds of results. However, they can be useful if you need to take more direct control over the responses sent to the client.

Sending a Specific HTTP Result Code

You can send a specific HTTP status code to the browser using the `HttpStatusCodeResult` class. There is no controller helper method for this, so you must instantiate the class directly, as shown in Listing 15-24.

Listing 15-24. Sending a Specific Status Code

```
using System;
using System.Web.Mvc;

namespace ControllersAndActions.Controllers {

    public class ExampleController : Controller {

        public ViewResult Index() {

            ViewBag.Message = "Hello";
            ViewBag.Date = DateTime.Now;

            return View();
        }

        public RedirectToRouteResult Redirect() {
            return RedirectToAction("Index", "Basic");
        }

        public HttpStatusCodeResult StatusCode() {
            return new HttpStatusCodeResult(404, "URL cannot be serviced");
        }
    }
}
```

The constructor parameters for `HttpStatusCodeResult` are the numeric status code and an optional descriptive message. In the listing, we have returned code 404, which signifies that the requested resource does not exist.

Sending a 404 Result

We can achieve the same effect as Listing 15-24 using the more convenient `HttpNotFoundResult` class, which is derived from `HttpStatusCodeResult` and can be created using the controller `HttpNotFound` convenience method, as shown in Listing 15-25.

Listing 15-25. Generating a 404 Result

```
...
public HttpStatusCodeResult StatusCode() {
    return HttpNotFound();
}
...
```

Sending a 401 Result

Another wrapper class for a specific HTTP status code is the `HttpUnauthorizedResult`, which returns the 401 code, used to indicate that a request is unauthorized. Listing 15-26 provides a demonstration.

Listing 15-26. Generating a 401 Result

```
...
public HttpStatusCodeResult StatusCode() {
    return new HttpUnauthorizedResult();
}
...
```

There is no helper method in the `Controller` class to create instances of `HttpUnauthorizedResult`, so you must do so directly. The effect of returning an instance of this class is usually to redirect the user to the authentication page, as you saw in Chapter 11.

UNIT TEST: HTTP STATUS CODES

The `HttpStatusCodeResult` class follows the pattern you have seen for the other result types, and makes its state available through a set of properties. In this case, the `StatusCode` property returns the numeric HTTP status code, and the `StatusDescription` property returns the associated descriptive string. The following test method is for the action method in Listing 15-26:

```
...
[TestMethod]
public void StatusCodeResultTest() {

    // Arrange - create the controller
    ExampleController target = new ExampleController();

    // Act - call the action method
    HttpStatusCodeResult result = target.StatusCode();

    // Assert - check the result
    Assert.AreEqual(401, result.StatusCode);
}
...
```

Summary

Controllers are one of the key building blocks in the MVC design pattern. In this chapter, you have seen how to create "raw" controllers by implementing the `IController` interface and more convenient controllers by deriving from the `Controller` class. You saw the role that actions methods play in MVC Framework controllers and how they ease unit testing. We showed you the different ways that you can receive input and generate output from an action method and demonstrated the different kinds of `ActionResult` that make this a simple and flexible process.

In the next chapter, we will go deeper into the controller infrastructure to show you the *filters* feature, which changes how requests are processed.

CHAPTER 16

■ ■ ■

Filters

Filters inject extra logic into MVC Framework request processing. They provide a simple and elegant way to implement *cross-cutting concerns*. This term refers to functionality that is used all over an application and doesn't fit neatly into any one place, where it would break the separation of concerns pattern. Classic examples of cross-cutting concerns are logging, authorization, and caching. In this chapter, we will show you the different categories of filters that the MVC Framework supports, how to create and use filters, and how to control their execution.

Using Filters

You have already seen an example of a filter in Chapter 11, when we applied authorization to the action methods of the SportsStore administration controller. We wanted the action method to be used only by users who had authenticated themselves, which presented us with a choice of approaches. We could have checked the authorization status of the request in each and every action method, as shown in Listing 16-1.

Listing 16-1. Explicitly Checking Authorization in Action Methods

```
namespace SportsStore.WebUI.Controllers {

    public class AdminController : Controller {

        // ... instance variables and constructor

        public ViewResult Index() {
            if (!Request.IsAuthenticated) {
                FormsAuthentication.RedirectToLoginPage();
            }
            // ...rest of action method
        }

        public ViewResult Create() {
            if (!Request.IsAuthenticated) {
                FormsAuthentication.RedirectToLoginPage();
            }
            // ...rest of action method
        }

        public ViewResult Edit(int productId) {
            if (!Request.IsAuthenticated) {
                FormsAuthentication.RedirectToLoginPage();
```

```
        }
            // ...rest of action method
        }

        // ... other action methods
    }
}
```

You can see that there is a lot of repetition in this approach, which is why we decided to use a filter instead, as shown in Listing 16-2.

Listing 16-2. Applying a Filter

```
namespace SportsStore.WebUI.Controllers {

    [Authorize]
    public class AdminController : Controller {

        // ... instance variables and constructor

        public ViewResult Index() {
            // ...rest of action method
        }

        public ViewResult Create() {
            // ...rest of action method
        }

        public ViewResult Edit(int productId) {
            // ...rest of action method
        }

        // ... other action methods
    }
}
```

Filters are .NET attributes that add extra steps to the request processing pipeline. We used the Authorize filter in Listing 16-2, which has the same effect as all of the duplicated checks in Listing 16-1.

.NET ATTRIBUTES: A REFRESHER

Attributes are special .NET classes derived from System.Attribute. You can attach them to other code elements, including classes, methods, properties, and fields. The purpose is to embed additional information into your compiled code that you can later read back at runtime.

In C#, attributes are attached by using a square-bracket syntax, and you can populate their public properties with a named parameter syntax (for example, [MyAttribute(SomeProperty=value)]). In the C# compiler's naming convention, if the attribute class name ends with the word Attribute, you can omit that portion (for example, you can apply AuthorizeAttribute by writing just [Authorize]).

Introducing the Four Basic Types of Filters

The MVC Framework supports four different types of filters. Each allows you to introduce logic at different points during request processing. The four filter types are described in Table 16-1.

Table 16-1. MVC Framework Filter Types

Filter Type	Interface	Default Implementation	Description
Authorization	IAuthorizationFilter	AuthorizeAttribute	Runs first, before any other filters or the action method
Action	IActionFilter	ActionFilterAttribute	Runs before and after the action method
Result	IResultFilter	ActionFilterAttribute	Runs before and after the action result is executed
Exception	IExceptionFilter	HandleErrorAttribute	Runs only if another filter, the action method, or the action result throws an exception

Before the MVC Framework invokes an action, it inspects the method definition to see if it has attributes that implement the interfaces listed in Table 16-1. If so, then at the appropriate point in the request pipeline, the methods defined by these interfaces are invoked. The framework includes default attribute classes that implement the filter interfaces. We will show you how to use these classes later in this chapter.

■ **Note** The ActionFilterAttribute class implements both the IActionFilter and IResultFilter interfaces. This class is abstract, which forces you to provide an implementation. The other classes, AuthorizeAttribute and HandleErrorAttribute, contain useful features and can be used without creating a derived class.

Applying Filters to Controllers and Action Methods

Filters can be applied to individual action methods or to an entire controller. In Listing 16-2, we applied the Authorize filter to the AdminController class, which has the same effect as applying it to each action method in the controller, as shown in Listing 16-3.

Listing 16-3. Applying a Filter to Action Methods Individually

```
namespace SportsStore.WebUI.Controllers {

    public class AdminController : Controller {

        // ... instance variables and constructor
        [Authorize]
        public ViewResult Index() {
            // ...rest of action method
        }
```

```
        [Authorize]
        public ViewResult Create() {
            // ...rest of action method
        }

        // ... other action methods
    }
}
```

You can apply multiple filters, and mix and match the levels at which they are applied—that is, whether they are applied to the controller or an individual action method. Listing 16-4 shows three different filters in use.

Listing 16-4. Applying Multiple Filters in a Controller Class

```
[Authorize(Roles="trader")] // applies to all actions
public class ExampleController : Controller {

    [ShowMessage]                    // applies to just this action
    [OutputCache(Duration=60)]       // applies to just this action
    public ActionResult Index() {
        // ... action method body
    }
}
```

Some of the filters in this Listing 16-take parameters. We will show you how these work as we explore the different kinds of filters.

▪ **Note** If you have defined a custom base class for your controllers, any filters applied to the base class will affect the derived classes.

Creating the Example Project

For this chapter we created a new MVC project called `Filters` using the `Empty` template option. We created a `Home` controller which has the action methods shown in Listing 16-5. We are only focused on controllers in this chapter, so we return string values from the action methods, rather than `ActionResult` objects—this has the effect of causing the MVC Framework to send the string value directly to the browser, by passing the Razor view engine. (We have done this for simplicity—we suggest you use views for real projects.)

Listing 16-5. The Home controller in the Filters project

```
using System;
using System.Collections.Generic;
using System.Linq;
using System.Web;
using System.Web.Mvc;

namespace Filters.Controllers {
    public class HomeController : Controller {

        public string Index() {
            return "This is the Index action on the Home controller";
        }
    }
}
```

If you start the example application the default routes that Visual Studio defines for an application will map the / URL requested by the browser to the Index action method in the Home controller, producing the result shown in Figure 16-1.

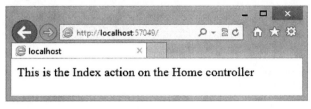

Figure 16-1. Running the example app

Using Authorization Filters

Authorization filters are the filters that are run first—before the other kinds of filters and before the action method is invoked. As the name suggests, these filters enforce your authorization policy, ensuring that action methods can be invoked only by approved users. Authorization filters implement the IAuthorizationFilter interface, which is shown in Listing 16-6.

Listing 16-6. The IAuthorizationFilter Interface

```
namespace System.Web.Mvc {

    public interface IAuthorizationFilter {
        void OnAuthorization(AuthorizationContext filterContext);
    }
}
```

You can, if you are so minded, create a class that implements the IAuthorizationFilter interface and create your own security logic. See our sidebar on why this is a really bad idea.

WARNING: WRITING SECURITY CODE IS DANGEROUS

We are always wary of writing our own security code. Programming history is littered with the wreckage of applications whose programmers thought they knew how to write good security code. That's actually a skill that very few people possess. There is usually some forgotten wrinkle or untested corner case that leaves a gaping hole in the application's security. If you do not believe us, just Google the term security bug and start reading through the top results.

Wherever possible, we like to use security code that is widely tested and proven. In this case, the MVC Framework has provided a full-featured authorization filter, which can be derived to implement custom authorization policies. We try to use this whenever we can, and we recommend that you do the same. At the very least, you can pass some of the blame to Microsoft when your secret application data is spread far and wide on the Internet.

A much safer approach is to create a subclass of the AuthorizeAttribute class which takes care of all of the tricky stuff and makes it easy to write custom authorization code. The best way to demonstrate this is create a custom filter and, to this end, we have added an Infrastructure folder to the example project and created a new class file within it called CustomAuthAttribute.cs. You can see the content of this file in Listing 16-7.

423

Listing 16-7. A custom authentication filter class

```
using System;
using System.Collections.Generic;
using System.Linq;
using System.Web;
using System.Web.Mvc;

namespace Filters.Infrastructure {
    public class CustomAuthAttribute : AuthorizeAttribute {
        private bool localAllowed;

        public CustomAuthAttribute(bool allowedParam) {
            localAllowed = allowedParam;
        }

        protected override bool AuthorizeCore(HttpContextBase httpContext) {
            if (httpContext.Request.IsLocal) {
                return localAllowed;
            } else {
                return true;
            }
        }
    }
}
```

This is a simple authorization filter. It allows you to prevent access to local requests (a local request is one where the browser and the application server are running on the same device, such as your development PC).

We have used the simplest approach to creating an authorization filter, which is to subclass the `AuthorizeAttribute` class and then override the `AuthorizeCore` method. This ensures that we benefit from the features built in to `AuthorizeAttribute`. The constructor for our filter takes a `bool` value, indicating whether local requests are permitted.

The interesting part of our filter class is the implementation of the `AuthorizeCore` method, which is how the MVC Framework checks to see if the filter will authorize access for a request. The argument to this method is an `HttpContextBase` object, through which we can get information about the request being processed. By taking advantage of the built-in features of the `AuthorizeAttribte` base class, we only have to focus on our authorization logic and return `true` from the `AuthorizeCore` method if we want to authorize a request and return `false` if we do not.

KEEPING AUTHORIZATION ATTRIBUTES SIMPLE

■ **Tip** The `AuthorizeCore` method is passed an `HttpContextBase` object, which provides access to information about the request, but not about the controller or action method that the authorization attribute has been applied to. The main reason that developers implement the `IAuthorizationFilter` interface directly is to get access to the `AuthorizationContext` passed to the `OnAuthorization` method, through which a much wider range of information can be obtained—including routing details and the current controller and action method.

We do not recommend this approach—and not just because we think writing your own security code is dangerous. Although authorization is a cross-cutting concern, building logic into your authorization attributes which is tightly coupled to the structure of your controllers undermines the separation of concerns and causes testing and maintenance problems. Keep your authorization attributes simple and focused on authorization based on the request—let the context of what is being authorized come from where the attribute is applied.

Applying the Custom Authorization Filter

To use our custom authorization filter, we simply apply an attribute to the action methods or controllers that we want to protect, as illustrated by Listing 16-8, which shows how we have applied the filter to the Index action method in the Home controller of the example project.

Listing 16-8. Applying a Custom Authorization Filter

```
using System;
using System.Collections.Generic;
using System.Linq;
using System.Web;
using System.Web.Mvc;
using Filters.Infrastructure;

namespace Filters.Controllers {
    public class HomeController : Controller {

        [CustomAuth(false)]
        public string Index() {
            return "This is the Index action on the Home controller";
        }
    }
}
```

We have set the constructor argument for the filter to false, which means that local requests will be denied access to the Index action method. You can test this by starting the application—the routing configuration will target the Index action method when the root URL is requested by the browser. If the browser making the request is on the machine running Visual Studio, then you will see the result in Figure 16-2. The filter will authorize the request if you make a request from a browser running on another computer (or if change the constructor argument for the filter to true and restart the application).

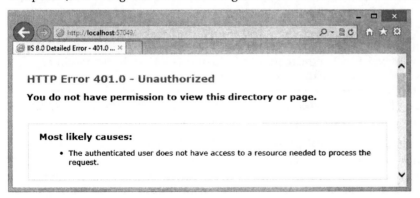

Figure 16-2. Access denied for a local request by the custom authorization filter

Using the Built-in Authorization Filter

Although we used the `AuthorizeAttribute` class as the base for our custom filter, it has its own implementation of the `AuthorizeCore` method which is useful for performing general purpose authorization tasks.

When using the `AuthorizeAttribute` directly, we can specify our authorization policy using two public properties of this class, as shown in Table 16-2.

Table 16-2. AuthorizeAttribute Properties

Name	Type	Description
Users	string	A comma-separated list of usernames that are allowed to access the action method.
Roles	string	A comma-separated list of role names. To access the action method, users must be in at least one of these roles.

Listing 16-9 shows how we can use the built-in filter to protect an action method with these properties.

Listing 16-9. Using the Built-in Authorization Filter

```
using System;
using System.Collections.Generic;
using System.Linq;
using System.Web;
using System.Web.Mvc;
using Filters.Infrastructure;

namespace Filters.Controllers {
    public class HomeController : Controller {

        [Authorize(Users = "adam, steve, jacqui", Roles = "admin")]
        public string Index() {
            return "This is the Index action on the Home controller";
        }
    }
}
```

We have specified both users and roles in the listing. This means that authorization won't be granted unless both conditions are met: the user's name is adam, steve, or jacqui *and* the user has the admin role. There is an implicit condition as well, which is that the request is authenticated. If we do not specify any users or roles, then any authenticated user can use the action method.

▓ **Tip** The `AuthorizeAttribute` deals with authorization, but doesn't have any responsibility for authentication. You can use any of the built-in ASP.NET authentication systems or develop your own (although, as noted previously, this is probably not a good idea). As long as the authentication system uses the standard ASP.NET APIs, then the `AuthorizeAttribute` will be able to restrict access to your controllers and actions.

For most applications, the authorization policy that `AuthorizeAttribute` provides is sufficient. If you want to implement something special, you can derive from this class as we did earlier in the chapter.

Using Exception Filters

Exception filters are run only if an unhandled exception has been thrown when invoking an action method. The exception can come from the following locations:

- Another kind of filter (authorization, action, or result filter)

- The action method itself

- When the action result is executed (see Chapter 15 for details on action results)

Creating an Exception Filter

Exception filters must implement the `IExceptionFilter` interface, which is shown in Listing 16-10.

Listing 16-10. The IExceptionFilter Interface

```
namespace System.Web.Mvc {

    public interface IExceptionFilter {
        void OnException(ExceptionContext filterContext);
    }
}
```

The `OnException` method is called when an unhandled exception arises. The parameter for this method is an `ExceptionContext` object, which is derived from `ControllerContext` and provides a number of useful properties that you can use to get information about the request, as shown in Table 16-3.

Table 16-3. ControllerContext Properties

Name	Type	Description
Controller	ControllerBase	Returns the controller object for this request
HttpContext	HttpContextBase	Provides access to details of the request and access to the response
IsChildAction	bool	Returns true if this is a child action (discussed briefly later in this chapter and fully in Chapter 18)
RequestContext	RequestContext	Provides access to the HttpContext and the routing data, both of which are available through other properties
RouteData	RouteData	Returns the routing data for this request

In addition to the properties inherited from the `ControllerContext` class, the `ExceptionContext` class defines some additional properties which are useful with dealing with exceptions, as shown in Table 16-4.

■ **Tip**   We have separated these tables out because there are other filter context classes which inherit from `ControllerContext`, which we will introduce as we go through this chapter.

Table 16-4. Additional ExceptionContext Properties

Name	Type	Description
ActionDescriptor	ActionDescriptor	Provides details of the action method
Result	ActionResult	The result for the action method; a filter can cancel the request by setting this property to a non-null value
Exception	Exception	The unhandled exception
ExceptionHandled	bool	Returns true if another filter has marked the exception as handled

The exception that has been thrown is available through the Exception property. An exception filter can report that it has handled the exception by setting the ExceptionHandled property to true. All of the exception filters applied to an action are invoked even if this property is set to true, so it is good practice to check whether another filter has already dealt with the problem, to avoid attempting to recover from a problem that another filter has resolved.

▓ **Note** If none of the exception filters for an action method set the ExceptionHandled property to true, the MVC Framework uses the default ASP.NET exception handling procedure which will display the dreaded "yellow screen of death."

The Result property is used by the exception filter to tell the MVC Framework what to do. The two main uses for exception filters are to log the exception and to display a suiTable 16-message to the user. To demonstrate how this all fits together, we have created a new class file called RangeExceptionAttribute.cs, which we added to the Infrastructure folder of our example project. The contents of this file are shown in Listing 16-11.

Listing 16-11. Implementing an Exception Filter

```
using System;
using System.Web.Mvc;

namespace Filters.Infrastructure {
    public class RangeExceptionAttribute : FilterAttribute, IExceptionFilter {

        public void OnException(ExceptionContext filterContext) {

            if (!filterContext.ExceptionHandled &&
                filterContext.Exception is ArgumentOutOfRangeException) {
                filterContext.Result
                    = new RedirectResult("~/Content/RangeErrorPage.html");
                filterContext.ExceptionHandled = true;
            }
        }
    }
}
```

This exception filter handles `ArgumentOutOfRangeException` instances by redirecting the user's browser to a file called `RangeErrorPage.html` in the `Content` folder.

Notice that we have derived the `RangeExceptionAttribute` class from the `FilterAttribute` class, in addition to implementing the `IExceptionFilter` interface. In order for a .NET attribute class to be treated as an MVC filter, the class has to implement the `IMvcFilter` interface. You can do this directly, but the easiest way to create a filter is to derive your class from `FilterAttribute`, which implements the required interface and provides some useful basic features, such as handling the default order in which filters are processed (which we will come to later in this chapter).

Applying the Exception Filter

We need to do some groundwork before we can test our exception filter. First, we need to create a `Content` folder in the example project and create the `RangeErrorPage.html` file within it. We are going to use this file to display as simple message, which you can see in Listing 16-12.

Listing 16-12. The contents of the RangeErrorPage.html file

```html
<!DOCTYPE html>
<html xmlns="http://www.w3.org/1999/xhtml">
<head>
    <title>Range Error</title>
</head>
<body>
    <h2>Sorry</h2>
    <span>One of the arguments was out of the expected range.</span>
</body>
</html>
```

Next, we need to add an action method to the `Home` controller which will throw the exception we are interested in. You can see the addition in Listing 16-13.

Listing 16-13. Adding a new action to the Home controller

```csharp
using System;
using System.Collections.Generic;
using System.Linq;
using System.Web;
using System.Web.Mvc;
using Filters.Infrastructure;

namespace Filters.Controllers {
    public class HomeController : Controller {

        [Authorize(Users = "adam, steve, jacqui", Roles = "admin")]
        public string Index() {
            return "This is the Index action on the Home controller";
        }

        public string RangeTest(int id) {
            if (id > 100) {
                return String.Format("The id value is: {0}", id);
            } else {
                throw new ArgumentOutOfRangeException("id", id, "");
            }
        }
    }
}
```

You can see the default exception handling if you start the application and navigate to the /Home/RangeTest/50 URL. The default routing that Visual Studio creates for an MVC project has a segment variable called id which will be set to 50 for this URL, triggering the response shown in Figure 16-3. (See Chapters 13 and 14 for details of routing and URL segments.)

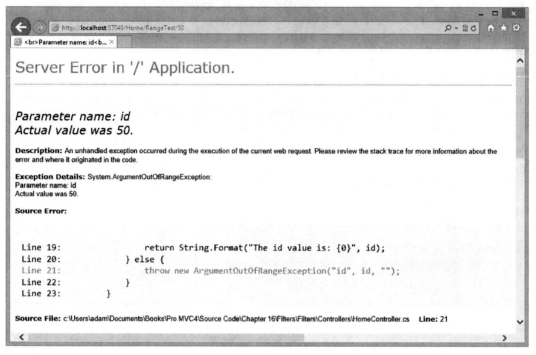

Figure 16-3. The default exception handling response

We can apply the exception filter to either controllers or individual actions, as shown in Listing 16-14.

Listing 16-14. Applying the filter

```
...
[RangeException]
public string RangeTest(int id) {
    if (id > 100) {
        return String.Format("The id value is: {0}", id);
    } else {
        throw new ArgumentOutOfRangeException("id");
    }
}
...
```

You can see the effect if you restart the application and navigate to the /Home/RangeTest/50 URL again, as shown in Figure 16-4.

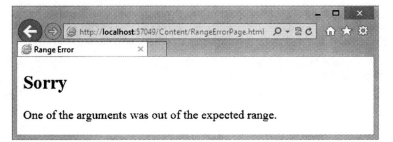

Figure 16-4. The effect of applying the exception filter

Using a View to Respond to an Exception

Depending on the exception you are dealing with, displaying a page of static content can be the simplest and safest thing to do—there is little chance of the process going wrong and causing additional problems. However, while you can be confident that the user will see the message, this approach is not especially useful to the user, who gets a generic warning and is dropped out of the application.

An alternative approach is to use a view to display details of the problem and present the user with some contextual information and options they can follow to sort things out. To do this, we have made some changes to the `RangeExceptionAttribute` class, as shown in Listing 16-15.

Listing 16-15. Returning a view from an exception filter

```
using System;
using System.Web.Mvc;

namespace Filters.Infrastructure {
    public class RangeExceptionAttribute : FilterAttribute, IExceptionFilter {

        public void OnException(ExceptionContext filterContext) {

            if (!filterContext.ExceptionHandled &&
                filterContext.Exception is ArgumentOutOfRangeException) {

                    int val = (int)(((ArgumentOutOfRangeException)
                        filterContext.Exception).ActualValue);
                    filterContext.Result = new ViewResult {
                        ViewName = "RangeError",
                        ViewData = new ViewDataDictionary<int>(val)
                    };
                    filterContext.ExceptionHandled = true;
            }
        }
    }
}
```

We create a `ViewResult` object and set the values of the `ViewName` and `ViewData` properties to specify the name of the view and the model object that will be passed to it. This is messy code because we are working with the `ViewResult` object directly, rather than relying on the `View` method defined by the `Controller` class that we use in action methods. We are not going to go into this code because we cover views in depth in Chapter 18 and the built-in exception filter, which we describe in the next section, can be used to achieve the same effect more elegantly—we just want to you see how things work behind the scenes.

Our `ViewResult` object specifies a view called `RangeError` and passes the `int` value of the argument that caused the exception as the view model object. We then added a `Views/Shared` folder to the Visual Studio project and created the `RangeError.cshtml` file within it, the contents of which you can see in Listing 16-16.

Listing 16-16. The contents of the RangeError.cshtml view file

```
@model int

<!DOCTYPE html>
<html>
<head>
    <meta name="viewport" content="width=device-width" />
    <title>Range Error</title>
</head>
<body>
    <h2>Sorry</h2>
    <span>The value @Model was out of the expected range.</span>
    <div>
        @Html.ActionLink("Change value and try again", "Index")
    </div>
</body>
</html>
```

The view file uses standard HTML and Razor tags to present a (slightly) more useful message to the user. Our example application is pretty limited, so there is not anything useful we can direct the user to do to resolve the problem, but we have used the `ActionLink` helper method to create a link that targets another action method, just to demonstrate that you have the full set of view features available. You can see the result if you restart the application and navigate to the `/Home/RangeTest/50` URL, as shown in Figure 16-5.

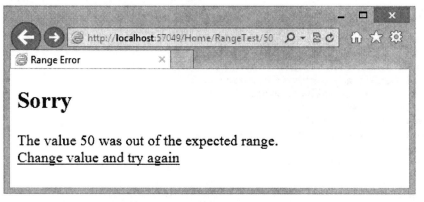

Figure 16-5. Using a view to display an error message from an exception filter

Avoiding the Wrong Exception Trap

The benefits of using a view to display an error are that you can use layouts to make the error message consistent with the rest of your application and generate dynamic content that will help the user understand what is going wrong and what they can do about it.

The drawback is that you must thoroughly test your view to make sure that you do not just generate another exception. We see this a lot, where the testing focus is on the main features of the application and does not properly cover the different error situations that can arise. As a simple demonstration, we have added a Razor code block to the `RangeError.cshtml` view that we know will throw an exception, as shown in Listing 16-17.

Listing 16-17. Adding code that will throw an exception to the view

```
@model int

@{
    var count = 0;
    var number = Model / count;
}

<!DOCTYPE html>
<html>
<head>
    <meta name="viewport" content="width=device-width" />
    <title>Range Error</title>
</head>
<body>
    <h2>Sorry</h2>
    <span>The value @Model was out of the expected range.</span>
    <div>
        @Html.ActionLink("Change value and try again", "Index")
    </div>
</body>
</html>
```

When the view is rendered, our code will generate a `DivideByZeroException`. If you start the application and navigate to the /Home/RangeTest/50 URL again, you will see the exception thrown while trying to render the view and not the one thrown by the controller, as shown in Figure 16-6.

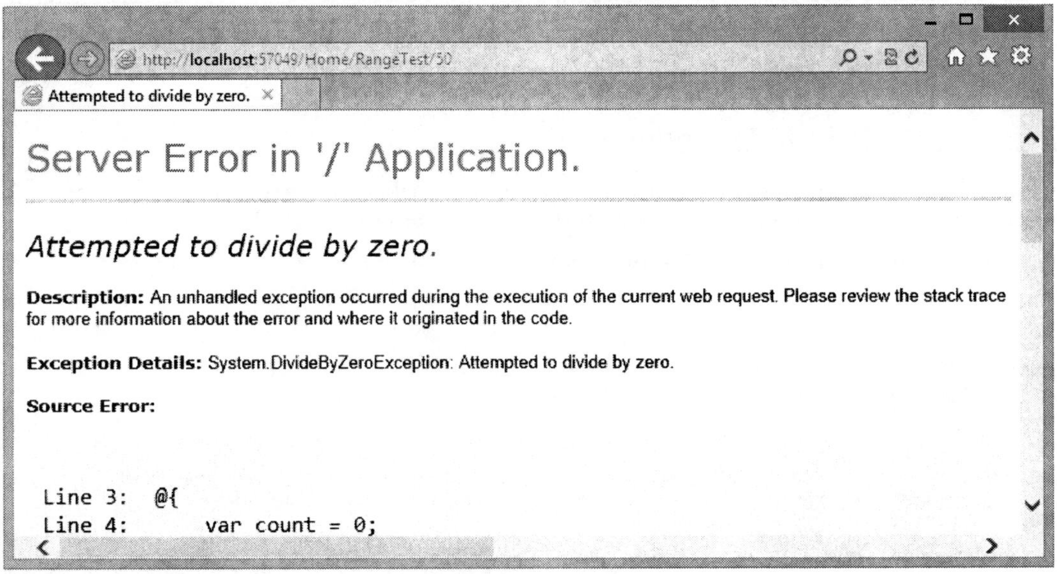

Figure 16-6. An exception thrown while rendering a view

This isn't a realistic scenario, but it demonstrates what happens when there are problems in the view—the user sees a bewildering error that does not even relate to the problem they encountered in the application. When using an exception filter that relies on a view, be careful to test that view very thoroughly.

Using the Built-In Exception Filter

We showed you how to create an exception filter because we think understanding what happens behind the scenes in the MVC Framework is a good thing. But you do not often need to create your own filters in real projects because Microsoft has included the `HandleErrorAttribute` in the MVC Framework, which is a built-in implementation of the `IExceptionFilter` interface. With it, you can specify an exception and the names of a view and layout using the properties described in Table 16-5.

Table 16-5. HandleErrorAttribute Properties

Name	Type	Description
ExceptionType	Type	The exception type handled by this filter. It will also handle exception types that inherit from the specified value, but will ignore all others. The default value is `System.Exception`, which means that, by default, it will handle all standard exceptions.
View	string	The name of the view template that this filter renders. If you do not specify a value, it takes a default value of `Error`, so by default, it renders `/Views/<currentControllerName>/Error.cshtml` or `/Views/Shared/Error.cshtml`.
Master	string	The name of the layout used when rendering this filter's view. If you do not specify a value, the view uses its default layout page.

When an unhandled exception of the type specified by `ExceptionType` is encountered, this filter will render the view specified by the `View` property (using the default layout or the one specified by the `Master` property).

Preparing to Use the Built-in Exception Filter

The `HandleErrorAttribute` filter works only when custom errors are enabled in the `Web.config` file, which we do by adding a `customErrors` attribute inside the `<system.web>` node, as shown in Listing 16-18.

Listing 16-18. Enabling custom error in the Web.config file

```
...
<system.web>
  <httpRuntime targetFramework="4.5" />
  <compilation debug="true" targetFramework="4.5" />
  <pages>
    <namespaces>
      <add namespace="System.Web.Helpers" />
      <add namespace="System.Web.Mvc" />
      <add namespace="System.Web.Mvc.Ajax" />
      <add namespace="System.Web.Mvc.Html" />
      <add namespace="System.Web.Routing" />
      <add namespace="System.Web.WebPages" />
```

```
    </namespaces>
  </pages>
  <customErrors mode="On"  defaultRedirect="/Content/RangeErrorPage.html"/>
</system.web>
...
```

The default value for the mode attribute is RemoteOnly, which means that during development, HandleErrorAttribute will not intercept exceptions, but when you deploy to a production server and make requests from another computer, HandleErrorAttribute will take effect. To see what end users are going to see, make sure you have set the custom errors mode to On. The defaultRedirect attribute specifies a default content page that will be displayed if all else fails.

Applying the Built-In Exception Filter

You can see how we have the HandleError filter to the Home controller in Listing 16-19.

Listing 16-19. Using the HandleErrorAttribute Filter

```
...
[HandleError(ExceptionType = typeof(ArgumentOutOfRangeException), View = "RangeError")]
public string RangeTest(int id) {
    if (id > 100) {
        return String.Format("The id value is: {0}", id);
    } else {
        throw new ArgumentOutOfRangeException("id", id, "");
    }
}
...
```

In this example, we have recreated the situation we had with our custom filter, which is that am ArgumentOutOfRangeException will be dealt with by displaying the RangeError view to the user.

When rendering a view, the HandleErrorAttribute filter passes a HandleErrorInfo view model object, which is a wrapper around the exception that provides additional information that you use in your view. Table 16-6 describes the properties defined by the HandleErrorInfo class.

Table 16-6. HandleErrorInfo Properties

Name	Type	Description
ActionName	string	Returns the name of the action method that generated the exception
ControllerName	string	Returns the name of the controller that generated the exception
Exception	Exception	Returns the exception

You can see how we have updated our RangeError.cshtml view to use this model object in Listing 16-20.

Listing 16-20. Using a HandleErrorInfo model object in the RangeError view

```
@model HandleErrorInfo

@{
    ViewBag.Title = "Sorry, there was a problem!";
```

```
}
```

```html
<!DOCTYPE html>
<html>
<head>
    <meta name="viewport" content="width=device-width" />
    <title>Range Error</title>
</head>
<body>
    <h2>Sorry</h2>
    <span>The value @(((ArgumentOutOfRangeException)Model.Exception).ActualValue)
        was out of the expected range.</span>
    <div>
        @Html.ActionLink("Change value and try again", "Index")
    </div>
    <div style="display: none">
        @Model.Exception.StackTrace
    </div>
</body>
</html>
```

We had to cast the value of the `Model.Exception` property to the `ArgumentOutOfRangeException` type to be able to read the `ActualValue` property because the `HandleErrorInfo` class is a general-purpose model object that is used to pass any exception to a view.

▓ **Caution**   There is an odd behavior that arises when using the `HandleError` filter where the view is not displayed to the user unless the value of the `Model.Exception.StackTrace` property is included in the view. We do not want to display the stack trace, so we have put the output in a div element whose CSS `display` property we have set to none, making it invisible to the user.

Using Action Filters

Action filters are filters that can be used for any purpose. The built-in class for creating this kind of filter, `IActionFilter`, is shown in Listing 16-21.

Listing 16-21. The IActionFilter Interface

```csharp
namespace System.Web.Mvc {

    public interface IActionFilter {
        void OnActionExecuting(ActionExecutingContext filterContext);
        void OnActionExecuted(ActionExecutedContext filterContext);
    }
}
```

This interface defines two methods. The MVC Framework calls the `OnActionExecuting` method *before* the action method is invoked. It calls the `OnActionExecuted` method *after* the action method has been invoked.

Implementing the OnActionExecuting Method

The OnActionExecuting method is called before the action method is invoked. You can use this opportunity to inspect the request and elect to cancel the request, modify the request, or start some activity that will span the invocation of the action. The parameter to this method is an ActionExecutingContext object, which subclasses the ControllerContext class and defines the two additional properties described in Table 16-7.

Table 16-7. ActionExecutingContext Properties

Name	Type	Description
ActionDescriptor	ActionDescriptor	Provides details of the action method
Result	ActionResult	The result for the action method; a filter can cancel the request by setting this property to a non-null value

You can use a filter to cancel the request by setting the Result property of the parameter to an action result. To demonstrate this, we have created our own action filter class called CustomActionAttribute in the Infrastructure folder of the example project, as shown in Listing 16-22.

Listing 16-22. Canceling a Request in the OnActionExecuting Method

```
using System.Web.Mvc;

namespace Filters.Infrastructure {
    public class CustomActionAttribute : FilterAttribute, IActionFilter {

        public void OnActionExecuting(ActionExecutingContext filterContext) {
            if (filterContext.HttpContext.Request.IsLocal) {
                filterContext.Result = new HttpNotFoundResult();
            }
        }

        public void OnActionExecuted(ActionExecutedContext filterContext) {
            // not yet implemented
        }
    }
}
```

In this example, we use the OnActionExecuting method to check whether the request has been made from the local machine. If it has, we return a 404–Not Found response to the user.

▓ **Note** You can see from Listing 16-22 that you do not need to implement both methods defined in the IActionFilter interface to create a working filter. Be careful not to throw a NotImplementedException, which Visual Studio adds to a class when you implement an interface—the MVC Framework calls both methods in an action filter and if an exception is thrown then you will trigger the exception filters. If you do not need to add any logic to a method, then just leave it empty.

You apply an action filter as you would any other attribute. To demonstrate the action filter we created in Listing 16-22, we have added a new action method to the Home controller, as shown in Listing 16-23.

Listing 16-23. Adding a new action to the Home controller

```
...
[CustomAction]
public string FilterTest() {
    return "This is the FilterTest action";
}
...
```

You can test the filter by starting the application and navigating to the /Home/FilterTest URL. If you have made the request from the local machine, then you will see the result shown in Figure 16-7, even though we know that the controller and action that the URL targets exists.

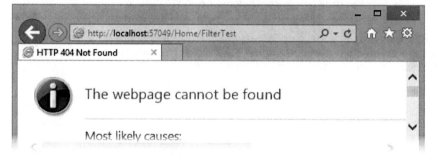

Figure 16-7. The effect of using an action filter

Implementing the OnActionExecuted Method

You can also use the filter to perform some task that spans the execution of the action method. As a simple example, we have created a new class called ProfileActionAttribute in the Infrastructure folder, which measures the amount of time that an action method takes to execute. You can see the code for this filter in Listing 16-24.

Listing 16-24. A More Complex Action Filter

```
using System.Diagnostics;
using System.Web.Mvc;

namespace Filters.Infrastructure {

    public class ProfileActionAttribute : FilterAttribute, IActionFilter {
        private Stopwatch timer;

        public void OnActionExecuting(ActionExecutingContext filterContext) {
            timer = Stopwatch.StartNew();
        }

        public void OnActionExecuted(ActionExecutedContext filterContext) {
            timer.Stop();
```

```
            if (filterContext.Exception == null) {
                filterContext.HttpContext.Response.Write(
                    string.Format("<div>Action method elapsed time: {0}</div>",
                        timer.Elapsed.TotalSeconds));
            }
        }
    }
}
```

In this example, we use the OnActionExecuting method to start a timer (using the high-resolution Stopwatch timer class in the System.Diagnostics namespace). The OnActionExecuted method is invoked when the action method has completed. Listing 16-25 shows how we applied the attribute to the Home controller (we removed the previous filter we created so that local requests are not redirected).

Listing 16-25. Applying the Action Filter to the Home Controller

```
...
[ProfileAction]
public string FilterTest() {
    return "This is the ActionFilterTest action";
}
...
```

If you start the application and navigate to the /Home/FilterTest URL, you will see the results illustrated by Figure 16-8.

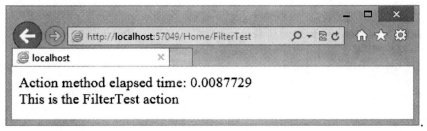

Figure 16-8. Using an action filter to measure performance

▪ **Tip**   Notice that the profile information is shown in the browser before the result of the action method. This is because the action filter is executed after the action method has completed but before the result is processed.

The parameter that is passed to the OnActionExecuted method is an ActionExecutedContext object. This class defines some additional properties, as shown in Table 16-8. The Exception property returns any exception that the action method has thrown, and the ExceptionHandled property indicates if another filter has dealt with it.

Table 16-8. ActionExecutedContext Properties

Name	Type	Description
ActionDescriptor	ActionDescriptor	Provides details of the action method
Canceled	bool	Returns **true** if the action has been canceled by another filter
Exception	Exception	Returns an exception thrown by another filter or by the action method
ExceptionHandled	bool	Returns **true** if the exception has been handled
Result	ActionResult	The result for the action method; a filter can cancel the request by setting this property to a non-**null** value

The Canceled property will return **true** if another filter has canceled the request (by setting a value for the Result property) since the time that the filter's OnActionExecuting method was invoked. Our OnActionExecuted method will still be called, but only so that we can tidy up and release any resources we were using.

Using Result Filters

Result filters are general-purpose filters which operate on the results produced by action methods. Result filters implement the IResultFilter interface, which is shown in Listing 16-26.

Listing 16-26. The IResultFilter Interface

```
namespace System.Web.Mvc {

    public interface IResultFilter {
        void OnResultExecuting(ResultExecutingContext filterContext);
        void OnResultExecuted(ResultExecutedContext filterContext);
    }
}
```

In Chapter 15, we explained how action methods return action results, allowing us to separate the intent of an action method from its execution. When we apply a result filter to an action method, the OnResultExecuting method is invoked when the action method has returned an action result but before the action result is executed. The OnResultExecuted method is invoked after the action result is executed.

The parameters to these methods are ResultExecutingContext and ResultExecutedContext objects, respectively, and they are very similar to their action filter counterparts. They define the same properties, which have the same effects (see Table 16-8).

To demonstrate a simple result filter, we created a new class file called ProfileResultAttribute.cs in the Infrastructure folder and used it to define the class shown in Listing 16-27.

Listing 16-27. A Simple Result Filter

```
using System.Diagnostics;
using System.Web.Mvc;

namespace Filters.Infrastructure {
```

```
public class ProfileResultAttribute : FilterAttribute, IResultFilter {
    private Stopwatch timer;

    public void OnResultExecuting(ResultExecutingContext filterContext) {
        timer = Stopwatch.StartNew();
    }

    public void OnResultExecuted(ResultExecutedContext filterContext) {
        timer.Stop();
        filterContext.HttpContext.Response.Write(
                string.Format("<div>Result elapsed time: {0}</div>",
                    timer.Elapsed.TotalSeconds));
    }
}
}
```

This result filter is the complement to the action filter we created in the previous section and measures the amount of time taken to execute the result. You can see how we applied this new filter to the Home controller in Listing 16-28.

Listing 16-28. Applying the Result Filter to the Home Controller

```
...
[ProfileAction]
[ProfileResult]
public string FilterTest() {
    return "This is the ActionFilterTest action";
}
...
```

Figure 16-9 shows the effect the starting the application and navigating to the /Home/FilterTest URL. You can see that both filters have added data to the response sent to the browser—the output from the result filter is shown after the result from the action method, of course, since the OnResultExecuted method cannot be executed by the MVC Framework until the result has been properly dealt with—which, in this case, means inserting a string value into the result.

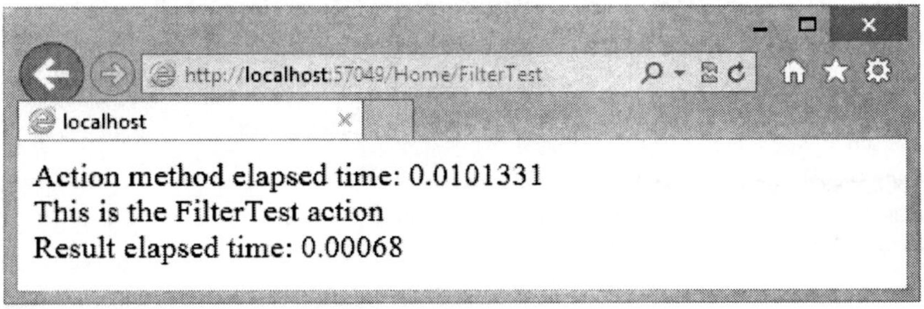

Figure 16-9. The effect of applying a result filter

Using the Built-In Action and Result Filter Class

The MVC Framework includes a built-in class that can be used to create both action and result filters. The class, called ActionFilterAttribute, is shown in Listing 16-29.

Listing 16-29. The ActionFilterAttribute Class

```
public abstract class ActionFilterAttribute : FilterAttribute, IActionFilter,
    IResultFilter{

        public virtual void OnActionExecuting(ActionExecutingContext filterContext) {
        }

        public virtual void OnActionExecuted(ActionExecutedContext filterContext) {
        }

        public virtual void OnResultExecuting(ResultExecutingContext filterContext) {
        }

        public virtual void OnResultExecuted(ResultExecutedContext filterContext) {
        }
    }
}
```

The only benefit to using this class is that you do not need to override and implement the methods that you do not intend to use—otherwise, there is no advantage over implementing the filter interfaces directly.

To demonstrate the use of the `ActionFilterAttribute` class we added a new class file called `ProfileAllAttribute.cs` to the `Infrastructure` folder of the example project and used it to define the class shown in Listing 16-30.

Listing 16-30. Using the ActionFilterAttribute Class

```
using System.Diagnostics;
using System.Web.Mvc;

namespace Filters.Infrastructure {
    public class ProfileAllAttribute : ActionFilterAttribute {
        private Stopwatch timer;

        public override void OnActionExecuting(ActionExecutingContext filterContext) {
            timer = Stopwatch.StartNew();
        }

        public override void OnResultExecuted(ResultExecutedContext filterContext) {
            timer.Stop();
            filterContext.HttpContext.Response.Write(
                    string.Format("<div>Total elapsed time: {0}</div>",
                        timer.Elapsed.TotalSeconds));
        }
    }
}
```

The `ActionFilterAttribute` class implements the `IActionFilter` and `IResultFilter` interfaces, which means that the MVC Framework will treat derived classes as both types of filters, even if not all of the methods are overridden. In our example, we have implemented only the `OnActionExecuting` method from the `IActionFilter` interface and the `OnResultExecuted` method from the `IResultFilter` interface, which allows us to continue our profiling theme and measure the time it takes for the action method to execute and the result to be processed as a single unit. Listing 16-31 shows how we applied the filter to the Home controller.

Listing 16-31. Applying the Filter to the Home Controller

```
...
[ProfileAction]
[ProfileResult]
[ProfileAll]
public string FilterTest() {
    return "This is the FilterTest action";
}
...
```

You can see the effect of all of these filters if you start the application and navigate to the /Home/FilterTest method. Figure 16-10 shows the result.

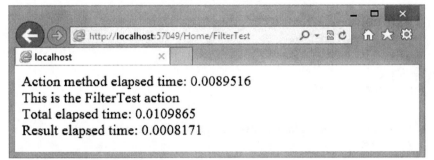

Figure 16-10. The effect of adding the ProfileAll filter

Using Other Filter Features

The previous examples have given you all the information you need to work effectively with filters. In the following sections, we will show you some of the advanced MVC Framework filtering capabilities, which are interesting but not as widely used.

Filtering Without Attributes

The normal way of using filters is to apply attributes, as we have demonstrated in the previous sections. However, there is an alternative—the Controller class implements the IAuthorizationFilter, IActionFilter, IResultFilter, and IExceptionFilter interfaces. It also provides empty virtual implementations of each of the OnXXX methods you have already seen, such as OnAuthorization and OnException. In Listing 16-32 we have updated the Home controller to use this feature and create a self-profiling controller class.

Listing 16-32. Using the Controller Filter Methods

```
using System;
using System.Collections.Generic;
using System.Linq;
using System.Web;
using System.Web.Mvc;
using Filters.Infrastructure;
using System.Diagnostics;

namespace Filters.Controllers {
```

```
public class HomeController : Controller {
    private Stopwatch timer;

    [Authorize(Users = "adam, steve, jacqui", Roles = "admin")]
    public string Index() {
        return "This is the Index action on the Home controller";
    }

    [HandleError(ExceptionType = typeof(ArgumentOutOfRangeException),
        View = "RangeError")]
    public string RangeTest(int id) {
        if (id > 100) {
            return String.Format("The id value is: {0}", id);
        } else {
            throw new ArgumentOutOfRangeException("id", id, "");
        }
    }

    public string FilterTest() {
        return "This is the FilterTest action";
    }

    protected override void OnActionExecuting(ActionExecutingContext filterContext) {
        timer = Stopwatch.StartNew();
    }

    protected override void OnResultExecuted(ResultExecutedContext filterContext) {
        timer.Stop();
        filterContext.HttpContext.Response.Write(
                string.Format("<div>Total elapsed time: {0}</div>",
                    timer.Elapsed.TotalSeconds));
    }
}
}
```

We have removed the filters from the FilterTest action method because they are no longer required—the Home controller will add the profile information to the response for any action method. Figure 16-11 shows the effect of starting the application and navigating to the /Home/RangeTest/200 URL, which targets the RangeTest action without causing the exception we set up to demonstrate the HandleError filter.

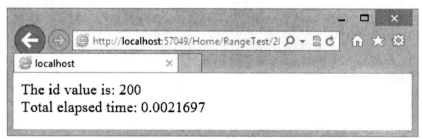

Figure 16-11. The effect of implementing filter methods directly in the controller

This technique is most useful when you are creating a base class from which multiple controllers in your project are derived. The whole point of filtering is to put code that is required *across* the application in one reusable location, so using these methods in a class that will not be used as a base for controllers does not make much sense.

■ **Tip**   For our projects, we prefer to use attributes. We like the separation between the controller logic and the filter logic. If you are looking for a way to apply a filter to all of your controllers, continue reading to see how to do that with global filters.

Using Global Filters

Global filters are applied to all of the action methods in all of the controllers in your application. We make a regular filter into a global filter through the `RegisterGlobalFilters` method defined in the `App_Start/FilterConfig.cs` file. Listing 16-33 shows how to change the `ProfileAll` filter we created in Listing 16-30 into a global filter.

Listing 16-33. Creating a Global Filter in the FilterConfig.cs File

```
using System.Web;
using System.Web.Mvc;
using Filters.Infrastructure;

namespace Filters {
    public class FilterConfig {
        public static void RegisterGlobalFilters(GlobalFilterCollection filters) {
            filters.Add(new HandleErrorAttribute());
            filters.Add(new ProfileAllAttribute());
        }
    }
}
```

The `RegisterGlobalFilters` method is called from the `Application_Start` method in the `Global.asax` file, which ensures that the global filters are registered when your MVC application starts.

■ **Note**   The first statement in the default `RegisterGlobalFilters` method created by Visual Studio sets up the default MVC exception handling policy. This will render the `/Views/Shared/Error.cshtml` view when an unhandled exception arises. This exception handling policy is disabled by default for development. See the "Creating an Exception Filter" section later in the chapter for a note on how to enable it in the `Web.config` file.

The parameter for the `RegisterGlobalFilters` method is a `GlobalFilterCollection`. You register global filters using the `Add` method, like this:

```
filters.Add(new ProfileAllAttribute());
```

Notice that you must refer to the filter by the full class name (`ProfileAllAttribute`), rather than the short name used when you apply the filter as an attribute (`ProfileAll`). Once you have registered a filter like this, it will apply to every action method.

To demonstrate the global filter, we have created a new controller called `Customer`, as shown in Listing 16-34. We have created a new controller because we want to use code to which we have not applied a filter in any of the earlier sections.

Listing 16-34. The Customer Controller

```
using System.Web.Mvc;

namespace Filters.Controllers {
    public class CustomerController : Controller {

        public string Index() {
            return "This is the Customer controller";
        }
    }
}
```

This is a very simple controller whose `Index` action returns a `string`. Figure 16-12 illustrates the effect of the global filter, which we achieved by starting the application and navigating to the /Customer URL. Even though we have not applied a filter directly to the controller, the global filter adds the profiling information shown in the figure.

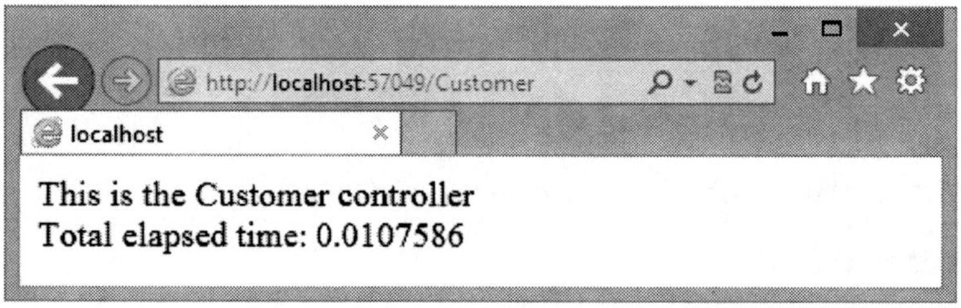

Figure 16-12. The Effect of a Global Filter

Ordering Filter Execution

We have already explained that filters are executed by type. The sequence is authorization filters, action filters, and then result filters. The framework executes your exception filters at any stage if there is an unhandled exception. However, within each type category, you can take control of the order in which individual filters are used.

Listing 16-35 shows a simple action filter class called `SimpleMessageAttribute` that we added to the `Infrastructure` folder to demonstrate ordering filter execution.

Listing 16-35. A Simple Action Filter

```
using System;
using System.Collections.Generic;
using System.Linq;
using System.Web;
using System.Web.Mvc;

namespace Filters.Infrastructure {
```

```
[AttributeUsage(AttributeTargets.Method, AllowMultiple=true)]
public class SimpleMessageAttribute : FilterAttribute, IActionFilter {

    public string Message { get; set; }

    public void OnActionExecuting(ActionExecutingContext filterContext) {
        filterContext.HttpContext.Response.Write(
            string.Format("<div>[Before Action: {0}]<div>", Message));
    }

    public void OnActionExecuted(ActionExecutedContext filterContext) {
        filterContext.HttpContext.Response.Write(
            string.Format("<div>[After Action: {0}]<div>", Message));
    }
}
}
```

This filter writes a message to the response when the `OnActionExecuting` and `OnActionExecuted` methods are invoked, part of which is specified using the `Message` property.

We can apply multiple instances of this filter to an action method, as shown in Listing 16-36 (notice that in the `AttributeUsage` attribute, we set the `AllowMultiple` property to `true`).

Listing 16-36. Applying Multiple Filters to an Action

```
using System.Web.Mvc;
using Filters.Infrastructure;

namespace Filters.Controllers {
    public class CustomerController : Controller {

        [SimpleMessage(Message="A")]
        [SimpleMessage(Message="B")]
        public string Index() {
            return "This is the Customer controller";
        }
    }
}
```

We have created two filters with different messages: the first has a message of A, and the other has a message of B. We could have used two different filters, but this approach allows us to create a simpler example. When you run the application and navigate to /Customer URL, you see the result shown in Figure 16-13.

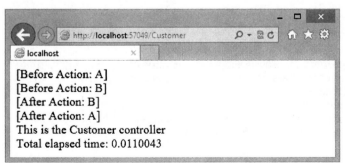

Figure 16-13. Multiple Filters on the Same Action Method

When we run this example, the MVC Framework executes the A filter before the B filter, but it could have been the other way around. The MVC Framework does not guarantee any particular order or execution. Most of the time, the order does not matter. When it does, you can use the Order property, as shown in Listing 16-37.

Listing 16-37. Using the Order Property in a Filter

```
...
[SimpleMessage(Message="A", Order=2)]
[SimpleMessage(Message="B", Order=1)]
public ActionResult Index() {
    Response.Write("Action method is running");
    return View();
}
...
```

The Order parameter takes an int value, and the MVC Framework executes the filters in ascending order. In the listing, we have given the B filter the lowest value, so the framework executes it first, as shown in Figure 16-14.

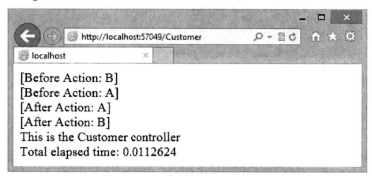

Figure 16-14. Specifying the order of filter execution

■ **Note** Notice that the OnActionExecuting methods are executed in the order we specified, but the OnActionExecuted methods are executed in the reverse order. The MVC Framework builds up a stack of filters as it executes them before the action method, and then unwinds the stack afterward. This unwinding behavior cannot be changed.

If we do not specify a value for the Order property, it is assigned a default value of -1. This means that if you mix filters so that some have Order values and others do not, the ones without these values will be executed first, since they have the lowest Order value.

If multiple filters of the same type (say, action filters) have the same Order value (say 1), then the MVC Framework determines the execution order based on where the filter has been applied. Global filters are executed first, then filters applied to the controller class, and then filters applied to the action method.

■ **Note** The order of execution is reversed for exception filters. If exception filters are applied with the same `Order` value to the controller and to the action method, the filter on the action method will be executed first. Global exception filters with the same `Order` value are executed last.

Using the Built-in Filters

The MVC Framework supplies some built-in filters, which we have described in Table 16-9.

Table 16-9. Built-In Filters

Filter	Description
RequireHttps	Enforces the use of the HTTPS protocol for actions
OutputCache	Caches the output from an action method
ValidateInput and ValidationAntiForgeryToken	Authorization filters related to security
AsyncTimeout NoAsyncTimeout	Used with asynchronous controllers
ChildActionOnlyAttribute	An authorization filter that supports the Html.Action and Html.RenderAction helper methods

Most of these are covered in other parts of the book. However, two filters—RequireHttps and OutputCache—do not really belong elsewhere, so we are going to explain their use here.

Using the RequireHttps Filter

The RequireHttps filter allows you to enforce the use of the HTTPS protocol for actions. It redirects the user's browser to the same action, but using the https:// protocol prefix.

You can override the HandleNonHttpsRequest method to create custom behavior when an unsecured request is made. This filter applies to only GET requests. Form data values would be lost if a POST request were redirected in this way.

■ **Note** If you are having problems controlling the order of filter execution when using the RequireHttps filter, it is because this is an authorization filter and not an action filter. See the "Ordering Filter Execution" section earlier in this chapter for details on how different types of filter are ordered.

Using the OutputCache Filter

The OutputCache filter tells the MVC Framework to cache the output from an action method so that the same content can be reused to service subsequent requests for the same URL. Caching action output can offer a significant increase in performance, because most of the time-consuming activities required to process a request (such as querying a database) are avoided. Of course, the downside of caching is that you are limited to producing the exact same response to all requests, which isn't suiTable 16-for all action methods.

The OutputCache filter uses the output caching facility from the core ASP.NET platform, and you will recognize the configuration options if you have ever used output caching in a Web Forms application.

The OutputCache filter can be used to control client-side caching by affecting the values sent in the Cache-Control header. Table 16-10 shows the parameters you can set for this filter.

Table 16-10. Parameters for the OutputCache Filter

Parameter	Type	Description
Duration	int	Required—specifies how long (in seconds) the output remains cached.
VaryByParam	string (semicolon-separated list)	Tells ASP.NET to use a different cache entry for each combination of Request.QueryString and Request.Form values matching these names. The default value, none, means "do not vary by query string or form values." The other option is *, which means "vary by all query string and form values." If unspecified, the default value of none is used.
VaryByHeader	string (semicolon-separated list)	Tells ASP.NET to use a different cache entry for each combination of values sent in these HTTP header names.
VaryByCustom	string	If specified, ASP.NET calls the GetVaryByCustomString method in Global.asax, passing this arbitrary string value as a parameter, so you can generate your own cache key. The special value browser is used to vary the cache by the browser's name and major version data.
VaryByContentEncoding	string (semicolon-separated list)	Allows ASP.NET to create a separate cache entry for each content encoding (e.g., gzip and deflate) that may be requested by a browser.

Parameter	Type	Description
Location	OutputCacheLocation	Specifies where the output is to be cached. It takes the enumeration value Server (in the server's memory only), Client (in the visitor's browser only), Downstream (in the visitor's browser or any intermediate HTTP-caching device, such as a proxy server), ServerAndClient (combination of Server and Client), Any (combination of Server and Downstream), or None (no caching). If not specified, it takes the default value of Any.
NoStore	bool	If true, tells ASP.NET to send a Cache-Control: no-store header to the browser, instructing the browser not to cache the page for any longer than necessary to display it. This is used only to protect very sensitive data.
CacheProfile	string	If specified, instructs ASP.NET to take cache settings from a particular section named <outputCacheSettings> in Web.config.
SqlDependency	string	If you specify a database/Table 16-name pair, the cached data will expire automatically when the underlying database data changes. This requires the ASP.NET SQL cache dependency feature, which can be quite complicated to set up. See http://msdn.microsoft.com/en-us/library/ms178604.aspx for further details.

One of the nice features of the OutputCache filter is that you can apply it to child actions. A *child action* is invoked from within a view using the Html.Action helper method. This allows you to be selective about which parts of a response are cached and which are generated dynamically. We discuss child actions fully in Chapter 18, but Listing 16-38 provides a simple demonstration in the form of a new controller called SelectiveCache.

Listing 16-38. The SelectiveCache Controller

```
using System;
using System.Web.Mvc;

namespace Filters.Controllers {
    public class SelectiveCacheController : Controller {
```

451

```
        public ActionResult Index() {
            Response.Write("Action method is running: " + DateTime.Now);
            return View();
        }

        [OutputCache(Duration = 30)]
        public ActionResult ChildAction() {
            Response.Write("Child action method is running: " + DateTime.Now);
            return View();
        }
    }
}
```

The controller in the Listing 16-defines two action methods:

- The ChildAction method has the OutputCache filter applied. This is the action method we will call from within the view.

- The Index action method will be the parent action.

Both action methods write the time that they were executed to the Response object. Listing 16-39 shows the Index.cshtml view (which is associated with the Index action method).

Listing 16-39. A View That Calls a Cached Child Action

```
@{
    ViewBag.Title = "Index";
}

<h2>This is the main action view</h2>

@Html.Action("ChildAction")
```

You can see that we call the ChildAction method at the end of the view. The view for the ChildAction method is shown in Listing 16-40.

Listing 16-40. The ChildAction.cshtml View

```
@{
    Layout = null;
}

<h4>This is the child action view</h4>
```

Start the application and navigate to the /SelectiveCache URL. The first time that you do this, you will see that the parent action and the child action both report the same time in the messages included in their response. If you reload the page (or navigate to the same URL using a different browser), you can see that the time reported by the parent action changes, but that the child action time stays the same. This tells us that we are seeing the cached output from the original invocation, as shown in Figure 16-15.

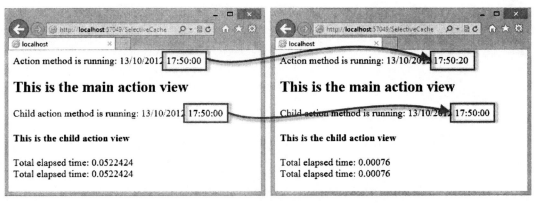

Figure 16-15. The effect of caching a child action

■ **Tip**   You may have to refresh the page one extra time before the caching starts—this is a facet of the way that views are compiled when an MVC Framework application first starts (and which we explain in Chapter 18).

Summary

In this chapter, you have seen how to encapsulate logic that addresses cross-cutting concerns as filters. We showed you the different kinds of filters available and how to implement each of them. You saw how filters can be applied as attributes to controllers and action methods, and how they can be applied as global filters. Filters are a means of extending the logic that is applied when a request is processed, without needing to include that logic in the action method. In the next chapter, we show you how to change and extend the way that the MVC Framework deals with controllers.

CHAPTER 17

■ ■ ■

Controller Extensibility

In this chapter, we are going to show you some of the advanced MVC features for working with controllers. We start this chapter by exploring the parts of the request processing pipeline that lead to the execution of an action method and demonstrating the different ways we can take control of this process. Figure 17-1 shows the basic flow of control between components.

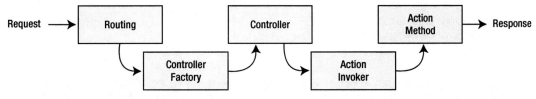

Figure 17-1. Invoking an action method

Our focus for the first part of this chapter is the *controller factory* and the *action invoker*. The names of these components suggest their purpose. The controller factory is responsible for creating instances of controllers to service a request and the action invoker is responsible for finding and invoking the action method in the controller class. The MVC Framework includes default implementations of both of these components, and we will show you how to conFigure 17-these to control their behavior. We will also show you how to replace these components entirely and use custom logic.

Creating the Example Project

For this chapter, we have created a new MVC project called `ControllerExtensibility` using the `Empty` template option. We need some simple controllers to work with in this chapter, so that we can demonstrate the different kinds of extensibility features that are available. To get set up, we created the `Result.cs` file in the `Models` folder and used it to define the `Result` class shown in Listing 17-1.

Listing 17-1. The Result Model Object

```
namespace ControllerExtensibility.Models {
    public class Result {
        public string ControllerName { get; set; }
        public string ActionName { get; set; }
    }
}
```

Our next step is to create the **/Views/Shared** folder and add a new view called `Result.cshtml`. This is the view that all of the action methods in our controller classes will render, and you can see the contents of this file in Listing 17-2.

Listing 17-2. The Contents of the Result.cshtml File

```
@model ControllerExtensibility.Models.Result

@{
    Layout = null;
}

<!DOCTYPE html>

<html>
<head>
    <meta name="viewport" content="width=device-width" />
    <title>Result</title>
</head>
<body>
    <div>Controller: @Model.ControllerName</div>
    <div>Action: @Model.ActionName</div>
</body>
</html>
```

This view uses the `Result` class that we defined in Listing 17-1 as its model and simply displays the values of the `ControllerName` and `ActionName` properties. Finally, we need to create some basic controllers. Listing 17-3 shows the `Product` controller.

Listing 17-3. The Product Controller

```
using ControllerExtensibility.Models;
using System.Web.Mvc;

namespace ControllerExtensibility.Controllers {
    public class ProductController : Controller {

        public ViewResult Index() {
            return View("Result", new Result {
                ControllerName = "Product",
                ActionName = "Index"
            });
        }

        public ViewResult List() {
            return View("Result", new Result {
                ControllerName = "Product",
                ActionName = "List"
            });
        }
    }
}
```

Listing 17-4 shows the `Customer` controller.

Listing 17-4. The Customer Controller

```
using ControllerExtensibility.Models;
using System.Web.Mvc;

namespace ControllerExtensibility.Controllers {
    public class CustomerController : Controller {

        public ViewResult Index() {
            return View("Result", new Result {
                ControllerName = "Customer",
                ActionName = "Index"
            });
        }

        public ViewResult List() {
            return View("Result", new Result {
                ControllerName = "Customer",
                ActionName = "List"
            });
        }
    }
}
```

Our controllers do not perform any useful actions other than to report that they have been called via the Result.cshtml view. That is all we need in this chapter, which is about how the MVC Framework allows us to customize the way that controllers and actions are managed.

Creating a Custom Controller Factory

As with much of the MVC Framework, the best way to understand how controller factories work is to create a custom implementation. We do not recommend that you do this in a real project, as there are easier ways to create custom behavior by extending the built-in factory—but this is a nice way to demonstrate how the MVC framework creates instances of controllers. Controller factories are defined by the IControllerFactory interface, which is shown in Listing 17-5.

Listing 17-5. The IControllerFactory Interface

```
using System.Web.Routing;
using System.Web.SessionState;

namespace System.Web.Mvc {
    public interface IControllerFactory {

        IController CreateController(RequestContext requestContext,
            string controllerName);

        SessionStateBehavior GetControllerSessionBehavior(RequestContext requestContext,
            string controllerName);

        void ReleaseController(IController controller);
    }
}
```

In the sections that follow, we will create a simple custom controller factory and walk you through the implementations we use for each of the methods in the IControllerFactory interface. We created an Infrastructure folder and created a new class file called CustomControllerFactory.cs. You can see the custom controller factory we defined in Listing 17-6.

Listing 17-6. The Contents of the CustomControllerFactory.cs File

```
using System;
using System.Web.Mvc;
using System.Web.Routing;
using System.Web.SessionState;
using ControllerExtensibility.Controllers;

namespace ControllerExtensibility.Infrastructure {

    public class CustomControllerFactory: IControllerFactory {

        public IController CreateController(RequestContext requestContext,
            string controllerName) {

            Type targetType = null;
            switch (controllerName) {
                case "Product":
                    targetType = typeof(ProductController);
                    break;
                case "Customer":
                    targetType = typeof(CustomerController);
                    break;
                default:
                    requestContext.RouteData.Values["controller"] = "Product";
                    targetType = typeof(ProductController);
                    break;
            }

            return targetType == null ? null :
                (IController)DependencyResolver.Current.GetService(targetType);
        }

        public SessionStateBehavior GetControllerSessionBehavior(RequestContext
            requestContext, string controllerName) {

            return SessionStateBehavior.Default;
        }

        public void ReleaseController(IController controller) {
            IDisposable disposable = controller as IDisposable;
            if (disposable != null) {
                disposable.Dispose();
            }
        }
    }
}
```

The most important method in the interface is `CreateController`, which the MVC Framework calls when it needs a controller to service a request. The parameters to this method are a `RequestContext` object, which allows the factory to inspect the details of the request, and a string, which contains the `controller` value from the routed URL. The `RequestContext` class defines the properties described in Table 17-1.

Table 17-1. RequestContext Properties

Name	Type	Description
HttpContext	HttpContextBase	Provides information about the HTTP request
RouteData	RouteData	Provides information about the route that matches the request

One of the reasons that we do not recommend creating a custom controller this way is that finding controller classes in the web application and instantiating them is complicated—you need to be able to locate controllers dynamically and consistently and deal with all sorts of potential problems, such as disambiguating between classes with the same name in different namespaces, constructor exceptions and a whole lot more.

We only have two controllers in our example project and we are going to instantiate them directly, which means hard-wiring the class names into the controller factory—something which is obviously not a good idea for a real project.

The purpose of the `CreateController` method is to create instances of controller classes that can handle the current request. There are no restrictions on how you do this—the only rule is that you *must* return an object that implements the `IController` interface as the method result.

The conventions that you have seen so far in this book exist because that's how the default controller factory has been written. As an example, we have implemented one of these conventions in our code— that when we receive a request for a controller, we append `Controller` to the class name, so that a request for `Product` leads to the `ProductController` class being instantiated.

You are free to follow the MVC Framework conventions when you write a controller factory or to discard them and create your own to suit your project needs. We do not think it is sensible to create your own conventions just for the sake of it, but it is useful to understand just how flexible the MVC Framework can be.

Dealing with the Fallback Controller

Custom controller factories must return an implementation of the `IController` interface as the result from the `CreateController` method—otherwise, an error will be displayed to the user. This means that you need to have a fallback position for when the request you are processing does not target any of the controllers in your project. You can create any policy you like for dealing with this situation: you could define a special controller that renders an error message, for example, or do as we have and map the request to a controller class that we know exists.

When we get a request that does not map to either of the controllers in our project, we target the `ProductController` class. This may not be the most useful thing to do in a real project, but it demonstrates that the controller factory has complete flexibility in how requests are interpreted. However, you do need to be aware of how the other points in the MVC Framework operate.

By default, the MVC Framework selects a view based on the `controller` value in the routing data, not the name of the controller class. So, in our example, if we want our fallback position to work with views that follow the convention of being organized by controller name, we need to change the value of the `controller` routing property, like this:

```
requestContext.RouteData.Values["controller"] = "Product";
```

This change will cause the MVC Framework to search for views associated with our fallback controller and not the controller that the user has requested.

There are two important points here: the first is that not only does the controller factory have sole responsibility for matching requests to controllers, but it can *change* the request to alter the behavior of subsequent steps in the request processing pipeline. This is pretty potent stuff and a critical characteristic of the MVC Framework.

The second point is that while you are free to follow whatever conventions you want in your controller factory, you still need to know what the conventions are for other parts of the MVC Framework—and, because those other components can be replaced with custom code as well (as we demonstrate for views in Chapter 18), it makes sense to follow as many of the conventions as possible to allow components to be developed and used independently of one another.

Instantiating Controller Classes

There are no rules about how you instantiate your controller classes, but it good practice to use the dependency resolver that we introduced in Chapter 6. This allows you to keep your custom controller factory focused on mapping requests to controller classes, and leaves issues like dependency inject to be handled separately and for the entire application. You can see how we used the `DependencyResolver` class to create our controllers instances:

```
return targetType == null ? null :
    (IController)DependencyResolver.Current.GetService(targetType);
```

The static `DependencyResolver.Current` property returns an implementation of the `IDependencyResolver` interface, which defines the `GetService` method. You pass a `System.Type` object to this method and get an instance of it in return. There is a strongly-typed version of the `GetService` method, but because we do not know what type we are dealing with in advance, we have to use the version that returns an `Object` and then perform an explicit case to `IController`.

▓ Tip   We have not checked that the object that we get back from the `GetService` method really is an implementation of `IController`, but it is a good idea to do so in real projects—especially if you other developers will be creating the classes you are trying to instantiate.

Implementing the Other Interface Methods

Two other methods are in the `IControllerFactory` interface:

- The `GetControllerSessionBehavior` method is used by the MVC Framework to determine if session data should be maintained for a controller. We will come back to this in the "Using Sessionless Controllers" section later in this chapter.

- The `ReleaseController` method is called when a controller object created by the `CreateController` method is no longer needed. In our implementation, we check to see if the class implements the `IDisposable` interface. If it does, we call the `Dispose` method to release any resources that can be freed.

Our implementations of the `GetControllerSessionBehaviour` and `ReleaseController` methods are suitable for most projects and can be used verbatim (although you should read the section on sessionless controllers later in this chapter to make sure you understand the options available).

Registering a Custom Controller Factory

We tell the MVC Framework to use our custom controller factory through the `ControllerBuilder` class. You need to register custom factory controllers when the application is started, which means using the `Application_Start` method in the `Global.asax.cs` file, as shown in Listing 17-7.

Listing 17-7. Registering a Custom Controller Factory

```
using System;
using System.Collections.Generic;
using System.Linq;
using System.Web;
using System.Web.Http;
using System.Web.Mvc;
using System.Web.Routing;
using ControllerExtensibility.Infrastructure;

namespace ControllerExtensibility {

    public class MvcApplication : System.Web.HttpApplication {
        protected void Application_Start() {
            AreaRegistration.RegisterAllAreas();

            WebApiConfig.Register(GlobalConfiguration.Configuration);
            FilterConfig.RegisterGlobalFilters(GlobalFilters.Filters);
            RouteConfig.RegisterRoutes(RouteTable.Routes);

            ControllerBuilder.Current.SetControllerFactory(new
                CustomControllerFactory());
        }
    }
}
```

Once the controller factory has been registered, it will be responsible for handling all of the requests that the application receives. You can see the effect of our custom factory simply by starting the application—the browser will request the root URL, which will be mapped to the Home controller by the routing system. Our custom factory will handle the request for the Home controller by creating an instance of the `ProductController` class, which will produce the result shown in Figure 17-2.

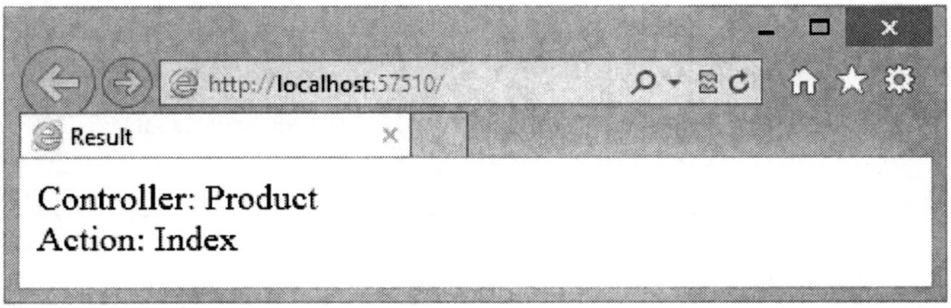

Figure 17-2. Using the custom controller factory

Working with the Built-In Controller Factory

We showed you how to create a custom controller factory because it is the most effective way of demonstrating what a controller factory does and how it functions. For most applications, however, the built-in controller factory class, called DefaultControllerFactory, is perfectly adequate. When it receives a request from the routing system, this factory looks at the routing data to find the value of the controller property (which we introduced in Chapter 13), and tries to find a class in the Web application that meets the following criteria:

- The class must be public.

- The class must be concrete (not abstract).

- The class must *not* take generic parameters.

- The name of the class must end with Controller.

- The class must implement the IController interface.

The DefaultControllerFactory class maintains a list of such classes in the application so that it does not need to perform a search every time a request arrives. If a suitable class is found, then an instance is created using the controller activator (we will come back to this in the upcoming "Customizing DefaultControllerFactory Controller Creation" section), and the job of the controller is complete. If there is no matching controller, then the request cannot be processed any further.

Notice how the DefaultControllerFactory class follows the convention-over-configuration pattern. You do not need to register your controllers in a configuration file, because the factory will find them for you. All you need to do is create classes that meet the criteria that the factory is seeking.

If you want to create custom controller factory behavior, you can conFigure 17-the settings of the default factory or override some of the methods. This way, you are able to build on the useful convention-over-configuration behavior without having to re-create it—a task which, we noted earlier, is pretty complicated and painful. In the sections that follow, we show you different ways to tailor controller creation.

Prioritizing Namespaces

In Chapter 14, we showed you how to prioritize one or more namespaces when creating a route. This was to address the ambiguous controller problem, where controller classes have the same name but reside in different namespaces. It is the DefaultControllerFactory that processes the list of namespaces and prioritizes them.

■ **Tip**   Global prioritization is overridden by route-specific prioritization. This means you can define a global policy, and then tailor individual routes as required. See Chapter 14 for details on specifying namespaces for individual routes.

If you have an application that has a lot of routes, it can be more convenient to specify priority namespaces globally, so that they are applied to all of your routes. Listing 17-8 shows how to do this in the Application_Start method of the Global.asax file (this is where we put these statements, but you can also use the RouteConfig.cs file in the App_Start folder if you prefer).

Listing 17-8. Global Namespace Prioritization

```
using System;
using System.Collections.Generic;
using System.Linq;
using System.Web;
using System.Web.Http;
using System.Web.Mvc;
using System.Web.Routing;
using ControllerExtensibility.Infrastructure;

namespace ControllerExtensibility {

    public class MvcApplication : System.Web.HttpApplication {
        protected void Application_Start() {
            AreaRegistration.RegisterAllAreas();

            WebApiConfig.Register(GlobalConfiguration.Configuration);
            FilterConfig.RegisterGlobalFilters(GlobalFilters.Filters);
            RouteConfig.RegisterRoutes(RouteTable.Routes);

            ControllerBuilder.Current.DefaultNamespaces.Add("MyControllerNamespace");
            ControllerBuilder.Current.DefaultNamespaces.Add("MyProject.*");
        }
    }
}
```

We use the static `ControllerBuilder.Current.DefaultNamespaces.Add` method to add namespaces that should be given priority. The order in which we add the namespaces does not imply any kind of search order or relative priority—all of the namespaces defined by the `Add` method are treated equally and the priority is relative to those namespaces which have not been specified by the `Add` method. This means that the controller factory will search the entire application if it can't find a suiTable 17-controller class in the namespaces defined by the `Add` method.

■ **Tip**   Notice that we used an asterisk character (*) in the second statement shown in bold in Listing 17-8. This allows us to specify that the controller factory should look in the `MyProject` namespace and any child namespaces that `MyProject` contains. Although this looks like regular expression syntax, it isn't; you can end your namespaces with `.*`, but you cannot use any other regular expression syntax with the `Add` method.

Customizing DefaultControllerFactory Controller Instantiation

There are a number of ways to customize how the `DefaultControllerFactory` class instantiates controller objects. By far, the most common reason for customizing the controller factory is to add support for DI. There are several different ways of doing this. The most suitable technique depends on how you are using DI elsewhere in your application.

Using the Dependency Resolver

The `DefaultControllerFactory` class will use a dependency resolver to create controllers if one is available. We covered dependency resolvers in Chapter 6 and showed you our `NinjectDependencyResolver` class, which implements the `IDependencyResolver` interface to provide Ninject DI support. We also demonstrated how to use the `DependencyResolver` class earlier in this chapter when we created our own custom controller factory.

The `DefaultControllerFactory` will call the `IDependencyResolver.GetService` method to request a controller instance, which gives you the opportunity to resolve and inject any dependencies.

Using a Controller Activator

You can also introduce DI into controllers by creating a *controller activator*. You create this activator by implementing the `IControllerActivator` interface, as shown in Listing 17-9.

Listing 17-9. The IControllerActivator Interface

```
namespace System.Web.Mvc {
    using System.Web.Routing;

    public interface IControllerActivator {
        IController Create(RequestContext requestContext, Type controllerType);
    }
}
```

The interface contains one method, called `Create`, which is passed a `RequestContext` object describing the request and a `Type` that specifies which controller class should be instantiated. Listing 17-10 shows a simple implementation of this interface.

Listing 17-10. Implementing the IControllorActivator Interface

```
using ControllerExtensibility.Controllers;
using System;
using System.Web.Mvc;
using System.Web.Routing;

namespace ControllerExtensibility.Infrastructure {
    public class CustomControllerActivator : IControllerActivator {

        public IController Create(RequestContext requestContext,
            Type controllerType) {

            if (controllerType == typeof(ProductController)) {
                controllerType = typeof(CustomerController);
            }

            return (IController)DependencyResolver.Current.GetService(controllerType);
        }
    }
}
```

Our `IControllerActivator` implementation is pretty simple—if the `ProductController` class is requested, it responds with an instance of the `CustomerController` class. This is not something you would want to do in a real project, but it demonstrates how you can use the `IControllerActivator` interface to intercept requests between the controller factory and the dependency resolver.

To use a custom activator, we need to pass an instance of our implementation class to the `DefaultControllerFactory` constructor and register the result in the `Application_Start` method of the `Global.asax` file, as shown in Listing 17-11.

Listing 17-11. Registering a Custom Activator

```
using System;
using System.Collections.Generic;
using System.Linq;
using System.Web;
using System.Web.Http;
using System.Web.Mvc;
using System.Web.Routing;
using ControllerExtensibility.Infrastructure;

namespace ControllerExtensibility {

    public class MvcApplication : System.Web.HttpApplication {
        protected void Application_Start() {
            AreaRegistration.RegisterAllAreas();

            WebApiConfig.Register(GlobalConfiguration.Configuration);
            FilterConfig.RegisterGlobalFilters(GlobalFilters.Filters);
            RouteConfig.RegisterRoutes(RouteTable.Routes);

            ControllerBuilder.Current.SetControllerFactory(new
                DefaultControllerFactory(new CustomControllerActivator()));
        }
    }
}
```

You can see the effect of the custom activator is you start the application and navigate to the /Product URL. The route will target the `Product` controller and the `DefaultControllerFactory` will ask the activator to instantiate the `ProductFactory` class—but our activator intercepts this request and creates an instance of the `CustomerController` class instead. You can see the result in Figure 17-3.

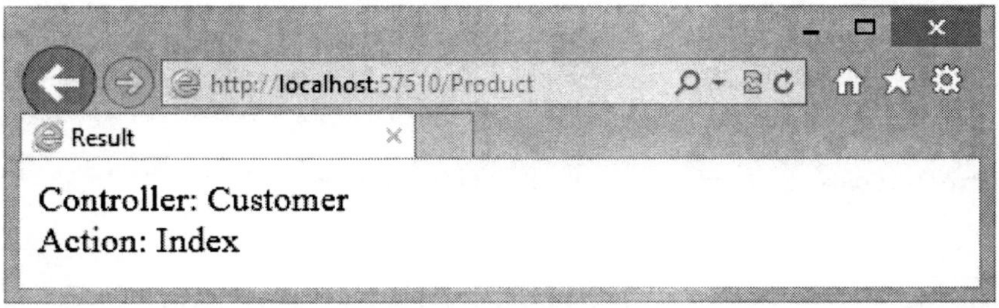

Figure 17-3. Intercepting instantiation requests using a custom controller activator

Overriding DefaultControllerFactory Methods

You can override methods in the `DefaultControllerFactory` class to customize the creation of controllers. Table 17-2 describes the three methods you can override, each of which performs a slightly different role.

Table 17-2. Overridable DefaultContollerFactory Methods

Method	Result	Description
CreateController	IController	The implementation of the CreateController method from the IControllerFactory interface. By default, this method calls GetControllerType to determine which type should be instantiated, and then gets a controller object by passing the result to the GetControllerInstance method.
GetControllerType	Type	Maps requests to controller types. This is where most of the criteria listed earlier in the chapter are enforced.
GetControllerInstance	IController	Creates an instance of a specified type.

Creating a Custom Action Invoker

Once the controller factory has created an instance of a class, the framework needs a way of invoking an action on that instance. If you derived your controller from the Controller class, then this is the responsibility of an *action invoker*, which is the subject of this section.

■ **Tip**   If you create a controller directly from the IController interface, then you are responsible for executing the action yourself—see Chapter 15 for details of both approaches to creating controllers. Action invokers are part of the functionality included in the Controller class.

An action invoker implements the IActionInvoker interface, which is shown in Listing 17-12.

Listing 17-12. The IActionInvoker Interface

```
namespace System.Web.Mvc {

    public interface IActionInvoker {

        bool InvokeAction(ControllerContext controllerContext, string actionName);
    }
}
```

The interface has only a single member: InvokeAction. The parameters are a ControllerContext object (which we described in Chapter 15) and a string that contains the name of the action to be invoked. The return value is a bool. A return value of true indicates that the action was found and invoked. A value of false indicates that the controller has no matching action.

Notice that we have not used the word *method* in this description. The association between actions and methods is strictly optional. Although this is the approach that the built-in action invoker takes, you are free to handle actions any way that you choose. Listing 17-13 shows an implementation of the IActionInvoker interface that takes a different approach.

Listing 17-13. A Custom Action Invoker

```
using System.Web.Mvc;

namespace ControllerExtensibility.Infrastructure {
    public class CustomActionInvoker : IActionInvoker {

        public bool InvokeAction(ControllerContext controllerContext,
                string actionName) {

            if (actionName == "Index") {
                controllerContext.HttpContext.
                    Response.Write("This is output from the Index action");
                return true;
            } else {
                return false;
            }
        }
    }
}
```

This action invoker doesn't care about the methods in the controller class. In fact, it deals with actions itself. If the request is for the Index action, then the invoker writes a message directly to the Response. If the request is for any other action, then it returns false, which causes a 404–Not found error to be displayed to the user.

The action invoker associated with a controller is obtained through the Controller.ActionInvoker property. This means that different controllers in the same application can use different action invokers. To demonstrate this, we have added a new controller to the example project called ActionInvoker, the definition of which you can see in Listing 17-14.

Listing 17-14. Using a Custom Action Invoker in a Controller

```
using ControllerExtensibility.Infrastructure;
using System.Web.Mvc;

namespace ControllerExtensibility.Controllers {
    public class ActionInvokerController : Controller {

        public ActionInvokerController() {
            this.ActionInvoker = new CustomActionInvoker();
        }
    }
}
```

There are no action methods in this controller. It depends on the action invoker to process requests. You can see how this works by starting the application and navigating to the /ActionInvoker/Index URL. The custom action invoker will generate the response shown in Figure 17-4. If you navigate to a URL that targets any other action on the same controller, you will see the 404 error page.

467

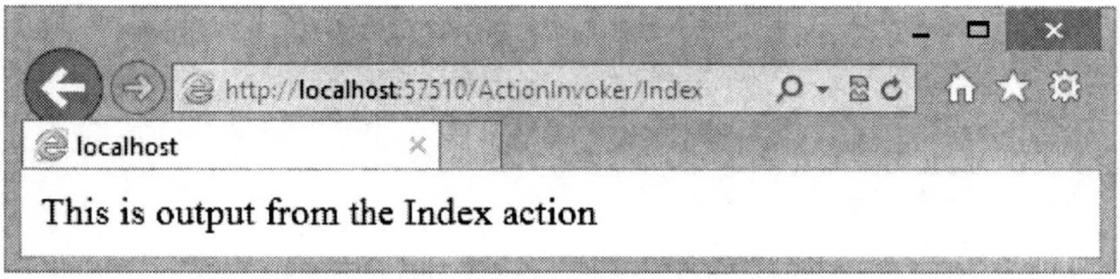

Figure 17-4. The effect of a custom action invoker

We are not suggesting that you implement your own action invoker. And, if you do, we do not suggest you follow this approach. Why? First, the built-in support has some very useful features, as you will see shortly. Second, our example has some problems: a lack of extensibility, poor separation of responsibilities, and a lack of support for views of any kind. But the example shows how the MVC Framework fits together and demonstrates, once again, that almost every aspect of the request processing pipeline can be customized or replaced entirely.

Using the Built-In Action Invoker

The built-in action invoker, which is the `ControllerActionInvoker` class, has some very sophisticated techniques for matching requests to actions. And, unlike our implementation in the previous section, the default action invoker operates on methods.

To qualify as an action, a method must meet the following criteria:

- The method must be `public`.

- The method must *not* be `static`.

- The method must *not* be present in `System.Web.Mvc.Controller` or any of its base classes.

- The method must *not* have a special name.

The first two criteria are simple enough. For the next, excluding any method that is present in the `Controller` class or its bases means that methods such as `ToString` and `GetHashCode` are excluded—as are the methods that implement the `IController` interface. This is sensible, because we do not want to expose the inner workings of our controllers to the outside world. The last criterion means that constructors, property and event accessors are excluded—in fact, no class member that has the `IsSpecialName` flag from `System.Reflection.MethodBase` will be used to process an action.

■ **Note** Methods that have generic parameters (such as `MyMethod<T>()`) meet all of the criteria, but the MVC Framework will throw an exception if you try to invoke such a method to process a request.

By default, the `ControllerActionInvoker` finds a method that has the same name as the requested action. So, for example, if the `action` value that the routing system produces is `Index`, then the `ControllerActionInvoker` will look for a method called `Index` that fits the action criteria. If it finds such a method, it will be invoked to handle the request. This behavior is exactly what you want almost all of the time, but as you might expect, the MVC Framework provides some opportunities to fine-tune the process.

Using a Custom Action Name

Usually, the name of an action method determines the action that it represents. The Index action method services requests for the Index action. You can override this behavior using the ActionName attribute, which we have applied to the Customer controller as shown in Listing 17-15.

Listing 17-15. Using a Custom Action Name

```
using ControllerExtensibility.Models;
using System.Web.Mvc;

namespace ControllerExtensibility.Controllers {
    public class CustomerController : Controller {

        public ViewResult Index() {
            return View("Result", new Result {
                ControllerName = "Customer",
                ActionName = "Index"
            });
        }

        [ActionName("Enumerate")]
        public ViewResult List() {
            return View("Result", new Result {
                ControllerName = "Customer",
                ActionName = "List"
            });
        }
    }
}
```

In this listing, we have applied the attribute to the List method, passing in a parameter value of Enumerate. When the action invoker receives a request for the Enumerate action, it will now use the List method to service it.

You can see the effect of the ActionName attribute by starting the application and navigating to the /Customer/Enumerate URL. You can see that the results shown by the browser in Figure 17-5 are those from the List method.

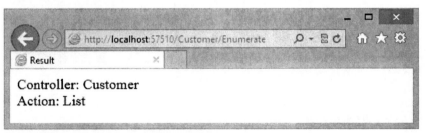

Figure 17-5. The effect of the ActionName attribute

Applying the attribute overrides the name of the action. This means that URLs which directly target the List method will no longer work, as shown in Figure 17-6.

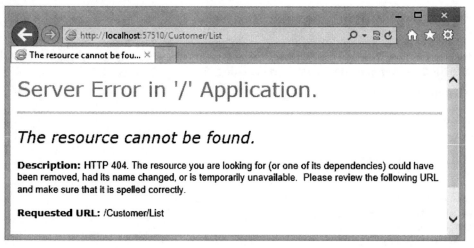

Figure 17-6. Using the method name as the action when the ActionName attribute has been applied

There are two main reasons why you might want to override a method name in this way:

- You can then accept an action name that wouldn't be legal as a C# method name (for example, [ActionName("User-Registration")]).

- If you want to have two different C# methods that accept the same set of parameters and should handle the same action name, but in response to different HTTP request types (for example, one with [HttpGet] and the other with [HttpPost]), you can give the methods different C# names to satisfy the compiler, but then use [ActionName] to map them both to the same action name.

One oddity that arises when using this attribute is that Visual Studio will use the original method name in the Add View dialog box. So, if you right-click the List method and select Add View, you see the dialog box shown in Figure 17-7.

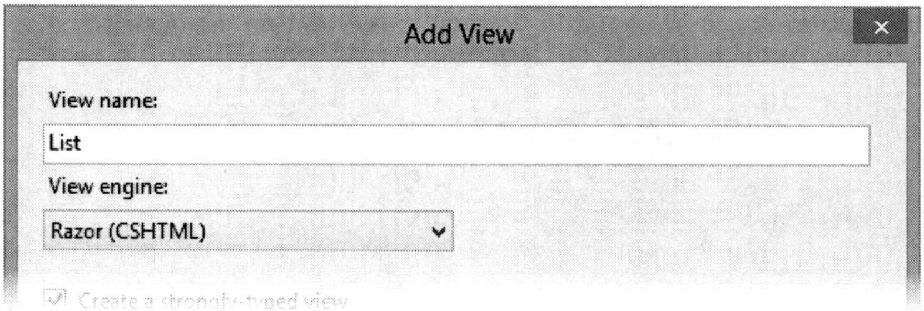

Figure 17-7. Visual Studio doesn't detect the ActionName attribute

This is a problem because the MVC Framework will look for the default views based on the action name, which is List in our example, as defined by the attribute. When creating the default view for an action method that use the ActionName attribute, you must make sure that the name matches the attribute value and not the C# method name.

Using Action Method Selection

It is often the case that a controller will contain several actions with the same name. This can be because there are multiple methods, each with different parameters, or because you used the ActionName attribute so that multiple methods represent the same action.

In these situations, the MVC Framework needs some help selecting the appropriate action with which to process a request. The mechanism for doing this is called *action method selection*. It allows you to define kinds of requests that an action is willing to process. You have already seen an example of action method selection when we restricted an action using the HttpPost attribute when we built the SportsStore application. We had two methods called Checkout in the Cart controller and we used the HttpPost attribute to indicate that one of them was to be used only for HTTP POST requests, as shown in Listing 17-16.

Listing 17-16. Using the HttpPost Attribute

```
using SportsStore.Domain.Abstract;
using SportsStore.Domain.Entities;
using SportsStore.WebUI.Models;
using System;
using System.Collections.Generic;
using System.Linq;
using System.Web;
using System.Web.Mvc;

namespace SportsStore.WebUI.Controllers {

    public class CartController : Controller {

        // ...other instance members omitted for brevity...

        [HttpPost]
        public ViewResult Checkout(Cart cart, ShippingDetails shippingDetails) {
            if (cart.Lines.Count() == 0) {
                ModelState.AddModelError("", "Sorry, your cart is empty!");
            }

            if (ModelState.IsValid) {
                orderProcessor.ProcessOrder(cart, shippingDetails);
                cart.Clear();
                return View("Completed");
            } else {
                return View(shippingDetails);
            }
        }

        public ViewResult Checkout() {
            return View(new ShippingDetails());
        }
    }

}
```

The action invoker uses action method selectors to resolve ambiguity when selecting an action. In Listing 17-16, there are two candidates for the Checkout action. The invoker gives preference to the actions that have selectors. In this case, the HttpPost selector is evaluated to see if the request can be processed. If it can, then this is the method that will be used. If not, then the *other* method will be used.

There are built-in attributes that work as selectors for the different kinds of HTTP requests: HttpPost for POST requests, HttpGet for GET requests, HttpPut for PUT requests, and so on. Another built-in attribute is NonAction, which indicates to the action invoker that a method that would otherwise be considered a valid action method should not be used. You can see how we have applied the NonAction attribute in Listing 17-17, where we have defined a new action method in the Customer controller.

Listing 17-17. Using the NonAction Selector

```
using ControllerExtensibility.Models;
using System.Web.Mvc;

namespace ControllerExtensibility.Controllers {
    public class CustomerController : Controller {

        // ...other action methods omitted for brevity...

        [NonAction]
        public ActionResult MyAction() {
            return View();
        }
    }
}
```

The MyAction method in the listing will not be considered as an action method, even though it meets all of the criteria that the invoker looks for. This is useful for ensuring that you do not expose the workings of your controller classes as actions. Of course, normally such methods should simply be marked private, which will prevent them from being invoked as actions; however, [NonAction] is useful if for some reason you must mark such as method as public. Requests for URLs that target NonAction methods will generate 404–Not Found errors, as shown in Figure 17-8.

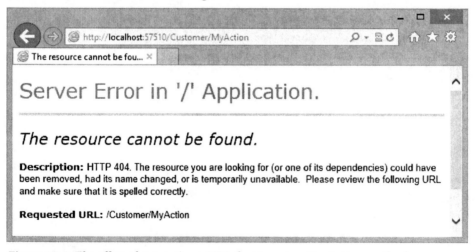

Figure 17-8. The effect of requesting a URL that targets a NonAction method

Creating a Custom Action Method Selector

Action method selectors are derived from the `ActionMethodSelectorAttribute` class, which is shown in Listing 17-18.

Listing 17-18. The ActionMethodSelectorAttribute Class

```
using System.Reflection;

namespace System.Web.Mvc {
    [AttributeUsage(AttributeTargets.Method, AllowMultiple = false, Inherited = true)]
    public abstract class ActionMethodSelectorAttribute : Attribute {

        public abstract bool IsValidForRequest(ControllerContext controllerContext,
            MethodInfo methodInfo);
    }
}
```

The `ActionMethodSelectorAttribute` is abstract and defines one abstract method: `IsValidForRequest`. The parameters for this method are a `ControllerContext` object, which allows you to inspect the request, and a `MethodInfo` object, which you can use to get information about the method to which your selector has been applied. You return `true` from `IsValidForRequest` if the method is able to process a request, and `false` otherwise. We created a simple custom action method selector called `LocalAttribute` in the `Infrastructure` folder of the example project, as shown in Listing 17-19.

Listing 17-19. A Custom Action Method Selector

```
using System.Reflection;
using System.Web.Mvc;

namespace ControllerExtensibility.Infrastructure {
    public class LocalAttribute : ActionMethodSelectorAttribute {

        public override bool IsValidForRequest(ControllerContext controllerContext,
            MethodInfo methodInfo) {

            return controllerContext.HttpContext.Request.IsLocal;
        }
    }
}
```

We have overridden the `IsValidForRequest` method so that it returns true when the request originates from the local machine. To demonstrate the custom action method selector, we have created a Home controller in the example project, as shown in Listing 17-20.

Listing 17-20. The Home Controller

```
using System.Web.Mvc;
using ControllerExtensibility.Infrastructure;
using ControllerExtensibility.Models;

namespace ControllerExtensibility.Controllers {
    public class HomeController : Controller {

        public ActionResult Index() {
```

```
            return View("Result", new Result {
                ControllerName = "Home", ActionName = "Index"
            });
        }

        [ActionName("Index")]
        public ActionResult LocalIndex() {
            return View("Result", new Result {
                ControllerName = "Home", ActionName = "LocalIndex"
            });
        }
    }
}
```

We have used the `ActionName` attribute to create a situation in which there are two `Index` action methods. At this point, the action invoker doesn't have any way to figure out which one should be used when a request for the /Home/Index URL arrives and will generate the error shown in Figure 17-9 when such a request is received.

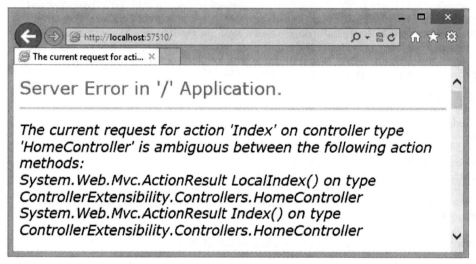

Figure 17-9. The error shown when there are ambiguous action method names

To resolve this situation, we can apply our method selection attribute to one of the ambiguous method, as shown in Listing 17-21.

Listing 17-21. Applying the Method Selection Attribute

```
...
[Local]
[ActionName("Index")]
public ActionResult LocalIndex() {
    return View("Result", new Result {
        ControllerName = "Home", ActionName = "LocalIndex"
    });
}
...
```

If you restart the application and navigate to the root URL from a browser running on the local machine, you will see that the MVC Framework takes the method selection attribute into account to resolve the ambiguity between the methods in the controller class, as shown in Figure 17-10.

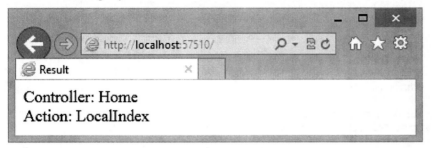

Figure 17-10. Using a method selection attribute to resolve action method ambiguity

---

THE ACTION METHOD DISAMBIGUATION PROCESS

Now that you have seen inside the action method selector base class, you can understand how the action invoker selects an action method. The invoker starts the process with a list of possible candidates, which are the controller methods that meet the action method criteria. Then it goes through the following process:

> The invoker discards any method based on name. Only methods that have the same name as the target action or have a suitable ActionName attribute are kept on the list.

> The invoker discards any method that has an action method selector attribute that returns false for the current request.

> If there is exactly one action method with a selector left, then this is the method that is used. If there is more than one method with a selector, then an exception is thrown, because the action invoker cannot disambiguate between the available methods.

> If there are no action methods with selectors, then the invoker looks at those without selectors. If there is exactly one such method, then this is the one that is invoked. If there is more than one method without a selector, an exception is thrown, because the invoker can't choose between them.

Handling Unknown Actions

If the action invoker is unable to find an action method to invoke, it returns false from its InvokeAction method. When this happens, the Controller class calls its HandleUnknownAction method. By default, this method returns a 404–Not Found response to the client. This is the most useful thing that a controller can do for most applications, but you can choose to override this method in your controller class if you want to do something special. Listing 17-22 provides a demonstration of overriding the HandleUnknownAction method in the Home controller.

Listing 17-22. Overriding the HandleUnknownAction Method

```
using System.Web.Mvc;
using ControllerExtensibility.Infrastructure;
using ControllerExtensibility.Models;

namespace ControllerExtensibility.Controllers {
    public class HomeController : Controller {

        // ...other action methods omitted for brevity...

        protected override void HandleUnknownAction(string actionName) {
            Response.Write(string.Format("You requested the {0} action", actionName));
        }
    }
}
```

If you start the application and navigate to a URL that targets a nonexistent action method, you will see the response shown in Figure 17-11.

Figure 17-11. Dealing with requests for action methods that do not exist

Improving Performance with Specialized Controllers

The MVC Framework provides two special kinds of controllers that may improve the performance of your MVC web applications. Like all performance optimizations, these controllers represent compromises, either in ease of use or with reduced functionality. In the follow sections, we will demonstrate both kinds of controllers and outline their benefits and shortcomings.

Using Sessionless Controllers

By default, controllers support *session state*, which can be used to store data values across requests, making life easier for the MVC programmer. Creating and maintaining session state is an involved process. Data must be stored and retrieved, and the sessions themselves must be managed so that they expire appropriately. Session data consumes server memory or space in some other storage location, and needing to synchronize the data across multiple Web servers makes it harder to run your application on a server farm.

In order to simplify session state, ASP.NET will process only one query for a given session at a time. If the client makes multiple overlapping requests, they will be queued up and processed sequentially by the server. The benefit is that you do not need to worry about multiple requests modifying the same data. The downside is that you do not get the request throughput you might like.

Not all controllers need the session state features. In such cases, you can improve the performance of your application by avoiding work involved in maintaining session state. You do this by using *sessionless controllers*. These are just like regular controllers, with two exceptions: the MVC Framework will not load or store session state when they are used to process a request, and overlapping requests can be processed simultaneously.

Managing Session State in a Custom IControllerFactory

At the start of this chapter, we showed you that the IControllerFactory interface contained a method called GetControllerSessionBehaviour, which returns a value from the SessionStateBehaviour enumeration. That enumeration contains four values that controls the session state configuration of a controller. The four values are described in Table 17-3.

Table 17-3. The Values of the SessionStateBehavior Enumeration

Value	Description
Default	Use the default ASP.NET behavior, which is to determine the session state configuration from the HttpContext.
Required	Full read-write session state is enabled.
ReadOnly	Read-only session state is enabled.
Disabled	Session state is disabled entirely.

A controller factory that implements the IControllerFactory interface directly sets the session state behavior for controllers by returning SessionStateBehavior values from the GetControllerSessionBehavior method. The parameters to this method are a RequestContext object and a string containing the name of the controller. You can return any of the four values shown in the table, and you can return different values for different controllers. We have changed the implementation of the GetControllerSessionBehavior method in the CustomControllerFactory class that we created earlier in the chapter, as shown in Listing 17-23.

Listing 17-23. Defining Session State Behavior for a Controller

```
...
public SessionStateBehavior GetControllerSessionBehavior(RequestContext
    requestContext, string controllerName) {

    switch (controllerName) {
        case "Home":
            return SessionStateBehavior.ReadOnly;
        case "Product":
            return SessionStateBehavior.Required;
        default:
            return SessionStateBehavior.Default;
    }
}
...
```

Managing Session State Using DefaultControllerFactory

When you are using the built-in controller factory, you can control the session state by applying the SessionState attribute to individual controller classes, as shown in Listing 17-24 where we have created a new controller called FastController.

Listing 17-24. Using the SessionState Attribute

```
using System.Web.Mvc;
using System.Web.SessionState;
using ControllerExtensibility.Models;

namespace ControllerExtensibility.Controllers {

    [SessionState(SessionStateBehavior.Disabled)]
    public class FastController : Controller {

        public ActionResult Index() {
            return View("Result", new Result {
                ControllerName = "Fast ",ActionName = "Index"
            });
        }
    }
}
```

The SessionState attribute is applied to the controller class and affects all of the actions in the controller. The sole parameter to the attribute is a value from the SessionStateBehavior enumeration (see Table 17-3). In the example, we have disabled session state entirely, which means that if we try to set a session value in the controller, like this:

```
Session["Message"] = "Hello";
```

or try to read back from the session state in a view, like this:

```
Message: @Session["Message"]
```

the MVC Framework will throw an exception when the action is invoked or the view is rendered.

■ **Tip**   When session state is Disabled, the HttpContext.Session property returns null.

If you have specified the ReadOnly behavior, then you can read values that have been set by other controllers, but you will still get a runtime exception if you try to set or modify a value. You can get details of the session through the HttpContext.Session object but trying to alter any values causes an error.

■ **Tip**   If you are simply trying to pass data from the controller to the view, consider using the View Bag feature instead, which is not affected by the SessionState attribute.

Using Asynchronous Controllers

The underlying ASP.NET platform maintains a pool of .NET threads that are used to process client requests. This pool is called the *worker thread pool*, and the threads are called *worker threads*. When a request is received, a worker thread is taken from the pool and given the job of processing the request.

When the request has been processed, the worker thread is returned to the pool, so that it is available to process new requests as they arrive. There are two key benefits of using thread pools for ASP.NET applications:

- By reusing worker threads, you avoid the overhead of creating a new one each time you process a request.

- By having a fixed number of worker threads available, you avoid the situation where you are processing more simultaneous requests than your server can handle.

The worker thread pool works best when requests can be processed in a short period of time. This is the case for most MVC applications. However, if you have actions that depend on other servers and take a long time to complete, then you can reach the point where all of your worker threads are tied up waiting for other systems to complete their work.

■ **Note** In this section, we assume that you are familiar with the Task Parallel Library (TPL). If you want to learn about the TPL, see Adam's book on the topic, called *Pro .NET Parallel Programming* in C# which is published by Apress.

Your server is capable of doing more work—after all, you are just waiting, which takes up very little of your resources—but because you have tied up all of your worker threads, incoming requests are being queued up. You will be in the odd state of your application grinding to a halt while the server is largely idle.

■ **Caution** At this point, some readers are thinking that they can write a worker thread pool that is tailored to their application. *Do not do it.* Writing concurrent code is easy. Writing concurrent code *that works* is difficult. If you are new to concurrent programming, then you lack the required skills. Our advice is to stick with the default pool. If you are experienced in concurrent programming, then you already know that the benefits will be marginal compared with the effort of coding and testing a new thread pool.

The solution to this problem is to use an *asynchronous controller*. This increases the overall performance of your application, but does not bring any benefits to the execution of your asynchronous operations.

■ **Note** Asynchronous controllers are useful only for actions that are I/O- or network-bound and *not* CPU-intensive. The problem you are trying to solve with asynchronous controllers is a mismatch between the pool model and the type of request you are processing. The pool is intended to ensure that each request gets a decent slice of the server resources, but you end up with a set of worker threads that are doing nothing. If you use additional background threads for CPU-intensive actions, then you will dilute the server resources across too many simultaneous requests.

Creating the Example

To begin our exploration of asynchronous controllers, we are going to show you an example of the kind of problem that they are intended to solve. Listing 17-25 shows a regular synchronous controller called RemoteData that we added to the example project.

Listing 17-25. A Problematic Synchronous Controller

```
using System.Web.Mvc;
using ControllerExtensibility.Models;

namespace ControllerExtensibility.Controllers {
    public class RemoteDataController : Controller {

        public ActionResult Data() {
            RemoteService service = new RemoteService();
            string data = service.GetRemoteData();
            return View((object)data);
        }
    }
}
```

This controller contains an action method, Data, which creates an instance of the model class RemoteService and calls the GetRemoteData method on it. This method is an example of a time-consuming, low-CPU activity. The RemoteService class is shown in Listing 17-26.

Listing 17-26. A Model Entity with a Time-Consuming, Low-CPU Method

```
using System.Threading;

namespace ControllerExtensibility.Models {
    public class RemoteService {

        public string GetRemoteData() {
            Thread.Sleep(2000);
            return "Hello from the other side of the world";
        }
    }
}
```

Okay, we admit it—we have faked the GetRemoteData method. In the real world, this method could be retrieving complex data across a slow network connection, but to keep things simple, we have used the Thread.Sleep method to simulate a two-second delay. We have also created a simple view, called Data.cshtml, as shown in Listing 17-27.

Listing 17-27. The Data View

```
@model string

@{
    Layout = null;
}

<!DOCTYPE html>
```

```html
<html>
<head>
    <meta name="viewport" content="width=device-width" />
    <title>Data</title>
</head>
<body>
    <div>
        Data: @Model
    </div>
</body>
</html>
```

When you run the application and navigate to the /RemoteData/Data URL, the action method is invoked, the RemoteService object is created, and the GetRemoteData method is called. After two seconds (simulating a real operation) the data is returned from the GetRemoteData method, passed to the view and rendered—as Figure 17-12.

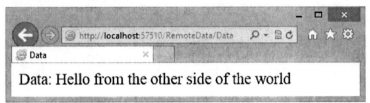

Figure 17-12. Navigating to the /RemoteData/Data URL

The problem here is that the worker thread that was handling our request was idle for two seconds—it wasn't doing anything useful, and it was not available for handling other requests while it was waiting.

Creating an Asynchronous Controller

Having shown you the problem we are going to solve, we can now move on to create the asynchronous controller. There are two ways to create an asynchronous controller. One is to implement the System.Web.Mvc.Async.IAsyncController interface, which is the asynchronous equivalent of IController. We are not going to demonstrate that approach, because it requires so much explanation of the .NET concurrent programming facilities.

■ **Tip** Not all actions in an asynchronous controller need to be asynchronous. You can include synchronous methods as well, and they will behave as expected.

We want to stay focused on the MVC Framework, which is why we will demonstrate the second approach: to derive your controller class from System.Web.Mvc.AsyncController, which implements IAsyncController for you. In previous version of the .NET Framework, creating asynchronous controllers was a complex process and required splitting the action into two methods. The new await and async keywords, which we described in Chapter 4, have simplified this process a lot: you create a new Task object and await its response, as shown in Listing 17-28.

■ **Tip** The old method of creating asynchronous action methods is still supported, although the approach we describe here is much more elegant and the one we recommend. One artifact of the old approach is that you can't use action method names that end with Async (e.g. IndexAsync) or Completed (e.g. IndexCompleted).

Listing 17-28. Creating an Asynchronous Controller without Modifying the Methods It Calls

```
using System.Web.Mvc;
using ControllerExtensibility.Models;
using System.Threading.Tasks;

namespace ControllerExtensibility.Controllers {
    public class RemoteDataController : AsyncController {

        public async Task<ActionResult> Data() {
            string data = await Task<string>.Factory.StartNew(() => {
                return new RemoteService().GetRemoteData();
            });

            return View((object)data);
        }
    }
}
```

We have highlighted the changes that are required to make the RemoteData controller asynchronous. In addition to changing the base class to AsyncController, we have refactored the action method so that it returns a Task<ActionResult>, applied the async and await keywords and created a Task<string>, which is responsible for calling the GetRemoteData method.

Consuming Asynchronous Methods in a Controller

You can also use an asynchronous controller to consume asynchronous methods elsewhere in your application. To demonstrate this, we have added an asynchronous method to the RemoteService class, as shown in Listing 17-29.

Listing 17-29. Adding an Asynchronous Method to the RemoteService Class

```
using System.Threading;
using System.Threading.Tasks;

namespace ControllerExtensibility.Models {
    public class RemoteService {

        public string GetRemoteData() {
            Thread.Sleep(2000);
            return "Hello from the other side of the world";
        }

        public async Task<string> GetRemoteDataAsync() {
            return await Task<string>.Factory.StartNew(() => {
                Thread.Sleep(2000);
                return "Hello from the other side of the world";
            });
        }
    }
}
```

The result from the GetRemoteDataAsync method is a Task<string>, which yields the same message as the synchronous method when it is completed. In Listing 17-30, you can see how we have consumed this asynchronous method in a new action method that we added to the RemoteData controller.

Listing 17-30. Consuming Asynchronous Methods in the RemoteData Controller

```
using System.Web.Mvc;
using ControllerExtensibility.Models;
using System.Threading.Tasks;

namespace ControllerExtensibility.Controllers {
    public class RemoteDataController : AsyncController {

        public async Task<ActionResult> Data() {
            string data = await Task<string>.Factory.StartNew(() => {
                return new RemoteService().GetRemoteData();
            });

            return View((object)data);
        }

        public async Task<ActionResult> ConsumeAsyncMethod() {
            string data = await new RemoteService().GetRemoteDataAsync();
            return View("Data", (object)data);
        }
    }
}
```

You can see that both action methods follow the same basic pattern and that the different is where the `Task` object is created. The result of calling either action method is that the worker thread is not tied up while we wait for the `GetRemoteData` call to complete—which means that the thread is available to process other requests, which can significantly improve the performance of your MVC Framework application.

Summary

In this chapter, you have seen how the MVC Framework creates controllers and invokes methods. We have explored and customized the built-in implementations of the key interfaces, and created custom versions to demonstrate how they work. You have learned how action method selectors can be used to differentiate between action methods and seen some specialized kinds of controllers that can be used to increase the request processing capability of your applications.

The underlying theme of this chapter is extensibility. Almost every aspect of the MVC Framework can be modified or replaced entirely. For most projects, the default behaviors are entirely sufficient. But having a working knowledge of how the MVC Framework fits together helps you to make informed design and coding decisions (and it is just plain interesting).

CHAPTER 18

■ ■ ■

Views

In Chapter 15, you saw how action methods can return **ActionResult** objects. As you learned, the most commonly used action result is **ViewResult**, which causes a view to be rendered and returned to the client.

You have seen views being used in many examples already, so you know roughly what they do. In this chapter, we will focus and clarify that knowledge. We will begin by showing you how the MVC Framework handles **ViewResults** using *view engines*, including demonstrating how to create a custom view engine. Next, we will describe techniques for working effectively with the built-in Razor View Engine. Then we will cover how to create and use partial views, child actions, and Razor sections. These are all essential topics for effective MVC development.

Creating a Custom View Engine

We are going to start this chapter by diving in at the deep end. We will create a custom view engine. You do not need to do this for most projects. The MVC Framework includes two built-in view engines that are full-featured and well-tested:

- The Razor engine, the one we have been using in this book, was introduced with MVC version 3. It has a simple and elegant syntax, which we described in Chapter 5.

- The legacy ASPX engine (also known as the Web Forms view engine) uses the ASP.NET Web Forms <%...%> tag syntax. This engine is useful for maintaining compatibility with older MVC applications.

The value in creating a custom view engine is to demonstrate how the request processing pipeline works and complete your knowledge of how the MVC Framework operates. This includes understanding just how much freedom view engines have in translating a **ViewResult** into a response to the client. View engines implement the **IViewEngine** interface, which is shown in Listing 18-1.

Listing 18-1. The IViewEngine Interface

```
namespace System.Web.Mvc {
    public interface IViewEngine {
        ViewEngineResult FindPartialView(ControllerContext controllerContext,
            string partialViewName, bool useCache);

        ViewEngineResult FindView(ControllerContext controllerContext,
            string viewName, string masterName, bool useCache);

        void ReleaseView(ControllerContext controllerContext, IView view);
    }
}
```

The role of a view engine is to translate requests for views into `ViewEngineResult` objects. The first two methods in the interface, `FindView` and `FindPartialView`, are passed parameters that describe the request and the controller that processed it (a `ControllerContext` object), the name of the view and its layout, and whether the view engine is allowed to reuse a previous result from its cache. These methods are called when a `ViewResult` is being processed. The final method, `ReleaseView`, is called when a view is no longer needed.

▓ **Note** The MVC Framework support for view engines is implemented by the `ControllerActionInvoker` class, which is the built-in implementation of the `IActionInvoker` interface, as described in Chapter 15. You will not have automatic access to the view engines feature if you have implemented your own action invoker or controller factory directly from the `IActionInvoker` or `IControllerFactory` interfaces.

The `ViewEngineResult` class allows a view engine to respond to the MVC Framework when a view is requested. We have shown the `ViewEngineResult` class in Listing 18-2.

Listing 18-2. The ViewEngineResult Class

```
using System.Collections.Generic;

namespace System.Web.Mvc {
    public class ViewEngineResult {

        public ViewEngineResult(IEnumerable<string> searchedLocations) {
            if (searchedLocations == null) {
                throw new ArgumentNullException("searchedLocations");
            }
            SearchedLocations = searchedLocations;
        }

        public ViewEngineResult(IView view, IViewEngine viewEngine) {
            if (view == null) { throw new ArgumentNullException("view");}
            if (viewEngine == null) { throw new ArgumentNullException("viewEngine");}
            View = view;
            ViewEngine = viewEngine;
        }

        public IEnumerable<string> SearchedLocations { get; private set; }
        public IView View { get; private set; }
        public IViewEngine ViewEngine { get; private set; }
    }
}
```

You express a result by choosing one of the two constructors. If your view engine is able to provide a view for a request, then you create a `ViewEngineResult` using this constructor:

```
...
public ViewEngineResult(IView view, IViewEngine viewEngine)
...
```

The parameters to this constructor are an implementation of the IView interface and a view engine (so that the ReleaseView method can be called later). If your view engine cannot provide a view for a request, then you use this constructor:

```
...
public ViewEngineResult(IEnumerable<string> searchedLocations)
...
```

The parameter for this version is an enumeration of the places searched you to find a view. This information is displayed to the user if no view can be found, as we will demonstrate later.

■ **Note** You are not alone if you think that the ViewEngineResult class is a little awkward. Expressing outcomes using different versions of a class constructor is an odd approach and does not really fit with the rest of the MVC Framework design. We do not know why the designers took this approach, but we are, sadly, stuck with it. We had hoped that this would be sorted out in the MVC 4 release, but sadly it was not.

The last building block of the view engine system is the IView interface, which is shown in Listing 18-3.

Listing 18-3. The IView Interface

```
using System.IO;

namespace System.Web.Mvc {
    public interface IView {
        void Render(ViewContext viewContext, TextWriter writer);
    }
}
```

We pass an IView implementation to the constructor of a ViewEngineResult object, which is then returned from our view engine methods. The MVC Framework calls the Render method. The ViewContext parameter gives us information about the request from the client and the output from the action method. The TextWriter parameter is for writing output to the client.

As we said earlier, the simplest way to see how this works—how IViewEngine, IView, and ViewEngineResult fit together—is to create a view engine. We are going to create a simple view engine that returns one kind of view. This view will render a result that contains information about the request and the view data produced by the action method. This approach lets us demonstrate the way that view engines operate without getting bogged down in parsing view templates.

Creating the Example Project

Our example project for this chapter is called Views and we created it using the Empty template option. We created a Home controller, which you can see in Listing 18-4.

Listing 18-4. The Home Controller in the Views Project

```
using System;
using System.Web.Mvc;

namespace Views.Controllers {
```

```
    public class HomeController : Controller {

        public ActionResult Index() {

            ViewData["Message"] = "Hello, World";
            ViewData["Time"] = DateTime.Now.ToShortTimeString();
            return View("DebugData");
        }

        public ActionResult List() {
            return View();
        }
    }
}
```

We have not created any views for this project because we are going to implement a custom view engine rather than relying on Razor.

Creating a Custom IView

We are going to start by creating our implementation of IView. We added an Infrastructure folder to the example project and created a new class file within it called DebugDataView, which is shown in Listing 18-5.

Listing 18-5. A Custom IView Implementation

```
using System.IO;
using System.Web.Mvc;

namespace Views.Infrastructure {
    public class DebugDataView : IView {

        public void Render(ViewContext viewContext, TextWriter writer) {

            Write(writer, "---Routing Data---");
            foreach (string key in viewContext.RouteData.Values.Keys) {
                Write(writer, "Key: {0}, Value: {1}",
                    key, viewContext.RouteData.Values[key]);
            }

            Write(writer, "---View Data---");
            foreach (string key in viewContext.ViewData.Keys) {
                Write(writer, "Key: {0}, Value: {1}", key,
                    viewContext.ViewData[key]);
            }
        }

        private void Write(TextWriter writer, string template, params object[] values) {
            writer.Write(string.Format(template, values) + "<p/>");
        }
    }
}
```

This view demonstrates the use of the two parameters to the Render method: we take values from the ViewContext and write a response to the client using the TextWriter. You will see how this class functions when we have created more of our custom view engine implementation.

Creating an IViewEngine Implementation

Remember that the purpose of the view engine is to produce an **ViewEngineResult** object that contains either an **IView** or a list of the places that searched for a suitable view. Now that we have an **IView** implementation to work with, we can create the view engine. We created a new class file called **DebugDataViewEngine.cs** in the Infrastructure folder, the content of which are shown in Listing 18-6.

Listing 18-6. A Custom IViewEngine Implementation

```
using System.Web.Mvc;

namespace Views.Infrastructure {
    public class DebugDataViewEngine : IViewEngine {

        public ViewEngineResult FindView(ControllerContext controllerContext,
                string viewName, string masterName, bool useCache) {

            if (viewName == "DebugData") {
                return new ViewEngineResult(new DebugDataView(), this);
            } else {
                return new ViewEngineResult(new string[]
                    { "No view (Debug Data View Engine)" });
            }
        }

        public ViewEngineResult FindPartialView(ControllerContext controllerContext,
                string partialViewName, bool useCache) {

            return new ViewEngineResult(new string[]
                { "No view (Debug Data View Engine)" });
        }

        public void ReleaseView(ControllerContext controllerContext, IView view) {
            // do nothing
        }
    }
}
```

We are going to support only a single view, which is called **DebugData**. When we see a request for that view, we will return a new instance of our custom **IView** implementation, like this:

```
...
return new ViewEngineResult(new DebugDataView(), this);
...
```

If we were implementing a more serious view engine, we would use this opportunity to search for templates, take into account the layout and provided caching settings. As it is, our simple example requires us to create only a new instance of the **DebugDataView** class. If we receive a request for a view other than **DebugData**, we return a **ViewEngineResult**, like this:

```
...
return new ViewEngineResult(new string[] { "No view (Debug Data View Engine)" });
...
```

The **IViewEngine** interface presumes that the view engine has places it needs to look to find views. This is a reasonable assumption, because views are typically template files that are stored as files in the project. In our case, we do not have anywhere to look, so we just return a dummy location which will indicate that we were asked for a view that we cannot deliver.

Our custom view engine doesn't support partial views, so we return a result from the `FindPartialView` method that indicates we do not have a view to offer. We will return to the topic of partial views and how they are handled in the Razor engine later in the chapter. We have not implemented the `ReleaseView` method, because there are no resources that we need to release in our `IView` implementation, which is the usual purpose of this method.

Registering a Custom View Engine

We register view engines in the `Application_Start` method of `Global.asax`, as shown in Listing 18-7.

Listing 18-7. Registering a Custom View Engine Using Global.asax

```
using System.Web.Http;
using System.Web.Mvc;
using System.Web.Routing;
using Views.Infrastructure;

namespace Views {
    public class MvcApplication : System.Web.HttpApplication {
        protected void Application_Start() {
            AreaRegistration.RegisterAllAreas();

            ViewEngines.Engines.Add(new DebugDataViewEngine());

            WebApiConfig.Register(GlobalConfiguration.Configuration);
            FilterConfig.RegisterGlobalFilters(GlobalFilters.Filters);
            RouteConfig.RegisterRoutes(RouteTable.Routes);
        }
    }
}
```

The static `ViewEngine.Engines` collection contains the set of view engines that are installed in the application. The MVC Framework supports the idea of there being several engines installed in a single application. When a `ViewResult` is being processed, the action invoker obtains the set of installed view engines and calls their `FindView` methods in turn.

The action invoker stops calling `FindView` methods as soon as it receives a `ViewEngineResult` object that contains an `IView`. This means that the order in which engines are added to the `ViewEngines.Engines` collection is significant if two or more engines are able to service a request for the same view name. If you want your view to take precedence, then you can insert it at the start of the collection, like this:

```
...
ViewEngines.Engines.Insert(0, new DebugDataViewEngine());
...
```

Testing the View Engine

We are now in a position to test our view engine. If we start the application, the browser will automatically navigate to the root URL for the project, which will be mapped to the `Index` action in our `Home` controller. The action method uses the `View` method to return a `ViewResult` that specifies the `DebugData` view. You can see the result of this in Figure 18-1.

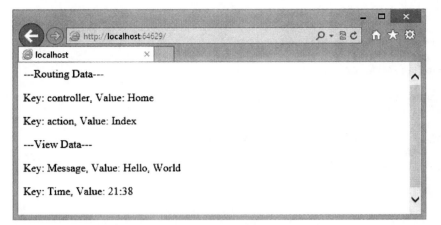

Figure 18-1. Using a Custom View Engine

This is the result of our `FindView` method being called for a view that we are able to process. If we navigate to the /Home/List URL, the MVC Framework will invoke the `List` action method, which calls the `View` method to request its default view—which is not one that we support. You can see the result in Figure 18-2.

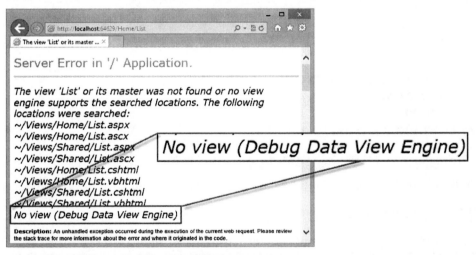

Figure 18-2. Requesting an unsupported view

You can see that our message is reported as one of the locations that have been searched for a view. Notice that Razor and ASPX views appear on the list as well—this is because those view engines are still being used. If we want to ensure that only our custom view engine is used, then we have to call the `Clear` method before we register our engine in the `Global.asax` file, as shown in Listing 18-8.

Listing 18-8. Removing the Other View Engines in the Example Application

```
using System.Web.Http;
using System.Web.Mvc;
using System.Web.Routing;
using Views.Infrastructure;
```

```
namespace Views {
    public class MvcApplication : System.Web.HttpApplication {
        protected void Application_Start() {
            AreaRegistration.RegisterAllAreas();

            ViewEngines.Engines.Clear();
            ViewEngines.Engines.Add(new DebugDataViewEngine());

            WebApiConfig.Register(GlobalConfiguration.Configuration);
            FilterConfig.RegisterGlobalFilters(GlobalFilters.Filters);
            RouteConfig.RegisterRoutes(RouteTable.Routes);
        }
    }
}
```

If we restart the application and navigate to /Home/List again, only our view engine will be used, as shown in Figure 18-3.

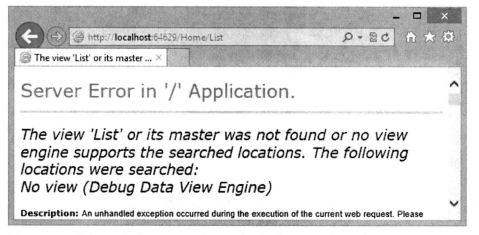

Figure 18-3. Using only the custom view engine in the example application

Working with the Razor Engine

In the previous section, we were able to create a custom view engine by implementing just two interfaces. Admittedly, we ended up with something very simple that generated very ugly views, but you saw how the concept of MVC extensibility continues throughout the request processing pipeline.

The complexity in a view engine comes from the system of view templates that include code fragments, support layouts, and are compiled to optimize performance. We did not do any of these things in our simple custom view engine, and we didn't need to, because the Razor engine takes care of all of that for us. The functionality that almost all MVC applications require is available in Razor. Only a vanishingly small number of projects need to go to the trouble of creating a custom view engine.

As a reminder, Razor is the view engine that was introduced with MVC 3 and replaced the previous view engine (known as the ASPX or Web Forms engine). You can still use the ASPX view engine but we recommend that you use Razor, as this is where Microsoft is investing its energy. We gave you a primer of the Razor syntax in Chapter 5. In this chapter, we are going to show you how to use other features to create and render Razor views. You will also learn how to customize the Razor engine.

Creating the Example Project

For this part of the chapter, we have created a new MVC project using the `Basic` template option. We called the project `WorkingWithRazor` and we created a `Home` controller, which is shown in Listing 18-9.

Listing 18-9. The Home Controller in the WorkingWithRazor Project

```
using System.Web.Mvc;

namespace WorkingWithRazor.Controllers {
    public class HomeController : Controller {

        public ActionResult Index() {
            string[] names = { "Apple", "Orange", "Pear" };
            return View(names);
        }
    }
}
```

We created a view called `Index.cshtml` for the `Home` controller, which was placed in the `/Views/Home` folder. You can see the contents of the view file in Listing 18-10.

Listing 18-10. The Contents of the View.cshtml File

```
@model string[]

@{
    ViewBag.Title = "Index";
}

This is a list of fruit names:

@foreach (string name in Model) {
    <span><b>@name</b></span>
}
```

Understanding Razor View Rendering

The Razor View Engine compiles the views in your applications to improve performance. The views are translated into C# classes, and then compiled, which is why you are able to include C# code fragments so easily. It is instructive to look at the source code that Razor views generate, because it helps to put many of the Razor features in context.

The views in an MVC application are not compiled until the application is started, so to see the classes that are created by Razor, you need to start the application and navigate to the `/Home/Index` action. The initial request to MVC application triggers the compilation process for all views. You can see the output from our request in Figure 18-4.

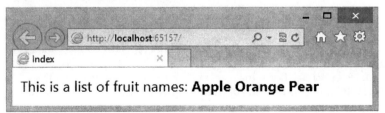

Figure 18-4. The output from the Index action method on the Home controller

Conveniently, classes generated from the view files are written to the disk as C# code files and then compiled, which means that you can see the C# statements that represent a view. You can find the generated files in c:\Users\<*yourLoginName*>\AppData\Local\Temp\Temporary ASP.NET Files on Windows 7 and Windows 8.

Finding the code file generated for a particular view requires a bit of poking around. There are usually a number of folders with cryptic names, and the names of the .cs files do not correspond to the names of the classes they contain. As an example, we found the generated class for the view in Listing 18-10 in a file called App_Web_cuymyfa4.0.cs in the root\bdd11980\ec057b05 folder. We have tidied up the class from our system to make it easier to read, as shown in Listing 18-11.

Listing 18-11. The Generated C# Class for a Razor View

```
namespace ASP {
    using System;
    using System.Collections.Generic;
    using System.IO;
    using System.Linq;
    using System.Net;
    using System.Web;
    using System.Web.Helpers;
    using System.Web.Security;
    using System.Web.UI;
    using System.Web.WebPages;
    using System.Web.Mvc;
    using System.Web.Mvc.Ajax;
    using System.Web.Mvc.Html;
    using System.Web.Optimization;
    using System.Web.Routing;


    public class _Page_Views_Home_Index_cshtml : System.Web.Mvc.WebViewPage<string[]> {

        public _Page_Views_Home_Index_cshtml() {
        }

        public override void Execute() {
            ViewBag.Title = "Index";
            WriteLiteral("\r\n\r\nThis is a list of fruit names:\r\n\r\n");

            foreach (string name in Model) {
                WriteLiteral("    <span><b>");
                Write(name);
                WriteLiteral("</b></span>\r\n");
            }
        }
    }
}
```

First, note that the class is derived from WebViewPage<T>, where T is the model type—WebViewPage<string[]> for our example. This is how strongly typed views are handled. Also notice the name of the class that has been generated: _Page_Views_Home_Index_cshtml. You can see how the path of the view file has been encoded in the class name. This is how Razor maps requests for views into instances of compiled classes.

In the Execute method, you can see how the statements and elements in the view have been handled. The code fragments that we prefixed with the @ symbol are expressed directly as C# statements. The HTML elements are handled with the WriteLiteral method, which writes the contents of the parameter to the result as they are given. This is opposed to the Write method, which is used for C# variables and encodes the string values to make them safe for use in an HTML page.

Both the Write and WriteLiteral methods write content to a TextWriter object. This is the same object that is passed to the IView.Render method, which you saw at the start of the chapter. The goal of a compiled Razor view is to generate the static and dynamic content and send it to the client via the TextWriter. This is useful to keep in mind when we look at HTML helper methods later in the chapter.

Configuring the View Search Locations

The Razor View Engine follows the convention established in earlier versions of the MVC Framework when looking for a view. For example, if you request the Index view associated with the Home controller, Razor looks through this list of views:

- ~/Views/Home/Index.cshtml

- ~/Views/Home/Index.vbhtml

- ~/Views/Shared/Index.cshtml

- ~/Views/Shared/Index.vbhtml

As you now know, Razor is not really looking for the view files on disk, because they have already been compiled into C# classes. Razor looks for the compiled class that represents these views. The .cshtml files are templates containing C# statements (the kind we are using), and the .vbhtml files contain Visual Basic statements.

You can change the view files that Razor searches for by creating a subclass of RazorViewEngine. This class is the Razor IViewEngine implementation. It builds on a series of base classes that define a set of properties that determine which view files are searched for. These properties are described in Table 18-1.

Table 18-1. *Razor View Engine Search Properties*

Property	Description	Default Value
ViewLocationFormats MasterLocationFormats PartialViewLocationFormats	The locations to look for views, partial views, and layouts	~/Views/{1}/{0}.cshtml, ~/Views/{1}/{0}.vbhtml, ~/Views/Shared/{0}.cshtml, ~/Views/Shared/{0}.vbhtml
AreaViewLocationFormats AreaMasterLocationFormats AreaPartialViewLocationFormats	The locations to look for views, partial views, and layouts for an area	~/Areas/{2}/Views/{1}/{0}.cshtml, ~/Areas/{2}/Views/{1}/{0}.vbhtml, ~/Areas/{2}/Views/Shared/{0}.cshtml, ~/Areas/{2}/Views/Shared/{0}.vbhtml

These properties predate the introduction of Razor, which why each set of three properties has the same values. Each property is an array of strings, which are expressed using the composite string formatting notation. The following are the parameter values that correspond to the placeholders:

- {0} represents the name of the view.

- {1} represents the name of the controller.

- {2} represents the name of the area.

To change the search locations, you create a new class that is derived from `RazorViewEngine` and change the values for one or more of the properties described in Table 18-1.

To demonstrate how to change the locations that are searched, we added an `Infrastructure` project in the example application and created a view engine called `CustomLocationViewEngine`, which is shown in Listing 18-12.

Listing 18-12. Changing the Search Locations in the Razor View Engine

```
using System.Web.Mvc;

namespace WorkingWithRazor.Infrastructure {
    public class CustomLocationViewEngine : RazorViewEngine {

        public CustomLocationViewEngine() {
            ViewLocationFormats = new string[]
                {"~/Views/{1}/{0}.cshtml", "~/Views/Common/{0}.cshtml"};
        }
    }
}
```

We have set a new value for the `ViewLocationFormats`. Our new array contains entries only for `.cshtml` files. In addition, we have changed the location we look for shared views to be `Views/Common`, rather than `Views/Shared`. We register our derived view engine using the `ViewEngines.Engines` collection in the `Application_Start` method of `Global.asax`, as shown in Listing 18-13.

Listing 18-13. Registering the Custom View Engine

```
using System.Web.Http;
using System.Web.Mvc;
using System.Web.Optimization;
using System.Web.Routing;
using WorkingWithRazor.Infrastructure;

namespace WorkingWithRazor {

    public class MvcApplication : System.Web.HttpApplication {
        protected void Application_Start() {
            AreaRegistration.RegisterAllAreas();

            ViewEngines.Engines.Clear();
            ViewEngines.Engines.Add(new CustomLocationViewEngine());

            WebApiConfig.Register(GlobalConfiguration.Configuration);
            FilterConfig.RegisterGlobalFilters(GlobalFilters.Filters);
            RouteConfig.RegisterRoutes(RouteTable.Routes);
            BundleConfig.RegisterBundles(BundleTable.Bundles);
        }
    }
}
```

Remember that the action invoker goes to each view engine in turn to see if a view can be found. By the time that we are able to add our view to the collection, it will already contain the standard Razor View Engine. To avoid competing with that implementation, we call the `Clear` method to remove any other view engines that may have been registered, and then call the `Add` method to register our custom implementation.

To demonstrate our change in locations, we created the **/Views/Common** folder and added a view file called List.cshtml. You can see the contents of this file in Listing 18-14.

Listing 18-14. The Contents of the /Views/Common/List.cshtml File

```
@{
    ViewBag.Title = "List";
}

<h3>This is the /Views/Common/List.cshtml View</h3>
```

To display this view, we have added a new action method to the Home controller, as shown in Listing 18-15.

Listing 18-15. Adding a New Action Method to the Home Controller

```
using System.Web.Mvc;

namespace WorkingWithRazor.Controllers {
    public class HomeController : Controller {

        public ActionResult Index() {
            string[] names = { "Apple", "Orange", "Pear" };
            return View(names);
        }

        public ActionResult List() {
            return View();
        }
    }
}
```

When we start the application and navigate to the /Home/List URL, our custom locations will be used to locate the List.cshtml view file in the /Views/Common folder, as shown in Figure 18-5.

Figure 18-5. The effect of custom locations in the view engine

Adding Dynamic Content to a Razor View

The whole purpose of views is to allow you to render parts of your domain model as a user interface. To do that, you need to be able to add *dynamic content* to views. Dynamic content is generated at runtime, and can be different for each and every request. This is opposed to *static content*, such as HTML, which you create when you are writing the application and is the same for each and every request. You can add dynamic content to views in the different ways described in Table 18-2.

Table 18-2. *Adding Dynamic Content to a View*

Technique	When to Use
Inline code	Use for small, self-contained pieces of view logic, such as `if` and `foreach` statements. This is the fundamental tool for creating dynamic content in views, and some of the other approaches are built on it. We introduced this technique in Chapter 5 and you have seen countless examples in the chapters since.
HTML helper methods	Use to generate single HTML elements or small collections of them, typically based on view model or view data values. The MVC Framework includes a number of useful HTML helper methods, and it is easy to create your own. HTML helper methods are the topic of Chapter 19.
Sections	Use for creating sections of content that will be inserted into layout at specific locations.
Partial views	Use for sharing subsections of view markup between views. Partial views can contain inline code, HTML helper methods, and references to other partial views. Partial views do not invoke an action method, so they cannot be used to perform business logic.
Child actions	Use for creating reusable UI controls or widgets that need to contain business logic. When you use a child action, it invokes an action method, renders a view, and injects the result into the response stream.

Two of these options are covered elsewhere in this book and we describe the others in the section that follow.

Using Sections

The Razor engine supports the concept of *sections*, which allow you to provide regions of content within a layout. Razor sections give greater control over which parts of the view are inserted into the layout and where they are placed. To demonstrate the sections feature, we have edited the /Views/Home/Index.cshtml file, as shown in Listing 18-16.

Listing 18-16. Defining a Section in a View

```
@model string[]

@{
    ViewBag.Title = "Index";
}

@section Header {
    <div class="view">
        @foreach (string str in new [] {"Home", "List", "Edit"}) {
            @Html.ActionLink(str, str, null, new { style = "margin: 5px" })
        }
    </div>
}
```

```
<div class="view">
    This is a list of fruit names:

    @foreach (string name in Model) {
        <span><b>@name</b></span>
    }
</div>

@section Footer {
    <div class="view">
        This is the footer
    </div>
}
```

We define sections using the Razor @section tag followed by a name for the section. In our example, we created sections called Header and Footer. The content of a section contains the usual mix of HTML markup and Razor tags.

You specify where in the layout you want your sections to be displayed using @RenderSection helper method. You can see how we have done this in Listing 18-17, which shows changes we have made to the ~/Views/Shared/_Layout.cshtml file.

■ **Tip**   Our custom view engine locations are still in use, which means that shared layouts are located in the /Views/Shared folder, even though shared views are located in the /Views/Common folder.

Listing 18-17. Using Sections in a Layout

```
<!DOCTYPE html>
<html>
<head>
    <meta charset="utf-8" />
    <meta name="viewport" content="width=device-width" />
    <style type="text/css">
        div.layout { background-color: lightgray;}
        div.view { border: thin solid black; margin: 10px 0;}
    </style>
    <title>@ViewBag.Title</title>
</head>
<body>
    @RenderSection("Header")

    <div class="layout">
        This is part of the layout
    </div>

    @RenderBody()

    <div class="layout">
        This is part of the layout
    </div>

    @RenderSection("Footer")
```

```
    <div class="layout">
        This is part of the layout
    </div>
</body>
</html>
```

When Razor parses the layout, the `RenderSection` helper method is replaced with the contents of the section in the view with the specified name. The parts of the view that are not contained with a section are inserted into the layout using the `RenderBody` helper.

You can see the effect of the sections by starting the application, as shown in Figure 18-6. We added some basic CSS styles to help make it clear which sections of the output are from the view and which are from the layout. This result is not pretty, but it neatly demonstrates how you can put regions of content from the view into specific locations in the layout.

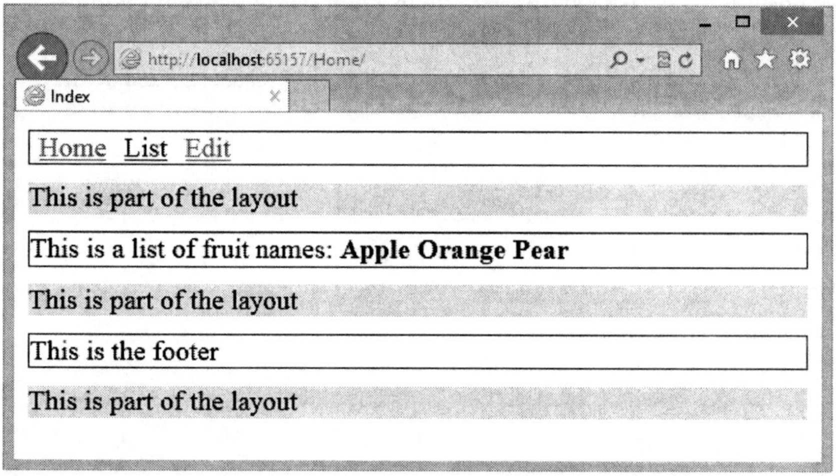

Figure 18-6. Using sections in a view to locate content in a layout

---

▒ **Note** A view can define only the sections that are referred to in the layout. The MVC Framework will throw an exception if you attempt to define sections in the view for which there is no corresponding `@RenderSection` helper call in the layout.

Mixing the sections in with the rest of the view is unusual. The convention is to define the sections at either the start or the end of the view, to make it easier to see which regions of content will be treated as sections and which will be captured by the `RenderBody` helper. Another approach, which we tend to use, is to define the view solely in terms of sections, including one for the body, as shown in Listing 18-18.

Listing 18-18. Defining a View in Terms of Razor Sections

```
@model string[]

@{
    ViewBag.Title = "Index";
}
```

```
@section Header {
    <div class="view">
        @foreach (string str in new [] {"Home", "List", "Edit"}) {
            @Html.ActionLink(str, str, null, new { style = "margin: 5px" })
        }
    </div>
}

@section Body {
    <div class="view">
        This is a list of fruit names:

        @foreach (string name in Model) {
            <span><b>@name</b></span>
        }
    </div>
}

@section Footer {
    <div class="view">
        This is the footer
    </div>
}
```

We find this makes for clearer views and reduces the chances of extraneous content being captured by RenderBody. To use this approach, we have to replace the call to the RenderBody helper with RenderSection("Body"), as shown in Listing 18-19.

Listing 18-19. Using RenderSection("Body") to Define a View

```
<!DOCTYPE html>
<html>
<head>
    <meta charset="utf-8" />
    <meta name="viewport" content="width=device-width" />
    <style type="text/css">
        div.layout { background-color: lightgray;}
        div.view { border: thin solid black; margin: 10px 0;}
    </style>
    <title>@ViewBag.Title</title>
</head>
<body>
    @RenderSection("Header")

    <div class="layout">
        This is part of the layout
    </div>

    @RenderSection("Body")

    <div class="layout">
        This is part of the layout
    </div>
```

```
    @RenderSection("Footer")

    <div class="layout">
        This is part of the layout
    </div>
</body>
</html>
```

Testing For Sections

You can check to see if a view has defined a specific section from the layout. This is a useful way to provide default content for a section if a view does not need or want to provide specific content. We have modified the _Layout.cshtml file to check to see if a Footer section is defined, as shown in Figure 18-20.

Listing 18-20. Checking Whether a Section Is Defined in a View

```
...
@if (IsSectionDefined("Footer")) {
    @RenderSection("Footer")
} else {
    <h4>This is the default footer</h4>
}
...
```

The IsSectionDefined helper takes the name of the section you want to check and returns true if the view you are rendering defines that section. In the example, we use this helper to determine if we should render some default content when the view does not define the Footer section.

Rendering Optional Sections

By default a view has to contain all of the sections for which there are RenderSection calls in the layout. If sections are missing, then the MVC Framework will report an exception to the user. To demonstrate this, we have added a new RenderSection call to the _Layout.cshtml file for a section called scripts, as shown in Listing 18-21—this is a section that Visual Studio adds to the layout by default when you create an MVC project using the Basic template option, but which we removed when we defined our initial content.

Listing 18-21. Adding a RenderSection Call to the Layout for which there is no Corresponding Section in the View

```
<!DOCTYPE html>
<html>
<head>
    <meta charset="utf-8" />
    <meta name="viewport" content="width=device-width" />
    <style type="text/css">
        div.layout { background-color: lightgray;}
        div.view { border: thin solid black; margin: 10px 0;}
    </style>
    <title>@ViewBag.Title</title>
</head>
<body>
    @RenderSection("Header")

    <div class="layout">
```

```
        This is part of the layout
    </div>

    @RenderSection("Body")

    <div class="layout">
        This is part of the layout
    </div>

    @if (IsSectionDefined("Footer")) {
        @RenderSection("Footer")
    } else {
        <h4>This is the default footer</h4>
    }

    @RenderSection("scripts")

    <div class="layout">
        This is part of the layout
    </div>
</body>
</html>
```

When we start the application and the Razor engine attempts to render the layout and the view, we see the error shown in Figure 18-7.

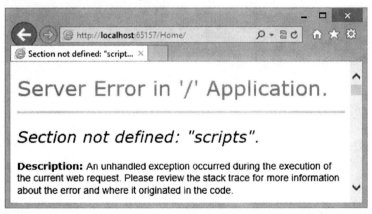

Figure 18-7. The error shown when there is a missing section

You can use the IsSectionDefined method to avoid making RenderSection calls for sections that the view does not define, but a more elegant approach is to use optional sections, which you do by passing an additional false value to the RenderSection method, as shown in Listing 18-22.

Listing 18-22. Making a Section Optional

```
...
@RenderSection("scripts", false)
...
```

This creates an optional section, the contents of which will be inserted into the result if the view defines it and which will not throw an exception otherwise.

Using Partial Views

We often want to use the same fragments of Razor tags and HTML markup in several different places in the application. Rather than duplicate the content, we can use *partial views*, which are separate view files that contain fragments of tags and markup that can be included in other views. In this section, we will show you how to create and use partial views, explain how they work, and demonstrate the techniques available for passing view data to a partial view.

Creating a Partial View

We start by creating a partial view called `MyPartial`. You create a partial view by right-clicking the `/Views/Shared` folder, selecting `Add` ➤ `View` from the pop-up menu, and making sure that the `Create as Partial View` option is checked, as shown in Figure 18-8.

Figure 18-8. Creating a partial view

A partial view is empty when it is created and we added the content you can see in Listing 18-23.

Listing 18-23. The Content of the MyPartial.cshtml File

```
<div>
    This is the message from the partial view.
    @Html.ActionLink("This is a link to the Index action", "Index")
</div>
```

We want to demonstrate that you can mix HTML markup and Razor tags, so we have defined a simple message and a call to the `ActionLink` helper method.

You consume a partial view by calling the `Partial` HTML helper method from within another view. To demonstrate this, we have made the changes to the `~/Views/Common/List.cshtml` view file shown in Listing 18-24.

Listing 18-24. Consuming a Partial View

```
@{
    ViewBag.Title = "List";
    Layout = null;
}

<h3>This is the /Views/Common/List.cshtml View</h3>

@Html.Partial("MyPartial")
```

We specify the name of the view file without the file extension. The view engine will look for the partial view that we have specified in the usual locations, which means the `/Views/Home` and `/Views/Shared` folders when we consume the partial view in a view that is being rendered for the `Home` controller. (We set the `Layout` variable to null so that we do not have to specify the sections we used earlier in the chapter.)

▪ **Tip**   The Razor View Engine looks for partial views in the same way that it looks for regular views (in the `~/Views/<controller>` and `~/Views/Shared` folders). This means that you can create specialized versions of partial views that are controller-specific and override partial views of the same name in the `Shared` folder. This may seem like an odd thing to do, but one of the most common uses of partial views is to render content in layouts, and this feature can be very handy.

You can see the effect of consuming the partial view by starting the application and navigating to the `/Home/List` URL, as shown in Figure 18-9.

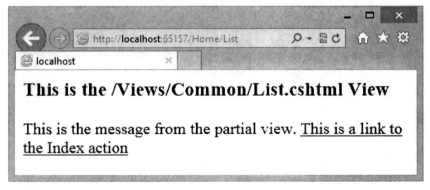

Figure 18-9. The effect of consuming a partial view

■ **Tip**   The call we made to the `ActionLink` helper method in the partial view takes its controller information from the request that is being processed. That means that when we specified the `Index` method, the a element will refer to the `Home` controller, since that was the controller that led to the partial view being rendered. If we consume the partial view in a view being rendered by another controller, then the `ActionLink` would generate a reference to that controller instead. We come back to the topic of HTML helper methods in Chapter 19.

Using Strongly Typed Partial Views

You can create strongly typed partial views, and then pass view model objects to be used when the partial view is rendered. To demonstrate this feature, we created a new strongly-typed partial view called `MyStronglyTypedPartial.cshtml` in the `/Views/Shared` folder. Creating a strongly typed partial is just like a regular partial, but you select or enter a type for the `Model` class option, as shown in Figure 18-10. We used the `IEnumerable<string>` type for our partial view.

Figure 18-10. Creating a strongly-typed partial view

You can see our additions to the partial view file that Visual Studio has created for us in Listing 18-25. When the file is created, it only contains the `@model` tag to specify the view model type.

Listing 18-25. Creating a Strongly Typed Partial View

```
@model IEnumerable<string>

<div>
    This is the message from the partial view.
    <ul>
        @foreach (string str in Model) {
            <li>@str</li>
        }
    </ul>
</div>
```

We use a Razor @foreach tag to display the contents of the view model object as items in an HTML list. To demonstrate the use of this partial view, we have updated the */Views/Common/List.cshtml* file, as shown in Listing 18-26.

Listing 18-26. Consuming a Strongly Typed Partial View

```
@{
    ViewBag.Title = "List";
    Layout = null;
}

<h3>This is the /Views/Common/List.cshtml View</h3>

@Html.Partial("MyStronglyTypedPartial", new [] {"Apple", "Orange", "Pear"})
```

The difference from the previous example is that we pass an additional argument to the Partial helper method which defines the view model object. You can see the strongly typed partial view in use by starting the application and navigating to the /Home/List URL, as shown in Figure 18-11.

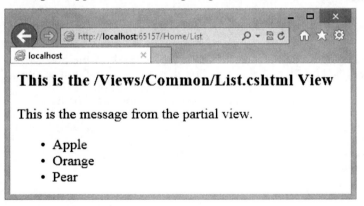

Figure 18-11. Consuming a strongly typed partial view

Using Child Actions

Child actions are action methods invoked from within a view. This lets you avoid repeating controller logic that you want to use in several places in the application. Child actions are to actions as partial views are to views.

You might want to use a child action whenever you want to display some data-driven widget that appears on multiple pages and contains data unrelated to the main action that is running. We used this technique in the SportsStore example to include a data-driven navigation menu on every page, without needing to supply the navigation data directly from every action method. The navigation data was supplied independently by the child action.

Creating a Child Action

Any action can be used as a child action. To demonstrate the child action feature, we have added a new action method to the Home controller, as shown in Listing 18-27.

Listing 18-27. Adding a Child Action to the Home Controller

```
using System.Web.Mvc;
using System;

namespace WorkingWithRazor.Controllers {
    public class HomeController : Controller {

        public ActionResult Index() {
            string[] names = { "Apple", "Orange", "Pear" };
            return View(names);
        }

        public ActionResult List() {
            return View();
        }

        [ChildActionOnly]
        public ActionResult Time() {
            return PartialView(DateTime.Now);
        }
    }
}
```

Our action method is called Time and it renders a partial view by calling the PartialView method (which we described in Chapter 15). The ChildActionOnly attribute ensures that an action method can be called only as a child method from within a view. An action method doesn't need to have this attribute to be used as a child action, but we tend to use this attribute to prevent the action methods from being invoked as a result of a user request.

Having defined an action method, we need to create the partial view that will be rendered when the action is invoked. Child actions are typically associated with partial views, although this is not compulsory. Listing 18-28 shows the /Views/Home/Time.cshtml view that we created for this demonstration. This is a strongly typed partial view whose view model is a DateTime object.

Listing 18-28. A Partial View for Use with a Child Action

```
@model DateTime

<p>The time is: @Model.ToShortTimeString()</p>
```

Rendering a Child Action

You invoke a child action using the `Html.Action` helper. With this helper, the action method is executed, the `ViewResult` is processed, and the output is injected into the response to the client. Listing 18-29 shows the changes we have made to the `/Views/Common/List.cshtml` file to render the child action.

Listing 18-29. Calling a Child Action from the List View

```
@{
    ViewBag.Title = "List";
    Layout = null;
}

<h3>This is the /Views/Common/List.cshtml View</h3>

@Html.Partial("MyStronglyTypedPartial", new [] {"Apple", "Orange", "Pear"})

@Html.Action("Time")
```

You can see the effect of the child action by starting the application and navigating to the `/Home/List` URL again, as shown in Figure 18-12.

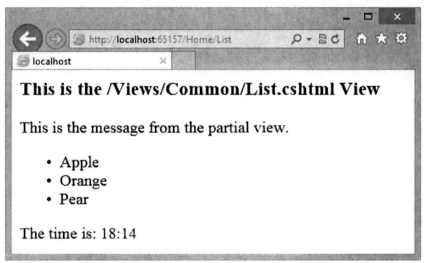

Figure 18-12. Using a child action

When we called the `Action` helper in Listing 18-29, we provided a single parameter that specified the name of the action method to invoke. This causes the MVC Framework to look for an action method in the controller that is handling the current request. To call action methods in other controllers, provide the controller name, like this:

```
...
@Html.Action("Time", "MyController")
...
```

You can pass parameters to action methods by providing an anonymously typed object whose properties correspond to the names of the child action method parameters. So, for example, if we have this child action:

```
...
[ChildActionOnly]
public ActionResult Time(DateTime time) {
    return PartialView(time);
}
...
```

then we can invoke it from a view as follows:

```
...
@Html.Action("Time", new { time = DateTime.Now })
...
```

Summary

In this chapter, we explored the details of the MVC view system and the Razor View Engine. You have seen how create a custom view engine, how to customize the behavior of the default Razor engine and the different techniques available for inserting dynamic content into a view. In the next chapter, we focus on helper methods, which assist in generating content that you can insert into your views.

CHAPTER 19

■ ■ ■

Helper Methods

In this chapter, we look at the *helper methods*, which allow you to package up chunks of code and markup so that they can be reused throughout an MVC Framework application. We start by showing you how to create your own helper methods. The MVC Framework comes with a wide-range of built-in helper methods, and we will explore them in this chapter and the chapters that follow, starting with the helper methods that you can use to create HTML `form`, `input` and `select` elements.

Creating the Example Project

For this chapter, we have created a new Visual Studio MVC project called `HelperMethods` using the `Basic` template option. We added a `Home` controller, which you can see in Listing 19-1

Listing 19-1. The Home Controller in the HelperMethods Project

```
using System.Web.Mvc;

namespace HelperMethods.Controllers {
    public class HomeController : Controller {

        public ActionResult Index() {

            ViewBag.Fruits = new string[] {"Apple", "Orange", "Pear"};
            ViewBag.Cities = new string[] { "New York", "London", "Paris" };

            string message = "This is an HTML element: <input>";

            return View((object)message);
        }
    }
}
```

We pass a pair of `string` arrays to the view via the view bag feature and set the model object to be a `string`. We created the `Index.cshtml` view file in the `/Views/Home` folder and you can see the contents of this file in Listing 19-2. This is a strongly typed view (where the model type is `string`) and we have not used a layout.

Listing 19-2. The Contents of the Index.cshtml File

```
@model string

@{
    Layout = null;
}

<!DOCTYPE html>
<html>
<head>
    <meta name="viewport" content="width=device-width" />
    <title>Index</title>
</head>
<body>
    <div>
        Here are the fruits:
        @foreach (string str in (string[])ViewBag.Fruits) {
            <b>@str </b>
        }
    </div>
    <div>
        Here are the cities:
        @foreach (string str in (string[])ViewBag.Cities) {
            <b>@str </b>
        }
    </div>
    <div>
        Here is the message:
        <p>@Model</p>
    </div>
</body>
</html>
```

You can see the way that the view is rendered by starting the application—the default routing configuration added to the project by Visual Studio will map the root URL requested automatically by the browser to the Index action on the Home controller, as shown in Figure 19-1.

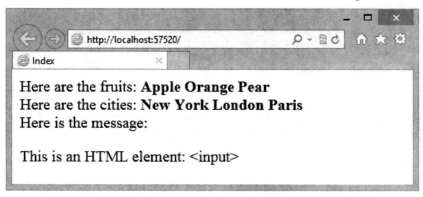

Figure 19-1. Running the example application

Creating Custom Helper Methods

We are going to follow the pattern we have established over the last few chapters and introduce you to helper methods by creating our own implementation. In the sections that follow, we will show you two different techniques for creating custom helper methods.

Creating an Inline Helper Method

The simplest kind of helper method is an *inline helper,* which is defined within a view. We can create an inline helper to simplify our example view using the @helper tag, as shown in Listing 19-3.

Listing 19-3. Creating an Inline Helper Method

```
@model string

@{
    Layout = null;
}

@helper ListArrayItems(string[] items) {
    foreach(string str in items) {
        <b>@str </b>
    }
}

<!DOCTYPE html>
<html>
<head>
    <meta name="viewport" content="width=device-width" />
    <title>Index</title>
</head>
<body>
    <div>
        Here are the fruits: @ListArrayItems(ViewBag.Fruits)
    </div>
    <div>
        Here are the cities: @ListArrayItems(ViewBag.Cities)
    </div>
    <div>
        Here is the message:
        <p>@Model</p>
    </div>
</body>
</html>
```

Inline helpers have names and parameters similar to regular C# methods. In the example, we defined a helper called ListArrayItems, which takes a string array as a parameter. Although an inline helper looks like a method, there is no return value. The contents of the helper body are processed and put into the response to the client.

■ **Tip**   Notice that we did not have to cast the dynamic properties from the ViewBag to string arrays when using the inline helper. One of the features of this kind of helper method is that it is happy to evaluate types at runtime.

The body of an inline helper follows the same syntax as the rest of a Razor view. Literal strings are regarded as static HTML, and statements that require processing by Razor are prefixed with the @ character. The helper in the example mixes static HTML and Razor tags to enumerate the items in the array, which produces the same output as our original view but has reduced the amount of duplicated code and markup.

The benefit of this approach is that we only have to make one change if we want to change the way that our array contents are displayed. As a simple example, in Listing 19-4 you can see how we have switched from just writing out the values to using the HTML unnumbered list elements.

Listing 19-4. Changing the Contents of a Helper Method

```
...
@helper ListArrayItems(string[] items) {
    <ul>
        @foreach(string str in items) {
            <li>@str</li>
        }
    </ul>
}
...
```

We only had to make the change in one place, which may seem like a trivial advantage in such a simple project, but this can be a useful way to keep your views simple and consistent in a real project. You can see the result of this change in Figure 19-2.

■ **Tip**   Notice that we had to prefix the foreach keyword with @ in this example but not in Listing 19-3. This is because the first element in our helper body changed to become an HTML element, which means we have to use @ to tell Razor that we are using a C# statement. In the previous example there was no HTML element, so Razor assumed the contents were code. It can be hard to keep track of these little parser quirks, but fortunately the Visual Studio will flag up errors like this for you.

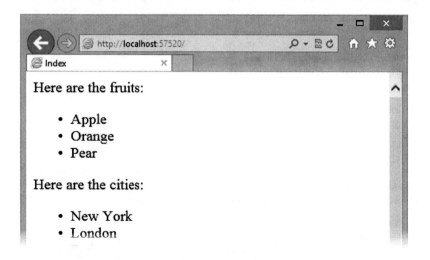

Figure 19-2. Changing the markup in a helper method

Creating an External Helper Method

Inline helpers are convenient, but they can be used only from the view in which they are declared and, if they are too complex, they can take over that view and make it hard to read.

The alternative is to create an external HTML helper method, which is expressed as a C# extension method. External helper methods can be used more widely, but are a little more awkward to write, because C# doesn't naturally handle HTML element generation very elegantly.

To demonstrate this feature, we have created an **Infrastructure** folder in the example project and created a new **CustomHelpers.cs** class file within it. You can see the contents of this file in Listing 19-5.

Listing 19-5. The Contents of the CustomerHelpers.cs File

```
using System.Web.Mvc;

namespace HelperMethods.Infrastructure {
    public static class CustomHelpers {

        public static MvcHtmlString ListArrayItems(this HtmlHelper html, string[] list) {

            TagBuilder tag = new TagBuilder("ul");

            foreach(string str in list) {
                TagBuilder itemTag = new TagBuilder("li");
                itemTag.SetInnerText(str);
                tag.InnerHtml += itemTag.ToString();
            }

            return new MvcHtmlString(tag.ToString());
        }
    }
}
```

The helper method we have created performs the same function as the inline helper in the previous example—it takes an array of strings and generates an HTML ul element, containing a li element for each string in the array.

The first parameter to the helper method is an **HtmlHelper** object, prefixed with the **this** keyword to tell the C# compiler that we are defining an extension method. The **HtmlHelper** provides access to information that can be useful when creating content, through the properties described in Table 19-1.

Table 19-1. Useful properties defined by the HtmlHelper class

Property	Description
RouteCollection	Returns the set of routes defined by the application
ViewBag	Returns the view bag data passed from the action method to the view that has called the helper method
ViewContext	Returns a ViewContext object, which provides access to details of the request and how it has been handled (and which we describe later in this chapter)

The `ViewContext` property is the most useful when you want to create content which adapts to the request being processed. In Table 19-2, we have described some of the most commonly used properties defined by the `ViewContext` class.

Table 19-2. Useful properties defined by the ViewContext class

Property	Description
Controller	Returns the controller processing the current request
HttpContext	Returns the `HttpContext` object that describes the current request
IsChildAction	Returns `true` if the view that has called the helper is being rendered by a child action (see Chapter 18 for details of child actions)
RouteData	Returns the routing data for the request
View	Returns the instance of the `IView` implementation that has called the helper method

The information you can get about the request is fairly comprehensive, but for the most part helper methods are simple and used to keep formatting consistent. You can use the built-in helper methods for generating requests specific content (we describe these helpers later in the chapter) and you can use partial views or child actions for more complex tasks (we provide guidance about which approach to use in next section of this chapter).

We do not need any information about the request in our example helper, but we do need to construct some HTML elements. The easiest way to create HTML in a helper method is to use the `TagBuilder` class, which allows you to build up HTML strings without needing to deal with all of the escaping and special characters. The `TagBuilder` class is part of the `System.Web.WebPages.Mvc` assembly but uses a feature called *type forwarding* to appear as though it is part of the `System.Web.Mvc` assembly. Both assemblies are added to MVC projects by Visual Studio, so you can use the `TagBuilder` class easily enough, but it does not appear in the Microsoft Developer Network (MSDN) API documentation.

We create a new `TagBuilder` instance, passing in name the HTML element we want to construct as the constructor parameter. We do not need to use the angle brackets (`<` and `>`) with the `TagBuilder` class, which means we can create a `ul` element, like this:

```
...
TagBuilder tag = new TagBuilder("ul");
...
```

The most useful members of the `TagBuilder` class are described in Table 19-3.

Table 19-3. Some Members of the TagBuilder Class

Member	Description
InnerHtml	A property that lets you set the contents of the element as an HTML string. The value assigned to this property will not be encoded, which means that is can be used to nest HTML elements.
SetInnerText(string)	Sets the text contents of the HTML element. The `string` parameter is encoded to make it safe to display (see the section on HTML string encoding earlier in the chapter for details).

Member	Description
AddCssClass(string)	Adds a CSS class to the HTML element.
MergeAttribute(string, string, bool)	Adds an attribute to the HTML element. The first parameter is the name of the attribute, and the second is the value. The bool parameter specifies if an existing attribute of the same name should be replaced.

The result of an HTML helper method is an MvcHtmlString object, the contents of which are written directly into the response to the client. For our example helper, we pass the result of the TagBuilder.ToString method to the constructor of a new MvcHtmlString object, like this:

```
...
return new MvcHtmlString(tag.ToString());
...
```

This statement generates the HTML fragment that contains our ul and li elements and returns them to the view engine so that it can be inserted into the response.

Using a Custom External Helper Method

Using a custom external helper method is a little different to using an inline one. In Listing 19-6, you can see the changes we have made to the /Views/Home/Index.cshtml file to replace our inline helper with the external one.

Listing 19-6. Using a Custom External Helper Method in the Index.cshtml view File

```
@model string
@using HelperMethods.Infrastructure

@{
    Layout = null;
}

<!DOCTYPE html>
<html>
<head>
    <meta name="viewport" content="width=device-width" />
    <title>Index</title>
</head>
<body>
    <div>
        Here are the fruits: @Html.ListArrayItems((string[])ViewBag.Fruits)
    </div>
    <div>
        Here are the cities: @Html.ListArrayItems((string[])ViewBag.Cities)
    </div>
    <div>
        Here is the message:
        <p>@Model</p>
    </div>
</body>
</html>
```

We need to ensure that the namespace that contains the helper extension method is in scope. We have done this using an @using tag, but if you are developing a lot of custom helpers then you will want to add the namespaces that contain them to the /Views/Web.config file so that they are always available in your views.

We refer to the helper using @Html.<helper>, where <helper> is the name of the extension method—in our case, this means that we use @Html.ListArrayItems. The Html part of this expression refers to a property defined by the view base class, which returns an HtmlHelper object—which is the type to which we applied our extension method in Listing 19-5.

We pass data to the helper method as we would for an inline helper or a C# method, although we must take care to cast from the dynamic properties of the ViewBag object to the type defined by the external helper—in this case, a string array. This syntax is not as elegant as using inline helpers, but it is part of the price that you must pay to create a helper that can be used in any view in your project.

KNOWING WHEN TO USE HELPER METHODS

Now that you have seen how helper methods work, you might be wondering when you should use them in preference to partial views or child actions—especially as there is overlap between what these features are capable of.

We only use helper methods to reduce the amount of duplication in views, just as we did in our example—and only for the simplest of content. For more complex markup and content we use partial views and we you need to perform any manipulation of model data, then we use a child action. We recommend that you follow the same approach and keep your use of helper methods as simple as possible (if our helpers contain more than a handful of C# statements—or more C# statements that HTML elements—then we tend to switch to a child action).

Managing String Encoding in a Helper Method

The MVC Framework makes an effort to protect you from malicious data by automatically encoding it so that it can be added to a Web page safely. You can see an example of this in our example application where we pass a potentially troublesome string to the view as the model object, as shown in Listing 19-7, where we have repeated the code for the Home controller.

Listing 19-7. The Home Controller in the Example Project

```
using System.Web.Mvc;

namespace HelperMethods.Controllers {
    public class HomeController : Controller {

        public ActionResult Index() {

            ViewBag.Fruits = new string[] { "Apple", "Orange", "Pear" };
            ViewBag.Cities = new string[] { "New York", "London", "Paris" };

            string message = "This is an HTML element: <input>";

            return View((object)message);
        }
    }
}
```

The model object contains a valid HTML element, but when the value is rendered by Razor, the following HTML is produced:

```
...
<div>
    Here is the message:
    <p>This is an HTML element: &lt;input&gt;</p>
</div>
...
```

This is a basic security precaution that prevents data values from being interpreted as valid markup by the browser—this is the foundation for a common form of Website attack in which malicious users will try to subvert the behavior of an application by trying to add their own HTML markup or JavaScript code.

Razor encodes data values automatically when they are used in a view, but helper methods need to be able to generate HTML and as a consequence they are given a higher level of trust by the view engine—and this can require some careful attention.

Demonstrating the Problem

To demonstrate the problem, we have created a new helper method in the CustomerHelpers class, as shown in Listing 19-8. This helper takes a string as a parameter and generates the same HTML that we included in the Index view.

Listing 19-8. Defining a New Helper Method

```
using System.Web.Mvc;
using System;

namespace HelperMethods.Infrastructure {
    public static class CustomHelpers {

        public static MvcHtmlString ListArrayItems(this HtmlHelper html, string[] list) {

            TagBuilder tag = new TagBuilder("ul");

            foreach(string str in list) {
                TagBuilder itemTag = new TagBuilder("li");
                itemTag.SetInnerText(str);
                tag.InnerHtml += itemTag.ToString();
            }

            return new MvcHtmlString(tag.ToString());
        }

        public static MvcHtmlString DisplayMessage(this HtmlHelper html, string msg) {
            string result = String.Format("This is the message: <p>{0}</p>", msg);
            return new MvcHtmlString(result);
        }
    }
}
```

We use the String.Format method to generate the HTML markup and pass the result as the argument to the MvcHtmlString constructor. In Listing 19-9, you can see how we have changed the /View/Home/Index.cshtml view to use the new helper method (we have also made some changes to emphasize the content that comes from the helper method).

Listing 19-9. Using the DisplayMessage Helper Method in the Index View

```
@model string
@using HelperMethods.Infrastructure

@{
    Layout = null;
}
<!DOCTYPE html>
<html>
<head>
    <meta name="viewport" content="width=device-width" />
    <title>Index</title>
</head>
<body>
    <p>This is the content from the view:</p>
    <div style="border: thin solid black; padding: 10px">
        Here is the message:
        <p>@Model</p>
    </div>

    <p>This is the content from the helper method:</p>
    <div style="border: thin solid black; padding: 10px">
        @Html.DisplayMessage(Model)
    </div>
</body>
</html>
```

You can see the effect our helper method has by starting the application, as shown in Figure 19-3.

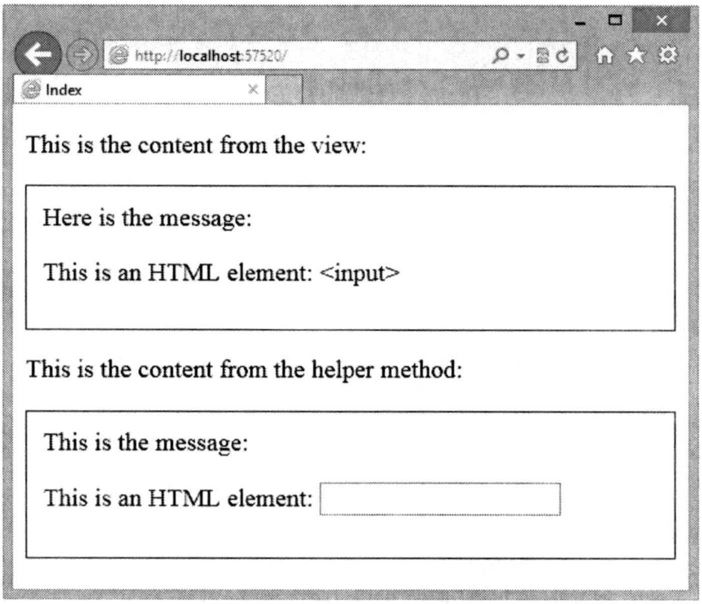

Figure 19-3. Comparing how data values are encoded

Our helper method is trusted to generate safe content, which is unfortunate because it leads to the browser displaying an input element, which is the kind of behavior that can be exploited to subvert an application.

Encoding Helper Method Content

There are a couple of different ways that we can solve this problem and the choice between them depends on the nature of the content that your helper method produces.

The simplest solution is to change the return type of the helper method to **string**, as shown in Listing 19-10. This alerts the view engine that your content is not safe and should be encoded before it is added to the view.

Listing 19-10. Ensuring that Razor Encodes the Content Generated by a Helper Method

```
using System.Web.Mvc;
using System;

namespace HelperMethods.Infrastructure {
    public static class CustomHelpers {

        public static MvcHtmlString ListArrayItems(this HtmlHelper html, string[] list) {

            TagBuilder tag = new TagBuilder("ul");

            foreach(string str in list) {
                TagBuilder itemTag = new TagBuilder("li");
                itemTag.SetInnerText(str);
                tag.InnerHtml += itemTag.ToString();
            }

            return new MvcHtmlString(tag.ToString());
        }

        public static string DisplayMessage(this HtmlHelper html, string msg) {
            return String.Format("This is the message: <p>{0}</p>", msg);
        }
    }
}
```

This technique causes Razor to encode all of the content that is returned by the helper, which is a problem when you are generating HTML elements as we are in our example helper but that is very convenient otherwise. You can see the effect in Figure 19-4.

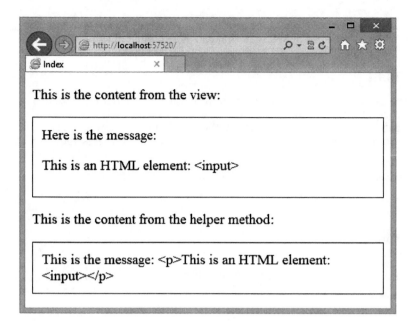

Figure 19-4. Ensuring that the view engine encodes the response from a helper method

We have solved the problem with the **input** element, but our **p** elements have been encoded as well, which is not what we need. In these situations, we need to be more selective and encode just the data values. You can see how we do this in Listing 19-11.

Listing 19-11. Selectively Encoding Data Values in a Helper Method

```
...
public static MvcHtmlString DisplayMessage(this HtmlHelper html, string msg) {
    string encodedMessage = html.Encode(msg);
    string result = String.Format("This is the message: <p>{0}</p>", encodedMessage);
    return new MvcHtmlString(result);
}
...
```

The **HtmlHelper** class defines an instance method called **Encode,** which solves our problem and encodes a string value so that it can be safely included in a view. The problem with this technique is that you have to remember to use it—we explicitly encode all of our data values at the start of the method as a reminder and we suggest that you adopt a similar approach.

You can see the result of this change in Figure 19-5, where you will see that the content generated by the external helper method matches that generated by using the model value directly in the view.

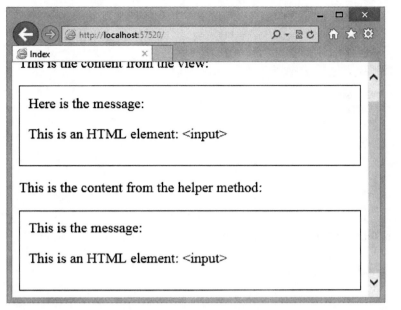

Figure 19-5. The effect of selectively encoding content in an external helper method

Using the Built-In Form Helper Methods

The MVC Framework includes a selection of built-in helper methods that help you manage the creating of HTML **form** elements. In the following sections, we will put these helpers in context and show you how they are used.

Creating Form Elements

One of the most common forms of interaction in a web application is the HTML form, which is the subject of a number of different helper methods. To demonstrate the form-related helpers, we have made some additions to the example project. We started by creating a new class file called **Person.cs** in the **Models** folder. You can see the contents of this file in Listing 19-12 - the **Person** type will be our view model class when we demonstrate the form-related helpers and the **Address** and **Role** types will help us showcase some more advanced features.

Listing 19-12. The Person Model Class

```
using System;

namespace HelperMethods.Models {

    public class Person {
        public int PersonId { get; set; }
        public string FirstName { get; set; }
        public string LastName { get; set; }
        public DateTime BirthDate { get; set; }
        public Address HomeAddress { get; set; }
        public bool IsApproved { get; set; }
        public Role Role { get; set; }
```

```
    }

    public class Address {
        public string Line1 { get; set; }
        public string Line2 { get; set; }
        public string City { get; set; }
        public string PostalCode { get; set; }
        public string Country { get; set; }
    }

    public enum Role {
        Admin,
        User,
        Guest
    }
}
```

We have also added new action methods to the Home controller to use the model objects, as shown in Listing 19-13.

Listing 19-13. Adding Action Methods to the Home Controller

```
using System.Web.Mvc;
using HelperMethods.Models;

namespace HelperMethods.Controllers {
    public class HomeController : Controller {

        public ActionResult Index() {

            ViewBag.Fruits = new string[] { "Apple", "Orange", "Pear" };
            ViewBag.Cities = new string[] { "New York", "London", "Paris" };

            string message = "This is an HTML element: <input>";

            return View((object)message);
        }

        public ActionResult CreatePerson() {
            return View(new Person());
        }

        [HttpPost]
        public ActionResult CreatePerson(Person person) {
            return View(person);
        }
    }
}
```

This is the standard two-method approach to dealing with HTML forms, where we rely on model binding so that the MVC Framework will create a `Person` object from the form data and pass it to the action method with the `HttpPost` attribute. (We explained the `HttpPost` attribute in Chapter 16 and model binding is the topic of Chapter 22.)

We are not processing the form data in any way because we are focused on how we generate elements in the view. Our HttpPost action method just calls the View method and passes the Person object that it received as a parameter, which has the effect of redisplaying the form data to the user.

We are going to start with a standard manual HTML form and show you how to replace different parts of it using helper methods. You can see the initial version of the form in Listing 19-14, which shows the CreatePerson.cshtml view file that we created in the /Views/Home folder.

Listing 19-14. The Initial Version of the HTML Form

```
@model HelperMethods.Models.Person

@{
    ViewBag.Title = "CreatePerson";
}

<h2>CreatePerson</h2>

<form action="/Home/CreatePerson" method="post">
    <div class="dataElem">
        <label>PersonId</label>
        <input name="personId" value="@Model.PersonId"/>
    </div>
    <div class="dataElem">
        <label>First Name</label>
        <input name="FirstName" value="@Model.FirstName"/>
    </div>
    <div class="dataElem">
        <label>Last Name</label>
        <input name="lastName" value="@Model.LastName"/>
    </div>
    <input type="submit" value="Submit" />
</form>
```

This view contains a very standard manually created form in which we have set the value of the value attribute of the input elements using the model object.

⬛ **Tip** Notice that we have set the name attribute on all of the input elements so that it corresponds to the model property that the input element displays. The name attribute is used by the MVC Framework default model binder to work out which input elements contain values for the model type properties when processing a post request and if you omit the name attribute your form will not work properly. We describe model binding fully in Chapter 22, including how you can change this behavior.

We have edited the contents of the /Views/Shared/_Layout.cshtml file, as shown in Listing 19-15, to keep this example as simple as possible. We have removed calls to the Razor @Scripts and @Styles tags, which we describe in Chapter 24.

Listing 19-15. Simplifying the Layout File

```
<!DOCTYPE html>
<html>
<head>
    <meta charset="utf-8" />
    <meta name="viewport" content="width=device-width" />
    <title>@ViewBag.Title</title>
    <link href="~/Content/Site.css" rel="stylesheet"/>
    <style type="text/css">
        label { display: inline-block; width: 100px;}
        .dataElem { margin: 5px;}
    </style>
</head>
<body>
    @RenderBody()
</body>
</html>
```

You can see the basic form functionality by starting the application and navigating to the /Home/CreatePerson URL. You can see the HTML form with some sample data in Figure 19-6. Because the form data is not used by the application in any way, clicking the Submit button will just cause whatever data is in the form to be redisplayed.

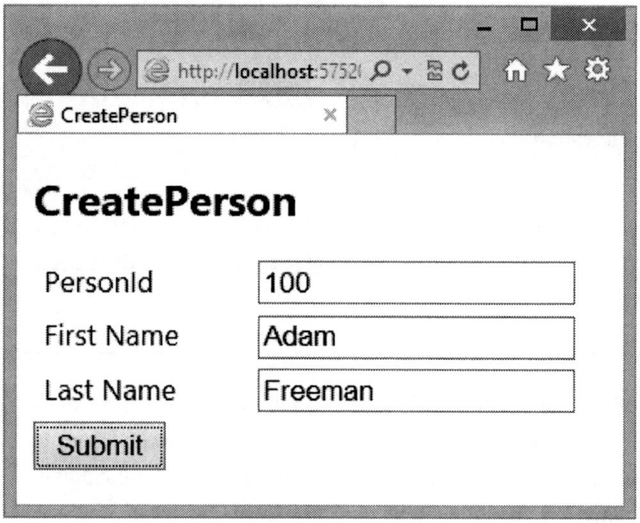

Figure 19-6. Using the simple HTML form in the example application

In Listing 19-16, you can see the HTML that the example MVC application has sent to the browser—we will use this to show you changes caused by helper methods.

Listing 19-16. The HTML Sent to the Browser for the Example Form

```
<!DOCTYPE html>
<html>
<head>
    <meta charset="utf-8" />
```

```
    <meta name="viewport" content="width=device-width" />
    <title>CreatePerson</title>
    <link href="/Content/Site.css" rel="stylesheet"/>
    <style type="text/css">
        label { display: inline-block; width: 100px;}
        .dataElem { margin: 5px;}
    </style>
</head>
<body>

<h2>CreatePerson</h2>

<form action="/Home/CreatePerson" method="post">
    <div class="dataElem">
        <label>PersonId</label>
        <input name="personId" value="0"/>
    </div>
    <div class="dataElem">
        <label>First Name</label>
        <input name="FirstName"/>
    </div>
    <div class="dataElem">
        <label>Last Name</label>
        <input name="lastName"/>
    </div>
    <input type="submit" value="Submit" />
</form>
</body>
</html>
```

■ **Note** Using the helper methods to generate HTML elements like form and input is not compulsory. If you prefer, you can code them using static HTML tags and populate values using view data or view model objects, just as we did in this section. The HTML that we generate from the helper methods in the following sections is very clean and there are no special attribute values or sneaky tricks that mean you have to use them—but they make it easy to ensure that the HTML is in sync with the application so that, for example, changes in touring configuration will be reflected automatically in your forms. The helpers are there for convenience, rather than because they create essential or special HTML and you do not have to use them if they do not suit your development style.

Creating Form Elements

Two of the most useful (and most commonly used) helpers are Html.BeginForm and Html.EndForm. These helpers create HTML form tags and generate a valid action attribute for the form that is based on the routing mechanism for the application.

There are 13 different versions of the BeginForm method, allowing you to be increasingly specific about how the resulting form element will be generated. We only need the most basic for our example application, which takes no arguments and creates a form element whose action attribute ensures that the form will be posted back to the same action method which led to the current view being generated. You can see how we have applied this overload of BeginForm and the EndForm helper in Listing 19-17—the EndForm helper has only one definition and it just closes the form element by adding </form> to the view.

Listing 19-17. Using the BeginForm and EndForm Helper Methods

```
@model HelperMethods.Models.Person

@{
    ViewBag.Title = "CreatePerson";
}
<h2>CreatePerson</h2>

@Html.BeginForm()
    <div class="dataElem">
        <label>PersonId</label>
        <input name="personId" value="@Model.PersonId"/>
    </div>
    <div class="dataElem">
        <label>First Name</label>
        <input name="FirstName" value="@Model.FirstName"/>
    </div>
    <div class="dataElem">
        <label>Last Name</label>
        <input name="lastName" value="@Model.LastName"/>
    </div>
    <input type="submit" value="Submit" />
@{Html.EndForm();}
```

Notice that we have had to treat the call to the EndForm helper method as a C# statement—this is because the EndForm method writes its tag directly to the output and does not return a result that can be inserted into the view like BeginForm does.

This is an ugly design choice, but it doesn't matter because the EndForm method is rarely used. A much more common approach is to use the approach shown in Listing 19-18, which wraps the call to the BeginForm helper method in a using expression. At the end of the using block, the .NET runtime calls the Dispose method on the object returned by the BeginForm method, which calls the EndForm method for you. (You can see how this works by downloading the source code for the MVC Framework and taking a look at the System.Web.Mvc.Html.FormExtensions class.)

Listing 19-18. Creating a Self-Closing Form

```
@model HelperMethods.Models.Person

@{
    ViewBag.Title = "CreatePerson";
}
<h2>CreatePerson</h2>

@using(Html.BeginForm()) {
    <div class="dataElem">
        <label>PersonId</label>
        <input name="personId" value="@Model.PersonId"/>
    </div>
    <div class="dataElem">
        <label>First Name</label>
        <input name="FirstName" value="@Model.FirstName"/>
    </div>
    <div class="dataElem">
```

```
    <label>Last Name</label>
    <input name="lastName" value="@Model.LastName"/>
</div>
<input type="submit" value="Submit" />
}
```

This approach, known as a self-closing form, is the one we use in our own projects—we like the way that the code block contains the form and makes it clear which elements will appear between the opening and closing form tags.

The other 12 variations for the BeginForm method allow you to change different aspects of the form element that is created. There is a lot of repetition in these overloads, as they allow you to be incrementally more specific about the details you provide. In Table 19-4 we have listed the most important overloads, which are the ones that you will use on a regular basis in an MVC application. The other overloads of the BeginForm method are provided for compatibility with version of the MVC Framework that were released before C# had support for creating dynamic objects.

Table 19-4. The overloads of the BeginForm helper method

Overload	Description
BeginForm()	Creates a form which posts back to the action method it originated from
BeginForm(**action, controller**)	Creates a form which posts back to the action method and controller, specified as strings
BeginForm(action, controller, **method**)	As for the previous overload, but allows you to specify the value for the method attribute using a value from the System.Web.Mvc.FormMethod enumeration.
BeginForm(action, controller, method, **attributes**)	As for the previous overload, but allows you to specify attributes for the form element an object whose properties are used as the attribute names.
BeginForm(action, controller, **routeValues**, method, attributes)	As for the previous overload, but allows you to specify values for the variable route segments in your application routing configuration as an object whose properties correspond to the routing variables.

We have shown you the simplest version of the BeginForm method, which is all we need for our example app, but in Listing 19-19 you can see the most complex, in which we specify additional information for how the form element should be constructed.

Listing 19-19. Using the Most Complex Overload of the BeginForm Method

```
@model HelperMethods.Models.Person

@{
    ViewBag.Title = "CreatePerson";
}
<h2>CreatePerson</h2>

@using (Html.BeginForm("CreatePerson", "Home",
    new { id = "MyIdValue" }, FormMethod.Post,
```

```
new { @class = "personClass", data_formType="person"})) {

    <div class="dataElem">
        <label>PersonId</label>
        <input name="personId" value="@Model.PersonId"/>
    </div>
    <div class="dataElem">
        <label>First Name</label>
        <input name="FirstName" value="@Model.FirstName"/>
    </div>
    <div class="dataElem">
        <label>Last Name</label>
        <input name="lastName" value="@Model.LastName"/>
    </div>
    <input type="submit" value="Submit" />
}
```

In this example, we have explicitly specified some details that would have been inferred automatically by the MVC Framework, such as the action name and the controller. We also specified that the form should be submitted using the HTTP POST method, which would have been used anyway.

The more interesting arguments are the ones that set values for the route variable and set attributes on the form element. We used the route values argument to specify a value for the `id` segment variable in the default route added by Visual Studio to the `/App_Start/RouteConfig.cs` file when the project was created and we defined `class` and a `data` attribute (data attributes are custom attributes which you can add to elements to make processing HTML content). Here is the HTML `form` tag that this call to `BeginForm` produces:

```
...
<form action="/Home/CreatePerson/MyIdValue" class="personClass" data-formType="person"
    method="post">
...
```

You can see that the value for the `id` attribute has been appended to the target URL and that our class and data attributes have been applied to the element. Notice that we specified an attribute called `data_formType` in our call to `BeginForm` but ended up with a `data-formType` attribute in the output—you cannot specify property names in a dynamic object that contain hyphens, so we use an underscore that is then automatically mapped to a hyphen in the output, neatly side-stepping a mismatch between the C# and HTML syntaxes. (And, of course, we had to prefix the property name `class` with a `@` so that we can use a C# reserved keyword as a property name for the `class` attribute.)

Specifying the Route Used by a Form

When you use the `BeginForm` method, the MVC Framework finds the first route in the routing configuration that can be used to generate a URL that will target the required action and controller—in essence, you leave the route selection to be figured out for you. If you want to ensure that a particular route is used, then you can use the `BeginRouteForm` helper method instead. To demonstrate this feature, we have added a new route to the `/App_Start/RouteConfig.cs` file, as shown in Listing 19-20.

Listing 19-20. Adding a New Route to the RouteConfig.cs File in the Example Application

```
using System;
using System.Collections.Generic;
using System.Linq;
using System.Web;
using System.Web.Mvc;
```

```
using System.Web.Routing;

namespace HelperMethods {
    public class RouteConfig {
        public static void RegisterRoutes(RouteCollection routes) {
            routes.IgnoreRoute("{resource}.axd/{*pathInfo}");

            routes.MapRoute(
                name: "Default",
                url: "{controller}/{action}/{id}",
                defaults: new { controller = "Home", action = "Index",
                    id = UrlParameter.Optional }
            );

            routes.MapRoute(
                name: "FormRoute",
                url: "app/forms/{controller}/{action}"
            );
        }
    }
}
```

If we call the BeginForm method with this routing configuration, we will end up with a form element whose action attribute contains a URL which is created from the default route. In Listing 19-21, you can see how we have specified that our new route should be used through the BeginRouteForm method.

Listing 19-21. Specifying Which Route Should Be Used When Creating a Form URL

```
@model HelperMethods.Models.Person

@{
    ViewBag.Title = "CreatePerson";
}
<h2>CreatePerson</h2>

@using(Html.BeginRouteForm("FormRoute", new {}, FormMethod.Post,
    new { @class = "personClass", data_formType="person"})) {

    <div class="dataElem">
        <label>PersonId</label>
        <input name="personId" value="@Model.PersonId"/>
    </div>
    <div class="dataElem">
        <label>First Name</label>
        <input name="FirstName" value="@Model.FirstName"/>
    </div>
    <div class="dataElem">
        <label>Last Name</label>
        <input name="lastName" value="@Model.LastName"/>
    </div>
    <input type="submit" value="Submit" />
}
```

This produces the following form tag, whose action attribute corresponds to the structure of our new route:

```
...
<form action="/app/forms/Home/CreatePerson" class="personClass"
    data-formType="person" method="post">
...
```

> ■ **Tip** There are a range of different overloads for the BeginRouteForm method allowing you to specify differing degrees of details for the form element, just as with the BeginForm method. These follow the same structure as their BeginForm counterparts—see the API documentation for details.

Using Input Helpers

An HTML form is no use unless you also create some input elements. Table 19-5 shows the basic helper methods that are available to create input elements and gives examples of the HTML they produce. For all of these helper methods, the first argument is used to set the value of the id and name attributes for the input element and the second argument is used to set the value attribute.

Table 19-5. Basic Input HTML Helpers

HTML Element	Example
Checkbox	Html.CheckBox("myCheckbox", false)
	Output:
	`<input id="myCheckbox" name="myCheckbox" type="checkbox" value="true" />` `<input name="myCheckbox" type="hidden" value="false" />`
Hidden field	Html.Hidden("myHidden", "val")
	Output:
	`<input id="myHidden" name="myHidden" type="hidden" value="val" />`
Radio button	Html.RadioButton("myRadiobutton", "val", true)
	Output:
	`<input checked="checked" id="myRadiobutton" name="myRadiobutton"` `    type="radio" value="val" />`
Password	Html.Password("myPassword", "val")
	Output:
	`<input id="myPassword" name="myPassword" type="password" value="val" />`
Text area	Html.TextArea("myTextarea", "val", 5, 20, null)
	Output:
	`<textarea cols="20" id="myTextarea" name="myTextarea" rows="5">` `    val</textarea>`

HTML Element	Example
Text box	`Html.TextBox("myTextbox", "val")`
	Output:
	`<input id="myTextbox" name="myTextbox" type="text" value="val" />`

Each of these helpers is overloaded. The table shows the simplest version, but you can provide an additional object argument that you use to specify HTML attributes, just as we did with the form element in the previous section.

■ **Note** Notice that the checkbox helper (`Html.CheckBox`) renders *two* input elements. It renders a checkbox and then a hidden input element of the same name. This is because browsers do not submit a value for checkboxes when they are not selected. Having the hidden control ensures that the MVC Framework will get a value from the hidden field when this happens.

You can see how we have used these basic input helper methods in Listing 19-22.

Listing 19-22. Using the Basic Input Element Helper Methods

```
@model HelperMethods.Models.Person

@{
    ViewBag.Title = "CreatePerson";
}
<h2>CreatePerson</h2>

@using(Html.BeginRouteForm("FormRoute", new {}, FormMethod.Post,
    new { @class = "personClass", data_formType="person"})) {

    <div class="dataElem">
        <label>PersonId</label>
        @Html.TextBox("personId", @Model.PersonId)
    </div>
    <div class="dataElem">
        <label>First Name</label>
        @Html.TextBox("firstName", @Model.FirstName)
    </div>
    <div class="dataElem">
        <label>Last Name</label>
        @Html.TextBox("lastName", @Model.LastName)
    </div>
    <input type="submit" value="Submit" />
}
```

You can see the HTML input elements that this view produces in Listing 19-23. The output is very similar to our original form element, but you can see some hints of the MVC Framework have appeared in the form of some data attributes which have been added to support form validation (which we introduced in Chapter 2 and which we revisit in Chapter 23).

Listing 19-23. The Input Elements Created by the Basic Input Helper Methods

```
<form action="/app/forms/Home/CreatePerson" class="personClass" data-formType="person"
    method="post">
    <div class="dataElem">
        <label>PersonId</label>
        <input data-val="true" data-val-number="The field PersonId must be a number."
            data-val-required="The PersonId field is required." id="personId"
            name="personId" type="text" value="0" />
    </div>
    <div class="dataElem">
        <label>First Name</label>
        <input id="firstName" name="firstName" type="text" value="" />
    </div>
    <div class="dataElem">
        <label>Last Name</label>
        <input id="lastName" name="lastName" type="text" value="" />
    </div>
    <input type="submit" value="Submit" />
</form>
```

■ **Tip**   We can the production of the `data` attributes that support form validation for the entire application by setting the value of `UnobtrusiveJavaScriptEnabled` to false in the `Web.config` file. We can disable the feature on individual views by calling `Html.EnableClientValidation(false)` within a Razor code block—you can see an example of this in Chapter 23 where we disable the `data` attributes so we can focus on the HTML elements generated by some more advanced helper methods.

Generating the Input Element from a Model Property

The helper methods we used in the previous section are fine, but we still have to ensure that the value we pass as the first argument corresponds to the model value we pass as the second argument—if they are not consistent, then the MVC Framework will not be able to reconstruct our model object from the form data because the `name` attributes and the forms values of the `input` elements will not match.

For each of the methods we listed in Table 19-5, there is an alternative overload which takes a `single` string argument, which we have used in Listing 19-24.

Listing 19-24. Generating the Input Element from the Model Property Name

```
@model HelperMethods.Models.Person

@{
    ViewBag.Title = "CreatePerson";
}
<h2>CreatePerson</h2>

@using(Html.BeginRouteForm("FormRoute", new {}, FormMethod.Post,
    new { @class = "personClass", data_formType="person"})) {

    <div class="dataElem">
        <label>PersonId</label>
```

```
        @Html.TextBox("PersonId")
    </div>
    <div class="dataElem">
        <label>First Name</label>
        @Html.TextBox("firstName")
    </div>
    <div class="dataElem">
        <label>Last Name</label>
        @Html.TextBox("lastName")
    </div>
    <input type="submit" value="Submit" />
}
```

The `string` argument is used to search the view data, `ViewBag`, and view model to find a corresponding data item that can be used as the basic for the input element. So, for example, if you call `@Html.TextBox("DataValue")`, the MVC Framework tries to find some item of data that corresponds with the key `DataValue`. The following locations are checked:

- `ViewBag.DataValue`

- `@Model.DataValue`

The first value that is found is used to set the `value` attribute of the generated HTML. (The last check, for `@Model.DataValue`, works only if the view model for the view contains a property or field called `DataValue`.)

If we specify a string like `DataValue.First.Name`, the search becomes more complicated. The MVC Framework will try different arrangements of the dot-separated elements, such as the following:

- `ViewBag.DataValue.First.Name`

- `ViewBag.DataValue["First"].Name`

- `ViewBag.DataValue["First.Name"]`

- `ViewBag.DataValue["First"]["Name"]`

Many permutations will be checked. Once again, the first value that is found will be used, terminating the search. There is an obvious performance consideration to this technique, but bear in mind that usually only a few items are in the view bag, so it does not take much time to search through them.

Using Strongly Typed Input Helpers

For each of the basic input helpers that we described in Table 19-5, there are corresponding strongly typed helpers. You can see these helpers in Table 19-6 along with samples of the HTML they produce. These helpers can be used only with strongly typed views. (Some of these helpers generate attributes that help with client-side form validation—we have omitted these from the Table 19-for brevity.)

Table 19-6. Strongly Typed Input HTML Helpers

HTML Element	Example
Checkbox	`Html.CheckBoxFor(x => x.IsApproved)`
	Output:
	`<input id="IsApproved" name="IsApproved" type="checkbox" value="true" />` `<input name="IsApproved" type="hidden" value="false" />`
Hidden field	`Html.HiddenFor(x => x.FirstName)`
	Output:
	`<input id="FirstName" name="FirstName" type="hidden" value="" />`
Radio button	`Html.RadioButtonFor(x => x.IsApproved, "val")`
	Output:
	`<input id="IsApproved" name="IsApproved" type="radio" value="val" />`
Password	`Html.PasswordFor(x => x.Password)`
	Output:
	`<input id="Password" name="Password" type="password" />`
Text area	`Html.TextAreaFor(x => x.Bio, 5, 20, new{})`
	Output:
	`<textarea cols="20" id="Bio" name="Bio" rows="5">Bio value</textarea>`
Text box	`Html.TextBoxFor(x => x.FirstName)`
	Output:
	`<input id="FirstName" name="FirstName" type="text" value="" />`

The strongly typed input helpers work on lambda expressions. The value that is passed to the expression is the view model object, and you can select the field or property that will be used to set the value attribute. You can see how we have used this kind of helper in the `CreatePerson.cshtml` view from the example application in Listing 19-25.

Listing 19-25. Using the Strongly Typed Input Helper Methods

```
@model HelperMethods.Models.Person

@{
    ViewBag.Title = "CreatePerson";
}
<h2>CreatePerson</h2>

@using(Html.BeginRouteForm("FormRoute", new {}, FormMethod.Post,
    new { @class = "personClass", data_formType="person"})) {
```

```
    <div class="dataElem">
        <label>PersonId</label>
        @Html.TextBoxFor(m => m.PersonId)
    </div>
    <div class="dataElem">
        <label>First Name</label>
        @Html.TextBoxFor(m => m.FirstName)
    </div>
    <div class="dataElem">
        <label>Last Name</label>
        @Html.TextBoxFor(m => m.LastName)
    </div>
    <input type="submit" value="Submit" />
}
```

The HTML generated by these helpers is not any different, but we use the strongly typed helper methods in our projects because they reduce the chances of causing an error by mistyping a property name.

Creating Select Elements

Table 19-7 shows the helper methods that can be used to create **select** elements. These can be used to select a single item from a drop-down list or present a multiple-item **select** element that allows several items to be selected. As with the other form elements, there are versions of these helpers that are weakly and strongly typed.

Table 19-7. HTML Helpers That Render Select Elements

HTML Element	Example

Drop-down list	`Html.DropDownList("myList", new SelectList(new [] {"A", "B"}), "Choose")`
	Output:
	`<select id="myList" name="myList">`
	`    <option value="">Choose</option>`
	`    <option>A</option>`
	`    <option>B</option>`
	`</select>`

Drop-down list	`Html.DropDownListFor(x => x.Gender, new SelectList(new [] {"M", "F"}))`
	Output:
	`<select id="Gender" name="Gender">`
	`    <option>M</option>`
	`    <option>F</option>`
	`</select>`

Multiple-select	`Html.ListBox("myList", new MultiSelectList(new [] {"A", "B"}))`
	Output:
	`<select id="myList" multiple="multiple" name="myList">`
	`    <option>A</option>`
	`    <option>B</option>`
	`</select>`

HTML Element	Example

Multiple-select	`Html.ListBoxFor(x => x.Vals, new MultiSelectList(new [] {"A", "B"}))`
	Output:
	`<select id="Vals" multiple="multiple" name="Vals">`
	`    <option>A</option>`
	`    <option>B</option>`
	`</select>`

The `select` helpers take `SelectList` or `MultiSelectList` parameters. The difference between these classes is that `MultiSelectList` has constructor options that let you specify that more than one item should be selected when the page is rendered initially.

Both of these classes operate on `IEnumerable` sequences of objects. In Table 19-7, we created inline arrays that contained the list items we wanted displayed, but a nice feature of `SelectList` and `MultiSelectList` is that they will extract values from objects, including the model object, for the list items. You can see how we have created a `select` element for the `Role` property of our `Person` model in Listing 19-26.

Listing 19-26. Creating a Select Element for the Person.Role Property

```
@model HelperMethods.Models.Person

@{
    ViewBag.Title = "CreatePerson";
}
<h2>CreatePerson</h2>

@using(Html.BeginRouteForm("FormRoute", new {}, FormMethod.Post,
    new { @class = "personClass", data_formType="person"})) {

    <div class="dataElem">
        <label>PersonId</label>
        @Html.TextBoxFor(m => m.PersonId)
    </div>
    <div class="dataElem">
        <label>First Name</label>
        @Html.TextBoxFor(m => m.FirstName)
    </div>
    <div class="dataElem">
        <label>Last Name</label>
        @Html.TextBoxFor(m => m.LastName)
    </div>
    <div class="dataElem">
        <label>Role</label>
        @Html.DropDownListFor(m => m.Role,
            new SelectList(Enum.GetNames(typeof(HelperMethods.Models.Role))))
    </div>
    <input type="submit" value="Submit" />
}
```

We defined our `Role` property so that it is a value from the `Role` enumeration defined in the same class file. Because the `SelectList` and `MultiSelectList` objects operate on `IEnumerable` objects, we have to use the `Enum.GetNames` method to be able to use the `Role` enum as the source for the `select` element. You can see the HTML that the latest version of our view creates, including the select element in Listing 19-27.

Listing 19-27. The HTML Generated by the CreatePerson View

```html
<!DOCTYPE html>
<html>
<head>
    <meta charset="utf-8" />
    <meta name="viewport" content="width=device-width" />
    <title>CreatePerson</title>
    <link href="/Content/Site.css" rel="stylesheet"/>
    <style type="text/css">
        label { display: inline-block; width: 100px;}
        .dataElem { margin: 5px;}
    </style>
</head>
<body>

<h2>CreatePerson</h2>

<form action="/app/forms/Home/CreatePerson" class="personClass" data-formType="person"
method="post">    <div class="dataElem">
        <label>PersonId</label>
        <input data-val="true" data-val-number="The field PersonId must be a number." data-val-
required="The PersonId field is required." id="PersonId" name="PersonId" type="text" value="0"
/>
    </div>
    <div class="dataElem">
        <label>First Name</label>
        <input id="FirstName" name="FirstName" type="text" value="" />
    </div>
    <div class="dataElem">
        <label>Last Name</label>
        <input id="LastName" name="LastName" type="text" value="" />
    </div>
    <div class="dataElem">
        <label>Role</label>
        <select data-val="true" data-val-required="The Role field is required."
                id="Role" name="Role">
            <option selected="selected">Admin</option>
            <option>User</option>
            <option>Guest</option>
        </select>
    </div>
    <input type="submit" value="Submit" />
</form>
</body>
</html>
```

Summary

In this chapter, we introduced the concept of helper methods, which you can use in views to generate chunks of content in a reusable way. We started by showing you how to create custom inline and external helpers and then showed you the helpers that are available to create HTML `form`, `input` and `select` elements. In the next chapter, we will continue on this theme and show you how to use *template helpers*.

CHAPTER 20

■ ■ ■

Templated Helper Methods

The HTML helpers that we looked at in the previous chapter, such as `Html.CheckBoxFor` and `Html.TextBoxFor` generate a specific type of element, which means that we have to decide in advance what kinds of elements should be used to represent model properties and to manually update our views if the type of a property changes.

In this chapter, we demonstrate the *templated helper methods*, with which we specify the property we want displayed and let the MVC Framework figure out what HTML elements are required. This is a more flexible approach to displaying data to the user, although it requires some initial care and attention to set up.

Reviewing the Example Project

In this chapter we are going to continue using the `HelperMethod` project that we created in Chapter 19. In the project, we created a `Person` model class along with a couple of supporting types. As a reminder, we have listed these in Listing 20-1.

Listing 20-1. The Person, Address, and Role Types

```
using System;

namespace HelperMethods.Models {

    public class Person {
        public int PersonId { get; set; }
        public string FirstName { get; set; }
        public string LastName { get; set; }
        public DateTime BirthDate { get; set; }
        public Address HomeAddress { get; set; }
        public bool IsApproved { get; set; }
        public Role Role { get; set; }
    }

    public class Address {
        public string Line1 { get; set; }
        public string Line2 { get; set; }
        public string City { get; set; }
        public string PostalCode { get; set; }
        public string Country { get; set; }
    }

    public enum Role {
```

```
        Admin,
        User,
        Guest
    }
}
```

The example project contains a very simple Home controller that we use to display forms and receive form posts—you can see the definition of the HomeController class in Listing 20-2.

Listing 20-2. The HomeController Class

```
using System.Web.Mvc;
using HelperMethods.Models;

namespace HelperMethods.Controllers {
    public class HomeController : Controller {

        public ActionResult Index() {

            ViewBag.Fruits = new string[] { "Apple", "Orange", "Pear" };
            ViewBag.Cities = new string[] { "New York", "London", "Paris" };

            string message = "This is an HTML element: <input>";

            return View((object)message);
        }

        public ActionResult CreatePerson() {
            return View(new Person());
        }

        [HttpPost]
        public ActionResult CreatePerson(Person person) {
            return View(person);
        }
    }
}
```

It is the two CreatePerson action methods that we will be using in this chapter, both of which render the /Views/Home/CreatePerson.cshtml view file. In Listing 20-3, you can see the CreatePerson view from the end of Chapter 19.

Listing 20-3. The CreatePerson View

```
@model HelperMethods.Models.Person

@{
    ViewBag.Title = "CreatePerson";
    Html.EnableClientValidation(false);
}
<h2>CreatePerson</h2>

@using(Html.BeginRouteForm("FormRoute", new {}, FormMethod.Post,
    new { @class = "personClass", data_formType="person"})) {
```

```
    <div class="dataElem">
        <label>PersonId</label>
        @Html.TextBoxFor(m => m.PersonId)
    </div>
    <div class="dataElem">
        <label>First Name</label>
        @Html.TextBoxFor(m => m.FirstName)
    </div>
    <div class="dataElem">
        <label>Last Name</label>
        @Html.TextBoxFor(m => m.LastName)
    </div>
    <div class="dataElem">
        <label>Role</label>
        @Html.DropDownListFor(m => m.Role,
            new SelectList(Enum.GetNames(typeof(HelperMethods.Models.Role))))
    </div>
    <input type="submit" value="Submit" />
}
```

We made one addition since Chapter 19, which we have marked in bold. By default, the helper methods will add data attributes to the HTML elements they generate to support the kind of form validation we showed you in Chapter 9 when we created the SportsStore application. We do not want those attributes in this chapter, so we have used the Html.EnableClientValidation method to disable them for the CreatePerson view. The client validation feature is still enabled for the rest of the application and we will explain how validation works in detail (including the purpose of the data attributes) in Chapter 23.

Using Templated Helper Methods

The first templated helper methods that we are going to look at are Html.Editor and Html.EditorFor. The Editor method takes a string argument that specifies the property for which we require an editor element—the helper follows the search process that we described in Chapter 18 to locate a corresponding property in the view bag and model object.

The EditorFor method is the strongly typed equivalent, which allows you to use a lambda expression to specify a model property that you want the editor element for.

In Listing 20-4, you can see how we have both the Editor and EditorFor helper methods to the CreatePerson view. As we mentioned in Chapter 19, we prefer to use the strongly-typed helpers because they reduce the changes of causing an error by mistyping the property name, but we have used both types in this listing just to demonstrate that you can mix and match as you see fit.

Listing 20-4. Using the Editor and EditorFor Helper Methods

```
@model HelperMethods.Models.Person

@{
    ViewBag.Title = "CreatePerson";
    Html.EnableClientValidation(false);
}
<h2>CreatePerson</h2>

@using(Html.BeginRouteForm("FormRoute", new {}, FormMethod.Post,
    new { @class = "personClass", data_formType="person"})) {
```

```
    <div class="dataElem">
        <label>PersonId</label>
        @Html.Editor("PersonId")
    </div>
    <div class="dataElem">
        <label>First Name</label>
        @Html.Editor("FirstName")
    </div>
    <div class="dataElem">
        <label>Last Name</label>
        @Html.EditorFor(m => m.LastName)
    </div>
    <div class="dataElem">
        <label>Role</label>
        @Html.EditorFor(m => m.Role)
    </div>
    <div class="dataElem">
        <label>Birth Date</label>
        @Html.EditorFor(m => m.BirthDate)
    </div>
    <input type="submit" value="Submit" />
}
```

The HTML elements that are created by the Editor and EditorFor methods are the same—the only difference is the way that you specify the property that the editor elements are created for. You can see the effect of the changes that we have made by starting the example application and navigating to the /Home/CreatePerson URL, as shown in Figure 20-1.

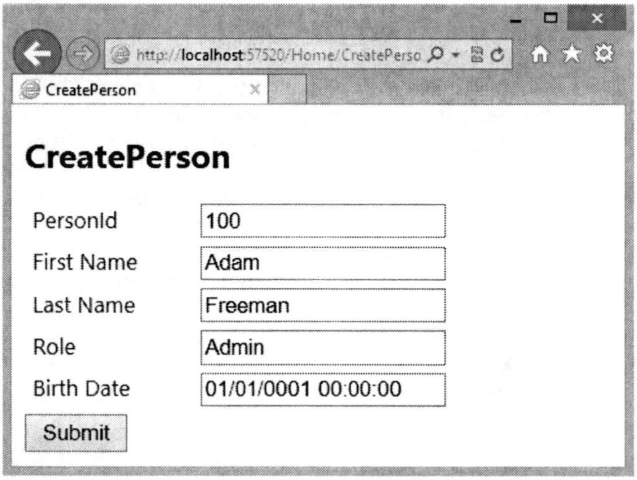

Figure 20-1. Using the Editor and EditorFor helper methods in a form

Other than the addition of the BirthDate property, this does not look different from the kind of form that we were creating in Chapter 19. However, there is a pretty substantial change, which you can see if you use a different browser. In Figure 20-2, you can see the same URL displayed in the Opera browser (which you can get from www.opera.com).

544

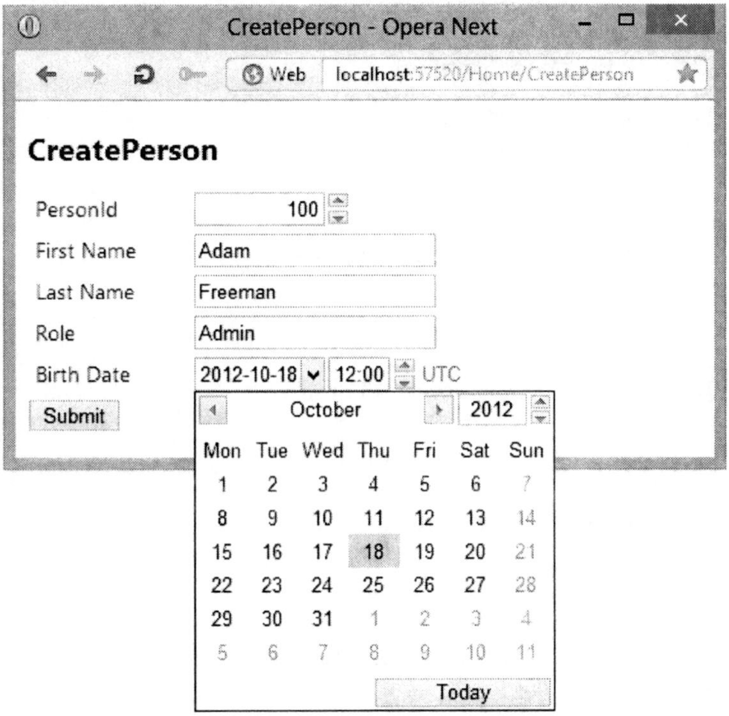

Figure 20-2. Displaying a form created using the Editor and EditorFor helper methods

Notice that the elements for the `PersonId` and `BirthDate` properties look different. The `PersonId` element has spinner arrows (allowing you to increment and decrement the value) and the `BirthDate` element is presented with a date picker.

The HTML5 specification defines different types of `input` element that can be used to edit common data types, such as numbers and dates. The `Helper` and `HelperFor` methods use the type of the property we want to edit to select one of those new types—you can see this in Listing 20-5, where we have shown the HTML that was generated for the form in Figures 20-1 and 20-2.

Listing 20-5. The HTML Input Elements Created by the Editor and EditorFor Helper Methods

```
<!DOCTYPE html>
<html>
<head>
    <meta charset="utf-8" />
    <meta name="viewport" content="width=device-width" />
    <title>CreatePerson</title>
    <link href="/Content/Site.css" rel="stylesheet"/>
    <style type="text/css">
        label { display: inline-block; width: 100px;}
        .dataElem { margin: 5px;}
    </style>
</head>
<body>

<h2>CreatePerson</h2>
```

```
<form action="/app/forms/Home/CreatePerson" class="personClass"
    data-formType="person" method="post">    <div class="dataElem">
        <label>PersonId</label>
        <input class="text-box single-line" id="PersonId" name="PersonId"
            type="number" value="0" />
    </div>
    <div class="dataElem">
        <label>First Name</label>
        <input class="text-box single-line" id="FirstName" name="FirstName"
            type="text" value="" />
    </div>
    <div class="dataElem">
        <label>Last Name</label>
        <input class="text-box single-line" id="LastName" name="LastName"
            type="text" value="" />
    </div>
    <div class="dataElem">
        <label>Role</label>
        <input class="text-box single-line" id="Role" name="Role"
            type="text" value="Admin" />
    </div>
    <div class="dataElem">
        <label>Birth Date</label>
        <input class="text-box single-line" id="BirthDate" name="BirthDate"
            type="datetime" value="01/01/0001 00:00:00" />
    </div>
    <input type="submit" value="Submit" />
</form>
</body>
</html>
```

The type attribute specifies which kind of input element should be displayed. The helper methods have specified the number and datetime types for the PersonId and BirthDate properties and the text type, which is the default for other the other properties. The reason that we only see these types in Opera is because the HTML5 features are still pretty new and not all browsers support them (including Internet Explorer 10, which is what we have been using for the figures throughout this book).

You can see that by using the templated helper methods we have been able to tailor the form elements to the content—although not in an especially useful way, in part because not all browsers can display the HTML5 input element types and in part because some properties, such as Role, are not displayed in a helpful way. We will show you how to provide the MVC Framework with additional information that will improve the HTML that the helper methods produce—but before we get into the detail, we are going to show you the other templated helpers that are available. You can see the complete set of helpers in Table 20-1 and we demonstrate each of them in the sections that follow.

Table 20-1. The MVC Templated HTML Helpers

Helper	Example	Description
Display	Html.Display("FirstName")	Renders a read-only view of the specified model property, choosing an HTML element according to the property's type and metadata

Helper	Example	Description
DisplayFor	Html.DisplayFor(x => x.FirstName)	Strongly typed version of the previous helper
Editor	Html.Editor("FirstName")	Renders an editor for the specified model property, choosing an HTML element according to the property's type and metadata
EditorFor	Html.EditorFor(x => x.FirstName)	Strongly typed version of the previous helper
Label	Html.Label("FirstName")	Renders an HTML <label> element referring to the specified model property
LabelFor	Html.LabelFor(x => x.FirstName)	Strongly typed version of the previous helper

Generating Label and Display Elements

To demonstrate the other helper methods, we are going to add a new to the example application which will display a read-only view of the data submitted from the HTML form. First, we have updated the HttpPost version of the CreatePerson action in the Home controller, as shown in Listing 20-6.

Listing 20-6. Specifying a Different View in the Home Controller

```
using System.Web.Mvc;
using HelperMethods.Models;

namespace HelperMethods.Controllers {
    public class HomeController : Controller {

        public ActionResult Index() {

            ViewBag.Fruits = new string[] { "Apple", "Orange", "Pear" };
            ViewBag.Cities = new string[] { "New York", "London", "Paris" };

            string message = "This is an HTML element: <input>";

            return View((object)message);
        }

        public ActionResult CreatePerson() {
            return View(new Person { IsApproved = true });
        }

        [HttpPost]
        public ActionResult CreatePerson(Person person) {
            return View("DisplayPerson", person);
        }
    }
}
```

We created the `DisplayPerson.cshtml` view file in the `/Views/Home` folder, and you can see the contents of this file in Listing 20-7.

Listing 20-7. The Contents of the DisplayPerson.cshtml File

```
@model HelperMethods.Models.Person

@{
    ViewBag.Title = "DisplayPerson";
}
<h2>DisplayPerson</h2>
<div class="dataElem">
    @Html.Label("PersonId")
    @Html.Display("PersonId")
</div>
<div class="dataElem">
    @Html.Label("FirstName")
    @Html.Display("FirstName")
</div>
<div class="dataElem">
    @Html.LabelFor(m => m.LastName)
    @Html.DisplayFor(m => m.LastName)
</div>
<div class="dataElem">
    @Html.LabelFor(m => m.Role)
    @Html.DisplayFor(m => m.Role)
</div>
<div class="dataElem">
    @Html.LabelFor(m => m.BirthDate)
    @Html.DisplayFor(m => m.BirthDate)
</div>
```

You can see the output that this new view produces by starting the application, navigating to the `/Home/CreatePerson` URL, filling in the form and clicking the Submit button. The result is shown in Figure 20-3 and you can see that we have taken a small step backward, because the `Label` and `LabelFor` helpers have just used the property names as the content for the labels.

Figure 20-3. Using helpers to generate a read only view of the Person object

You can see the output that these helper methods produce in Listing 20-8. Notice that the `Display` and `DisplayFor` methods do not generate an HTML element by default—they just emit the value of the property they operate on.

Listing 20-8. The HTML Generated from the DisplayPerson View

```
<!DOCTYPE html>
<html>
<head>
    <meta charset="utf-8" />
    <meta name="viewport" content="width=device-width" />
    <title>DisplayPerson</title>
    <link href="/Content/Site.css" rel="stylesheet"/>
    <style type="text/css">
        label { display: inline-block; width: 100px;}
        .dataElem { margin: 5px;}
    </style>
</head>
<body>

<h2>DisplayPerson</h2>
<div class="dataElem">
    <label for="PersonId">PersonId</label>
    100
</div>
<div class="dataElem">
    <label for="FirstName">FirstName</label>
    Adam
</div>
<div class="dataElem">
    <label for="LastName">LastName</label>
    Freeman
</div>
<div class="dataElem">
    <label for="Role">Role</label>
    Admin
</div>
<div class="dataElem">
    <label for="BirthDate">BirthDate</label>
    01/01/0001 00:00:00
</div>

</body>
</html>
```

Although these helpers may not seem especially useful at the moment, we will show you how to change their behavior shortly in order to produce output that is much more the kind of thing that you would want to display to users.

Using Whole-Model Template Helpers

We have been using templated helpers which generate output for a single property, but the MVC Framework also defines helpers that operate on the entire objects—a process known as *scaffolding*. There are scaffolding helpers available, as shown in Table 20-2.

Table 20-2. The MVC Scaffolding Templated Helper methods

Helper	Example	Description
DisplayForModel	Html.DisplayForModel()	Renders a read-only view of the entire model object
EditorForModel	Html.EditorForModel()	Renders editor elements for the entire model object
LabelForModel	Html.LabelForModel()	Renders an HTML <label> element referring to the entire model object

In Listing 20-9, you can see how we have used the LabelForModel and EditorForModel helper methods to simplify the CreatePerson.cshtml view.

Listing 20-9. Using the Scaffolding Helper Methods in the CreatePerson View

```
@model HelperMethods.Models.Person

@{
    ViewBag.Title = "CreatePerson";
    Html.EnableClientValidation(false);
}

<h2>CreatePerson: @Html.LabelForModel()</h2>

@using(Html.BeginRouteForm("FormRoute", new {}, FormMethod.Post,
    new { @class = "personClass", data_formType="person"})) {

    @Html.EditorForModel()

    <input type="submit" value="Submit" />
}
```

You can see the effect of the scaffold helpers in Figure 20-4. Once again, you can see what the helpers are trying to do but that things are not quite right yet. The LabelForModel helper has not generated a useful label and although more properties from the Person model object are being shown than we defined manually in previous examples, not everything is visible (such as the Address property) and what is visible is not always useful (such as the Role property, which would be more usefully expressed as a select instead of an input element).

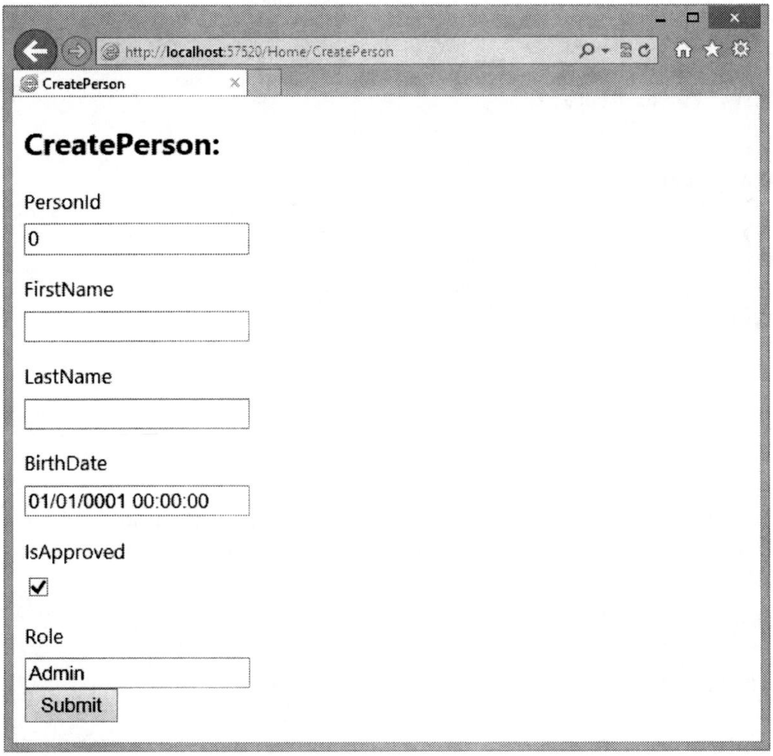

Figure 20-4. Using the scaffolding helpers to create an editor for the Person model object

Part of the problem is that the HTML that the scaffolding helpers generate doesn't correspond to the CSS styles that we added to the /Views/Shared/_Layout.cshtml file in Chapter 19. Here is an example of the HTML generated to edit the FirstName property:

```
...
<div class="editor-label">
    <label for="FirstName">FirstName</label>
</div>
<div class="editor-field">
    <input class="text-box single-line" id="FirstName" name="FirstName"
        type="text" value="" />
</div>
...
```

We can tidy up the appearance of view by making simple changes to our styles so that they correspond to the CSS class values added to the div and input elements by the scaffolding helpers. In Listing 20-10, you can see the changes we have made to the _Layout.cshtml file.

Listing 20-10. Making Changes to the CSS Styles Defined in the _Layout.cshtml File

```
<!DOCTYPE html>
<html>
<head>
    <meta charset="utf-8" />
    <meta name="viewport" content="width=device-width" />
```

551

```
    <title>@ViewBag.Title</title>
    <link href="~/Content/Site.css" rel="stylesheet"/>
    <style type="text/css">
        label { display: inline-block; width: 100px;}
        .dataElem { margin: 5px;}
        h2 > label {width: inherit;}
        .editor-label, .editor-field {float: left;}
        .editor-label, .editor-label label, .editor-field input {height: 20px;}
        .editor-label {clear: left;}
        .editor-field { margin-left: 10px; margin-top: 10px;}
        input[type=submit] { float: left; clear: both; margin-top: 10px;}
        .column { float: left; margin: 10px;}
    </style>
</head>
<body>
    @RenderBody()
</body>
</html>
```

These new styles produce something that is more in keeping with the layout we used in earlier examples, as shown in Figure 20-5. (We also added some styles that we will need later in the chapter—you will see where they are applied shortly.)

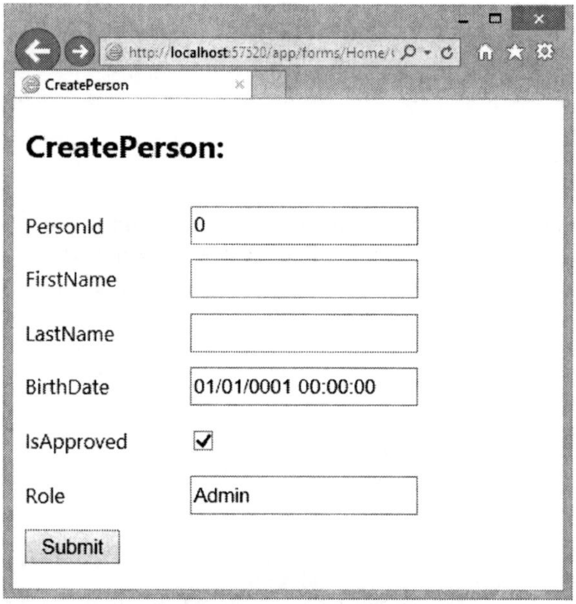

Figure 20-5. The effect of styling elements using the classes defined by the scaffolding helper methods

Using Model Metadata

As you have seen, the templated helpers have no special knowledge about our application and its model data types, and so we end up with HTML that is not what we require. We want the benefits that come with simpler views, but we need to get improve the quality of the output that the helper methods generate before we can use them seriously.

We cannot blame the templated helpers in these situations; the HTML that is generated is based on a best-guess about what we want. Fortunately, we can use model metadata to provide guidance to the helpers about how to handle our model types. Metadata is expressed using C# attributes, where attributes and parameter values provide a range of instructions to the view helpers. The metadata is applied to the model class, which the helper methods consult when they generate HTML elements. In the following sections, we will show you how to use metadata to provide directions to the helpers for labels, displays, and editors.

Using Metadata to Control Editing and Visibility

In our `Person` class, the `PersonId` property is one that we do not want the user to be able to see or edit. Most model classes have at least one such property, often related to the underlying storage mechanism—a primary key that is managed by a relational database, for example, which we demonstrated when we created the `SportsStore` application.

We can use the `HiddenInput` attribute, which causes the helper to render a hidden input field. You can see how we have applied the `HiddenAttribute` to our `Person` class in Listing 20-11.

Listing 20-11. Using the HiddenInput Attribute

```
using System;
using System.Web.Mvc;

namespace HelperMethods.Models {

    public class Person {
        [HiddenInput]
        public int PersonId { get; set; }
        public string FirstName { get; set; }
        public string LastName { get; set; }
        public DateTime BirthDate { get; set; }
        public Address HomeAddress { get; set; }
        public bool IsApproved { get; set; }
        public Role Role { get; set; }
    }
    // ...other types omitted from Listing 20-for brevity...
}
```

When this attribute has been applied, the `Html.EditorFor` and `Html.EditorForModel` helpers will render a read-only view of the decorated property (which is the term used to describe a property to which an attribute has been applied), as shown in Figure 20-6, which shows the effect of starting the application and navigating to the `/Home/CreatePerson` URL.

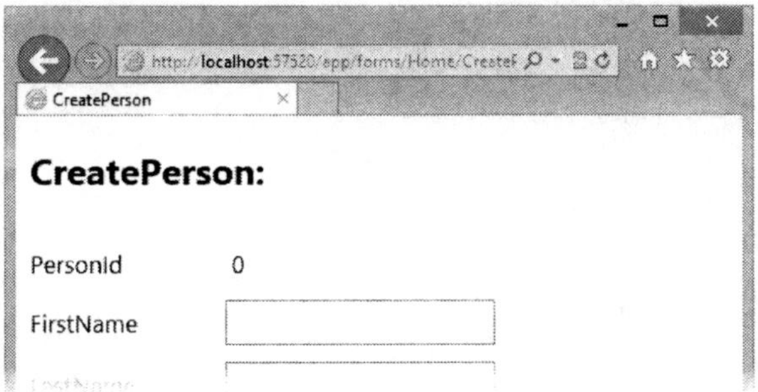

Figure 20-6. Creating a read-only representation of a property in an editor

The value of the PersonId property is shown, but the user cannot edit it. The HTML that is generated for the property is as follows:

```
...
<div class="editor-field">
    0
    <input id="PersonId" name="PersonId" type="hidden" value="0" />
</div>
...
```

The value of the property (0 in this case) is rendered literally, but the helper also includes a hidden input element for the property, which is helpful for HTML forms because it ensures that a value for the property is submitted when the form is submitted—this is something we will return to when we look at model binding in Chapter 22 and model validation in Chapter 23. If we want to hide a property entirely, then we can set the value of the DisplayValue property in the DisplayName attribute to false, as shown in Listing 20-12.

Listing 20-12. Using the HiddenInput Attribute to Hide a Property

```
...
public class Person {
    [HiddenInput(DisplayValue=false)]
    public int PersonId { get; set; }
    public string FirstName { get; set; }
    public string LastName { get; set; }
    public DateTime BirthDate { get; set; }
    public Address HomeAddress { get; set; }
    public bool IsApproved { get; set; }
    public Role Role { get; set; }
}
...
```

When we use the Html.EditorForModel helper on a Person object, a hidden input will be created so that the value for the PersonId property will be included in any form submissions, but the label and the literal value will be omitted. This has the effect of hiding the PersonId property from the user, as shown by Figure 20-7.

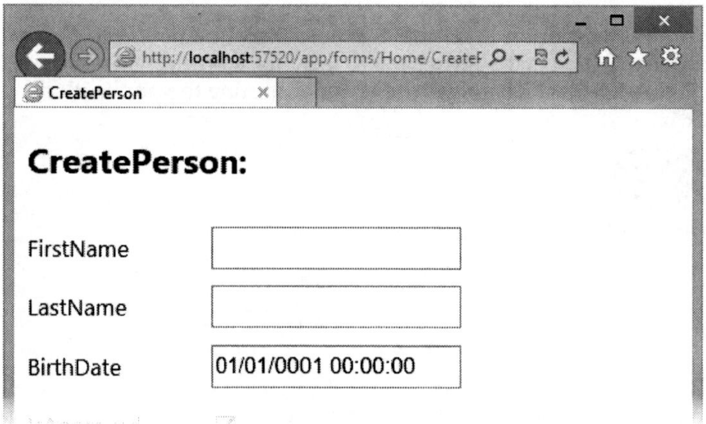

Figure 20-7. Hiding model object properties from the user

If we have chosen to render HTML for individual properties, we can still create the hidden input for the `PersonId` property by using the `Html.EditorFor` helper, like this:

```
...
@Html.EditorFor(m => m.PersonId)
...
```

The `HiddenInput` property is detected, and if `DisplayValue` is `true`, then the following HTML is generated:

```
...
<input id="PersonId" name="PersonId" type="hidden" value="1" />
...
```

EXCLUDING A PROPERTY FROM SCAFFOLDING

If we want to exclude a property from the generated HTML, we can use the `ScaffoldColumn` attribute. Whereas the `HiddenInput` attribute includes a value for the property in a hidden input element, the `ScaffoldColumn` attribute allows us to mark a property as being entirely off limits for the scaffolding process. Here is an example of the attribute in use:

```
...
[ScaffoldColumn(false)]
public int PersonId { get; set; }
...
```

When the scaffolding helpers see the `ScaffoldColumn` attribute, they skip over the property entirely; no hidden `input` elements will be created, and no details of this property will be included in the generated HTML. The appearance of the generated HTML will be the same as if we had used the `HiddenInput` attribute, but no value will be returned for the property during a form submission—this has an effect on model binding, which we discuss later in the chapter. The `ScaffoldColumn` attribute doesn't have an effect on the per-property helpers, such as `EditorFor`. If we call `@Html.EditorFor(m => m.PersonId)` in a view, then an editor for the `PersonId` property will be generated, even when the `ScaffoldColumn` attribute is present.

Using Metadata for Labels

By default, the `Label`, `LabelFor`, `LabelForModel`, and `EditorForModel` helpers use the names of properties as the content for the `label` elements they generate. For example, if we render a label like this:

```
...
@Html.LabelFor(m => m.BirthDate)
...
```

the HTML element that is generated will be as follows:

```
...
<label for="BirthDate">BirthDate</label>
...
```

Of course, the names we give to our properties are often not what we want to be displayed to the user. To that end, we can apply the DisplayName attribute from the System.ComponentModel.DataAnnotations namespace, passing in the value we want as a value for the Name property. Listing 20-13 demonstrates this attribute applied to the Person class.

Listing 20-13. Using the DisplayName Attribute to Define a Label

```
using System;
using System.Web.Mvc;
using System.ComponentModel.DataAnnotations;
using System.ComponentModel;

namespace HelperMethods.Models {

    [DisplayName("New Person")]
    public class Person {
        [HiddenInput(DisplayValue=false)]
        public int PersonId { get; set; }

        [Display(Name="First")]
        public string FirstName { get; set; }

        [Display(Name = "Last")]
        public string LastName { get; set; }

        [Display(Name = "Birth Date")]
        public DateTime BirthDate { get; set; }

        public Address HomeAddress { get; set; }

        [Display(Name="Approved")]
        public bool IsApproved { get; set; }
        public Role Role { get; set; }
    }

    // ...other types omitted from Listing 20-for brevity...
}
```

When the label helpers render a label element for the BirthDate property, they will detect the Display attribute and use the value of the Name parameter for the inner text, like this:

```
<label for="BirthDate">Birth Date</label>
```

The helpers also recognize the DisplayName attribute, which can be found in the System.ComponentModel namespace. This attribute has the advantage of being able to be applied to classes, which allows us to use the Html.LabelForModel helper—you can see how we have applied this attribute to the Person class in the listing. (We can apply the DisplayName attribute to properties as well, but we tend to use this attribute only for model classes, for no reason other than habit.) You can see the effect of the Display and DisplayName attributes in Figure 20-8.

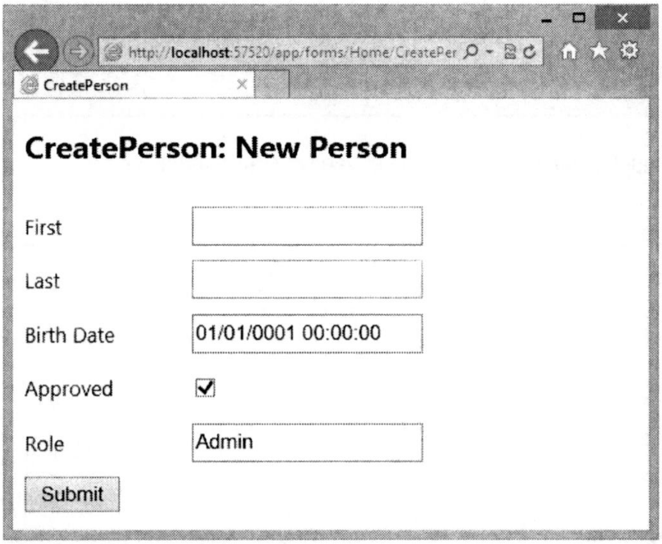

Figure 20-8. Using the Display and DisplayName attributes to control labels

Using Metadata for Data Values

We can also use metadata to provide instructions about how a model property should be displayed—we can use this to deal with the fact that our `BirthDate` property is displayed with a time when we really just want a date, for example. We control the way that data values are displaying using the `DataType` attribute, which you can see applied to the `Person` class in Listing 20-14.

Listing 20-14. Applying the DataType Attribute to the Person Class

```
...
[DisplayName("New Person")]
public class Person {
    [HiddenInput(DisplayValue=false)]
    public int PersonId { get; set; }

    [Display(Name="First")]
    public string FirstName { get; set; }

    [Display(Name = "Last")]
    public string LastName { get; set; }

    [Display(Name = "Birth Date")]
    [DataType(DataType.Date)]
    public DateTime BirthDate { get; set; }

    public Address HomeAddress { get; set; }

    [Display(Name="Approved")]
    public bool IsApproved { get; set; }
    public Role Role { get; set; }
}
...
```

The DataType attribute takes a value from the DataType enumeration as a parameter. In the example we have specified the DataType.Date value, which causes the templated helpers to render the value of the BirthDate property as a date without a time component, as shown in Figure 20-9.

■ **Tip**   The change is more pronounced when the application is viewed using a Web browser that has better support for the HTML5 input element types.

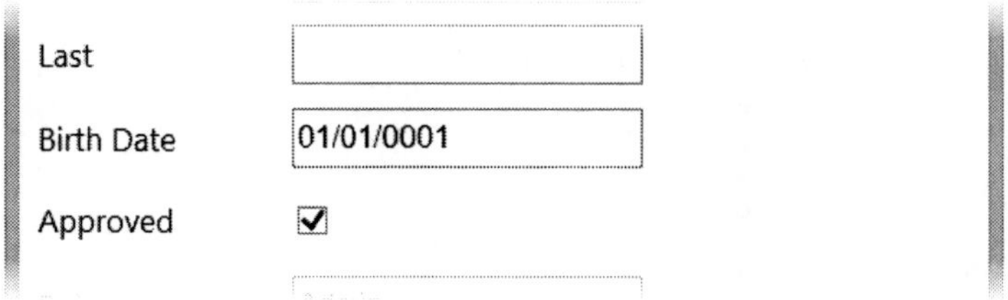

Last	
Birth Date	01/01/0001
Approved	✓

Figure 20-9. Using the DataType attribute to control the display of a DateTime value

Table 20-3 describes the most useful values of the DataType enumeration.

Table 20-3. The Values of the DataType Enumeration

Value	Description
DateTime	Displays a date and time (this is the default behavior for System.DateTime values)
Date	Displays the date portion of a DateTime
Time	Displays the time portion of a DateTime
Text	Displays a single line of text
PhoneNumber	Displays a phone number
MultilineText	Renders the value in a textarea element
Password	Displays the data so that individual characters are masked from view
Url	Displays the data as a URL (using an HTML a element)
EmailAddress	Displays the data as an e-mail address (using an a element with a mailto href)

The effect of these values depends on the type of the property they are associated with and the helper we are using. For example, the MultilineText value will lead those helpers that create editors for properties to create an HTML textarea element but will be ignored by the display helpers. This makes sense—the textarea element allows the user to edit a value, which doesn't make sense when we are displaying the data in a read-only form. Equally, the Url value has an effect only on the display helpers, which render an HTML a element to create a link.

Using Metadata to Select a Display Template

As their name suggests, templated helpers use display templates to generate HTML. The template that is used is based on the type of the property being processed and the kind of helper being used. We can use the UIHint attribute to specify the template we want to use to render HTML for a property, as shown in Listing 20-15.

Listing 20-15. Using the UIHint Attribute

```
...
[DisplayName("New Person")]
public class Person {
    [HiddenInput(DisplayValue=false)]
    public int PersonId { get; set; }

    [Display(Name="First")]
    [UIHint("MultilineText")]
    public string FirstName { get; set; }

    [Display(Name = "Last")]
    public string LastName { get; set; }

    [Display(Name = "Birth Date")]
    [DataType(DataType.Date)]
    public DateTime BirthDate { get; set; }

    public Address HomeAddress { get; set; }

    [Display(Name="Approved")]
    public bool IsApproved { get; set; }
    public Role Role { get; set; }
}
...
```

In the listing, we specified the MultilineText template, which renders an HTML textarea element for the FirstName property when used with one of the editor helpers, such as EditorFor or EditorForModel. Table 20-4 shows the set of built-in templates that the MVC Framework includes.

Table 20-4. The Built-In MVC Framework View Templates

Value	Effect (Editor)	Effect (Display)
Boolean	Renders a checkbox for bool values. For nullable bool? values, a select element is created with options for True, False, and Not Set.	As for the editor helpers, but with the addition of the disabled attribute, which renders read-only HTML controls.
Collection	Renders the appropriate template for each of the elements in an IEnumerable sequence. The items in the sequence do not have to be of the same type.	As for the editor helpers.
Decimal	Renders a single-line textbox input element and formats the data value to display two decimal places.	Renders the data value formatted to two decimal places.

Value	Effect (Editor)	Effect (Display)
DateTime	Renders an input element whose type attribute is datetime and which contains the complete date and time.	Renders the complete value of a DateTime variable.
Date	Renders an input element whose type attribute is dateand that contains the date component (but not the time).	Renders the date component of a DateTime variable
EmailAddress	Renders the value in a single-line textbox input element.	Renders a link using an HTML a element and an href attribute that is formatted as a mailto URL.
HiddenInput	Creates a hidden input element.	Renders the data value and creates a hidden input element.
Html	Renders the value in a single-line textbox input element.	Renders a link using an HTML a element.
MultilineText	Renders an HTML textarea element that contains the data value.	Renders the data value.
Number	Renders an input element whose type attribute is set to number.	Renders the data value
Object	See explanation after this table.	See explanation after this table.
Password	Renders the value in a single-line textbox input element so that the characters are not displayed but can be edited.	Renders the data value—the characters are not obscured.
String	Renders the value in a single-line textbox input element.	Renders the data value.
Text	Identical to the String template.	Identical to the String template
Tel	Renders an input element whose type attribute is set to tel.	Renders the data value
Time	Renders an input element whose type attribute is time and which contains the time component (but not the date).	Renders the time component of a DateTime variable
Url	Renders the value in a single-line textbox input element.	Renders a link using an HTML a element. The inner HTML and the href attribute are both set to the data value.

> ■ **Caution** Care must be taken when using the UIHint attribute. We will receive an exception if we select a template that cannot operate on the type of the property we have applied it to—for example, applying the Boolean template to a string property.

The Object template is a special case—it is the template used by the scaffolding helpers to generate HTML for a view model object. This template examines each of the properties of an object and selects the most suitable template for the property type. The Object template takes metadata such as the UIHint and DataType attributes into account.

Applying Metadata to a Buddy Class

It is not always possible to apply metadata to an entity model class. This is usually the case when the model classes are generated automatically, like sometimes with ORM tools such as the Entity Framework (although not the way we used Entity Framework in the SportsStore application). Any changes we apply to automatically generated classes, such as applying attributes, will be lost the next time the classes are updated or regenerated.

The solution to this problem is to ensure that the model class is defined as partial and to create a second partial class that contains the metadata. Many tools that generate classes automatically create partial classes by default, including the Entity Framework. Listing 20-16 shows the Person class modified such that it could have been generated automatically—there is no metadata, and the class is defined as partial.

Listing 20-16. A Partial Model Class

```
using System;
using System.ComponentModel.DataAnnotations;

namespace HelperMethods.Models {

    [MetadataType(typeof(PersonMetaData))]
    public partial class Person {
        public int PersonId { get; set; }
        public string FirstName { get; set; }
        public string LastName { get; set; }
        public DateTime BirthDate { get; set; }
        public Address HomeAddress { get; set; }
        public bool IsApproved { get; set; }
        public Role Role { get; set; }
    }

    // ...other types omitted from listing for brevity...
}
```

We tell the MVC Framework about the buddy class through the MetadataType attribute, which takes the type of the buddy class as its argument. Buddy classes must be defined in the same namespace and must also be partial classes. To demonstrate how this works, we have added a new folder to the example project called Models/Metadata. In this folder, we created a new class file called PersonMetadata.cs, the contents of which are shown in Listing 20-17.

Listing 20-17. Defining the Metadata Buddy Class

```
using System;
using System.ComponentModel;
using System.ComponentModel.DataAnnotations;
using System.Web.Mvc;

namespace HelperMethods.Models {

    [DisplayName("New Person")]
    public partial class PersonMetaData {
        [HiddenInput(DisplayValue=false)]
        public int PersonId { get; set; }

        [Display(Name="First")]
        public string FirstName { get; set; }

        [Display(Name = "Last")]
        public string LastName { get; set; }

        [Display(Name = "Birth Date")]
        [DataType(DataType.Date)]
        public DateTime BirthDate { get; set; }

        [Display(Name="Approved")]
        public bool IsApproved { get; set; }
    }
}
```

The buddy class only needs to contain properties that we want to apply metadata to—we do not have to replicate all of the properties of the `Person` class, for example.

■ **Tip**   Take particular care to change the namespace that Visual Studio adds to the new class file—the buddy class must be in the same namespace as the model class, which is `HelperMethods.Models` for our example application.

Working with Complex Type Properties

The templating process relies on the `Object` template that we described in the previous section. Each property is inspected, and a template is selected to render HTML to represent the property and its data value.

You may have noticed that the `HomeAddress` property was not rendered as part of the `Person` class when we used the `EditorForModel`. This happens because the `Object` template operates only on *simple types*—which means those types that can be parsed from a `string` value using the `GetConverter` method of the `System.ComponentModel.TypeDescriptor` class. The supported types include the intrinsic C# types such as `int`, `bool`, and `double` and many common framework types including `Guid` and `DateTime`.

The result is that scaffolding helpers are not recursive. Given an object to process, a scaffolding templated helper method will generate HTML only for simple property types and will ignore any properties that are complex objects.

Although it can be inconvenient, this is a sensible policy; the MVC Framework does not know how our model objects are created, and if the `Object` template was recursive, then we could easily end up triggering our ORM lazy-loading feature, which would lead us to read and render every object in our underlying database. If we want to render HTML for a complex property, we have to do it explicitly by making a separate call to a templated helper method. You can see how we have done this in Listing 20-18, which shows the changes we have made to the `CreatePerson.cshtml` method.

Listing 20-18. Dealing with a Property that Is a Complex Type

```
@model HelperMethods.Models.Person

@{
    ViewBag.Title = "CreatePerson";
    Html.EnableClientValidation(false);
}
<h2>CreatePerson: @Html.LabelForModel()</h2>

@using(Html.BeginRouteForm("FormRoute", new {}, FormMethod.Post,
    new { @class = "personClass", data_formType="person"})) {

    <div class="column">
        @Html.EditorForModel()
    </div>
    <div class="column">
        @Html.EditorFor(m => m.HomeAddress)
    </div>
    <input type="submit" value="Submit" />
}
```

To display the `HomeAddress` property, we added a call to the strongly-typed `EditorFor` helper method. (We also added some `div` elements to provide structure to the HTML that is generated, relying on the CSS style we defined for the `column` class back in Listing 20-10.) You can see the result in Figure 20-10.

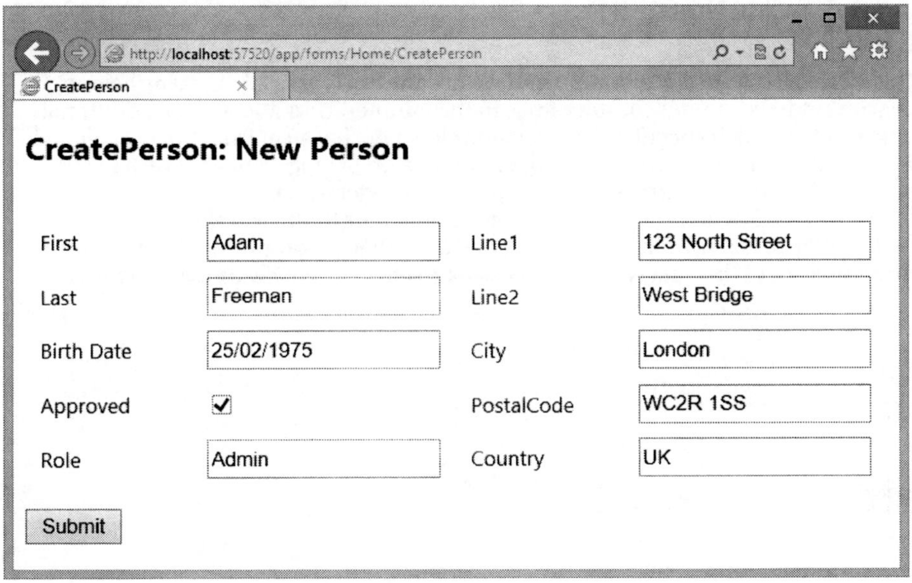

Figure 20-10. Displaying a complex property

■ **Tip**　　The HomeAddress property is typed to return an Address object, and we can apply all of the same metadata to the Address class as we did to the Person class. The Object template is invoked explicitly when we use the EditorFor helpers on the HomeAddress property, and so all of the metadata conventions are honored.

Customizing the Templated View Helper System

We have shown you how to use metadata to shape the way that the templated helpers render data, but this is the MVC Framework and so there are some advanced options that let us customize the templated helpers entirely. In the following sections, we will show you how to can supplement or replace the built-in support to create very specific results.

Creating a Custom Editor Template

One of the easiest ways of customizing the templated helpers is to create a custom template. This allows us to render exactly the HTML we want for a model property.

To demonstrate how this feature works, we are going to create a custom template for the Role property in our Person class. This property is typed to be a value from the Role enumeration, but the way that this is rendered by default is problematic because the templated helpers just create a regular input element that allows the user to enter any value and not just the values defined by the enumeration.

The MVC Framework looks for custom editor templates in the /Views/Shared/EditorTemplates folder, so we added this folder to the example project and then created a new strongly typed partial view called Role.cshtml within it. You can see the contents of this file in Listing 20-19.

Listing 20-19. The Contents of the Role.cshtml File

```
@model HelperMethods.Models.Role

@Html.DropDownListFor(m => m,
    new SelectList(Enum.GetNames(Model.GetType()),
        Model.ToString()))
```

The model type for this view is the Role enumeration and we use the Html.DropDownListFor helper method to create a select with option elements for the values in the enumeration. We pass an additional value to the SelectList constructor, which specifies the selected value, which we get from the view model object. The DropDownListFor method and the SelectList object operate on string values, so we have to make sure that we convert the values in the enumeration and the view model value.

When we use any of the templated helper methods to generate an editor for the Role type, our /Views/Shared/EditorTemplates/Role.cshtml file will be used, ensuring that we get present the user with a consistent and usable representation of the data type. You can see the effect of the custom template in Figure 20-11.

Figure 20-11. The effect of a custom template for the Role enumeration

UNDERSTANDING THE TEMPLATE SEARCH ORDER

Our `Role.cshtml` template works because the MVC Framework looks for custom templates for a given C# type before it uses one of the built-in templates. In fact, there is a very specific sequence that the MVC Framework follows to find a suitable template:

1. The template passed to the helper—for example, `Html.EditorFor(m => m.SomeProperty, "MyTemplate")` would lead to `MyTemplate` being used.
2. Any template that is specified by metadata attributes, such as `UIHint`.
3. The template associated with any data type specified by metadata, such as the `DataType` attribute.
4. Any template that corresponds to the.NET class name of the data type being processed.
5. The built-in `String` template if the data type being processed is a simple type.
6. Any template that corresponds to the base classes of the data type.
7. If the data type implements `IEnumerable`, then the built-in `Collection` template will be used.If all else fails, the `Object` template will be used—subject to the rule that scaffolding is not recursive.

Some of these steps rely on the built-in templates, which are described in Table 20-4. At each stage in the template search process, the MVC Framework looks for a template called `EditorTemplates/<name>` for editor helper methods or `DisplayTemplates/<name>` for display helper methods. For our `Role` template, we satisfied step 4 in the search process; we created a template called `Role.cshtml` and placed it in the `/Views/Shared/EditorTemplates` folder.

Custom templates are found using the same search pattern as regular views, which means we can create a controller-specific custom template and place it in the `~/Views/<controller>/EditorTemplates` folder to override the templates found in the `~/Views/Shared` folder. In Chapter 18, we explained more about the way that views are located.

Creating a Generic Template

We are not limited to creating type-specific templates. We can, for example, create a template that works for all enumerations and then specify that this template be selected using the `UIHint` attribute. If you look at the template search sequence in the "Understanding the Template Search Order" sidebar, you will see that templates specified using the `UIHint` attribute take precedence over type-specific ones.

To demonstrate how this works, we have created a new view file called `Enum.cshtml` in the `/Views/Shared/EditorTemplates` folder. The contents of this file are shown in Listing 20-20.

Listing 20-20. The Contents of the Enum.cshtml

```
@model Enum

@Html.DropDownListFor(m => m, Enum.GetValues(Model.GetType())
    .Cast<Enum>()
    .Select(m => {
        string enumVal = Enum.GetName(Model.GetType(), m);
        return new SelectListItem() {
            Selected = (Model.ToString() == enumVal),
            Text = enumVal,
            Value = enumVal
        };
    }))
```

The model type for this template is Enum, which allows us to work with any enumeration. For variety, we have used some LINQ to generate the strings that are required to create the select and option elements.

We can then apply the UIHint attribute. Our example project defines a metadata buddy class, so we have applied the attribute to the PersonMetadata class, as shown in Listing 20-21. (As a reminder, you can find this class defined in the /Models/Metadata/PersonMetadata.cs file.)

Listing 20-21. Using the UIHint Attribute to Specify a Custom Template

```
using System;
using System.ComponentModel;
using System.ComponentModel.DataAnnotations;
using System.Web.Mvc;

namespace HelperMethods.Models {

    [DisplayName("New Person")]
    public partial class PersonMetaData {
        [HiddenInput(DisplayValue=false)]
        public int PersonId { get; set; }

        [Display(Name="First")]
        public string FirstName { get; set; }

        [Display(Name = "Last")]
        public string LastName { get; set; }

        [Display(Name = "Birth Date")]
        [DataType(DataType.Date)]
        public DateTime BirthDate { get; set; }

        [Display(Name="Approved")]
        public bool IsApproved { get; set; }

        [UIHint("Enum")]
        public Role Role { get; set; }
    }
}
```

This approach gives a more general solution that you can apply throughout an application to ensure that all Enum properties are displayed using a select element. We tend to prefer to create model type-specific custom templates, but it can be more convenient to have one template that you can apply widely.

Replacing the Built-in Templates

If we create a custom template that has the same name as one of the built-in templates, the MVC Framework will use the custom version in preference to the built-in one. Listing 20-22 shows the contents of the Boolean.cshtml file that we created in the /Views/Shared/EditorTemplates folder. This view replaces the built-in Boolean template which is used to render bool and bool? values.

Listing 20-22. Replacing a Built-In Template

```
@model bool?

@if (ViewData.ModelMetadata.IsNullableValueType && Model == null) {
    @:(True) (False) <b>(Not Set)</b>
} else if (Model.Value) {
    @:<b>(True)</b> (False) (Not Set)
} else {
    @:(True) <b>(False)</b> (Not Set)
}
```

In this view, we display all of the possible values and highlight the one that corresponds to the model object. You can see the effect of this template in Figure 20-12.

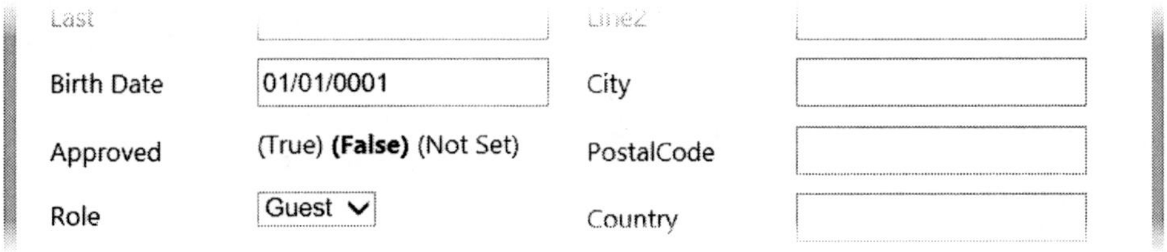

Figure 20-12. The effect of overriding a built-in editor template

You can see the flexibility that custom templates offer, even if the example we have shown you is not especially useful and does not let the user change the property value. As you have seen, there are a number of different ways that you can control how your model properties and displayed and edited, and you can pick the approach that suits your programming style and application best.

Summary

In this chapter, we have shown you the system of model templates that are accessible through the templated view helper methods. It can take a little while to set up the metadata and to create custom templates, but the result is closely tailored to your application and gives you complete flexibility in how your view model data is displayed and edited.

CHAPTER 21

▓ ▓ ▓

URL and Ajax Helper Methods

In this chapter, we are going to complete our coverage of the MVC Framework helper methods by showing you those methods, which are able to generate URLs, links, and Ajax-enabled elements. Ajax is a key feature of any rich Web application and the MVC Framework includes some useful features that are based on the jQuery library. We'll show you how this works and demonstrate how you can use it to create Ajax-enabled forms and links.

▓ **Note** You will need to clear the browser history as you go from one example in this chapter to the next—this is because we build out our features incrementally and isn't something you would need to worry about in a real project. We have added notes to remind you at key points in the chapter, but if you don't get the result you are expecting from an example then the first thing to try is clearing the history.

Reviewing and Preparing the Example Project

We are going to continue using the `HelperMethods` project that we created in Chapter 19 and added to in Chapter 20. Some of our examples in this chapter will use the routing information we defined in the project that, as a reminder, is shown in Listing 21-1.

Listing 21-1. The Contents of the /App_Start/RouteConfig.cs File

```
using System;
using System.Collections.Generic;
using System.Linq;
using System.Web;
using System.Web.Mvc;
using System.Web.Routing;

namespace HelperMethods {
    public class RouteConfig {
        public static void RegisterRoutes(RouteCollection routes) {
            routes.IgnoreRoute("{resource}.axd/{*pathInfo}");

            routes.MapRoute(
                name: "Default",
                url: "{controller}/{action}/{id}",
                defaults: new { controller = "Home", action = "Index",
                    id = UrlParameter.Optional }
```

569

```
        );

        routes.MapRoute(
            name: "FormRoute",
            url: "app/forms/{controller}/{action}"
        );
    }
  }
}
```

Our routing configuration is pretty simple. It consists of the default route added by Visual Studio when the project was created and an additional route called FormRoute that has two static segments.

For this chapter, we have created a new controller called People, as shown in Listing 21-2. This controller defines a collection of Person model objects that we will use to demonstrate different helper features.

Listing 21-2. The People Controller

```
using System;
using System.Collections.Generic;
using System.Linq;
using System.Web;
using System.Web.Mvc;
using HelperMethods.Models;

namespace HelperMethods.Controllers {
    public class PeopleController : Controller {
        private Person[] personData = {
            new Person {FirstName = "Adam", LastName = "Freeman", Role = Role.Admin},
            new Person {FirstName = "Steven", LastName = "Sanderson", Role = Role.Admin},
            new Person {FirstName = "Jacqui", LastName = "Griffyth", Role = Role.User},
            new Person {FirstName = "John", LastName = "Smith", Role = Role.User},
            new Person {FirstName = "Anne", LastName = "Jones", Role = Role.Guest}
        };

        public ActionResult Index() {
            return View();
        }

        public ActionResult GetPeople() {
            return View(personData);
        }

        [HttpPost]
        public ActionResult GetPeople(string selectedRole) {
            if (selectedRole == null || selectedRole == "All") {
                return View(personData);
            } else {
                Role selected = (Role)Enum.Parse(typeof(Role), selectedRole);
                return View(personData.Where(p => p.Role == selected));
            }
        }
    }
}
```

We have not used any new techniques in this controller. The Index action method returns the default view. We will use the two GetPeople action methods to handle a simple form. The new features in this chapter appear in the views, which we will create as we demonstrate different helper methods.

We also need to add some new CSS styles to project. In earlier chapters, we demonstrated that you can define styles in individual views or in layouts, but we are going to define the styles we need in the /Content/Site.css file, for which there is a link element in the /Views/Shared/_Layout.cshtml file. You can see the styles we have added to Site.css in Listing 21-3. We will define the elements they apply to as we go through the chapter.

Listing 21-3. Adding Styles to the Site.css File

```
...
table, td, th {
    border: thin solid black; border-collapse: collapse; padding: 5px;
    background-color: lemonchiffon; text-align: left; margin: 10px 0;
}
div.load {color: red; margin: 10px 0; font-weight: bold;}
div.ajaxLink {margin-top: 10px;margin-right: 5px;float: left;}
...
```

Creating Basic Links and URLs

One of the most fundamental tasks in a view is to create a link or URL that the user can follow to another part of the application. In previous chapters, you saw most of the helper methods that you can use to create links and URLs, but we want to take a moment to recap before moving on to some of the more advanced helpers that are available. Table 21-1 describes the available HTML helpers and it shows examples of each of them.

■ **Tip** As a reminder, the benefit of using these helpers to generate links and URLs is that the output is derived from the routing configuration, which means that a change in routes is automatically reflected in the links and URLs.

Table 21-1. HTML Helpers That Render URLs

Description	Example
Application-relative URL	Url.Content("~/Content/Site.css") Output: /Content/Site.css
Link to named action/controller	Html.ActionLink("My Link", "Index", "Home") Output: <a href="/">My Link</a>
URL for action	Url.Action("GetPeople", "People") Output: /People/GetPeople

Description	Example
URL using route data	`Url.RouteUrl(new {controller = "People", action="GetPeople"})`
	Output:
	`/People/GetPeople`
Link using route data	`Html.RouteLink("My Link", new {controller = "People", action="GetPeople"})`
	Output:
	`<a href="/People/GetPeople">My Link</a>`
Link to named route	`Html.RouteLink("My Link", "FormRoute", new {controller = "People", action="GetPeople"})`
	Output:
	`<a href="/app/forms/People/GetPeople">My Link</a>`

To demonstrate these helpers in action, we created the /People/Index.cshtml view file, the contents of which you can see in Listing 21-4.

Listing 21-4. The Contents of the /People/Index.cshtml File

```
@{
    ViewBag.Title = "Index";
}
<h2>Basic Links & URLs</h2>
<table>
    <thead><tr><th>Helper</th><th>Output</th></tr></thead>
    <tbody>
        <tr>
            <td>Url.Content("~/Content/Site.css")</td>
            <td>@Url.Content("~/Content/Site.css")</td>
        </tr>
        <tr>
            <td>Html.ActionLink("My Link", "Index", "Home")</td>
            <td>@Html.ActionLink("My Link", "Index", "Home")</td>
        </tr>
        <tr>
            <td>Url.Action("GetPeople", "People")</td>
            <td>@Url.Action("GetPeople", "People")</td>
        </tr>
        <tr>
            <td>Url.RouteUrl(new {controller = "People", action="GetPeople"})</td>
            <td>@Url.RouteUrl(new {controller = "People", action="GetPeople"})</td>
        </tr>
        <tr>
            <td>Html.RouteLink("My Link", new {controller = "People",
                action="GetPeople"})</td>
            <td>@Html.RouteLink("My Link", new {controller = "People",
                action="GetPeople"})</td>
        </tr>
```

```
        </tr>
        <tr>
            <td>Html.RouteLink("My Link", "FormRoute", new {controller = "People",
                action="GetPeople"})</td>
            <td>@Html.RouteLink("My Link", "FormRoute", new {controller = "People",
                action="GetPeople"})</td>
        </tr>
    </tbody>
<///table>
```

This view contains the same set of helper calls that we have listed in Table 21-1 and presents the results in an HTML table, as shown in Figure 21-1. We have included this example because it makes it easy to experiment with routing changes and immediately see the effect.

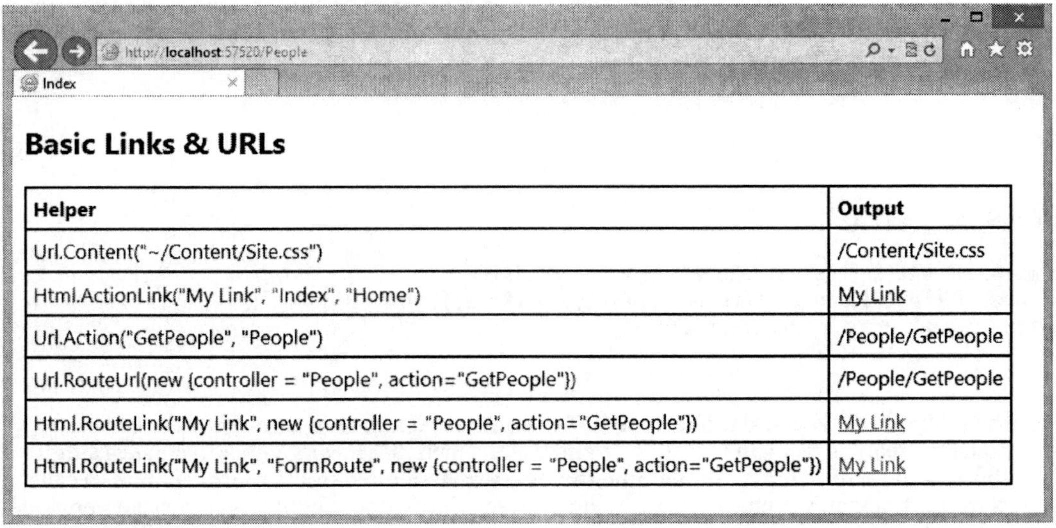

Figure 21-1. Using helpers to create links and URLs

Using MVC Unobtrusive Ajax

Ajax (often referred to as AJAX) is shorthand for *Asynchronous JavaScript and XML*. As we will see, the XML part is not as significant as it used to be, but the asynchronous part is what makes Ajax useful—it is a model for requesting data from the server in the background, without having to reload the Web page.

The MVC Framework contains built-in support for *unobtrusive* Ajax, which means that you use helper methods to define your Ajax features, rather than having to add blocks of code throughout your views.

■ **Tip**   The MVC Framework unobtrusive Ajax feature is based on jQuery. If you are familiar with the way that jQuery handles Ajax, then you will understand the MVC feature very quickly.

Creating the Synchronous Form View

We are going to begin this section by creating the view for the GetPeople action in our controller, which we created as the /Views/People/GetPeople.cshtml file. You can see the contents of this file in Listing 21-5.

Listing 21-5. The Contents of the GetPeople.cshtml View File

```
@using HelperMethods.Models
@model IEnumerable<Person>
@{
    ViewBag.Title = "GetPeople";
}
<h2>Get People</h2>
<table>
    <thead><tr><th>First</th><th>Last</th><th>Role</th></tr></thead>
    <tbody>
        @foreach (Person p in Model) {
            <tr>
                <td>@p.FirstName</td>
                <td>@p.LastName</td>
                <td>@p.Role</td>
            </tr>
        }
    </tbody>
</table>

@using (Html.BeginForm()) {
    <div>
        @Html.DropDownList("selectedRole", new SelectList(
            new [] {"All"}.Concat(Enum.GetNames(typeof(Role)))))
        <button type="submit">Submit</button>
    </div>
}
```

This is a strongly-typed view whose model type is `IEnumerable<Person>`. We enumerate the `Person` objects in the model to create rows in an HTML table and use the `Html.BeginForm` helper to create a simple form that posts back to the action and controller that the view was generated by. The form contains a call to the `Html.DropDownList` helper, which we use to create a `select` element that contains `option` elements for each of the values defined by the `Role` enumeration, plus the value `All`. (We have used LINQ to create the list of values for the `option` elements by concatenating the values in the `enum` with an array that contains a single `All` string).

The form contains a button that submits the form. The effect is that you can use the form to filter the `Person` objects that we defined in the controller in Listing 21-2, as shown in Figure 21-2.

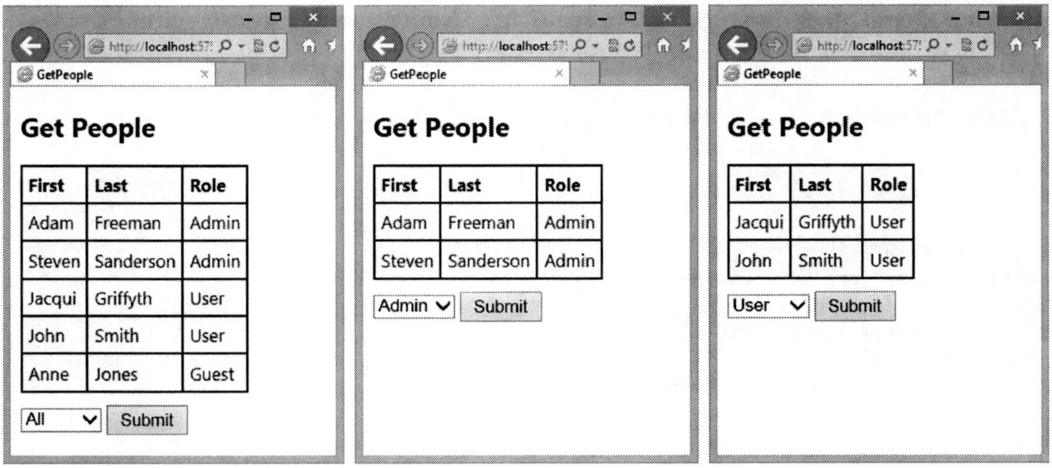

Figure 21-2. A simple synchronous form

This is a simple demonstration of a fundamental limitation in HTML forms, which is that the entire page is reloaded when the form is submitted. It means that the entire content of the Web page has to be regenerated and loaded from the server (which can be an expensive operation for complex views) and while this is happening, users cannot perform any task with the application. They have to wait until the new page is generated, loaded, and then displayed by the browser.

For a simple application like this one, where the browser and server are running on the same machine, the delay is hardly noticeable—but for real applications over real internet connections, synchronous forms can make using a Web application frustrating for the user and expensive in terms of server bandwidth and processing power.

Preparing the Project for Unobtrusive Ajax

The unobtrusive Ajax feature is set up in two places in the application. First, in the **/Web.config** file (the one in the root folder of the project) the **configuration/appSettings** element contains an entry for the **UnobtrusiveJavaScriptEnabled** property, which must be set to **true**, as shown in Listing 21-6. (This property is set to **true** by default when Visual Studio creates the project).

Listing 21-6. Enabling the Unobtrusive Ajax Feature in the Web.config File

```
...
<configuration>
  <!-- other elements omitted for brevity -->
  <appSettings>
    <add key="webpages:Version" value="2.0.0.0" />
    <add key="webpages:Enabled" value="false" />
    <add key="PreserveLoginUrl" value="true" />
    <add key="ClientValidationEnabled" value="true" />
    <add key="UnobtrusiveJavaScriptEnabled" value="true" />
  </appSettings>
  <!-- other elements omitted for brevity -->
</configuration>
...
```

In addition to checking the **Web.config** setting, we need to add references to the jQuery JavaScript libraries that implement the unobtrusive Ajax functionality. You can reference the libraries from

575

individual views, but a more common approach is to do this in a layout file so that it affects all of the views that use that layout. In Listing 21-7, you can see how we have added references for two JavaScript libraries to the /Views/Shared/_Layout.cshtml file.

Listing 21-7. Adding References for the Unobtrusive Ajax JavaScript Libraries to the _Layout.cshtml File

```
<!DOCTYPE html>
<html>
<head>
    <meta charset="utf-8" />
    <meta name="viewport" content="width=device-width" />
    <title>@ViewBag.Title</title>
    <link href="~/Content/Site.css" rel="stylesheet"/>
    <style type="text/css">
        label { display: inline-block; width: 100px;}
        h2 > label {
            width: inherit;
        }
        .dataElem { margin: 5px;}
        .editor-label, .editor-field {float: left;}
        .editor-label, .editor-label label, .editor-field input {height: 20px;}
        .editor-label {clear: left;}
        .editor-field { margin-left: 10px; margin-top: 10px;}
        input[type=submit] { float: left; clear: both; margin-top: 10px;}
        .column {
            float: left;
            margin: 10px;
        }
    </style>
    <script src="~/Scripts/jquery-1.7.1.min.js" type="text/javascript"></script>
    <script src="~/Scripts/jquery.unobtrusive-ajax.min.js"
        type="text/javascript"></script>
</head>
<body>
    @RenderBody()
</body>
</html>
```

The files that have references with our `script` elements are added to the project's `Scripts` folder by Visual Studio when you create a new MVC project using the `Basic` template option. The `jquery-1.7.1.min.js` file contains the core jQuery library and the `jquery.unobtrusive-ajax.min.js` file contains the Ajax functionality (which relies on the main jQuery library). The `.min` extension means that these are the *minified* versions of the libraries, which are smaller than the versions without the `.min` extension, but which are impossible to debug with. We tend to develop with the non-`.min` versions and then switch for the final release of our projects.

■ **Tip** jQuery is a well-maintained library and new releases are made often. It is worth checking to ensure that you are using the latest versions. We will use the versions that come with the initial release of Visual Studio 2012, but as we write this, jQuery version 1.8.2 is available from `http://jquery.com`.

Creating an Unobtrusive Ajax Form

We are now ready to start applying unobtrusive Ajax features to our example application, starting with an unobtrusive Ajax form. In the sections that follow, we will go through the process of replacing a regular synchronous form with an Ajax equivalent and explain how the unobtrusive Ajax feature works.

Preparing the Controller

Our goal is that only the data in the HTML `table` element is replaced when the user clicks on the `Submit` button in our example application. That means that the first thing that we need to do is refactor the action methods in our `People` controller so that we can get just the data we want through a child action. You can see the changes we have made to the `People` controller in Listing 21-8.

Listing 21-8. Refactoring the Action Methods in the People Controller

```
using System;
using System.Collections.Generic;
using System.Linq;
using System.Web;
using System.Web.Mvc;
using HelperMethods.Models;

namespace HelperMethods.Controllers {
    public class PeopleController : Controller {
        private Person[] personData = {
            new Person {FirstName = "Adam", LastName = "Freeman", Role = Role.Admin},
            new Person {FirstName = "Steven", LastName = "Sanderson", Role = Role.Admin},
            new Person {FirstName = "Jacqui", LastName = "Griffyth", Role = Role.User},
            new Person {FirstName = "John", LastName = "Smith", Role = Role.User},
            new Person {FirstName = "Anne", LastName = "Jones", Role = Role.Guest}
        };

        public ActionResult Index() {
            return View();
        }

        public PartialViewResult GetPeopleData(string selectedRole = "All") {
            IEnumerable<Person> data = personData;
            if (selectedRole != "All") {
                Role selected = (Role)Enum.Parse(typeof(Role), selectedRole);
                data = personData.Where(p => p.Role == selected);
            }
            return PartialView(data);
        }

        public ActionResult GetPeople(string selectedRole = "All") {
            return View((object)selectedRole);
        }
    }
}
```

We have added a `GetPeopleData` action that selects the `Person` objects that we need to display, and passes them to the `PartialView` method to generate the table rows that we require. Because the selection of the data is handled in the `GetPeopleData` action method, we have been able to drastically simplify the

GetPeople action method and remove the HttpPost version entirely. The purpose of this method is to pass the selected role as a string to its view.

We created a new partial view file, /Views/People/GetPeopleData.cshtml, for the new GetPeopleData action method. You can see the contents of the view in Listing 21-9. This view is responsible for generating the tr elements that will populate the table using the enumeration of Person objects that are passed from the action method.

Listing 21-9. The Contents of the GetPeopleData.cshtml View

```
@using HelperMethods.Models
@model IEnumerable<Person>

@foreach (Person p in Model) {
    <tr>
        <td>@p.FirstName</td>
        <td>@p.LastName</td>
        <td>@p.Role</td>
    </tr>
}
```

We also had to update the /Views/People/GetPeople.cshtml view, which you can see in Listing 21-10.

Listing 21-10. Updating the GetPeople.cshtml View

```
@using HelperMethods.Models
@model string
@{
    ViewBag.Title = "GetPeople";
}
<h2>Get People</h2>
<table>
    <thead><tr><th>First</th><th>Last</th><th>Role</th></tr></thead>
    <tbody>
        @Html.Action("GetPeopleData", new {selectedRole = Model })
    </tbody>
</table>

@using (Html.BeginForm()) {
    <div>
        @Html.DropDownList("selectedRole", new SelectList(
            new [] {"All"}.Concat(Enum.GetNames(typeof(Role)))))
        <button type="submit">Submit</button>
    </div>
}
```

We have changed the view model type to string, which we pass to the Html.Action helper method to invoke the GetPeopleData child action. This renders the partial view and gives us the table rows.

Creating the Ajax Form

We still have a synchronous form in our application after these changes, but we have separated out the functionality in the controller so that we can request just the table rows through the GetPeopleData action. This new action method will be the target of our Ajax request and the next step is to update the GetPeople.cshtml view so that posting the form is handled through Ajax, as shown in Listing 21-11.

Listing 21-11. Creating an Unobtrusive Ajax form in the GetPeople.cshtml View

```
@using HelperMethods.Models
@model string
@{
    ViewBag.Title = "GetPeople";
    AjaxOptions ajaxOpts = new AjaxOptions {
        UpdateTargetId = "tableBody"
    };
}
<h2>Get People</h2>
<table>
    <thead><tr><th>First</th><th>Last</th><th>Role</th></tr></thead>
    <tbody id="tableBody">
        @Html.Action("GetPeopleData", new {selectedRole = Model })
    </tbody>
</table>

@using (Ajax.BeginForm("GetPeopleData", ajaxOpts)) {
    <div>
        @Html.DropDownList("selectedRole", new SelectList(
            new [] {"All"}.Concat(Enum.GetNames(typeof(Role)))))
        <button type="submit">Submit</button>
    </div>
}
```

As you can see, then changes are relatively minor and we have not had to insert blocks of code around the view to make everything work.

At the heart of the MVC Framework support for Ajax forms is the **Ajax.BeginForm** helper method, which takes an **AjaxOptions** object as its argument. We like to create our **AjaxOptions** objects at the start of the view in a Razor code block, but you can create them inline when you call **Ajax.BeginForm** if you prefer.

The **AjaxOptions** class, which is in the **System.Web.Mvc.Ajax** namespace, defines properties that let us configure how the asynchronous request to the server is made and what happens to the data that we get back—these properties are described in Table 21-2.

Table 21-2. AjaxOptions Properties

Property	Description
Confirm	Sets a message to be displayed to the user in a confirmation window before making the Ajax request.
HttpMethod	Sets the HTTP method that will be used to make the request—must be either Get or Post.
InsertionMode	Specifies the way in which the content retrieved from the server is inserted into the HTML. The three choices are expressed as values from the InsertionMode enum: InsertAfter, InsertBefore and Replace (which is the default).
LoadingElementId	Specifies the ID of an HTML element that will be displayed while the Ajax request is being performed.

Property	Description
LoadingElementDuration	Specifies the duration of the animation used to reveal the element specified by LoadingElementId.
UpdateTargetId	Sets the ID of the HTML element into which the content retrieved from the server will be inserted.
Url	Sets the URL that will be requested from the server.

In the listing, we have set the UpdateTargetId property to tableBody. This is the id we assigned to the tbody HTML element in the view in Listing 21-11. When the user clicks the Submit button, an asynchronous request will be made to the GetPeopleData action method and the HTML fragment that is returned is used to replace the existing elements in the tbody.

■ **Tip**   The AjaxOptions class also defines properties that allow us to specify callbacks for different stages in the request life cycle—see the "Working with Ajax Callbacks" section later in this chapter for details.

That's all there is to it: we replace the Html.BeginForm method with Ajax.BeginForm and ensure that we have a target for our new content. Everything else happens automatically and we get an asynchronous form.

Understanding How Unobtrusive Ajax Works

When we call the Ajax.BeginForm helper method, the options that we specify using the AjaxOptions object are transformed into attributes applied to the form element. Our view in Listing 21-11 produces the following form element:

```
...
<form action="/People/GetPeopleData" data-ajax="true" data-ajax-mode="replace"
    data-ajax-update="#tableBody" id="form0" method="post">
...
```

When the HTML page rendered from the GetPeople.cshtml view is loaded by the browser, the JavaScript in the jquery.unobtrusive-ajax.js library scans the HTML elements and identifies the Ajax form by looking for elements that have a data-ajax attribute with a value of true.

The other attributes whose names start with data-ajax contain the values we specified using the AjaxOptions class. These configuration options are used to configure jQuery, which has built-in support for managing Ajax requests.

■ **Tip**   You don't have to use the MVC Framework support for unobtrusive Ajax. There are plenty of alternatives available, including using jQuery directly. That said, pick a technique and stick to it—we recommend against mixing the MVC Framework unobtrusive Ajax support with other techniques and libraries in the same view, as there can be some unfortunate interactions, such as duplicated or dropped Ajax requests.

Setting Ajax Options

We can fine-tune the behavior of our Ajax requests by setting values for the properties of the `AjaxOptions` object that we pass to the `Ajax.BeginForm` helper method. In the following sections, we explain what each of these options does and why they can be useful.

Ensuring Graceful Degradation

When we set up our Ajax-enabled form in Listing 21-11, we passed in the name of the action method that we wanted to be called asynchronously. In our example, this was the `GetPeopleData` action, which generates a partial view containing a fragment of HTML.

One problem with this approach is that it doesn't work well if the user has disabled JavaScript (or is using a browser that doesn't support it). In such cases, when the user submits the form, the browser display discards the current HTML page and replaces it with the fragment returned by the target action method. The effect can be seen in Figure 21-3.

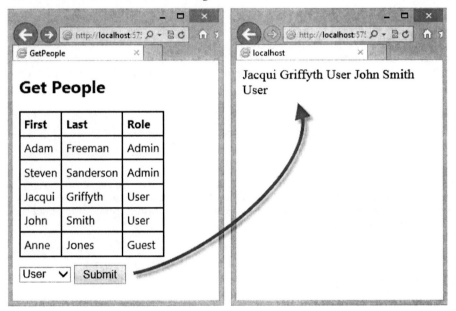

Figure 21-3. The effect of using the Ajax.BeginForm helper without browser JavaScript support

The simplest way to address this problem is to use the `AjaxOptions.Url` property to specify the target URL for the asynchronous request rather than specifying the action name as an argument to the `Ajax.BeginForm` method, as shown in Listing 21-12.

Listing 21-12. Using the AjaxOptions.Url Property to Ensure Gracefully Degrading Forms

```
@using HelperMethods.Models
@model string
@{
    ViewBag.Title = "GetPeople";
    AjaxOptions ajaxOpts = new AjaxOptions {
        UpdateTargetId = "tableBody",
        Url = Url.Action("GetPeopleData")
```

581

```
        };

    }
    <h2>Get People</h2>
    <table>
        <thead><tr><th>First</th><th>Last</th><th>Role</th></tr></thead>
        <tbody id="tableBody">
            @Html.Action("GetPeopleData", new {selectedRole = Model })
        </tbody>
    </table>

    @using (Ajax.BeginForm(ajaxOpts)) {
        <div>
            @Html.DropDownList("selectedRole", new SelectList(
                new [] {"All"}.Concat(Enum.GetNames(typeof(Role)))))
            <button type="submit">Submit</button>
        </div>
    }
```

We have used the `Url.Action` helper method to create a URL that will invoke the `GetPeopleData` action, and used the version of the `Ajax.BeginForm` method that takes only an `AjaxOptions` parameter. This has the effect of creating a `form` element that posts back to the originating action method if JavaScript isn't enabled, like this:

```
...
<form action="/People/GetPeople" data-ajax="true" data-ajax-mode="replace"
    data-ajax-update="#tableBody" data-ajax-url="/People/GetPeopleData" id="form0"
    method="post">
...
```

If JavaScript is enabled, then the unobtrusive Ajax library will take the target URL from the `data-ajax-url` attribute, which refers to our child action. If JavaScript is disabled, then the browser will use the regular form posting technique, which takes the target URL from the `action` attribute, which points back at the action method that will generate a complete HTML page.

▨ **Caution** You might be wondering why we are making such a big deal about users who have disabled JavaScript. After all, who does that? In fact, it is surprisingly prevalent in two groups of users. The first group consists of those users who take their IT security very seriously and disable anything that could be used as the basis for an attack—something that JavaScript has been known for over the years. The second group is users in large corporations, which apply incredibly restrictive policies in the name of IT security (although, in our experience, corporate PCs are so poorly set up that security is nonexistent and the restrictions just annoy the users). You can ignore graceful degradation if you feel you can ignore IT security experts and people who work for big companies—but, since these can be affluent and tech-savvy users, we always take the time to make sure we support them.

Providing the User with Feedback While Making an Ajax Request

One drawback of using Ajax is that it isn't obvious to the user that something is happening, because the request to the server is made in the background. We can inform the user that a request is being performed by using the `AjaxOptions.LoadingElementId` and `AjaxOptions.LoadingElementDuration` properties. Listing 21-13 shows how we have applied these properties in the `GetPerson.cshtml` view file.

Listing 21-13. Giving Feedback to the User with the LoadingElementId Property

```
@using HelperMethods.Models
@model string
@{
    ViewBag.Title = "GetPeople";
    AjaxOptions ajaxOpts = new AjaxOptions {
        UpdateTargetId = "tableBody",
        Url = Url.Action("GetPeopleData"),
        LoadingElementId = "loading",
        LoadingElementDuration = 1000,
    };

}
<h2>Get People</h2>

<div id="loading" class="load" style="display:none">
    <p>Loading Data...</p>
</div>

<table>
    <thead><tr><th>First</th><th>Last</th><th>Role</th></tr></thead>
    <tbody id="tableBody">
        @Html.Action("GetPeopleData", new {selectedRole = Model })
    </tbody>
</table>

@using (Ajax.BeginForm(ajaxOpts)) {
    <div>
        @Html.DropDownList("selectedRole", new SelectList(
            new [] {"All"}.Concat(Enum.GetNames(typeof(Role)))))
        <button type="submit">Submit</button>
    </div>
}
```

The AjaxOptions.LoadingElementId property specifies the id attribute value of a hidden HTML element that will be shown to the user while an Ajax request is performed. To demonstrate this feature, we added a div element to the view that we hid from the user by setting the CSS display property to none. We gave this div element an id attribute of loading and used this id as the value for the LoadingElementId property and the unobtrusive Ajax feature will display the element to the user for the duration of the request, as shown in Figure 21-4. The LoadingElementDuration property specifies the duration of the animation that is used to reveal the loading element to the user. We specified a value of 1000, which denotes one second.

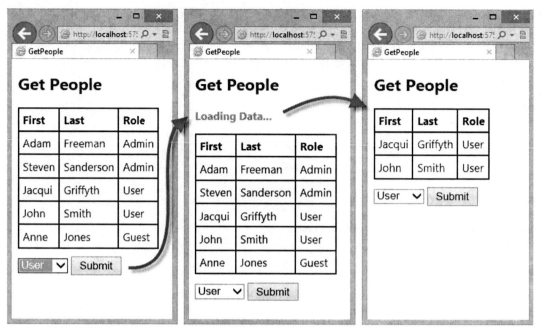

Figure 21-4. Providing the user with feedback during an Ajax request

Prompting the User Before Making a Request

The `AjaxOptions.Confirm` property lets us specify a message that will be used to prompt the user before each asynchronous request. The user can elect to proceed with or cancel the request. Listing 21-14 shows how we have applied this property to the `GetPerson.cshtml` file.

Listing 21-14. Promoting the User Before Making an Asynchronous Request

```
...
@{
    ViewBag.Title = "GetPeople";
    AjaxOptions ajaxOpts = new AjaxOptions {
        UpdateTargetId = "tableBody",
        Url = Url.Action("GetPeopleData"),
        LoadingElementId = "loading",
        LoadingElementDuration = 1000,
        Confirm = "Do you wish to request new data?"
    };
}
...
```

With this addition, the user is prompted each time they submit the form, as shown in Figure 21-5. The user is prompted for *every* request, which means that this feature should be used sparingly to avoid irritating the user.

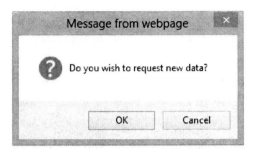

Figure 21-5. Prompting the user before making a request

Creating Ajax Links

In addition to forms, we can use unobtrusive Ajax to create a elements that will be followed asynchronously. The mechanism for this is very similar to the way that Ajax forms work. You can see how we have added Ajax links to the GetPeople.cshtml view in Listing 21-15.

Listing 21-15. Creating Ajax-Enabled Links

```
@using HelperMethods.Models
@model string
@{
    ViewBag.Title = "GetPeople";
    AjaxOptions ajaxOpts = new AjaxOptions {
        UpdateTargetId = "tableBody",
        Url = Url.Action("GetPeopleData"),
        LoadingElementId = "loading",
        LoadingElementDuration = 1000,
        Confirm = "Do you wish to request new data?"
    };
}
<h2>Get People</h2>

<div id="loading" class="load" style="display:none">
    <p>Loading Data...</p>
</div>

<table>
    <thead><tr><th>First</th><th>Last</th><th>Role</th></tr></thead>
    <tbody id="tableBody">
        @Html.Action("GetPeopleData", new {selectedRole = Model })
    </tbody>
</table>

@using (Ajax.BeginForm(ajaxOpts)) {
    <div>
        @Html.DropDownList("selectedRole", new SelectList(
            new [] {"All"}.Concat(Enum.GetNames(typeof(Role)))))
        <button type="submit">Submit</button>
    </div>
}
```

```
<div>
    @foreach (string role in Enum.GetNames(typeof(Role))) {
        <div class="ajaxLink">
            @Ajax.ActionLink(role, "GetPeopleData",
                new {selectedRole = role},
                new AjaxOptions {UpdateTargetId = "tableBody"})
        </div>
    }
</div>
```

We have used a foreach loop to call the Ajax.ActionLink helper for each of the values defined by the Role enumeration, creating a set of Ajax-enabled a elements. The a elements that are produced have the same kind of data attributes we saw when working with forms, like this:

```
...
<a data-ajax="true" data-ajax-mode="replace" data-ajax-update="#tableBody"
    href="/People/GetPeopleData?selectedRole=Guest">Guest</a>
...
```

Our routing configuration does not have an entry for the selectedRole variable, so the URL that has been generated for the href attribute specifies the role that the link represents using the query string component of the URL.

You can see the links we added to the view in Figure 21-6. Clicking one of these links will call the GetPersonData action method and replace the contents of the tbody element with the HTML fragment that is returned. This creates the same effect of filtering the data that we achieved using the Ajax-enabled form earlier in the chapter.

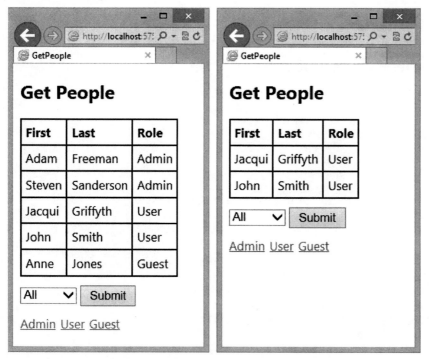

Figure 21-6. Adding Ajax-enabled links to a view

> ■ **Tip**   You may have to clear your browser history to see the changes for this example.

Ensuring Graceful Degradation for Links

We face the same problem with the Ajax-enabled links as we did with the forms—when there is no JavaScript support on the browser, clicking one of the links will just display the HTML fragment that the GetPeopleData action method generates.

We address this using the AjaxOptions.Url property to specify the URL for the Ajax request, and we specify the GetPeople action to the Ajax.ActionLink helper method, as shown in Listing 21-16.

Listing 21-16. Creating Graceful Ajax-Enabled Links

```
...
<div>
    @foreach (string role in Enum.GetNames(typeof(Role))) {
        <div class="ajaxLink">
            @Ajax.ActionLink(role, "GetPeople",
                new {selectedRole = role},
                new AjaxOptions {
                    UpdateTargetId = "tableBody",
                    Url = Url.Action("GetPeopleData", new {selectedRole = role})
                })
        </div>
    }
</div>
...
```

This is why we create a new AjaxOptions object for each of the links we require rather than use the one we created in the Razor code block for the form element. Independent AjaxOptions allow us to specify a different value for the Url property for each link and support graceful degradation for non-JavaScript browsers.

Working with Ajax Callbacks

The AjaxOptions class defines a set of properties that allow us to specify JavaScript functions that will be called at various points in the Ajax request life cycle—these properties are described in Table 21-3.

Table 21-3. AjaxOptions Callback Properties

Property	jQuery Event	Description
OnBegin	beforeSend	Called immediately prior to the request being sent.
OnComplete	complete	Called if the request is successful.
OnFailure	error	Called if the request fails.
OnSuccess	success	Called when the request has completed, irrespective of whether the request succeeded or failed.

Each of the `AjaxOptions` callback properties correlates to an Ajax event supported by the jQuery library. We have listed the jQuery events in Table 21-3 for those readers who have used jQuery before. You can get details on each of these events and the parameters that will be passed to your functions at http://api.jquery.com/jQuery.ajax.

In Listing 21-17, you can see how we have used a `script` element to define some basic JavaScript functions that will report on the progress of the Ajax request and use the properties shown in Table 21-3 to specify our functions as handlers for the Ajax events.

Listing 21-17. Using the Ajax Callbacks

```
@using HelperMethods.Models
@model string
@{
    ViewBag.Title = "GetPeople";
    AjaxOptions ajaxOpts = new AjaxOptions {
        UpdateTargetId = "tableBody",
        Url = Url.Action("GetPeopleData"),
        LoadingElementId = "loading",
        LoadingElementDuration = 1000,
        Confirm = "Do you wish to request new data?"
    };
}

<script type="text/javascript">
    function OnBegin() {
        alert("This is the OnBegin Callback");
    }

    function OnSuccess(data) {
        alert("This is the OnSuccessCallback: " + data);
    }

    function OnFailure(request, error) {
        alert("This is the OnFailure Callback:" + error);
    }

    function OnComplete(request, status) {
        alert("This is the OnComplete Callback: " + status);
    }
</script>

<h2>Get People</h2>

<div id="loading" class="load" style="display:none">
    <p>Loading Data...</p>
</div>

<table>
    <thead><tr><th>First</th><th>Last</th><th>Role</th></tr></thead>
    <tbody id="tableBody">
        @Html.Action("GetPeopleData", new {selectedRole = Model })
    </tbody>
</table>
```

```
@using (Ajax.BeginForm(ajaxOpts)) {
    <div>
        @Html.DropDownList("selectedRole", new SelectList(
            new [] {"All"}.Concat(Enum.GetNames(typeof(Role)))))
        <button type="submit">Submit</button>
    </div>
}

<div>
    @foreach (string role in Enum.GetNames(typeof(Role))) {
        <div class="ajaxLink">
            @Ajax.ActionLink(role, "GetPeople",
                new {selectedRole = role},
                new AjaxOptions {
                    UpdateTargetId = "tableBody",
                    Url = Url.Action("GetPeopleData", new {selectedRole = role}),
                    OnBegin = "OnBegin",
                    OnFailure = "OnFailure",
                    OnSuccess = "OnSuccess",
                    OnComplete = "OnComplete"
                })
        </div>
    }
</div>
```

We have defined four functions, one for each of the callbacks. For this example, we have kept things very simple and we simply display a message to the user in each of the functions. With these changes, clicking one of the links will display a sequence of alters that report on the progress of the Ajax request, as shown in Figure 21-7.

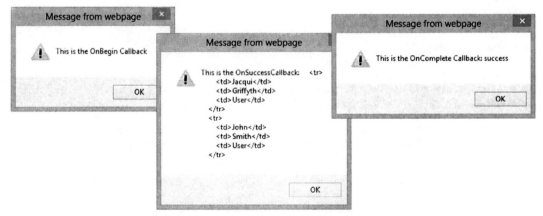

Figure 21-7. The series of dialog boxes shown in response to the Ajax callbacks

Displaying dialog boxes to the user for each callback isn't the most useful thing to do with the Ajax callbacks, but it does demonstrate the sequence in which they are called. We can do anything we like in these JavaScript functions—manipulate the HTML DOM, trigger additional requests, and so forth. One of the most useful things we can do with the callbacks is handle JSON data, which we describe in the next section.

589

Working with JSON

In our Ajax examples so far, the server has rendered fragments of HTML and sent them to the browser. This is a perfectly acceptable technique, but it is verbose (because we are sending the HTML elements along with the data) and it limits what we can do with the data at the browser.

One way to address both of these issues is to use the *JavaScript Object Notation* (JSON) format, which is a language-independent way of expressing data. It emerged from the JavaScript language, but has long since taken on a life of its own and is very widely used. In this section, we'll show you how to create an action method that returns JSON data, as well as how to process that data in the browser.

■ **Tip**   In Chapter 25, we describe the Web API feature, which is an alternative approach for creating Web services.

Adding JSON Support to the Controller

The MVC Framework makes creating an action method that generates JSON data rather than HTML very simple. You can see how we have added such an action method to the People controller in Listing 21-18.

Listing 21-18. An Action Method That Returns JSON Data

```
using System;
using System.Collections.Generic;
using System.Linq;
using System.Web;
using System.Web.Mvc;
using HelperMethods.Models;

namespace HelperMethods.Controllers {
    public class PeopleController : Controller {
        private Person[] personData = {
            new Person {FirstName = "Adam", LastName = "Freeman", Role = Role.Admin},
            new Person {FirstName = "Steven", LastName = "Sanderson", Role = Role.Admin},
            new Person {FirstName = "Jacqui", LastName = "Griffyth", Role = Role.User},
            new Person {FirstName = "John", LastName = "Smith", Role = Role.User},
            new Person {FirstName = "Anne", LastName = "Jones", Role = Role.Guest}
        };

        public ActionResult Index() {
            return View();
        }

        private IEnumerable<Person> GetData(string selectedRole) {
            IEnumerable<Person> data = personData;
            if (selectedRole != "All") {
                Role selected = (Role)Enum.Parse(typeof(Role), selectedRole);
                data = personData.Where(p => p.Role == selected);
            }
            return data;
```

```
    }

    public JsonResult GetPeopleDataJson(string selectedRole = "All") {
        IEnumerable<Person> data = GetData(selectedRole);
        return Json(data, JsonRequestBehavior.AllowGet);
    }

    public PartialViewResult GetPeopleData(string selectedRole = "All") {
        return PartialView(GetData(selectedRole));
    }

    public ActionResult GetPeople(string selectedRole = "All") {
        return View((object)selectedRole);
    }
    }
}
```

Since we want to present the same data in two different formats (HTML and JSON), we have refactored our controller so that there is a common (and `private`) GetData method that is responsible for performing the filtering.

We have added a new action method called GetPeopleDataJson, which returns a JsonResult object. This is a special kind of ActionResult that tells the view engine that we want to return JSON data to the client, rather than HTML. (You can learn more about the ActionResult class and the role it plays in the MVC Framework in Chapter 15).

We create a JsonResult by calling the Json method in the action method, passing in the data that we want converted to the JSON format, like this:

```
...
return Json(data, JsonRequestBehavior.AllowGet);
...
```

In this case, we have also passed in the AllowGet value from the JsonRequestBehavior enumeration. By default, JSON data will only be sent in response to POST requests, but by passing this value as a parameter to the Json method, we tell the MVC Framework to respond to GET requests as well.

■ **Caution**   You should only use JsonRequestBehavior.AllowGet if the data you are returning is not private. Due to a security issue in many Web browsers, it's possible for third-party sites to intercept JSON data that you return in response to a GET request, which is why JsonResult will not respond to GET requests by default. In most cases, you will be able to use POST requests to retrieve the JSON data instead, avoiding the problem. For more information, see http://haacked.com/archive/2009/06/25/json-hijacking.aspx.

Processing JSON in the Browser

To process the JSON we retrieve from the MVC Framework application server, we specify a JavaScript function using the OnSuccess callback property in the AjaxOptions class. In Listing 21-19, you can see how we have updated our GetPerson.cshtml view file to remove the handler functions we defined in the last section and use the OnSuccess callback to process the JSON data.

Listing 21-19. Working with JSON Data in the GetPerson View

```
@using HelperMethods.Models
@model string
@{
    ViewBag.Title = "GetPeople";
    AjaxOptions ajaxOpts = new AjaxOptions {
        UpdateTargetId = "tableBody",
        Url = Url.Action("GetPeopleData"),
        LoadingElementId = "loading",
        LoadingElementDuration = 1000,
        Confirm = "Do you wish to request new data?"
    };
}

<script type="text/javascript">
    function processData(data) {
        var target = $("#tableBody");
        target.empty();
        for (var i = 0; i < data.length; i++) {
            var person = data[i];
            target.append("<tr><td>" + person.FirstName + "</td><td>"
                + person.LastName + "</td><td>" + person.Role + "</td></tr>");
        }
    }
</script>

<h2>Get People</h2>

<div id="loading" class="load" style="display:none">
    <p>Loading Data...</p>
</div>

<table>
    <thead><tr><th>First</th><th>Last</th><th>Role</th></tr></thead>
    <tbody id="tableBody">
        @Html.Action("GetPeopleData", new {selectedRole = Model })
    </tbody>
</table>

@using (Ajax.BeginForm(ajaxOpts)) {
    <div>
        @Html.DropDownList("selectedRole", new SelectList(
            new [] {"All"}.Concat(Enum.GetNames(typeof(Role)))))
        <button type="submit">Submit</button>
    </div>
}

<div>
    @foreach (string role in Enum.GetNames(typeof(Role))) {
        <div class="ajaxLink">
            @Ajax.ActionLink(role, "GetPeople",
                new {selectedRole = role},
                new AjaxOptions {
```

```
            Url = Url.Action("GetPeopleDataJson", new {selectedRole = role}),
            OnSuccess = "processData"
        })
    </div>
    }
</div>
```

We have defined a new function called processData, which contains some basic jQuery code that processes the JSON objects and uses them to create the tr and td elements needed to populate the table.

■ **Tip**   We don't go into jQuery in this book because it is a topic in and of itself. We love jQuery though, and if you want to learn more about it, then Adam has written *Pro jQuery* (Apress, 2012).

Notice that we have removed the value for the UpdateTargetId property from the AjaxOptions objects we created for the links. If you forget to do this, the unobtrusive Ajax feature will try and treat the JSON data it retrieves from the server as HTML. You can usually tell this is happening because the contents of the target element will be removed but not replaced with any new data.

You can see the result of the switch to JSON by starting the application, navigating to the /People/GetPerson URL, and clicking one of the links. As Figure 21-8 shows, we don't get quite the right result—in particular, the information displayed in the Role column of the table isn't correct. We will explain why this happens and show you how to make it right in the next section.

Figure 21-8. Working with JSON data instead of HTML fragments

Preparing Data for Encoding

When we called the Json method from within the GetPeopleDataJson action method, we left the MVC Framework to figure out how to encode our People objects in the JSON format. The MVC Framework doesn't have any special insights into our models, and so it makes a best-effort guess about what it needs to do. Here is how the MVC Framework expresses a single Person object in JSON:

```
...
{"PersonId":0,"FirstName":"Adam","LastName":"Freeman",
    "BirthDate":"\/Date(62135596800000)\/","HomeAddress":null,"IsApproved":false,"Role":0}
...
```

593

It looks like a bit of a mess, but the result is actually pretty clever—it just isn't quite what we require. First, all the properties defined by the Person class are represented in the JSON, even though we did not assign values to some of them in the People controller. In some cases, the default value for the type has been used (false is used for IsApproved, for example) and in others null has been used (such as for HomeAddress). Some values are converted into a form that can be readily interpreted by JavaScript, such as the BirthDate property, but others are not handled as well—such as using 0 for the Role property, rather than Admin.

VIEWING JSON DATA

It can be useful to see what JSON data your action methods return and the easiest way to do this is to enter a URL that targets the action in the browser, like this:

```
http://localhost:57520/People/GetPeopleJson?selectedRole=Admin
```

You can do this in pretty much any browser, but most will force you to save and open a text file before you can see the JSON content. We like to use the Google Chrome browser for this because it helpfully displays the JSON data in the main browser window, which makes the process slightly quicker and means you don't end up with dozens of open text file windows. We also recommend Fiddler (www.fiddler2.com), which is an excellent Web debugging proxy that allows you to dig right into the details of the data sent between the browser and the server.

The MVC Framework has made a good attempt, but we end up sending properties to the browser that we don't subsequently use and the Role value isn't useful to us. This is a typical situation when relying on the default JSON encoding and some preparation of the data you want to send the client is usually required.

In Listing 21-20, you can see how we have revised the GetPersonDataJson action method in the People controller to prepare the data we pass to the Json method.

Listing 21-20. Preparing Data Objects for JSON Encoding

```
...
public JsonResult GetPeopleDataJson(string selectedRole = "All") {
    var data = GetData(selectedRole).Select(p => new {
        FirstName = p.FirstName,
        LastName = p.LastName,
        Role = Enum.GetName(typeof(Role), p.Role)
    });
    return Json(data, JsonRequestBehavior.AllowGet);
}
...
```

We have used LINQ to create a sequence of new objects that contain just the FirstName and LastName properties from our Person objects, along with the string representation of the Role value. The effect of this change is that we get JSON data that contains just the properties we want, expressed in a way that is more useful to our jQuery code, like this:

```
...
{"FirstName":"Adam","LastName":"Freeman","Role":"Admin"}
...
```

Figure 21-9 shows the change in the output displayed in the browser. You can't tell the unused properties are not sent, of course, but you can see that the Role column contains the right values.

Figure 21-9. The effect of preparing the data objects for JSON encoding

---

■ **Tip**   You may have to clear your browser history to see the changes for this example.

Detecting Ajax Requests in the Action Method

Our controller presently contains two action methods so that we can support requests for HTML and JSON data. This is usually how we build our controllers, because we like lots of short and simple actions, but you don't have to work this way. The MVC Framework provides a simple way of detecting Ajax requests, which means that you can create a single action method that handles multiple data formats. In Listing 21-21, you can see how we have refactored the Person controller to contain a single action that handles both JSON and HTML.

Listing 21-21. Creating a Single Action Method That Handles JSON and HTML Requests

```
using System;
using System.Collections.Generic;
using System.Linq;
using System.Web;
using System.Web.Mvc;
using HelperMethods.Models;

namespace HelperMethods.Controllers {
    public class PeopleController : Controller {
        private Person[] personData = {
            new Person {FirstName = "Adam", LastName = "Freeman", Role = Role.Admin},
            new Person {FirstName = "Steven", LastName = "Sanderson", Role = Role.Admin},
            new Person {FirstName = "Jacqui", LastName = "Griffyth", Role = Role.User},
```

595

```
            new Person {FirstName = "John", LastName = "Smith", Role = Role.User},
            new Person {FirstName = "Anne", LastName = "Jones", Role = Role.Guest}
        };

        public ActionResult Index() {
            return View();
        }

        public ActionResult GetPeopleData(string selectedRole = "All") {
            IEnumerable<Person> data = personData;
            if (selectedRole != "All") {
                Role selected = (Role)Enum.Parse(typeof(Role), selectedRole);
                data = personData.Where(p => p.Role == selected);
            }
            if (Request.IsAjaxRequest()) {
                var formattedData = data.Select(p => new {
                    FirstName = p.FirstName,
                    LastName = p.LastName,
                    Role = Enum.GetName(typeof(Role), p.Role)
                });
                return Json(formattedData, JsonRequestBehavior.AllowGet);
            } else {
                return PartialView(data);
            }
        }

        public ActionResult GetPeople(string selectedRole = "All") {
            return View((object)selectedRole);
        }
    }
}
```

We used the `Request.IsAjaxRequest` method to detect Ajax requests and deliver the JSON format if the result is `true`. There are a couple limitations that you should be aware of before you follow this approach.

First, the `IsAjaxRequest` methods returns `true` if the browser has included the `X-Requested-With` header in its request and set the value to `XMLHttpRequest`. This is a widely used convention, but it isn't universal and so you should consider whether your users are likely to make requests that require JSON data without setting this header.

The second limitation is that it assumes that all Ajax requests require JSON data. Your application may be better served by separating the way that a request has been made from the data format that the client seeks. This is our preferred approach and the reason we tend to define separate action methods for data formats.

We also need to make two changes to our `GetPerson.cshtml` view to support the single action method, as shown in Listing 21-22.

Listing 21-22. Changing the GetPerson.cshtml View to Support a Single Data Action Method

```
@using HelperMethods.Models
@model string
@{
    ViewBag.Title = "GetPeople";
    AjaxOptions ajaxOpts = new AjaxOptions {
        Url = Url.Action("GetPeopleData"),
        LoadingElementId = "loading",
```

```
            LoadingElementDuration = 1000,
            OnSuccess = "processData"
    };
}

<script type="text/javascript">
    function processData(data) {
        var target = $("#tableBody");
        target.empty();
        for (var i = 0; i < data.length; i++) {
            var person = data[i];
            target.append("<tr><td>" + person.FirstName + "</td><td>"
                + person.LastName + "</td><td>" + person.Role
                + "</td></tr>");
        }
    }
</script>

<h2>Get People</h2>

<div id="loading" class="load" style="display:none">
    <p>Loading Data...</p>
</div>

<table>
    <thead><tr><th>First</th><th>Last</th><th>Role</th></tr></thead>
    <tbody id="tableBody">
        @Html.Action("GetPeopleData", new {selectedRole = Model })
    </tbody>
</table>

@using (Ajax.BeginForm(ajaxOpts)) {
    <div>
        @Html.DropDownList("selectedRole", new SelectList(
            new [] {"All"}.Concat(Enum.GetNames(typeof(Role)))))
        <button type="submit">Submit</button>
    </div>
}

<div>
    @foreach (string role in Enum.GetNames(typeof(Role))) {
        <div class="ajaxLink">
            @Ajax.ActionLink(role, "GetPeople",
                new {selectedRole = role},
                new AjaxOptions {
                    Url = Url.Action("GetPeopleData", new {selectedRole = role}),
                    OnSuccess = "processData"
                })
        </div>
    }
</div>
```

The first change is to the `AjaxOptions` object we use for the Ajax-enabled `form`. Because we are no longer able to receive an HTML fragment via an Ajax request, we have had to use the same `processData` function to handle the JSON server response that we created for the Ajax-enabled links. The second change is to the value of the `Url` property for the `AjaxOptions` objects we create for the links. The `GetPeopleDataJson` action no longer exists and we target the `GetPeopleData` action instead.

Summary

In this chapter, we looked at the MVC Framework's unobtrusive Ajax feature, which lets us take advantage of the functionality of the jQuery library in a simple and elegant way and without needing to add lots of code to our views. If you are able to with HTML fragments, then you don't need to add any JavaScript code to your views at all—but we like working with JSON, which means that we tend to need small JavaScript functions that use jQuery to process the data and generate the HTML elements we require. In the next chapter, we will look at one of the most interesting and useful aspects of the MVC Framework: model binding.

CHAPTER 22

■ ■ ■

Model Binding

Model binding is the process of creating .NET objects using the data sent by the browser in an HTTP request. We have been relying on the model binding process each time we have defined an action method that takes a parameter—the parameter objects are created by model binding. In this chapter, we'll show you how the model binding system works and demonstrate the techniques required to customize it for advanced use.

Preparing the Example Project

For this chapter, we have created a new Visual Studio MVC project called `MvcModels` using the `Basic` template option. We will be using the same model class that you have seen in previous chapters, so create a new class file called `Person.cs` in the `Models` folder and ensure that the contents match, as shown in Listing 22-1.

Listing 22-1. The Contents of the /Models/Person.cs Class File

```
using System;

namespace MvcModels.Models {

    public class Person {
        public int PersonId { get; set; }
        public string FirstName { get; set; }
        public string LastName { get; set; }
        public DateTime BirthDate { get; set; }
        public Address HomeAddress { get; set; }
        public bool IsApproved { get; set; }
        public Role Role { get; set; }
    }

    public class Address {
        public string Line1 { get; set; }
        public string Line2 { get; set; }
        public string City { get; set; }
        public string PostalCode { get; set; }
        public string Country { get; set; }
    }

    public enum Role {
        Admin,
        User,
        Guest
    }
}
```

599

We have also defined a Home controller, as shown in Listing 22-2. This controller defines some sample Person objects and defines the Index action, which allows us to select a single Person by the value of the PersonId property.

Listing 22-2. The Home Controller

```
using System;
using System.Collections.Generic;
using System.Linq;
using System.Web;
using System.Web.Mvc;
using MvcModels.Models;

namespace MvcModels.Controllers {
    public class HomeController : Controller {
        private Person[] personData = {
            new Person {PersonId = 1, FirstName = "Adam", LastName = "Freeman",
                Role = Role.Admin},
            new Person {PersonId = 2, FirstName = "Steven", LastName = "Sanderson",
                Role = Role.Admin},
            new Person {PersonId = 3, FirstName = "Jacqui", LastName = "Griffyth",
                Role = Role.User},
            new Person {PersonId = 4, FirstName = "John", LastName = "Smith",
                Role = Role.User},
            new Person {PersonId = 5, FirstName = "Anne", LastName = "Jones",
                Role = Role.Guest}
        };

        public ActionResult Index(int id) {
            Person dataItem = personData.Where(p => p.PersonId == id).First();
            return View(dataItem);
        }
    }
}
```

We have created a view file called /Views/Home/Index.cshtml to support the action method. You can see the contents of this file in Listing 22-3. We have used the templated display helper to show some of the property values of the Person view model.

Listing 22-3. The Contents of the /Views/Home/Index.cshtml File

```
@model MvcModels.Models.Person
@{
    ViewBag.Title = "Index";
}
<h2>Person</h2>
<div><label>ID:</label>@Html.DisplayFor(m => m.PersonId)</div>
<div><label>First Name:</label>@Html.DisplayFor(m => m.FirstName)</div>
<div><label>Last Name:</label>@Html.DisplayFor(m => m.LastName)</div>
<div><label>Role:</label>@Html.DisplayFor(m => m.Role)</div>
```

Finally, we added some CSS styles to the /Content/Site.css file, as shown in Listing 22-4.

Listing 22-4. Additional Styles for the Site.css File

```
...
label { display: inline-block; width: 100px; font-weight:bold; margin: 5px;}
form  label { float: left;}
input.text-box { float: left; margin: 5px;}
button[type=submit] { margin-top: 5px; float: left; clear: left;}
form  div {clear: both;}
...
```

Understanding Model Binding

Model binding is an elegant bridge between the HTTP request and the C# methods that define our actions methods. Most MVC Framework applications rely on model binding to some extent, including the simple example application that we created in the previous section. To see the model binding at work, start the application and navigate to /Home/Index/1. The result is illustrated in Figure 22-1.

Figure 22-1. A simple demonstration of model binding

Our URL contained the value of the PersonId property of the Person object we wanted to view, like this:

/Home/Index/**1**

The MVC Framework translated that part of the URL and used it as the argument when it called on the Index method in the Home controller class to service the request:

```
...
public ActionResult Index(int id) {
...
```

The process by which the URL segment was converted into the int method argument is an example of model binding. In the sections that follow, we show the process that this simple demonstration initiated, and then move on to explain some of the more complex model binding features. The process that leads to model binding begins when the request is received and processed by the routing engine. We have not changed the routing configuration for the example application, and the default route that Visual Studio adds to the /App_Start/RouteConfig.cs file was used to process the request. As a reminder, you can see the default route in Listing 22-5.

Listing 22-5. The Default Route Added to MVC Applications by Visual Studio

```
using System;
using System.Collections.Generic;
using System.Linq;
using System.Web;
using System.Web.Mvc;
using System.Web.Routing;

namespace MvcModels {
    public class RouteConfig {
        public static void RegisterRoutes(RouteCollection routes) {
            routes.IgnoreRoute("{resource}.axd/{*pathInfo}");

            routes.MapRoute(
                name: "Default",
                url: "{controller}/{action}/{id}",
                defaults: new { controller = "Home", action = "Index",
                    id = UrlParameter.Optional }
            );
        }
    }
}
```

We described how routes are defined and how they work in detail in Chapter 13, so we aren't going to repeat that information here. For the model binding process, the important part is the `id` optional segment variable. When we navigated to the `/Home/Index/1` URL, the last segment of our URL, which specifies the `Person` object we are interested in, is assigned to the `id` routing variable.

The action invoker, which we introduced in Chapter 15, used the routing information to figure out that the `Index` action method was required to service the request, but it couldn't call the `Index` method until it had some useful values for the method argument.

The default action invoker, `ControllerActionInvoker`, (which we introduced in Chapter 15), relies on *model binders* to generate the data objects that are required to invoke the action. Model binders are defined by the `IModelBinder` interface, which is shown in Listing 22-6. We'll come back to this interface later in the chapter when we should you how to create a custom model binder.

Listing 22-6. The IModelBinder Interface

```
namespace System.Web.Mvc {

    public interface IModelBinder {
        object BindModel(ControllerContext controllerContext,
            ModelBindingContext bindingContext);
    }
}
```

There can be multiple model binders in an MVC application, and each binder can be responsible for binding one or more model types. When the action invoker needs to call an action method, it looks at the parameters that the method defines and finds the responsible model binder for the type of each one.

For our simple example, the action invoker would examine the `Index` method and find that it has one `int` parameter. It would then locate the binder responsible for `int` values and call its `BindModel` method.

The model binder is responsible for providing an `int` value that can be used to call the `Index` method. This usually means transforming some element of the request data (such as form or query string values), but the MVC Framework doesn't put any limits on how the data is obtained.

We will show you some examples of custom binders later in this chapter. We will also show you some of the features of the `ModelBindingContext` class, which is passed to the `IModelBinder.BindModel` method.

Using the Default Model Binder

Although an application can define custom model binders, most just rely on the built-in binder class, `DefaultModelBinder`. This is the binder that is used by the action invoker when it cannot find a custom binder to bind the type. By default, this model binder searches four locations, shown in Table 22-1, for data matching the name of the parameter being bound.

Table 22-1. The Order in Which the DefaultModelBinder Class Looks for Parameter Data

Source	Description
Request.Form	Values provided by the user in HTML form elements.
RouteData.Values	The values obtained using the application routes.
Request.QueryString	Data included in the query string portion of the request URL.
Request.Files	Files that have been uploaded as part of the request (see Chapter 11 for a demonstration of uploading files).

The locations are searched in order. For example, in our simple example, the `DefaultModelBinder` looks for a value for our `id` parameter as follows:

1. `Request.Form["id"]`
2. `RouteData.Values["id"]`
3. `Request.QueryString["id"]`
4. `Request.Files["id"]`

The search is stopped as soon as a value is found. In our example, the form data is searched without success, but a routing variable is found with the right name. This means that the query string and the names of uploaded files will not be searched at all.

■ **Tip**   When replying on the default model binder, it is important that the parameters for your action method match the data property you are looking for. Our example application works because the name of our action method parameter corresponds to the name of a routing variable. If we had named our action method parameter `personId`, for example, the default model binder would not have been able to locate a matching data value and our request would have failed.

Binding to Simple Types

When dealing with simple parameter types, the `DefaultModelBinder` tries to convert the string value, which has been obtained from the request data into the parameter type using the `System.ComponentModel.TypeDescriptor` class. If the value cannot be converted—for example, if we have supplied a value of `apple` for a parameter that requires an `int` value, then the `DefaultModelBinder` won't be able to bind to the model.

You can see the problem that this creates by starting the example application and navigating to the URL `/Home/Index/apple`. Figure 22-2 illustrates the response from the server.

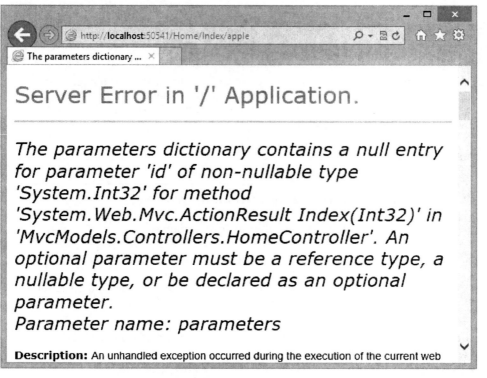

Figure 22-2. An error processing a model property

The default model binder is a little dogged—it sees that an `int` value is required and it tries to convert the value we provided, `apple`, into an `int`, which causes the error shown by the figure.

We can make things easier for the model binder by using a `nullable` type, which provides a fallback position. Instead of requiring a numeric value, a nullable `int` parameter gives the model binder the choice of setting the action method argument to `null` when invoking the action. You can see how we have applied a nullable type to the `Index` action in Listing 22-7.

Listing 22-7. Using a Nullable Type for an Action Method Parameter

```
...
public ActionResult Index(int? id) {
    Person dataItem = personData.Where(p => p.PersonId == id).First();
    return View(dataItem);
}
...
```

If you run the application and navigate to `/Home/Index/apple`, you can see that we have solved only part of the problem, as shown by Figure 22-3.

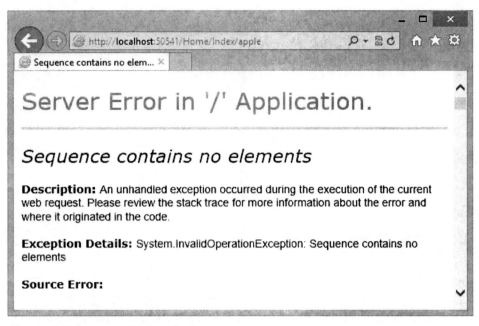

Figure 22-3. A request for a null value

We have changed the nature of the problem—the model binder is able to use null as the value for the id argument to the Index method, but the code inside the action method doesn't check for null values.

We could fix that by explicitly checking for null values, but we can also set a default value for the parameter that will be used instead of null. You can see how we have applied a default parameter value to the Index action method in Listing 22-8.

Listing 22-8. Applying a Default Parameter Value to the Index Action Method

```
...
public ActionResult Index(int id = 1) {
    Person dataItem = personData.Where(p => p.PersonId == id).First();
    return View(dataItem);
}
...
```

Whenever the model binder is unable to find a value for the id parameter, the default value of 1 will be used instead, which has the effect of selecting the Person object whose PersonId property has a value of 1, as shown in Figure 22-4.

Figure 22-4. The effect of using a default parameter value in an action method

■ **Tip**   Bear in mind that we have solved the problem of non-numeric values for the model binder, but that we can still get `int` values for which there are no valid `Person` objects defined by the `Home` controller. For example, the model binder will happily convert the final segment of the URLs /Home/Index/-1 and /Home/Index/500 to `int` values. This will allow the action method to call the `Index` method with a real value, but will still result in an error because we don't perform any additional checks in our example code. We recommend you pay attention to the range of parameter values your action method may receive, and test accordingly.

CULTURE-SENSITIVE PARSING

The `DefaultModelBinder` class use different culture settings to perform type conversions from different areas of the request data. The values that are obtained from URLs (the routing and query string data) are converted using culture-insensitive parsing, but values obtained from form data are converted taking culture into account.

The most common problem that this causes relates to `DateTime` values. Culture-insensitive dates are expected to be in the universal format yyyy-mm-dd. Form date values are expected to be in the format specified by the server. This means that a server set to the UK culture will expected dates to be in the form dd-mm-yyyy, whereas a server set to the US culture will expect the format mm-dd-yyyy, though in either case yyyy-mm-dd is acceptable too.

A date value won't be converted if it isn't in the right format. This means that we must make sure that all dates included in the URL are expressed in the universal format. We must also be careful when processing date values that users provide—the default binder assumes that the user will express dates in using the format of the server culture, something that unlikely to always happen in an MVC application that has international users.

Binding to Complex Types

When the action method parameter is a complex type (i.e., any type which cannot be converted using the TypeConverter class), then the DefaultModelBinder class uses reflection to obtain the set of public properties and then binds to each of them in turn.

To demonstrate how this works, we have added two new action methods to the Home controller, as shown in Listing 22-9.

Listing 22-9. Adding New Action Methods to the Home Controller

```csharp
using System;
using System.Collections.Generic;
using System.Linq;
using System.Web;
using System.Web.Mvc;
using MvcModels.Models;

namespace MvcModels.Controllers {
    public class HomeController : Controller {
        private Person[] personData = {
            new Person {PersonId = 1, FirstName = "Adam", LastName = "Freeman",
                Role = Role.Admin},
            new Person {PersonId = 2, FirstName = "Steven", LastName = "Sanderson",
                Role = Role.Admin},
            new Person {PersonId = 3, FirstName = "Jacqui", LastName = "Griffyth",
                Role = Role.User},
            new Person {PersonId = 4, FirstName = "John", LastName = "Smith",
                Role = Role.User},
            new Person {PersonId = 5, FirstName = "Anne", LastName = "Jones",
                Role = Role.Guest}
        };

        public ActionResult Index(int id = 1) {
            Person dataItem = personData.Where(p => p.PersonId == id).First();
            return View(dataItem);
        }

        public ActionResult CreatePerson() {
            return View(new Person());
        }

        [HttpPost]
        public ActionResult CreatePerson(Person model) {
            return View("Index", model);
        }
    }
}
```

The CreatePerson overload without any parameters creates a new Person object and passes it to the view method, which has the effect of rendering the /Views/Home/CreatePerson.cshtml view, which you can see in Listing 22-10.

Listing 22-10. The CreatePerson.cshtml View File

```
@model MvcModels.Models.Person
@{
    ViewBag.Title = "CreatePerson";
}
<h2>Create Person</h2>
@using(Html.BeginForm()) {
    <div>@Html.LabelFor(m => m.PersonId)@Html.EditorFor(m=>m.PersonId)</div>
    <div>@Html.LabelFor(m => m.FirstName)@Html.EditorFor(m=>m.FirstName)</div>
    <div>@Html.LabelFor(m => m.LastName)@Html.EditorFor(m=>m.LastName)</div>
    <div>@Html.LabelFor(m => m.Role)@Html.EditorFor(m=>m.Role)</div>
    <button type="submit">Submit</button>
}
```

This view renders a simple set of labels and editors for the properties in the `Person` object that we are working with, and contains a form element that posts the editor data back to the `CreatePerson` action method decorated with the `HttpPost` attribute. This reuses the `/Views/Home/Index.cshtml` view to display the data that the form contained. You can see how the new action methods work by starting the application and navigating to `/Home/CreatePerson`, as shown in Figure 22-5.

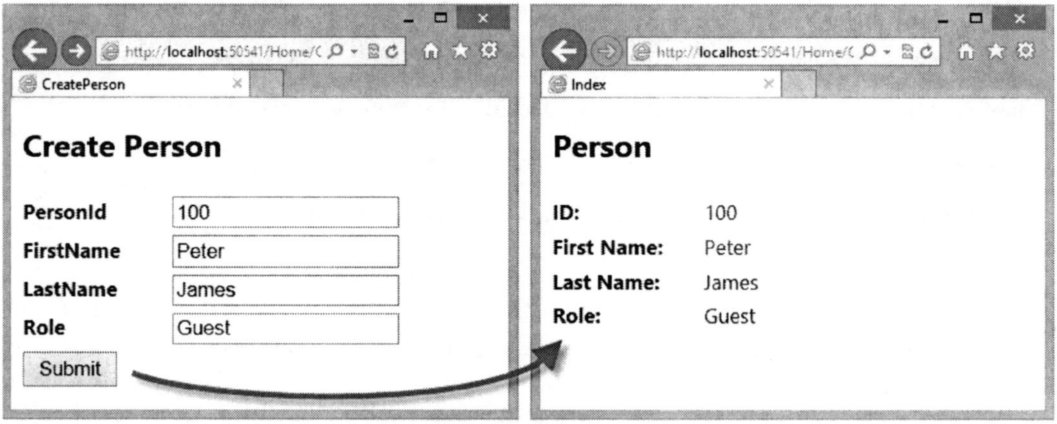

Figure 22-5. Using the CreatePerson action methods

We create a different kind of model binding situation when we post the form back to the `CreatePerson` method. The default model binder discovers that our action method requires a `Person` object and process each of the properties in turn. For each simple type property, the binder tries to locate a request value, just as it did in the previous example. So, for example, when it encounters the `PersonId` property, the binder will look for a `PersonId` data value, which it finds in the form data in the request.

If a property requires another complex type, then the process is repeated for the new type—the set of public properties are obtained and the binder tries to find values for all of them. The difference is that the property names are nested. For example, the `HomeAddress` property of the `Person` class is of the `Address` type, which is shown in Listing 22-11.

Listing 22-11. A Nested Model Class

```
...
public class Address {
    public string Line1 { get; set; }
    public string Line2 { get; set; }
    public string City { get; set; }
    public string PostalCode { get; set; }
    public string Country { get; set; }
}
...
```

When looking for a value for the Line1 property, the model binder looks for a value for HomeAddress.Line1—as in the name of the property in the model object combined with the name of the property in the property type.

Creating Easily-Bound HTML

The use of prefixes means that we have to design views that take them into account—although the helper methods make this a relatively easy thing to do. In Listing 22-12, you can see how we have updated the CreatePerson.cshtml view file so that we capture some of the properties for the Address type.

Listing 22-12. Updating the CreatePerson.cshtml View to Capture Address Details

```
@model MvcModels.Models.Person
@{
    ViewBag.Title = "CreatePerson";
}
<h2>Create Person</h2>
@using(Html.BeginForm()) {
    <div>@Html.LabelFor(m => m.PersonId)@Html.EditorFor(m=>m.PersonId)</div>
    <div>@Html.LabelFor(m => m.FirstName)@Html.EditorFor(m=>m.FirstName)</div>
    <div>@Html.LabelFor(m => m.LastName)@Html.EditorFor(m=>m.LastName)</div>
    <div>@Html.LabelFor(m => m.Role)@Html.EditorFor(m=>m.Role)</div>
    <div>
        @Html.LabelFor(m => m.HomeAddress.City)
        @Html.EditorFor(m=> m.HomeAddress.City)
    </div>
    <div>
        @Html.LabelFor(m => m.HomeAddress.Country)
        @Html.EditorFor(m=> m.HomeAddress.Country)
    </div>
    <button type="submit">Submit</button>
}
```

We have used the strongly-typed EditorFor helper method, and specified the properties we want to edit from the HomeAddress property. The helper automatically sets the name attributes of the input elements to match the format that the default model binder uses, as follows:

```
...
<input class="text-box single-line" id="HomeAddress_Country" name="HomeAddress.Country"
    type="text" value="" />
...
```

As a consequence of this neat feature, we don't have to take any special action to ensure that the model binder can create our Address object for the HomeAddress property. We can demonstrate this by editing the /Views/Home/Index.cshtml view to display the HomeAddress properties when they are submitted from the form, as shown in Listing 22-13.

Listing 22-13. Displaying the HomeAddress.City and HomeAddress.Country Properties

```
@model MvcModels.Models.Person
@{
    ViewBag.Title = "Index";
}
<h2>Person</h2>
<div><label>ID:</label>@Html.DisplayFor(m => m.PersonId)</div>
<div><label>First Name:</label>@Html.DisplayFor(m => m.FirstName)</div>
<div><label>Last Name:</label>@Html.DisplayFor(m => m.LastName)</div>
<div><label>Role:</label>@Html.DisplayFor(m => m.Role)</div>
<div><label>City:</label>@Html.DisplayFor(m => m.HomeAddress.City)</div>
<div><label>Country:</label>@Html.DisplayFor(m => m.HomeAddress.Country)</div>
```

If you start the application and navigate to the /Home/CreatePerson URL, you can enter values for the City and Country properties, and check that they are being bound to the model object by submitting the form, as shown in Figure 22-6.

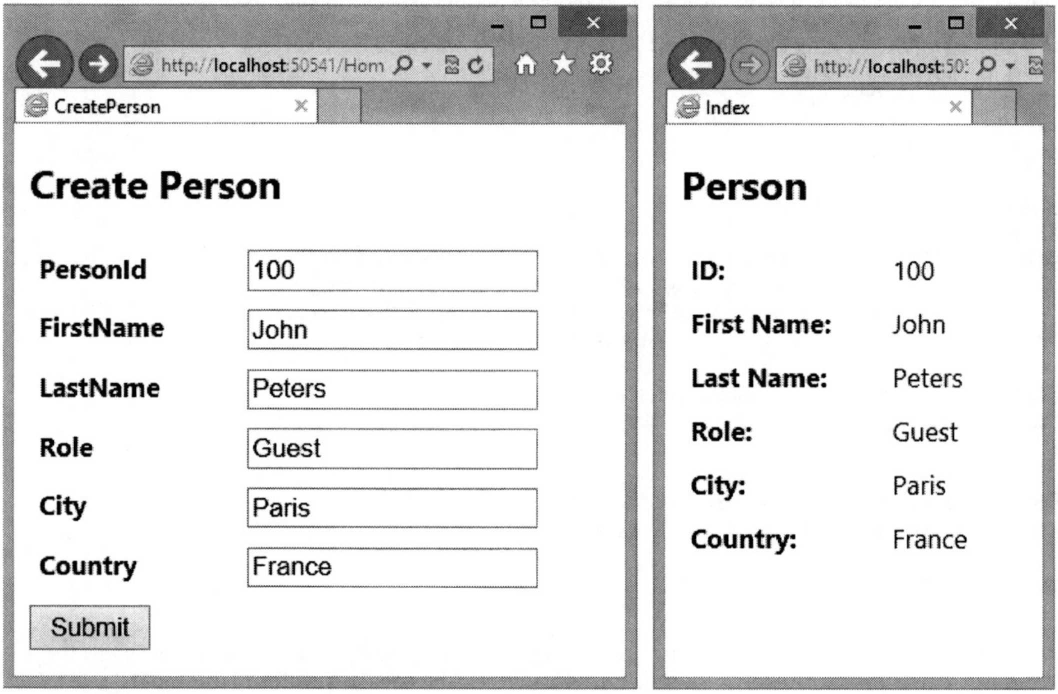

Figure 22-6. Binding to properties in complex objects

Specifying Custom Prefixes

There are occasions when the HTML you generate relates to one type of object, but you want to bind it to another. This means that the prefixes containing the view won't correspond to the structure that the model binder is expecting and your data won't be properly processed.

To demonstrate this situation, we have created a new class file called `AddressSummary.cs` in the `Models` folder. You can see the contents of this file in Listing 22-14.

Listing 22-14. The Contents of the AddressSummary.cs Class File

```
namespace MvcModels.Models {
    public class AddressSummary {
        public string City { get; set; }
        public string Country { get; set; }
    }
}
```

We have added a new action method in the `Home` controller that uses the `AddressSummary` class, as shown in Listing 22-15.

Listing 22-15. Adding a New Action Method to the Home Controller

```
using System;
using System.Collections.Generic;
using System.Linq;
using System.Web;
using System.Web.Mvc;
using MvcModels.Models;

namespace MvcModels.Controllers {
    public class HomeController : Controller {

        // ...other statements omitted from listing for brevity...

        public ActionResult DisplaySummary(AddressSummary summary) {
            return View(summary);
        }
    }
}
```

Our new action method is called `DisplaySummary`. It has an `AddressSummary` parameter, which it passes to the `View` method. The view for this method is called `DisplaySummary.cshtml`. We created it in the `/Views/Home` folder. You can see the contents of this view in Listing 22-16.

Listing 22-16. The DisplaySummary.cshtml View

```
@model MvcModels.Models.AddressSummary
@{
    ViewBag.Title = "DisplaySummary";
}
<h2>Address Summary</h2>
<div><label>City:</label>@Html.DisplayFor(m => m.City)</div>
<div><label>Country:</label>@Html.DisplayFor(m => m.Country)</div>
```

This is a very simple view that just displays the values of the two properties defined by the `AddressSummary` class. To demonstrate the problem with prefixes when binding to different model types, we will change the call to the `BeginForm` helper method in the `/Views/Home/CreatePerson.cshtml` file so that the form is submitted back to the new `DisplaySummary` action method, as shown in Listing 22-17.

Listing 22-17. Changing the Target of the Form in the CreatePerson.cshtml View

```
@model MvcModels.Models.Person
@{
    ViewBag.Title = "CreatePerson";
}
<h2>Create Person</h2>
@using(Html.BeginForm("DisplaySummary", "Home")) {
    <div>@Html.LabelFor(m => m.PersonId)@Html.EditorFor(m=>m.PersonId)</div>
    <div>@Html.LabelFor(m => m.FirstName)@Html.EditorFor(m=>m.FirstName)</div>
    <div>@Html.LabelFor(m => m.LastName)@Html.EditorFor(m=>m.LastName)</div>
    <div>@Html.LabelFor(m => m.Role)@Html.EditorFor(m=>m.Role)</div>
    <div>
        @Html.LabelFor(m => m.HomeAddress.City)
        @Html.EditorFor(m=> m.HomeAddress.City)
    </div>
    <div>
        @Html.LabelFor(m => m.HomeAddress.Country)
        @Html.EditorFor(m=> m.HomeAddress.Country)
    </div>
    <button type="submit">Submit</button>
}
```

You can see the problem if you start the application and navigate to the /Home/CreatePerson URL. When you submit the form, the values that you entered for the City and Country properties are not displayed in the HTML generated by the DisplaySummary view.

The problem is that the name attributes in the form have the HomeAddress prefix, which is not what the model binder is looking for when it tries to bind the AddressSummary type. We can fix this by applying the Bind attribute to the action method parameter, which we use to tell the binder which prefix it should look for, as shown in Listing 22-18.

Listing 22-18. Applying the Bind Attribute to an Action Method Parameter

```
...
public ActionResult DisplaySummary([Bind(Prefix="HomeAddress")]AddressSummary summary) {
    return View(summary);
}
...
```

The syntax is a bit nasty, but the effect is very useful. When populating the properties of our AddressSummary object, the model binder will look for HomeAddress.City and HomeAddress.Country data values in the request. In this example, we displayed editors for properties of the Person object, but used the model binder to create an instance of the AddressSummary class when the form data was posted, as shown in Figure 22-7. This may seem like a long setup for a simple problem, but the need to bind to a different kind of object is surprisingly common and you are likely to need this technique in your projects.

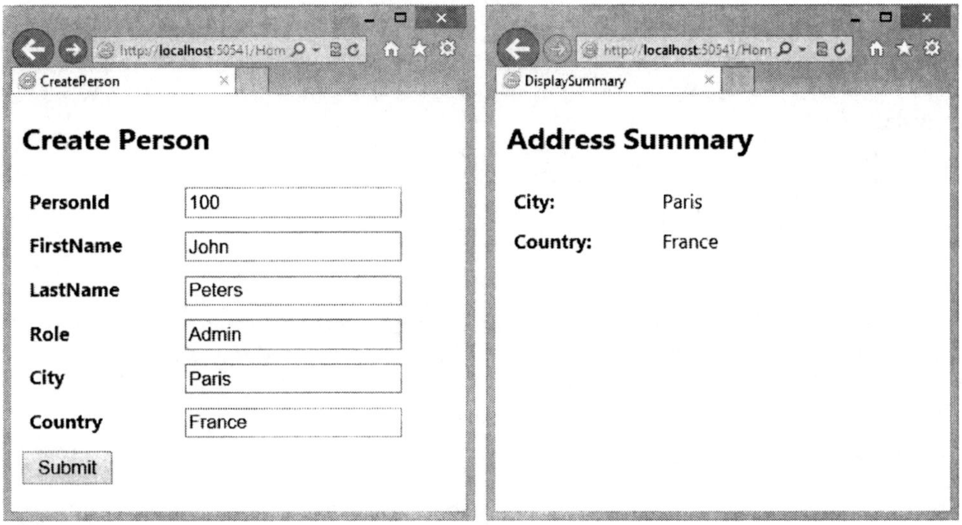

Figure 22-7. Binding to the properties of a different object type

Selectively Binding Properties

Imagine that the `Country` property of the `AddressSummary` class is especially sensitive and we don't want the user to be able to specify values for it. The first thing we can do is prevent the user from seeing the property or even prevent the property from being included in the HTML sent to the browser using the attributes we showed you in Chapter 20, or simply by not adding editors for that property to the view.

However, a nefarious user could simply edit the form data sent to the server when submitting the form data and pick the value for the `Country` property that suits them. What we really want to do is tell the model binder not to bind a value for the `Country` property from the request, which we can do by using the `Bind` attribute on the action method parameter. In Listing 22-19, you can see how we have used the attribute to prevent the user from providing a value for `Country` property in the `DisplaySummary` action method in the `Home` controller.

Listing 22-19. Excluding a Property from Model Binding

```
...
public ActionResult DisplaySummary(
    [Bind(Prefix="HomeAddress", Exclude="Country")]AddressSummary summary) {
    return View(summary);
}
...
```

The `Exclude` property of the `Bind` attribute allows you to exclude properties from the model binding process. You can see the effect by navigating to the `/Home/CreatePerson` URL, entering some data and submitting the form. You will see that there is no data displayed for the `Country` property. (As an alternative, you can use the `Include` property to specify only those properties that should be bound in the model; all other properties will be ignored).

When the `Bind` attribute is applied to an action method parameter, it only affects instances of that class that are bound for that action method; all other action methods will continue to try and bind all the properties defined by the parameter type. If you want to create a more widespread effect, then you can apply the `Bind` attribute to the model class itself, as shown in Listing 22-20, where we have applied the `Bind` method to the `AddressSummary` class so that only the `City` property is included in the bind process.

Listing 22-20. Applying the Bind Attribute to the Model Class

```
using System.Web.Mvc;

namespace MvcModels.Models {
    [Bind(Include="City")]
    public class AddressSummary {
        public string City { get; set; }
        public string Country { get; set; }
    }
}
```

When the `Bind` attribute is applied to the model class *and* to an action method parameter, a property will be included in the bind process only if neither application of the attribute excludes it. This means that the policy applied to the model class cannot be overridden by applying a less restrictive policy to the action method parameter.

Binding to Arrays and Collections

The default model binder includes some nice support for binding request data to arrays and collections. We demonstrate these features in the following sections, before we move on to show you how to customize the model binding process.

Binding to Arrays

One elegant feature of the default model binder is how it supports action method parameters that are arrays. To demonstrate this, we have added a new method to the Home controller called `Names`, which you can see in Listing 22-21.

Listing 22-21. Adding the Names Action Method to the Home Controller

```
using System;
using System.Collections.Generic;
using System.Linq;
using System.Web;
using System.Web.Mvc;
using MvcModels.Models;

namespace MvcModels.Controllers {
    public class HomeController : Controller {

        // ...other statements omitted from listing for brevity

        public ActionResult Names(string[] names) {
            names = names ?? new string[0];
            return View(names);
        }
    }
}
```

The `Names` action method takes a `string` array parameter called `names`. The model binder will look for any data item that is called `names` and create an array that contains those values.

■ **Tip**   Notice that we have to check to see if the parameter is null in the action method for this example. You can only use constant or literal values as defaults for parameters.

In Listing 22-22, you can see the /Views/Home/Names.cshtml view file, which we created to show array binding.

Listing 22-22. The Content of the Names.cshtml File

```
@model string[]
@{
    ViewBag.Title = "Names";
}
<h2>Names</h2>
@if (Model.Length == 0) {
    using(Html.BeginForm()) {
        for (int i = 0; i < 3; i++) {
            <div><label>@(i + 1):</label>@Html.TextBox("names")</div>
        }
        <button type="submit">Submit</button>
    }
} else {
    foreach (string str in Model) {
        <p>@str</p>
    }
    @Html.ActionLink("Back", "Names");
}
```

This view displays different content based on the number of items there are in the view model. If there are no items, then we display a form that contains three identical **input** elements, like this:

```
...
<form action="/Home/Names" method="post">
    <div><label>1:</label><input id="names" name="names" type="text" value="" /></div>
    <div><label>2:</label><input id="names" name="names" type="text" value="" /></div>
    <div><label>3:</label><input id="names" name="names" type="text" value="" /></div>
    <button type="submit">Submit</button>
</form>
...
```

When we submit the form, the default model binder sees that our action method requires a string array and looks for data items that have the same name as the parameter. For our example, this means that the contents of all of our **input** elements is gathered together. You can see how the action method and view operate in Figure 22-8.

615

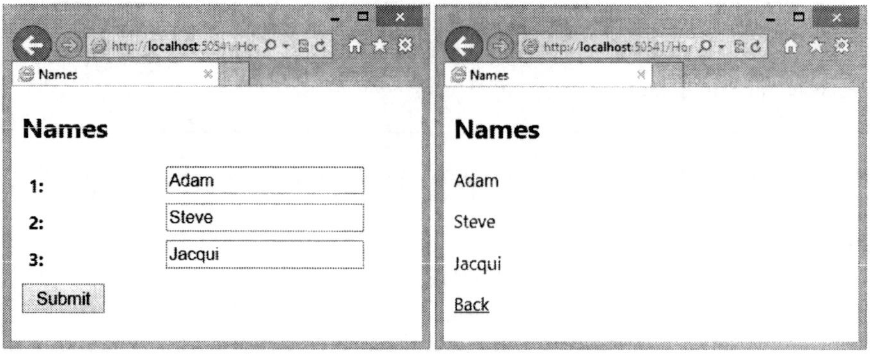

Figure 22-8. Model binding for arrays

Binding to Collections

It isn't just arrays that we can bind to—we can also use the .NET collection classes. In Listing 22-23, you can see how we have changed the type of the **Names** action method parameter to be a strongly-typed list.

Listing 22-23. Using a Strongly-Typed Collection As an Action Method Parameter

```
...
public ActionResult Names(IList<string> names) {
    names = names ?? new List<string>();
    return View(names);
}
...
```

Notice that we have used the **IList** interface. We didn't even need to specify a concrete implementation class (although we could have if we preferred). In Listing 22-24, you can see how we have modified the **Names.cshtml** view file to use the new model type.

Listing 22-24. Using a Collection As the Model Type in the Names.cshtml View

```
@model IList<string>
@{
    ViewBag.Title = "Names";
}
<h2>Names</h2>
@if (Model.Count == 0) {
    using(Html.BeginForm()) {
        for (int i = 0; i < 3; i++) {
            <div><label>@(i + 1):</label>@Html.TextBox("names")</div>
        }
        <button type="submit">Submit</button>
    }
} else {
    foreach (string str in Model) {
        <p>@str</p>
    }
    @Html.ActionLink("Back", "Names");
}
```

The functionality of the **Names** action is unchanged, but we are now able to work with a collection class rather than an array.

Binding to Collections of Custom Model Types

We can also bind individual data properties to an array of custom types, such as our **AddressSummary** model class. In Listing 22-25, you can see that we have added a new action method called **Address**, which has a strongly-typed collection parameter that relies on a custom model class.

Listing 22-25. Defining an Action Method with a Collection of Custom Model Types

```
using System;
using System.Collections.Generic;
using System.Linq;
using System.Web;
using System.Web.Mvc;
using MvcModels.Models;

namespace MvcModels.Controllers {
    public class HomeController : Controller {

        // ...other statements omitted from listing for brevity...

        public ActionResult Address(IList<AddressSummary> addresses) {
            addresses = addresses ?? new List<AddressSummary>();
            return View(addresses);
        }
    }
}
```

The view that we created for this action method is the **/Views/Home/Address.cshtml** file, which you can see in Listing 22-26.

Listing 22-26. The Contents of the Address.cshtml View File

```
@using MvcModels.Models
@model IList<AddressSummary>
@{
    ViewBag.Title = "Address";
}
<h2>Addresses</h2>
@if (Model.Count() == 0) {
    using (Html.BeginForm()) {
        for (int i = 0; i < 3; i++) {
            <fieldset>
                <legend>Address @(i + 1)</legend>
                <div><label>City:</label>@Html.Editor("[" + i + "].City")</div>
                <div><label>Country:</label>@Html.Editor("[" + i + "].Country")</div>
            </fieldset>
        }
        <button type="submit">Submit</button>
    }
} else {
    foreach (AddressSummary str in Model) {
        <p>@str.City, @str.Country</p>
    }
    @Html.ActionLink("Back", "Address");
}
```

This view renders a `form` element if there are no items in the model collection. The `form` consists of pairs of `input` elements whose `name` attributes are prefixed with an array index, like this:

```
...
<fieldset>
    <legend>Address 1</legend>
    <div>
        <label>City:</label>
        <input class="text-box single-line" name="[0].City" type="text" value="" />
    </div>
    <div>
        <label>Country:</label>
        <input class="text-box single-line" name="[0].Country" type="text" value="" />
    </div>
</fieldset>
<fieldset>
    <legend>Address 2</legend>
    <div>
        <label>City:</label>
        <input class="text-box single-line" name="[1].City" type="text" value="" />
    </div>
    <div>
        <label>Country:</label>
        <input class="text-box single-line" name="[1].Country" type="text" value="" />
    </div>
</fieldset>
...
```

When the `form` is submitted, the default model binder realizes that it needs to create a collection of `AddressSummary` objects and uses the array index prefixes in the `name` attributes to obtain values for the object properties. The properties prefixed with `[0]` are used for the first `AddressSumary` object; those prefixed with `[1]` are used for the second object, and so on.

Our `Address.cshtml` view defines `input` elements for three such indexed objects and displays them when the model collection contains items. Before we can demonstrate this, we need to remove the `Bind` attribute from the `AddressSummary` model class, as shown in Listing 22-27; otherwise, the model binder will ignore the `Country` property.

Listing 22-27. Removing the Bind Attribute from the AddressSummary Model Class

```
using System.Web.Mvc;

namespace MvcModels.Models {
    // This attribute has been commented out
    //[Bind(Include="City")]
    public class AddressSummary {
        public string City { get; set; }
        public string Country { get; set; }
    }
}
```

You can see how the binding process for custom object collections works by starting the application and navigating to the /Home/Address URL. Enter some cities and countries, and then click the Submit button to post the form to the server. The model binder will find and process the indexed data values and use them to create the collection of `AddressSummary` objects that are then passed back to the view and displayed to you, as shown in Figure 22-9.

Figure 22-9. Binding collections of custom objects

Manually Invoking Model Binding

The model binding process is performed automatically when an action method defines parameters, but we can take direct control of the process if we want to. This gives us more explicit control over how model objects are instantiated, where data values are obtained from, and how data parsing errors are handled. Listing 22-28 demonstrates how we have changed our **Address** action method in the **Home** controller to manually invoke the binding process.

Listing 22-28. Manually Invoking the Model Binding Process in the Address Action Method

```
...
public ActionResult Address() {
    IList<AddressSummary> addresses = new List<AddressSummary>();
    UpdateModel(addresses);
    return View(addresses);
}
...
```

The **UpdateModel** method takes a model object that we were previously defining as a parameter and tries to obtain values for its public properties using the standard binding process.

When we manually invoke the binding process, we can restrict the binding process to a single source of data. By default, the binder looks in four places—form data, route data, the query string, and any uploaded files. Listing 22-29 shows how we can restrict the binder to searching for data in a single location—in this case, the form data.

Listing 22-29. Restricting the Binder to the Form Data

```
...
public ActionResult Address() {
    IList<AddressSummary> addresses = new List<AddressSummary>();
    UpdateModel(addresses, new FormValueProvider(ControllerContext));
    return View(addresses);
}
...
```

This version of the UpdateModel method takes an implementation of the IValueProvider interface, which becomes the sole source of data values for the binding process. Each of the four default data locations is represented by an IValueProvider implementation, as shown in Table 22-2.

Table 22-2. The Built-in IValueProvider Implementations

Source	IValueProvider **Implementation**
Request.Form	FormValueProvider
RouteData.Values	RouteDataValueProvider
Request.QueryString	QueryStringValueProvider
Request.Files	HttpFileCollectionValueProvider

Each of the classes listed in Table 22-2 takes a ControllerContext constructor parameter, which we obtain through the property called ControllerContext that is defined by the Controller class, as shown in the listing.

The most common way of restricting the source of data is to look only at the form values. There is a neat binding trick that we can use so that we don't have to create an instance of FormValueProvider, as shown in Listing 22-30.

Listing 22-30. Restricting the Binder Data Source

```
...
public ActionResult Address(FormCollection formData) {
    IList<AddressSummary> addresses = new List<AddressSummary>();
    UpdateModel(addresses, formData);
    return View(addresses);
}
...
```

The FormCollection class implements the IValueProvider interface, and if we define the action method to take a parameter of this type, the model binder will provide us with an object that we can pass directly to the UpdateModel method.

■ **Tip**   There are other overloaded versions of the UpdateModel method that allow us to specify a prefix to search for and which model properties should be included in the binding process.

Dealing with Binding Errors

Users will inevitably supply values that cannot be bound to the corresponding model properties—invalid dates or text for numeric values, for example. When we invoke model binding explicitly, we are responsible for dealing with any such errors. The model binder expresses binding errors by throwing an InvalidOperationException. Details of the errors can be found through the ModelState feature, which we describe in Chapter 23, but when using the UpdateModel method, we must be prepared to catch the exception and use the ModelState to express an error message to the user, as shown in Listing 22-31.

Listing 22-31. Dealing with Model Binding Errors

```
...
public ActionResult Address(FormCollection formData) {
    IList<AddressSummary> addresses = new List<AddressSummary>();
    try {
        UpdateModel(addresses, formData);
    } catch (InvalidOperationException ex) {
        // provide feedback to user
    }
    return View(addresses);
}
...
```

As an alternative approach, we can use the TryUpdateModel method, which returns true if the model binding process is successful and false if there are errors, as shown in Listing 22-32.

Listing 22-32. Using the TryUpdateModel Method

```
...
public ActionResult Address(FormCollection formData) {
    IList<AddressSummary> addresses = new List<AddressSummary>();
    if (TryUpdateModel(addresses, formData)) {
        // proceed as normal
    } else {
        // provide feedback to user
    }
    return View(addresses);
}
...
```

The only reason to favor TryUpdateModel over UpdateModel is if you don't like catching and dealing with exceptions. There is no functional difference in the model binding process.

■ **Tip**   When model binding is invoked automatically, binding errors are not signaled with exceptions. Instead, we must check the result through the ModelState.IsValid property. We explain ModelState in Chapter 23.

Customizing the Model Binding System

We have shown you the default model binding process. As you might expect by now, there are some different ways in which we can customize the binding system. We show you some examples in the following sections.

Creating a Custom Value Provider

By defining a custom value provider, we can add our own source of data to the model binding process. Value providers implement the `IValueProvider` interface, which is shown in Listing 22-33.

Listing 22-33. The IValueProvider Interface

```
namespace System.Web.Mvc {
    public interface IValueProvider {

        bool ContainsPrefix(string prefix);

        ValueProviderResult GetValue(string key);
    }
}
```

The `ContainsPrefix` method is called by the model binder to determine if the value provider can resolve the data for a given prefix. The `GetValue` method returns a value for a given data key, or `null` if the provider doesn't have any suitable data.

We have added an `Infrastructure` folder to the example project and created a new class file called `CountryValueProvider.cs`, which we will use to provide values for the `Country` property. You can see the contents of this file in Listing 22-34.

Listing 22-34. The Contents of the CountryValueProvider.cs File

```
using System.Globalization;
using System.Web.Mvc;

namespace MvcModels.Infrastructure {
    public class CountryValueProvider : IValueProvider {

        public bool ContainsPrefix(string prefix) {
            return prefix.ToLower().IndexOf("country") > -1;
        }

        public ValueProviderResult GetValue(string key) {
            if (ContainsPrefix(key)) {
                return new ValueProviderResult("USA", "USA",
                    CultureInfo.InvariantCulture);
            } else {
                return null;
            }
        }
    }
}
```

This value provider only responds to requests for values for the `Country` property and it always returns the value `USA`. For all other requests, we return `null`, indicating that we cannot provide data.

We have to return our data value as a `ValueProviderResult` class. This class has three constructor parameters. The first is the data item that we want to associate with the requested key. The second parameter is a version of the data value that is safe to display. The final parameter is the culture information that relates to the value; we have specified the `InvariantCulture`.

To register our value provider with the application, we need to create a factory class that will create instances of our provider. This class be derived from the abstract `ValueProviderFactory` class. In Listing

22-35, you can see the contents of the `CustomValueProviderFactory.cs` class file that we created in the `Infrastructure` folder.

Listing 22-35. The Contents of the CustomValueProviderFactory.cs File

```
using System.Web.Mvc;

namespace MvcModels.Infrastructure {
    public class CustomValueProviderFactory : ValueProviderFactory {

        public override IValueProvider GetValueProvider(ControllerContext
                controllerContext) {
            return new CountryValueProvider();
        }
    }
}
```

The `GetValueProvider` method is called when the model binder wants to obtain values for the binding process. Our implementation simply creates and returns an instance of the `CountryValueProvider` class, but you can use the data provided through the `ControllerContext` parameter to respond to different kinds of requests by creating different value providers.

We need to register the factory class with the application, which we do in the `Application_Start` method of `Global.asax`, as shown in Listing 22-36.

Listing 22-36. Registering a Value Provider Factory

```
using System;
using System.Collections.Generic;
using System.Linq;
using System.Web;
using System.Web.Http;
using System.Web.Mvc;
using System.Web.Optimization;
using System.Web.Routing;
using MvcModels.Infrastructure;

namespace MvcModels {


    public class MvcApplication : System.Web.HttpApplication {
        protected void Application_Start() {
            AreaRegistration.RegisterAllAreas();

            ValueProviderFactories.Factories.Insert(0, new CustomValueProviderFactory());

            WebApiConfig.Register(GlobalConfiguration.Configuration);
            FilterConfig.RegisterGlobalFilters(GlobalFilters.Filters);
            RouteConfig.RegisterRoutes(RouteTable.Routes);
            BundleConfig.RegisterBundles(BundleTable.Bundles);
        }
    }
}
```

We register our factory class by adding an instance to the static `ValueProviderFactories.Factories` collection. The model binder looks at the value providers in sequence, which means we have to use the `Insert` method to put our factory at the first position in the collection of value providers maintained by the application if we want to take precedence over the built-in providers.

If we wanted our provider to be a fallback that is used when the other providers cannot supply a data value, then we can use the `Add` method to append our factory class to the end of the collection, like this:

```
...
ValueProviderFactories.Factories.Add(new CustomValueProviderFactory());
...
```

We want our value provider to be used before any other provider, and so we have used in the `Insert` method in the example. We need to modify the `Address` action method before we can test our value provider, so that the model binder doesn't just look at the form data for model property values. In Listing 22-37, you can see how we have removed the restriction on the source for values in the call to the `TryUpdateModel` method.

Listing 22-37. Removing the Restriction on the Sources of Model Property Values

```
...
public ActionResult Address() {
    IList<AddressSummary> addresses = new List<AddressSummary>();
    UpdateModel(addresses);
    return View(addresses);
}
...
```

You can see our custom value provider at work if you start the application and navigate to the `/Home/Address` URL. Enter city and country data, and then press the `Submit` button. You will see that our custom value provider, which has precedence over the built-in providers, has been used to generate values for the `Country` property in each of the `AddressSummary` objects that the model binder has created, as shown in Figure 22-10.

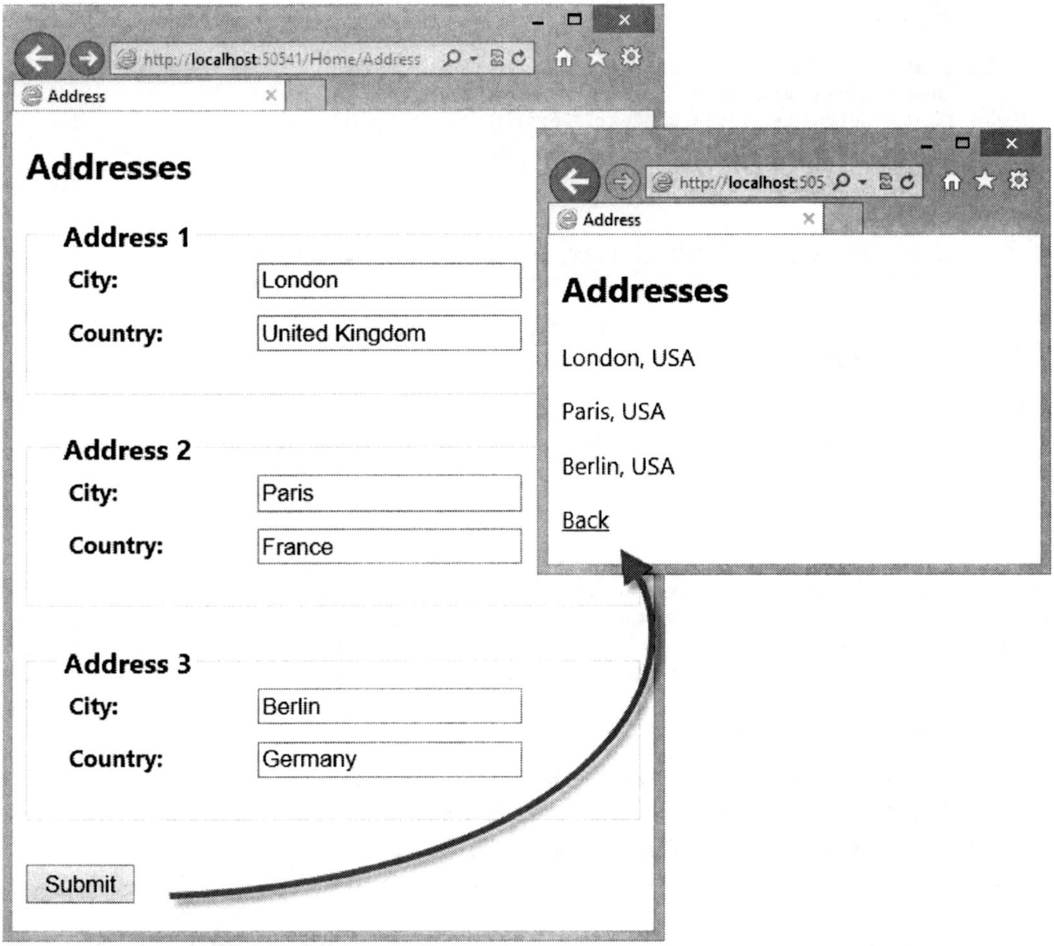

Figure 22-10. The effect of the custom value provider

Creating a Custom Model Binder

We can override the default binder's behavior by creating a custom model binder for a specific type. Custom model binders implement the `IModelBinder` interface, which we showed you earlier in the chapter. To demonstrate how to create a custom binder, we have added the `AddressSummaryBinder.cs` file to the `Infrastructure` folder, the contents of which you can see in Listing 22-38.

Listing 22-38. The Contents of the AddressSummaryBinder.cs Class File

```
using MvcModels.Models;
using System.Web.Mvc;

namespace MvcModels.Infrastructure {
    public class AddressSummaryBinder : IModelBinder {

        public object BindModel(ControllerContext controllerContext,
```

```
                ModelBindingContext bindingContext) {

        AddressSummary model = (AddressSummary)bindingContext.Model
            ?? new AddressSummary();
        model.City = GetValue(bindingContext, "City");
        model.Country = GetValue(bindingContext, "Country");
        return model;
    }

    private string GetValue(ModelBindingContext context, string name) {
        name = (context.ModelName == "" ? "" : context.ModelName + ".") + name;

        ValueProviderResult result = context.ValueProvider.GetValue(name);
        if (result == null || result.AttemptedValue == "") {
            return "<Not Specified>";
        } else {
            return (string)result.AttemptedValue;
        }
    }
    }
  }
}
```

The MVC Framework will call the BindModel method when it wants an instance of the model type that the binder supports. We'll show you how to register a model binder shortly, but our AddressSummaryBinder class will only be used to create instances of the AddressSummary class, which makes the code a lot simpler (you can create custom binders that support multiple types, but we prefer one binder for each type).

■ **Tip**   We don't perform any input validation in this model binder—meaning that we blithely assume that the user has provided valid values for all of the Person properties. We discuss validation in Chapter 23, but for the moment, we want to focus on the basic model binding process.

The parameters to the BindModel method are a ControllerContext object that you can use to get details of the current request and a ModelBindingContext object, which provides details of the model object that is sought, as well as access to the rest of the model binding facilities in the MVC application. In Table 22-3, we have described the most useful properties defined by the ModelBindingContext class.

Table 22-3. The Most Useful Properties Defined by the ModelBindingContext Class

Property	Description
Model	Returns the model object passed to the UpdateModel method if binding has been invoked manually.
ModelName	Returns the name of the model that is being bound.
ModelType	Returns the type of the model that is being created.
ValueProvider	Returns an IValueProvider implementation that can be used to get data values from the request.

Our custom model binder is very simple. When the BindModel method is called, we check to see if the Model property of the ModelBindingContext object has been set. If it has, this is the object that we will generate data value for, and if not, then we create a new instance of the AddressSummary class. We get the values for the City and Country properties by calling the GetValue method we defined, and then return the populated AddressSummary object.

In the GetValue method, we use the IValueProvider implementation obtained from the ModelBindingContext.ValueProvider property to get values for the model object properties.

The ModelName property tells us if there is a prefix we need to append to the property name we are looking for. You will recall that our action method is trying to create a collection of AddressSummary objects, which means that the individual input elements will have name attribute values that are prefixed [0] and [1]. The values we are looking for in the request will be [0].City, [0].Country, and so on. As a final step, we supply a default value of <Not Specified> if we can't find a value for a property or the property is the empty string (which is what is sent to the server when the user doesn't enter a value in the input elements in the form).

Registering the Custom Model Binder

We have to register our model binder so that the MVC application knows which types it can support. We do this in the Application_Start method of Global.asax, as demonstrated by Listing 22-39.

Listing 22-39. Registering a Custom Model Binder

```
using System;
using System.Collections.Generic;
using System.Linq;
using System.Web;
using System.Web.Http;
using System.Web.Mvc;
using System.Web.Optimization;
using System.Web.Routing;
using MvcModels.Infrastructure;
using MvcModels.Models;

namespace MvcModels {


    public class MvcApplication : System.Web.HttpApplication {
        protected void Application_Start() {
            AreaRegistration.RegisterAllAreas();

            // This statement has been commented out
            //ValueProviderFactories.Factories.Insert(0,
            //        new CustomValueProviderFactory());

            ModelBinders.Binders.Add(typeof(AddressSummary), new AddressSummaryBinder());

            WebApiConfig.Register(GlobalConfiguration.Configuration);
            FilterConfig.RegisterGlobalFilters(GlobalFilters.Filters);
            RouteConfig.RegisterRoutes(RouteTable.Routes);
            BundleConfig.RegisterBundles(BundleTable.Bundles);
        }
    }
}
```

We register our binder through the `ModelBinders.Binders.Add` method, passing in the type that our binder supports and an instance of the binder class. Notice that we have removed the statement that registers the custom value provider. You can test the custom model binder by starting the application, navigating to the `/Home/Address` URL, and filling in only some of the form elements. When you submit the form, our custom model binder will use `<Not Specifed>` for all of the properties for which you didn't enter a value, as shown in Figure 22-11.

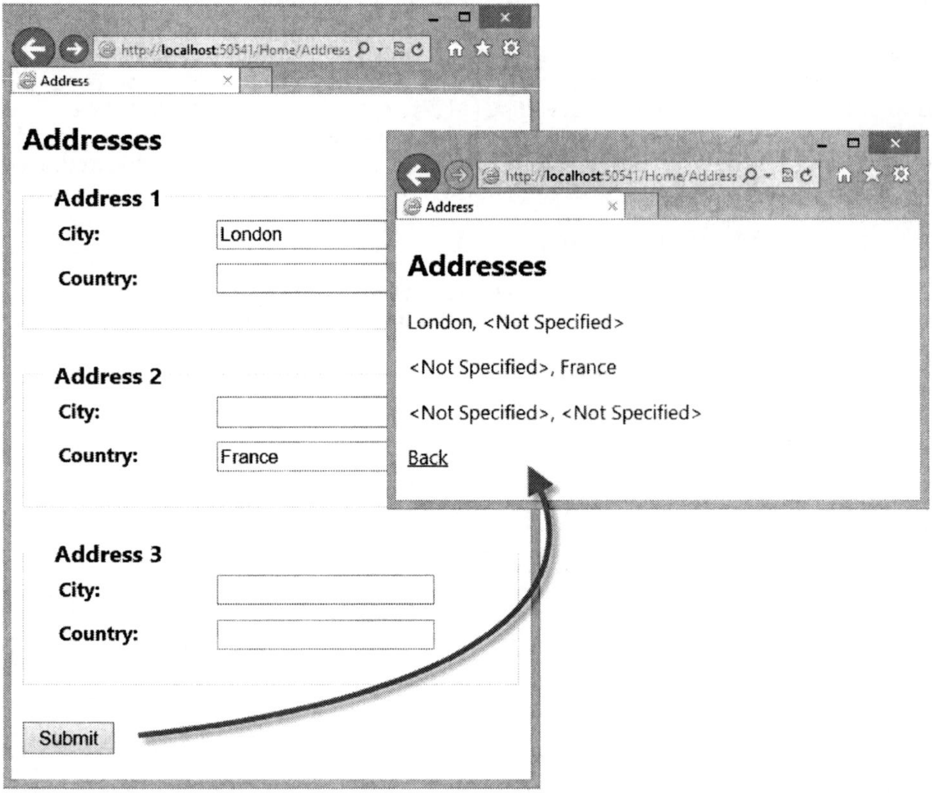

Figure 22-11. The effect of using a custom model binder

■ **Tip**   As an alternative, you can specify custom model binders by decorating the model class with the `ModelBinder` attribute.

Summary

In this chapter, we introduced you to the workings of the model binding process, showing you how the default model binder operates and the different ways in which the process can be customized. Many MVC Framework applications will only need the default model binder, which works nicely to process the HTML that the helper methods generate, but for more advanced applications, it can be useful to use custom binders that create model objects in a more efficient or specific way. In the next chapter, we will show you how to validate model objects and how to present the user with meaningful errors when invalid data is received.

CHAPTER 23

■ ■ ■

Model Validation

In the previous chapter, we showed you how the MVC Framework creates model objects from HTTP requests through the model binding process. Throughout that chapter, we worked on the basis that the data the user supplied was valid. The reality is that users will often enter data that we cannot work with, which leads us to the topic of this chapter—*model validation*.

Model validation is the process of ensuring the data we receive is suitable for binding to our model and, when this is not the case, providing useful information to the user that will help explain the problem.

The first part of the process—checking the data we receive—is one of the ways we preserve the integrity of our domain model. By rejecting data that doesn't make sense in the context of our domain, we prevent odd and unwanted states arising in our application. The second part—helping the user correct the problem—is equally important. If we do not provide the user with the information and tools they need to interact with our application the way we need them to, then they will become frustrated and confused. In public-facing applications, this means users will simply stop using the application. In corporate applications, this means we will be hindering our user's workflow. Neither outcome is desirable. Fortunately, the MVC Framework provides extensive support for model validation. We will show you how to use the basic features and then demonstrate some advanced techniques to fine-tune the validation process.

Creating the Example Project

Before we can start, we need to create a simple MVC application to which we can apply different model validation techniques. We created a new MVC project called **ModelValidation** using the **Basic** template option. We created a new model class file called **Appointment.cs**, which you can see in Listing 23-1.

Listing 23-1. The Appointment Model Class

```
using System;
using System.ComponentModel.DataAnnotations;

namespace ModelValidation.Models {
    public class Appointment {

        public string ClientName { get; set; }

        [DataType(DataType.Date)]
        public DateTime Date { get; set; }

        public bool TermsAccepted { get; set; }
    }
}
```

Our `Appointment` model class defines three properties and we have used the `DataType` attribute to indicate that the `Date` property should be expressed as a date without a time component.

We created a `Home` controller for the example project and defined action methods that operate on the `Appointment` model class, as shown in Listing 23-2.

Listing 23-2. The Home Controller in the ModelValidation Project

```
using System;
using System.Web.Mvc;
using ModelValidation.Models;

namespace ModelValidation.Controllers {
    public class HomeController : Controller {

        public ViewResult MakeBooking() {
            return View(new Appointment { Date = DateTime.Now });
        }

        [HttpPost]
        public ViewResult MakeBooking(Appointment appt) {

            // statements to store new Appointment in a
            // repository would go here in a real project

            return View("Completed", appt);
        }
    }
}
```

As you have seen in previous chapters, we have defined two versions of the `MakeBooking` action method. The one that will interest us in this chapter is the version to which the `HttpPost` attribute has been applied, since this is the version where model binding will be used to construct the `Appointment` parameter object.

Notice that we have added some comments to indicate where, in a real application, statements would be placed to store the details of the `Appointment` object that the model binder will create. We are not going to create a repository in our example because we want to focus on the model binding and validation process; but it is important to bear in mind that the reason that we validate a model is to prevent bad or meaningless data from being placed in the repository and causing problems (either when we try to store the data or when we try to process the data later).

To complete our example application, we need to create a couple of views to support the action methods, both of which are located in the `/Views/Home` folder. In Listing 23-3, you can see the contents of the `MakeBooking.cshtml` file, which contains a form that allows the user to create a new appointment.

Listing 23-3. The Contents of the MakeBooking.cshtml File

```
@model ModelValidation.Models.Appointment
@{
    ViewBag.Title = "Make A Booking";
}
<h4>Book an Appointment</h4>

@using (Html.BeginForm()) {
    <p>Your name: @Html.EditorFor(m => m.ClientName)</p>
    <p>Appointment Date: @Html.EditorFor(m => m.Date)</p>
    <p>@Html.EditorFor(m => m.TermsAccepted) I accept the terms & conditions</p>
    <input type="submit" value="Make Booking" />
}
```

When the form is posted back to the application, the MakeBooking action method displays the details of the appointment that the user has created using the Completed.cshtml view, which you can see in Listing 23-4.

Listing 23-4. The Contents of the Completed.cshtml File

```
@model ModelValidation.Models.Appointment
@{
    ViewBag.Title = "Completed";
}
<h4>Your appointment is confirmed</h4>
<p>Your name is: <b>@Html.DisplayFor(m => m.ClientName)</b></p>
<p>The date of your appointment is: <b>@Html.DisplayFor(m => m.Date)</b></p>
```

As you may have gathered, our example for this chapter is based around creating appointments. You can see how it works by starting the application and navigating to the /Home/MakeBooking URL. Entering details into the form and clicking the Submit button will send the data to the server, which performs the model-binding process to create an Appointment object, the details of which are then rendered using the Completed.cshtml view, as shown in Figure 23-1.

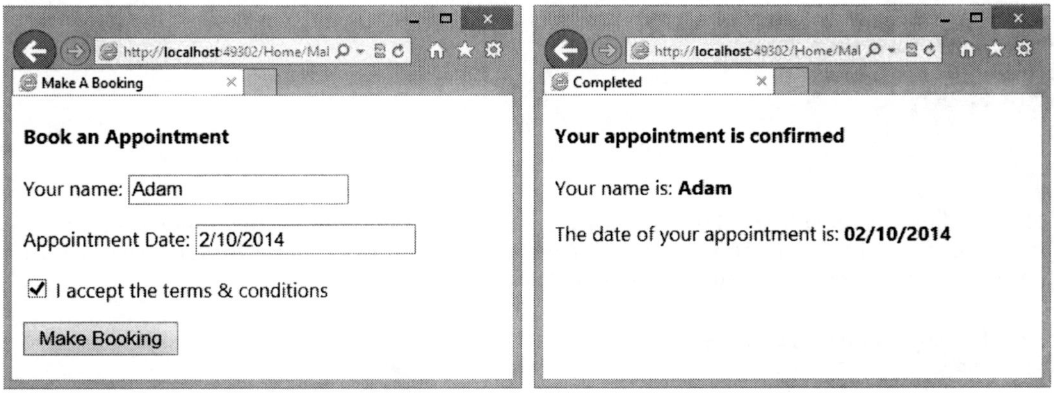

Figure 23-1. Using the example application

As it stands, our application will accept any data the user submits, but to preserve the integrity of our application and domain model, we require three things to be true before we accept an Appointment that the user has submitted:

- The user must provide a name.

- The user must provide a date (in the mm/dd/yyyy format) that is in the future.

- The user must have checked the check box to accept the terms and conditions.

Model validation is the process of enforcing these requirements. In the following sections, we will show you the different techniques available for checking the data that the user has provided and how we can give the user feedback when we cannot use the data they have submitted.

Explicitly Validating a Model

The most direct way of validating a model is to do so in the action method. Listing 23-5 shows how we have added explicit checks for each property defined by the Appointment class in the HttpPost version of the MakeBooking action method.

Listing 23-5. Explicitly Validating a Model

```
...
[HttpPost]
public ViewResult MakeBooking(Appointment appt) {

    if (string.IsNullOrEmpty(appt.ClientName)) {
        ModelState.AddModelError("ClientName", "Please enter your name");
    }

    if (ModelState.IsValidField("Date") && DateTime.Now > appt.Date) {
        ModelState.AddModelError("Date", "Please enter a date in the future");
    }

    if (!appt.TermsAccepted) {
        ModelState.AddModelError("TermsAccepted", "You must accept the terms");
    }

    if (ModelState.IsValid) {
        // statements to store new Appointment in a
        // repository would go here in a real project
        return View("Completed", appt);
    } else {
        return View();
    }
}
...
```

We check the values that the model binder has assigned to the properties of the parameter object and register any errors we find with the ModelState property, which our controller inherits from its base class. As an example, consider how we check the ClientName property:

```
...
if (string.IsNullOrEmpty(appt.ClientName)) {
    ModelState.AddModelError("ClientName", "Please enter your name");
}
...
```

We want a value from the user for this property, so we use the static string.IsNullOrEmpty method to check the property. If we have not received a value, we use the ModelState.AddModelError method to specify the name of the property for which there is a problem (ClientName) and a message that should be displayed to the user to help them correct the problem (Please enter your name).

We can check to see whether the model binder was able to assign a value to a property by using the ModelState.IsValidField property. We do this for the Date property to make sure that the model binder was able to parse the value the user submitted; there is no point performing additional checks or reporting additional errors if no value could be parsed from the request data.

After we have validated all the properties in the model object, we read the ModelState.IsValid property to see whether there were errors. This method returns true if we called the Model.State.AddModelError method during our checks or if the model binder had any problems creating the Appointment object.

```
...
if (ModelState.IsValid) {
    // statements to store new Appointment in a
    // repository would go here in a real project
    return View("Completed", appt);
```

```
} else {
    return View();
}
...
```

We know we have a valid `Appointment` object if there are no problems reported by the `IsValid` property and we can render the `Completed.cshtml` view (and, in a real project, store the `Appointment` object in the repository). If the `IsValue` property returns false, then we know that we have a problem, which we deal with by calling the `View` method to render the default view.

Displaying Validation Errors to the User

It may seem odd to deal with a validation error by calling the `View` method, but the templated view helpers that we used to generate input elements in the `MakeBooking.cshtml` view check the view model for validation errors.

The helper adds a CSS class called `input-validation-error` to the `input` element if an error has been reported for the corresponding property. The `~/Content/Site.css` file contains a default definition for this style, which is as follows:

```
...
.input-validation-error {
    border: 1px solid #f00;
    background-color: #fee;
}
...
```

This has the effect of setting a red border and a pink background on any element for which there is an error. We can test our explicit validation approach by starting the application, navigating to the `/Home/MakeBooking` URL, and clicking the `Make Booking` button without entering any data in the form. You can see the result in Figure 23-2.

▓ **Tip**   If you want to write your own helper methods that support validation, then you should look at the source code for the `System.Mvc.Web.Html.InputExtensions` class to see how it is done. The short version is that the `System.Web.Mvc.HtmlHelper` class defines a `GetModelStateValue` method that lets you see if there are validation errors for a particular property. There are additional methods that let you easily obtain the CSS and error messages that you need if you want to display warnings to the user.

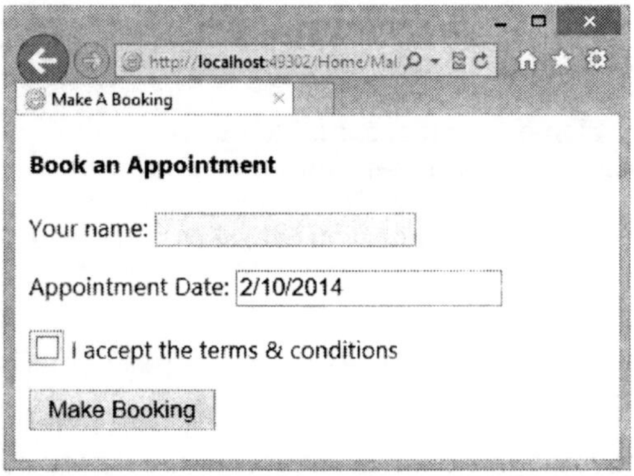

Figure 23-2. Errors result in highlighted elements

STYLING CHECK BOXES

Some browsers, including Chrome and Firefox, ignore styles applied to check boxes, which leads to inconsistent visual feedback. The solution to this is to replace the Boolean editor template by creating a custom template in `~/Views/Shared/EditorTemplates/Boolean.cshtml` and to wrap the check box in a `div` element. Here is a template that we use, which you can tailor to your own application:

```
@model bool?

@if (ViewData.ModelMetadata.IsNullableValueType) {
    @Html.DropDownListFor(m => m, new SelectList(new [] {"Not Set", "True", "False"},
Model))
} else {
    ModelState state = ViewData.ModelState[ViewData.ModelMetadata.PropertyName];
    bool value = Model ?? false;

    if (state != null && state.Errors.Count > 0) {
        <div class="input-validation-error" style="float:left">
            @Html.CheckBox("", value)
        </div>
    } else {
        @Html.CheckBox("", value)
    }
}
```

This template will wrap a check box in a `div` element to which the `input-validation-error` style has been applied if there are any model errors associated with the property that the template has been applied to. You can learn more about replacing editor templates in Chapter 20.

When you submit the form without any data, errors are highlighted for the `ClientName` and `TermsAccepted` properties. The default value that we display for the `Date` property is a valid date, so there is no validation error.

The user will not be shown the `Completed.cshtml` view until the form is submitted with data that can be parsed by the model browser and which passes our explicit validation checks in the `MakeBooking` action method. Until that happens, submitting the form will cause the `MakeBooking.cshtml` view to be rendered with the current validation errors.

Displaying Validation Messages

The CSS styles that the templated helper methods apply to `input` elements indicate that there are problems with a field, but they do not tell the user what the problem is. Fortunately, there are some convenient helper methods that assist us in doing this. Listing 23-6 shows one of these helper methods, which we have applied to the `MakeBooking` view (since this is where the validation errors are shown to the user).

Listing 23-6. Using the Validation Summary Helper Method

```
@model ModelValidation.Models.Appointment
@{
    ViewBag.Title = "Make A Booking";
}
```

```
<h4>Book an Appointment</h4>

@using (Html.BeginForm()) {
    @Html.ValidationSummary()
    <p>Your name: @Html.EditorFor(m => m.ClientName)</p>
    <p>Appointment Date: @Html.EditorFor(m => m.Date)</p>
    <p>@Html.EditorFor(m => m.TermsAccepted) I accept the terms & conditions</p>
    <input type="submit" value="Make Booking" />
}
```

The `Html.ValidationSummary` helper adds a summary of the validation errors we have registered to the page displayed to the user. If there are no errors, then the helper doesn't generate any HTML. Figure 23-3 demonstrates the validation summary in use. We produced this effect by clearing the data fields and submitting the form.

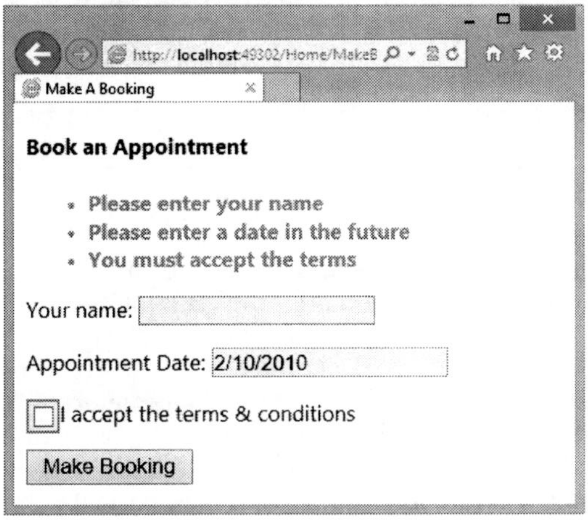

Figure 23-3. Displaying a validation summary

■ **Note** The values that we have shown for the `Date` property in this chapter follow the US date format of month/day/year. If you are in a different locale, then you can either enter valid dates in your local format (such as day/month/year, which is used widely in Europe) or add `<globalization culture="en-US" uiCulture="en-US"/>` to the `system.web` element in the `Web.config` file for the example project to force the MVC application to use US date formats.

The validation summary displays the error messages that we registered with the `ModelState` in our `MakeBooking` action method. Here is the HTML that the helper method generates:

```
...
<div class="validation-summary-errors" data-valmsg-summary="true">
    <ul>
        <li>Please enter your name</li>
        <li>Please enter a date in the future</li>
        <li>You must accept the terms</li>
    </ul>
</div>
...
```

The errors are expressed as a list contained in a `div` element, to which the `validation-summary-errors` style is applied. This style is defined in `~/Content/Site.css` and can be changed as needed. The default style makes the text of the errors bold and red:

```
...
.validation-summary-errors {
    font-weight: bold;
    color: #f00;
}
...
```

There are a number of overloaded versions of the `ValidationSummary` method; Table 23-1 shows the most useful. Some of the overloads of the `ValidationSummary` helper method allow us to specify that only *model-level errors* should be displayed. The errors that we have registered with `ModelState` so far have been *property-level errors*, meaning there is a problem with the value supplied for a given property and changing that value can address the problem.

Table 23-1. Useful Overloads of the ValidationSummary Helper Method

Overloaded Method	Description
`Html.ValidationSummary()`	Generates a summary for all validation errors.
`Html.ValidationSummary(bool)`	If the bool parameter is true, then only model-level errors are displayed (see the explanation after the table). If the parameter is false, then all errors are shown.
`Html.ValidationSummary(string)`	Displays a message (contained in the string parameter) before a summary of all the validation errors.
`Html.ValidationSummary(bool, string)`	Displays a message before the validation errors. If the bool parameter is true, only model-level errors will be shown.

By contrast, model-level errors can be used when there is some problem arising from an interaction between two or more property values. As a simple example, let's imagine that customers named Joe cannot make appointments on Mondays. Listing 23-7 shows how we can enforce this rule with an explicit validation check in the `MakeBooking` action method and report problems as model-level validation errors.

Listing 23-7. A Model-Level Validation Error

```
...
[HttpPost]
public ViewResult MakeBooking(Appointment appt) {

    if (string.IsNullOrEmpty(appt.ClientName)) {
        ModelState.AddModelError("ClientName", "Please enter your name");
    }

    if (ModelState.IsValidField("Date") && DateTime.Now > appt.Date) {
        ModelState.AddModelError("Date", "Please enter a date in the future");
    }

    if (!appt.TermsAccepted) {
        ModelState.AddModelError("TermsAccepted", "You must accept the terms");
```

```
    }

    if (ModelState.IsValidField("ClientName") && ModelState.IsValidField("Date")
        && appt.ClientName == "Joe" && appt.Date.DayOfWeek == DayOfWeek.Monday) {
        ModelState.AddModelError("", "Joe cannot book appointments on Mondays");
    }

    if (ModelState.IsValid) {
        // statements to store new Appointment in a
        // repository would go here in a real project
        return View("Completed", appt);
    } else {
        return View();
    }
}
...
```

Before we check to see whether Joe is trying to book on a Monday, we use the
`ModelState.IsValidField` method to ensure that we have valid `ClientName` and `Date` values to work with.
This means we will not generate a model-level error unless the previous checks on the properties have
been successful. We register a model-level error by passing the empty string (`""`) as the first parameter to
the `ModelState.AddModelError` method, like this:

```
...
ModelState.AddModelError("", "Joe cannot book appointments on Mondays");
...
```

We can then update the `MakeBooking.cshtml` view file to use the version of the `ValidationSummary`
helper method that takes a `bool` parameter to display only the model-level errors, as shown in Listing 23-8.

Listing 23-8. Updating the MakeBooking.cshtml View to Display Only Model-Level Errors

```
@model ModelValidation.Models.Appointment
@{
    ViewBag.Title = "Make A Booking";
}
<h4>Book an Appointment</h4>

@using (Html.BeginForm()) {
    @Html.ValidationSummary(true)
    <p>Your name: @Html.EditorFor(m => m.ClientName)</p>
    <p>Appointment Date: @Html.EditorFor(m => m.Date)</p>
    <p>@Html.EditorFor(m => m.TermsAccepted) I accept the terms & conditions</p>
    <input type="submit" value="Make Booking" />
}
```

You can see the result of these changes in Figure 23-4, where we have entered the name Joe and
specified a date, which is a Monday.

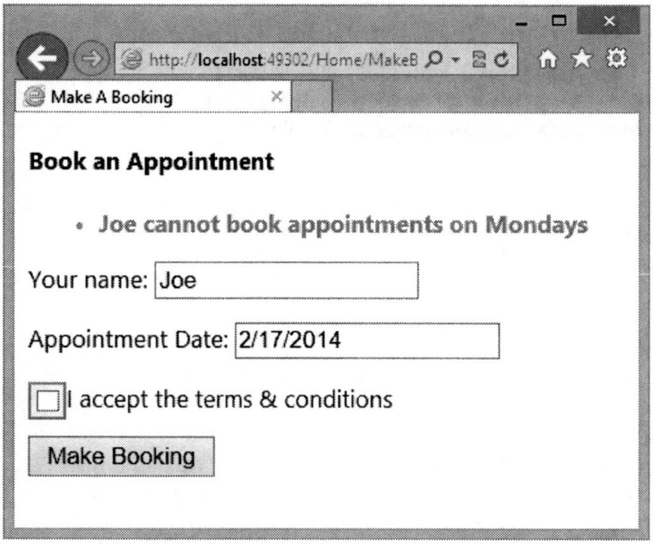

Figure 23-4. Displaying validation summary information for model-level errors

You can see from the figure that there are two validation errors. The first is the model-level error that arises from Joe trying to get a Monday appointment. The second is that the terms and conditions check box is unchecked. Since we are displaying only model-level errors in the validation summary, the user will not see any information about this problem in the summary.

Displaying Property-Level Validation Messages

The reason we might want to restrict the validation summary to model-level errors is that we can display property-level errors alongside the fields themselves. If we do this, then we do not want to duplicate the property-specific messages. Listing 23-9 shows how we updated the MakeBooking.cshtml view to display model-level errors in the summary and to display property-level errors alongside the corresponding input field.

Listing 23-9. Using Property-Specific Validation Error Messages

```
@model ModelValidation.Models.Appointment
@{
    ViewBag.Title = "Make A Booking";
}
<h4>Book an Appointment</h4>

@using (Html.BeginForm()) {
    @Html.ValidationSummary(true)
    <p>@Html.ValidationMessageFor(m => m.ClientName)</p>
    <p>Your name: @Html.EditorFor(m => m.ClientName)</p>
    <p>@Html.ValidationMessageFor(m => m.Date)</p>
    <p>Appointment Date: @Html.EditorFor(m => m.Date)</p>
    <p>@Html.ValidationMessageFor(m => m.TermsAccepted)</p>
    <p>@Html.EditorFor(m => m.TermsAccepted) I accept the terms & conditions</p>
    <input type="submit" value="Make Booking" />
}
```

The `Html.ValidationMessageFor` helper displays validation errors for a single model property. You can see the effect it has on the `MakeBooking` view in Figure 23-5.

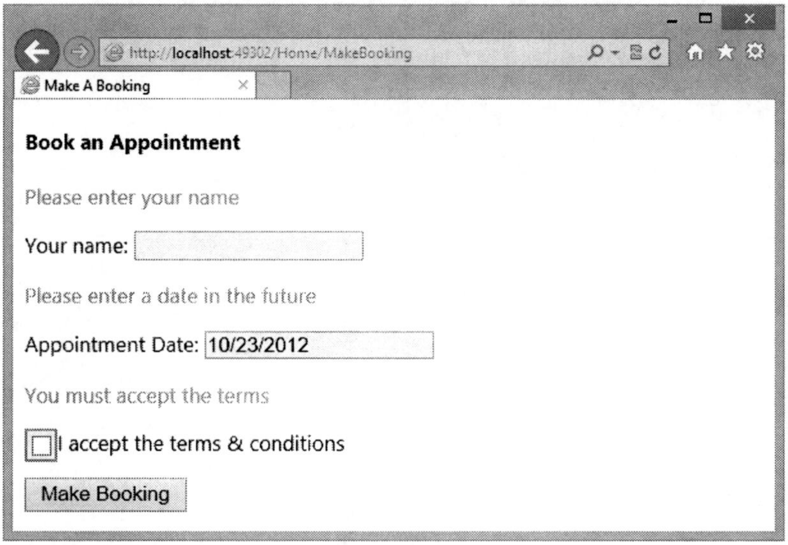

Figure 23-5. Using the per-property validation message helper

Using Alternative Validation Techniques

Performing model validation in the action method is only one of the validation techniques available in the MVC Framework. In the following sections, we will show you how to use some different approaches.

Performing Validation in the Model Binder

The default model binder performs validation as part of the binding process. As an example, Figure 23-6 shows what happens if we clear the `Date` field and submit the form.

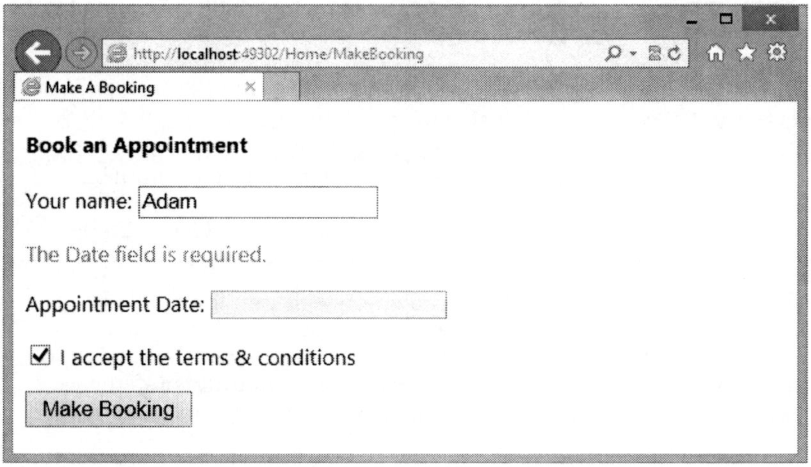

Figure 23-6. A validation message from the model binder

The error displayed for the Date field has been added by the model binder because it wasn't able to create a DateTime object from the empty field we posted in the form. The model binder performs some basic validation for each of the properties in the model object. If a value has not been supplied, the message shown in Figure 23-6 will be displayed. If we supply a value that cannot be parsed into the model property type, then a different message is displayed, as shown in Figure 23-7.

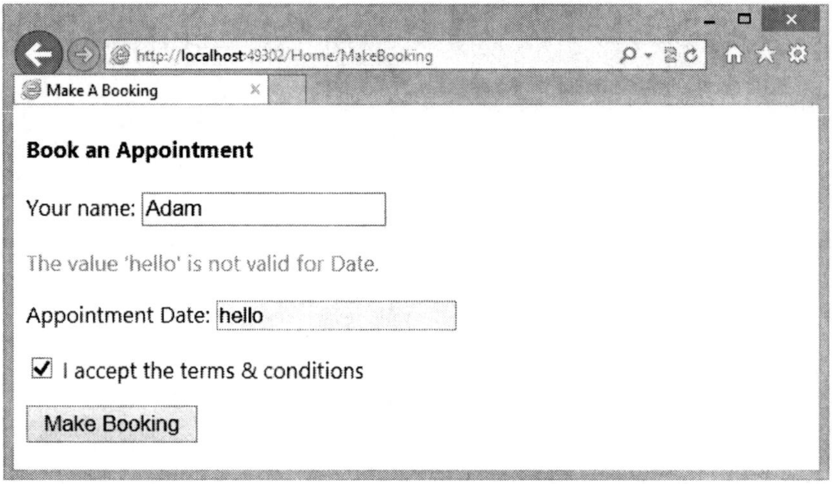

Figure 23-7. A format validation error displayed by the model binder

The built-in default model binder class, DefaultModelBinder, provides us with some useful methods that we can override to add validation to a binder. Table 23-2 describes these methods.

Table 23-2. DefaultModelBinder Methods for Adding Validation to the Model Binding Process

Method	Description	Default Implementation
OmModelUpdated	Called when the binder has tried to assign values to all of the properties in the model object	Applies the validation rules defined by the model metadata and registers any errors with ModelState. We describe the use of metadata for validation later in this chapter.
SetProperty	Called when the binder wants to apply a value to a specific property	If the property cannot hold a null value and there was no value to apply, then the The <name> field is required error registered with ModelState (see Figure 23-6). If there is a value but it cannot be parsed, then the The value <value> is not valid for <name> error is registered (see Figure 23-7).

We can override the methods shown in Table 23-2 to push our validation logic into the binding process when creating a custom model binder, which we demonstrated in Chapter 22. This is not a technique we like, however, because it feels like the wrong place in the MVC pattern to put the validation logic—although, as with so much in an MVC application, it is a matter of personal taste and preference. We prefer to handle validation using metadata applied to the model class, which we demonstrate in the next section.

Specifying Validation Rules Using Metadata

The MVC Framework supports the use of metadata to express model validation rules. The advantage of using metadata is that our validation rules are enforced anywhere that the binding process is applied throughout the application, not just in a single action method. The validation attributes are detected and enforced by the built-in default model binder class, `DefaultModelBinder`, which we described in Chapter 22. In Listing 23-10, you can see how we have applied some validation attributes to the `Appointment` model class.

Listing 23-10. Using Attributes to Define Validation Rules for the Appointment Model Class

```
using System;
using System.ComponentModel.DataAnnotations;

namespace ModelValidation.Models {
    public class Appointment {

        [Required]
        public string ClientName { get; set; }

        [DataType(DataType.Date)]
        [Required(ErrorMessage="Please enter a date")]
        public DateTime Date { get; set; }

        [Range(typeof(bool), "true", "true", ErrorMessage = "You must accept the terms")]
        public bool TermsAccepted { get; set; }
    }
}
```

We have used two validation attributes in the listing—**Required** and **Range**. The **Required** attribute specifies that it is a validation error if the user doesn't submit a value for a property. The **Range** attribute specifies that only a subset of values is acceptable. Table 23-3 shows the set of built-in validation attributes available in an MVC application.

Table 23-3. The Built-in Validation Attributes

Attribute	Example	Description
Compare	[Compare("MyOtherProperty")]	Two properties must have the same value. This is useful when you ask the user to provide the same information twice, such as an e-mail address or a password.
Range	[Range(10, 20)]	A numeric value (or any property type that implement `IComparable`) must not lie beyond the specified minimum and maximum values. To specify a boundary on only one side, use a `MinValue` or `MaxValue` constant—for example, `[Range(int.MinValue, 50)]`.

Attribute	Example	Description
RegularExpression	[RegularExpression("pattern")]	A string value must match the specified regular expression pattern. Note that the pattern has to match the *entire* user-supplied value, not just a substring within it. By default, it matches case sensitively, but you can make it case insensitive by applying the (?i) modifier—that is, [RegularExpression("(?i)mypattern")].
Required	[Required]	The value must not be empty or be a string consisting only of spaces. If you want to treat whitespace as valid, use [Required(AllowEmptyStrings = true)].
StringLength	[StringLength(10)]	A string value must not be longer than the specified maximum length. We can also specify a minimum length: [StringLength(10, MinimumLength=2)].

All of the validation attributes allow us to specify a custom error message by setting a value for the ErrorMessage property, like this:

```
...
[Required(ErrorMessage="Please enter a date")]
...
```

If we do not supply a custom error message, then the default messages will be used, such as the ones we saw in Figures 23-6 and 23-7. The built-in validation attributes are pretty basic, and they only allow us to do property-level validation. Even so, we still have to use some sleight of hand to get things working consistently. As an example, consider the validation attribute we applied to the TermsAccepted property:

```
...
[Range(typeof(bool), "true", "true", ErrorMessage="You must accept the terms")]
...
```

We want to make sure that the user checks the box to accept the terms. We cannot use the Required attribute, because the templated helper for bool values generates a hidden HTML element to ensure that we get a value even when the box isn't checked. To work around this, we use a feature of the Range attribute that lets us provide a Type and specify the upper and lower bounds as string values. By setting both bounds to true, we create the equivalent of the Required attribute for bool properties that are edited using check boxes.

■ **Tip** The DataType attribute cannot be used to validate user input—only to provide hints for rendering values using the templated helpers (described in Chapter 20). So, for example, do not expect the DataType(DataType.EmailAddress) attribute to enforce a specific format.

Creating a Custom Property Validation Attribute

The trick of using the Range attribute to re-create the behavior of the Required attribute is a little awkward. Fortunately, we aren't limited to just the built-in attributes; we can also create our own by deriving from the ValidationAttribute class and implementing our own validation logic. This is a lot more useful and to demonstrate how this works, we have added an Infrastructure folder to the example project and created a class file called MustBeTrueAttribute.cs within in. Listing 23-11 shows the contents of the new class file.

Listing 23-11. A Custom Property Validation Attribute

```
using System.ComponentModel.DataAnnotations;

namespace ModelValidation.Infrastructure {
    public class MustBeTrueAttribute : ValidationAttribute {

        public override bool IsValid(object value) {
            return value is bool && (bool)value;
        }
    }
}
```

Our class file defined a new attribute that we have called MustBeTrueAttribute and which overrides the IsValid method of the base class. This is the method that the model binder will call to validate properties to which the attribute is applied, passing in the value that the user has provided as the parameter.

Our validation logic is simple; a value is valid if it is a **bool** that has a value of **true**. We indicate that a value is valid by returning **true** from the IsValid method. In Listing 23-12, you can see how we have replaced the Range attribute with our custom MustBeTrue attribute in the Appointment class.

Listing 23-12. Applying a Custom Validation Attribute to a Model Class

```
using System;
using System.ComponentModel.DataAnnotations;
using ModelValidation.Infrastructure;

namespace ModelValidation.Models {
    public class Appointment {

        [Required]
        public string ClientName { get; set; }

        [DataType(DataType.Date)]
        [Required(ErrorMessage="Please enter a date")]
        public DateTime Date { get; set; }

        [MustBeTrue(ErrorMessage="You must accept the terms")]
        public bool TermsAccepted { get; set; }
    }
}
```

This is neater and easier to make sense of than abusing the Range attribute. You can see the effect of our custom model validation attribute in Figure 23-8.

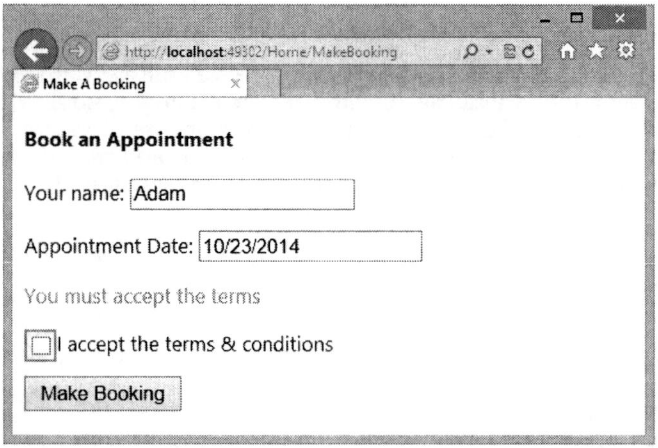

Figure 23-8. The error message from a custom validation attribute

Deriving from the Built-In Validation Attributes

In the previous example, we built a simple validation attribute from scratch, but we can derive new classes from the built-in attributes, which gives us the ability to extend their behavior. In Listing 23-13, you can see the contents of a new class file called **FutureDateAttribute.cs** that we added to the **Infrastructure** folder.

Listing 23-13. The Contents of the FutureDateAttribute.cs Class File

```
using System;
using System.ComponentModel.DataAnnotations;

namespace ModelValidation.Infrastructure {
    public class FutureDateAttribute : RequiredAttribute {

        public override bool IsValid(object value) {
            return base.IsValid(value) && ((DateTime)value) > DateTime.Now;
        }
    }
}
```

We have derived our new **FutureDataAttribute** class from **RequiredAttribute** and overridden the **IsValid** method to validate that the date is in the future. Since we have called the base implementation of the **IsValid** method, our custom attribute will perform all of the basic validation steps contained in the **Required** attribute. You can see how we have applied our new attribute to the **Appointment** model class in Listing 23-14.

Listing 23-14. Applying a Custom Model Validation Attribute to the Appointment Class

```
using System;
using System.ComponentModel.DataAnnotations;
using ModelValidation.Infrastructure;
using System.Web.Mvc;

namespace ModelValidation.Models {
```

```
public class Appointment {

    [Required]
    public string ClientName { get; set; }

    [DataType(DataType.Date)]
    [FutureDate(ErrorMessage="Please enter a date in the future")]
    public DateTime Date { get; set; }

    [MustBeTrue(ErrorMessage="You must accept the terms")]
    public bool TermsAccepted { get; set; }
}
}
```

Creating a Model Validation Attribute

The custom validation attributes we created so far are applied to individual model properties. This means they are only able to raise property-level validation errors. We can use attributes to validate the entire model as well, which allows us to raise model-level errors. As a demonstration, we have created the NoJoeOnMondaysAttribute.cs class file in the Infrastructure folder. The contents of the new file are shown in Listing 23-15.

Listing 23-15. Creating a Custom Model Validation Attribute

```
using System;
using System.ComponentModel.DataAnnotations;
using ModelValidation.Models;

namespace ModelValidation.Infrastructure {
    public class NoJoeOnMondaysAttribute : ValidationAttribute {

        public NoJoeOnMondaysAttribute() {
            ErrorMessage = "Joe cannot book appointments on Mondays";
        }

        public override bool IsValid(object value) {
            Appointment app = value as Appointment;
            if (app == null || string.IsNullOrEmpty(app.ClientName) ||
                    app.Date == null) {
                // we don't have a model of the right type to validate, or we don't have
                // the values for the ClientName and Date properties we require
                return true;
            } else {
                return !(app.ClientName == "Joe" &&
                    app.Date.DayOfWeek == DayOfWeek.Monday);
            }
        }
    }
}
```

When we apply a validation attribute to the model class, as opposed to a single property, the object parameter that the model binder will pass to the IsValid method will be the model object – an Appointment in this example. Our validation attribute checks to make sure that we really do have an Appointment object and, if we do, that we have values for the ClientName and Date properties that we can work with. If so, we make sure that Joe isn't trying to get a booking on a Monday. In Listing 23-16, you can see how we have applied the custom attribute to the Appointment class.

Listing 23-16. Applying a Model-Level Custom Validation Attribute to the Model Class

```
using System;
using System.ComponentModel.DataAnnotations;
using ModelValidation.Infrastructure;

namespace ModelValidation.Models {
    [NoJoeOnMondays]
    public class Appointment {

        [Required]
        public string ClientName { get; set; }

        [DataType(DataType.Date)]
        [FutureDate(ErrorMessage="Please enter a date in the future")]
        public DateTime Date { get; set; }

        [MustBeTrue(ErrorMessage="You must accept the terms")]
        public bool TermsAccepted { get; set; }
    }
}
```

At this point, we are performing the same kinds of validation in the action method and using validation attributes, which means that the user will see two similar error messages for the same validation problem. To resolve this, we have removed the explicit validation checks from the MakeBooking action method in the Home controller, as shown in Listing 23-17, which has the effect of making the validation attributes solely responsible for performing our custom validation checks.

Listing 23-17. Removing the Explicit Validation Checks from the MakeBooking Action Method

```
using System;
using System.Web.Mvc;
using ModelValidation.Models;

namespace ModelValidation.Controllers {
    public class HomeController : Controller {

        public ViewResult MakeBooking() {
            return View(new Appointment { Date = DateTime.Now });
        }

        [HttpPost]
        public ViewResult MakeBooking(Appointment appt) {
            if (ModelState.IsValid) {
                // statements to store new Appointment in a
                // repository would go here in a real project
                return View("Completed", appt);
            } else {
                return View();
            }
        }
    }
}
```

On important point to note is that model-level validation attributes will not be used when a property-level problem is detected. To see how this works, start the application and navigate to the /Home/MakeBooking URL. Enter **Joe** as the name, **2/17/2014** as the date, and leave the check box unchecked. When you submit the form, you will see only the warning about the check box. Check the box and submit again. Only now will you see the model-level error, as illustrated in Figure 23-9.

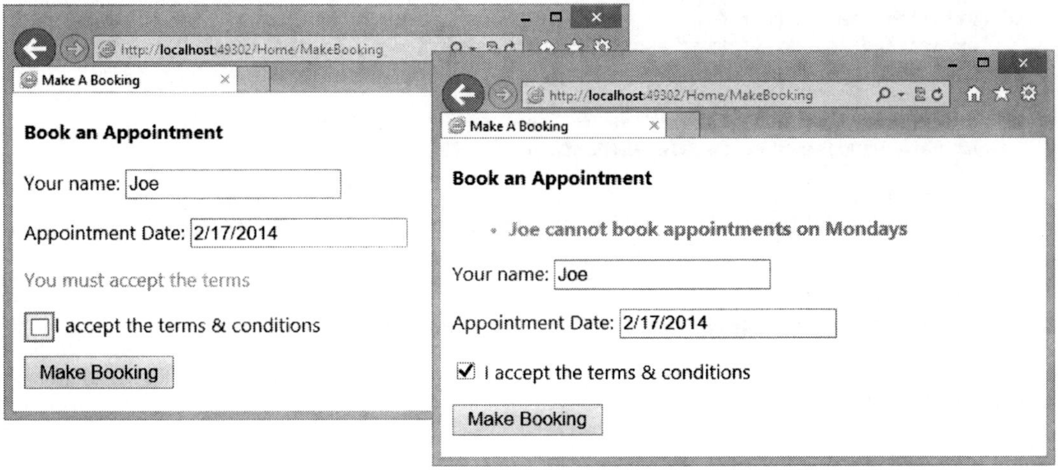

Figure 23-9. Property-levels errors being displayed before model-level errors

The problem from the user's perspective is that we implicitly accepted the name and data values by not flagging up errors for them in the first panel. This may seem like a minor issue, but it is worth paying careful attention to any situation that may frustrate users.

Defining Self-Validating Models

Another validation technique is to create *self-validating models*, where the validation logic is part of the model class. We denote a self-validating model class by implementing the IValidatableObject interface, as shown in Listing 23-18.

Listing 23-18. A Self-Validating Model Class

```
using System;
using System.Collections.Generic;
using System.ComponentModel.DataAnnotations;
using ModelValidation.Infrastructure;

namespace ModelValidation.Models {
    public class Appointment : IValidatableObject {

        public string ClientName { get; set; }

        [DataType(DataType.Date)]
        public DateTime Date { get; set; }

        public bool TermsAccepted { get; set; }

        public IEnumerable<ValidationResult> Validate(ValidationContext
                validationContext) {
```

```csharp
            List<ValidationResult> errors = new List<ValidationResult>();

            if (string.IsNullOrEmpty(ClientName)) {
                errors.Add(new ValidationResult("Please enter your name"));
            }

            if (DateTime.Now > Date) {
                errors.Add(new ValidationResult("Please enter a date in the future"));
            }

            if (errors.Count == 0 && ClientName == "Joe"
                && Date.DayOfWeek == DayOfWeek.Monday) {

                errors.Add(
                    new ValidationResult("Joe cannot book appointments on Mondays"));
            }

            if (!TermsAccepted) {
                errors.Add(new ValidationResult("You must accept the terms"));
            }

            return errors;
        }

    }
}
```

The IValidatableObject interface defines one method, Validate. This method takes a ValidationContext parameter, although this type isn't MVC-specific and isn't a great deal of use. The result of the Validate method is an enumeration of ValidationResult objects, each of which represents a validation error.

If our model class implements the IValidatableObject interface, then the Validate method will be called after the model binder has assigned values to each of the model properties. This approach has the benefit of combining the flexibility of putting the validation logic in the action method, but with the consistency of being applied any time the model binding process creates an instance of our model type. We also benefit by combining the model- and property-level validation in one place, which means that all of the errors are displayed together, as shown in Figure 23-10. Some programmers don't like putting the validation logic in the model class, but we think it sits nicely in the MVC design pattern—and we like the flexibility and consistency, of course.

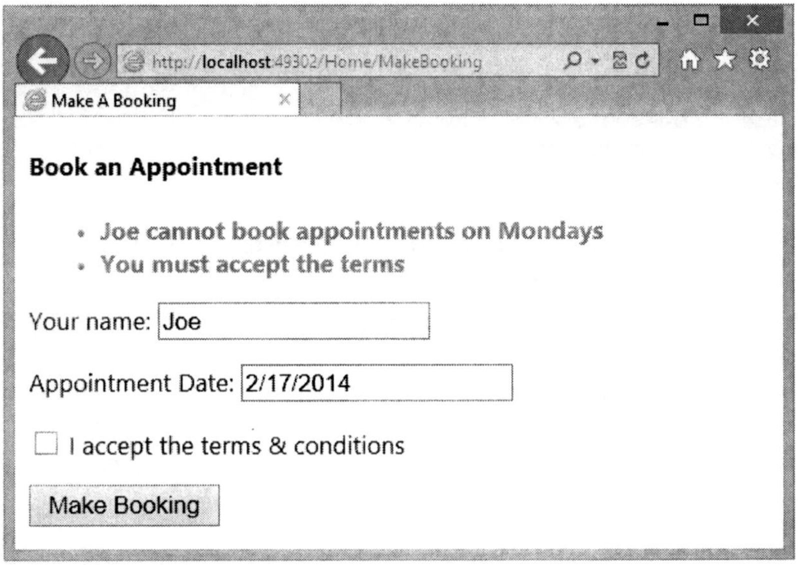

Figure 23-10. The effect of a self-validating model class

Performing Client-Side Validation

The validation techniques we have demonstrated so far have all been examples of *server-side validation*. This means the user submits their data to the server, and the server validates the data and sends back the results of the validation (either success in processing the data or a list of errors that need to be corrected).

In Web applications, users typically expect immediate validation feedback—without having to submit anything to the server. This is known as *client-side validation* and is usually implemented using JavaScript. The data that the user has entered is validated before being sent to the server, providing the user with immediate feedback and an opportunity to correct any problems.

The MVC Framework supports *unobtrusive client-side validation*. The term *unobtrusive* means that validation rules are expressed using attributes added to the HTML elements that we generate. These attributes are interpreted by a JavaScript library that is included as part of the MVC Framework that, in turn, relies configures the jQuery Validation library, which does the actual validation work. In the following sections, we will show you how the built-in validation support works and demonstrate how we can extend the functionality to provide custom client-side validation.

■ **Tip**   Client-side validation is focused on validating individual properties. In fact, it is hard to set up model-level client-side validation using the built-in support that comes with the MVC Framework. To that end, most MVC applications use client-side validation for property-level issues and rely on server-side validation for the overall model.

Enabling and Disabling Client-Side Validation

Client-side validation is controlled by two settings in the Web.config file, as shown in Listing 23-19.

Listing 23-19. Controlling Client-Side Validation

```
...
  <appSettings>
    <add key="ClientValidationEnabled" value="true"/>
    <add key="UnobtrusiveJavaScriptEnabled" value="true"/>
  </appSettings>
...
```

Both of these settings must be true for client-side validation to work. When you first created your MVC project, Visual Studio created these entries and set them to true.

▓ **Tip**   You can also configure client-side validation on a per-view basis by setting the HtmlHelper.
ClientValidationEnabled and HtmlHelper.UnobtrusiveJavaScriptEnabled in a razor code block.

We must also ensure that there are three JavaScript libraries referenced in the HTML sent to the browser for client validation to work:

- /Scripts/ jquery-1.7.1.min.js
- /Scripts/ jquery.validate.min.js
- /Scripts/ jquery.validate.unobtrusive.min.js

The easiest way to add these JavaScript files to a view is using the new *script bundles* feature. This is a new addition to MVC 4, which we describe in Chapter 24. We will not explain how this new feature works in this chapter, but you can see the change that we made to the /Views/Shared/_Layout.cshtml file in Listing 23-20, which makes the scripts we want available. (We could have made the same change to the MakeBooking view, but we like to import script files in layouts so we don't remember to make changes to all of our views).

Listing 23-20. Adding the JavaScript Libraries Required for Client-Side Validation to the Layout

```
<!DOCTYPE html>
<html>
<head>
    <meta charset="utf-8" />
    <meta name="viewport" content="width=device-width" />
    <title>@ViewBag.Title</title>
    @Styles.Render("~/Content/css")
    @Scripts.Render("~/bundles/modernizr")
</head>
<body>
    @RenderBody()

    @Scripts.Render("~/bundles/jquery")
    @Scripts.Render("~/bundles/jqueryval")
    @RenderSection("scripts", required: false)
</body>
</html>
```

Using Client-Side Validation

Once we have enabled client-side validation and ensured that the JavaScript libraries are referenced in our layout, we can start to perform client-side validation. The simplest way of doing this is to apply the metadata attributes that we previously used for server-side validation, such as **Required, Range**, and **StringLength**. Listing 23-21 shows our **Appointment** model class with these annotations applied (we have removed the implementation of the **IValidatableObject** interface, which has no effect on client-side validation).

Listing 23-21. Validation Attributes Applied to the Appointment Model Object

```
using System;
using System.ComponentModel.DataAnnotations;

namespace ModelValidation.Models {
    public class Appointment {

        [Required]
        [StringLength(10, MinimumLength = 3)]
        public string ClientName { get; set; }

        [DataType(DataType.Date)]
        public DateTime Date { get; set; }

        public bool TermsAccepted { get; set; }
    }
}
```

That's all we have to do to get the basic client-side validation working. We have applied a slightly different mix of the built-in validation attributes so that we can demonstrate some of the client-side validation features, but once you have the JavaScript libraries included in the HTML that is sent to the client, everything just starts to work.

You can see the effect of the client-side validation by starting the application, navigating to the /Home/MakeBooking URL and entering the letter X into the name field. Hit the tab key or click one of the other input elements and you will immediately see a validation message produced by the JavaScript running the browser, as shown in Figure 23-11.

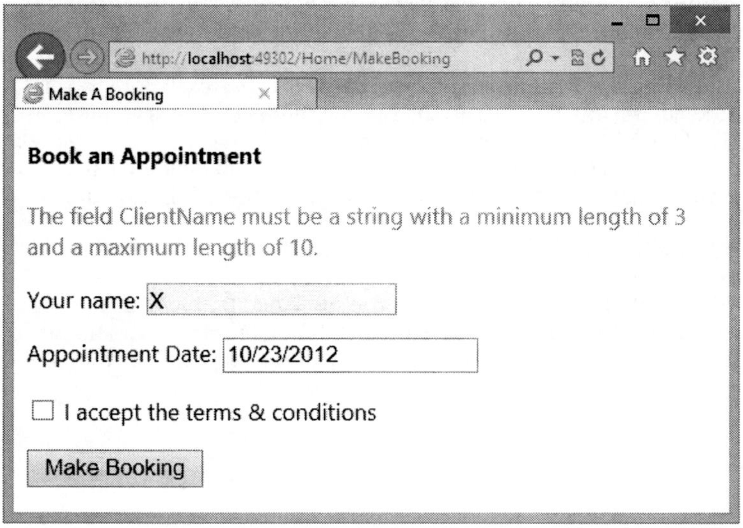

Figure 23-11. Immediate feedback from the client-side validation feature

We applied the `StringLength` validation attribute to the `Appointment` class in Listing 23-21 and it is the error message from that attribute that you can see in the figure. The feedback presented in the browser is immediate and no request has been made to the server. In fact, the JavaScript code that is performing the validation will prevent the form from being submitted until there are no outstanding validation errors.

The feedback is as immediate when the user corrects the error. If you return to the name property and keep typing, the validation error will be removed when the name you have entered is three or more characters long. But if you keep typing until you get to the eleventh character, you will see the error reappear. This is because we specified a minimum length of three characters and a maximum length of ten for the `ClientName` property with the `StringLength` attribute.

Understanding How Client-Side Validation Works

One of the benefits of using the MVC Framework client-side validation feature is that we do not have to write any JavaScript. Instead, the validation rules are expressed using HTML attributes. Here is the HTML that is rendered by the `Html.EditorFor` helper for the `ClientName` property when client-side validation is disabled:

```
...
<input class="text-box single-line" id="ClientName" name="ClientName" type="text"
    value="" />
...
```

And here is the HTML rendered for the same property when client-side validation is switch on:

```
...
<input class="text-box single-line" data-val="true"
    data-val-length="The field ClientName must be a string with a minimum length of 3 and
        a maximum length of 10." data-val-length-max="10" data-val-length-min="3"
    data-val-required="The ClientName field is required." id="ClientName"
    name="ClientName" type="text" value="" />
...
```

The MVC client-side validation support doesn't generate any JavaScript or JSON data to direct the validation process; like much of the rest of the MVC Framework, we rely on convention. The first attribute that was added is `data-val`. The jQuery Validation library identifies those fields that require validation by looking for this attribute.

Individual validation rules are specified using an attribute in the form `data-val-<name>`, where `name` is the rule to be applied. So, for example, the `Required` attribute we applied to the model class has resulted in a `data-val-required` attribute in the HTML. The value associated with the attribute is the error message associated with the rule. Some rules require additional attributes; you can see this with the length rule, which has `data-val-length-min` and `data-val-length-max` attributes to let us specify the minimum and maximum string lengths that are allowed.

The interpretation of the required and length validation rules is provided by the jQuery Validation library, on which the MVC client validation features are built.

One of the nice features about the MVC client-side validation is that the same attributes we use to specify validation rules are applied at the client *and* at the server. This means that data from browsers that do not support JavaScript are subject to the same validation as those that do, without requiring us to make any additional effort.

```
┌─────────────────────────────────────────────────────────────────┐
│         MVC CLIENT VALIDATION VS. JQUERY VALIDATION               │
└─────────────────────────────────────────────────────────────────┘
```

The MVC client-validation features are built on top of the jQuery Validation library. If you prefer, you can use the Validation library directly and ignore the MVC features. The Validation library is very flexible and feature-rich; it is well worth exploring, if only to understand how to customize the MVC features to take best advantage of the available validation options. Adam covers the jQuery Validation library in depth in his *Pro jQuery* book (Apress, 2012).

Performing Remote Validation

The last validation feature we will look at in this chapter is *remote validation*. This is a client-side validation technique that invokes an action method on the server to perform validation.

A common example of remote validation is to check whether a username is available in applications when such names must be unique; the user submits the data, and the client-side validation is performed. As part of this process, an Ajax request is made to the server to validate the username that has been requested. If the username has been taken, a validation error is displayed so that the user can enter another value.

This may seem like regular server-side validation, but there are some benefits to this approach. First, only some properties will be remotely validated; the client-side validation benefits still apply to all the other data values that the user has entered. Second, the request is relatively lightweight and is focused on validation, rather than processing an entire model object. This means we can minimize the performance impact that the requests generate.

The third difference is that the remote validation is performed in the background. The user doesn't have to click the submit button and then wait for a new view to be rendered and returned. It makes for a more responsive user experience, especially when there is a slow network between the browser and the server.

That said, remote validation is a compromise; it allows us to strike a balance between client-side and server-side validation, but it does require requests to the application server, and it is not as quick to validate as normal client-side validation.

The first step toward using remote validation is to create an action method that can validate one of our model properties. We are going to validate the Date property of our Appointment model to ensure that the requested appointment is in the future (this is one of the original validation rules we used at the start of the chapter, but which isn't possible to validate using the standard client-side validation features). In Listing 23-22, you can see the ValidateDate action method that we added to the Home controller.

Listing 23-22. Adding a Validation Action Method in the Home Controller

```
using System;
using System.Web.Mvc;
using ModelValidation.Models;

namespace ModelValidation.Controllers {
    public class HomeController : Controller {

        public ViewResult MakeBooking() {
            return View(new Appointment { Date = DateTime.Now });
        }

        [HttpPost]
        public ViewResult MakeBooking(Appointment appt) {
```

```
        if (ModelState.IsValid) {
            // statements to store new Appointment in a
            // repository would go here in a real project
            return View("Completed", appt);
        } else {
            return View();
        }
    }

    public JsonResult ValidateDate(string Date) {
        DateTime parsedDate;

        if (!DateTime.TryParse(Date, out parsedDate)) {
            return Json("Please enter a valid date (mm/dd/yyyy)",
                JsonRequestBehavior.AllowGet);
        } else if (DateTime.Now > parsedDate) {
            return Json("Please enter a date in the future",
                JsonRequestBehavior.AllowGet);
        } else {
            return Json(true, JsonRequestBehavior.AllowGet);
        }
    }
}
}
```

Actions methods that support remote validation must return the JsonResult type, which tells the MVC Framework that we are working with JSON data. In addition to the result, validation action methods must define a parameter that has the same name as the data field being validated. This is Date for our example. We make sure that we can parse a DateTime object from the value that the user has submitted and, if we can, check to see that the date is in the future.

■ **Tip**   We could have taken advantage of model binding so that the parameter to our action method would be a DateTime object, but doing so would mean that our validation method wouldn't be called if the user entered a nonsense value like apple, for example. This is because the model binder wouldn't have been able to create a DateTime object from apple and throws an exception when it tries. The remote validation feature doesn't have a way to express that exception and so it is quietly discarded. This has the unfortunate effect of *not* highlighting the data field and so creating the impression that the value that the user has entered is valid. As a general rule, the best approach to remote validation is to accept a string parameter in the action method and perform any type conversion, parsing, or model binding explicitly.

We express validation results using the Json method, which creates a JSON-formatted result that the client-side remote validation script can parse and process. If the value that we are processing meets our requirements, then we pass true as the parameter to the Json method, like this:

```
...
return Json(true, JsonRequestBehavior.AllowGet);
...
```

If we are unhappy with the value, we pass the validation error message that the user should see as the parameter, like this:

```
...
return Json("Please enter a date in the future", JsonRequestBehavior.AllowGet);
...
```

In both cases, we must also pass the `JsonRequestBehavior.AllowGet` value as a parameter. This is because the MVC Framework disallows GET requests that produce JSON by default, and we have to override this behavior. Without this additional parameter, the validation request will quietly fail, and no validation errors will be displayed to the client.

To use the remote validation method, we apply the Remote attribute to the property we want to validate in the model class. In Listing 23-23, you can see how we have applied the attribute to the Date property.

Listing 23-23. Using the Remote Attribute on the Model Class

```
using System;
using System.ComponentModel.DataAnnotations;
using System.Web.Mvc;

namespace ModelValidation.Models {
    public class Appointment {

        [Required]
        [StringLength(10, MinimumLength = 3)]
        public string ClientName { get; set; }

        [DataType(DataType.Date)]
        [Remote("ValidateDate", "Home")]
        public DateTime Date { get; set; }

        public bool TermsAccepted { get; set; }
    }
}
```

The arguments for the attribute are the name of the action and the controller that should be used to generate the URL that the JavaScript validation library will call to perform the validation; in our case, the `ValidateDate` action on the Home controller.

You can see how the remote validation works by starting the application, navigating to the /Home/MakeBooking URL, and entering a date that is in the past. As you type, you will see the validation message appear, as shown in Figure 23-12.

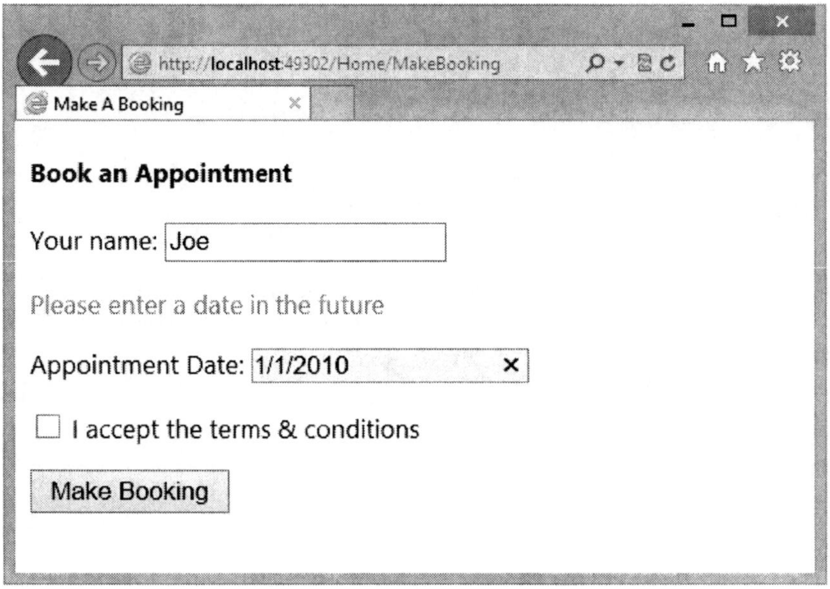

Figure 23-12. Performing remote validation

■ **Caution** The validation action method will be called when the user first submits the form and then again each time he or she edits the data. In essence, every keystroke will lead to a call to our server. For some applications, this can be a significant number of requests and must be taken into account when specifying the server capacity and bandwidth that an application requires in production. Also, you might choose *not* to use remote validation for properties that are expensive to validate (for example, if you have to query a slow Web service to determine whether a username is unique).

Summary

In this chapter, we examined the wide range of techniques available to perform model validation, ensuring that the data that the user has provided is consistent with the constraints that we have imposed on our data model.

Model validation is an important topic, and getting the right validation in place for our applications is essential to ensuring that our users have a good and frustration-free experience. Equally important is the fact that we preserve the integrity of our domain model and do not end up with low-quality or problematic data in our system.

■ ■ ■

CHAPTER 24

Bundles and Display Modes

In this chapter, we are going to look at two features that the MVC Framework provides to make developing the client-side part of a Web application simpler and easier. The first feature, called *bundles*, allows us to organize and optimize the CSS and JavaScript files that our views and layouts cause the browser to request from the server. The second feature, *display modes*, allows us to target different types of devices with different views.

Understanding the Default Script Libraries

Some of the features that we show you in this chapter relate to the management of JavaScript files. When you create an MVC project with any of the template options other than **Empty**, Visual Studio adds a set of JavaScript libraries to the **Scripts** folder. These libraries are some of the most widely used for developing rich client-side functionality for client-side applications, which we have described in Table 24-1.

Table 24-1. The Client-Side Development Libraries in the Scripts Folder

File Name	Description
jquery-1.7.1.js	The jQuery library makes working with HTML elements in the browser simple and easy, especially when compared to the built-in APIs that are part of the HTML standards.
jquery-ui-1.8.20.js	The jQuery UI library creates rich user controls from HTML elements, creating slick-looking UIs for Web apps. jQuery UI is built on jQuery.
jquery.mobile-1.1.0.js	The jQuery Mobile library creates rich user controls for mobile devices. jQuery Mobile is built on jQuery and will only be added to projects that are created using the Mobile template option.
jquery-validate.js	The jQuery Validation library performs input validation for HTML **form** elements.
knockout-2.1.0.js	Knockout applies the Model-View-ViewModel pattern to the client-side part of Web apps, which separates the data in client-side Web applications from the elements that display it to the user. Knockout is often referred to as MVC for the browser.
modernizr-2.5.3.js	Modernizr detects support for HTML5 and CSS3 features in browsers, allowing you to use the latest capabilities when they are available and to gracefully fall back when they are not.

We are not going to show you how to use these libraries in this book, in part because this is a book about a server-side framework and in part because these are serious libraries that are topics in their own right. We strongly recommend getting to know these libraries because we think they are super and make Web app development easier and more robust.

> ■ **Note** We have to admit that we are biased. Steve created the Knockout library and Adam has written extensively about these libraries (and about client-side Web development in general) in his books *Pro jQuery* (Apress, 2012) and *Pro JavaScript for Web App Development* (Apress, 2012). There are alternatives to all of these JavaScript libraries, and despite our fondness for the ones that Microsoft includes in new MVC projects, we are pretty sure that you can find an alternative that will suit you if you can't get along with one of those shown in the table.

In addition to the popular libraries shown in Table 24-1, the `Scripts` folder contains additional libraries that contain Visual Studio- or MVC-specific functionality. We have described these in Table 24-2.

Table 24-2. The Visual Studio- and MVC-specific libraries in the Scripts folder

File Name	Description
`jquery-1.7.1.intellisense.js`	Allows Visual Studio to provide function name completion when writing jQuery code in view files.
`jquery.unobtrusive-ajax.js`	Provides the MVC Framework unobtrusive Ajax feature that we described in Chapter 21. Relies on jQuery.
`jquery.validate-vsdoc.js`	Allows Visual Studio to provide function name completion when writing code that uses the jQuery validation library.
`jquery.validate.unobtrusive.js`	Provides the MVC Framework unobtrusive validation feature that we described in Chapter 23. Relies on the jQuery Validation library.

You do not have to do anything special with the script files that support the Visual Studio code completion. Visual Studio finds and uses them automatically when they are in the application project. We described the unobtrusive Ajax and validation libraries in Chapter 21 and Chapter 23. They act as a nice bridge between the MVC Framework and the jQuery functionality that they rely on.

There are two versions in the `Scripts` folder of many of the files we described in Table 24-1 and Table 24-2—the regular and minified versions. The regular versions contain JavaScript code with comments, whitespace, and meaningful function and variable names. These are great for debugging because you can read through the source code and figure out where the problem is (one of the nice things about JavaScript is that it is easy to read the source code because JavaScript files are not compiled until they reach the browser).

The problem with regular JavaScript files is that they are large. Those helpful comments and meaningful variable and function names all require space in a file, which means longer downloads and more bandwidth demands on your server to deliver the JavaScript code.

The minified files contain the same functionality defined in the corresponding regular file, but all the human-readable names, comments, and whitespace are stripped out to make the file smaller. To give you an idea of the effect, the regular jQuery library that Visual Studio adds to new project is 252KB and the minified version is 92KB. You might be wondering why anyone would care about a difference of 160KB, but if you are serving millions of requests a day, the difference starts to accumulate—both in terms of the time your user has to wait to get the JavaScript code and the amount of bandwidth you need to buy for your servers.

▓ **Tip** Minified JavaScript files still contain text, but it is very hard to read. To see what we mean, just open one of the minified libraries and take a look at the contents, which Visual Studio will display quite happily.

The drawback of minified files is that they make it hard to debug problems, which is why development is usually done with the regular files that are then replaced with minified versions when the application is deployed.

The minified versions of files are usually denoted with .min; for example, the minified version of the jQuery-1.7.1.js file is jQuery-1.7.1.min.js. Not all libraries follow this convention, however; for example, the knockout-2.1.0.js file is the minified file while knockout-2.1.0.debug.js contains the human-readable code.

The MVC Framework contains some useful features that help you manage the JavaScript files that your application uses. Now that you know what these files are and what they do, we can move on to creating the example application, which will then allow us to demonstrate these management features.

Preparing the Example Application

For this chapter, we have created a new MVC project called ClientFeatures using the Basic template option. We are going to create a variation on the application that we used in the previous chapter, so we started by creating a new class file called Appointment.cs in the Models folder.

You can see the contents of this file in Listing 24-1.

Listing 24-1. The Appointment Model Class

```
using System;
using System.ComponentModel.DataAnnotations;

namespace ClientFeatures.Models {
    public class Appointment {

        [Required]
        public string ClientName { get; set; }

        [DataType(DataType.Date)]
        public DateTime Date { get; set; }

        public bool TermsAccepted { get; set; }
    }
}
```

We created a Home controller that operates on the Appointment model class, as shown in Listing 24-2.

Listing 24-2. The Home Controller in the ClientFeatures Application

```
using System;
using System.Web.Mvc;
using ClientFeatures.Models;

namespace ClientFeatures.Controllers {
```

```
public class HomeController : Controller {

    public ViewResult MakeBooking() {
        return View(new Appointment {
            ClientName = "Adam",
            Date = DateTime.Now.AddDays(2),
            TermsAccepted = true
        });
    }

    [HttpPost]
    public JsonResult MakeBooking(Appointment appt) {
        // statements to store new Appointment in a
        // repository would go here in a real project
        return Json(appt, JsonRequestBehavior.AllowGet);
    }
}
}
```

There are two version of the MakeBooking method in this controller. The version with no parameters creates an Appointment object and passes it to the View method to render the default view. The HttpPost version of the MakeBooking method relies on the model binder to create an Appointment object and uses the Json method to encode the Appointment and send it back to the client in the JSON format.

We are focused on the MVC Framework features that support client-side development in this chapter, so we have taken some shortcuts in the controller that wouldn't be sensible or useful in a real project. Most importantly, we do not perform any kind of validation when we receive a HTTP POST request and just sent the details of the object created by the model binder back to the browser as JSON (with no support for HTML responses to POST requests).

We want to make it as easy as possible to use the Ajax-enabled form element that we have defined in the /Views/Home/MakeBooking.cshtml file, which you can see in Listing 24-3. Our interest is in the script and link elements in the view and the interaction with the application is far less important.

Listing 24-3. The MakeBooking View

```
@model ClientFeatures.Models.Appointment

@{
    ViewBag.Title = "Make A Booking";
    AjaxOptions ajaxOpts = new AjaxOptions {
        OnSuccess = "processResponse"
    };
}
<h4>Book an Appointment</h4>

<link rel="stylesheet" href="~/Content/CustomStyles.css" />
<script src="~/Scripts/jquery-1.7.1.min.js"></script>
<script src="~/Scripts/jquery.validate.js"></script>
<script src="~/Scripts/jquery.validate.unobtrusive.js"></script>
<script src="~/Scripts/jquery.unobtrusive-ajax.js"></script>

<script type="text/javascript">
    function processResponse(appt) {
        $('#successClientName').text(appt.ClientName);
        $('#successDate').text(processDate(appt.Date));
```

```
        switchViews();
    }

    function processDate(dateString) {
        return new Date(parseInt(dateString.substr(6,
            dateString.length - 8))).toDateString();
    }

    function switchViews() {
        var hidden = $('.hidden');
        var visible = $('.visible');
        hidden.removeClass("hidden").addClass("visible");
        visible.removeClass("visible").addClass("hidden");
    }

    $(document).ready(function () {
        $('#backButton').click(function (e) {
            switchViews();
        });
    });
</script>

<div id="formDiv" class="visible">
    @using (Ajax.BeginForm(ajaxOpts)) {
        @Html.ValidationSummary(true)
        <p>@Html.ValidationMessageFor(m => m.ClientName)</p>
        <p>Your name: @Html.EditorFor(m => m.ClientName)</p>
        <p>@Html.ValidationMessageFor(m => m.Date)</p>
        <p>Appointment Date: @Html.EditorFor(m => m.Date)</p>
        <p>@Html.ValidationMessageFor(m => m.TermsAccepted)</p>
        <p>@Html.EditorFor(m => m.TermsAccepted) I accept the terms & conditions</p>
        <input type="submit" value="Make Booking" />
    }
</div>
<div id="successDiv" class="hidden">
    <h4>Your appointment is confirmed</h4>
    <p>Your name is: <b id="successClientName"></b></p>
    <p>The date of your appointment is: <b id="successDate"></b></p>
    <button id="backButton">Back</button>
</div>
```

In this view, there are two div elements. The first is shown to the user when the view is first rendered and contains an Ajax-enabled form. When the form is submitted, we respond to the server's response to the Ajax request by hiding the form and revealing the other div element, which we use to display details of the appointment confirmation.

We included a number of the standard JavaScript libraries from the Scripts folder and defined a local script element that contains some simple jQuery code that is specific to this view. We also added a link element that loads a CSS file from the /Content folder called CustomStyles.css, which you can see in Listing 24-4.

Listing 24-4. The Contents of the CustomStyles.css File

```
div.hidden { display: none;}
div.visible { display: block;}
```

We want to create a typical scenario for a complex view file without needing to create a complex application, which is why we have added a CSS file that only contains two styles and why we are using a bunch of jQuery libraries for a very simple view. The key idea is that there are lots of files to be managed. When you are writing real applications, you will be struck by just how many script and style files you have to deal with in your views.

You can see how our example application works by starting the application and navigating to the /Home/MakeBooking URL. The form is pre-populated with data so that you can just click the Make Booking button to submit the form data to the server using Ajax. When the response is received, you will see a summary of the Appointment object that was created by the model binder from the form data, along with a button element that will return you to the form, as illustrated in Figure 24-1.

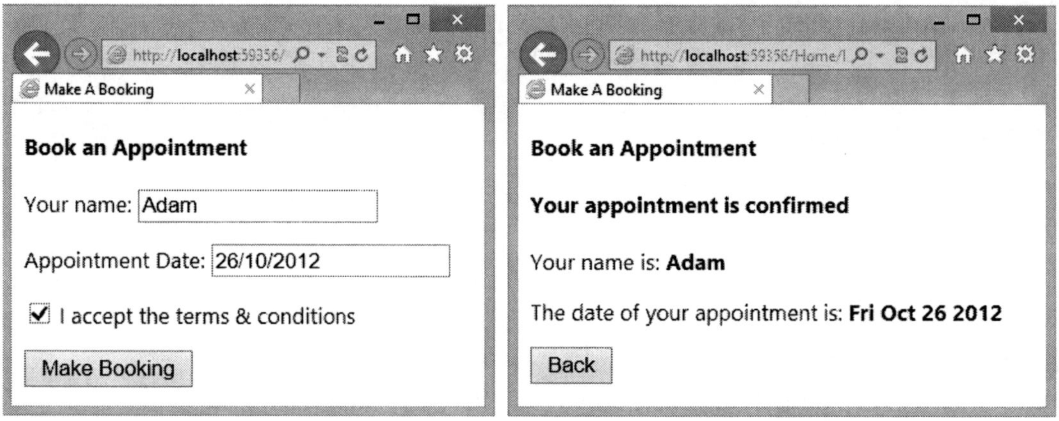

Figure 24-1. Using the example application

Managing Scripts and Style Sheets

The view that we created in Listing 24-3 is typical of the MVC projects that we see in the wild. There is a mix of libraries from the Scripts folder, CSS style sheets from the Content folder, local script elements, and of course, HTML and Razor markup.

Developers tend to write view files just as they would write HTML pages, which is fine but isn't the most effective approach. As we will show you in the sections that follow, there are some hidden problems in our MakeBooking.cshtml view file. We can make a number of improvements in the way that we manage our scripts and style sheets.

Profiling Script and Style Sheet Loading

When considering any kind of optimization in any kind of project, you need to start by taking some measurements. We are all for efficient and optimized applications, but our experience is that people rush to optimize problems that don't have much impact, and in doing so, make design decisions that cause problems later.

For the problems that we are going to look at in this chapter, we are going to perform our measurements using the Internet Explorer 10 *F12 tools* (so called because you access them by pressing the F12 key). Load the application, navigate to the /Home/MakeBooking URL, and then press the F12 key. When the tools window opens, navigate to the Network tab and click the Start Capturing button. Reload the contents of the browser tab (right-click in the browser window and select Refresh), and you will see the results shown in Figure 24-2.

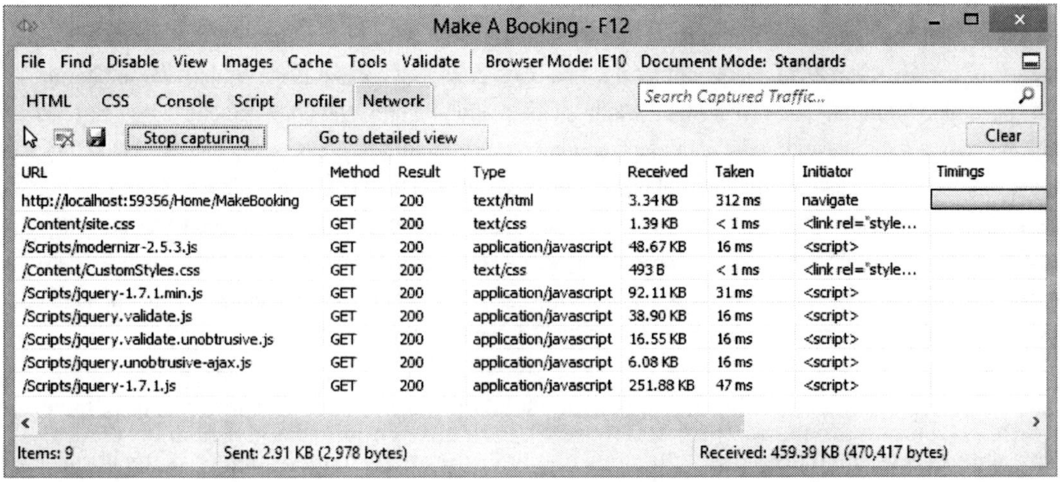

Figure 24-2. Profiling script and style sheet loading for the example application

The F12 tools in IE10 allow you to profile the network requests that your application makes. (There are other tools available if you are not using Internet Explorer. Our favorite is Fiddler, which you can get for free from www.fiddler2.com).

So that we can compare the optimizations that we make in this chapter, we will use the data shown in Figure 24-2 as our baseline. Here are the key figures:

- The browser made nine requests for the /Home/MakeBooking URL.

- There were two requests for CSS files.

- There were six requests for JavaScript files.

- A total of 2,978 bytes were sent from the browser to the server.

- A total of 470,417 bytes were sent from the server to the browser

This is the worst-case profile for our application because we cleared the browser's cache before we reloaded the view. We have done this because it allows us to easily create a measurable starting point, even though we know that real-world use would be improved by the browser caching files from previous requests.

If we reload the /Home/MakeBooking URL without clearing the cache, then we get the following results:

- The browser made nine requests for the /Home/MakeBooking URL.

- There were two requests for CSS files.

- There were six requests for JavaScript files.

- A total of 2,722 bytes were sent from the browser to the server.

- A total of 6,302 bytes were sent from the server to the browser.

This is our best-case scenario, where all the requests for CSS and JavaScript files were able to be serviced using previously cached files.

■ **Note** In a real project, we would stop at this point and try to understand if we have a problem that needs to be solved. It may seem that 470K is a lot of bandwidth for a simple Web page, but context is everything. We might be developing an application for Intranet use where bandwidth is cheap and plentiful, and optimizations of any sort are outweighed by the cost of the developer, who could be working on more-important projects. Equally, we could be writing an application that operates over the Internet with high-value customers in countries with low-speed connections—in which case it is worth spending the time to optimize every aspect of the application. Our point is that you shouldn't automatically assume that you have to squeeze every optimization into every application— there will often be better things you could be doing. (This is *always* the case if you are sneakily optimizing your application without telling anyone. Stealth optimization is a bad idea and will catch up with you eventually).

If you look at the list of JavaScript files that are downloaded for the view, you will notice that we have re-created two very common problems. The first is that we have a mix of minified and regular JavaScript files. This isn't a huge issue, but it does mean that we won't have the ability to easily debug all the library code during development.

The second problem is that we have downloaded both the minified and regular versions of the jQuery library. This has happened because the layout is loading some JavaScript and CSS files as well, and our lack of coordination means that we are forcing the browser to download code that it already has.

We see both of these problems often. We will show you the MVC Framework features that help you get script and CSS files under control. More broadly, we will also show you how to reduce the number of requests that the browser has to make to the server and the amount of data that has to be downloaded.

Using Script and Style Bundles

Our first step will be to organize our JavaScript and CSS files into *bundles,* which allows us to treat them as a single unit. Bundles are defined in the `/App_Start/BundleConfig.cs` file. We have listed the default contents of this file, as created by Visual Studio, in Listing 24-5.

Listing 24-5. The Default Contents of the BundleConfig.cs File

```
using System.Web;
using System.Web.Optimization;

namespace ClientFeatures {
    public class BundleConfig {
        public static void RegisterBundles(BundleCollection bundles) {

            bundles.Add(new ScriptBundle("~/bundles/jquery").Include(
                    "~/Scripts/jquery-{version}.js"));

            bundles.Add(new ScriptBundle("~/bundles/jqueryui").Include(
                    "~/Scripts/jquery-ui-{version}.js"));

            bundles.Add(new ScriptBundle("~/bundles/jqueryval").Include(
                    "~/Scripts/jquery.unobtrusive*",
                    "~/Scripts/jquery.validate*"));

            bundles.Add(new ScriptBundle("~/bundles/modernizr").Include(
                    "~/Scripts/modernizr-*"));
```

```
        bundles.Add(new StyleBundle("~/Content/css").Include("~/Content/site.css"));

        bundles.Add(new StyleBundle("~/Content/themes/base/css").Include(
                "~/Content/themes/base/jquery.ui.core.css",
                "~/Content/themes/base/jquery.ui.resizable.css",
                "~/Content/themes/base/jquery.ui.selectable.css",
                "~/Content/themes/base/jquery.ui.accordion.css",
                "~/Content/themes/base/jquery.ui.autocomplete.css",
                "~/Content/themes/base/jquery.ui.button.css",
                "~/Content/themes/base/jquery.ui.dialog.css",
                "~/Content/themes/base/jquery.ui.slider.css",
                "~/Content/themes/base/jquery.ui.tabs.css",
                "~/Content/themes/base/jquery.ui.datepicker.css",
                "~/Content/themes/base/jquery.ui.progressbar.css",
                "~/Content/themes/base/jquery.ui.theme.css"));
        }
    }
}
```

The static `RegisterBundles` method is called from the `Application_Start` method in `Global.asax` when the MVC Framework application first starts. The `RegisterBundles` method takes a `BundleCollection` object, which we use to register new bundles of files through the `Add` method.

▪ **Tip**   The classes that are used for creating bundles are contained in the `System.Web.Optimization` namespace and, as we write this, the MSDN API documentation for this namespace isn't easy to find. You can navigate directly to http://msdn.microsoft.com/en-us/library/system.web.optimization.aspx if you want to learn more about the classes in this namespace.

We can create bundles for script files and for style sheets and it is important that we keep these types of file separate because the MVC Framework optimizes the files differently. Styles are represented by the `StyleBundle` class and scripts are represented by the `ScriptBundle` class.

When you create a new bundle, you create an instance of either `StyleBundle` or `ScriptBundle`, both of which take a single constructor argument that is the path that the bundle will be referenced by. The path is used as a URL for the browser to request the contents of the bundle, so it is important to use a scheme for your paths that won't conflict with the routes your application supports. The safest way to do this is to start your paths with ~/bundles or ~/Content. (The importance of this will become apparent as we explain how bundles work).

Once you have created the `StyleBundle` or `ScriptBundle` objects, you use the `Include` method to add details of the style sheets or script files that the bundle will contain. There are some nice features available for making your bundles flexible. To help us demonstrate this, we have edited and simplified the bundles our example application supports in the `BundleConfig.cs` file, as shown in Listing 24-6. We added a new bundle, edited one of the existing ones, and removed all of the ones that we do not need.

Listing 24-6. Customizing the Bundle Configuration

```
using System.Web;
using System.Web.Optimization;

namespace ClientFeatures {
    public class BundleConfig {
        public static void RegisterBundles(BundleCollection bundles) {
```

```
bundles.Add(new StyleBundle("~/Content/css").Include("~/Content/*.css"));

bundles.Add(new ScriptBundle("~/bundles/clientfeaturesscripts")
    .Include("~/Scripts/jquery-{version}.js",
            "~/Scripts/jquery.validate.js",
            "~/Scripts/jquery.validate.unobtrusive.js",
            "~/Scripts/jquery.unobtrusive-ajax.js"));

    }
  }
}
```

We started by modifying the StyleBundle with the ~/Content/css path. We want this bundle to include all the CSS files in our application, so we changed the argument passed to the Include method from ~/Content/site.css (which refers to a single file) to ~/Content/*.css. The asterisk (*) character is a wild card, which means that our bundle now refers to all of the CSS files in the /Content folder of our project. This is an excellent way of ensuring that files in a directory are automatically included in a bundle and where the order in which the files are loaded isn't important. The order in which the browser loads our CSS files isn't important, so using a wildcard is just fine; but if you are relying on the CSS style precedence rules, then you need to list the files individually to ensure a specific order.

The addition to the BundleConfig.cs file is a ScriptBundle whose path we set to ~/bundles/clientfeaturesscripts. You will see the paths for both of these bundles again when we apply them in our application shortly. We used the Include method for this bundle to specify individual JavaScript files, separated by commas, because we only require some of the files in the Scripts folder and we care about the order in which the browser loads and executes the code.

Notice how we specified the jQuery library file:

```
...
~/Scripts/jquery-{version}.js
...
```

The {version} part of the file name is pretty handy because it matches any version of the file specified and it uses the configuration of the application to select either the regular or minified version of the file. MVC 4 comes with version 1.7.1 of the jQuery library, which means that our bundle will include /Scripts/jquery-1.7.1.js during development and /Scripts/jquery-1.7.1.min.js when deployment.

■ **Tip**　The decision between the regular and minified version is driven by the compilation element in the Web.config file. The regular version is used when the debug attribute is set to true and the minified version is used when debug is false. We will switch our application from debug to deployment mode later in the chapter so you can see how it is done.

The benefit of using {version} is that you can update the libraries you use to new versions without having to redefine your bundles. The drawback is that the {version} token isn't able to differentiate between two versions of the same library in the same directory. So, for example, if we were to add the jquery-1.7.2.js file in our Scripts folder, we would end up with both the 1.7.1 and 1.7.2 files being shipped to the client. Since this would undermine our optimization, we must ensure that only one version of the library is in the /Scripts folder.

> ■ **Tip** The MVC Framework is smart enough to ignore the IntelliSense files when processing {version} in a bundle, but we always check what is being requested by the browser because it is so easy to include unwanted files. You will see how we do this shortly.

Applying Bundles

The first thing we need to do when applying bundles is prepare the view. Our first step is optional, but it will allow the MVC Framework to perform maximum optimization for our application. We have created a new /Scripts/Home folder and added a new JavaScript file called MakeBooking.js within it. This is the convention that we follow to keep our per-page JavaScript files organized by controller. You can see the contents of the MakeBooking.js file in Listing 24-7.

Listing 24-7. The Contents of the MakeBooking.js File

```javascript
function processResponse(appt) {
    $('#successClientName').text(appt.ClientName);
    $('#successDate').text(processDate(appt.Date));
    switchViews();
}

function processDate(dateString) {
    return new Date(parseInt(dateString.substr(6,
        dateString.length - 8))).toDateString();
}

function switchViews() {
    var hidden = $('.hidden');
    var visible = $('.visible');
    hidden.removeClass("hidden").addClass("visible");
    visible.removeClass("visible").addClass("hidden");
}

$(document).ready(function () {
    $('#backButton').click(function (e) {
        switchViews();
    });
});
```

This is the same code that we used previously—we have just moved it into a separate file. The next step is to change the /Views/Home/MakeBooking.cshtml view file to remove the link and script elements for which we have created a bundle, as shown in Listing 24-8. We only want the browser to request the files it needs; leaving those elements in place will lead to duplicate requests. The only script element that remains is the one that refers to the view-specific MakeBooking.js file we created in Listing 24-7.

Listing 24-8. Removing the Script and Link Elements from the MakeBooking.cshtml View File

```
@model ClientFeatures.Models.Appointment

@{
    ViewBag.Title = "Make A Booking";
```

```
    AjaxOptions ajaxOpts = new AjaxOptions {
        OnSuccess = "processResponse"
    };
}
<h4>Book an Appointment</h4>

<script src="~/Scripts/Home/MakeBooking.js" type="text/javascript"></script>

<div id="formDiv" class="visible">
    @using (Ajax.BeginForm(ajaxOpts)) {
        @Html.ValidationSummary(true)
        <p>@Html.ValidationMessageFor(m => m.ClientName)</p>
        <p>Your name: @Html.EditorFor(m => m.ClientName)</p>
        <p>@Html.ValidationMessageFor(m => m.Date)</p>
        <p>Appointment Date: @Html.EditorFor(m => m.Date)</p>
        <p>@Html.ValidationMessageFor(m => m.TermsAccepted)</p>
        <p>@Html.EditorFor(m => m.TermsAccepted) I accept the terms & conditions</p>
        <input type="submit" value="Make Booking" />
    }
</div>
<div id="successDiv" class="hidden">
    <h4>Your appointment is confirmed</h4>
    <p>Your name is: <b id="successClientName"></b></p>
    <p>The date of your appointment is: <b id="successDate"></b></p>
    <button id="backButton">Back</button>
</div>
```

You can refer to bundles in view files, but we tend to create bundles only for content that is shared across multiple views, and that means we apply bundles in the layout files. In Listing 24-9, you can see the /Views/Shared/_Layout.cshtml file that Visual Studio added to the project.

Listing 24-9. The Layout Added to the Project by Visual Studio

```
<!DOCTYPE html>
<html>
<head>
    <meta charset="utf-8" />
    <meta name="viewport" content="width=device-width" />
    <title>@ViewBag.Title</title>

    @Styles.Render("~/Content/css")
    @Scripts.Render("~/bundles/modernizr")
</head>
<body>
    @RenderBody()

    @Scripts.Render("~/bundles/jquery")

    @RenderSection("scripts", required: false)
</body>
</html>
```

Bundles are added using the @Scripts.Render and @Styles.Render helper methods. You can see that the layout already contains three bundles, which we have marked in bold. The two calls to @Scripts.Render explain some of the initial profile data. The ~/bundles/jquery bundle is the reason that we ended up with two copies of the jQuery library being requested by the browser. The ~/bundles/modernizr bundle makes the browser request a library that we do not use in our simple application.

In fact, only the ~/Content/css bundle was any help to us because it loaded the /Content/Site.css file in the original bundle definition and will now load all the CSS files in the /Content folder following the change we made in Listing 24-9. To get the behavior we want, we have edited the _Layout.cshtml file to use our newly defined bundles and remove the references that we do not want, as shown in Listing 24-10.

Listing 24-10. Ensuring the Right Bundles Are Using the _Layout.cshtml File

```
<!DOCTYPE html>
<html>
<head>
    <meta charset="utf-8" />
    <meta name="viewport" content="width=device-width" />
    <title>@ViewBag.Title</title>
    @Styles.Render("~/Content/css")
</head>
<body>
    @RenderBody()

    @Scripts.Render("~/bundles/clientfeaturesscripts")

    @RenderSection("scripts", required: false)
</body>
</html>
```

You can see the HTML that these helper methods generate by starting the application, navigating to the /Home/MakeBooking URL, and viewing the page source. Here is the output produced by the Styles.Render method for the ~/Content/css bundle:

```
...
<link href="/Content/CustomStyles.css" rel="stylesheet"/>
<link href="/Content/Site.css" rel="stylesheet"/>
...
```

And here is the output produced by the Scripts.Render method:

```
...
<script src="/Scripts/jquery-1.7.1.js"></script>
<script src="/Scripts/jquery.unobtrusive-ajax.js"></script>
<script src="/Scripts/jquery.validate.js"></script>
<script src="/Scripts/jquery.validate.unobtrusive.js"></script>
...
```

Using the Scripts Section

We have one more thing to do. Our view-specific JavaScript contained in the /Scripts/Home/MakeBooking.js file depends on jQuery to set up the event handler for the button. This means that we have to make sure that the jQuery file is loaded before the MakeBooking.js file. If you look at the layout in Listing 24-10, you will see that the call to the RenderBody method is before the call to Scripts.Render, which means that the script element in the view appears before the script elements in the layout and our button code won't work. (It will either fail quietly or report a JavaScript error, depending on the browser being used.)

669

We could fix this by moving the `Scripts.Render` call to the `head` element in the view; in fact, this is what we usually do. However, we can also take advantage of the optional `scripts` section that is defined in the `_Layout.cshtml` file and which you can see in Listing 24-10. In Listing 24-11, you can see how we have updated the `MakeBooking.cshtml` view to use this section.

Listing 24-11. Using the Optional Scripts Section in the View

```
@model ClientFeatures.Models.Appointment

@{
    ViewBag.Title = "Make A Booking";
    AjaxOptions ajaxOpts = new AjaxOptions {
        OnSuccess = "processResponse"
    };
}
<h4>Book an Appointment</h4>
@section scripts {
    <script src="~/Scripts/Home/MakeBooking.js" type="text/javascript"></script>
}
<div id="formDiv" class="visible">
    @using (Ajax.BeginForm(ajaxOpts)) {
        @Html.ValidationSummary(true)
        <p>@Html.ValidationMessageFor(m => m.ClientName)</p>
        <p>Your name: @Html.EditorFor(m => m.ClientName)</p>
        <p>@Html.ValidationMessageFor(m => m.Date)</p>
        <p>Appointment Date: @Html.EditorFor(m => m.Date)</p>
        <p>@Html.ValidationMessageFor(m => m.TermsAccepted)</p>
        <p>@Html.EditorFor(m => m.TermsAccepted) I accept the terms & conditions</p>
        <input type="submit" value="Make Booking" />
    }
</div>
<div id="successDiv" class="hidden">
    <h4>Your appointment is confirmed</h4>
    <p>Your name is: <b id="successClientName"></b></p>
    <p>The date of your appointment is: <b id="successDate"></b></p>
    <button id="backButton">Back</button>
</div>
```

The `scripts` section appears after the call to `Scripts.Render` in the layout, which means that our view-specific script won't be loaded until after jQuery, and our button element will work the way we intended. This is an incredibly common mistake to make when using bundles, which is why we have demonstrated it explicitly.

Profiling the Changes

We have defined our own bundles, removed the unwanted JavaScript references, and generally tidied up our use of scripts and style sheets. It is now time to profile our changes and get a handle on the difference.

To do this, we cleared the browser cache and navigated to the /Home/MakeBooking URL, and monitored the requests the browser makes using the F12 tools. You can see the results in Figure 24-3.

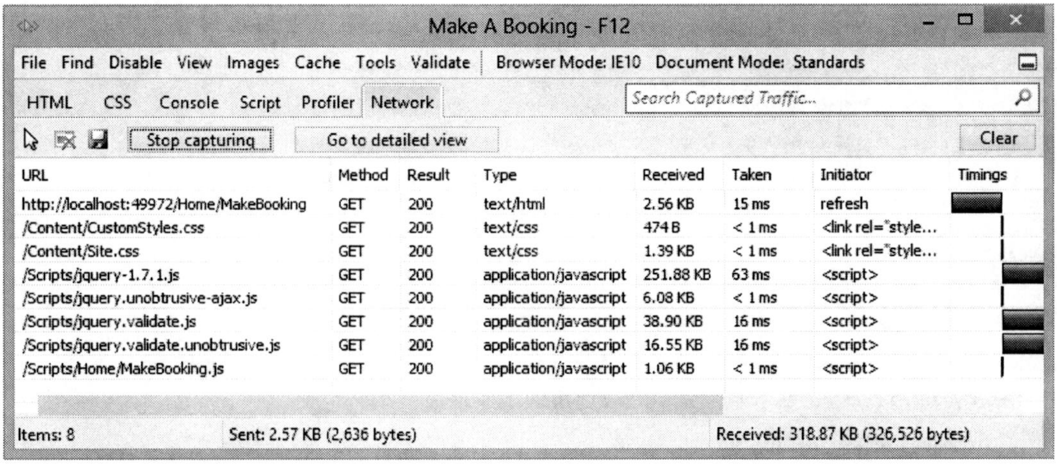

Figure 24-3. Profiling with bundles

Here is the summary of the profile information:

- The browser made eight requests for the /Home/MakeBooking URL.

- There were two requests for CSS files.

- There were five requests for JavaScript files.

- A total of 2,638 bytes were sent from the browser to the server.

- A total of 326,549 bytes were sent from the server to the browser.

That's not bad. We have shaved about 30 percent off the amount of data that is sent to the browser. But we should get even greater benefits when we switch the application from its debugging to deployment configuration, which we do by setting the debug attribute on the compilation element in the Web.config file to false, as shown in Listing 24-12.

Listing 24-12. Disabling Debug Mode in the Web.config File

```
...
<system.web>
    <httpRuntime targetFramework="4.5" />
    <compilation debug="true" targetFramework="4.5" />
...
```

Once we have made this change, we restart the application, clear the browser cache, and profile the network requests again. You can see the results in Figure 24-4.

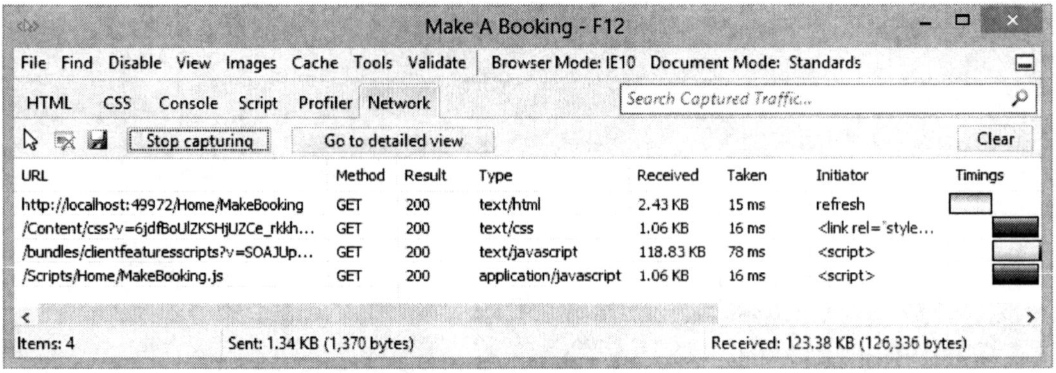

Figure 24-4. Profiling with bundles in the deployment configuration

Here is the summary of the profile information:

- The browser made four requests for the /Home/MakeBooking URL.

- There was one request for CSS.

- There were two requests for JavaScript files.

- A total of 1,372 bytes were sent from the browser to the server.

- A total of 126,340 bytes were sent from the server to the browser.

You might be wondering why there are fewer requests for CSS and JavaScript files. The reason is that the MVC Framework concatenates and minifies the style sheets and JavaScript files in the deployment mode so that all the content in a bundle can be loaded in a single request. You can see how this works if you look at the HTML that the application renders. Here is the HTML that the Styles.Render method has produced:

```
...
<link href="/Content/css?v=6jdfBoUlZKSHjUZCe_rkkh4S8jotNCGFDO9DYm7kBWE1"
    rel="stylesheet"/>
...
```

And here is the HTML produced by the Scripts.Render method:

```
...
<script   src="/bundles/clientfeaturesscripts?v=SOAJUpvGwNrOXsILBsLrEwEpdyIziIN9frqxIjgTyWE1">
</script>
...
```

These long URLs are used to request the contents of a bundle in a single blob of data. The MVC Framework minifies CSS data differently from JavaScript files, which is why we have to keep style sheets and scripts in different bundles.

The impact of the optimizations we have applied is significant. We have far fewer requests from the browser, which reduces the amount of data sent to the client. And we have less data sent in return; in fact, we have sent about 27 percent of the volume of data that we recorded when we profiled the application at the start of the chapter.

This is the point where we stop optimizing the requests. We could add our MakeBooking.js file to a bundle to eliminate another request and have the MVC Framework minify the code, but we have reached the point where our returns are diminished and we start mixing up the content that is view-specific with the code that is in the layout, which we prefer not to do. If we had a more complex application, we might well create a second script bundle that contains more custom code, but we have a simple application and our final rule of optimization is to know where to stop. For this application, we have reached that point.

Targeting Mobile Devices

You will often want to target mobile devices with your MVC Framework application, and that means tailoring the content you present to the user to take advantage of the available device features and limitations. There are lots of differences between mobile and desktop devices, but the two that cause the most trouble are touch interactions and restricted screen size. Every view that you render for a mobile client must be useable through touch interaction, which requires larger elements and enough space to allow accurate fingertip selection. Equally, you need to make sure that you present your content so that it can be read or understood on a physically small screen.

We are not going to go into the details of mobile device development, but we are going to show you how the MVC Framework helps you to support both traditional and mobile clients in an application.

■ **Tip**   There is a Mobile template option available when you create a new MVC Framework project, but it is just a variation on the Internet template that adds support for the jQuery Mobile library. We really like jQuery Mobile and, as you might have guessed by now, Adam has covered it in depth in his other books. We do not like the Mobile template, however, because it adds some default views and controllers for authentication that we do not think are very good. Instead, we recommend that you install jQuery Mobile and any other JavaScript library you require using NuGet.

Taking Stock of the Application

The best way to target mobile devices is do so from the very start of a development project. We are going to do this opposite here, which is to add support to our existing example ClientFeatures application, which we created to show you how to use bundles.

We start by understanding how our application appears on a range of mobile devices. We like to use the Opera Mobile Emulator for this, which is freely available from www.opera.com/developer/tools/mobile. There is no substitute for testing mobile applications on a representative range of real mobile hardware, but for quickly taking stock of where you stand, the Opera Mobile Emulator is a good place to start. It is free, it provides a faithful emulator of the Opera Mobile browser that is used on a lot of mobile devices, and it lets you test different hardware profiles and capabilities.

■ **Tip**   There are other emulators around, including ones for Windows Phone, Android, and the Blackberry. These tend to be pretty slow and painful to use because they are emulating the entire mobile operating system and not just the browser. We have yet to find anything that will sensibly emulate the iPhone on a Windows PC. There are plenty of products that claim that they can, but they typically use the Windows version of Safari, which isn't the same as the iOS version and looks like it has been retired by Apple.

In Figure 24-5, you can see how our /Home/MakeBooking view is displayed by the mobile browser. We have used the HTC Hero profile for the emulator, which simulates a typical, but not outstanding, mobile device with a 320×480–pixel touch display at 180 pixels per inch.

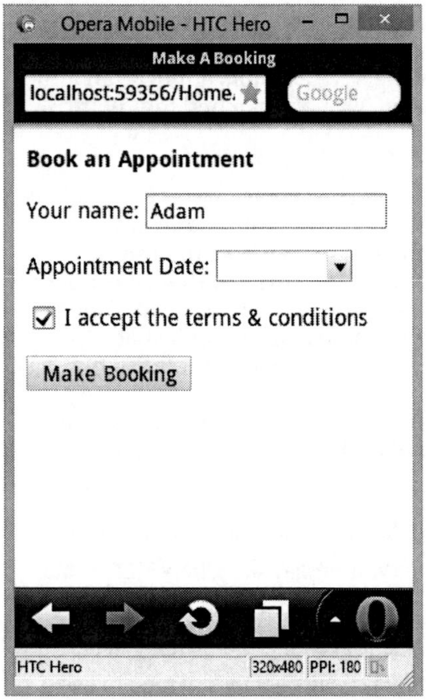

Figure 24-5. Displaying the application in the mobile browser

This is such a simple application that we do not have any truly hideous problems to solve. The worst we can say is that we haven't presented the content in a way that is easy to use on a touch screen. A real application that has been developed and tested for desktop browsers generally looks pretty terrible on a mobile browser.

Using Mobile Specific Layouts and Views

In the sections that follow, we are going to show you how to create mobile-specific versions of your views and layouts so that you can tailor your content to a range of devices. It is a pleasantly simple process, and to get basic support, all you need to do is create versions of your views and layouts with **.Mobile** in their name. This takes advantage of the built-in support for display modes.

As an example, we have created a new view file called /Views/Home/MakeBooking.Mobile.cshtml. Note the addition of **.Mobile** before the file extension. You can see the contents of the new view in Listing 24-13.

Listing 24-13. The Contents of the /Views/Home/MakeBooking.Mobile.cshtml

```
@model ClientFeatures.Models.Appointment

@{
    ViewBag.Title = "Make A Booking";
    AjaxOptions ajaxOpts = new AjaxOptions {
        OnSuccess = "processResponse"
    };
}
<h4>This is the MOBILE View</h4>
@section scripts {
    <script src="~/Scripts/Home/MakeBooking.js" type="text/javascript"></script>
```

```
}
<div id="formDiv" class="visible">
    @using (Ajax.BeginForm(ajaxOpts)) {
        @Html.ValidationSummary(true)
        <p>@Html.ValidationMessageFor(m => m.ClientName)</p>
        <p>Name:</p><p>@Html.EditorFor(m => m.ClientName)</p>
        <p>@Html.ValidationMessageFor(m => m.Date)</p>
        <p>Date:</p><p>@Html.EditorFor(m => m.Date)</p>
        <p>@Html.ValidationMessageFor(m => m.TermsAccepted)</p>
        <p>@Html.EditorFor(m => m.TermsAccepted) Terms & Conditions</p>
        <input type="submit" value="Make Booking" />
    }
</div>
<div id="successDiv" class="hidden">
    <h4>Your appointment is confirmed</h4>
    <p>Your name is: <b id="successClientName"></b></p>
    <p>The date of your appointment is: <b id="successDate"></b></p>
    <button id="backButton">Back</button>
</div>
```

We have made some minor adjustments to the view so that the labels for the input elements are displayed on their own, and to make it obvious which view is being displayed, we have changed the content of the h4 title element.

The MVC Framework applies our mobile view automatically. If you start the application and navigate to the /Home/MakeBooking URL in a desktop browser, you will be shown the HTML rendered from the /Views/Home/MakeBooking.cshtml view. But if you visit the same URL with the mobile browser emulator, you will see the HTML rendered from the /Views/Home/MakeBooking.Mobile.cshtml view, as illustrated in Figure 24-6.

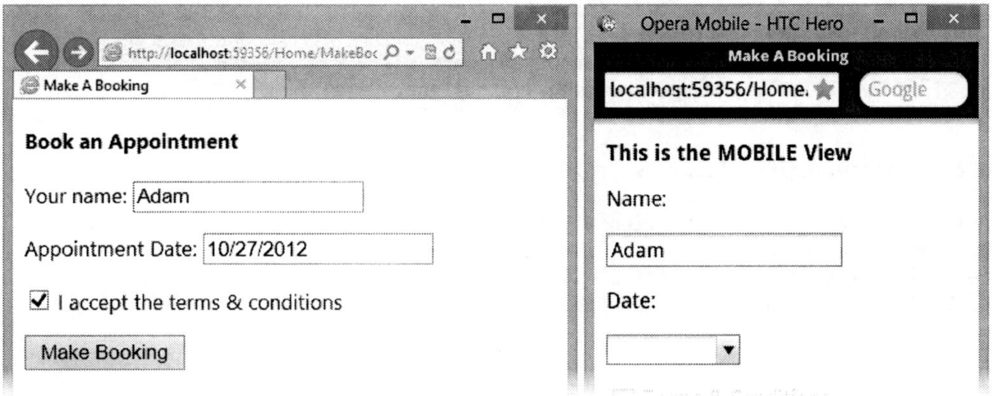

Figure 24-6. The same URL viewed in desktop and mobile browsers

The way that mobile browsers are detected is a little odd and relies on a set of text files that are included with the .NET Framework. On our system, we found the text files in C:\Windows\Microsoft.NET\Framework\v4.0.30319\Config\Browsers, but the exact location may vary on your system. In this directory, there are a series of files, each of which identifies a mobile browser—including Opera Mobile. When the MVC Framework received the request from the mobile emulator, it used the user-agent string that all browsers send and it determined that the request was from a mobile device, leading to the MakeBooking.Mobile.cshtml view being used.

Creating Custom Display Modes

By default, the MVC Framework only detects mobile devices and treats everything else as a single category. If you want to be very specific about how you respond to different kinds of device, then you can create your own display modes.

To demonstrate this, we are going to use the Amazon Kindle Fire profile, which comes with the Opera Mobile Emulator. The user agent string that Opera Mobile sends when it is installed on a table device doesn't match what the .NET Framework expects from Opera Mobile, and so the device is presented with the standard MakeBooking.cshtml view.

In Listing 24-14, you can see how we have modified the Global.asax file to create a new display mode for the Opera Tablet browser.

Listing 24-14. Creating a New Display Mode in the Global.asax File

```
using System;
using System.Collections.Generic;
using System.Linq;
using System.Web;
using System.Web.Http;
using System.Web.Mvc;
using System.Web.Optimization;
using System.Web.Routing;
using System.Web.WebPages;

namespace ClientFeatures {

    public class MvcApplication : System.Web.HttpApplication {
        protected void Application_Start() {

            DisplayModeProvider.Instance.Modes.Insert(0,
                new DefaultDisplayMode("OperaTablet") {
                ContextCondition = (context => context.Request.UserAgent.IndexOf
                    ("Opera Tablet", StringComparison.OrdinalIgnoreCase) >= 0)
            });

            AreaRegistration.RegisterAllAreas();

            WebApiConfig.Register(GlobalConfiguration.Configuration);
            FilterConfig.RegisterGlobalFilters(GlobalFilters.Filters);
            RouteConfig.RegisterRoutes(RouteTable.Routes);
            BundleConfig.RegisterBundles(BundleTable.Bundles);
        }
    }
}
```

The static DisplayModeProvider.Instance.Modes property returns a collection that we can use to define custom display modes, which are created by instantiating the DefaultDisplayMode object and setting the ContextCondition property to a lambda expression that receives an HttpContextBase object and returns a boolean value. The constructor argument for the DefaultDisplayMode class is the name of the display mode, which will be used to find views and layouts that have been customized for a particular kind of device. We have specified OperaTablet, which means that the MVC Framework will look for views such as /Views/Home/MakeBooking.OperaTable.cshtml.

▨ **Tip** Notice that we used the Insert method to place our DefaultDisplayMode object at index zero in the collection returned by the DisplayModeProvider.Instance.Modes property. The MVC Framework checks each display mode in turn, and stops looking when it finds one whose ContextCondition expression returns true. There is a default fallback display mode that will match any request and use the default views (i.e., with no OperaTable or Mobile addition). We need to make sure that our display mode is queried before the fallback.

We use the HttpContextBase object to decide if the request that we have received matches the display mode we are looking for. We have read the Request.UserAgent property and check to see if it contains the phrase Opera Tablet, and return true if it does.

To take advantage of this display mode, we have created a new view file called /Views/Home/MakeBooking.OperaTablet.cshtml, which you can see in Listing 24-15.

Listing 24-15. The Contents of the MakeBooking.OperaTablet.cshtml File

```
@model ClientFeatures.Models.Appointment

@{
    ViewBag.Title = "Make A Booking";
    AjaxOptions ajaxOpts = new AjaxOptions {
        OnSuccess = "processResponse"
    };
}
<h4>This is the OPERA TABLET View</h4>
@section scripts {
    <script src="~/Scripts/Home/MakeBooking.js" type="text/javascript"></script>
}

<div id="formDiv" class="visible">
    @using (Ajax.BeginForm(ajaxOpts)) {
        @Html.ValidationSummary(true)
        <p>@Html.ValidationMessageFor(m => m.ClientName)</p>
        <p>Name:</p><p>@Html.EditorFor(m => m.ClientName)</p>
        <p>@Html.ValidationMessageFor(m => m.Date)</p>
        <p>Date:</p><p>@Html.EditorFor(m => m.Date)</p>
        <p>@Html.ValidationMessageFor(m => m.TermsAccepted)</p>
        <p>@Html.EditorFor(m => m.TermsAccepted) Terms & Conditions</p>
        <input type="submit" value="Make Booking" />
    }
</div>
<div id="successDiv" class="hidden">
    <h4>Your appointment is confirmed</h4>
    <p>Your name is: <b id="successClientName"></b></p>
    <p>The date of your appointment is: <b id="successDate"></b></p>
    <button id="backButton">Back</button>
</div>
```

The only change that we have made is to the text in the h4 element, which lets us see which view is being used. If we start an Opera Mobile Emulator window using the Kindle File profile and navigate to the /Home/MakeBooking URL, we can see our new view being used, as illustrated in Figure 24-7.

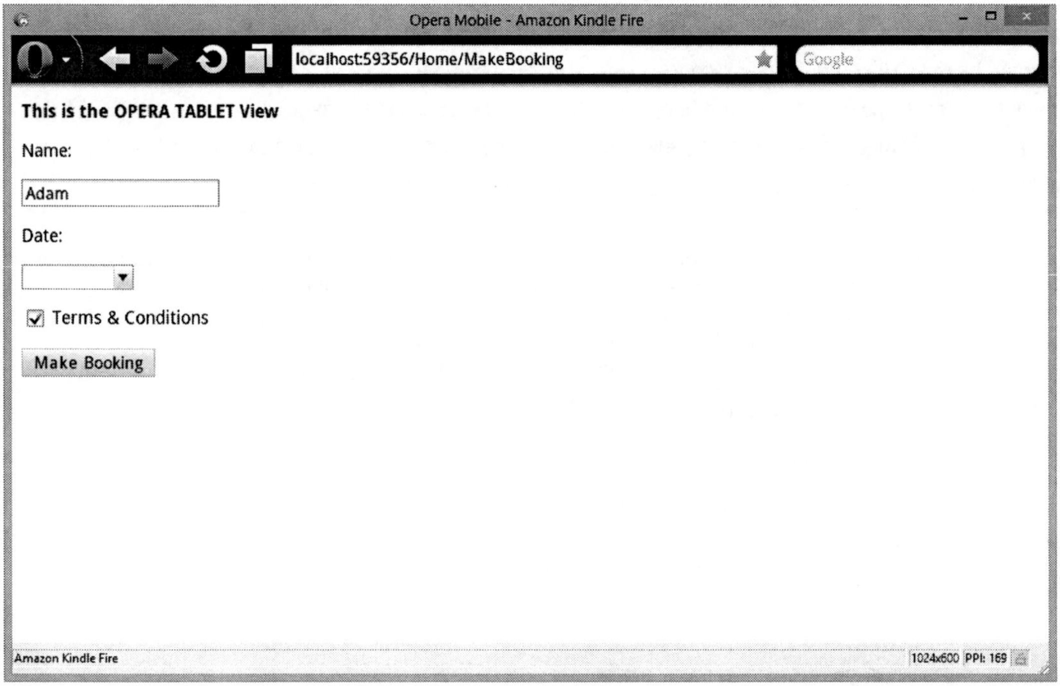

Figure 24-7. The result of creating a custom display mode

Obviously, in a real project we would want to do a little more to take advantage of the screen size and touch capabilities of the tablet; but it is enough for this chapter to demonstrate how we can use custom display modes to provide fine-grain control over which views are used to satisfy requests from the client.

■ **Caution**   Be careful when creating custom display modes. It is very easy to capture requests from the wrong clients or to miss some subtle variations between different versions of a browser running on a particular client type. We recommend thorough testing with a range of devices.

Summary

In this chapter, we showed you the bundles and display modes features, which can be useful when developing the client-side part of a Web application. In the next chapter, we will show you the Web API, which makes it easy to create Web services that clients can consume.

CHAPTER 25

■■■

Web API

In this chapter, we describe the Web API feature, which is a new addition to the ASP.NET platform that allows you to quickly and easily create Web services that provide an API to HTTP clients, known as *Web APIs*.

The Web API feature is based on the same foundation as regular MVC Framework applications, but is not part of the MVC Framework. Instead, Microsoft has taken some key classes and characteristics that are associated with the `System.Web.Mvc` namespace and duplicated them in the `System.Web.Http` namespace. The idea is that Web API is part of the core ASP.NET platform and can be used in other types of Web applications or used as a stand-alone Web services engine.

The good news is that we already understand the Web API underpinnings because we have described them in the previous chapters. We show you how to add a Web API to a regular MVC Framework application project in this chapter. This process is so simple that we end up spending most of our time listing the JavaScript code that we wrote to use the API we created.

That is not to take away from the way that Web API simplifies creating Web services (and it is a huge improvement over the other Microsoft Web service technologies that have been appearing over the last decade or so). We like the Web API and we think you should use it for your projects, but mainly because it is simple and built on the same design that the MVC Framework uses.

Understanding the Web API

The Web API feature is based on adding a special kind of controller to an MVC Framework application. This kind of controller, called an *API Controller*, has two distinctive characteristics:

1. Action methods return model, rather than `ActionResult`, objects

2. Action methods selected based on the HTTP method used in the request

The model objects that are returned from an API controller action method are encoded as JSON and sent to the client. API controllers are designed to deliver Web data services, so they do not support views, layouts, or any of the other features that we have been using to generate HTML for browsers to display.

API controller can support any Web-enabled client, but the most frequent use is to service Ajax requests from Web applications, which is what we will be demonstrating in this chapter.

As we demonstrated in Chapter 21, you can create action methods in regular controllers that return JSON data to support Ajax, but the API controller offers an alternative approach that separates the data-related actions in your application from the view-related actions, and makes creating a general-purpose Web API quick and simple.

░ **Tip**   Like pretty much all of the MVC Framework features, you do not have to use API controllers. We mix and match the techniques we used in Chapter 21 with API controllers in our projects. We tend to find API controllers useful when we are creating lots of actions that return JSON or when we are working on a project that doesn't have an HTML component and just provides data services.

The easiest way to explain how API controllers work is to create an MVC Framework application that uses one, which is what we will do in this chapter. However, the Web API feature is pretty simple and it relies on many of the same MVC features that we have explored in detail in earlier chapters, so we will spend a lot more time setting up the rest of the application and then just drop the API controller in at the end.

In a way, this is a good thing. It means that you already know all of the foundation features that an API controller relies on. But it does make for an odd example because we have a lot of standard MVC plumbing to create before we get to the API controller. It also means that we need to write some JavaScript code that makes Ajax requests. We will use jQuery for this task, and although we won't explain jQuery in detail, we will explain what each section of the code does and how it interacts with the Web service we will create.

Creating the Web API Application

As we explained, a Web API application is just a regular MVC Framework application with the addition of a special kind of controller. For our example application, we created a new MVC Framework project called `WebServices` using the `Basic` template option. In the sections that follow, we will add all of the regular components of an MVC Framework application—model objects, a repository, controllers, and views—and then add the API Controller.

░ **Tip**   There is a `WebAPI` template option available, but it just creates a normal MVC Framework project and adds a couple example controllers. As you will have gathered by now, we favor the `Empty` and `Basic` template options and think that the other options just add generic code that you are better off not using.

Creating the Model and Repository

For this example application, we have created an especially simple model class called `Reservation`, which we defined in a class file called `Reservation.cs` that we placed in the `Models` folder. You can see the definition of the model class in Listing 25-1.

Listing 25-1. The Reservation Model Class

```
using System.ComponentModel.DataAnnotations;

namespace WebServices.Models {
    public class Reservation {
        public int ReservationId { get; set; }
        public string ClientName { get; set; }
        public string Location { get; set; }
    }
}
```

The `ReservationId` property uniquely identifies each model object. The `ClientName` and `Location` properties contain the model data values. We don't really care about the meaning of these properties in this chapter because are focused on the Web API that we are going to create, so we have chosen something that is simple and generic.

In the last few chapters, we created example applications where the model data is created inside a controller. We did this because we were focused on different aspects of the MVC Framework that didn't relate to storing model data. In this chapter, we are going to create a repository interface and a simple implementation. We are taking the time to do this because one of the most striking aspects of an API controller is just how simple it is—and we do not want to undermine that effect.

We created a new interface called `IReservationRepository` in the `IReservationRepository.cs` file in the `Models` folder, as shown in Listing 25-2.

Listing 25-2. The IReservationRepository Interface

```
using System.Collections.Generic;

namespace WebServices.Models {

    public interface IReservationRepository {

        IEnumerable<Reservation> GetAll();

        Reservation Get(int id);

        Reservation Add(Reservation item);

        void Remove(int id);

        bool Update(Reservation item);
    }
}
```

This is a very standard repository interface that defines methods that allow model objects to be retrieved (either individually by `ReservationId` or as a collection), added, updated, and deleted.

We also created the `ReservationRepository` class, which we defined in the `ReservationRepository.cs` file in the `Models` folder. This class implements the `IReservationRepository` interface and defines some example in-memory model objects. This is not an approach that you would take in a real application, but it is suitable for our purposes in this chapter. You can see the repository class in Listing 25-3.

Listing 25-3. The ReservationRepository Class

```
using System;
using System.Collections.Generic;
using System.Linq;
using System.Web;

namespace WebServices.Models {
    public class ReservationRepository : IReservationRepository {
        private List<Reservation> data = new List<Reservation> {
            new Reservation {ReservationId = 1,  ClientName = "Adam",
                Location = "London"},
            new Reservation {ReservationId = 2,  ClientName = "Steve",
                Location = "New York"},
```

```
        new Reservation {ReservationId = 3,  ClientName = "Jacqui",
            Location = "Paris"},
    };

    private static ReservationRepository repo = new ReservationRepository();
    public static IReservationRepository getRepository() {
        return repo;
    }

    public IEnumerable<Reservation> GetAll() {
        return data;
    }

    public Reservation Get(int id) {
        var matches = data.Where(r => r.ReservationId == id);
        return matches.Count() > 0 ? matches.First() : null;
    }

    public Reservation Add(Reservation item) {
        item.ReservationId = data.Count + 1;
        data.Add(item);
        return item;
    }

    public void Remove(int id) {
        Reservation item = Get(id);
        if (item != null) {
            data.Remove(item);
        }
    }

    public bool Update(Reservation item) {
        Reservation storedItem = Get(item.ReservationId);
        if (storedItem != null) {
            storedItem.ClientName = item.ClientName;
            storedItem.Location = item.Location;
            return true;
        } else {
            return false;
        }
    }
}
}
```

There is no persistence of changes in this repository, so the model data will be reset to the three sample objects each time that the application is restarted.

Creating the Home Controller

You can freely mix regular controllers and API controllers in a project. In fact, you will usually need to if you want to support HTML clients because API controllers will only return object data and will not render a view. So that we can start using our application, we have created a Home controller whose Index action method will render the default view. We do not pass any model objects to the view because we want to take a totally Web service approach to getting the data we require from the API controller. You can see the Home controller in Listing 25-4.

Listing 25-4. The Home Controller in the WebServices Project

```
using System.Web.Mvc;

namespace WebServices.Controllers {
    public class HomeController : Controller {

        public ActionResult Index() {
            return View();
        }
    }
}
```

Creating the View and the CSS

We have added some CSS styles to the /Content/Site.css file to support the HTML elements that we will present when the Index action is invoked. You can see these additions in Listing 25-5.

Listing 25-5. Additions to the Site.css File for the Example Application

```
table { margin: 10px 0;}
th { text-align: left;}

.nameCol {width: 100px;}
.locationCol {width: 100px;}
.selectCol {width: 30px;}
.display { float: left; border: thin solid black; margin: 10px; padding: 10px;}
.display label {display: inline-block;width: 100px;}
```

The view that we render when the Index action on the Home controller is invoked is the /Views/Home/Index.cshtml file, which you can see in Listing 25-6. We have not set a value for the Layout property in the view, which means that the default layout will be used. This means that our CSS styles and the jQuery library (on which we will rely later) will be loaded by the browser automatically when the view is rendered. We have added a script element in the scripts section for the unobtrusive Ajax library, which we will use later.

Listing 25-6. The Index.cshtml

```
@{ ViewBag.Title = "Index";}
@section scripts {
    <script src="~/Scripts/jquery.unobtrusive-ajax.js"></script>
}
<div id="summaryDisplay" class="display">
    <h4>Reservations</h4>
    <table>
        <thead>
            <tr>
                <th class="selectCol"></th>
                <th class="nameCol">Name</th>
                <th class="locationCol">Location</th>
            </tr>
```

```
            </thead>
            <tbody id="tableBody">
                <tr><td colspan="3">The data is loading</td></tr>
            </tbody>
        </table>
        <div id="buttonContainer">
            <button id="refresh">Refresh</button>
            <button id="add">Add</button>
            <button id="edit">Edit</button>
            <button id="delete">Delete</button>
        </div>
    </div>

    <div id="addDisplay" class="display">
        <h4>Add New Reservation</h4>
        @{
            AjaxOptions addAjaxOpts = new AjaxOptions {
                // options will go here
            };
        }
        @using (Ajax.BeginForm(addAjaxOpts)) {
            @Html.Hidden("ReservationId", 0)
            <p><label>Name:</label>@Html.Editor("ClientName")</p>
            <p><label>Location:</label>@Html.Editor("Location")</p>
            <button type="submit">Submit</button>
        }
    </div>

    <div id="editDisplay" class="display">
        <h4>Edit Reservation</h4>
        <form id="editForm">
            <input id="editReservationId" type="hidden" name="ReservationId"/>
            <p><label>Name:</label><input id="editClientName" name="ClientName" /></p>
            <p><label>Location:</label><input id="editLocation" name="Location" /></p>
        </form>
        <button id="submitEdit" type="submit">Save</button>
</div>
```

There are three sections to the HTML that this view produces. Each section is defined in a div element of the display class, and for the moment at least, all three are shown to the user (we will change the visibility of these elements when we write our JavaScript code later in the chapter).

You can see how the HTML appears in the browser if you start the application. None of the buttons will work and no data will be displayed, but you can get a sense of the structure and layout, as shown in Figure 25-1.

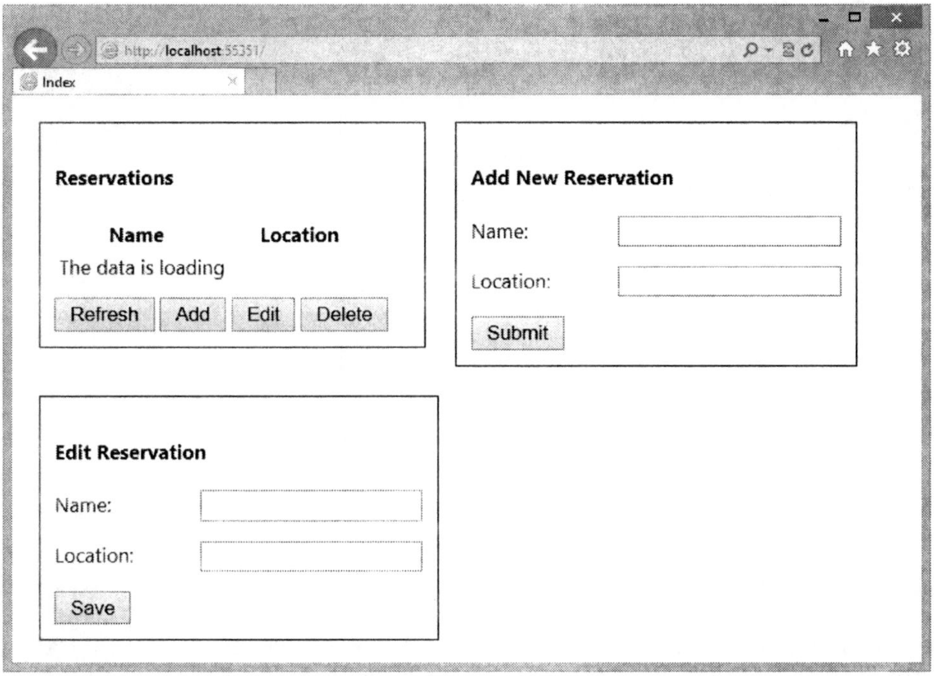

Figure 25-1. The initial appearance of the HTML rendered by the Index.cshtml view

When we have finished this application, only the Reservations section will be shown to the user. We will load the model data from the server and use it to populate the table element.

The Add New Reservation section contains an unobtrusive Ajax-enabled form that will post data back to the server to create new Reservation objects in the repository. The AjaxOptions object that we will use to configure the Ajax request doesn't have any options defined at the moment, but we will come back and sort that out once we have the rest of the application in place.

The Edit Reservation section will allow the user to change an existing Reservation object in the repository. We haven't used an unobtrusive Ajax form for this section of the application because we intend to use the jQuery Ajax support directly (which is what the unobtrusive Ajax library uses anyway) for variety.

Creating the API Controller

We have reached the point in our example application where we are ready to define the Web API that we will use in our JavaScript code to interact with the contents of the repository. In this section, we will add a new API Controller to the project and explains how it works.

To create the controller, right-click the Controllers folder in the Solution Explorer and select Add ↗ Controller from the pop-up menu. Change the Controller name field to ReservationController and select Empty API controller from the Template drop-down menu, as shown in Figure 25-2.

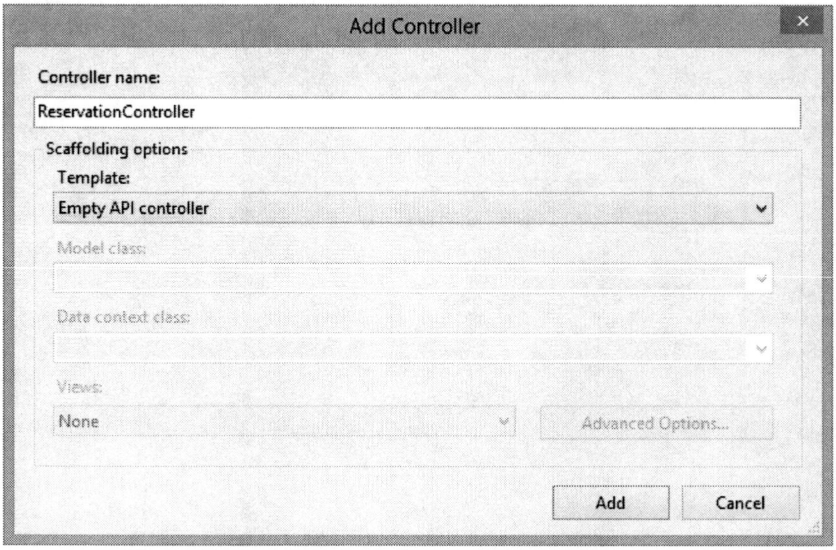

Figure 25-2. Adding a new API Controller to the example project

The `Empty API controller` option creates an API controller without any action methods. There are a couple other options available in the drop-down list that will create API controllers with template action methods that you can fill in, but we prefer to start with an empty class and define the features we need. You can see the initial controller class that Visual Studio creates in Listing 25-7.

Listing 25-7. The Controller Created by Visual Studio When the Empty API Controller Option Is Selected

```
using System;
using System.Collections.Generic;
using System.Linq;
using System.Net;
using System.Net.Http;
using System.Web.Http;

namespace WebServices.Controllers {
    public class ReservationController : ApiController {

    }
}
```

We have highlighted the base class for the `Reservation` because it signifies the differences from a regular controller. The `System.Web.Http.ApiController` implements the `IController` interface that we described in Chapter 15, but takes an entirely different approach to processing requests than the regular `System.Web.Mvc.Controller` class that has been the base for all the other examples in this book (except where we created our own custom `IController` implementation). In Listing 25-8, you can see how we added a repository to the `Reservation` controller and defined the action methods we need to define a Web API for accessing `Reservation` objects.

Listing 25-8. Completing the Reservation API Controller

```
using System.Collections.Generic;
using System.Web.Http;
using WebServices.Models;

namespace WebServices.Controllers {
    public class ReservationController : ApiController {
        IReservationRepository repo = ReservationRepository.getRepository();

        public IEnumerable<Reservation> GetAllReservations() {
            return repo.GetAll();
        }

        public Reservation GetReservation(int id) {
            return repo.Get(id);
        }

        public Reservation PostReservation(Reservation item) {
            return repo.Add(item);
        }

        public bool PutReservation(Reservation item) {
            return repo.Update(item);
        }

        public void DeleteReservation(int id) {
            repo.Remove(id);
        }
    }
}
```

That is all that is required to create a Web API. We created an instance of our demo repository class and a set of five action methods that provide access to the Reservation model objects that the repository contains.

■ **Tip**   Notice that we obtain an IReservationRepository by calling the static ReservationRepository.getRepository method. New instances of controllers are created to service API requests and our changes wouldn't be reflected in the data sent to the client if we were to create a new ReservationRepository object in the controller itself. This is a facet of our in-memory repository and does not occur when you are working with real repositories with persistent data stores.

Testing the API Controller

We will explain how the API controller works shortly, but first we are going to perform a simple test. Start the application. Once the browser loads the root URL for the project, navigate to the **/api/reservation** URL. The result that you see will depend on the browser that you are using. If you are using Internet Explorer 10, then you will be prompted to save or open a file that contains the following JSON data:

```
[{"ReservationId":1,"ClientName":"Adam","Location":"London"},
 {"ReservationId":2,"ClientName":"Steve","Location":"New York"},
 {"ReservationId":3,"ClientName":"Jacqui","Location":"Paris"}]
```

If you navigate to the same URL using a different browser, such as Google Chrome or Mozilla Firefox, then the browser will display the following XML data:

```
<ArrayOfReservation>
    <Reservation>
        <ClientName>Adam</ClientName>
        <Location>London</Location>
        <ReservationId>1</ReservationId>
    </Reservation>
    <Reservation>
        <ClientName>Steve</ClientName>
        <Location>New York</Location>
        <ReservationId>2</ReservationId>
    </Reservation>
    <Reservation>
        <ClientName>Jacqui</ClientName>
        <Location>Paris</Location>
        <ReservationId>3</ReservationId>
    </Reservation>
</ArrayOfReservation>
```

There are a couple interesting things to note here. The first is that our request for the /api/reservation URL has produced a list of all of our model objects and their properties, from which we can infer that our GetAllReservations action method in the Reservation controller was called.

The second point to note is that different browsers received different data formats. You might get different results if you try this yourself because later versions of the browsers may change the way they make requests, but you can see that one of requests has produced JSON and the other has produced XML. (You can also see why JSON has largely replaced XML for Web services. XML is more verbose and harder to process, especially when you are using JavaScript).

The different data formats are used because the Web API uses the HTTP Accept header contained in the request to work out what data type the client would prefer to work with. Internet Explorer got JSON because this is the Accept header it sends:

```
...
Accept: text/html, application/xhtml+xml, */*
...
```

The browser specified that it would like text/html content most of all, and then application/xhtml+xml. The final part of the Accept header is */*, which means the browser will accept any data type if the first two are not available.

The Web API supports JSON and XML, but it gives preference to JSON, which is what it used to respond to the */* part of the IE Accept header. Here is the Accept header that Google Chrome sent:

```
...
Accept:text/html,application/xhtml+xml,application/xml;q=0.9,*/*;q=0.8
...
```

We have highlighted the important part: Chrome has said that it prefers to receive application/xml data in preference to the */* catchall. The Web API honored this preference and delivered the XML data.

We mention this because a common problem with Web API is getting an undesired data format. This happens because the Accept header gives unexpected preference to a format—or it is missing from the request entirely.

Understanding How the API Controller Works

You will understand a lot more about how the API controller works by navigating to the /api/reservation/3 URL. You will see the following JSON (or the equivalent XML if you are using another browser):

```
{"ReservationId":3,"ClientName":"Jacqui","Location":"Paris"}
```

This time, our request has returned details of the `Reservation` object whose `ReservationId` value corresponds to the last segment of the URL we requested. The format of the URL and the use of the URL segment should remind you of Chapter 13, where we explained how MVC Framework routes work.

API controllers have their own routing configuration, which is completely separate from the rest of the application. You can see the default configuration that Visual Studio creates for new projects by looking at the /App_Start/WebApiConfig.cs file, which we have shown in Listing 25-9.

Listing 25-9. The Contents of the Default WebApiConfig.cs File

```csharp
using System;
using System.Collections.Generic;
using System.Linq;
using System.Web.Http;

namespace WebServices {
    public static class WebApiConfig {
        public static void Register(HttpConfiguration config) {
            config.Routes.MapHttpRoute(
                name: "DefaultApi",
                routeTemplate: "api/{controller}/{id}",
                defaults: new { id = RouteParameter.Optional }
            );
        }
    }
}
```

The `WebApiConfig.cs` file contains the routes used for API Controllers, but uses different classes from the regular MVC routes that we define in the `RouteConfig.cs` file. The Web API feature is implemented as a stand-alone ASP.NET feature and it can be used outside of the MVC Framework, which means that Microsoft has duplicated some key MVC Framework functionality in the `System.Web.Http` namespace to keep MVC and Web API features separate. (This seems oddly duplicative when writing an MVC Framework application but makes sense since Microsoft is trying to target non-MVC developers with Web API, too).

The static `Register` method is called from the `Application_Start` method in `Config.asax` when the application is started and is used to register Web API routes. The `Register` method receives an `HttpConfiguration` object that is provides access to routing through its `Routes` property. Routes are created using the `MapHttpRoute` method.

Understanding API Controller Action Selection

The default Web API route, which you can see in Listing 25-9, has a static `api` segment, and `controller` and `id` segment variables, the latter being optional. They key difference from a regular MVC route is that there is no `action` segment variable—and this is where we start to see the behavior of API controllers take shape.

When a request comes in to the application that matches a Web API route, the action is determined from the HTTP method used to make the request. When we tested the API controller by requesting /api/reservation using the browser, the browser specified the GET method.

The ApiController class, which is the base for API controllers, knows which controller it needs to target from the route and uses the HTTP method to look for suitable action methods.

The convention when naming API controller action methods is to prefix the name with the action method that it supports and include some reference to the model type that it operates on. But this is just a convention because Web API will match any action method whose name contains the HTTP method used to make the request.

For our example, that means that a GET request results in a choice between the GetAllReservations and GetReservation but method names like DoGetReservation or just ThisIsTheGetAction would also be matched.

To decide between the two action methods, the controller looks at the arguments that the contenders accept and uses the routing variables to make the best match. When requesting the /api/reservation API, there we no routing variable except for controller, and so the GetAllReservations method was selected because it has no arguments. When we requested the /api/reservation/3 URL, we supplied a value for the optional id segment variable, which made the GetReservation the better match because it accepts an id argument.

We target the other actions in our Reservation API controller using other HTTP methods: POST, DELETE, and PUT. This is the foundation for the *Representation State Transfer* (REST) style of Web API, known more commonly as a *RESTful* service, where an operation is specified by the combination of a URL and the HTTP method used to request it.

■ **Note**   REST is a style of API rather than a well-defined specification and there is disagreement about what exactly makes a Web service RESTful. One point of contention is that purists do not consider Web services that return JSON as being RESTful. Like any disagreement about an architectural pattern, the reasons for the disagreement are arbitrary and dull. We try to be pragmatic about how patterns are applied and JSON services are RESTful as far as we are concerned.

Mapping HTTP Methods to Action Methods

We explained that the ApiController base class uses the HTTP method to work out which action methods to target. It is a nice approach, but it does mean that you end up with some unnatural method names that are inconsistent with conventions you might be using elsewhere. For example, the PutReservation method might be more naturally called UpdateReservation. Not only would UpdateReservation make the purpose of the method more obvious, but it may allow for a more direct mapping between the actions in your controller and the methods in your repository.

■ **Tip**   You might be tempted to derive your repository class from ApiController and expose the repository methods directly as a Web API. We recommend against that and strongly suggest you create a separate controller, even if as simple as the one we created in the example. At some point, the methods you want to offer via your API and the capabilities of your repository will diverge, and having a separate API controller class will make that easier to manage.

The System.Web.Http namespace contains a set of attributes that you can use to specify which HTTP methods an action should be used for. You can see how we have applied two of these attributes in Listing 25-10 to create a more natural set of method names.

Listing 25-10. Applying Attributes to Specify the HTTP Methods That an Action Supports

```
using System.Collections.Generic;
using System.Web.Http;
using WebServices.Models;

namespace WebServices.Controllers {
    public class ReservationController : ApiController {
        IReservationRepository repo = ReservationRepository.getRepository();

        public IEnumerable<Reservation> GetAllReservations() {
            return repo.GetAll();
        }

        public Reservation GetReservation(int id) {
            return repo.Get(id);
        }

        [HttpPost]
        public Reservation CreateReservation(Reservation item) {
            return repo.Add(item);
        }

        [HttpPut]
        public bool UpdateReservation(Reservation item) {
            return repo.Update(item);
        }

        public void DeleteReservation(int id) {
            repo.Remove(id);
        }
    }
}
```

You can see the duplication between the MVC Framework features we showed you in Chapter 17 and the Web API. The HttpPost and HttpPut attributes that we used in Listing 25-10 have the exact same purpose as the attributes with the same name that we used in Chapter 17, but they are defined in the System.Web.Http namespace and not System.Web.Mvc. Duplication aside, the attributes work in the same way and we have ended up with more useful method names that will still work for the POST and PUT HTTP methods. (There are, of course, attributes for all of the HTTP methods, including GET, DELETE and so on).

Writing the JavaScript Code to Use the Web API

We have created our API controller and explained how a URL like /api/reservation/3 is mapped to an action method using the HTTP method. Now it is time to write the JavaScript code that will allow us to consume the Web API we created. We will be using jQuery to manipulate the HTML elements that the /Views/Home/Index.cshtml view renders and to handle the Ajax requests that we will make to target actions in the Reservation controller.

jQuery is an excellent and feature-rich JavaScript library that we use extensively in our own projects and we recommend that you do the same. But we do not have the space in this book to provide a jQuery tutorial, so we are going to build up our JavaScript functionality by telling you what each code block does but without going into detail of how the jQuery functions work. For more information about jQuery, you see the jquery.com Web site or Adam's *Pro jQuery* book.

Creating the Basic Functionality

We started by creating a /Scripts/Home folder and adding a new JavaScript file called Index.js to it (as we mentioned in Chapter 24, this is the convention we follow to keep per-view scripts organized). Before we do anything else, we add a script element to the definition of the scripts section of the /Views/Home/Index.cshtml view file that loads our JavaScript code, as shown in Listing 25-11.

Listing 25-11. Adding a Script Element for the Index.js File to the Index.cshtml View

```
...
@{ ViewBag.Title = "Index";}
@section scripts {
    <script src="~/Scripts/jquery.unobtrusive-ajax.js"></script>
    <script src="~/Scripts/Home/Index.js"></script>
}
...
```

Next, we add the basic functionality that we require to the Index.js file, as shown in Listing 25-12.

Listing 25-12. Adding the Basic Functionality to the Index.js File

```
function selectView(view) {
    $('.display').not('#' + view + "Display").hide();
    $('#' + view + "Display").show();
}

function getData() {
    $.ajax({
        type: "GET",
        url: "/api/reservation",
        success: function (data) {
            $('#tableBody').empty();
            for (var i = 0; i < data.length; i++) {
                $('#tableBody').append('<tr><td><input id="id" name="id" type="radio"'
                    + 'value="' + data[i].ReservationId + '" /></td>'
                    + '<td>' + data[i].ClientName + '</td>'
                    + '<td>' + data[i].Location + '</td></tr>');
            }
            $('input:radio')[0].checked = "checked";
            selectView("summary");
        }
    });
}

$(document).ready(function () {
    selectView("summary");
    getData();
    $("button").click(function (e) {
        var selectedRadio = $('input:radio:checked')
```

```
switch (e.target.id) {
    case "refresh":
        getData();
        break;
    case "delete":
        break;
    case "add":
        selectView("add");
        break;
    case "edit":
        selectView("edit");
        break;
    case "submitEdit":
        break;

    }
    });
});
```

We have defined three functions. The first, selectView, changes the visibility of the div elements in the display class so that only one set of elements is displayed. The second function, getData, uses the jQuery Ajax support to make a GET request to the /api/reservation URL. The JSON array of objects is used to add rows to the table element in the view, replacing the The data is loading placeholder that was visible in Figure 25-1. Each row in the table contains a radio button with which the user will select a Reservation for editing or deleting.

The final function is passed to the jQuery ready function, which means that it won't be executed until the page contents have been loaded and processed by the browser. We call the selectView function to display only the contents of the summaryDisplay element and call the getData function to load the data from the /api/reservation URL, which as we demonstrated previously, will result in the GetAllReservations method in the Reservation controller being called.

We also set up an event handler function that will be executed when any of the buttons in the page are clicked. We have used a switch statement to differentiate between the button elements based on the value of the id attribute. It is in the case statements of the switch that we will build out the different requests we will make to the server.

At the moment, we respond to the Refresh button by calling the getData function to reload the data from the server, and respond to the Edit and Add buttons by calling the selectView function to show the elements that are required to create and edit model objects.

If you start the application and navigate to the root URL, you can see the changes that our basic JavaScript code creates, as illustrated by Figure 25-3.

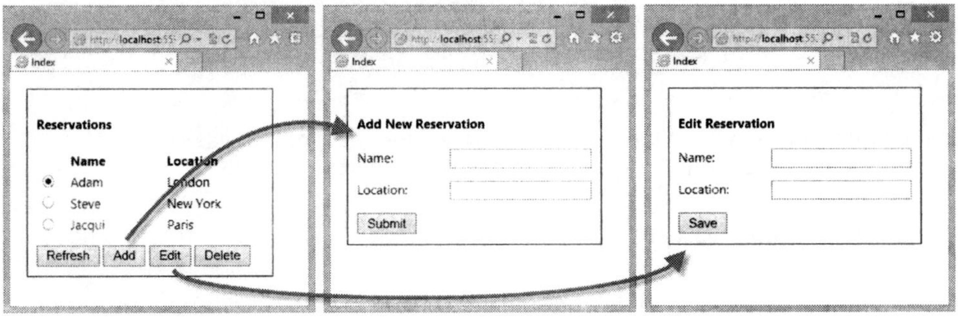

Figure 25-3. The effect of the basic JavaScript functionality

Adding Support for Editing New Reservations

We want to target all the action methods in our Reservation controller, so we are going to take a slightly odd approach to editing Reservation records. We already have the data that we need in the HTML document to be able to edit a Reservation, but we are going to start by making a request to the server for a single Reservation object so that we can target the GetReservation object. In Listing 25-13, you can see how we have added statements to the Index.js file to respond when the Edit button is clicked.

Listing 25-13. Responding to the Edit Button

```
...
$(document).ready(function () {
    selectView("summary");
    getData();
    $("button").click(function (e) {
        var selectedRadio = $('input:radio:checked')
        switch (e.target.id) {
            case "refresh":
                getData();
                break;
            case "delete":
                break;
            case "add":
                selectView("add");
                break;
            case "edit":
                $.ajax({
                    type: "GET",
                    url: "/api/reservation/" + selectedRadio.attr('value'),
                    success: function (data) {
                        $('#editReservationId').val(data.ReservationId);
                        $('#editClientName').val(data.ClientName);
                        $('#editLocation').val(data.Location);
                        selectView("edit");
                    }
                });
                break;
            case "submitEdit":
                break;
        }
    });
});
...
```

When we created the table rows in the getData function, we used the value of the ReservationId property of each Reservation object to set the value of the radio button element, like this:

```
...
<input name="id" id="id" type="radio" value="3"/>
...
```

When the user clicks the Edit button, we find the selected radio button and use the value attribute to build the URL we request from the server. If the user had selected the radio button shown earlier, then we would request the URL /api/reservation/3. We tell jQuery that we want a GET request and the combination of the URL and the HTTP method targets the `GetReservation` action method in the `Reservation` controller.

We use the JSON data that we get back to set the value of the `input` elements in the `editDisplay` section of the page and then call the `selectView` function to display them to the user, as shown in Figure 25-4.

Figure 25-4. Selecting a reservation to edit

To allow the user to save their changes, we need to fill out the `case` block that deals with the `submitEdit` button `id`, as shown in Listing 25-14.

Listing 25-14. Saving Changes to the Server

```
$(document).ready(function () {
    selectView("summary");
    getData();
    $("button").click(function (e) {
        var selectedRadio = $('input:radio:checked')
        switch (e.target.id) {
            case "refresh":
                getData();
                break;
            case "delete":
                break;
            case "add":
                selectView("add");
                break;
            case "edit":
                $.ajax({
                    type: "GET",
                    url: "/api/reservation/" + selectedRadio.attr('value'),
                    success: function (data) {
                        $('#editReservationId').val(data.ReservationId);
                        $('#editClientName').val(data.ClientName);
                        $('#editLocation').val(data.Location);
                        selectView("edit");
```

```
                       }
                });
                break;
            case "submitEdit":
                $.ajax({
                    type: "PUT",
                    url: "/api/reservation/" + selectedRadio.attr('value'),
                    data: $('#editForm').serialize(),
                    success: function (result) {
                        if (result) {
                            var cells = selectedRadio.closest('tr').children();
                            cells[1].innerText = $('#editClientName').val();
                            cells[2].innerText = $('#editLocation').val();
                            selectView("summary");
                        }
                    }
                });
                break;
        }
    });
});
```

We use the same URL that gets the Reservation object, /api/reservation/3, but we use the HTTP PUT method, which means that the PutReservation action method in the Reservation controller will be used to service the request. As a reminder, here is the action method we defined:

```
...
public bool PutReservation(Reservation item) {
    return repo.Update(item);
}
...
```

Notice that the argument for this action method is a Reservation object. API controllers benefit from the same kind of model binding that we described in Chapter 22, which means that we don't have to take responsibility for converting the request data into a model object.

Adding Support for Deleting Reservations

You can see the pattern we have established and how the HTTP method changes the action method that our request targets, even if we are using the same URL. In Listing 25-15, you can see how we have added support for deleting reservations, which we do by using the HTTP DELETE method.

Listing 25-15. Adding Support for Deleting Reservations

```
...
case "delete":
    $.ajax({
        type: "DELETE",
        url: "/api/reservation/" + selectedRadio.attr('value'),
        success: function (data) {
            selectedRadio.closest('tr').remove();
        }
    });
    break;
...
```

We delete the row in the `table` element that contains the data for the reservation that has been deleted. We do this irrespective of the result we get from the server, which is not something that would be sensible in real project.

Adding Support for Creating Reservations

We have taken a slightly different approach for creating new reservations. It is easier to use the jQuery Ajax support directly when making `PUT` or `DELETE` requests, but the MVC Framework unobtrusive Ajax forms feature can be used without any problems for POST and GET requests. All we have to do to add support for creating new data objects is to configure the `AjaxOptions` object that we use with the `Ajax.BeginForm` helper method in the `Index.cshtml` listing, as shown in Listing 25-16.

■ **Tip** If you want to use the Ajax forms for all of your requests or you want to consume a RESTful service from a browser that only supports GET and POST methods, you can use the `Html.HttpMethodOverride` helper to add a hidden element to the form, which will be interpreted by the API controller and used to target action methods. You can only override POST requests, but it can be a helpful fallback technique, especially for older browsers.

Listing 25-16. Configuring Ajax Options to Create New Model Objects

```
...
<div id="addDisplay" class="display">
    <h4>Add New Reservation</h4>
    @{
        AjaxOptions addAjaxOpts = new AjaxOptions {
            OnSuccess = "getData",
            Url = "/api/reservation"
        };
    }
    @using (Ajax.BeginForm(addAjaxOpts)) {
        @Html.Hidden("ReservationId", 0)
        <p><label>Name:</label>@Html.Editor("ClientName")</p>
        <p><label>Location:</label>@Html.Editor("Location")</p>
        <button type="submit">Submit</button>
    }
</div>
...
```

The `form` will be submitted using the POST method by default and we do not have to build a URL dynamically because the `PostReservation` action method does not rely on segment variables for parameters (it takes a `Reservation` object, which we rely on the model binder to create). When the user submits the form to the server, the `PostReservation` action method is called and a new `Reservation` is created in the repository. When the request has finished, we call the `getData` method to refresh the client data and switch to the summary view. We don't do this to keep our JavaScript code as simple as possible, even though the server sends back a JSON representation of the newly created `Reservation` that we could have used to append a new row to the `table` element. You can see the effect of creating a new `Reservation` in Figure 25-5.

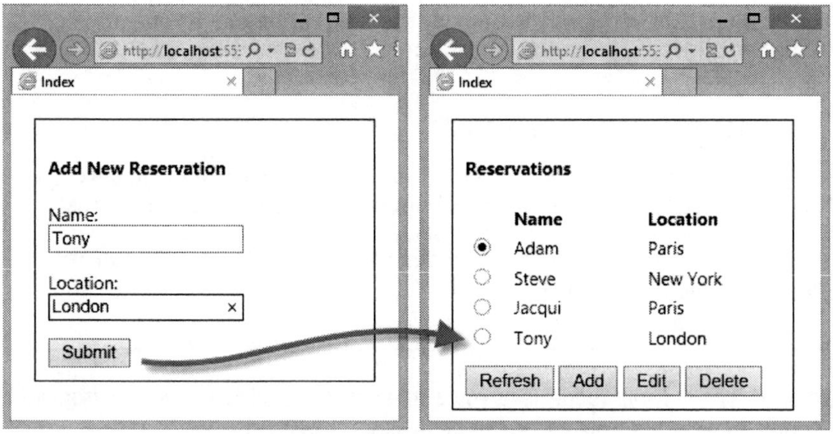

Figure 25-5. Adding a new reservation

And that is all the code we need to complete our Web API and the simple application that uses it. As we said earlier in the chapter, the Web API feature is pretty simple and the time is taken creating and testing the client that uses the API. The process of creating just the API consists of creating a new controller that is derived from `ApiController` and creating action methods whose names correspond to the HTTP methods you want to target them.

Summary

In this chapter, we showed you how to use the Web API feature to create RESTful Web services that can be consumed by HTTP clients. While not really part of the MVC Framework, the Web API is modeled so closely on the nature and structure of MVC that it is familiar to MVC developers, and as we demonstrated, Web API controllers can be added alongside regular MVC controllers in an application. In Chapter 26, we finish this book by showing you how to deploy your MVC applications.

CHAPTER 26

∎∎∎

Deployment

In this chapter, we will show you how to prepare your application for deployment and perform an example deployment.

There are lots of different ways to deploy MVC Framework applications and there is a wide range of deployment targets. You can deploy to a Windows Server machine running Internet Information Services (IIS), which you run and manage locally; you can deploy to a remote hosting service that manages servers for you; or, increasingly, you can deploy to a cloud infrastructure platform that provisions and scales your application to seamlessly meet demand.

We debated for some time about how to create a useful example deployment in this chapter. We ruled out showing you how to deploy directly to IIS because the server configuration process is long and complicated, and most MVC Framework developers that are targeting local servers rely on an IT operations group to perform configuration and deployment tasks. We also ruled out demonstrating deployment to a managed hosting company because each has its own custom deployment processes and no one company sets the standard for hosting.

So, somewhat by default, we settled on demonstrating a deployment to Windows Azure, which is Microsoft's cloud platform and which has some nice support for MVC applications. We are not suggesting that Azure is suitable for all deployments, but we like the way it works and using it in this chapter allows us to focus on the deployment process rather than getting bogged down in configuring issues. There is a free 90-day trial available on Azure as we write this (and some MSDN subscriptions include Azure), which means that you should be able to follow the example in this chapter, even if you don't intend to use Azure to host your application. We start this chapter by showing you how to prepare your application for deployment and then work through the deployment itself.

∎ **Caution** We recommend that you practice deployment using a test application and server before attempting to deploy a real application into a production environment. Like every other aspect of the software development life cycle, the deployment process benefits from testing. We both have horror stories of project teams who have destroyed operational applications through overly hasty and poorly tested deployment procedures. It is not that the ASP.NET deployment features are especially dangerous—they are not—but rather, any interaction that involves a running application with real user data deserves careful thought and planning.

Deploying a Web application used to be a tedious and error-prone process, but Microsoft has put a lot of effort into improving the deployment tools in Visual Studio; so even if you need to deploy to a different kind of infrastructure, you will find that Visual Studio is able to do a lot of the heavy lifting for you.

Preparing an Application for Deployment

We are going to deploy the SportsStore application that we created in Part 1 of this book. We chose SportsStore because it has a database, and ensuring that the database is set up and working properly is a big part of any deployment process.

▓ **Tip**   When we talk about deploying the SportsStore application, we are referring to the SportsStore.WebUI project. We do not need to separately deploy the other two projects that we created. The output from the SportsStore.Domain project is included in the WebUI project, and the unit tests contained in the SportsStore.UnitTests project are not required in production.

Detecting View Errors

As we explained in Chapter 18, Razor views are compiled by the server when the application is started, not when we perform a project build in Visual Studio. Normally, the only way to detect compiler errors is to systematically visit every action to cause each view to be rendered. This is a tedious and not always successful technique, especially if different views are rendered based on different model states.

We can enable a special project option that will compile our views and report any compiler errors. This is not a feature that we can enable from within Visual Studio, so use Notepad to open the SportsStore/WebUI/SportsStore.WebUI.csproj file. Search for the MvcBuildViews element and change its contents to true, as shown in Listing 26-1.

Listing 26-1. Enabling the MvcBuildViews Option

```
...
   <PropertyGroup>
     ... other settings omitted ...

     <MvcBuildViews>true</MvcBuildViews>

     ... other settings omitted ...

   </PropertyGroup>
...
```

Save the changes and return to Visual Studio, which will prompt you to reload the project. Now when you compile the project, the view files will be compiled and any errors reported. To demonstrate how this works, we have added an error to the */Views/Product/List.cshtml* view file, as shown in Listing 26-2.

Listing 26-2. Introducing an Error into a View File

```
@model SportsStore.WebUI.Models.ProductsListViewModel

@{
    ViewBag.Title = "Products";
}
```

```
@Model.NotARealProperty

@foreach (var p in Model.Products) {
    Html.RenderPartial("ProductSummary", p);
}

<div class="pager">
    @Html.PageLinks(Model.PagingInfo, x => Url.Action("List",
        new {page = x, category = Model.CurrentCategory}))
</div>
```

Normally, our attempt to render a property would not show up until we ran the application and navigated to a URL that renders the List.cshtml view, but with the MvcBuildViews option enabled, we see an error when we build the project, as shown in Figure 26-1.

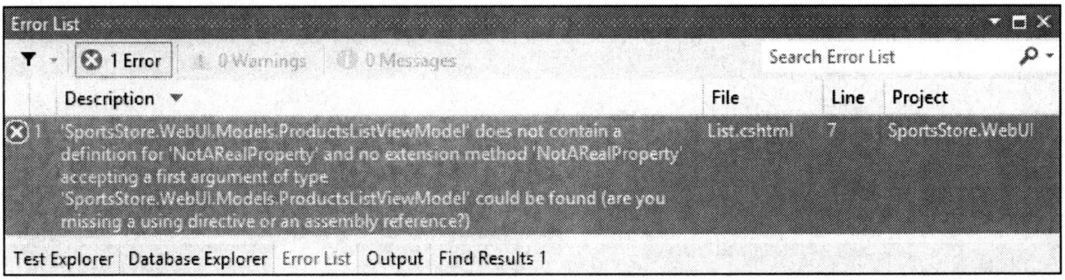

Figure 26-1. A compiler error for problems in a view

This technique detects compiler errors only. It does not detect logic errors and is not a substitute for a serious testing regime, but it is a helpful precaution that we always take before deploying an application. We are not able to deploy the application with the error in the view, so we have restored the view to its problem-free state, as shown in Listing 26-3.

Listing 26-3. Removing the Error from the List.cshtml View

```
@model SportsStore.WebUI.Models.ProductsListViewModel

@{
    ViewBag.Title = "Products";
}

@foreach (var p in Model.Products) {
    Html.RenderPartial("ProductSummary", p);
}

<div class="pager">
    @Html.PageLinks(Model.PagingInfo, x => Url.Action("List",
        new {page = x, category = Model.CurrentCategory}))
</div>
```

■**Tip**   You may see an error message that tells you that it is an `error to use a section registered as` `allowDefinition='MachineToApplication'` `beyond application level`. This is a bug that occurs after you have deployed an application. The only reliable way we have found to clear the problem is to clean the project in `Debug` mode, clean the project in `Release` mode, and then build the application in `Debug` mode.

Disabling Debug Mode

One of the most important `Web.config` settings that you should pay attention to when deploying an application is `compilation`, as shown in Listing 26-4.

Listing 26-4. The Compilation Setting in Web.config

```
...
<system.web>
  <httpRuntime targetFramework="4.5" />
  <compilation debug="true" targetFramework="4.5" />
  <authentication mode="Forms">
    <forms loginUrl="~/Account/Login" timeout="2880">
...
```

When the debug attribute is set to `true`, the behavior of the compiler and the application are designed to support the development process. For example, the compiler does the following:

- Omits some code optimizations so that the compiler can step through the code line-by-line.

- Compiled each view as it is requested, rather than compiling all the views in a single batch.

- Disables request timeouts so that we can spend a long time in the debugger.

- Limits the way that browsers will cache content.

In addition, if you have used bundles to group your CSS and JavaScript files together, the browser will be instructed to obtain each file individually and it will not receive the minified versions of those files. (We explained bundles in Chapter 24).

These are all useful features when we are developing the application, but they hinder performance in deployment. As you might imagine, the solution is to change the value of the `debug` setting to `false`, like this:

```
...
 <compilation debug="false" targetFramework="4.5" />
...
```

You do not usually need to make this change to perform a deployment because the Visual Studio deployment tools that offer you a choice about the configuration for your app or the value in the `Web.config` file will be overridden by the configuration of the IIS application server.

However, since the application behaves differently when the `debug` attribute is set to `false`, it is important that you run your testing program with debug mode disabled before you perform your deployment. You should check that your views render the way that you expect and that any bundles defined in your application that use the {version} token specify files that exist and are available on the server.

Removing Unused Connection Strings

One of the most error-prone parts of a deployment is getting the database connections working properly. In our experience, most problems are caused by having details of unused databases in the Web.config file. Knowing that databases are problematic, the developers of deployment tools try to automate the process of setting up databases, but they always seem to get hung up with the default configuration information that Visual Studio adds to a project. We can head off these problems by editing the Web.config file. In Listing 26-5, you can see the two sets of data connection information that exist in the Web.config file in the SportsStore.WebUI project. The entry whose name attribute is DefaultConnection was created by Visual Studio to help get a new project started, and we do not use it in the SportsStore application. The other entry, EFDbContext, is the one we created, used, and need to keep in the deployed project.

Listing 26-5. The Connection Strings in the Web.config File

```
...
<configuration>
  <configSections>
    <section name="entityFramework"
        type="System.Data.Entity.Internal.ConfigFile.EntityFrameworkSection,
            EntityFramework, Version=5.0.0.0, Culture=neutral,
            PublicKeyToken=b77a5c561934e089" requirePermission="false" />
  </configSections>
  <connectionStrings>
    <add name="DefaultConnection" providerName="System.Data.SqlClient"
        connectionString="Data Source=(LocalDb)\v11.0;Initial Catalog=aspnet-
        SportsStore.WebUI-20121003232522;Integrated
        Security=SSPI;AttachDBFilename=|DataDirectory|\aspnet-SportsStore.WebUI-
            20121003232522.mdf" />

    <add name="EFDbContext" connectionString="Data Source=(localdb)\v11.0;Initial
        Catalog=SportsStore;Integrated Security=True"
        providerName="System.Data.SqlClient"/>
  </connectionStrings>
...
```

You could just comment out the connections you do not need, but we like to be definite about this because we have spent so many hours debugging deployment problems caused by unused connection details. In Listing 26-6, you can see the edit we have made, leaving only the EFDbContext entry in the Web.config file.

Listing 26-6. Removing Unused Connection Details from the Web.config File

```
...
<configuration>
  <configSections>
    <section name="entityFramework"
        type="System.Data.Entity.Internal.ConfigFile.EntityFrameworkSection,
            EntityFramework, Version=5.0.0.0, Culture=neutral,
            PublicKeyToken=b77a5c561934e089" requirePermission="false" />
  </configSections>
```

```
<connectionStrings>
  <add name="EFDbContext" connectionString="Data Source=(localdb)\v11.0;Initial
      Catalog=SportsStore;Integrated Security=True"
      providerName="System.Data.SqlClient"/>
</connectionStrings>
...
```

Preparing Windows Azure

Once we have prepared and tested the application, we can prepare the hosting environment. You have to create an account before you can use Azure, which you can do by going to www.windowsazure.com. At the time of writing, Microsoft is offering free trial accounts, and some MSDN packages include Azure services. Once you have created your account, you can manage your Azure services by going to http://manage.windowsazure.com to provide your credentials. When you start, you will see the summary view we have shown in Figure 26-2.

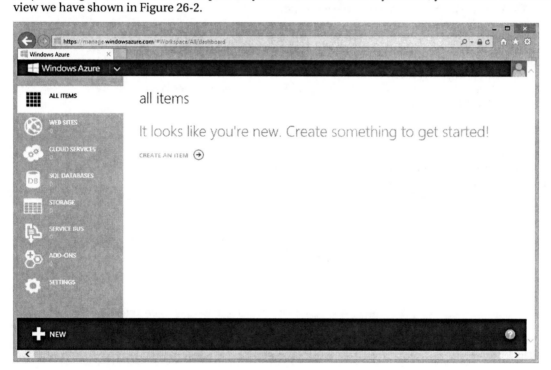

Figure 26-2. The Azure portal

■ **Caution**   At the time of writing, the Azure portal only works with Internet Explorer. Other browsers won't display all the pop-up windows or the Silverlight app that is required for configuring the database.

Creating the Web Site and Database

We start by creating a new Web site and database service. Click the large plus sign in the bottom-left corner of the portal window and select Compute ↗ Web Site ↗ Create With Database. You will see the form illustrated in Figure 26-3.

■ **Tip**   At the time of writing, the Web Site feature is available as a preview. You can enable the feature by clicking the link that is presented when you click the Compute option.

Figure 26-3. Creating a new Web site and database

We need to select a URL for our application. For the free and basic Azure services, we are restricted to names in the azurewebsites.net domain. We have chosen the name mvc4sportsstore, but you will have to choose your own name since each Azure Web site requires a unique name.

Select the region that you want your application deployed to and ensure that the Create a new SQL database option is selected for the Database field (Azure can use MySql, which our application is not set up to use, so we want the option that gives us a SQL Server database).

Set the DB Connection String Name field to EFDbContext. This is the name the SportsStore application uses to get a database connection, and by using this name in the Azure service, we ensure that our application code works in deployment without modification.

When you have filled out the form, click the arrow button to proceed to the form shown in Figure 26-4.

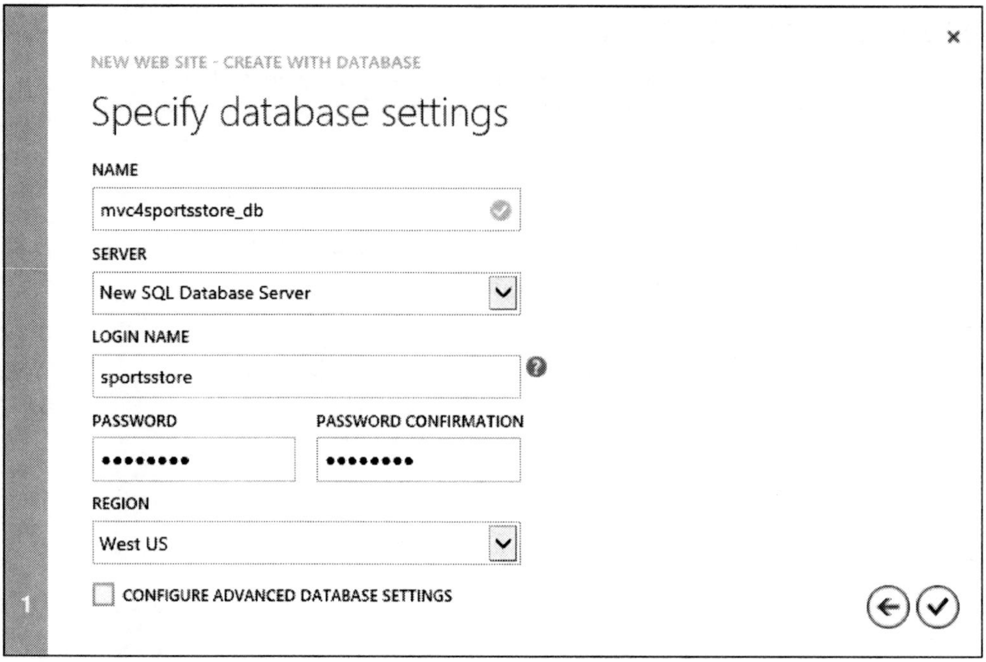

NEW WEB SITE - CREATE WITH DATABASE

Specify database settings

NAME

mvc4sportsstore_db

SERVER

New SQL Database Server

LOGIN NAME

sportsstore

PASSWORD   PASSWORD CONFIRMATION

••••••••   ••••••••

REGION

West US

☐ CONFIGURE ADVANCED DATABASE SETTINGS

Figure 26-4. Configuring the database

Select the New SQL Data Server option for the Server field and enter a login name and password. We specified a name of sportsstore and followed the guidance provided by the form to select a password containing mixed-case letters and numbers. Make a note of the username and password you use because you will need them in the next section. Click the check mark button to complete the set up process. Azure will create new Web site and database services, which can take a few minutes. You will be returned to the overview when setup is complete and you will see that the Web Sites and SQL Databases categories each report one item, as shown in Figure 26-5.

Figure 26-5. The effect of creating a Web site with a database

Preparing the Database for Remote Administration

The next step is to configure the Azure database so that it contains the same schema and data that we used in Chapter 7. Click the SQL Databases link in the Azure summary page and then click the entry that appears in the SQL Databases table (if you accepted the default values, the database will be called mvc4sportsstore_db).

The portal will show you details of the database and its performance, which will be empty because there is no content and no queries have been received. Click the Manage allowed IP addresses link in the Quick Glance section and you will see the form shown in Figure 26-6.

Figure 26-6. Enabling firewall access for configuration

Azure restricts access to databases so that they can only be accessed by other Azure services. We need to grant access to our development machine, which we do by clicking Add to Allowed IP Addresses and then clicking the Save button, which appears at the bottom of the browser window.

■ **Tip**   You will need to add the IP addresses of all the client machines that you want to be able to administer your Azure database.

Click the Dashboard link at the top of the page and then click the link displayed under Manage URL. This will open a new browser window and load a Silverlight database administration tool.

■ **Tip**   You will need to install Silverlight at this point if you do not already have it. The browser will prompt you to perform the installation and walk you through the process automatically.

Leave the Database field blank and enter the credentials you created in the previous section to administer the database. If you see a message telling you that there was an error connecting to the server, then wait a few minutes and try again. This happens because the firewall rule that grants access to your machine can take a few minutes to propagate through the Azure infrastructure.

Creating the Schema

Our next step is to create the schema for our database. Click the Administration button and you will see an item in the main part of the browser window that represents the database we created previously (which will be called mvc4sportsstore.db if you accepted the default name).

There are a number of small buttons at the bottom of the database item. Find and click the Query button, which will display an empty text area. This is where we are going to provide the SQL command that will create the database table we need.

Getting the Schema Command

We can get the SQL command we need from Visual Studio. Open the Database Explorer window and expand the items it contains until you reach the entry for the Products table. Right-click the table and select Open Table Definition, as shown in Figure 26-7.

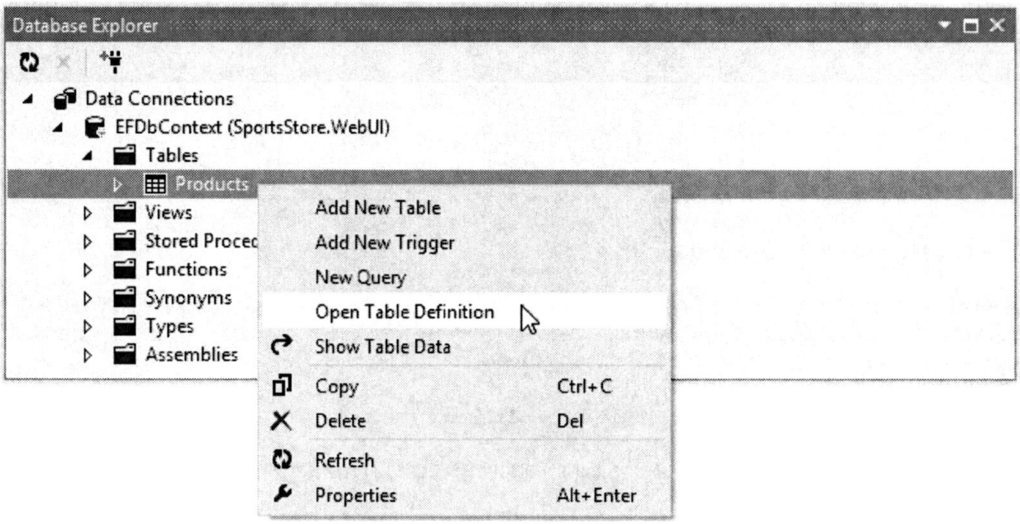

Figure 26-7. Obtaining the table definition in the Data Explorer window

The editor for the table schema will be opened. In the T-SQL table, you will see the SQL shown in Listing 26-7.

Listing 26-7. The Statement to Create the Products Table

```
CREATE TABLE [dbo].[Products] (
    [ProductID]     INT            IDENTITY (1, 1) NOT NULL,
    [Name]          NVARCHAR (100) NOT NULL,
    [Description]   NVARCHAR (500) NOT NULL,
    [Category]      NVARCHAR (50)  NOT NULL,
    [Price]         DECIMAL (16, 2) NOT NULL,
    [ImageData]     VARBINARY (MAX) NULL,
    [ImageMimeType] VARCHAR (50)    NULL,
    PRIMARY KEY CLUSTERED ([ProductID] ASC)
);
```

Copy the SQL from Visual Studio, paste it into the text area in the browser, and click the Run button at the top of the browser window. After a second, you will see the message Command(s) completed successfully, which indicates that our Azure database contains a Product database using the same schema as we defined in the SportsStore application.

Adding the Table Data

Now that we have created the table, we can populate it with the product data that we used in Chapter 7. Return to the Products entry in the Database Explorer window, right-click, and select Show Table Data from the pop-up menu. You will find a Script button at the top of the window that is opened, as shown in Figure 26-8.

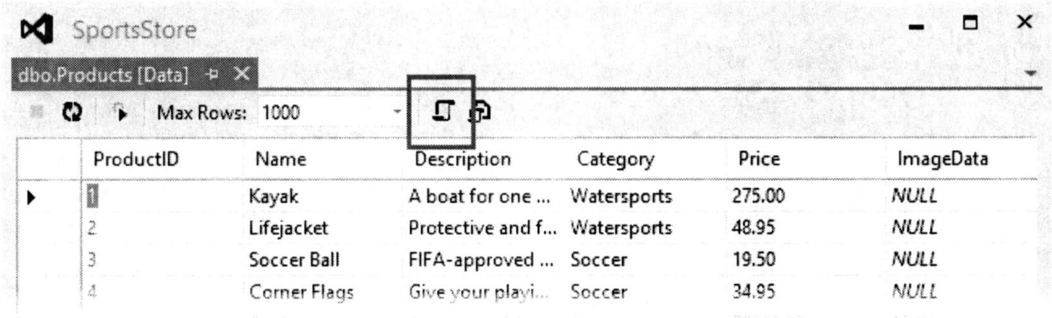

Figure 26-8. The script button in the table data display

A new window will open containing another SQL statement, which we have shown in Listing 26-8.

Listing 26-8. The SQL Statement to Add Data to the Products Table

```
SET IDENTITY_INSERT [dbo].[Products] ON
INSERT INTO [dbo].[Products] ([ProductID], [Name], [Description], [Category], [Price],
[ImageMimeType]) VALUES (1, N'Kayak', N'A boat for one person', N'Watersports', CAST(275.00 AS
Decimal(16, 2)), NULL)
INSERT INTO [dbo].[Products] ([ProductID], [Name], [Description], [Category], [Price],
[ImageMimeType]) VALUES (2, N'Lifejacket', N'Protective and fashionable', N'Watersports',
CAST(48.95 AS Decimal(16, 2)), NULL)
INSERT INTO [dbo].[Products] ([ProductID], [Name], [Description], [Category], [Price],
[ImageMimeType]) VALUES (3, N'Soccer Ball', N'FIFA-approved size and weight', N'Soccer',
CAST(19.50 AS Decimal(16, 2)), NULL)
INSERT INTO [dbo].[Products] ([ProductID], [Name], [Description], [Category], [Price],
[ImageMimeType]) VALUES (4, N'Corner Flags', N'Give your playing field a professional touch',
N'Soccer', CAST(34.95 AS Decimal(16, 2)), NULL)
INSERT INTO [dbo].[Products] ([ProductID], [Name], [Description], [Category], [Price],
[ImageMimeType]) VALUES (5, N'Stadium', N'Flat-packed 35,000-seat stadium', N'Soccer',
CAST(79500.00 AS Decimal(16, 2)), NULL)
INSERT INTO [dbo].[Products] ([ProductID], [Name], [Description], [Category], [Price],
[ImageMimeType]) VALUES (6, N'Thinking Cap', N'Improve your brain efficiency by 75%', N'Chess',
CAST(16.00 AS Decimal(16, 2)), N'image/jpeg')
```

```
INSERT INTO [dbo].[Products] ([ProductID], [Name], [Description], [Category], [Price],
[ImageMimeType]) VALUES (7, N'Unsteady Chair', N'Secretly give your opponent a disadvantage',
N'Chess', CAST(29.95 AS Decimal(16, 2)), NULL)
INSERT INTO [dbo].[Products] ([ProductID], [Name], [Description], [Category], [Price],
[ImageMimeType]) VALUES (9, N'Human Chess Board', N'A fun game for the family', N'Chess',
CAST(75.00 AS Decimal(16, 2)), NULL)
INSERT INTO [dbo].[Products] ([ProductID], [Name], [Description], [Category], [Price],
[ImageMimeType]) VALUES (10, N'Bling-Bling King', N'Gold-plated, diamond-studded King',
N'Chess', CAST(1200.00 AS Decimal(16, 2)), NULL)
SET IDENTITY_INSERT [dbo].[Products] OFF
```

Clear the text area in the Azure browser window and paste the SQL shown in the listing in its place. Click the Run button. The script will be executed and add the data to the table.

Deploying the Application

Now that the setup is complete, deploying the application is relatively simple. Return to the main Azure portal and click the Web Sites button. Click the mvc4sportsstore Web site to open the dashboard page and click the Download publish profile link in the Quick Glance section. Save this file in a prominent location.

For our Azure service, the file is called mvc4sportsstore.azurewebsites.net.PublishSettings. We saved it to the desktop. This file contains the details that Visual Studio needs to publish your app to the Azure infrastructure.

Right-click the SportsStore.WebUI project in the Solution Explorer and select Publish from the pop-up menu. You will see the Publish Web dialog window, as illustrated in Figure 26-9.

Figure 26-9. The Publish Web dialog

Click the Import button and locate the file that you downloaded from the Azure portal. Visual Studio will process the file and display the details of your Azure service configuration, as shown in Figure 26-10. Your details will reflect the name you selected for your Web site.

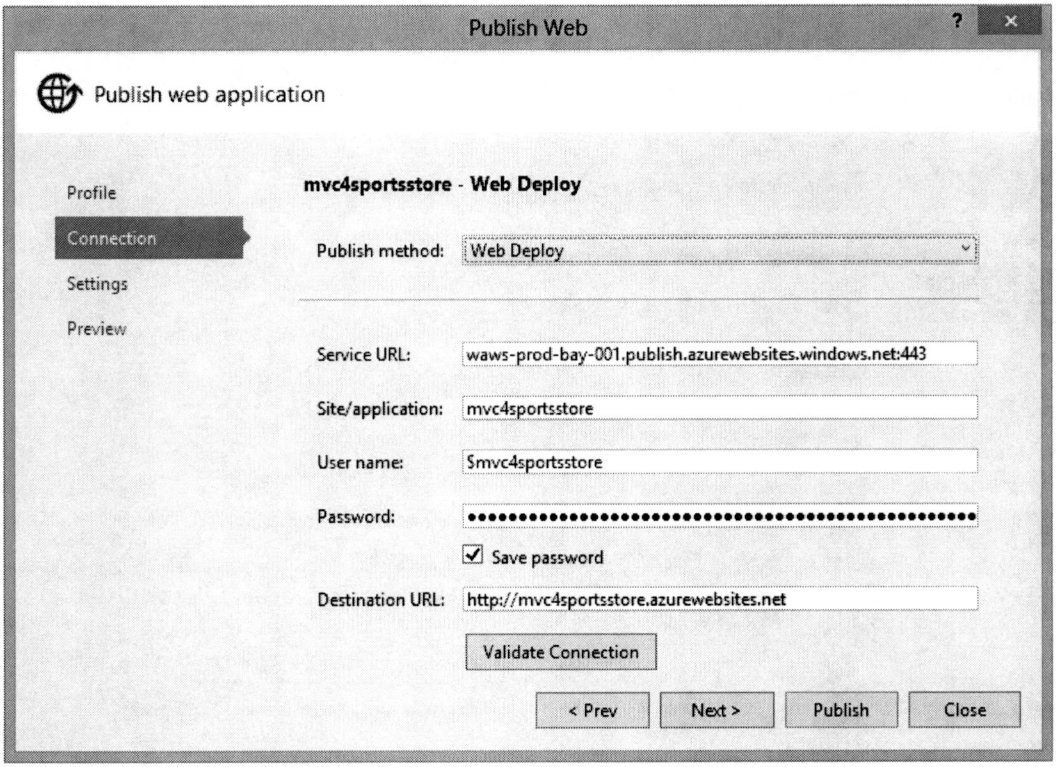

Figure 26-10. Details of the Azure service that the application will be deployed to

There is no need to change any of the values that are displayed. Click the Next button to move to the next stage of the deployment process, which you can see in Figure 26-11.

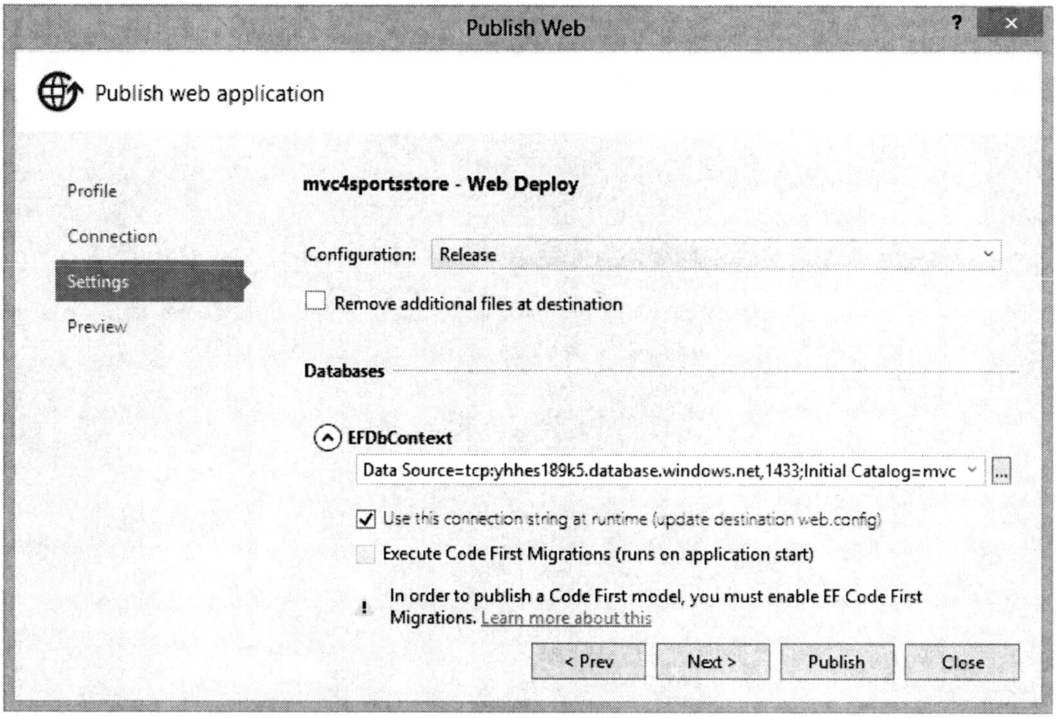

Figure 26-11. Settings for the deployed application

You can choose the configuration that will be used in deployment. This will usually be Release, but you can select Debug if you intend to test your application on the Azure infrastructure and want the debug settings for the compiler and your application bundles.

The other part of this process is configuring database connections. Visual Studio gives you the opportunity to create mappings between the database connections defined in your project and the databases that are associated with your Azure Web site. We made sure that our Web.config file contained only one set of details—and since we only created one Azure database, the default mapping is fine. If you have multiple databases in your application, you should take care to ensure that the right Azure database is associated with each of your application connections.

Click the Next button to preview the effect of your deployment, as shown in Figure 26-12. When you click the Start Preview button, Visual Studio walks through the deployment process, but does not actually send the files to the server. If you are upgrading an application that is already deployed, this can be a useful check to ensure that you are only replacing the files that you expect.

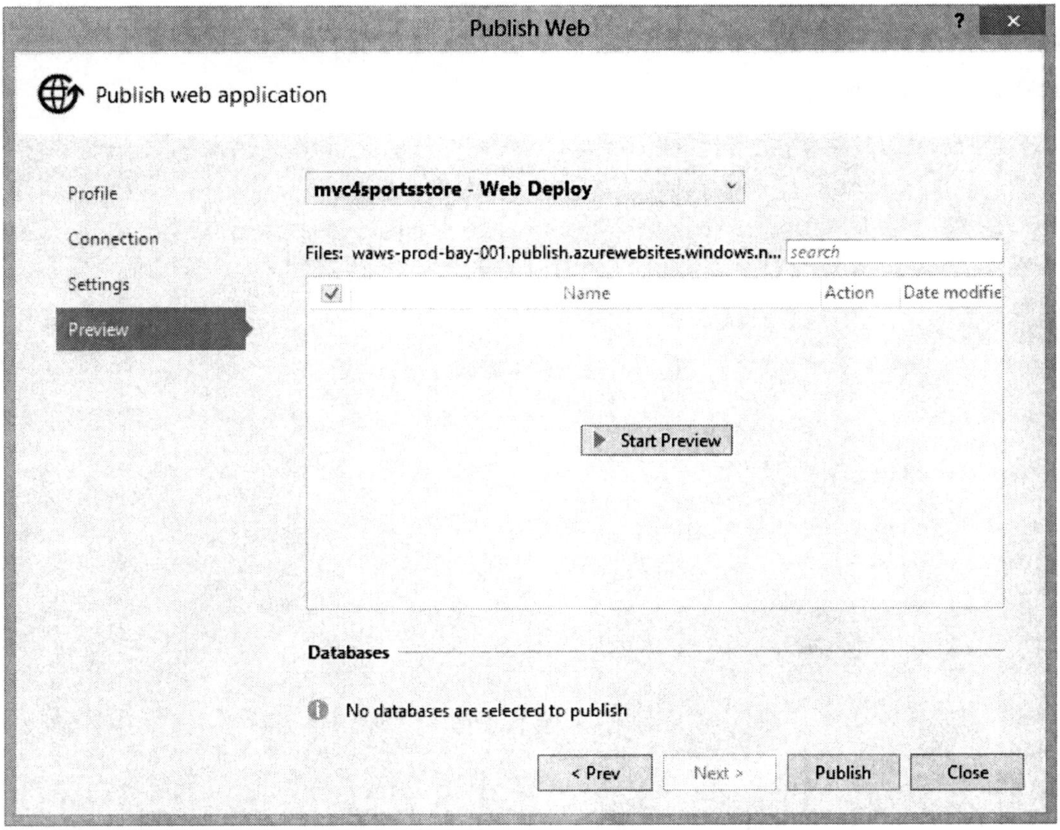

Figure 26-12. The Preview section of the Publish Web dialog

This is the first time that we have deployed our application, so all the files in the project will appear in the preview window, as shown in Figure 26-13. Notice that each file has a check box next to it. You can prevent individual files from being deployed, although you should be careful when doing this. We are pretty conservative in this regard and we would rather deploy files that we do not need rather than forget to deploy one that we do.

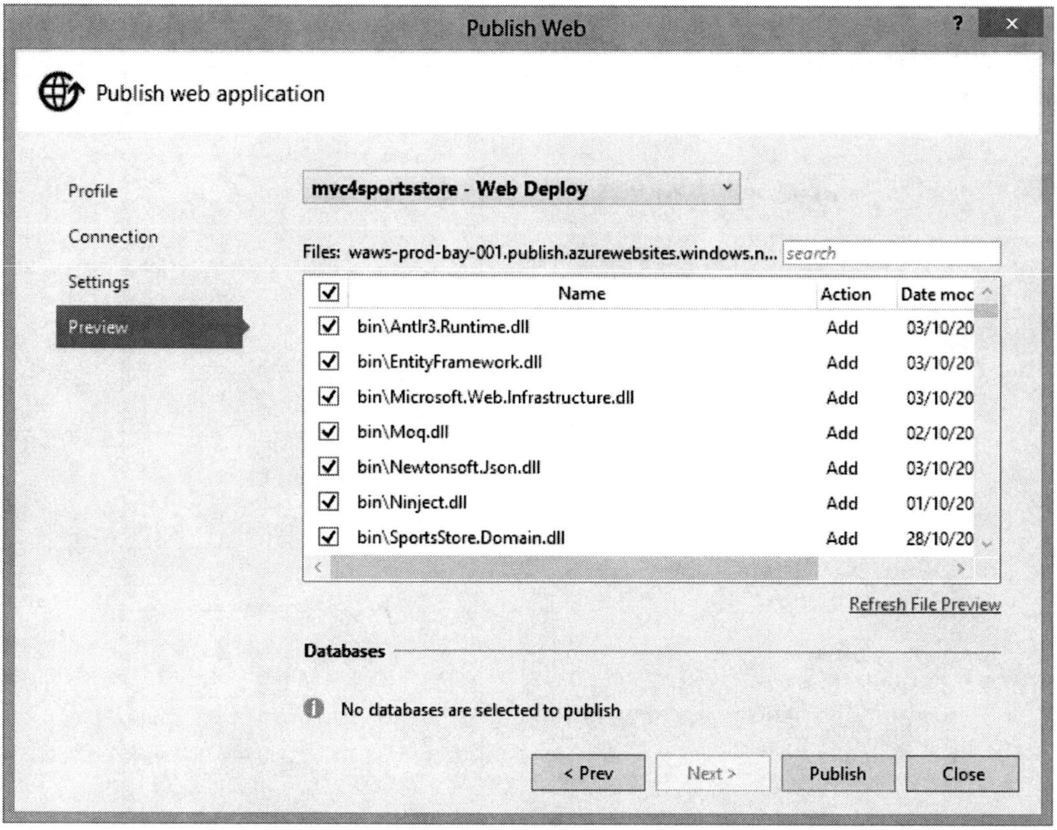

Figure 26-13. Previewing the deployment changes

Click the Publish button to deploy your application to the Azure platform. The Publish Web dialog window will close and you will be able to see details of the deployment progress in the Visual Studio Output window, as shown in Figure 26-14.

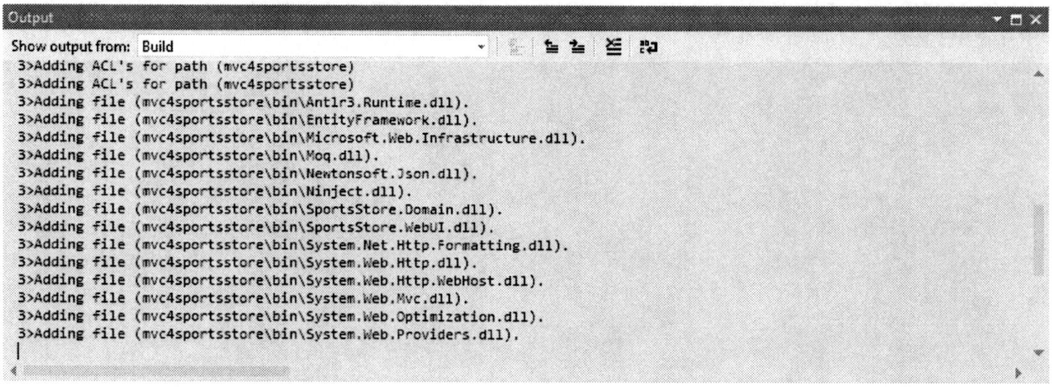

Figure 26-14. Deploying an application to the Azure platform

■ **Tip**   You may see an error message that tells you that it is an `error to use a section registered as` `allowDefinition='MachineToApplication'` beyond application level. This is a bug that occurs after you have deployed an application. The only reliable way we have found to clear the problem is to clean the project in `Debug` mode, clean the project in `Release` mode, and then build the application in `Debug` mode. Once you have rebuilt the project, you can repeat the deployment. The Publish Web dialog remembers your deployment settings and it will jump straight to the preview part of the process.

It can take a few minutes to deploy an application, but then the process is complete. Visual Studio will open a browser window that navigates to the URL of your Azure Web site. For us, this URL is `http://mvc4sportsstore.azurewebsites.net`, as shown in Figure 26-15.

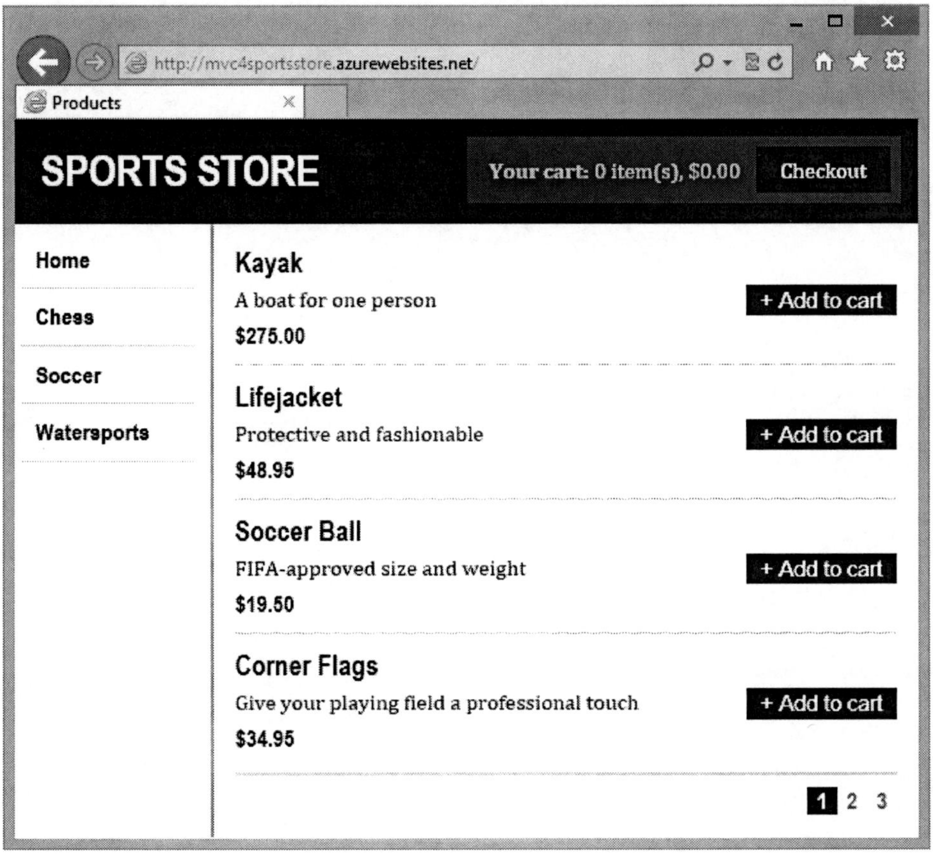

Figure 26-15. The SportsStore application running on the Windows Azure platform

Summary

In this chapter, we have shown you how to prepare your application for deployment, as well as how to create a simple Windows Azure service and deploy an application to it. There are many different ways to deploy applications and many different platforms that you can target, but the process we shown you in this chapter is representative of what you can expect, even if you don't use Azure.

And that is all we have to teach you about the MVC Framework. We started by creating a simple application, and then took you on a comprehensive tour of the different components in the framework and showed you how they can be configured, customized, or replaced entirely.

We wish you every success in your MVC Framework projects and we can only hope that you have enjoyed reading this book as much as we enjoyed writing it.

Index

A

B

C

D

N

O, P, Q

R

CPSIA information can be obtained at www.ICGtesting.com
Printed in the USA
LVOW052102271212

313485LV00004BA/4/P

9 781430 242369